Patriots and Paupers

Patriots and Paupers

HAMBURG, 1712–1830

Mary Lindemann

New York   Oxford
Oxford University Press
1990

Oxford University Press

Oxford   New York   Toronto
Delhi   Bombay   Calcutta   Madras   Karachi
Petaling Jaya   Singapore   Hong Kong   Tokyo
Nairobi   Dar es Salaam   Cape Town
Melbourne   Auckland

and associated companies in
Berlin   Ibadan

Library of Congress Cataloging-in-Publication Data
Lindemann, Mary.
Patriots and paupers : Hamburg, 1712–1830 / Mary Lindemann.
p. cm   Includes bibliographical references.
ISBN 0-19-506140-3
1 Public welfare—Germany (West)—Hamburg—History—18th century.
2. Charities—Germany (West)—Hamburg—History—18th century.
3. Middle classes—Germany (West)—Hamburg—Political activity-
-History—18th century.   I. Title.
HV280.H3L56   1990   89-16302
361.6′0943′51509033—dc20

2 4 6 8 9 7 5 3 1

Printed in the United States of America
on acid-free paper

ACKNOWLEDGMENTS

I do not think I will ever be able to thank adequately all those people who have, over the years, supported me, cajoled me, admonished me, raised my courage, argued with me, and in numerous other ways contributed to my finishing this book. My debts are professional and personal, and as it is so difficult to disentangle the two, I will not even try.

My first, and perhaps greatest, debt is to Martin Ewald, archivist at the Staatsarchiv Hamburg, where the vast majority of research for this book was carried out in the years 1978–80. He patiently coped with my bumbling German, guided me through archival mazes, and was both mentor and friend. I cannot thank him and his wife, Bertha Ewald, enough for the many kindnesses they have extended to me over the years. However, I can truthfully say that without his assistance this book would never have been written.

Otis C. Mitchell was my dissertation advisor at the University of Cincinnati, and he has waited many years to see this project completed. Guido Ruggiero, now at the University of Connecticut-Storrs, probably never expected to see this work in print. He read the manuscript in various incarnations and never wavered (at least visibly!) in his faith that I would—eventually—produce a book. Perhaps even more important, it was Guido who taught me (whether he realized it or not) what it was to be a historian, and for that I am very grateful. My debts to both Guido and Kris Ruggiero are also personal: they are friends as well as fellow historians.

Chapters 3 and 4 were written in the fall of 1985 while I was a Visiting Fellow at the Shelby Cullom Davis Center for Historical Studies at Princeton University. I would like to thank Lawrence and Jeanne Fawtier Stone for their interest and hospitality while I was there. My semester at Princeton gave me a much-needed respite from teaching as well as time to think and write in a stimulating intellectual atmosphere. Joan Daviduk likewise did much to make my stay at Princeton pleasant and profitable.

Franklin Kopitzsch is frequently cited in the following pages, but even these numerous citations cannot convey the importance of his own work to my understanding of Hamburg's history. He corrected misconceptions, guided me to materials, clarified my thinking on numerous points, and was the very soul of generosity in sharing his encyclopedic knowledge not only of Hamburg but of German history in general. He and Ursula Stephan were my good friends and comrades as well as intellectual companions. Peter Albrecht was an unfailing fount of information on poor relief, and he, too, went to great lengths to help me in my research, ferreting out obscure references, locating rare materials, and giving pertinent advice. A very special thank you is owed to Jill and Jochen Bepler. In Germany, they housed me and fed me, lent me their car, ferried me off to England for holidays, corrected my German, laughed and cried with me, and did all the things friends do to help preserve the sanity of someone writing a book and hunting for a job.

But this only touches on my many obligations. I owe much more to many other friends in the United States, England, and Germany. I only hope they forgive me for listing them without further specific thanks. Be assured I shall never forget the many pleasant hours we spent together, or their readiness to answer questions, to listen to me talk about my project, their advice, and their many kindnesses: Kathleen Berkeley, William Boehart, Bob Cage, Darius and Vivian Conger, Natalie Zemon Davis, Geoff Eley, Jürgen Ellermeyer, Richard Evans, Peter Freimark, Maria-Elisabeth Hilger, Frederick Marquardt, Barbara Musselman, William Olejniczak, Dennis Romano, Christoph Sachße, Donna Schroth, Jan Steinberg, Florian Tennstedt, and Joachim Whaley.

I would also like to take this opportunity to express my appreciation to the staffs and librarians at the following institutions: the Staatsarchiv Hamburg; the Staats- und Universitätsbibliothek Hamburg; the Commerzbibliothek Hamburg; Widener Library and the Kress Library, Harvard University; and Bird Library, Syracuse University. Francie Mrkich and the Interlibrary Loan service at Hunt Library, Carnegie-Mellon University, located material for me rapidly and cheerfully. I wish to thank my colleagues and friends in the history departments at the University of North Carolina at Wilmington, LeMoyne College in Syracuse, Syracuse University, and Carnegie-Mellon University. Lori Cole, who prepared most of this manuscript on a word processor, worked with speed, accuracy, and a smile (or was it a grimace?).

My final thank you must go to Michael Miller, who, like all academic spouses, suffered the most. There is nothing in the marriage contract that requires you to read a manuscript of 711 pages four times, as he did! It was his fine sense of style and his knowledge of how to construct a historical argument that probably make this book more readable and more sensible than it might otherwise have been. Despite his objection, I insisted on retaining the word "architectonics," for which I ask his forgiveness. As always, of course, he and those many others who lent their assistance are by no means responsible for any faults and errors, which, despite their best efforts to purge them from the manuscript, still remain.

I would like to thank Rowohlt Verlag GmbH (Reinbek), CURIO Verlag, Erziehung and Wissenschaft (Hamburg), and Franklin Kopitzsch and the Patriotische Gesellschaft in Hamburg for permission to use material in this book from three earlier publications ["Bürgerliche Karriere und patriotische Philanthropie: Armenpolitik in Hamburg vor und nach der Armenreform von 1788," *Jahrbuch der Sozialarbeit* 4 (1982): 157–80; "Unterschichten und

Sozialpolitik in Hamburg, 1799–1814," pp. 61–70, in Arno Herzig, Dieter Langewiesche, and Arnold Swottek, eds., *Arbeiter in Hamburg* (Hamburg, 1983); and "The *Allgemeine Armenanstalt* and the Non-Registered Poor," pp. 37–45, in Erich Braun and Franklin Kopitzsch, eds., *Zwangsläufig oder Abwendbar? 200 Jahre Hamburgische Allgemeine Armenanstalt* (Hamburg, 1990). Likewise, I would like to acknowledge Yale University Press for giving me permission to quote from Marc Raeff, *The Well-Ordered Police State: Social and Institutional Change through Law in the Germanies and Russia, 1600–1800* (New Haven, Conn., 1983).

Syracuse, N.Y.   M.L.
May 1990

CONTENTS

Patriots and Paupers

INTRODUCTION

No one who visited Hamburg in the eighteenth century departed unimpressed. Even sober businessmen and worldly travelers marveled at an affluence and economic vigor still uncommon in Europe in the closing decades of the century. Hamburg served as a commercial nerve center for half the continent.

> The importance of business in Hamburg and the variety of things connected with it are so great that one could profitably spend an entire year here and learn something new each day. There are few European seaports which Hamburg's ships do not enter, and there is no seafaring people in this part of the world which does not traffic with Hamburg. Its superb location has made the city the emporium of all Germany. . . . The Elbe and the canals . . . are almost blanketed over with ships. The assembly on the Stock Exchange is one of the largest [in Europe] and the place teems with negotiants. In a word, one finds here a perpetual motion of all nations and peoples caught up in the business of money-making.[1]

Yet Hamburg was no economic parvenu. Ever since the sixteenth century, the city on the Elbe had enjoyed a reputation as the "florentissimum Emporium totius Germaniae." Its wealth was built on a fortuitous combination of commerce and manufacturing. Commerce had always dominated the partnership, but never as thoroughly as it did in the eighteenth century, when Hamburg's seemingly boundless prosperity rested almost entirely on the strength of its position in the world market. While production for domestic consumption declined steadily, manufacturing for export expanded greatly, so that by the 1790s Hamburg had lost most characteristics of an artisanal center.

This economic metamorphosis, and the population explosion that accompanied it, radically altered and disrupted traditional social structures while simultaneously shaking the foundations of a political order that had known almost a century of serenity. These upheavals within the context of the social, economic, and political life of Hamburg during the period 1712–1830 are examined in this book. So intertwined are these strands that to write the history of one necessitates an understanding of the others as well. My subject is poor relief from a political as well as a socioeconomic perspective. Perhaps in no other way can the complex interplay of socioeconomic and political forces be better understood than by observing the relationships between patriots and paupers after 1712.

3

By the middle of the eighteenth century, changing economic and social conditions began to eat away at a political structure assembled two centuries earlier, when the parish had emerged as the basic unit of city government. Participation in parish governing bodies, and especially in parish poor relief, became the sine qua non of a future career in municipal politics. Such had been the consequences of an urban reform movement set into motion by the Reformation's stress on the revival of Christian community and sustained by the demands of many well-to-do burghers for more political influence. The numbers of people directly engaged in formulating policy, or even involved in municipal administration, remained limited; they were selected by lengthy and convoluted electoral procedures. Despite this restricted access to power and the endless complexities generated by a minutely detailed constitution, the system ran surprisingly well; in fact, it functioned more expeditiously than might be expected. This accomplishment can be attributed to a homogeneity of origins and interests among the ruling elite, a city small enough to be governed on a personal and ad hoc basis, and a great deal of backdoor politicking that sliced through Gordian knots of cross-jurisdictional hassles.

In the eighteenth century, however, the size of Hamburg's population, its highly mobile and more foreign character, and the physical sprawl of the city itself weakened this reign of "fathers and uncles." Governing techniques that performed adequately when Hamburg was a fishing village inhabited by few thousands, or even a medium-sized town of twenty thousand (in 1550), collapsed under the pressures of a population exceeding ninety thousand. Hamburg was (after Vienna and Berlin) the third largest city in central Europe.[2] Simply keeping track of the growing number of taxpayers (or tax dodgers!), for example, turned into a bookkeeping nightmare for a city possessing virtually no bureaucracy. As the city grew, the very bases of communal unity—the parishes—either lost their central importance or, as in the case of poor relief, were swamped by tasks never envisioned in the sixteenth century.

It was in this environment that poverty was identified as the city's major social problem for the first time since the Reformation. Hamburg's growth had snapped many links with the past, and the traditional agents of poor relief—the parishes and the almshouses—no longer sufficed in themselves to deal with a qualitatively different and numerically overwhelming "new poor." Most of Hamburg's inhabitants now depended for their livelihoods on the uninterrupted flow of overseas trade. Disturbances such as embargoes, high import tariffs, recessions, and wars jeopardized the very existence of thousands. This group of mostly unpropertied, unskilled workers had become a normal part of the urban landscape. Hamburg's prosperity was no longer imaginable without them. A new vocabulary arose to describe them. One now spoke of the poor (die *Arme*) and the workers (die *Arbeiter*) in the same breath, applying the phrase *die arbeitende Arme* to the whole multitude of laborers and their families living in Hamburg. Their presence, and not the "ubiquitous plague of beggars" prominently noted in every traveler's account, led to a reassessment of traditional relief practices and institutions and effected a restructuring of poor relief in the 1780s.

The impetus for poor relief reform, however, matured within the context of far bigger problems generated by the end of the Seven Years' War. Most disturbing of these was the beginning of a long economic depression that persisted into the 1780s. In 1765, in this climate of anxiety and even fear, Johann Ulrich Pauli penned a famous appeal to "All True Hamburg Patriots," calling on his fellow citizens to form a society dedicated to fostering renewed economic and commercial expansion and to promoting the common good in every way.[3] The Hamburg Society for the Promotion of the Arts and Useful Crafts, known as the Patriotic Society and founded in the same year, was the result. The Patriotic Society cultivated an "inwardly directed patriotism" designed to turn "each fruit of human knowledge and invention" toward solving the dilemmas of everyday life. The society expressed a strong antipathy to vain and futile *Projektmacherei* and actually took little interest in scientific research per se. It concentrated instead on applying the results of scientific discoveries to social and economic problems.[4] Yet despite the apolitical stance avowed in its constitution, the Patriotic Society and its members, like Hamburg's elite in general, never clearly differentiated between the public and private spheres; in their minds the two were one and indivisible. Patriots' own inclinations and the positions they held in their community ensured that the separation between public and private sectors, like that existing between economics and politics, could only by nominal. Pauli phrases it this way: "[O]ur republic . . . [is] nothing more than a commercial state, in which each and every thing draws its politics, raison d'être, and its very essence from commerce."[5]

Thus, Hamburg's patriots, whether or not they actually belonged to the Patriotic Society, fit the mold of eighteenth-century patriotism, which Harvey Chisick defined as

> primarily a social, and not, as it was in antiquity and was again to become, a political concept. In contrast to nineteenth-century nationalism which was forged in international conflict and [was] essentially exclusivist, the patriotism of the Enlightenment was positively oriented toward assuring the well-being of the whole community. . . . Typically, the "patriot" of eighteenth-century France was a man who had done something to promote the common good, such as, for example, writing a book on agriculture, or education, or ethics, or who had performed a signal act of beneficence. . . .[6]

Chisick, of course, was writing about France, and the French Enlightenment and the German Aufklärung were not identical. Yet there was a commonality of purpose and perspective here, an emphasis on community and, to a lesser extent, on cosmopolitanism that transcended political boundaries and national interests. To be sure, the German version of the Enlightenment worked within a different political framework: It was distinguished by a commitment to gradual meliorism and to political paternalism.[7] And the Patriotic Society in Hamburg clearly represented this Enlightenment. In the present study, however, the rubric of patriot has been applied to a broader group of people who were generally sympathetic to the goals of the society, even if they were not members, or who were otherwise active and influential in the traditional circles of government and communal affairs. This is a fairly loose definition, but it facilitates a better understanding of the role patriots played in a great city's laborious passage from town to metropolis.

It is not, therefore, odd that the Patriotic Society, in its concern for Hamburg's future, should address the issue of poor relief reform. In the 1770s and 1780s, the society created or lent its support to several organizations designed to alleviate or prevent impoverishment. By far the most splendid of the Society's projects was the Allgemeine Armenanstalt (General Poor Relief), which was chartered in 1788. As we shall see, the General Poor Relief dealt almost exclusively with the problems of the new poor and was principally concerned not with charity but with the more general objectives of social improvement. Though in strictly legal terms a private association, the General Poor Relief functioned as an arm of government. Not surprisingly, poor relief in Hamburg faced the same obstacles that had stymied effective government in the late eighteenth century: obtaining accurate information on Hamburg's inhabitants, controlling population movements, and whetting the appetites of citizens for greater involvement in public affairs. Poor relief reform nicely illustrates how Hamburg's elites came to perceive the deficiencies of their society and how they began to rethink the purpose and redefine the range of government action. The obsolescence of traditional institutions clearly evidenced itself in the obvious failure of the parishes and the almshouses to manage the poor. It also was distressingly apparent in the city's inability to bounce back from a shattering economic crisis, to overcome chronic shortages in its Treasury, and to lessen the pressure felt by almost every municipal official. These problems bespoke a city skidding out of the control of its traditional masters.

Slowly, and ultimately incompletely, outdated administrative procedures were discarded or streamlined as the city was forced to cope more efficiently, more rapidly, and, inevitably, less personally with its subjects and citizens. Few people questioned the essential rightness of Hamburg's constitution. Despite their willingness to experiment, reformers sought to preserve as much as they altered, or, rather, hoped to channel inescapable change in the right direction. They attempted to forestall catastrophic upheavals by tinkering with the "good old ways" only as much as they dared, and by seeking to revive civic virtues through appeals to public duty and noblesse oblige. Still, a decaying avuncular rule could only be propped up, and not saved. Poor relief was the first casualty, because of the demands placed upon it during the French occupation of 1806–14. The Relief that rose from the ashes in 1815 differed dramatically from that of 1788. It now operated according to the nineteenth-century liberal maxim in the area of social policy that less was more. Gone were the optimism, dirigisme, and generosity of the 1790s; they were supplanted by pessimism, laissez-faire, and parsimony. The political structure of Hamburg's government survived the crisis, at least for a while, testifying to lingering reserves of strength and resilience. But the same ethos that reshaped poor relief in 1815 was eventually to triumph in government as well.

Although the Patriotic Society, the General Poor Relief, and the men who guided them—Hamburg's patriots—play central roles in this book, they are not the only actors. To better understand the events that triggered the redefinition of poverty in the 1780s, it is necessary to observe how government in Hamburg functioned and how poor relief and parish organs overlapped with other municipal offices. Equally germane to a proper comprehension of how shifts in that economy's architectonics revolutionized the composition of the urban population is an analysis of what happened to Hamburg's economy in the crucial middle decades of the eighteenth century. How Hamburg's government strove to overcome the problems generated by the masses of the new or laboring poor living within the city's perimeter provides a clue to how closely poor relief was woven into the fabric of political and civic life. This is the subject of my opening chapters. Subsequent chapters reveal how contemporaries grappled with the transformations in their world, not only reevaluating the role of poor relief but redefining the meaning of community and reshaping their perceptions of who belonged in their city, of who were insiders and who outsiders.

My approach, therefore, is essentially political. This book illustrates how poor relief was an integral part of the governance of Hamburg in the eighteenth century and how, in turn, experiences with the new poor at first augmented and then, (after 1815) diminished the range of legitimate government action. This study examines politics and elites, patriots and politicians, as well as poor relief and paupers. Even though there may appear to be more concern with policymakers than the beneficiaries of that policy, it is also my intention to show that the poor were not uninfluential in determining what was done to them. Unfortunately, while the archival evidence in Hamburg (as in most places) reveals much about how the poor were regarded by their "betters," only seldom does it unambiguously present the opinion the poor held of the latter. Some might find that this documentary bias has unduly shaped my argument. I think not yet admit that I am sympathetic to the patriots of the eighteenth century. Their dedication to policies geared to the welfare of the city as a whole was only seldom preempted by the lure of material gain or crass self-interest. Their political paternalism also preserved an older sense of responsibility for the community and dictated a government composed of nonspecialists whose agenda ranged from military defense to sumptuary legislation.[8] Though I try to present their story with understanding, I do not accept their prejudices, nor excuse their blind spots. They were *always* ambivalent about the poor and never totally resolved the conflict between seeing poverty as the inevitable consequence of individual moral flaws or failings, on the one hand, or the result of external societal forces overwhelming individuals on the other. Even in their most compassionate moments, these patriots still remained skeptical about whether *all* forms of impoverishment could be attributed to the impersonal workings of the economy. Still, they were far more willing than their nineteenth-century liberal successors to seek solutions to poverty by engineering social change and vigorously pursuing social improvements. Unlike their descendants and heirs, they did more than merely preach the virtues of self-help. Nor did they slavishly commit themselves to the law of supply and demand as the ultimate panacea for all socioeconomic imbalances. Admittedly, they were hardly social or political revolutionaries. They firmly believed in their traditions of governance and their ideas of self-government never veered in the direction of nineteenth-century republicanism or democracy. The city was best governed by the merchants, politicians, and patriots who had long been its rulers. They admitted no contradiction between a distinct limitation of political and civic rights and a quest for social justice and fair government. Yet it must be stressed that this was never merely empty rhetoric camouflaging personal greed and selfishness. Not everyone, of course, recognized or fulfilled the creed of civic service, nor did all patriots eschew money-grubbing. But those who did were the movers and shakers in Hamburg after 1750. They sustained the spirit of commitment to public service and the public good that epitomized eighteenth-century patriotism.

This patriotism was lost, or at least drastically altered, by 1815. Earlier, poor relief was always tied to the larger concerns of governing. Later, it was increasingly cast adrift and moved, for the better part of the century, out of the direct range of *public* affairs. Before 1815, Hamburg's patriots always tuned poor relief policies to broader social, economic, and political issues. However, these larger frameworks were precisely what had changed dramatically in the eighteenth century. As the population grew, and as the economy expanded at an accelerated rate, the city's governors confronted several novel problems that forced them to make new decisions to achieve a balance between innovation and tradition.

The final question addressed in this book concerns what eventually caused the shift from patriotism and paternalism to liberalism and social laissez-faire policy. Was it the inevitable socioeconomic transformations that had gathered steam in the eighteenth century, or was it the impact of the French Revolution, Napoleon, and war that crushed and discredited the older forms of governing and demonstrated to Hamburg's elite that social policies, such as poor relief, could and should no longer be concerns of the municipality as a whole? It is hard to answer with any degree of certainty since we cannot repeat the experiment. The generally accepted response credits the French Revolution and the Napoleonic occupation with this crucial reworking of Hamburg's administration and, to a lesser degree, its politics. However, it is my position that it is here that the pressures of social and economic change and population growth were equally determinant. For a while the patriotism and renewed civic initiatives of the period after 1765 successfully dealt with these upheavals. Their achievements in the 1780s and 1790s were, of course, nourished by an almost unexampled economic prosperity. The traditional government of Hamburg had perhaps even then already passed its zenith, and it is difficult to believe that the rule of fathers and uncles in its older form could have successfully carried the city into the modern, industrialized world of the nineteenth century. Yet without the violence and despair of that first fifteen years of the new century, perhaps more of the older patriotic spirit would have merged with early liberalism and given it a greater sense of social responsibility than it possessed.

This transition from paternalism to liberalism inevitably leads to larger debates in German (and European) history concerning class formation in the late eighteenth and early nineteenth centuries, the contours of middle-class culture, and the pervasiveness of social control. Influencing these debates has been the argument that Germany followed a special path (*Sonderweg*) separate from other Western societies, that, in essence, its premodern elites remained strong, its bourgeoisie politically weak, and that the nation, once formed, suffered from a deficit of what has been called "middle classness" (*Bürgerlichkeit*). This Sonderweg thesis has generated a mountain of literature, much of it valuable, but one that most historians have rummaged through, picking up bits and pieces. Some have circumvented it entirely, arguing that similarities rather than differences most closely define the relationship between imperial Germany and states like Edwardian England, and that "we should not speak of German peculiarity, but of British, French, and German *particularities.*"[9]

Yet if few historians ever adopted the Sonderweg thesis in its entirety, many—perhaps even most—assimilated parts of it. And while discussion on the origins of the German Sonderweg has mainly centered on the nineteenth century (especially the Kaiserreich), historians have also looked back to the eighteenth century for the roots of a political and social evolution that, on the one hand, led to the "deficits" of the German middle classes in the nineteenth and twentieth centuries, while, on the other, facilitated the birth of liberalism. Thus, historians have seen in this earlier period not only the basis for German liberalism but the foundation of the latter "illiberal" antimodernity of the German *Bürgertum*.[10] Not surprisingly, the Bürgertum stands at the heart of this dialogue: How did it develop? Why did it evolve the way it did? Was it peculiar? The debate about the German Sonderweg has renewed interest in the middle classes and in middle-class culture among historians.[11]

Where, then, does a history of one city and of social policies within that city fit into these larger issues, and how does it contribute to current debates in German history? To a large extent, it would appear that the path taken by Hamburg into the modern world diverged from that followed by the rest of Germany. Hamburg has repeatedly been described as a *Sonderfall,* a special case in German history, an exception to an exception. This singularity seems especially striking when we consider Hamburg's government, its middle classes, and its bourgeois culture in the seventeenth and eighteenth centuries. When Percy Ernst Schramm and other earlier historians spoke of Hamburg's "peculiarity," they said it proudly and meant it positively. To them Hamburg was freer, richer, and happier than the other German cities or territories. In the eighteenth century, Hamburg's *Bürger* considered themselves a breed apart.[12] They lived in a free city owing no allegiance to a higher authority (except a tenuous one to the Holy Roman Empire). The city ruled itself and, according to one observer, "citizens govern citizens." There was no legally defined patriciate. Hamburg's elite proved quite receptive to newcomers. After the promulgation of the 1712 constitution, Hamburg suffered no serious bouts of civic unrest. Its inner peace was apparently untroubled by tussles between burghers and patricians that had so badly disrupted life in Frankfurt and other cities.[13] Many admired Hamburg's constitution as a masterpiece, a fortuitous mélange of aristocratic and democratic principles that had produced a degree of social harmony and economic prosperity few cities could emulate. There is in this positive valuation, of course, a good deal of Hamburg boosterism. Yet many outsiders also professed enthusiasm for Hamburg's evident peace and very real affluence. There was also sharp criticism of Hamburg's wealth, or rather its greed. Some viewed its existence as detrimental to the welfare of other German cities and territories and, increasingly in the nineteenth century, as even "un-German."

This "myth of Hamburg" (like the very similar "myth of Renaissance Venice" a city with which Hamburg has often been compared) stubbornly refuses to die. Some viewed Hamburg's free trading stance and capitalist mentality as its salvation. Others quite rightly pointed out that much of Hamburg's vaunted religious toleration, social justice, and civic peace was only superficial and will not stand the test of rigorous historical inquiry.[14] Still, not all myth is fantasy. Hamburg *was* different, and not just on the surface. For example, if one examines Hamburg's middle classes, few of the standard categories that have been profitably exploited to analyze civil society in other German cities work very well for the metropolis on the Elbe. The gulf between the politically powerful and the economically puissant but politically impotent existed throughout the Germanies except in Hamburg. Whereas in the German territories princely and ducal governments reigned with the assistance of a portion of the middle classes—the civil servants (Germany's famous *Beamten*)—and merchants were politically mute, in Hamburg there were few civil servants and merchants were sovereign. In Hamburg, unlike many other German cities, no upper class of patricians existed to thwart or stifle the political ambitions of the merchant class. Hamburg's elite was composed of merchants, whose sons had often studied law, of the owners of large manufactories producing goods (calico, refined sugar, and tobacco) for export, of Lutheran pastors, and of a handful of academics. Only academics and non-Lutherans were unable to participate in government. Guilds and guildmasters—groups that in other cities comprised another segment of the Bürgertum and often struggled violently with an upper class of merchants or patricians—here had some political expressions (in the *Bürgerschaft,* or Citizens' Assembly) but little political clout in eighteenth-century Hamburg. In a city the wealth of which resided in overseas commerce, guildsmen tended to lose out. Therefore, in eighteenth-century Hamburg, there is little reason to speak of the weakness of the middle classes. For the most part, their economic dominance was equaled by their political preeminence.

The story of the "rise of the middle class," however, involves more than an analysis of its composition; it also requires an examination of its connections to other groups and classes. In Hamburg, of course, there was no nobility or patriciate. But an investigation of the middle class also necessitates a study of its rapport—or lack of it—with the laboring classes. To a large extent, a modern laboring class emerged in the eighteenth century.

Moreover, this laboring class was also the class of the laboring poor, or, to employ Jean Gutton's felicitous phrase, the "potential poor." This trend was most pronounced and occurred earliest in cities, like Hamburg, where the working classes depended on employment in the areas of large-scale manufacturing for export, trade (especially overseas commerce), and, only much later, industry.[15]

Historians have grappled with the dynamics of the middle-class relationship to this new social group. Since Michel Foucault's provocative and incisive studies on madness and civilization, the birth of the clinic, and the rise of the prison, historians have often reduced this complex interplay to one of social control or disciplining, arguing that philanthropic endeavors like poor relief were merely more sophisticated or "softer" ways (to paraphrase Pierre Bourdieu's *violence symbolique* or *violence douce*) of exerting force over indolent, potentially disruptive, or dangerous groups.[16] It is hard to refute the idea that social policies always harbored motives ulterior to altruism. It is indeed the very existence of these deeper motivations that makes social welfare policies such good "windows" into the workings of a society. As we shall see, Hamburg's patriots were by no means squeamish about applying force (*ouverte* or *douce*) to punish malefactors or to inculcate behavior patterns they felt were desirable for the laboring poor. There are instances here in which social control and social disciplining models are useful and instructive. For example, the education and make-work projects of the General Poor Relief clearly fit well, into social control models even if Hamburg's elites rejected most experiments in Foucault's "Great Confinement." Still, social control and social disciplining arguments are all too frequently unnecessarily reductionist. One might, of course, argue that *all* social interactions are merely expressions of social control or disciplining, but this definition becomes uncomfortably amorphous and unwieldly when we try to apply it. If we accept social control and social disciplining as the *single* organizing framework for understanding poor relief, we run the risk of making social welfare and labor policies sui generis, that is, as special cases that somehow proceed by rules other than the more general ones governing various social relationships, such as the exercise of political power. Another objection to this type of interpretive model is that it tends to render the laboring classes unrealistically passive. A different approach seems possible here. My interpretation centers on the problems of governance and urbanization in a particular environment at a given historical moment. My argument is that poor relief functioned as an integral part of a larger governing process that was substantially modified by massive social and economic changes in the eighteenth and early nineteenth centuries. These changes dictated modifications in *intra*- as well as in *inter*-class dynamics. This is especially true for a city the constitution of which locked poor relief into the interstices of government. Poor relief was always intimately, indeed, structurally linked to larger concerns of governing, especially to policies of population and labor regulation; the shifting definitions of citizens, inhabitants, and aliens; the ordering (or reordering) of urban space; and marketing and commercial needs.

It seems to me that this linkage pertained everywhere. But its details were quite different, conditioned by variables that reappeared in numerous combinations and multifarious guises: religion, civic traditions, the derivation of wealth, the size of the city, its rate of growth, its location—all could vary. These, then, were the determinants of poor relief. Humanitarianism, social disciplining, and social learning were constants with protean configurations. To some readers this argument, and my perceptions of what happened in the city of Hamburg from 1712 to 1830, will seem theoretically careless, methodologically irresolute, and "too descriptive." Others might argue that Hamburg's peculiarity makes it an interesting case study but not very suitable for broader historical comparisons. It is my position, however, that while Hamburg's particularity is real, its peculiarity has been overstated. First, Hamburg possessed an economy in which masses of the laboring poor had come to dominate the labor landscape. Guild workers played a steadily declining role not because guilds were forcibly stripped of their monopolies (as they were in some places) but because the course of the economy undercut them. Second, Hamburg's economy, while not industrialized in the normal sense of the term, showed characteristics common to those of early industrialized societies: the numbers of the working poor, massive yet volatile economic expansion, speculation in property and goods, and urbanization. While its evolution in the last half of the eighteenth century by no means typified German cities, Hamburg's experience approximated what was happening in other large, commercial cities (like Amsterdam and Antwerp) and what would eventually occur in German cities like Barmen and Elberfeld under the impact of industrialization and urban growth. In fact, when one reads the accounts of the genesis of the Elberfelder system of poor relief in the 1840s, one is struck not only by the replication of the Hamburg model of 1788 but also by the fact that the necessity for reform in poor relief was motivated by industrial immiserization, whose descriptions parallel those drawn of the impoverishment and distress existing in Hamburg in the 1780s.[17]

Finally, the question of what urbanization and population growth meant in psychological and moral terms as well as in a purely physical sense will be addressed in this book. The physical problems associated with urban growth are fairly self-evident, but urban expansion also dictated modifications in how people would perceive their living space and those who inhabited it. They had to learn new skills in living together in close quarters and were forced to redefine their sense of community—if indeed a sense of community could be preserved. In Hamburg the city had to come to terms with a series of changes that eluded the control of a traditional government of fathers and uncles. That older style of governing had succeeded in Hamburg as long as the city remained small and uncomplicated, and it would continue to work for other cities well into the nineteenth century, but not for those convulsed by industrialization.

1

Politics and Poverty

By the middle of the eighteenth century, poor relief in Hamburg was approaching a crisis. Until then the patchwork of institutions inherited from the preceding three centuries had fulfilled satisfactorily (if not altogether flawlessly) the heterogeneous tasks of social welfare assigned to them. The parish distributed alms, bread, and clothing to the poor at the door of the chruch. The *Zuchthaus* provided shelter to the destitute, indiscriminately crowding children, adults, delinquents, and drunkards together within its vast halls. The *Pesthof* served as a Hôtel-Dieu, domiciling the invalid, the insane, and the aged alike. "Spitals," many of them dating back to the Middle Ages when hospitals for lepers and the syphilitic were needed, now served as final havens for pensioners whose few possessions or modest savings enabled them to "buy in" for life. The *Waisenhaus* offered refuge to orphans, while several dozen "Ragged Schools" drilled religion and learning into the heads of pauper children. Meanwhile hundreds of private legacies, testaments, and family-run charities dispersed their moneys among the lower classes widely, if not always wisely. Each of these organizations constituted an independent body with its own personnel, funds, and administration. Yet the hodge-podge worked well as long as poverty itself remained limited and thus of minor concern. With some exceptions, this had been the situation since the Reformation. But especially by the latter half of the eighteenth century the very conditions of poverty were changing, provoking a prolonged crisis in the social welfare system and raising the question whether a decentralized and informal network of institutions could adequately respond to new challenges. To understand how this crisis and the issue of decentralization were to mold the debate over poor relief by the 1780s, it is necessary first to examine more closely the character of welfare in the previous two centuries, looking at how its institutional history intertwined not only with the long-term and short-term fluctuations in the economy but also with the very nature of political life in Hamburg.[1]

The Legacy of the Reformation

Properly told, the story antedates the Reformation. Formed jointly by Catholic traditions, humanist theory, Protestantism, and the city's own history, social welfare policies evolved in Hamburg in the fifteenth and sixteenth centu-

13

ries in the same ways and under many of the same conditions as they had in other urban centers. Humanists like Juan Luis Vives and John Major, Roman Catholic clerics like Johannes Geiler von Kayserberg, and religious reformers like Martin Luther, Johann Bugenhagen, Martin Bucer, and Wenzeslaus Linck had all accepted three points as basic to a Christian exercise of charity. First, they wanted secular authority to replace the Church as the prime executor of all forms of welfare. Second, they established the principle of reciprocity by which the poor received alms only in exchange for honest labor according to the Pauline dictum that "he who does not work, shall not eat." Third, they condemned begging as parasitic ("a clear breach of Divine order") and almsgiving as un-Christian. They argued that putting these principles into practice necessitated a massive reorganization of poor relief in order to clear away the remnants of the capricious, wasteful, and ineffectual Catholic relief system as it had existed until that time. This relief system was to be replaced with a more rigorously structured edifice characterized by a strict work ethic, a fiercely prosecuted war on mendicancy, and a tighter administration controlled by the secular authorities and dependent on the active participation of all members of the Christian community. They also drew up guidelines to separate the worthy from the unworthy poor, in biblical terms sorting out the Lord's sheep from the "stinking he-goats." At the same time, they determined criteria for appointing guardians of the poor to investigate the claims of supplicants and to oversee the distribution of alms. The guardians were to play a dual role, acting, on the one hand, as spokesmen for the poor and, on the other, as watchdogs over the resources of the parish. They thereby fulfilled their several civic duties as Christians, parish officers, and citizens, while their selection as guardians affirmed their status in the community as upright, God-fearing, and honorable men.[2] Limits were also set on what the legitimate functions of poor relief were to be. Most accepted Luther's dictum that the poor should neither freeze nor starve as sufficient; sixteenth-century poor relief rarely aimed at achieving more than this.[3] At the same time, poor relief supported a social order of poor, middling, and rich bound together by an unwritten social contract that apportioned to each his rights and obligations.

Just how the Reformation shaped this process is difficult to evaluate. Historians now agree that most of the innovations in social welfare policy supposedly spawned by the Protestant Reformation drew on earlier precedents established in the late medieval cities. The assertion that the Reformation single-handedly secularized poor relief has proved particularly shaky. Well before the sixteenth century, laymen were regularly running what nominally remained ecclesiastical charities. Recently the revolution in poor relief, once facilely labeled "reformed," has been attributed to a much slower transformation spanning at least two centuries. A pattern of change in social legislation that began in the fourteenth century only culminated in the Reformation.[4]

Social welfare policies in Hamburg went through a similar process. In the Middle Ages the *Rat* (city council) had slowly, but perceptibly, rolled back the influence of the Roman Catholic church on poor relief and, on the eve of the Reformation, exercised an almost absolute stewardship over the financial affairs of the city's major beneficent institutions. The penetration of the medieval Rat into matters once reserved for the church or considered the domain of private individuals laid the basis for the appearance in the sixteenth and seventeenth centuries of "semipublic" foundations, which became standard features of municipal life and determined, in form and style, the model social welfare practice followed well into the eighteenth century. These were hybrid institutions, which were created by grafting private initiative onto public benefit, and they fulfilled the tasks of asylums, hospitals, orphanges, almshouses, and workhouses. They also funneled private resources into public channels by offering individuals social recognition and a certain degree of power in return for their financial support and their sacrifices of time and energy as the honorary administrators of these institutions. Likewise, they provided opportunities to express piety.[5]

However, lest we commit the error of banishing the Reformation from the history of poor relief altogether, we must realize how closely poor relief reform was woven into Hamburg's constitution during the Reformation.[6] Simply put, the restructuring of poor relief not only accompanied but actually laid the groundwork for a thorough reorganization of government, which opened more opportunities for citizens to participate in communal affairs and augmented to some degree the strength of the *Bürgerschaft* (Citizens' Assembly) in relation to the Rat. This was to happen during the Reformation as ancient and relatively impotent parish councils[7] spawned three new collegial bodies—the Oberalten, the Forty-Eight, and the One Hundred Forty-Four (with the addition of a fifth municipal parish in 1685, the last two became, respectively, the Sixty and the One Hundred Eighty). These were originally designed to supervise all parish affairs, including poor relief, but soon became permanent governmental organs whose very existence seemingly signaled the end of the unchallenged suzerainty of the Rat. Social revolution and violence neither proceeded nor followed this reshuffling of political power, which merely granted a larger share of governmental influence to men who were hardly different in their socioeconomic backgrounds from those already sitting in the Rat. This gentle shift in the municipal balance of power and not the posited secularization of poor relief or even the introduction of reformed ideas of charity constitutes one true link between the Reformation and poor relief in Hamburg.[8]

As early as 1522, reformed teachings had penetrated Hamburg and sunk deep roots in the parishes.[9] By 1527, three of the city's four principal pastors were Lutheran sympathizers. The parish officers of St. Nikolai had taken decisive steps toward recasting parish life in a reformed mode by creating a *Gotteskasten,* or parish chest, which was modeled after *der Gemeine Kasten* favored by Luther and Bugenhagen, a full two years before Bugenhagen's Evangelical Church Order was promulgated for Hamburg. They designed their Gotteskasten to hold "all the fruits of Christian charity," designating these moneys for the salaries of schoolmasters, pastors, and catechists, for the maintenance of church properties and, primarily, for the benefit of the parish poor who had sunk into destitution "through no fault of their own, but rather as the result of God's inscrutable will." From their own ranks, the parish officers chose twelve men as deacons or *Gotteskastenverwalter* (whom Catholics spoofed as "box men") to dispense the Gotteskasten funds and to advise the parish on the appointment of pastors and schoolteachers.[10] A few months later, in December 1527, the three other parishes—St. Petri, St. Katharinen, and St. Jakobi—followed the same example, establishing their own Gotteskasten and electing their own deacons, thereby raising the total number of deacons in the city to forty-eight. The next step was to marshal these "devout men" into a permanent collegial body, the Forty-Eight. At first charged only with superintending parish affairs, the Forty-Eight soon gained the right of advising the Rat on "all matters touching on the prosperity and tranquility of our good city."[11]

Each parish also selected twenty-four subdeacons and it was from this larger body that the deacons picked their successors. The forty-eight deacons and the ninety-six subdeacons then combined in a second, more cumbersome, collegial body, the One Hundred Forty-Four. Its size meant that it participated little in the daily business of governing yet its importance exceeded that of merely a pool of candidates for the more exalted post of deacon. In most cases, a man first embarked on a career in public life with his election as subdeacon and from there he ascended the *cursus honorum,* with membership in the One Hundred Forty-Four (later, after the addition of St. Michaelis as the fifth metropolitan parish, the One Hundred Eighty) determining his eligibility for appointment to positions in Hamburg's government and to any one of the many deputations and collegia that became the substance of political life. Indeed, it was rare for a man *not* to begin his civic career with a parish post.[12] The twelve senior deacons—three from each parish—formed an elite group, the Oberalten which, as the most powerful of the collegial bodies, mediated directly between the Rat and Bürgerschaft.[13]

At first the Rat regarded the collegial bodies with great skepticism and even outright hostility, distrusting in equal measure their political ambitions, social presumption, and religious persuasions. As a body, the Rat had shown little early enthusiasm for the new religious teachings, yielding only slowly to intense pro-Reformation sentiment in the city. Because the Rat viewed itself as sovereign and the only legitimate executor of secular authority, it feared the collegial bodies as rivals. Yet under the circumstances the Rat found it impossible to resist their demands for expression and, in the Long Recess of 1529, acknowledged the right of burghers to check and balance its power. For itself, the Rat reserved absolute control over military and foreign affairs, and, temporarily, over finances. In 1563, however, the burghers forced the Rat to agree to an independent, burgher-controlled financial administration, the Treasury (*Kämmerei*). In the long term, however, apprehensions of the Rat proved exaggerated. By the eighteenth century, the Rat had regained most of the powers it relinquished in the sixteenth and seventeenth centuries and could rely on the Oberalten and the collegial bodies as collaborators and corulers over the vast majority of Hamburg's inhabitants. Even in the short term, the willingness of both sides to compromise mitigated the Rat's loss of power. This was no novelty but rather a recurring situation: In the fifteenth century, negotiations between the Rat and ad hoc committees of burghers had generated several recesses (in 1410, 1458, 1482, and 1483), which had defused potentially explosive situations and had likewise redefined or reinterpreted the ways in which the city was to be governed. The creation of permanent collegial bodies during the Reformation, therefore, only institutionalized a pattern of conciliation that had become by then a political convention.[14].

As in other cities, the Reformation in Hamburg breathed fresh life into old and almost moribund communal associations, which revived a perhaps flagging sense of corporate identity.[15] The collegial bodies offer the clearest proof of this resurgence of civic spirit, but poor relief fits the model equally well since it called on all burghers to take up new missions in life as active Christians, citizens, and patriots. The mandate bestowed on the One Hundred Forty-Four in 1528 testified, and not only rhetorically, to "the great wickedness of the times . . . the uproar, discord, and confusion," which raged unchecked and threatened "perpetual ruin." The collegial bodies were to soothe a fractious society by drawing contentious burghers closer to one another, braking their drift toward violence. Their work in the parishes and among the poor was to cement the community together through a combination of Christian duty, civic pride, and good neighborliness.[16]

Poor Relief and Communal Life

In this spirit, the poor relief ordinances of 1550 completed the rebuilding of parish life begun in 1527–28, defining the duties of the deacons and subdeacons and delegating to them the real burden of parish relief. Each subdeacon, in turn, was to pass the collection plate (the *Klingbeutel* or bag) during services and conduct the biweekly distributions of bread and alms on the church steps. Each month the deacons were to enter the dwellings of the poor to investigate in minute detail their living conditions, family circumstances, and needs. Then they were to meet to discuss their findings and decide on the best allocation of Gotteskasten moneys. Parish relief was to replicate in microcosm a smoothly running Christian community in which each member extended a hand to his fellows and cheerfully and piously assumed his civic duties. Yet this construct sought as well to eliminate the whimsy of charity by erecting a tribunal of deacons to determine who was or was not worthy of assistance. Included among the deserving were the sick, invalids, widows (especially those with young children), orphans, respectable spinsters, and déclassé. A shield of anonymity protected the latter sparing them the ignomiy of being listed among common paupers. The special protection afforded them suggests that even poverty had its social hierarchy, that poverty had not yet come to be defined in solely economic terms, and that "the poor" were not yet equated with the laboring classes as a whole.[17]

Normally parish relief excluded all those perceived as alien to the community, or regarded as undesirables, namely, beggars, transients, and pilgrims.

Likewise young, healthy males (and often females) could expect little assistance from the parish. It was hoped that the parish would find ways to employ all the able-bodied poor, extending alms only in supplement of wages. This principle of reciprocity was the foundation on which parish relief was to rest, and, while the intention was excellent, the achievement was dismal. While the collegial bodies solidified their positions, expressing a true renewal of civic spirit in the realm of politics, parish-based social welfare policies succeeded less brilliantly. Either the charitable manifestation of a revived civic spirit never fully flowered or else it soon wilted as mundane chores wore the bloom off initial enthusiasm. Finding work for the poor proved infeasible, and by the end of the sixteenth century even the cardinal feature of parish relief—the deacons' regular detailed investigation of each pauper at home—had fallen by the wayside. All that survived of a once ambitious program was a scattering of alms and occasional handouts of bread, clothing, and fuel.[18]

Johann Georg Büsch, a major advocate of poor relief reform in the 1770s and 1780s, labeled the theory embodied in parish relief "capital" but found considerably less to praise in its practice. He traced the source of failure primarily to a faulty assignment of duties. He noted that the burden of administration fell primarily on the Oberalten, mostly elderly men who lacked the energy to pursue the matter with the requisite vigor. Heavy governmental responsibilities so totally monopolized the Sixty that they, too, had precious few moments to spare for a time-consuming, thorough visitation of the poor. Finally, the weight of empty ceremony immobilized the whole apparatus of parish relief. Büsch diagnosed the most serious flaw as an insufficiency of personnel. Parish relief depended on too few men, or on men too involved in more pressing governmental tasks.[19] But the simple solution of hiring people to carry out the quotidian demands of poor relief, like the creation of a paid bureaucracy, was never seriously advanced as a viable alternative to the tradition of voluntarism (or voluntary office-holding) that had prevailed in Hamburg ever since the sixteenth century.

Voluntarism was the inviolable principle of Hamburg's government. With few exceptions, policy-making positions at most levels were voluntary or honorary (*ehrenamtlich*). Only those holding very demanding offices, such as the members of the Rat, the syndics and secretaries to the Rat, and the Oberalten, received honoraria in addition to tax exemptions. The entire middle range of Hamburg's government, therefore, was staffed by unpaid nonprofessionals. Only lesser officials, the notaries, secretaries, city apothecary, the foremen who managed public construction and fortification repairs, and the almoners of hospitals and almhouses purchased or leased their posts. Still fewer were hired outright and paid a salary. The common practice of selling or leasing a position to the highest bidder had all too often produced unhappy results. Graft and corruption were less common problems than the bidding up of prices and sheer incompetence. Furthermore, that officials worked for money supposedly impaired their ability to come to impartial and balanced decisions. In contrast, "pious, Christian, honorable, true, upright . . . indefatigable,"[20] and prosperous men served out of a sense of commitment to God and community, not in hopes of gain. Ideally these men seamlessly integrated their private and public lives, seeing no difference between the good of the commune and their own good, since the first inevitably secured the second. Good government in Hamburg appeared unthinkable without these pillars of the community, who willingly sacrificed their time, leisure, and, on occasion, their wealth in the service of the city. In return, the municipality held out some admittedly enticing rewards, offering them status, pleasing rituals, connections, deference, and, of course, power. Their wealth supposedly mitigated the temptation of lining their own pockets at the expense of the city (and, in fact, cases of corruption were rare), while their reputations supposedly ensured that they would not abuse their authority.[21]

Wealth could be interpreted as the visible manifestation of God's favor. Wealth as an unspoken criterion for public office also represented the belief that those who had the most to lose were the best conservators of discipline and order. It seemed just as obvious to contemporaries that those honored by God and man, and blessed in their earthly lives, should willingly serve their community, thus keeping their part of an unwritten celestial and social bargain. Therefore, those who aspired to stations of prestige were expected to participate in parish life, to assist in the administration of poor relief, and to assume the burdens of public office, in addditon to meeting the more passive civic duties incumbent on all citizens of paying taxes and obeying the law. This was what noblesse oblige was all about in an early modern urban milieu. Such considerations explain the preference for maintaining a low ratio of paid to honorary officeholders. When seen against this backdrop, the necessity of paying people to run the government appeared lamentable proof that civic spirit had succumbed to rampant self-interest. The city was proud that "in Hamburg citizens govern citizens," and this rule of equals seemed commensurate with Hamburg's status as a free republic. Civic harmony appeared more readily attainable when neighbors, fellow parishioners, customers, partners, friends, and perhaps even relatives, portioned out among themselves the tasks of government. Naturally, reality proved less rosy. Still, voluntarism was the ideal and, at least after 1712, Hamburg exhibited an unusual degree of political equilibrium and civic peace widely believed to be based on its ability to traverse a golden middle road between absolutism and mobocracy, avoiding the tyranny of the one and the anarchy of the other.[22]

The Governing Elite

The collegial bodies steadied this delicate balance. The Oberalten formed an elite drawn almost exclusively from prosperous mercantile families. Many enjoyed kinship ties to members of the Rat and were frequently elected into the Rat themselves. From 1528 (when the first Oberalten were chosen) until 1712, the Rat selected 58 Oberalten (of a total of 254) as senators, that is, as members of the Rat. Apparently the Rat had developed its own method of dampening burgher opposition by co-opting prominent opponents. The burghers, understandably angered by the easy defection of their spokesmen, sought to make the Oberalten less cautious in their dealings with the Rat and less susceptible to such "bribery" by having them declared ineligible for selection as senators. And this the Bürgerschaft achieved, if only briefly, during the tumultuous closing decades of the seventeenth century. Peace was restored in the city with the Principal Recess of 1712, which de jure divided sovereignty equally between Rat and Bürgerschaft; however, de facto the Rat's authority went virtually unquestioned. Although the Principal Recess of 1712 made no provision for the exclusion of the Oberalten, after 1720 no Oberalte ever again entered the Rat. Certainly the Rat no longer had to disarm a burgher opposition that was by then defunct. The once suspect collegial bodies had become its allies.[23]

The Oberalten remained powerful, however; their presence in almost every influential governmental deputation was an accepted fact, even though they no longer voiced burgher opposition. Ex officio they sat on fourteen major councils of which at least two, the Deputation for the Admission of Aliens and the council of the General Poor Relief, will be of special concern to us later. In addition, the Oberalten headed evangelical poor relief as trustees of a fifth parish chest (the *Haupt-Kiste,* literally a strongbox stored in the otherwise deserted cloister of St. Marien-Magdalenen), which was to combine the charitable contributions from all four (later five) parishes.[24]

By 1720, then, the *cursus honorum* had split in twain. One branch remained rooted in the parish and culminated in the office of the Oberalte. The other branch terminated in the Rat and had fewer direct ties to the parish. At the time of their election, the Oberalten tended to be considerably older than the senators and they were, as a group, generally more conservative in matters of religion. The Oberalten were almost all merchants or manufacturers, while the Rat consisted of merchants and jurists in about equal proportions. In other ways, however, the two groups differed not at all.[25]

It must be remembered that the number of people active in the major councils of government in Hamburg was very small. A recent estimate suggests that in the late eighteenth century, when Hamburg's population exceeded 100,000 only 300–350 men governed (about 3,000–4,000 were eligible for public office).[26] In the sixteenth and seventeenth centuries, the percentages were probably similar. Still, Hamburg's government was not patrician. Access to citizenship and office was open to newcomers and no legal strictures (except those based on religion) barred even those of the most humble origins from attaining the city's most exalted post of Bürgermeister. This fact did not, of course, prevent power from gravitating to certain places, particularly to prominent mercantile families and, increasingly, with the doctors and licentiates of law as the legal complexities of government multiplied. The Principal Recess of 1712 set quotas of jurists and merchants for some offices. Of the twenty-four senators, half were to be jurists, but three of the four Bürgermeister and all the syndics and secretaries, had to be. In the seventeenth and eighteenth centuries, the nonjurist members of the Rat, almost without exception, came from mercantile backgrounds. Although nothing in municipal law prohibited the elevation of artisans to the Rat, only one, the rich brewer Nicolaus Krull in 1676, ever broke through to that inner circle of power.[27]

In fact the merchant class dominated Hamburg. Besides their numerical superiority among the nonjurist members of the Rat, they controlled practically every other position of influence. For example, of the 185 Oberalten who took office between 1600 and 1725, all but 10 were merchants and merchants enjoyed a similar predominance of numbers in the Sixty and the One Hundred Eighty. In the seventeenth century, more than 700 nonjurists held public office but only 23 were not merchants. The only office in which artisans and tradesmen outnumbered merchants was that of militia captain. The predominant representation of the merchants is partially explained by their wealth, since their assured incomes permitted them to accept obligations that frequently pulled them away from their businesses.[28] Yet it is a bit simplistic to believe that economics alone can explain oligarchic tendencies. The partiality for voluntarism and, thus, the concomitant reliance on the wealthy expressed a widely accepted belief about who was most capable of assessing the needs of the city, of knowing when to uphold tradition and when to abandon it, and of mapping out policies for the future. In the opinion of most contemporaries, there were natural leaders—the merchants and the lawyers—who emerged with astonishing regularity in certain families. And, of course, once the preeminence was established, it was almost impossible to break.[29]

Among the most politically active families were the Anckelmanns, Spreckelsens, Klefekers, Sievekings, Rentzels, Doormanns, and later, the Kellinghusens, Hüdtwalckers, and Westphalens.[30] Two examples, the Anckelmanns and the Rentzels, may serve to illustrate how the tradition of communal service took root and grew. Joachim Anckelmann was an emigrant from Schwäbisch Hall who settled in Hamburg in the fifteenth century. His son, Tolen, a zealous partisan of reformed ideas, was one of the original twelve Oberalten elected in 1528. In the course of the next three centuries, three other Anckelmanns became Oberalten. Yet another, Diedrich (1602–43), actively participated in communal affairs, filling several offices in rapid succession. He, too, seemed destined for greater glories when he died at age forty-one. In addition, five Anckelmanns were elected senators and one became a syndic, while other sons and daughters married into families with members in the Rat and Oberalten. Almost every male Anckelmann assumed some role in communal politics. Although the Anckelmanns were primarily businessmen, in the seventeenth and eighteenth centuries an increasing number of sons studied jurisprudence and at least nine (from 1650 to 1853) were awarded the doctorate or licentiate of law.[31] Before the University of Göttingen was founded in 1737, most of Hamburg's native sons, including the Anckelmanns, studied in Halle. Both institutions enjoyed great prestige as centers of cameralist teaching, and the lawyers educated there were probably responsible for the quite substantial infusion of cameralist thought into government and social policies in eighteenth-century Hamburg.[32]

The Rentzels could also boast of many generations of community service.

Peter Rentzel, the progenitor of the Hamburg Rentzels, served as a senator in the sixteenth century (although he was forced to resign in 1596 because of debts). One son, Hermann (1576–1657), served first as an Oberalte and later as a senator. Three other Rentzels assumed equally influential posts in government: Hermann (son of Hermann, 1612–82) as an Oberalte; Joachim (1694–1768), a licentiate of law; and Eduard (1772–1832), a doctor of jurisprudence—the latter two as senators. Here again, as with the Anckelmanns, we find the staggered generational pattern of merchants and lawyers that characterized many eminent Hamburg lineages and that made them doubly suited to the business of government and doubly eligible for public office. Both the Anckelmanns and the Rentzels represented well-established commercial firms commanding large reserves of capitals and engaging in extensive overseas trade primarily with the Iberian peninsula, and in colonial products. The Rentzels in the seventeenth century ranked among the richest families in Hamburg. When Hermann Rentzel died in 1682, he left a truly princely legacy of 400,000 marks, including a handsome bequest of 76,000 marks to be divided among the *Waisenhaus, Pesthof, Zuchthaus,* and *Spinnhaus*—the last a prison that had been endowed many years earlier by his older brother, Peter.[33]

A Great Confinement?

The institutions Hermann's magnanimity enriched were all founded during the seventeenth century. Contemporaries tended to lump them together under the misleading rubric of poorhouses (*Armenhäuser*). As a group, these represented the totality of Hamburg's experience with what Michel Foucault has labeled "The Great Confinement," that is, the substitution of incarceration for outdoor relief.[34] Hamburg's poorhouses handled those persons the parish could not, or would not, assist and thus supplemented parish relief rather than supplanting it. In other words, the founding of the several poorhouses did not rationalize poor relief but further decentralized it by setting up yet other independent institutions charged with executing a part of social welfare policy that was, however, not always well defined. Confinement promised to solve the vexatious problem of how to put the poor to work, which the parishes had never been able to accomplish. Moreover, parish relief had not swept beggars off Hamburg's streets despite the draconian threats raised against them. Many now looked to internment as the most practical way to deal with mendicants as well.[35]

Interestingly enough, the first such institution built in Hamburg was an orphanage and had little or nothing to do with either penning up beggars or employing paupers. Still, the orphanage's founding articles, while justifying on humanitarian grounds the need for such an institution, advanced a detailed and harsh critique of parish relief as it then existed. As is clear from this document, the orphanage was to spearhead a broader attack on poverty and the social problems associated with it. The most insistently raised complaint was about how the growing number of beggars disrupted municipal peace.

The "foreign rabble" among them, it was argued, might simply be banished from the city (which was easier said than done). Local beggars presented other and more formidable problems closely linked to the demands of the labor market. The statute included a plan for exploiting this previously untapped labor pool. According to this plan, a physical capacity for doing work, and not necessarily "worthiness," became the essential criterion for differentiating between the various groups of the poor and assigning responsibility for them. The "Methuselahs, the invalid, and the very young" counted as lost causes and, except for the young, were thought best relegated to the parish or to one of the hospitals to be "fed to death" (*todgefüttert*). A much more sizable group of "healthy males and females older than ten" presented the best opportunities for converting laboring potential into reality. Although the statute did not actually suggest building a house of industry, it did express a desire for a supervised mobilization of the poor within the parishes. It was argued that the best supervisors would be the deacons and subdeacons, who by virtue of their office knew everyone in their parish and could personally arrange for suitable employment or apprenticeship of adolescent beggars. Clearly, these men were to act in loco parentis, and the success of the project hinged on the personal concern shown by the supervisors for their wards.[36] This nicely paralleled a governmental style that continued to function on a face-to-face basis and was predicated on a close personal relationship between ruler and ruled.

Guild work according to this plan, represented the employment of choice, indicating how strong traditional values and attitudes toward work were and how the small workshop remained the dominant unit of production throughout the seventeenth century. And yet the same paragraphs document a momentous if still embryonic transformation occurring in Hamburg as early manufactories emerged to compete with the guilds. As illustration, the statute turned to the example of an unnamed manufacturer of a sergelike cloth called *Sayen*. This manufacturer reputedly employed more than two hundred persons in the surrounding countryside. The manufacturing of textiles and especially of fabrics fashioned from wool and flax all required scores of workers to complete the many time-consuming steps in the production process. Why, it was queried, could not similar manufactories be set up in Hamburg "with the sole intent of allowing paupers a chance to earn their bit of bread?" Obviously, this involved nurturing enterprises that engaged workers whose lack of skill or whose illegitimate birth disqualified them from guild work. Not accidentally, this scheme would at the same time provide more workers for established manufactories. This was clearly an attempt to eliminate poverty by generating jobs. Exactly how this goal was to be achieved remained unclear. The authors of this document felt that some of the poor might well be trusted to spin or weave on their own, receiving raw materials on commission and then delivering the finished products back to their employers. The "less dependable" would require a taskmaster supervising them to ensure their continued industriousness, to protect equipment from willful or inadvertent damage, and to prevent the misappropriation or theft of raw materials.[37]

Hopes for a supervised mobilization of the poor moved a step closer to fulfillment with the establishment of a workhouse, the Zuchthaus, in 1622. The Hamburger Zuchthaus fits neatly into a European-wide pattern of *enfermement* simultaneously evidenced in the Dutch *tuchthuizen,* the French *hôpitaux généraux,* and the English bridewells. According to Foucault, these institutions were intended to transform superfluous and disruptive groups of social parasites into a "docile and profitable labor force."[38] Bremen and Lübeck in 1613, Hamburg in 1622, and Danzig in 1629 erected the first Zuchthäuser in central Europe. Only much later, toward the end of the century, did other central European cities and territorial states follow their lead.[39] Certainly the geographic proximity of Amsterdam and the presence of many Dutch immigrants after 1567 in part explain the early decision to build a Zuchthaus in Hamburg. Other factors contributed to its longevity as a public institution. In the seventeenth century, Hamburg, not unlike other prosperous cities, attracted people of various backgrounds. Transients looking for work and refugees fleeing war or religious persecution found a haven (if they were Protestant) and sometimes their fortunes in Hamburg. Not surprisingly, the problem of poverty also grew and became more threatening. At the same time, Hamburg with 36,000 inhabitants (in 1600) was already the most populous city in northern Germany and one of the richest in Europe. Hamburg's size and economic vitality had allowed the maintenance of a Zuchthaus even though the expense involved had soon forced many other cities to close the doors of their Zuchthäuser. The first mention of a Zuchthaus in Hamburg was in connection with the reformation of malingerers. The Zuchthaus also represented those early endeavors to reform penal justice, which advocated a turn away from capital and corporal punishments toward imprisonment as a more efficient and humane way of dealing with lawbreakers.[40]

In typical fashion, Hamburg's Zuchthaus fulfilled multiple roles; often these roles appear perplexingly heterogeneous to modern observers, but their apparent inconsistencies did not trouble the people of that time. The Zuchthaus was a house of correction for petty thieves, disobedient wives, unruly offspring, spendthrifts, and others whose actions embarrassed their families. A stay in the Zuchthaus was to improve their behavior while preventing their eventual criminalization. The Zuchthaus also served as a house of industry designed to employ the poor and, simultaneously, to diminish the number of beggars on the streets. The grouping of inmates echoed the several missions of the Zuchthaus "to honor God, to protect the righteous, to frighten those who contemplate evil, and to minister to the poor." House rules divided them into two broad categories, using the standard of *labore nutrior, labore plector.* The first—"I am one who labors for my bread"—referred to the poor, while the second—"I am one who is chastened by work"—referred to the petty thieves and beggars. The first category accommodated those who were no longer able to survive in the outside world as well as those whose "indolent natures" supposedly inclined them to prefer charity and handouts to honest work. The others were the malefactors and "the sturdy, godless, lazy, rude, lewd, disobedient beggars and rogues, the drunkards and beerbellies, male and female" who shamelessly solicited alms. The house rules excluded the aged, the ill, the infirm of limb, and the very young, viewing these as "well deserving of charity" and again designated the Gotteskasten, the orphanage, and the hospitals for their relief.[41]

A physical ability to work was the major criterion restricting, or rather allowing, admission to the Zuchthaus. This guideline soon proved impracticable, however, and was ignored. Soon so many children crowded the Zuchthaus that it was necessary to hire a schoolteacher and a catechist to instruct them. These youngsters were not sent to the orphanage partly because of a reluctance to separate families and partly because the orphanage—itself overcrowded, understaffed, and poorly financed—opposed admitting them especially if their legitimate birth could not be verified. At least at first, the Zuchthaus officials endeavored to provide children with a rudimentary education and some religious instruction. In addition, there was an attempt to teach boys skills useful to them in future careers as artisans while girls were taught to spin and sew so they could be placed as servants in good homes. By the eighteenth century, however, this minimal education and scanty vocational training, like the daily labor supposedly required of all inmates, had practically disappeared. Reportedly almost everyone in the Zuchthaus lived "in idleness and ignorance," that is, poverty and neglect. And this was severely condemned by eighteenth-century poor relief reformers who viewed work and education in tandem as the only panaceas for poverty.[42]

In addition, the Zuchthaus gradually became a final refuge for the elderly and the infirm. The old plague hospital, the Pesthof, suffered from chronic overcrowding, housing in its labyrinth of buildings all of society's castaways; it had no room for more. Most of the other institutions had similarly long since abandoned their original raison d'être as hospitals for lepers and syphilitics, or as hospices for pilgrims and travellers. They now reserved their places for those able to exchange their few worldly possessions or meager savings for a roof over their heads and the promise of a decent burial. Thus, alterations in other institutions forced the Zuchthaus to admit willy-nilly the ill, invalid, senile, and mentally incompetent.[43]

Many paupers voluntarily petitioned for a place in the Zuchthaus. If admitted, they were accorded privileges that beggars and delinquents were not; the greatest of these privileges was the freedom to depart essentially at will. It is true that work was compulsory, but they were paid a wage as well as being fed, lodged, and, if necessary, clothed. They might be granted a leave of absence to visit relatives, attend church, search for other work, or perhaps to take advantage of seasonal employment in the shipping and construction industries. Some families regularly migrated into the Zuchthaus in the fall and out again as warm weather approached; however, beggars received no such dispensations. The beggars who were apprehended were immediately brought before one of the magistrates and, on simple testimony of their captors, summarily sentenced to the Zuchthaus. Initially, the magistrates alone determined the length of their sentence, but later it was standardized at four weeks for a first offense, and then doubled or tripled for recidivists. In the eighteenth century many came to question the efficacy of a four-week, or even an eight-week incarceration. They pointed out that it rewarded rather than punished mendicancy by permitting idle beggars to loaf (*faulenzen*) in the Zuchthaus at the city's expense. Moreover, no rehabilitative program, however fine, could be expected to work in a month or two. Finally, few beggars ever served even a four-week term. Especially in the winter, when the Zuchthaus was often overcrowded with more than a thousand inmates, beggars sentenced one day were often released the next.[44]

The founders of the Zuchthaus had intended it to bustle with industry, prayer, and song. Work was to regulate the daily routine and each person was to be assigned a particular task. Criminals often sawed valuable dyewoods and animal horn, which the Zuchthaus sold at a profit. Unfortunately, because this work demanded a robust constitution, it was suitable only for a few strong men. Both the poor and the beggars, as well as the weaker men and the women, were allotted other jobs including wool-carding, weaving, spinning, reeling silk, and sewing; however, there was never much work done in the Zuchthaus, and only the dyewoods consistently sold well. All cities and states, with few exceptions, quickly discovered that such institutions were bothersome to manage and almost impossible to run profitably. On the one hand, the labor was unskilled, feeble, sick, or intransigent, while on the other, the government had to take care not to pauperize independent artisans by fostering unfair competition. In addition, Zuchthaus products, such as the cloth woven for the garrison in Hamburg, were frequently inferior in quality to those available on the free market and could only be disposed of at a loss if at all. Still, the criticisms eighteenth-century reformers launched at the Zuchthaus did not target its inability to turn a profit, but rather its failure to busy the "idle" hands of the poor and its inefficiency in supplying a pedagogically valuable work experience.[45]

The administration of the Zuchthaus followed the paradigm of voluntarism, harnessing private energy to public benefit. A Large Council of thirteen members—including a Bürgermeister and two senators as patrons plus eight governors and two emeritus governors—made all major decisions. Everyday business fell to a Small Council composed of all the governors, but the senior governor assumed real responsibility for day-to-day affairs. The governors were usually chosen from the One Hundred Eighty and remained in office for ten years. The Zuchthaus administration, unlike the collegial bodies and the deputations, was legally defined as an independent corporation, but like them formed a branch of communal self-government. Of course, an enterprise of such size and diversity could not exist without the support of a large corps of hirelings. The members of this group ranged from the almoner and his wife down to the cooks and scullery maids, including, among others, a schoolmaster, catechist, carpenters, masons, workmasters, and instructors (usually female) in sewing, spinning, and weaving. A huge gulf separated the prestigious voluntary office of governor from the lowly paid positions and, as we have seen, the split rested on considerations other than the obvious ones setting apart all masters and servants, employers and employees.[46]

Civil War and Plague

By the middle of the seventeenth century, almost all elements of what served Hamburg as a social welfare system were in place; though decentralized and poorly coordinated, they functioned adequately under normal circumstances. However, the period from 1680 to 1715 was definitely not normal. In quick succession, a series of pronounced internal crises jeopardized the social order and crippled the economy. On several occasions the imminent threat of foreign intervention reminded the city–state how precarious its independence was and how much its freedom depended on adroitly playing off the competing greed of its enemies. The old yet still festering feud between the Rat and Bürgerschaft repeatedly erupted into open warfare in 1663, 1682–83, and most furiously in the 1690s. The quarrel dated from the Reformation and revolved around the single issue of sovereignty: Did it lie with the Rat, with the Bürgerschaft, or with both indivisibly? As we know, the Rat in fact emerged triumphant by 1712 but this final victory was hardly so self-evident ten years earlier. Any dissension in the city quickly attracted the attention of others, which was by no means altruistic. Hamburg's chronic inability to order its own house prompted the Holy Roman Emperor to intervene as Hamburg's overlord, while Christian V of Denmark sought to exploit whenever possible Hamburg's internecine bickerings. An uprising of burghers in 1682–86, which was led by Cord Jastram and Hieronymous Snitger, encouraged the Danish monarch to attempt reasserting his contested hegemony over the city. Unfortunately for Christian, the plan backfired; as the Danes bombarded Hamburg's outer fortifications, all support in the city for Jastram and Snitger collapsed. Civic peace was restored if all too briefly.[47]

In the 1690s, a religious controversy again turned political life topsy-turvy. The defenders of Lutheran orthodoxy had launched a barrage of pamphlets against those clergymen in the city who flirted with "dangerous Spenerian heresies," that is, with Pietism. The preachers' squabble rapidly became politicized because the Rat tended to be more sympathetic, or less rabidly opposed, to Pietism than the more conservative burghers and ministers thought proper. This was only a pretext for stirring up the still smoldering embers of constitutional conflict. In the years of upheaval that ensued, the burghers wrenched power away from the Rat and tried to rule themselves; consequently, anarchy soon reigned. This turn of events alarmed the imperial resident, Freiherr von Kurzrock. Apprehensive that continued unrest might result in the loss of the city to the Danes, he communicated fear of this possibility in his dispatches to Vienna. Prodded out of his lethargy by Kurzrock's warnings, Joseph I sent troops to quell the disturbances and subsequently empaneled an imperial commission to mediate between the warring factions. It took the commission four years of wearisome negotiations to restore civic order and to reorganize Hamburg's constitution, essentially to everyone's satisfaction.[48] The commission ended more than 150 years of constitutional strife with the promulgation of the Principal Recess of 1712 as Hamburg's "perpetual, immutable, and irrevocable fundamental law," which remained valid and virtually unchanged until 1859. More importantly, it upheld the role of the collegial bodies as intermediaries between Rat and Bürgerschaft and, although it placed sovereignty in the hands of the Rat and Bürgerschaft—"inseparabili nexu conjunctim"—it did not prevent the Rat from attaining a position of almost unchallenged supremacy on most issues that lasted for more than 150 years.[49]

As the constitutional crisis consumed the attention of Hamburg's leaders, another danger loomed. The new foe was biological. Disease, in this case plague, like war, famine, and civil strife, could shake or even topple a social order. Yet such crises could also strengthen the bonds of society and foster bursts of communal initiative. Faced with disaster, communities often mustered enough courage and incentive to jettison administrative procedures that had become calcified with age and to innovate, at least until the danger passed.

Several times in the sixteenth and seventeenth centuries, plague had raged in Hamburg, but never as violently or as protractedly as in 1712–14, when nine to ten thousand people died. Hamburg responded like other early modern polities, quarantining goods and persons, restricting contacts with the outside world, and intensifying its supervision of beggars and transients. Physicians and city fathers were convinced of a link between poverty and epidemic disease, having "learned from experience . . . that such contagions spring from the poor and are spread by wandering rabble." In 1596, the City Physician, Johannes Böckel, warned against beggars who carried the "plague seed," transmitting it to those who "goodheartedly" gave them alms or sheltered them in their homes. The progress of the 1712–14 epidemic produced much additional evidence to support these theories because the most impoverished sections of the city were the first to succumb to plague.[50]

The plague approached slowly, silently stealing its way westward across the continent from the Eurasian heartland. Its slow march led to many months of anxiety yet it also gave the city time to mount its defenses. As early as 1705, the leaders of Hamburg and Altona had conferred on a strategy for dealing with the plague. In 1707, Hamburg issued its first plague degrees, strengthening their effect with each passing month. Hamburg applied standard *cordon sanitaire* measures, requiring travelers to procure health passes, refusing to admit persons or goods from suspicious areas, fumigating letters, bales of cotton, wool, and furs, and tightening the control over those aliens regarded as especially dangerous—singling out the "Polish and other begging Jews." The Rat also created a special Board of Health empowered to coordinate all aspects of fighting the epidemic. The board's members included two senators (one of whom, Garlieb Sillem—the syndic and subsequently Bürgermeister— acted as president), numerous burghers, and the two City Physicians as medical experts. The board was an unusual and unusually forceful body. For the duration of the emergency, it exercised almost dictatorial powers, in many cases circumventing the normal, much slower, channels of government. It implemented all the usual steps to check the plague, placing extra guards at the gates of the city, sealing plague-infested houses, creating temporary plague hospitals, and marshaling teams of nurses and gravediggers. But the board also pioneered new techniques in monitoring and controlling paupers, transients, and strangers.[51]

The plague years severely disrupted trade and industry. Such recessions always struck hardest at those least able to bear the strain, namely, the common laborers and the poor. This was no exception. During the harsh winter of 1712–13, thousands of starvelings swarmed into the city displaced by the ravages of the Great Northern War, aggravating the misery of the indigenous poor by competing with them for jobs, housing, bread, fuel, and charity. The plague's impact on economic life was nearly catastrophic, and the very measures intended to protect the city hamstrung commerce. Since 1707, Hamburg had interdicted all communication with suspicious areas and the city's trading partners quickly retaliated, instituting equally severe countermeasures. For many months no ship entered or departed the port, idling thousands of dock workers and even more thousands whose livelihoods depended on imported raw materials. According to one estimate, by September 1712 about forty thousand people (of a total population of about seventy thousand) were unemployed, and not until the summer of 1714 did the economy rally. These circumstances contributed to widespread impoverishment as well as increasing concerns about the poor;[52] poor relief soon became a pressing part of the business of the Board of Health. The Improved Poor Relief Ordinance of 1711, which provded a temporary centralization of poor relief efforts under the board, was primarily a form of plague prophylaxis. It also prefigured attempts later in the century to wrest poor reflief from parish control, to centralize funds, and to provide an integrated system based on a more rigorous supervision and control of the registered poor, aliens, transients, and mendicants. The board was the first in a line of special commissions having the power to cut through tangles of administrative red tape. It was, in many ways, a bureaucratic Great Leap Forward, yet it also preserved the principle of voluntarism.[53]

In other ways as well the ordinance of 1711 mixed tradition and innovation. It spoke the new language of cameralism, emphasizing that "widespread mendicancy is incompatible with a good police and intolerable in a well-ordered republic" while restating the old admonitions against begging and almsgiving. Furthermore, the ordinance differentiated between the various groups of the poor, which was in itself no novelty. Still, when combined with more methodical means of surveillance, supervision, and investigation, this careful sorting of the poor promised to combat the "problem of poverty" more forcefully. Poor relief was no longer to be passive and neutral, but instead active and judgmental. The very real dangers threatening the city appeared to justify the energy and money expended on a detailed inquiry concerning the poor as individuals and as a group. The board forbade innkeepers and tavern owners to lodge anyone who could not produce a valid health pass and ordered the militia captains to canvas house-to-house for unreported plague cases. In addition, each captain was also to mount a general visitation of his company (each parish was divided into several companies) to count "the number of honest Christian poor or rogues and sturdy beggars" and ascertain where they lived and with whom. The militia colonel then was to compile a master list to be forwarded to the board. Thus, the municipality embarked on an active campaign to ferret out and register the poor.[54] Previously only beggars had been the objects of such aggressive measures. Now poverty itself could no longer be safely regarded as a personal, parish, or even a Christian matter, involving a relatively private arrangement between an individual petitioner and a near and familiar benefactor. Under the threat of plague, poverty rapidly became an issue of state and a matter of public record, which was closely tied in theory and practice to the expansion of governmental competencies overall and especially linked to the use of statistics as a tool of government—although these were still inchoate tendencies in the early eighteenth century.

The ordinance of 1711 also improved the financing of poor relief. The expense of ministering to the sick and assisting the needy was great and, although much was given to charity, it never seemed enough. Because "Honoratioren" (notables) managed the city, Hamburg's government preferred to depend on private beneficence to support charity rather than on tax moneys. Unfortunately, private charity was notoriously unpredictable. Precisely when misery was greatest, during economic recession, pestilence, famine, civil war, or invasion, people had less to give. Income from church collections varied enormously and thus making it next to impossible to budget resources realistically. Individual generosity ebbed and flowed with events (e.g., a particularly stirring sermon or the happy resolution of a family crisis), which did not necessarily correspond to the degree of deprivation in the city. Special collections to assist the poor during severe weather or to aid the survivors of disasters sometimes overcame these bottlenecks but did not obviate the need for more reliable ways of funding poor relief. The 1711 ordinance initiated a subscription whereby representatives of the board of health visited each house carrying special ledgers in which they recorded pledges. It was certainly more difficult to refuse a neighbor and a fellow citizen than simply to avoid slipping a coin or two into the collection plate or poor box. The idea behind the subscription sought to centralize funds and to ensure a more rational allotment of these moneys through an agency—the board of health—cognizant as it was supposed to be of the real needs of paupers.[55]

The extraordinary circumstances engendered by civil war and plague had perhaps lessened the pain of experimentation. Once the dangers had subsided, however, energy became sloth and generosity niggardliness. The threat of plague receded in early 1714 while the economic recession continued. Thus, the financial commitment required to maintain a board of health seemed indefensibly great and the board was dissolved in 1714. With it vanished most of the innovations in poor relief if not the sometimes exaggerated memory of their successes. The administration of poor relief was again decentralized, involving the Gotteskasten, the magistrates, and the almshouses. However, the board did not disappear without a final flurry of activity. During its last days, the board's president, Garlieb Sillem, drafted a proposal for a permanent improvement of Hamburg's poor relief. He based his plan on the ordinance of 1711 and on the precedents set by the board, incorporating his own ideas of how to employ the poor. In preparation for the reform that never happened (at least not in his lifetime), Sillem and his colleagues personally interviewed all the registered poor to ascertain what they lacked and what work they might reasonably be expected to do.[56] It is not clear why Sillem's proposal was tabled. Undoubtedly the expense of the project frightened many. Some felt that once the economy recovered, poverty would disappear or dwindle to a point where the existing institutions could adequately cope with it. The presumption that alms and make-work projects only sanctioned lives of "indolence and frivolity" always created opposition to efforts like the one Sillem sponsored. The board of health was gone, but not forgotten, and it would be one of the models to which reformers turned when poor relief approached a major crisis in the 1770s and 1780s.

One of the major flaws of poor relief after 1715 was a decentralization that established no firm jurisdictional boundaries, pursued no clear goals, and enjoyed no reliable source of funding. These very same difficulties troubled Hamburg's government. Yet, on the other hand, diffusion of authority allowed a more personalized style in government and considerably more flexibility in the execution of policy. It was an arrangement that worked well as long as the city was relatively small and compact. In the previous pages, we have traced the erratic development of poor relief in Hamburg, observing just how often new institutions, ad hoc methods, and temporary expedients compensated for deficiencies while never violating the sacrosanct tradition of voluntarism and only occasionally straying from a pattern of decentralization. Nothing clearly separated the various agents of relief from one another and there was, from the perspective of the reformers of the 1780s, no foolproof way to discourage the poor from soliciting and receiving alms from several sources at once. The close personal contacts between men who faced each other daily in a variety of public and private circumstances was presumed adequate to mitigate disputes. Moreover, the Rat saw itself as the ultimate mediator able to resolve any serious jurisdictional altercations.

The Rat also possessed a formal means of supervision. Two members of the Rat—the praetors (*Präturen*) or magistrates—assumed a more direct control over some important branches of poor relief.[57] All poorhouses were under their personal surveillance and the praetors often worked parallel to normal channels of relief, disbursing discretionary funds to aid the poor in any number of ways. They might, for instance, arrange free lying-in for a needy expectant mother or finance a pauper's funeral.[58] Thus, the praetors to some extent informally coordinated the disparate areas of social policy and represented most clearly the avuncular side of Hamburg's government. Other attempts to open up better lines of communication, to circumscribe more narrowly the duties of each institution, or to draw less ambiguous rules on procedures, were not truly successful until 1788.

Despite these problems, many admired Hamburg for the richness of its charity. A late seventeenth-century English atlas reported that "hardly any great city in Europe . . . can shew more public hospitals, and larger allowances for the maintenance of the miserable, than this town."[59] And so it was. In the opening decades of the eighteenth century, Hamburg possessed an enviable range of social welfare institutions and the amount of money expended on charity was vast. Most importantly, the entire panoply of institutions functioned reasonably well except in crisis situations. Since the Reformation, Hamburg's government had settled into a similar pattern of decentralization and voluntarism, which proved satisfactory for a city still knowable and therefore governable by individuals. This older style of paternalism, which was based on an essentially immediate relationship between ruler and ruled, held on tenaciously throughout the eighteenth century. But it was fighting a rearguard action.

Hamburg changed drastically in the eighteenth century; its population rose to more than one hundred thousand and changed in composition. At the same time, the decay of the artisanal trades, the shift in manufacturing, and the rising dominance of international trade recast the economic bases of the city. In turn, these alterations disrupted the labor market, unsettling or destroying traditional patterns of employment. Hamburg's voluntarist government still operated, but ever more slowly and the burdens on many officeholders became crushing. In fundamental ways, the city's government had lost sight of, and therefore control over, much of its population. Some recognized what was happening and responded with piecemeal measures to tighten up methods of monitoring and control, often seeking statistical solutions to complex social problems. But the principle of voluntarism remained a constant. Indeed, poor relief reform in the 1770s and 1780s aspired to improve poor relief by reviving civic spirit. The reformers upheld the venerable tradition of voluntarism, holding open Pandora's box while all the evils of modernity escaped.

We must now look at the eighteenth century to see how Hamburg was metamorphosed by the same socioeconomic trends that were reshaping Europe. Even more important, we must try to understand what contemporaries thought of these portentous changes in their world and how they struggled to master them.

2

A German Amsterdam

Hamburg in the eighteenth century witnessed a period of political quiescence and economic ferment. In the hundred years after 1715, Hamburg experienced alternating waves of great prosperity and deep depression as the city groped for its place in an immature and still highly unstable world economy. Underneath the surface of civil peace ran forces of economic change that transformed the urban environment, ruptured older social bonds, and, in the next century, upended the traditional political balance. By the 1770s, Hamburg had become a principal trade entrepôt in northern Europe, engaging in extensive overseas commerce on a scale unimagined fifty years earlier. It had over the decades shed much though certainly not all of its former character as an artisanal and manufacturing center. The city grew, population diversified, prices rose precipitously, cheap housing became scarce, established government practices staggered under the strain of new tasks, and shifts in the labor market caused bouts of unemployment and worrisome if still rather muted rumblings of labor unrest. Not the least salient feature of the new Hamburg was the presence of a large, mobile, economically indispensable class of the working poor. These mostly nonguilded workers inhabited the fragile economic ground between subsistence and destitution and their very existence denoted a major shift in the labor structure that forced a rethinking of social policies. This latter trend was especially pronounced in the last third of the century.

The Preeminence of Commerce

Hamburg has always been sustained by commerce. As early as the sixteenth century, the city enjoyed a European-wide reputation as the "florentissimum Emporium totius Germaniae."[1] By the eighteenth century Hamburg's commercial ties spanned the globe. In particular, its trade with the Netherlands, Italy, England, and the Iberian peninsula made the city and its merchant bankers the envy of all Europe. Hamburg had already become the grain transshipping center of northern Europe; this position was further consolidated in the nineteenth century. Equally important for Hamburg's economic growth was the fall of Antwerp in 1564, which drove the first wave of Dutch refugees to Hamburg where the Rat allowed them to settle under favorable economic circumstances. The Lutherans among them rapidly achieved positions of power within communal government. The Dutch brought with them a sizable share of Antwerp's trade, but also contributed much to Hamburg's commerce, industry, technology, art, and social policies. For example, it was these new residents who formed the first insurance companies in Hamburg. Germany's first stock exchange (and the fourth in Europe) was founded in Hamburg in 1558 on the Antwerp model. The Dutch immigrants taught Hamburg's inhabitants how to fashion new fabrics from silk and wool (thereby spawning Hamburg's first textile industry), how to draw out the fine threads of gold and silver for brocades, and probably also imparted the profitable secret of refining sugar.[2]

Another legacy of the Dutch was the rise of investment banking, which paved the way for the founding of the Hamburg Bank in 1619. The bank acted as a clearing house and helped Hamburg avoid the worst of the widespread currency devaluation that rocked northern Europe in the first quarter of the seventeenth century. Just as central to the economic life of the city was the creation in 1665 of the Hamburg Chamber of Commerce (*Commerz-Deputation*). The Chamber of Commerce represented the merchant-bankers in politics, keeping abreast of commercial trends, informing the Rat of its observations, and making its wishes known. Though technically only an advisory body, the Chamber of Commerce functioned as a powerful lobby.[3]

During the first half of the seventeenth century, the Netherlands, followed by Spain and Portugal, were Hamburg's most valuable trading partners. At the same time, however, Hamburg was forging new commercial ties to France. These connections flourished in the period after the Thirty Years' War when the Barbary pirates impeded trade with the Mediterranean littoral and the Iberian peninsula. France soon became, and remained throughout the eighteenth century, Hamburg's foremost trade associate. Through Hamburg France shipped wine, sugarcane, vinegar, salt, fruits, colonial wares such as indigo (which also found a market in Hamburg because the dye was essential to the calico printing industry), and manufactured articles such as paper, silk, glass, and fine stockings. Through Hamburg France received grain, wood, metals, and natural products especially beeswax, meat, and furs. Most of the goods destined for France came from Russia, Scandinavia, and the Baltic Increasingly, Hamburg was able to satisfy a large part of the European appetite for textiles, velvets, silk, spices, sugar, and popular luxury items like coffee, tea, chocolate, and tobacco. Continental merchandise such as linen from Silesia and Westphalia, metal implements from Saxony and Bohemia, wood and grain from Brandenburg, flowed through Hamburg en route to markets in western Europe, England, and the New World.[4]

By the eighteenth century, Hamburg had become firmly locked into a global trade network and thus suffered through the cycles of economic crisis and recovery that typified this pubescent yet precocious world economy. In eighteenth-century Hamburg there were periods of great opulence and also some of the darkest days in its economic chronicle. The recessions of 1720 and 1793 were brief and, a buoyant economy quickly rebounded. The crises of

1763 and 1799, however, marked the advent of long and deep depressions from which it took years to regain lost ground. Moreover, the specter of inflation haunted the last three decades of the century.[5]

During the Seven Years' War, Hamburg thrived as perhaps never before. However, the end of the war and the European-wide depression that soon followed severely disrupted trade. The crisis of 1763 also resulted from irresponsible speculation and bill discounting (a perennial problem in eighteenth-century Hamburg) that triggered at least ninety-seven bankruptcies in the city. Throughout the 1760s, 1770s, and into the 1780s, Hamburg struggled to overcome the aggressive mercantilist policies of the surrounding states, especially those of Frederician Prussia. So menacing was the economic threat posed by depression and shrinking markets that Hamburg's elites began to discuss among themselves not only various measures to revitalize the ailing economy but also the irksomely persistent problem of poverty. Solutions that they proposed will be discussed later.[6]

Growth resumed in the late 1770s, although slowly and accompanied by an inflation that reduced the real wages of workers. The rise in prices that began in the 1770s (and that was most acute during the French occupation from 1806 to 1814) continued throughout the *Vormärz*. Staple prices (e.g., of bread, potatoes, butter, milk) more than doubled between 1792 and 1800 while rents tripled. In the 1780s as commerce accelerated, inflation more than kept pace. By the 1790s, as Hamburg was swept along in the wake of an unprecedented economic surge, the pressure of rising prices still created hardships for wage earners and the marginally employed.[7] Several events combined to catapult Hamburg into the economic limelight: the gradual disappearance of the Dutch as commercial rivals (culminating in the fall of Amsterdam in 1795), the favorable trade agreement concluded with the French in 1769, the continued hunger for colonial products in Europe, England's new status as a grain importer (Hamburg was a major intermediary in the east–west grain trade), and the profitable commercial links formed with the infant American republic after 1783. At first Hamburg was only to benefit from the turmoil unleashed by the revolutionary wars.[8]

Much of this expansion rested on solid foundations, but the same sort of commercial euphoria that led firms like Voght and Sieveking to extend themselves into world trade successfully, "bring[ing] coffee from Mocha, tobacco from Baltimore, cacao from Surinam and rubber from Africa," drew the less adroit, or less lucky into economic disaster. A frenzy of building and a flurry of dubious investments attended the economic boom. Speculation in goods and futures became volatile. Merchants stockpiled and gambled on later profits. But the severe winter of 1798–99 put their dreams of untold wealth on ice. The port closed down for months, idling forty to forty-five thousand navvies, stevedores, teamsters, lightermen, and others who lived directly from the harbor. Prices plummeted and the speculative fortunes constructed on shaky credit crumbled, ruining 152 firms; the speculators often dragging down with them some of the oldest and most respected houses in Hamburg. The economy rallied from 1800 to 1803. The renewed English blockade of the Elbe in 1803, the occupation of the city in 1806, and the imposition of the Continential System in 1807 gradually but inexorably devastated Hamburg's commerce. Many firms fled the city or established branches in other places (especially St. Petersburg), returning, if at all, only after Hamburg's liberation in 1814.[9]

In this environment, politics had to reflect the needs and affairs of business, with particular sensitivity to the vicissitudes of commerce. The Rat, the merchant-bankers, and the Chamber of Commerce all embraced the doctrine of free trade, which certainly benefited commerce and the industries that manufactured for export but also undoubtedly harmed the guilds and those who produced solely for domestic consumption. These producers suffered the most from the high price of food and other necessities that free-trade policies entailed. The problem of how to protect the guilds and simultaneously foster free trade led to a peculiar duality in Hamburg's economic policies, which did not trouble smaller towns. Free-trade policies fed the disgruntlement of guildsmen who were alternately protected and then exposed to foreign competition. Particularly in the eighteenth century, this issue assumed another dimension as the guilded trades could no longer supply the demands of a swelling population. Indeed, the number of nonguilded artisans multiplied partly because the Rat did not strictly enforce policies governing their activities.[10]

Guilds and Guildsmen

Only in the tumultuous period from 1680 to 1710 had Hamburg's guilds exercised much political influence. In the eighteenth century, artisans were poorly represented in the collegial bodies and deputations and their economic position was being irreversibly eroded by the rising power of new branches of manufacturing. One contemporary observer noted that "although the number of guilds [in Hamburg] is considerable, their importance [is] minimal."[11] This decline in the economic significance of the guilds forms a crucial part in the story of how Hamburg's economy changed in the eighteenth century.

To comprehend these events, we must first see how the guilds were organized. Most artisans belonged to one of several associations: the *Ämter,* the *Brüderschaften,* or a third group that had no particular name.[12] The Ämter, the oldest of the three associations, included the barbers and barber-surgeons, glovers, wooden bucket makers, coopers, bookbinders, furriers (two different Ämter), lathe turners, fish salters, white-bread bakers, fishermen, goldsmiths, glaziers, knitters of coarse stockings, house carpenters, hatters, grocers, one sort of butchers, tin founders and pewterers, brass casters, candle makers, tanners, linen weavers, tinsmiths, confectioners, masons, clothiers producing Brandenburg cloth, house painters, needle makers, trimmers, harness markers, rope plaiters, tailors, shoemakers, bung and spigot makers, farriers and locksmiths, saddlers, ships' carpenters, swordsmiths, potters, cabinetmakers or joiners, and cloth finishers. In the sixteenth century, the Brüderschaften joined guildsmen from other cities whose trade was not acknowledged as guilded in Hamburg. At first persecuted, then tolerated, they eventually won the right to form their own organizations. By the eighteenth century, no concrete advantages elevated the Ämter over the Brüderschaften. Both were equally privileged and enjoyed (at least on paper) trade monopolies guaranteed by municipal law. In the Brüderschaften could be found sailors, brewers, brewers' assistants, weavers (of velvet, velveteen, and silk), groats bakers, dark bread bakers, "house" butchers, crane workers, pocketwatch makers, basket weavers, tanners, shepherds, wheelwrights and cartwrights, Spanish needle makers, another group of butchers, quarrymen, and pavers. The last unnamed group of guilded handworkers included carters, pinmakers, coppersmiths, dyers, silk spoolers, spursmiths, stonecutters, and wine coopers. Sone artisans were designated "free artists" (*freie Künstler*). These formed a heterogeneous and unorganized group of printers, engravers, painters and draftsmen, piano and harpsichord builders, gold and silver thread makers, jewelers, sculptors, mirror polishers, gold platers, paperhangers and upholsterers, brushbinders, chimney sweeps, distillers, starch and powder makers, yeast preparers, knife and scissors grinders, truss makers, chocolatiers, cleaners, bellrope makers, enamelers, music note printers, and dentists.[13]

The Règlement promulgated in 1710—intended to squelch the "excesses" of the guilds during the civil strife of the late seventeenth century—continued to regulate guild life for the next 150 years. It prohibited the formation of more Ämter and Brüderschaften while promising existing guilds official protection. The Règlement also decreed that all guild members must acquire citizenship. Despite this complicated and seemingly rigidly structured guild framework, Hamburg had by no means a closed economy. In the seventeenth century, and even more markedly in the eighteenth, it became evident that the guilds were often unable to fulfill the requirements of the home market. Even the Règlement had acknowledged this predicament by permitting some journeymen to practice as "free masters" (*Freimeister*) upon producing their indentures, after paying a fee to the relevant guild, and upon becoming citizens. Freimeister were prohibited from employing journeymen or apprentices.[14] Especially in the eighteenth century, the number of Freimeister multiplied rapidly. Near the end of the century, for example, 103 master smiths belong to the guild of smiths and farriers. In addition, however, between 1796 and 1808 about 62 Freimeister had won permission to ply their trade, which meant that at least one third, and probably far more, of all smiths in Hamburg were not guild members;[15] this ratio reflect the situation in many other guilds as well.

In addition to the Freimeister, whom the guilds grudgingly endured, Hamburg harbored a large population of other artisans known as "ground rabbits" (*Bönhasen*) who led an independent, illegal, and vulnerable existence. In the seventeenth century, as guild mastership became increasingly difficult and expensive to attain and as the city's population soared, the rabbits increased their numbers dramatically, breeding prolifically in the tailoring, shoemaking, and linenweaving crafts. Demand for the products of these trades was great and the tools were inexpensive to procure and easy to transport, quickly if need be. The guilds, of course, complained incessantly about the ground rabbits, and did everything in their power to eliminate their competition. In the seventeenth century, the guildsmen, especially the journeymen and apprentices, hunted the rabbits mercilessly, hounding them in their dwellings and workplaces, insulting, even fondling their wives and daughters on the streets, brutally attacking them and destroying their property in outbursts of self-righteous fury. The Règlement proscribed such behavior in strong terms, defining when, where, and how the rabbits might be pursued. These restraints prevented the guilds from exercising a sort of vigilante justice and allowed the proliferation of the ground rabbits to the point where they became a permanent feature of Hamburg's economy; flushed out only occasionally and often only pro forma. Guildsmen themselves often hired ground rabbits when they required extra workers. The Règlement, as well as the Rat, expressed more anxiety over the possible excesses of the guilds than over the putative damage done by the ground rabbits in undermining the guilds' prerogatives.[16]

Clearly the ground rabbits rarely lacked employment, although their lives could be made wretched by the guildsmen and their livelihoods were unsure at best. The Règlement forbade the inhabitants of the city (with the exception of the almshouses, hospitals, and other charitable foundations) to patronize nonguilded labor, or to purchase goods from ground rabbits. That stricture stopped few, especially as the municipal government was relatively lax about investigating abuses and imposing fines. The ground rabbits worked cheaply and were most popular among the lower classes. Because they often resided outside the city proper—many in the suburb of St. Georg—each guild sought to prevent their wares from entering Hamburg illegally by stationing its own gatekeeper to search for contraband goods clandestinely being carried into the city. This did not deter the ground rabbits, nor did it effectively hinder the residents of Hamburg from purchasing the cheaper articles fabricated in Altona, Ottensen, Wandsbek, and Bergedorf.[17]

Despite the competition of the Freimeister and ground rabbits, as well as the free-trade stance of the Rat, many guilds held their own throughout the eighteenth century. Not unexpectedly, bakers and butchers conducted a brisk business in a city with an expanding population, while carpenters and masons profited from the construction boom of the late 1700s. Other guilds succumbed to changes in fashion or to the tough new competition resulting from freer trade. The decline in the numbers of Brandenburg clothiers from 400 looms in 1700 to only 10 at the end of the century provides a dramatic illustration of how shifting styles could devastate old occupations. Similarly, as velvet and silk garments disappeared in the wake of the great calico craze of the eighteenth century, these once thriving guilds atrophied. In 1700 there were 300 silk spoolers in Hamburg; in 1810–11 there were only 3. The whole trade had suffered not only from changing tastes but also from the importation of lower priced and higher quality silk from France. Hatters, haberdashers, and stocking knitters could not compete with the imports from France, England, the Brabant, and from other parts of central Europe that poured into Hamburg in the late eighteenth century as the city developed into an open market unrivaled anywhere in northern Europe.[18]

The guilds that retained their economic viability were in general those most closely wedded to commerce or construction. Still numerous and prosperous until the end of the century were the coopers, lathe turners (for furniture), glaziers, smiths and locksmiths, house carpenters (even in the crisis-laden years of the French occupation, there was employment for 27 masters, 160 journeymen, and about 200 foreign journeymen, while in the 1790s the number of foreign journeymen had fluctuated between 500 and 600), masons (39 masters, 329 journeymen, 23 apprentices, and 93 foreign journeymen in 1811, while during the 1790s there were usually 700 foreign journeymen in Hamburg), house painters, ropemakers (during the 1790s there were only 14 masters, but each engaged between 50 and 60 journeymen as well as a large number of day laborers), ships' carpenters (there were 13 guild masters and 152 journeymen in 1810–11, and more than 180 foreign journeymen had worked in the city in the 1790s), and cabinetmakers and joiners (in 1810–11 there were 190 guild masters, 174 free masters, 102 journeymen, and 108 apprentices, but during the 1790s an additional 150 to 200 persons were employed). Some guilds that produced exclusively for export—the furriers and goldsmiths, for example—also did very well in the booming 1790s.[19]

The tailor and shoemaker guilds were the largest and poorest, because these trades had always nourished the greatest number of Freimeister and ground rabbits. In 1810–11, for the 158 master tailors there were also 350 Freimeister, 400 to 450 journeymen, and hundreds of others, including ground rabbits and seamstresses, who eked out a miserable living. Much the same was true for the shoemakers. In 1810–11 the guild rolls carried 200 masters, 320 journeymen, and 40 apprentices. Contemporary estimates added "and innumerable ground rabbits."[20]

Thus, it is not correct to see a state of unrelieved decline in Hamburg's guilds in the late eighteenth century. Some guilds vanished almost overnight while others—those most intimately tied to commerce—flourished and faltered with the inevitable oscillations of trade. Yet the labor structure had changed, incorporating ever more Freimeister and ground rabbits as perennial features of Hamburg's economic life. These formed an army of transient, or semitransient workers whose labor proved indispensable in normal times, but whose presence became undesirable whenever the economy lagged. The genesis of this class reflects with remarkable fidelity previous developments in late medieval and early modern textile centers and the later growth of an industrial laboring class in the nineteenth century.

Manufacturing Workers, Domestic Servants, and Casual Laborers

The growth of three major industries in Hamburg added to the number of wage earners whose fortunes rose and fell synchronously with the expansion and contraction of commerce. In the 1600s, two industries—calico printing and sugar refining—had appeared in Hamburg for the first time and rapidly developed into major producers for the export market. In the eighteenth century, they were joined by tobacco processing. These industries alone sustained many thousands. Semiskilled or unskilled, often poorly paid, and protected by no guilds, workers in these industries (along with the Freimeister, the members of the poorest guilds, the ground rabbits, and the casual laborers) comprised a major part of the working poor in eighteenth-century Hamburg.[21]

Calico was the dernier cri of the eighteenth century.[22] Everywhere one saw maidservants and their mistresses garbed in the bright, crisp fabric, and chintz-upholstered furniture decorated even modest homes. In the seventeenth century the finished cloth had been imported from India. Europeans, however, soon discovered for themselves the secret of printing calico cloth and by the middle of the century calico was a well-established industry in France. Huguenot merchants—driven out of France as much by the royal decree of October 1686 prohibiting calico printing as by the revocation of the Edict of Nantes—settled in Hamburg (and also in Geneva, Basel, Frankfurt, Amsterdam, and London) bearing their trade secrets with them. In the 1700s, Hamburg's printing shops turned out between fourteen and seventeen and a half million yards of calico annually. In the late seventeenth and early eighteenth century, Hamburg purchased raw cotton from the English and the Dutch, who brought it from Asia.[23] Calico printing in these years was still not a large-scale industry. Johann Georg Büsch compared the cheapness of calico in the late eighteenth century to the more expensive calico he had known as a boy. He remembered that then "calico was a luxury . . . and only the wealthiest ladies had frocks made of it."[24] Although calico printing was introduced into Hamburg sometime before 1690, the first major workshop dated from about 1730. Between 1730 and 1758, seventeen new print shops were established. By 1784, there were eighteen in Hamburg, eight in the countryside surrounding the city, and another six in neighboring Danish territories working largely on commission from Hamburg merchants. From 1790 to 1797, Hamburg's calico industry experienced its greatest period of prosperity, rolling out between five and six hundred thousand pieces of printed cloth each year.[25]

Calico printing was to some extent a seasonal industry, in that ice on the large dyeing vats could suspend work until a thaw set in. The severe winter of 1798–99 slowed production to a crawl. Many workshops closed down entirely, laying off their workers while waiting for a break in the weather. Some never reopened. The return of a sort of normalcy in 1801–2 and for part of 1803 allowed business to pick up again. Yet the revival was short-lived, lasting only until the effects of the renewed blockade of the Elbe took hold. Necessary materials, such as bituminous coal and dyestuffs, became scarce and very expensive before disappearing entirely from the market. Still, even after the imposition of the Continental System, the calico printers managed to survive for a while by drawing cloth and raw materials from Saxony and Denmark; however, they fought a losing battle. In 1811, the Chamber of Commerce reported that in the calico industry, "no work is being done" ("es wird nicht mehr gearbeitet!").[26]

Some calico merchants amassed vast wealth and the power and influence that accompanied it. Among the largest calico printers we find prominent Hamburg families, as represented, for example, in the firm of Nicolas and J. W. Burmester.[27] A brief look at the establishment of the brothers Hermann and Gabriel von Rahusen (a Mennonite family that originally came from Antwerp) suggests how lucrative the trade in calico could be. Their workshops dated from sometime in the late 1730s or early 1740s. In 1749, they contracted with an Augsburg textile manufacturer named Johann Heinrich Schülte to print his cloth. This first contract netted the von Rahusens more than 175,000 gulden.[28] Such deals were typical in the calico printing industry. Merchants imported the cloth, then arranged with printers to have it worked up according to specifications. Many Hamburg merchants also put out their cloth for finishing to a calico penciling shop in Altona that employed 93 workers and produced 10,000 pieces of calico in 1786.[29] The size of the printing works varied. We have some idea about how many employees the von Rahusens or Burmesters required in their enterprises, as well as a rough approximation of how big the shops tended to be. Of the 27 printeries active in 1797, one had 70 "tables" (for each table, there was a printer and a helper, plus an additional assistant for every 4 tables) and about 157 to 158 workers, 3 operated with 60 tables, 3 with 55, 2 with 50, 5 with 45, 4 with 35, 1 with 30, 3 with 25, 2 with 20, and 1 with 15 tables. A shop, therefore, might average anywhere from 34 to 160 printers, plus any number of *Schildermädchen,* the young women who penciled dyes onto designs traced on the cloth. In addition, there were 24 *Gelb-Druckereien,* which only printed patterns in yellow. Each of these had 8 tables and about 18 workers. Using this crude measure, Jonas Ludwig von Heß calculated that about 3,000 workers were normally employed in calico printing. If one counts the Schildermädchen and all those engaged in such auxiliary industries as cotton beating and bleaching, then the number of persons whose livelihood was tied to calico printing in Hamburg must have totaled about 5,500 to 5,600. All depended on the unabated success of an export industry.[30]

The importance of sugar refining, however, far exceeded that of calico printing. Apart from commerce itself, the sugar refineries were the biggest employers in the city. With the importation of large quantities of sugarcane to Europe from Madeira, St. Tomé, the Canary Islands, the French West Indies, and Mexico, sugar refining had become a widespread European industry. Refineries were established early in the sixteenth century in the ports of Seville, Antwerp, and Lisbon. Emigrants, fleeing the troubles at Antwerp (1566–86), settled in Amsterdam and Hamburg, bringing with them the skill of sugar refining. Hamburg's first refinery dated from 1585. By 1700 Hamburg's sugar, in the forms of sugar loaves, "hats," candies, and "English" lump sugar, had conquered northern European markets. Consumers in Scandinavia, around the Baltic, in Russia, in France, and throughout central Europe prized Hamburg's sugar for its purity, taste, and price. With the eighteenth century came the heyday of Hamburg's refining industry, which was caused by the fortuitous conjunction of two events: the colonial success of the French West Indies and the growing demand for sugar throughout Europe to sweeten the once exotic beverages of coffee, tea, and chocolate. In 1750 there were 365 refineries in Hamburg; by 1807 they had increased to 428.[31].

In the 1790s, just before the outbreak of the War of the Second Coalition, Hamburg imported 80 million *Pfund* (weighing a little more than an English pound) of raw sugar each year from the French colonies, principally through the ports of Bordeaux, Nantes, and Le Havre. Hamburg exported 8 million Pfund of refined sugar to St. Petersburg alone.[32] The amount of money and corresponding business generated by sugar refining was enormous. Besides the profit to the importer on the sale of cane sugar to refiners, and to the refiner himself, the industry created jobs for thousands in the refineries and for hundreds more in transporting the raw materials and refined products. Wages alone totaled more than 175,000 marks each year. There was also a factory solely engaged in the manufacture of the characteristic blue paper used to wrap sugar. The refiners spent about 300,000 marks for coals, and another 680,000 for tinder, oxblood (a vital ingredient in the refining process), paper, twine, and quicklime. Another 15,000,000 marks of capital was invested in 40,000 crates and barrels. Toward the end of the century, therefore, a total capital investment of 32,800,000 marks yielded some 3,391,500 marks annually in profits, fees, and wages.[33]

Sugar refining was big business, but individual refineries were small. Sugar refining remained for the most part an enterprise that was family owned and operated, each refinery rarely exceeding a maximum of five workers. Many refiners, especially those that produced syrup or candies, made do with fewer hands. Yet despite the modest size of individual refineries, the total number of workers was large, between 15,000 and 16,000 in the 1790s. Of these, 7,000 to 8,000 were engaged in the actual refining process. Even in the harsh years under the French yoke, about 5,000 persons continued to be involved directly in refining and the industry must have supported almost 8,000 people.[34] Refiners thrived as well, often amassing enviable fortunes. Among the wealthier refiners, we find some of the most respected Hamburg families. The Amsincks had built their fortune in refining. Claes Bartels, one of the most venerated of the Oberalten and a prominent figure in poor relief reform in 1780s, was a refiner by trade. So, too, originally were the Nothnagels, the Jencquels, the Kellinghusens, and the Pehmöllers—families all distinguished by service to the commune in various capacities.[35]

Sugar refining was a highly competitive, capital-intensive industry. Production secrets were closely and jealously guarded.[36] In the seventeenth century, Hamburg had successfully competed with the Dutch for markets. By the eighteenth century, the Austrians, Russians, Prussians, Danes, Norwegians, and Swedes were constructing their own refineries. Still, because of the superiority of Hamburg's sugar, this rivalry initially cost Hamburg little. The mercantilist policies adopted by many European states after mid-century hurt more, as did the general depression that struck all branches of Hamburg's economy after 1763. Fluctuations in sugar prices clearly reflected the economic roller-coaster: an era of prosperity during the Seven Years' War; the postwar depression; the boom of the 1790s; and the post-1799 economic debacle.[37]

Hamburg's refining industry suffered most from the economic barriers erected by Prussia. In 1751, Frederick II closed Prussia's borders to foreign sugar and in 1760 granted one "Herr Splittgerber" a sugar monopoly. This cut into Hamburg's export trade, but since sugar was 15 to 20 percent more expensive in Prussia than in Hamburg, it was smuggled into Prussia in vast quantities, dulling the impact of the ban and undercutting the monopoly. By 1789 the Splittgerber concern had failed. In 1760, the Habsburgs awarded a refining monopoly to the Dutch Fiumer Company, which by 1787 was operating two refineries. Austria collected a 30 percent import duty on foreign sugar and, in 1787, stopped its importation into the Bohemian lands altogether. This too damaged, but hardly destroyed, Hamburg's trade with central Europe in refined sugar. When Joseph II lifted the embargo and reduced the tariff, Hamburg flooded Austrian and Bohemian markets with its products. Much the same story can be told about the trade with Russia. Early in the eighteenth century, Peter the Great had established a refinery (typically employing Dutch *suykerbakkers*). Sugar from Hamburg remained incomparably better than that from Russia. In the late eighteenth century, Russia began to protect its own infant refining industry by imposing in 1797 a 7 percent duty on all imported sugar. Since Hamburg's sugar cost about 20 to 25 percent less than Russian sugar, the 7 percent impost did little to deter Russians from purchasing the superior and still cheaper Hamburg product. Indeed, throughout the eighteenth century, Russia and the Scandinavian countries continued to be Hamburg's most reliable customers for sugar.[38]

At least until the crisis of 1799, when sugar prices dropped more than 35 percent within a year, Hamburg's refining industry flourished, although there is no denying that the post-1763 depression and the economic policies of other states did some damage. The Elbe blockade, the French occupation, and the Continental System disrupted all trade. Sugarcane importation and the exportation of refined sugar were no exceptions. It was not until 1809, however, when Napoleon interdicted the import of all colonial goods, that the movement of raw cane sugar into Hamburg practically ceased. Sugarcane was an unlikely product to attract smugglers' attention. In 1803, for example, Hamburg exported 16.5 million Pfund to Russia, in 1804 17.5 million, in 1805 19 million, in 1806 10.5 million. By 1810 the trade had altogether ceased. Many Hamburg refiners emigrated to Russia and put their skills to profitable use in Russian refineries, which were supplied directly from the Americas, though not without difficulty.[39]

The manufacture of "Havana" cigars, cigarillos, cigarettes, and (to a lesser extent) snuff, was a third major industry. Hamburg tobacco merchants obtained leaves and stems from Puerto Rico, Cuba, Virginia, and from "plantations" in Jutland and Mecklenburg. The raw tobacco was cut, cured, rolled, and packaged, then exported to central and eastern Europe along the Elbe and Oder waterways. At the end of the eighteenth century, forty-five processors offered a wide range of tobacco products. Cigars were especially popular. The largest processor employed as many as fifty-six people, although this was atypical. Most processing plants were tiny, either home industries or hole-in-the-wall enterprises with three or four workers, mostly young boys. Still, probably 800 to 1,000 people derived their income from tobacco processing and almost all of these jobs vanished after 1809.[40]

For all these industries, however, the 1780s and 1790s were heady days of great profits and rapid expansion. The same years were not so happy for many of Hamburg's older industries. Declining industries such as brewing, shipbuilding, and textiles had once employed thousands but now no longer. In the Middle Ages beer had been the city's prime export. The general shift of emphasis to overseas commerce and, in particular, the maturation of the colonial trade converted European tastes to other, more genteel beverages, such as coffee, tea, and wine. Hamburg's beer was no longer consumed either at home or elsewhere. Competition from Danzig and Berlin further cut into the native brewing industry. By the end of the eighteenth century, only seventeen breweries were active, employing fewer than 150 workers.[41]

A similar fate had befallen shipbuilding. In the fifteenth century, Hamburg had constructed its own ships as well as many for the other members of the Hanseatic League. Deforestation around the city, however, soon compelled Hamburg to import wood. In the seventeenth century, competitors—especially the Dutch—shouldered their way into Hamburg's business, and Hamburg, while building fewer seafaring vessels, sold or transshipped more lumber. This remunerative trade perished when Frederick II imposed a tax on the transport of goods along the Elbe, thereby severing Hamburg's lifeline to her chief suppliers, Electoral Saxony and Saxon-Anhalt. This essentially eliminated the remnants of Hamburg's shipbuilding as well. In the last decades of the century, Hamburg shippers preferred to contract for ships with dockyards in Altona, Eckernförde, and Flensburg, where both wages and the price of raw materials were low.[42]

In the seventeenth and early eighteenth centuries, textiles had been a mainstay of Hamburg's economy. With the significant exception of calico printing, this was no longer true after mid-century. All the other branches of a once vigorous industry failed to withstand the pressure of changes in fashion and intensified foreign competition. Such luxury fabrics as silk, brocades, and velveteen had always been produced by guildsmen, and we have already seen how the demand for these dwindled. Other textiles—linen, wool, say, linsey-woolsey, and hosiery—had once flourished as putting-out industries that kept large numbers of the poorer classes busy in Hamburg.

Stocking knitting is an excellent example of a domestic industry that had once assumed considerable dimensions but that stagnated in the closing half of the eighteenth century. Although there was a hosiers' guild, most hosiery fabricated in Hamburg was produced by domestic, nonguilded labor. At one time the knitting of coarse woolen stockings, as well as the spinning of wool for them, occupied thousands in and around Hamburg. Until the middle of the 1760s, merchants purchased coarse shearlings from Mecklenburg and finer wool from Holstein for finishing. They then contracted with peasants in Hamburg's neighboring Marschland to spin the wool into yarn. According to one source, these spinners earned a total of more than 50,000 marks annually in wages. Once the spinners returned the yarn, it was sorted and then put out once more to men and women in the city who knitted the stockings. Hamburg's hosiery, especially the thick woolen stockings worn with wooden clogs, was popular at the Frankfurt fair where most such wares were marketed. Guild masters, on a smaller scale, also farmed out their yarn to be knitted, subcontracting within the city as well. In 1726, as we shall discuss in more detail later, the city experimented with a new form of poor relief, negotiating with local merchants to employ the poor in the manufacture of hosiery. The plan noted that merchants already employed "thousands" in the countryside. If they were assured of finding enough laborers in the city, they could, it was postulated, hire as many as thirty to fifty thousand, boosting the economy while lessening the burden on the relief rolls. Soon after the middle of the century, the market for Hamburg's hosiery petered out, contributing to the ruin of the "new" poor relief as well as destituting many who lived, however meanly, from knitting. Most destructive of the native industry were the cheap, "Mecklenburg" stockings peddled on the streets. What happened to the hosiers' guild may be taken as indicative of the deterioration of the industry as a whole. In the 1750s and 1760s, there were twenty masters, numerous journeymen, a flock of apprentices, and hundreds of domestic workers. In 1792, there were only seven masters, three journeymen, a single apprentice, and a handful of knitters.[43]

Other failing industries included dyeing, fulling, and finishing (which, of course, faded as large-scale textile manufacturing waned), whaling, vinegar distilling, wax bleaching, and tanning, among others. With the exception of the textile-related trades and possibly whaling, none of these had ever played much of a role in the economy as employers. To be sure, new industries sprang up in the closing decades of the century. But the manufacture of wallpaper, playing cards, enamels, powder, starch, straw hats, twine, precision instruments, umbrellas, bedding, and corks (while perhaps demonstrating the rise of some sort of consumer culture) never involved more than a fraction of the total working population.[44]

Domestic servants, shopkeepers, peddlers, and casual laborers filled the bottom tiers of the labor pyramid. Domestics were almost always female; only very few bourgeois households could afford, or wanted, liveried servants, major domos, or valets. In the last half of the century, twelve to fifteen thousand maidservants, cooks, scullery girls, and wet nurses lived in Hamburg.[45] Married former servants often accepted temporary positions as day servants, or were hired to assist a household move, clean, mourn, or celebrate. The whole underbelly of Hamburg's economy presented men and women with a broad if not particularly attractive (or lucrative) range of possibilities. The bustling port generated thousands of pickup jobs and required casual laborers by the hundreds on a per diem basis. New construction and the repair and modernization of ancient walls and fortifications opened up yet more opportunities for laborers. Large-scale projects commonly lured hundreds of workers into the city during warm weather. Simply supplying needed services to an urban environment created jobs for both sexes while demanding only the ability to carry water, sweep streets, swing a pick, push carts, and shoulder hods. Innumerable others, often pensioned, furloughed, or invalided soldiers, rented tiny shops merchandising milk and green groceries or vending sweets and novelties. These enterprises were notoriously ephemeral "open today, shut tomorrow, today selling tea, tomorrow quills."[46] Peddlers hawked similar wares in the open air, leaving the more profitable trade in rags and waste paper to the Jews. The night watchmen and soldiers of the garrison also lived shadowy existences, frequently supplementing their pitiful pay (which was, moreover, often months in arrears) with spinning, weaving, and cobbling. Many begged to complete the patchwork of jobs that sustained them.

The structure of Hamburg's economy, and the transformations that economy underwent in the eighteenth century, shaped the contours of its laboring population. Until the middle of the century, Hamburg successfully mixed manufacturing for export, production for the domestic market, and commerce. The proportions were always uneven and commerce always dominated, but beginning in the late seventeenth century, and even more obviously in the next hundred years, overseas commerce muscled the other branches of the economy into the background. Hamburg's economy and its working population became increasingly dependent on the vagaries of world trade and tremulously sensitive to any wavering in its progress. The composition of the working class had changed as well. Commerce, the export trades, and the booming construction industry, relied on masses of unskilled or semiskilled laborers. The city's growing population, in turn, demanded an increasing number of goods and services that the guilds could no longer supply, thus allowing nonguilded artisans a wider place in the market. The working class that existed after 1750 included more recent immigrants, more transients, and more persons who lived outside of Hamburg in what later would become worker suburbs. The fortunes of both the old and the new working classes came to be more intimately bound to something they could not control: commerce.[47]

Such truly momentous shifts in the economy sent shock waves rippling through all layers of society. Among guildsmen, and especially among the journeymen and apprentices who watched their futures darken as guilds closed off the path to mastership and independence, the mood was one of growing frustration. In the eighteenth century, such discontent boiled over into frightening, though still rather subdued outbursts of labor unrest. There were few major incidents in the first half of the eighteenth century. After 1750, the violence mounted sharply. Most serious of the "strikes" in the second half of the century involved various groups of journeymen and apprentices: the cabinetmakers in 1750, the tailors in 1753, the sugar refiners in 1766, and, finally, the locksmiths in 1791 who precipitated a series of disturbances that lasted several days before being suppressed. Although little blood was shed (and almost all of it that of journeymen), the tumult threw a good scare into respectable citizens, who feared for their property and perhaps for their lives as well. In the 1790s, the government passed several ordinances designed to establish tighter controls over the journeymen's associations and imposed stiffer penalties on "troublemakers and agitators."[48]

Overt violence in the form of strikes, riots, and protests, however, did not seriously threaten social or political stability in eighteenth-century Hamburg. Far more pressing causes for concern were the quantitative and qualitative changes in the city's population. Contemporaries saw in their city not only more people, but more strangers, more criminals, and more paupers than ever before. The following chapters will address the question of how the city sought ways to define, monitor, and assimilate (or perhaps eliminate) those persons who were the inevitable by-products of the economic evolution traced here.

3

Citizens, Inhabitants,
and Others

Massive population growth was an eighteenth-century fact of life nowhere more evident and ultimately, nowhere more disturbing than in the cities. Like London and Paris—but on a smaller scale—Hamburg assumed truly metropolitan proportions between 1700 and 1800. Everywhere in Europe these new cities evoked extravagant forebodings. Critics contrasted their faults with the virtues of rural life, branding them modern Molochs, destroyers of men and defilers of morals.[1] Josiah Tucker castigated them as "the bane of mankind in every sense," Rousseau as "the burial pits of the human species." Even Samuel Johnson, whose most famous bon mot celebrated the richness of urban life, could paint a gloomier picture in the poem "London" where the city "sucks in the dregs of each corrupted state."[2] The city seemed to consume people in very real ways as deaths exceeded births, infant mortality soared, and epidemics raged among densely packed city dwellers. Some medical men, like Johann Jakob Rambach, Hamburg's City Physician, believed cities actually exhaled a noxious poison, blaming the destruction of the very "materia" of the air on the "transpirations, perspirations, and evacuations of more than 100,000 beings, all crowded together."[3]

The city showed a less Caliban side as well. Urban centers like London, Paris, Edinburgh, Amsterdam, and Hamburg formed the "nurseries of enlightened thought," and size, to some extent, determined whether a city innovated or merely copied the fashions set by others.[4] Parallel to the imagery of evil and cancerous gigantism ran brighter visions of strength, resilience, and hope. Caspar Voght, despite gushing sentimentality for his own country estate, Klein Flottbek, could describe the city as an "oak forest." "Where plants find nourishment, air, and space," he continued, "they thrive [and] though thousands sicken and suffocate, the forest survives, still standing strong after a hundred years."[5] Eighteenth-century conurbations presented a bewildering set of contrarieties, being as much "the arenas of human misery as of luxury" home to a poverty "much more terrible" than any in the countryside but also to a new plutocracy that possessed and flaunted an almost unimagined wealth. This sense of contrast—rich and poor, good and evil, beauty and deformity, coexisting and feeding on one another—underlay eighteenth-century equivocality on city life.[6]

Yet the city could not be wished away, nor did many people genuinely yearn for a return to a more bucolic existence. The elite of eighteenth-century Hamburg were eminently urbanites, who were imbued with an old sense of civic pride, but increasingly aware that they must come to terms with an urban, commercialized center that was shaped as much by the dictates of modern life as by tradition. They wanted to tame the city, but not dismantle it, to control the influx of population, but not throttle it. Thus, population policies, which had always been part of the way the city governed itself, seemed more difficult to formulate after 1750.

Policing in Hamburg

When we speak of population policies in the eighteenth century, we enter the realm of what was then considered part of a policy of good policing (*Polizei*). The most common way historians have dealt with the complicated concept of Polizei is to equate it with internal concerns or domestic policies as distinct from foreign and military affairs. This brief characterization, while serviceable and even correct, is far too austere to catch the deeper implications of "policing" and of the "police state" for early modern Europe. Polizei was not simply synonymous with domestic policy. Moreover, the police state was not merely a refined organ for social control but eudaemonistic in its objectives, seeking "to elevate society to a higher level . . . by promoting the common good."[7] Marc Raeff has reevaluated the historical role of the "well-ordered police state" by placing it on "the road to modernity." For Raeff, it embodied "society's conscious desire to maximize all its resources and to use this new potential dynamically for the enlargement and improvement of its way of life."[8] Police laws, as defined by Johann Klefeker, the eighteenth-century Hamburg legalist, guaranteed "that civil life will pass in a tranquil and Christian manner [and] according to the judicious rules prescribed by the magistracy."[9]

The highest authority (*Obrigkeit*) in any polity—in Hamburg, it was the Rat—ultimately determined police laws and policies. Although in Hamburg three fundamental statutes outlined the basic duties of police, it was the daily decisions of the Rat—written down and preserved in thousands of "Conclusa et Commissoria"[10]—that actually shaped policing. Each "Conclusum et Commissiorum" fell into one of three broad categories: those regulating economic life, those affecting rules of social conduct, and those concerned with demographic matters, including population control, medical practice, and public health. Such a neat tripartite division, however, while heuristically sound, denies the central reality of the police state: its holism. No police law worked alone or had but one purpose; each was synchronously tuned to all other police laws, and woven tightly into a fabric of rules that governed city life as an entity.[11]

The agents of policing both carried out police laws and molded policies as daily decisions became precedents directing future actions. In Hamburg, the agents of policing most intimately involved in controlling the population in a broad sense, as well as in administering what might loosely be termed social policies—including poor relief—were the Wedde and the two praetors. It should be kept in mind, however, that almost every part of Hamburg's government exercised some police powers, and, moreover—as we shall see when we consider the General Poor Relief at length in subsequent chapters—even such "private" organizations could and did engage in policing.[12]

The Wedde in the eighteenth century was composed of four senators and was responsible for a miscellany of policing activities. It monitored markets, checked weights and measures for accuracy, decided on the eligibility of couples to affiance and wed, examined credentials for citizenship, and, in conjunction with other members of the government, comprised the Deputation for the Admission of Aliens.[13] The praetors approximated what other cities termed police magistrates. They were senators and functioned primarily as the delegates of the Rat on Hamburg's lower court, the *Niedergericht.* Just as weighty, however, were their powers *in publicis,* that is, their police powers. According to law, "in the exercise of their office and also outside the courts [they are] to see that public and private . . . vices and transgressions, such as immorality, whoring, adultery, blasphemy, stabbings, brawling, usury, other similar disorders and forbidden acts are punished with due severity."[14] They wielded this authority summarily, at their own discretion, and in the absence of a formal legal process. Although by the end of the eighteenth century their once extensive discretionary authority had been significantly reduced, their police powers continued to be vitally important in quotidian governing. It was their responsibility to see that beggars and vagabonds were cleaned from the streets, that prostitutes and those "caught thieving from ships" were punished, and that public order was upheld. In addition, the praetors mediated domestic quarrels, matrimonial disputes, and paternity cases. All members of the municipality's official medical corps—the City Physician and his assistant, the city's Barber-Surgeon and Midwife—came under the direct surveillance of the praetors. Furthermore, they supervised the city's various charitable institutions, often supplementing the normal channels of relief by providing immediate assistance to the disabled, the aged, the ill, and the destitute on an ad hoc basis. As we have seen, they frequently distributed extraordinary alms, arranged free lying-in, or financed a pauper's funeral.[15]

It was precisely these agencies—institutions inherited from a time when Hamburg was much smaller and the bonds of community more tightly drawn—that wobbled the most under the burden of population growth. Neither the Wedde nor the praetors bore up well under the pressure of duties that now fell to them, leading one praetor to complain that his "was the most miserable job in Germany," while the Wedde protested that it, too, could no longer satisfactorily fulfill its role "since Hamburg has become so extremely populous."[16] In sum, Hamburg's ruling elites struggled with a political conundrum partly of their own making. Hamburg's government of amateurs was losing its ability to manage the problems of a new urban order. The organs of government, like the Wedde and the praetors, were strikingly defective when they were called upon to deal with such familiar social problems as poverty in a new environment that was radically altering both the qualitative and quantitative dimensions of these tasks. Hamburg's elites did not easily abandon their ideals of communal responsibility and yet they could not deny that government as it existed (and had existed since the sixteenth century) was failing in critical ways to meet the challenges presented by a eighteenth-century metropolis. The story of the Enlightenment in Hamburg is to a large extent the story of how Hamburg's patriots toiled to resolve some of these incongruities. They refused to tamper with the fundament of a social order that appeared to them both God-given and rational. Yet within the boundaries of their own social prejudices and Hamburg's political structure, they strove to eliminate waste and maximize efficiency. Poor relief fitted within a latticework of enlightened reforms that cherished two goals: preservation of what was good and improvement of what was less good. Reformers agreed that nothing could (or should) be done to assist "each individual member of society to become wealthy or even wealthier"; nor should they try to guarantee a "middling" income for all. Each society, they contended, needed a pool of "indigent but industrious, capable, and honest workers."[17] Johann Georg Büsch best voiced a widely shared sentiment when he wrote in 1785, "I cannot believe that a state, be it large or small, can be adjudged fortunate if populated with many inhabitants who, although they neither beg nor steal, can barely squeeze out a wretched existence. But there is no harm in it when next to the citizen who drinks in the fullness and richness of life's pleasures [there are] thousands who live only most frugally."[18]

Population Policies and the Laboring Poor

It was Büsch's "thousands," however, who created perplexing new problems for Hamburg. Attitudes toward them were always ambivalent. Many healthy, industrious workers—laborers willing to sweat for low wages—were an obvious asset to any prosperous commercial center, as masses of the ill, the aged, and the invalid—like hordes of beggars, criminals, and economic derelicts—were not. Unfortunately, no one understood how to entice the former and discourage the latter because the two groups overlapped and intermingled in so many ways. The very same workers whom employers wooed in times of economic growth, all too quickly became hungry and potentially disruptive troublemakers when business slackened. Those seemingly draconian early modern prohibitions against begging, which had never worked satisfactorily, were now outdated in theory as well. The population problems of eighteenth-century Hamburg transcended simple judgments on "insiders" and "outsiders," or even on "desirables" and "undesirables," and now turned on more complex socioeconomic calculations, which were themselves crucially influenced by an economy locked into the cycles of world trade. Not surprisingly, the influx of people into Hamburg corresponded to economic shifts, waxing and waning in rough sequence with periods of expansion and contraction. Hamburg had been a labor magnet at least since the fifteenth century and had often assimilated waves of refugees, like the Dutch, who fled wars, revolutions, famines, and religious persecution in search of the peace neutral Hamburg seemed to offer. The migrants of the late seventeenth and eighteenth centuries were qualitatively different and much more numerous. Periodic spurts of refugees swelled into torrents of newcomers. The increasing wealth of Hamburg's merchant-bankers and manufacturers developed a market for domestic servants, while the unprecedented upsurge in commerce and construction multiplied the demand for casual laborers. Hopes of employment—perhaps even dreams of fortunes to be gained—enticed many to Hamburg from an overpopulated and hunger-ridden countryside. However, the rather unpredictable periods of economic growth and decline, as well as the slow deterioration of older manufactures and the rise of new ones, impaired the ability of the labor market to adjust smoothly to the inrush of workers.[19]

Population growth in Hamburg in the last two decades of the century was especially dramatic. Hamburg became literally crowded. In the streets, contemporaries observed that there was "no end to the movement [of people] on foot and in conveyances of all types, no end to the hustle and bustle. The crowd masses so thickly that it drives itself to a standstill, [then] strains back and forth until it once more finds room to maneuver."[20] Even though Hamburg's population had grown more rapidly in the seventeenth than for most of the eighteenth century, it was in the eighteenth century that Hamburg's population reached critical levels—levels that strained, indeed threatened to tumble, existing political and social structures. In 1787 Hamburg's population exceeded 100,000 inhabitants. If one included the areas outside the walls, the figure approached 130,000. Population in the city itself reached 130,000 by 1800, although about one third of this increment (10,000–20,000) can be attributed to the French who fled to Hamburg after 1794. In 1811, the French government of occupation conducted the first census in Hamburg, tallying 100,192 people in the city and the two major suburbs of St. Pauli and St. Georg. Because the French census underestimated the population by about 13 percent, a figure of about 120,000 for 1800 is more plausible. Population had declined somewhat from the high in 1800 since many French expatriates went home again after 1799, while the economic crunch of the early 1800s impelled some inhabitants of Hamburg to seek their fortunes elsewhere.[21]

It would be useful, of course, to know what portion of this population can be classified as the poor or the laboring poor. There is no direct way to measure the extent of impoverishment, particularly because Hamburg's tax lists, which dated from the fifteenth century, were destroyed by the French in 1813. In 1787 when the General Poor Relief conducted its first investigations, it uncovered 3,903 poor families, a total of 7,391 individuals or about 7 percent of the population.[22] This did not include, however, the inmates of the orphanage, the almshouses, and the hospitals, resulting in at least another 2,000, maybe even 3,000, persons. Moreover, these numbers represented only the destitute—that is, those requiring "immediate assistance"—and not the much broader class of the laboring poor. The size of the former group could, as we have seen, fluctuate enormously with the often quite unexpected reversions in Hamburg's economy, setbacks that at times left thousands bereft of all employment. There is some indirect evidence, however, that suggests how many laboring poor lived in Hamburg. We know that St. Michaelis parish—the parish with the highest concentration of laborers and traditionally viewed as the poorest of the five metropolitan parishes—grew most rapidly in these years, comprising 25.54 percent of the total population in 1764 and 31.49 percent in 1811.[23] Although St. Michaelis was almost certainly the most impoverished parish, the four other parishes were not without their poor, since poverty in Hamburg did not cluster in neighborhoods.

Another way to measure the relative degree of impoverishment and to estimate, if crudely, the size of the laboring population is to examine the types of housing inhabitants occupied. People lived in *Häuser, Buden, Etagen, Kellern, Sählen*. The most affluent—the merchant-bankers, sugar refiners, calico printers, tobacco processors, some professionals, and some, though very few, of the artisans—representing less than one third of the population in 1811, occupied houses or *Etagenwohnungen* (spacious flats within houses that were reached by an internal staircase). Artisans, grocers, brokers, and the like, representing about one fifth of the population, inhabited Buden (smaller, one-story structures opening onto courtyards or secondary streets rather than onto main avenues, as houses did). Alternatively, they occupied the "better" cellars, which had plastered walls, planked floors, and windows, and, most crucially, were situated on ground high enough to avoid flooding. Hamburg's poorest inhabitants were housed in subterranean dwellings (damp and unhealthy holes-in-the-ground, which were swamped by every heavy rainfall) or they huddled together in Sählen, which were perhaps worse if somewhat drier. The Sähle (also called *Boden*) were wooden upper stories perched on top of Buden, or sometimes added as third or fourth stories above houses. A steep external stairway tacked to the side of the building provided access. They were narrow, had low ceilings, and were cold—not only unheated, but often unheatable. Needless to add, they were firetraps. In 1811, 45 percent of Hamburg's population dwelled in such Sählen. We must also take into account that some cellars, especially in the low-lying parish of St. Michaelis, were only rented by the poor. Thus, if we assume that the wealthy lived in houses, the lower middle classes in Buden or cellars, and the poor in Sählen or the least desirable cellars, then at least 45 percent and probably almost 50 percent of Hamburg's population in 1811 belonged to the class of the laboring poor. The city's population as a whole undoubtedly suffered greater impoverishment in 1811 than one or two decades earlier. Still, because little new housing was constructed after 1790 and much of the old housing was demolished to make way for warehouses (causing a severe shortage of cheap dwellings), these figures probably represent with at least fair reliability the conditions of the 1790s.[24]

The remarkable growth in population was joined to a steady differentiation of social classes but also to an increasing homogenization of occupations at the lower end of the labor hierarchy. The great intricacy and abundance of these variations became too complex for a personal understanding by any individual or group. Everything about population had become ambiguous. Even the dimensions of the quantitative fluctuations were confusing. Yet people did correctly, if imperfectly, perceive that the shift occurring was not only in numbers but also, and more troubling, in the *nature* of the laboring classes. Exactly what was changing, in what direction, how rapidly, and why, eluded them. A new way of "knowing" seemed necessary, one that would reduce tangled realities to simpler categories. Statistics promised to be the guide that government could use to lead it through the quantitative and qualitative mazes generated by population growth and economic transformation in eighteenth-century Hamburg.

"Counting the people," in one form or another, probably dates back to the very dawn of society, although modern periodic censuses first appeared in the mid-seventeenth century. Conducting a census became a regular task of government in the nineteenth century, but even during the eighteenth century collecting population data had become recognized by some as "an exigent and indispensable activity" of the state.[25] "A wise government," it was argued, "must know all those governed by it. Ergo, it must be cognizant of the true number of people within its jurisdiction."[26] Earlier enumerations frequently omitted "marginal" sectors of the population, for example, women, the poor, and non-taxpayers. The information gathered remained largely unpublicized—often locked away as closely guarded state secrets. Most "precursors of the modern census were almost wholly executive operations discharging essential functions of government such as military recruitment or taxation."[27]

The eighteenth century altered these goals. The increasingly convoluted tasks of administration within a modern state had bred a sense of desperation and futility. Statistics seemed to offer one answer to these dilemmas. As the utility of figures supplanted the magic of numbers, the desire to count and therefore to "know" became positively maniacal. Everything from ships to souls, apple trees to illegitimate births was zealously enumerated. "As a form of intellectual activity," the statistical method "fitted easily and logically in the inquiring spirit of the Enlightenment. . . . The comprehensive view that vital statistics could illuminate many of the dark corners of society harmonized with the idea that men and society could be improved by projects devised for that purpose."[28] Not only were more statistics collected in the eighteenth century than ever before, but the information thus obtained was put to a greater variety of uses, not the least of which was to evaluate how mankind was progressing and how that progress might be stimulated or redirected.[29] Poverty became one of the favored objects of statistical inquiry. As we shall see in later chapters, hard evidence was sought in order to gauge more accurately the extent of impoverishment as well as to calculate the amount of support based on "objectively determined" subsistence levels.

Thus, long before the French introduced the census into Hamburg, the city had developed its own set of cruder statistical tools. The privately compiled and published *Hamburgisches Diarium,* which appeared between 1701 and 1715, tabulated by weeks those "Born, Married, and Deceased."[30] In 1749, the Rat ordered all Lutheran pastors to report those they "Christened,

Joined in Matrimony, Communicated, and Buried," and requested similar lists from the Jewish communities. Hamburg's most widely circulated newspaper, the *Hamburgischer Correspondent*, published statistical profiles twice a year.[31] The city's citizens' militia conducted its own survey every six months to compose its muster rolls. Since their rostering led them into almost every home, the Rat often charged the militia captains "in conjunction with their regular inventory" to note additional information that was then placed at the disposal of the Treasury to use in making up tax rolls, or provided to the Wedde and the praetors to help in identifying strangers in the city. As in 1732, the Rat repeatedly ordered the captains to list "any aliens residing [in their company], especially soldiers in foreign service." The job of compiling the lists for the head tax (*Kopf-Geld*), the most universal form of taxation, fell to the captains as well. In 1753, the Rat directed them to record the names "of each and every one . . . without distinction and exclude no one even if he lives *notorie* from charity." In hopes of standardizing and improving the accuracy of the information the captains provided, the Rat issued in 1782 a six-part questionnaire to guide the captains in their inquiries: Who lived in the dwelling? What did he do? Was he married? Did he have any children, were they his? How many servants, journeymen, coachmen, maids, governesses, and wet nurses did he employ? Who else resided in the building? The captains also received vague instructions to "record the names of the poor at the same time," although the Rat neglected to explain what constituted poverty. Apparently no one felt it necessary to define so familiar a phenomenon. This assumption reflected the mentality of a government that still believed it could base its policies on the personal knowledge of citizens rather than on objective classifications and bureaucratic proficiency. The captains tallied the poor many times in the eighteenth century. Thus, in 1787, when the General Poor Relief wished to compile a reliable guide on the extent of poverty in the city, the Rat once again called on the captains, this time to provide "another, separate list of all paupers living in their companies."[32]

Throughout the eighteenth century, the Rat, the Treasury, and the Wedde sought to improve the quality and reliability of these and other statistical compilations that promised to lighten the tasks of governing. One prominent member of the Treasury, Franz Nicolaus Lütkens, argued in 1768 that such demographic information was indispensable: "No one can be a sound financier, unless he knows how many people live in the city, what sort they are, if [their numbers] are increasing or diminishing, the work they do and much more."[33] In the midst of a severe financial crisis with rapidly dwindling revenues, Lütkens and others like him perceived that a large population could be a source of great strength to a government, but only if it were correctly "balanced" and "utilized." Moreover, one could not rely on guesses if plans for the future were to be framed realistically. Such projections could also not be based on the fragments of statistical information (of dubious accuracy) that Hamburg's government possessed at that time. Not only must statistics be collected; they must also be preserved, analyzed, and applied. Lütkens did not deny that "from time to time, many such vital tasks are well and properly executed," however, all too often "the papers are lost [or] . . . and end up eternally imprisoned in the archive where they are of little use to anyone."[34]

What they knew or thought they knew troubled them deeply. These men were never merely concerned with issues of population size alone, but also traced unsettling trends in the nature of Hamburg's population. The principal issues were the health and morality—both broadly conceived—of the thousands inhabiting Hamburg. How would these affect the traditional framework of civic life? And what kinds of controls might still be exerted over such a fluid and unfamiliar population? The answers to these questions would crucially influence the formulation of such social policies as poor relief. Hamburg's governing elites explicitly identified conditions in public health and moral standards (e.g. illegitimacy) with the types and to some extent with the numbers of people occupying Hamburg. Hamburg's leaders felt whirled about, at least temporarily, in a maelstrom of uncertainties that obscured older points of reference. They sensed that they were slowly losing control over the city's population, that the city harbored an increasing number of foreigners, as well as an ever greater number of easily impoverished laborers who were needed and useful, but who brought problems with them—problems that seemed to defy the efforts and wisdom of a government of fathers and uncles. The statistics that they had available indicated that their city was slipping away from them; these changes reflected what they interpreted as a social pathology. Even more unambiguously these statistics suggested that the older population of citizens was being buried under an avalanche of new inhabitants, many of whom remained "unknowns." Existing mechanisms for control and integration—the varied forms of citizenship—were no longer working. New methods were needed and poor relief, in this context, increasingly became a mechanism for reestablishing stability. It was clearly an important part of the response to the failure of older forms of social welfare (that had virtually collapsed under the pressure of numbers), but it was also an answer to the breakdown of an older machinery that apparently had ensured a relatively integrated and homogeneous community for so long.

By mid-century, Lütkens and others desired to know not only how many but what kind of people then made up Hamburg's population. Unfortunately, too many of the answers that they finally got troubled them deeply: something was rotten in Hamburg. First, despite the obvious population increase, the excess of deaths over births formed an even then recognized and much lamented municipal fact of life for all cities.[35] In analyzing "Some Causes of the Greater Mortality in Cities," the eighteenth-century demographer Johann Peter Süssmilch pointed out that thousands died each year from the city's "natural insalubrity," the "frail constitutions" and "degeneracy" of urban parents, a "murderous" reliance on wet nurses among the wealthy, rampant prostitution, alcoholism, and the wildfire spread of diseases among dense populations.[36] Even if some figures suggested that Hamburg's environment might well have been less pathological than that of other large cities,[37] Hamburg's elites viewed the situation in quite a different light. The statistics on

"Births, Marriages, and Deaths" published in the *Hamburgisches Diarium* and later in the *Hamburgischer Correspondent* painted a grim picture of decay. Anyone who cared to tote up the figures (here from 1701 to 1715 and from 1767 to 1780) soon came to the conclusion that Hamburg lay dying. For the two-year period 1766–67, Lütkens in his "Computation of the Number of Inhabitants in the City" reckoned the margin of death's victory at 512 lives. Others confirmed this dreary opinion with their own hardly more propitious calculations. An annually repeated excess of births over deaths, however small, only became the norm much later (Tables 3.1, 3.2).[38]

Indicative to contemporaries of "urban disease" were high infant mortality rates and the large number of stillbirths. Of each 1,000 deaths in Hamburg (1794–1801), 209 were reported as those of children less than two years old and 291 less than six years old; for the period 1801–10, stillbirths and mortality for children under ten years of age was 46.25 percent.[39] This high infant and child mortality seemed most pronounced among the poor and particularly among illegitimate children. Thus, high infant mortality rates appeared as yet another sobering indicator of social disintegration. Equally alarming was the number of illegitimate births, which ostensibly multiplied as rapidly as the population increased.[40] The author of one topographical survey produced the statistics in Table 3.4 to support this claim. Although Hamburg's "illegitimacy problem" was neither unique nor excessive, many drew from these numbers the facile conclusion that population growth and immorality were inextricably linked.[41]

One hastens to explain that the relatively good record Hamburg might

Table 3.1 Births, Marriages, and Deaths in Hamburg, 1701–1715

Year	Born*	Married	Died	Gain/Loss
1701	2,033	284	1,856	+177
1702	3,310	491	3,338	−28
1703	3,287	595	2,817	+470
1704	3,479	495	3,016	+463
1705	3,010	560	3,127	−117
1706	3,333	542	3,257	+76
1707	2,900	558	2,827	+73
1708	3,042	656	2,948	+94
1709	2,849	552	3,295	−446
1710	2,885	554	2,914	−29
1711	2,374	449	2,618	−244
1712	3,018	601	4,124	−1,106
1713	2,758	838	10,956	−8,198
1714	2,726	1,142	3,976	−1,250
1715	3,012	793	4,281	−1,269
Totals	44,016	9,110	55,350	−11,334

Source: StAHbg, Senat, Cl. VII, Lit. De, no. 6, vol. 6, and "Summarische Specification des Hamb. Diarii," in *Hamburgisches Diarium,* no. 52 (1715). StAHbg, Bibliothek.

For city and one suburb (St. Georg)

*baptized; includes neither Mennonites nor Jews.

Table 3.2 Births, Marriages, and Deaths in Hamburg, 1767–1790

Year	Born	Married	Died	Gain/Loss
1767	2,752	—	2,473	+279
1768	2,817	1,052	2,902	−85
1769	2,918	932	3,625	−707
1770	2,764	923	2,259	+505
1771	2,690	869	3,158	−468
1772	2,354	824	3,220	−866
1773	2,472	935	2,418	+54
1774	2,742	870	2,959	−217
1775	2,606	866	2,420	+186
1776	2,602	885	2,299	+303
1777	2,633	842	2,689	−56
1778	2,591	911	2,880	−289
1779	2,780	947	2,496	+284
1780	2,726	937	2,598	+128
1781	2,675	962	2,810	−135
1782	2,735	936	2,734	+1
1783	2,723	972	2,938	−215
1784	2,737	1,070	3,514	−777
1785	3,051	965	3,169	−118
1786	2,644	971	3,416	−772
1787	2,901	925	3,138	−237
1788	2,787	917	3,048	−261
1789	2,641	905	3,162	−521
1790	2,792	910	3,715	−923
Totals	65,133		70,040	−4,907

Source: StAHbg, Senat Cl. VII, Lit. Nc, no. 1.

1767–68, 1789–90: Information available only for Lutherans.

1778–88: Lutheran, Roman Catholic, German Reformed, Mennonites; does not include Jews, French Reformed, Anglican (English Court).

present to the outside world had little impact on home-grown moralists and policymakers. Other influences played a role as well. The sentiment that "illegitimate children must be regarded as more dishonorable . . . in free cities, where morals need be purer than in monarchies"[42] could cancel statistical realities or kaleidoscope them into something quite the opposite. However, it was not only, or even primarily, a question of slackening morals that confronted city fathers. Illegitimate children were believed more likely than their legitimate compeers to become burdens on the city's corporate resources, straining already strapped charitable resources to the breaking point. Furthermore, high illegitimacy rates struck an uncomfortable contrast to the apparently low, and still falling, fertility among citizens. It was Süssmilch who first noted a particularly weak marital fertility rate for Hamburg, and a whole series of local commentators echoed his concerns. Von Heß bemoaned the "general decline of the number of marriages among citizens" and deplored the many childless couples. Lütkens, in his "Treasury Meditations," took into account that for Hamburg one could only estimate 150 existing marriages for every 1,000 people, whereas in most other places one could expect 175.[43]

Table 3.3 Mortality: Age Distributions in Hamburg, 1801–1810

Age Range	Number of Deaths	Percentage
Stillbirths	2,933	6.95[a]
Unknown	3,754	8.89
Less than 1 year	9,521	22.56[b]
1–10	7,066	16.74[c]
10–20	945	2.24
20–30	2,268	5.37
30–40	2,738	6.49
40–50	2,802	6.64
50–60	2,933	6.95
60–70	3,219	7.63
70–80	2,839	6.73
80–90	1,081	2.56
90–100	104	.25
more than 100	4	.01

Source: von Heß, *Hamburg* (2nd ed.), vol. 3. p. 460.

Infant mortality (under 10 years) = a + b + c = 6.95

$$
\begin{array}{r}
6.95 \\
22.56 \\
16.74 \\
\hline
47.25\%
\end{array}
$$

Table 3.4 Illegitimacy Rates in Hamburg, 1701–1715, 1780–1811

Years	Illegitimate/All Births	Percentage Illegitimate
1701–1715	1:16	6.25
1780–1790	1:11	9.09
1790–1800	1:9	11.11
1800–1811	1:7	14.29

Source: Rambach, *Versuch,* p. 252.

These statistical realities, or perceived realities—the excess of deaths over births, the diminished fertility rates among citizens, and soaring illegitimacy among the poor—placed native Hamburg residents in the unenviable position of being, or seeing themselves becoming, a vanishing minority in their own city. That the population irrefutably continued to expand—and expand rapidly—they could only attribute to that "great flood of foreigners" streaming into the city, which had forever altered older population structures. Rambach estimated that there were at least 9,000 immigrants living in Hamburg in 1801. Von Heß thought that "an incomparable mass of strangers" flowed in and out of Hamburg and that their numbers were "perhaps greater here than anywhere in Europe except in London and Paris." Lütkens realized that the settling of so many "foreigners" typified all large cities, yet believed that the "influx of so many outsiders" engendered an "unhealthy state" in the population as a whole.[44] Newcomers bred other, more political problems. Allegedly they claimed more than their share of attention from city authorities. One exasperated praetor fumed in frustration: "I have had no end of trouble with these people and have squandered much precious time on them."[45]

Citizens and Others

Such alterations in the social composition of Hamburg's population upset traditional political balances in several ways. Clearly, they put pressure on the old legal definitions of citizens, quasi citizens, inhabitants, and aliens. The slow shift in the meaning of citizen—from a privileged inhabitant of a city whose legal status derived from a contractual relationship in which a sense of responsibility for the city's honor and general welfare was expected, to the modern, unitary interpretation of the word common in the nineteenth and twentieth centuries—began earlier. Before 1800, no European government apart from that of France seriously proposed introducing a general and uniform citizenship encompassing all estates or classes without distinction.[46] For most of Europe, this was a metamorphosis first completed in the nineteenth century, which was propelled into being by massive political upheavals. In the 1820s and 1830s, one indication of Hamburg's drift toward liberalism was its (admittedly slow) revision of citizenship requirements in just this direction.[47] Another, already completed by 1815–16, was the thorough reconstruction of poor relief (to be analyzed in a later chapter). The perception current in Hamburg after mid-century was that older legal definitions were no longer working. This would lead Hamburg's elites to think more as well about the kind of population Hamburg possessed and about the ways in which other cherished parts of municipal life were also in danger of collapsing. Hamburg's "new" population represented, therefore, not only greater numbers of people but people less well integrated into city life and hence far more vulnerable to economic shifts.

Differences between citizens or burghers (*Bürger*)[48] and quasi citizens—often known as *Schutzbürger* or, as in Hamburg, as *Schutzverwandten,* who possessed fewer civil and no political rights—existed in every early modern city. In Hamburg, the distinction was apparently first drawn in the thirteenth century. The delimitation between citizens and quasi citizens normally paralleled socioeconomic categories but could also rest on matters of lineage and kin ties. In the late Middle Ages, bondsmen, serfs, and villagers entered the cities in large numbers diluting the concentration of burghers. When cities allowed these newcomers to remain, they usually settled them as "inhabitants" or "residents" (*Einwohner* or *Beÿsassen* are the two most common terms) rather than granting them access to citizenship. Besides being politically disenfranchised, they lacked full economic privileges as well as being denied the right to acquire property or participate in communal affairs such as parish governance and poor relief.[49]

Cities varied enormously in their willingness to admit newcomers to the civic family—or to use the now antiquated legal phrase—to the communal *nexus.* Towns caught in economic backwaters erected strong barriers to discourage immigration, preventing interlopers from strong-arming their way into the municipality. Such "home-towns" (to employ Mack Walker's imagery) kept to themselves as much as possible. Politically, "all the classes bind themselves to each other [through elaborate sets of] laws and ordinances," while economically, "all capital flows in an unending circle" by sealing off any escape to the outside. These towns presented a hardened carapace of tradition to the rest of the world; their social organization was difficult for outsiders to comprehend and even more difficult to penetrate. They neither needed nor wanted free trade. Competition from without or even from "capitalistic" upstarts within foreshadowed their demise as a community and an end to their way of life. By fiercely guarding their citizens' most vital commodity—the burgher's livelihood (*bürgerliche Nahrung*)—they discouraged all innovation and any "novelties" that broke with their sense of moral economy. Thus, they also doomed themselves to economic stagnation. They regarded outsiders with a mixture of ill-concealed hostility and fear. "Outsiders," snorted the "home-towners," "what can we expect, await, demand from these? That they will serve our community better for its money?"[50] The obvious answer was no.

Hamburg was different. It was neither economically backward nor especially fearful of the competition of others. The "webs and walls" that sheltered "home-towners" could only stifle Hamburg's thriving merchant capitalism. Thus, when Johann Carl Daniel Curio, one of Hamburg's prominent patriots and educational reformers, himself an immigrant to the city, claimed that "we have no nobles [here], no patricians, no slaves, no, not even subjects. All true Hamburgers belong to and acknowledge only one class, that of burgher, nothing more and nothing less," he did not merely flatter his adopted home. Although Curio's praise ignored the crucial disparities of wealth and political power separating citizens from noncitizens, he nevertheless had a point. In contrast to other Hanseatic cities, like Bremen and Lübeck, Hamburg tolerated no legally defined patriciate nor recognized anything resembling the noblelike fraternities that reigned in Frankfurt, Rottweil, Nuremberg, and Strasbourg, nor even accepted a closed circle of families that functioned so unofficially.[51] Admittedly, some families built dynasties of influence and power, and names like Amsinck, Bartels, Jencquel, Kirchhof, Mattiessen, Moller, Schuback, and Sieveking appear several times each on the *Ratsrolle* and even more frequently in the lesser councils of government. Nonetheless, these families never clung together as an impenetrable elite. New families, talented men, foresighted and ambitious entrepreneurs, moved in and up, and often with astonishing speed. Hamburg's dynamic yet turbulent economy ensured that few commercial houses held on to their wealth for more than a couple of generations. Far more significant than any sort of patriciate for Hamburg's social and political structure was the unwavering dominance of mercantile interests.[52]

Hamburg readily accepted and even encouraged the immigration of "desirable" individuals and groups. It particularly welcomed those who supplied capital, offered trade secrets, or proposed new branches of manufacturing. For these immigrants, the city smoothed the path to citizenship in explicit acknowledgment that "a great number of inhabitants undeniably contributes much to the expansion of commerce and to the prosperity of the Republic . . . [and] therefore, we must not place obstacles in the path of those who wish to establish residence here and become citizens." The author of this statement, however, emphasized that "one prefers to augment the number of citizens rather than merely [add to] the number of inhabitants."[53] Hamburg's Chamber of Commerce agreed, petitioning the Rat in 1745 for a decision requiring "each person, who in the future desires to set up business here, to become a citizen, so that commerce flows into the hands of citizens and not into the pockets of others."[54] Clearly a large proportion of citizens, in comparison to other inhabitants, promised the most gain for the municipality. In return, the city permitted only citizens to exercise a burgher's livelihood, which embraced all forms of commercial activity "in distinction to the scholarly professions," and included retailing, skilled trades, tavernkeeping, and even some forms of peddling.[55] All burghers, however, were not created equal. There were Small Burghers, Large Burghers, and Propertied Burghers, all of whom received unequal slices of the political, social, and economic pies. Only the Propertied Burghers who "possessed unencumbered property [of a certain value] either within the city itself or in its territories" exercised full political rights. They formed a core of citizens permitted to vote in the sessions of the Bürgerschaft; in 1800, this group numbered between 3,000 and 4,000 men. Other persons "regardless of what property they own" were also allowed to attend the meetings of the Bürgerschaft: the members of the One Hundred Eighty, the Sixty, the Treasury, the militia captains, the guild elders, and those who held or had once held any major communal office. Despite this lengthy list of eligibles, the 200-member quorum necessary for valid decision-making often failed to appear. Hamburg's constitution excluded some Propertied Burghers from appearing in the Bürgerschaft as well as from holding office: all non-Lutherans, those in the service of foreign governments, bankrupts, and those employed by the city or the Rat as well as those "who do not actually maintain a hearth within the walls."[56]

Other legal distinctions separated the Large from the Small Burghers, although these had become so blurred over time as to be almost meaningless by the eighteenth century. Technically, the amount of business one did set the boundary between those required to become Large Burghers and those who needed only to pay for the substantially cheaper status of Small Burgher. According to the Recess of 1603, all merchants "who engage in substantial trade, or who run a public warehouse" must become Large Burghers, while those who "have only an ordinary business, like retailing or tavern-keeping" could satisfy their legal obligations by becoming Small Burghers. Constitutional modifications in the late seventeenth century required the status of Large Burgher for all guild masters, as well as of those "who use the large scale and especially the flour dealers," if they wished to practice their livelihoods.[57] As early as the sixteenth century, economic factors had impelled Hamburg to allow some other groups to settle in the city under particularly advantageous circumstances, despite their inabilty to fulfill all the normal criteria for citizenship. In 1567, for instance, the Rat practically invited the Merchant Adventurers, or English Court, to take up residence in the city and conduct its business. Early in the next century, the city extended similar dispensations to other economically desirable groups, such as the Dutch, the Portuguese Jews, and the Mennonites. These, of course, with the exception of those Dutch who were Lutherans, did not become citizens and enjoyed no political rights.[58]

The *Schutzverwandten*

Lesser forms of citizenship accommodated those perched on the lower rungs of Hamburg's economic ladder. Manual labor, like domestic service, fell outside the protected province of a burgher's livelihood. Hamburg's constitution disencumbered "day laborers, nonguilded craftsmen, publicans, sailors, peddlers, valets, others [practicing] petty professions" and domestic servants of the obligations and costs of full citizenship although in no way barring them from citizenship.[59] These people, however, were not totally free from nexus obligations. A special category of quasi citizenship (*Schutzverwandschaft*) pertained to them. Assuming the status of Schutzverwandschaft was a trifling formality. The applicant appeared before the senior member of the Wedde, sealed a pledge of loyalty to the city and promised obedience to its laws with a handclasp, and laid down as surety the first of the annually renewable fees, the *Schutzthaler.* In return, the new *Schutzverwandte* obtained a certificate, the *Schutzbrief,* as proof of his status as well as less tangible but far more consequential benefits such as the right to reside in the city and contract a marriage if he wished. Although the conditions of Schutzverwandschaft specifically denied him the privilege of a burgher's livelihood, all other forms of employment now stood open to him. His restricted citizenship exempted him from standing watch with the militia, although he was liable to taxation, if only to a limited degree.[60]

At least since the sixteenth century, the Schutzverwandschaft had, on the one hand, allowed individuals of small means, mostly laborers (many of whom first entered the city as "impecunious migrants"), to settle in Hamburg, while, on the other hand, drawing them into the nexus.[61] Thus, theoretically, unskilled workers and domestic servants trickled into the city in a thin stream without discombobulating the sociopolitical equilibrium. In others ways as well, the Schutzverwandschaft was quintessentially a part of the personalized governing style of fathers and uncles that continued to exist in Hamburg. It required little bureaucratic apparatus, and was based, at least partially, on the individual's own willingness to come forward and register, or on the knowledge that the community's surveillance would make it impossible for outsiders to escape notice. This system probably never achieved everything expected of it; for example, the city was constantly losing track of its Schutzverwandten population. Still, as long as the city's population grew only slowly, this problem remained negligible. By the middle of the eighteenth century (and actually even before then), however, the once negligible issue generated a knotty complex of problems for city government in general and for the Wedde and the Treasury in particular. The Schutzverwandschaft seemed to have outlasted its usefulness because it was no longer able to cope with basic alterations in the size and composition of Hamburg's population. As the population expanded and diversified, the Schutzverwandten literally vanished, disappearing into a nameless, anonymous crowd. As they melted away so did the fees and taxes they were supposed to pay. Moreover, both in and outside of government circles, they had come to be perceived as the largest reservoir of the poor. The post-1763 economic crisis, which plunged the Treasury into severe financial troubles, also brought the whole nexus system—particularly the Schutzverwandschaft—under closer scrutiny and opened it up to strong criticism on fiscal grounds.[62]

Within the framework of this debate broader issues of population policy now surfaced. Discussion centered on the problem of how to combine quantitative and qualitative characteristics in the most favorable and utilitarian ways. It was axiomatic that smaller cities held together better and were more easily governed than sprawling metropolises. Yet it was also quite clear that such parochialism contradicted the very foundations of Hamburg's economic and social life. Senator Schuback, writing in 1769, confessed his intuitive preference for a tightly knit community of modest size, but acknowledged that Hamburg's "felicitous location . . . abundance of housing, and massive fortifications" allowed for greater populousness, and "the needs of our militia" and of the economy perhaps dictated it. Still, he felt uneasy about the quality of an expanded (and expanding) population. He found no place in his ideal social world for what he termed "less welcome elements," that is, peddlers, grocers, and shopkeepers: "What can our city anticipate from these save disorder, dissipation, and bankruptcies?" For Schuback and many other influential figures, these people all too quickly slid down into "that mass of beggars roaming Hamburg's streets as nowhere else in the world."[63]

It is at this point that the basic contradictions that bedeviled population policies in Hamburg reappeared. How did one cater to economic growth yet not totally destroy any remaining sense of community as this flood of newcomers threatened to do? Schuback's convictions represent the general philosophy (if such a word can be applied to a point of view by no means based on theoretical reflection) behind the evolution of Hamburg's nexus policies in the last decades of the eighteenth century. Everyone realized that the nexus could be manipulated to regulate population, although the exact mechanism and even the goals of such manipulation were never clearly worked out. Rather, they became an issue of bitter dispute between advocates of expansionism and proponents of retrenchment. The result was that the city pursued no consistent population policy. Instead, it responded to momentary needs without committing itself to any single strategy.[64] This flexibility was one of the strongest points of the reign of fathers and uncles but it also generated inconsistency and encouraged the proliferation of contradictory policies.

For example, as we have already seen, by the middle of the eighteenth century the guilds had long since forfeited whatever monopoly they had ever had on production because the number of Freimeister and ground rabbits kept pace with the demands of a growing population. Similar economic realities recast older policies regarding the employment of casual and unskilled laborers. In the 1730s, the Rat had forbidden weavers of woolens and calico printers to hire those who neither resided in Hamburg nor could produce a Schutzbrief complete with records of their paid fees. Apparently these protoindustrialists busied thousands of persons who "come through the gates on Monday morning and leave again on Saturday night, lodging in hostels" during the workweek. The Rat modified such restrictions several times in the course of the eighteenth century. In 1769, for instance, the Rat relaxed legal requirements for workers hired by the "Fabriken und Manufacturen" in what appears to be a deliberate attempt to prop up faltering industries hit hard by the depression of 1763 and shaken by the mercantilist policies of other states. Furthermore, the Rat sanctioned the special labor requirements of large-scale manufacturers who must, it insisted, be permitted "to hire and employ outsiders" freely.[65] Such dispensations facilitated the search for workers, while reaching out "a patriotic helping hand to those men whose businesses furnish[ed] a living for the numerous poor" and whose taxes enlarged the revenues of the state.[66] Thus, when the city's manufactures could absorb more workers, or perhaps in order to cheapen labor costs and pump some life into a sluggish economy, nexus rules could be relaxed. Not all agreed, of course. The guilds adamantly opposed any slackening of traditional nexus policies as antithetical to their economic well-being. The same economic logic, in reverse, could be employed to justify the tightening of restrictions. Writing in 1805, in the midst of an almost totally prostrated economy, another senator recommended that any stranger who could not prove his ability to support himself and his family should be refused permission to settle in Hamburg. He conceded that "to many this sounds unduly harsh," but felt that the "current unhappy circumstances of our city" condoned such severity. Moreover, as he pointed out, such policies could always be reversed. When times improved, so, too, "can we drop our vigilance."[67] One area in which the Rat did not bend its rules was in the hiring of workers for public works projects, such as the walls and fortifications, which always drew thousands of seasonal workers into the city. The city refused to "take on any laborer who did not actually produce his Schutzbrief." The Rat further specified that "no migrants . . . be hired on public works" nor were they to be recruited as soldiers or night watchmen.[68] These rules, like so many others, however, were more often broken than observed.

Yet these oscillations in policy should not obscure the gradual change in attitude toward the Schutzverwandschaft, which came to be regarded as a major pecuniary liability and a serious sociopolitical problem that was closely correlated with the growing impoverishment in the city.[69] The Schutzverwandten created the biggest headaches for the Treasury during the course of the century, even though fees from citizenship and the Schutzverwandten never comprised much of the total municipal income (rarely more than 1.5 percent). The average annual income from Schutzthaler and citizenship fees,

Table 3.5 Income from *Schutzverwandten* Fees, 1751–1770

Year	Fees from Existing *Schutzverwandten* (marks)	Fees from New *Schutzverwandten** (marks)
1751	9,550	732
1752	9,289	881
1753	9,376	906
1754	9,195	998
1755	9,519	944
1756	9,102	764
1757	8,448	596
1758	7,089	974
1759	9,426	708
1760	8,727	760
1761	7,668	848
1762	8,730	800
1763	14,508	864
1764	11,925	878
1765	—	—
1766	13,155	898
1767	—	—
1768	—	—
1769	11,346	752
1770	11,571	732

Source: StAHbg, Senat Cl. VII, Lit. Db, no. 8, vol. 6.

* minus percentage subtracted for officials

however, declined from a high of 19,000 marks in the period from 1700 to 1709 to about 14,000 marks in the period from 1740 to 1749, and then plummeted to a paltry 8,000 marks in 1768 (Tables 3.5, 3.6) while the size of the population, especially that of the lower classes, increased.[70] But the problem did not end there. Schutzverwandten who did not pay their Schutzthaler usually did not pay their taxes, and thus much of the discussion on reforming Schutzverwandschaft that took place after mid-century centered on ways to enforce their compliance to tax laws. Also it was believed that many of the Schutzverwandten were perfectly capable of affording citizenship and of "shouldering a larger share of the civil onera." Lütkens complained of "flagrant abuses": "We presently have two *medici* as Schutzverwandten, one of whom lives from his investments!"[71] In 1759, when the Treasury evaluated the lists that it had ordered the militia captains to compile, it discovered 4,000 Schutzverwandten and 330 persons "unrelated" to the city. Of the Schutzverwandten, more than 220 were seriously behind in the payment of their Schutzthaler, and only 300 of the 4,000 could prove that they had ever paid any taxes whatsoever. The situation among the unrelated was even worse: Only 35 had ever paid taxes.[72]

The predicament worsened as the proportion of noncitizens—the Schutzverwandten and those outside the nexus entirely—expanded. Both became increasingly unknown elements within the population. A twentieth-century

Table 3.6 Income from Bürger and Schutzverwandten Fees, 1626–1800

Year	Fees (marks)	Total Municipal Income	Percentage in Fees
1626	14,500	872,628	1.7
1659	18,881	1,409,991	1.3
1686	7,761	2,020,740	0.4
1716	24,940	3,098,478	0.8
1746	30,136	2,502,266	1.2
1775	12,980	3,292,849	0.4
1800	65,997	5,853,511	1.1

Source: Mauersberg, *Wirtschafts- und Sozialgeschichte,* p. 463.

analysis suggests that half of Hamburg's inhabitants in the early nineteenth century were not citizens and that in 1759 the size of the noncitizen population made up at least 40 percent of the total population;[73] furthermore, the city government possessed only inaccurate and dated information about this population. The results of enumerations varied enormously, often creating wildly different estimations and interpretations of what the situation must have been. In 1603–4, according to the best figures available, there were 14,565 citizens, 650 aliens, and 7,282 Schutzverwandten in the city. A tax assessment of 1759 uncovered about 4,000 Schutzverwandten, 9,000 citizens, and 3,300 miscellaneous "others." A twentieth-century search of the extant Wedde registers for 1732 counted 2,020 newly admitted Schutzverwandten as compared to 1,246 fee defaulters. In 1740, the register recorded only 34 new admissions. In 1750, according to this same source, the total number of Schutzverwandten had reached 4,500 and by 1797 more than 5,000 were on the books, although only a trifling number of these paid their fees annually.[74] All this proves that the government was, as Lütkens had observed in 1768, very uncertain about how many Schutzverwandten resided in the city at any one time and totally ignorant about the number of "others."

From the government's point of view, worse still was the growing inability of the city to exert influence over most of these people; little could be done to tax them or to compel them to pay their Schutzthaler. Near the end of the century, even after the Wedde and Treasury had attempted to eliminate the most glaring abuses, a representative of the Treasury still had to admit that "the entire system is in a very bad way and continues to deteriorate." Of the estimated 7,000–8,000 Schutzverwandten then living somewhere in the city, even among those who "have dwelled here for 5, 8, 10, 12, 16, or even 20 years," few had paid their fees more than once or twice.[75] No one appeared to be able to say with certainty just how many Schutzbriefe were still valid. Many had lapsed "because the possessor is either destitute, or, in light of how often the common people move from lodging to lodging, simply can no longer be located."[76] Searching out individual Schutzverwandten presented formidable logistical problems in a city generally without street names or any form of house identification, such as numbers, and that resembled a labyrinth of twisted thoroughfares, often unexpectedly bisected by incredibly narrow canals. In 1787, when the militia captains went about trying to compose lists of "all the poor," the chore had not become any less arduous. Captain Johann Hinrich Meyer reported of his company in St. Michaelis parish:

> [I]t is really impossible to assess the number of poor with any accuracy, especially as everyone who comes into [Hamburg] over the Elbe lodges here in my company because housing is so cheap. The annual rents of 6, 7, 8, 9 thaler are collected at seven-day intervals. . . . [The people] move in and then out again, almost every week. Many are driven away, and so it goes. [And] there are houses here with as many as ten dwellings in each.[77]

In 1754, as the Treasury struggled to compose more accurate tax lists, the parish clerks (*Kirchspiel-Lauffer*) charged with the task begged for more time because "we need at least fourteen days unencumbered by all other duties to complete the survey of an entire parish."[78] The Schutzverwandten, like the lower classes of which they formed a major part, not only floated from one job to another and from one cheap dwelling to another, but also flowed in and out of the city searching for employment. Some lived lives of almost permanent transience.

The documentation available on the Schutzverwandten affords only tantalizingly brief glimpses of the sort of existence they must have led. By combining three sources—a 1795 memorandum to the Rat from the Wedde, the Wedde registers from 1698 to 1750, and a series of lists compiled by the militia captains in 1741—we can piece together a fairly representative list of their vocations.[79] They fall into the broad categories of artisans, manufacturing workers, and casual laborers. Almost without exception, the artisans belonged to the poorest trades, such as cobbling and tailoring, or were apprentices or journeymen with little hope of becoming masters, or were Freimeister or ground rabbits. Workers in the manufactories—in calico printing, sugar refining, and tobacco processing, and, to a lesser extent, in the tiny industries producing powder, wallpaper, enamels, playing cards, and bedding—comprised a second grouping. The term laborer included almost all of the unskilled workers involved in construction, engaged on the repair of walls and fortifications, or employed as casual laborers in the thousands of activities attending commerce and shipping; this term also includes stevedores, water carriers, street cleaners, lamplighters, and the like. Another group not included in other classifications were peddlers of vegetables, milk, and notions, gardeners, and boatmen. Other occupations less well represented were clerks, petty municipal officials, post runners, messengers, servants (live-in or day servants, including some liveried servants), sailors, soldiers in either Hamburg's service or that of other powers (especially Denmark) and, finally, night watchmen. Sprinkled in among these were a scattering of language teachers, dancing and fencing masters, artists, French hairdressers, an occasional *Musicus* or *Studiosus,* a few schoolmasters, oculists, barber-surgeons, and regimental drummers. Although it is impossible to determine what the percentages of each occupation the Schutzverwandten were, we can get a rough idea of the composition of a neighborhood or part of a parish. In 1741, of the fifty

Schutzverwandten living in Captain Lorenz Poppe's company in St. Jakobi parish, twenty-two gave their occupations as laborers, six as sailors, six as cobblers, four as minor tax officials, three as tailors, two worked for calico printers, and there was one sand hauler, one clerk, one milk peddler, one ribbon maker, one sailcloth weaver, one lighterman, and one fisherman among them.

A peek into the investigations conducted by the militia captains produces some idea of the common lot of those who lived *in* Hamburg but *outside* the nexus. In 1732, the Rat ordered the captains to query all aliens in their companies and to be particularly assiduous in investigating the circumstances under which Danish soldiers resided there. Although these soldiers may seem an eccentric choice—a particularly atypical group—nothing could be further from the truth. For most of them, soldiering was very much a part-time job. Their real lives, like their homes and their families, were in Hamburg. Thus, the information amassed by the captains offers more details on some members of the working classes in eighteenth-century Hamburg. Most of the soldiers questioned had been in Hamburg on extended furlough for quite some time, as long as nineteen years in one case. Some were natives of Hamburg. Most were married. All of them clung tenuously to respectability while living on the brink of poverty. With the exception of one self-proclaimed noble, their occupations corresponded to those of the Schutzverwandten examined earlier. Unless prevented by age or infirmities, in most cases both husband and wife worked. Some couples had children, although families with more than two or three offspring were rare and childless couples fairly common. Few paid more than a minimal four to eight shillings in taxes; most paid nothing. Several husbands were "clandestine" buttonmakers, tailors, and shoemakers, that is, were ground rabbits. Some worked for calico printers, tobacco processsors, or sugar refiners. Many others were casual laborers whose wives contributed to the family economy by knitting stockings, sewing, taking in laundry, or going out to clean house. For example, Hinrich Kott—a Danish soldier born in Hanover—took whatever work he could find, as did his wife. They had been in Hamburg for six years, for four of which he had been a Danish soldier, "but only when called out on maneuvers." He paid no taxes. Twenty-five-year-old Hinrich Ludwig Riemschneider, a native of Hamburg, had resided continuously in the city for four years and was married to the daughter of a Hamburg workman. They had one child. When queried as to why he remained in Hamburg if he served the Danish crown, he explained that he and his wife carved buttons for a manufacturer in Altona. He paid nothing to the city except four shillings quarterly in taxes.[80]

The most disturbing and deeply ingrained "habit" of these people, and of the Schutzverwandten in general, observers agreed, was their "propensity" for sinking into poverty. The many workers who "entered the city and joined the nexus as *Schutzverwandten* in the summer, when employment is plentiful," either disappeared again once the work ran out, or, more frequently, became public charges.[81] Such a chain of events led contemporaries to equate the Schutzverwandten with the people historians have identified as the potential poor. It was a perception closely allied to reality because the two groups indeed overlapped. The frequent, brief notations in the Wedde registers— "enjoys public relief," "languishes in the hospital," "is in the workhouse," or simply, poignantly, "is old and has nothing"—wrote the civil obituary for many once respectable folk who had been sucked down into a substratum of destitution from which they rarely reemerged. In the debates surrounding nexus reform that occupied so much of the time of the Treasury, the Wedde, and the Rat between 1760 and the end of the century, several purported traits of the Schutzverwandten were routinely paraded out as the avoidable causes of their impoverishment, namely, their lack of marketable skills, their inability to plan for the future, and, most especially, their "rash and imprudent" marriages.

Marriage restrictions indicate how the city used legal tactics to try to alleviate the overburdening of the city's charitable resources. They reflect equally well the interplay of morality and fiscal practicality that was characteristic of the reign of fathers and uncles. Part of the municipality's duty to preserve order in the community and to ensure that "civic life be . . . passed in tranquility and in a Christian manner" extended to the definition of proper marriages, while discouraging those "frequent, thoughtless, and foolish" unions that, purportedly, accounted for so much destitution. If people refrained from or could be prevented from marrying until they were able to support a family, then, theoretically at least, one cause of impoverishment should be eliminated.[82] All municipalities legally defined the right of their subjects and citizens to marry; this was one of their oldest policing functions. In Hamburg, the ultimate arbiter in conjugal and parental matters was the secular authority of the Rat, and not the church-governing body, the Reverend Ministerium. It was the Wedde, however, that determined the right of couples to affiance, granted them permission to wed, limited the size and ostentation of marital festivities, and collected marriage fees. Various Wedde ordinances outlined major points of municipal matrimonial policy. They forbade marriages in certain degrees of consanguinity, "secret betrothals," and "having the nuptials performed by pastors other than those ordained in the city."[83]

Besides working to assure civic tranquility, propriety, and promote Christian life, marriage laws were closely tied to nexus policies in other ways. Only the Schutzbrief opened the gates of the "earthly paradise of wedded bliss," and no one received permission to enter "without presenting the appropriate documentation in full." This right prodded many to join the nexus in the first place, or at least so it was believed. It was, however, just these Schutzverwandten whom contemporaries regarded as most likely to conclude "irresponsible unions" or sire illegitimate children if they chose not to wed. Municipal officials repeatedly portrayed the Schutzverwandschaft as "this all too simple way of becoming part of the community," holding it answerable for "on the one hand, luring all sorts of rabble to the city, and, on the other, expediting marriages among people of small means."[84] The charge was less an expression of moral censure than disapproval based on economics. In the long run, such unconsidered marriages were seen as the root of much destitution.[85]

Following this line of reasoning, then, the ease with which a person became a Schutzverwandte could seduce the "incautious and the unwise" into taking the matrimonial plunge. Not only did such matches prove "very tragic for the state," but they were supposedly just as unhappy for the couples involved. These "either soon separate or have nothing better to do than embitter one another's lives." Considering the frequency with which domestic strife spilled out onto the streets, this last concern coincided with matters of public order as well.[86] More importantly, many saw these marriages as a tragedy for the state in that all too often the families thus "improvidently" created, later proved economically inviable. The arrival of children quickly completed the process of pauperizing a working family. Such families were seen as the breeding grounds of the new generations of beggars and criminals that crowded Hamburg's almshouses and prisons, "exhausting their resources." Servants, it was thought, ran special risks. Once having accustomed themselves to a "life of leisure[!]" in the households of their masters, "they are never quite able to accept the privations and belt-tightening" required to make tiny family economies succeed.[87]

From this perspective, municipal elites associated the system of Schutzverwandschaft with the increased poverty that they observed with growing apprehension in the 1760s, 1770s, and 1780s. Very little masked the official insinuation that the only reason people bothered with the legal formality of Schutzverwandschaft at all was to obtain legal sanction for their marriages. Some, "mostly the common people," circumvented marriage laws in other ways, "speaking their vows in churches outside the city, without seeking the permission of the Wedde and without paying the normal fees." However, the result was the same since these people "forthwith set up housekeeping in the city and carry out their businesses or trades without entering the nexus," and "all too quickly they end up as burdens on the local charities and almshouses." That the city proscribed such marriages and denied them validity deterred few.[88]

The Schutzverwandschaft was repeatedly held responsible for the financial crisis of the city, for the great proliferation in the numbers of the poor after 1763, and indeed—in the words of one man, hyperbolically—for being "the very fount of mendicancy."[89] One solution proposed several times to the Treasury and to the Rat suggested that citizenship be required of all those who wanted to settle in the city. The Schutzverwandschaft would be eliminated. The French, in fact, introduced a unitary citizenship in Hamburg in 1811. For most of the intervening time, the desirability of a cheap labor supply apparently overrode the possible advantages to be gleaned from a more restrictive policy. Lütkens, in the 1760s, remarked that "although it would be salutary if all Hamburg's inhabitants accommodated themselves to citizenship," he felt other considerations outweighed the putative benefits. He believed that "the continued affluence of so great a commercial center" dictated that the settlement of many outsiders be "expedited as much as is feasible."[90] In 1769, the Treasury agreed that "many inhabitants enhance business . . . and add to the revenues" of the city. Thus, it was an essential task of government to ensure "that many laborers are here to be found." The necessity of a plentiful labor supply made unrealistic any plans to abolish the Schutzverwandschaft. It seemed entirely sufficient to refuse to admit to Schutzverwandschaft "soldiers in foreign service, and people who do not even live in the city, who consume little or nothing here."[91] Although schemes for revamping the nexus categories continued to be proposed throughout the century,[92] the strategies advanced always stuck on such obstacles. At the very end of the century and at the beginning of the next, however, the number of Schutzverwandten declined sharply. As economic life stagnated during the Elbe blockade and later ground to a halt during the French occupation, the city simply created ever fewer Schutzverwandten. Of course, at the same time the demand for workers dried up and the burdens placed on poor relief intensified proportionally. Many manufactories shut down completely and commerce died, eliminating the earlier circumstances contraindicating the introduction of a "citizenship only" policy. After 1799, economic adversities and the highly charged political atmosphere combined to generate an official unwillingness to admit people to the Schutzverwandschaft. Admission to citizenship, meanwhile, suffered less, although the number of new citizens also declined measurably after 1802. For example, in 1795, 598 persons became Schutzverwandten, whereas in 1799 only 196 did. In the years between 1800 and 1809, only about 34 persons a year were added to the nexus as Schutzverwandten (Table 3.7).[93]

Manipulating the nexus was, of course, not the most direct way the city sought to control population movements. Hamburg also attempted to stop "foreign elements" from lodging in the city undetected. Along with their semiannual muster, the militia captains recorded the names and circumstances of all "logierende" aliens.[94] Numerous mandates[95] prohibited the "creeping in" of outsiders, while requiring ordinary citizens to report boarders and guests lodging with them directly to the militia captains. They were to be especially vigilant for "obviously pregnant" women and large families. Those

Table 3.7 Admission to the Nexus, 1800–1809

Year	Citizens	Schutzverwandten	Fremden-Kontrakt	Total
1800	1,447	33	36	1,516
1801	873	51	34	958
1802	1,004	75	40	1,119
1803	912	33	18	963
1804	835	44	26	905
1805	710	38	11	759
1806	834	7	12	853
1807	690	16	12	718
1808	634	25	6	665
1809	626	18	3	647
	8,565	340	198	9,103
	(94.09%)	(3.74%)	(2.18%)	

Source: Report "In den bürgerlichen Nexus der Stadt getretene von 1800 an." StAHbg,Senat Cl. VII, Lit. Nc, no. 12, vol. 5a.

who failed to register such suspicious persons with the authorities promptly were threatened with monetary fines or, in the case of abandoned children or pregnant women, with paying for their care.[96] Because the records of the lower court are no longer extant, it is impossible to say just how often, if ever, such penalties were applied. One suspects seldom. Still, the underlying motivation is clear enough. The main purpose of such mandates was not (at least not until 1793) to prevent seditious foreigners from stirring up trouble, or even to uncover criminals, but quite simply to do what they said: to prevent aliens from settling in the city, from taking work away from locals, and from falling onto the city's already overburdened charities. At times, other motives dominated. The prevention of plague, for example, triggered a spate of ordinances passed in the period from 1710 to 1713, which prohibited sheltering even overnight any newcomers who lacked valid health passes.[97]

Poor relief, therefore, can never be disengaged from the broader issues of population and politics discussed in this chapter. According to contemporary analyses, loopholes in the formulation and execution of nexus policies—in particular, those involving the Schutzverwandten—nurtured poverty. Furthermore, concerns over the Schutzverwandschaft impressed on Hamburg's elites the more general problems the city confronted after mid-century: population growth and diversification, the increasing vulnerability of the working poor to destitution, and the inadequacy of the existing administrative machinery. The rethinking and eventual restructuring of poor relief policies after mid-century would be influenced greatly by all these considerations. But the character of this reformulation would also reflect the pull in two directions that Hamburg's elites felt. On one side, they were not prepared to sever the flow of cheap labor into the city despite the poverty it inevitably seemed to entail, because that would have been economic suicide. They understood, however, that some nexus policies, in particular the Schutzverwandschaft, very probably nourished poverty. On the other side, they recognized the necessity of improving the ways in which the city was governed, yet here, too, they were faced with a dilemma: how could they promote efficiency and yet not relinquish the traditional, informal, and voluntarist ways of governing that they had always known and continued to revere. Despite much discussion, the Treasury, the Rat, and the Wedde could never strike a balance between these two equally desirable but apparently mutually unattainable goals. It was not until poverty was redefined and poor relief reorganized that Hamburg—partly and for a time—resolved some of these contradictions. New forms of poor relief promised to promote efficiency in government without eroding traditional ties of community or undoing the bonds of civic duty upon which government in Hamburg had always depended.

4

Patriots and the Redefinition
of Poverty, 1712–1785

The redefinition of poverty in the eighteenth century makes sense only when considered within the context of the two great historical events that spawned it. The first was the Enlightenment and the second was the massive economic and demographic changes that, while affecting most of Europe gradually and selectively, were rapidly transforming Hamburg into a modern commercial giant. Older historiography has tended to lump poor relief reform into a neat package of enlightened reform projects that touched all parts of society.[1] One would be foolish to suggest that the current of enlightened thought that washed over almost all European states somehow ebbed before reaching Hamburg. But it is hazardous as well to ignore the European Enlightenment as a protean and amorphous movement with various manifestations that by no means shared a clearly articulated or closely defined theory or program of action. If the philosophes all agreed on the essential dignity and goodness of man and on the value of reason in shaping social relationships, they haggled over how society might best be reconstructed, tailoring their ideas to suit specific times and localities. Still, without dismissing the importance of what may be termed generally enlightened views on the reorganization of poor relief in the eighteenth century, it is not necessary to succumb to a vague sort of humanitarian determinism by underestimating the role played by socioeconomic change. It was the latter that molded the Enlightenment itself in Hamburg, lending it the characteristically pragmatic stamp that became its hallmark after mid-century. Nor should one overlook the authority of civic traditions that had emerged in previous centuries and continued to exert formative powers on society and government at least until the mid-1800s. All these in combination brought about a poor relief reform in Hamburg in the last quarter of the century that, while perhaps radical in its extension and enlightened in its rhetoric, was at the same time firmly rooted in older civic traditions and conditioned by the peculiar economic and demographic realities of a pacesetter economy.

The Cameralist Heritage

The Enlightenment itself can boast little claim to originality in the realm of social and economic policies; it owed much to its cameralist antecedents. At the base of cameralism lay a holistic approach to the welfare of the state anchored in the "well-ordered police state," that is, in a state guided by rational rather than arbitrary principles. Only such a polity ensured the general well-being of the state as well as the felicity of its individual members, rich, middling, or poor.[2] Cameralism was in most of its forms quintessentially statist, vesting economic control and planning in the hands of the central government, thus generating the system usually known as mercantilism. It was essentially practical in its orientation, preferring to deal with the concrete realities of economic life, to move in the realm of the possible, and to eschew utopian dreams. Finally, it was "scientific" in its search for an exact knowledge (here, for the first time, equated with statistics) that would unlock the secrets of economic prosperity or misery and aid in the formulation of effective policies in all areas of human endeavor.[3] In the field of poor relief, the cameralists refused to separate poverty from broader economic issues. They successfully disseminated a concept of economically based poverty that would allow others to develop structural definitions and pioneer inventive new approaches to social welfare planning and practice later in the eighteenth century.[4]

The cameralist heritage greatly influenced Enlightenment thought on poor relief, whether or not the reformers involved accepted or rejected (as they did in Hamburg) mercantilist methods. In defining poverty as "economic inefficiency," the cameralists acknowledged that poverty could no longer be facilely interpreted as merited punishment for sin or as the end result of egregious moral flaws. They traced the sources of poverty not to the malevolence of paupers, but located them instead in the impersonal workings of the economy. "Obstacles" and "obstructions" arising from economic change—even, paradoxically, from economic growth—caused poverty. Such global perturbations eluded the control of the individual, subjecting the laborer to an impoverishment that he was unable to control, unable to combat, unable, without assistance, to overcome. Thus, it was here clearly the duty of the state to intervene.

Most cameralists favored the creation of workhouses, in the sense of "houses of industry," as the best means to busy the unproductive poor while simultaneously gearing up the productive capacity of the state.[5] The early cameralist thinker Johann Becher regarded the workhouse both as a school in which a "work methodology" and a new work ethic would be imparted to individuals, and as a laboratory where "manufacturing [techniques] would be discovered and [then] introduced" on a wider scale throughout the territory.[6] Almost all cameralists, and a majority of the adherents of Enlightenment— especially those in territorial states—advocated similar, statist solutions designed to assail the problem of poverty at its base by supporting government-sponsored manufactories (often physically located in workhouses and orphanages) fitted to undertake the task of school of industry for those unwilling to work and of voluntary workhouse for the willing.[7]

The cameralists also, however, stripped away from poverty some of the stigma that clung to it ever since the sixteenth century. "Incarceration in a workhouse," the cameralist author Johann von Justi insisted, "must have no shame adhering to it, [must] impart neither disgrace nor dishonor."[8] If the cameralists no longer found poverty contemptible and no longer blamed the individual for his economic plight, it was because they no longer viewed poverty as a personal flaw. The cameralists widened the definition of the deserving poor by couching it in economic rather than in purely moral or religious terms. This is not to suggest, however, that they lifted the moral responsibility for impoverishment totally from the shoulders of its victims. For beggars—those "shirkers" who preferred to live from alms—they evinced no sympathy.[9]

The eighteenth-century cameralists and their heirs, the German philosophes, regarded the increased impoverishment of their day as a barometer that accurately assessed the economic backwardness of the German territories. This economic malaise they diagnosed as a direct result of an inappropriate exploitation of labor and of a lack of jobs. Until these flaws were corrected, the economies of most territorial states would never exceed subsistence levels. To alleviate this vicious cycle of underemployment and impoverishment, they wanted to foster manufactures that drew on a pool of workers that until then had been inadequately utilized: the laboring poor. In a partnership of manufactories and workhouses, then, the cameralists saw a panacea for the sluggish, underdeveloped economies of the German territorial states.[10]

Simply in drawing these connections, the cameralists moved poor relief out of the province of either private or religious initiative and elevated it to a primary concern of the state. The first unmistakable declaration of the priority of the "secular competencies" (*weltlich-obrigkeitlicher Instanzen*) in poor relief is found in the writings of Becher, who advocated discarding private and ecclesiastical charity in favor of a universal poor tax (*Armensteuer*). Furthermore, he insisted that almsgiving be banned and almsgivers themselves fined "in the [amount] which they give to the poor annually."[11] Even if not all cameralists welcomed the idea of a tax to support the poor, almost complete unanimity reigned on the advantages to be gained by rationalizing and bureaucratizing the institutions of charity and philanthrophy.[12] Far too much money, they charged, had been squandered on the poor in the form of alms and inexpedient bequests, which had done little or nothing to relieve poverty but much to abet idleness. Too little had been spent purposefully for constructing houses of industry or promoting manufactures.[13]

The problem of poverty, however, had become increasingly complex in the eighteenth century. It soon exceeded the ability of any single person to evaluate either the need or the worthiness of each and every supplicant for assistance. Moreover, a scattering of alms could never achieve the almost universal results expected from houses of industry. For these reasons, the cameralists linked "purposeful poor relief" not only to well-managed institutions but also to careful investigations of individual cases of poverty to verify the extent of want and to discern the best ways in which funds might be expended. Their painstakingly careful scrutinies of society and social relationships carried over into poor relief as a desire for meticulous, methodical inquiries, and equally careful accounting of incomes and expenditures.[14]

In conclusion, then, we have seen that by proposing sweeping strategies to deal with the profound issue of economic torpor the cameralists by no means advocated purely negative, repressive measures for combating poverty.[15] Cure fundamental ills of underproduction and underemployment, they seemed to say, and the enigma of poverty would, if not quite solve itself, at least open itself to amelioration. Although the solutions the cameralists put forth, even when implemented, never produced, nor could have produced, the economic prosperity they so desired (nor, obviously, did they vanquish poverty), still they introduced the ideas and methods the Enlightenment would later adopt. It is a ticklish task to try to disentangle the two movements since there simply is no one point at which cameralism ended and the Enlightenment commenced. The one faded almost imperceptibly into the other and they often coexisted quite harmoniously. It is perhaps a bit simple to understand the Enlightenment as merely a culmination of cameralism, but this interpretation does explain the contradictory impulses toward control and liberation that characterized enlightened reforms.

Yet it does not quite work to see the Enlightenment in Hamburg as a form of cameralism. Nourished by territorial rulers anxious to augment control over their principalities, cameralism flourished in the German states in the seventeenth and eighteenth centuries. Cameralists were typically trained in law and in the *Kameral- und Polizeiwissenschaften,* with their education intended to create capable administrators, who would become the functionaries necessary to the task of constructing absolutism.[16] Hamburg was unlike any territorial state: Its politics, social composition, and economy all differed. Hamburg was a paragon of what the eighteenth century termed a republic. Its social composition was not rigidly defined by estates; its economy was an ebullient merchant capitalism that depended in no direct way on agriculture or hothouse industries. It is especially this last difference that is most pronounced. Hamburg's great if somewhat vulnerable prosperity, which was based on a fortunate combination of economic events and a stroke of geographic luck, set the city apart from the other German territories. Even bustling ports like Bremen and Lübeck, or, on a much smaller scale, Altona and Glückstadt, could only palely imitate Hamburg. Whereas the cameralists and enlightened bureaucrats in territorial states could adopt and promote as "progressive" programs of enlightened absolutism and mercantilist calculation, in Hamburg these same policies ran counter to time-honored municipal traditions and radically clashed with the central economic reality: Hamburg's economic puissance fed on the free flow of trade. Still many of the leaders of the Enlightenment in Hamburg—many of those who governed the city (especially after 1760)—had been educated at universities like Göttingen, which had strong cameralist curricula. The social theories to which they were exposed as students and the systematic legalistic approach they had learned, like the social policies they later embraced, never seemed alien or even unfamiliar to their counterparts—the enlightened bureaucrats, teachers, professors, and pastors—who worked to achieve the same goals albeit in the quite different setting of the territorial state. All accepted the basic view of a society divided into several groups. Each group, if no longer located in a hierarchy of rigorously defined and hermetically sealed estates, possessed its peculiar sources of dignity and its particular rights and privileges.[17] Yet while drawing heavily on the cameralist traditions of their youthful training, the residents of Hamburg adjusted for their own native circumstances modeling their own brand of Enlightenment and their own social policies to fit Hamburg's unique situation. We will want to keep in mind both these continuities and discontinuities, for neither the Enlightenment nor poor relief reform nor the changes in governing Hamburg can be understood unless seen as acting within these conplementary spheres of influence.

Specific events also shaped the content and concerns of the Enlightenment in Hamburg. During the eighteenth century, Hamburg twice experienced crises that drew from its elites prolonged analyses of the problems and their solutions. Both emergencies, one vaguely political, the other clearly economic, evoked feelings of disorientation and anxiety. Both resulted in a new form of public expression: the patriotic society. These societies responded to perceived inadequacies in communal governance with programs that, while boldly utilitarian in tone, never really crossed conservative political, social, and religious boundaries. Each addressed the broader issues of population growth and economic transformation discussed earlier. What will interest us here is how enlightened opinion, as expressed in the patriotic societies and among the elite of Hamburg (to a great degree, overlapping categories), came to grips with these problems, thrashed out proposals for their amelioration, and implemented their solutions.[18]

The Patriot

Hamburg in the 1720s was the scene of political and psychological retrenchment and reorientation. The Recess of 1712 had ended decades of civil strife. Now the city faced an uncertain, if vaguely promising future. It was still burdened with the tasks of soothing festering civic wounds, of learning to live with a new constitution, and of developing a civic identity that blended old values and new aspirations. Although the Haupt-Recess proved in many ways a tremendously successful political document because it halted further political upheaval, its weaknesses had been all too palpably exposed by the plague-induced crisis of 1712–14 and by the dislocations of the Great Northern War, which engulfed the city even if the actual fighting did not. Both emergencies taxed the ingenuity of the existing government to the point that it found itself forced to initiate extradordinary commissions (e.g., the *Sanitäts-Collegium*) to deal with truly extraordinary problems. Another response was the founding of Hamburg's first Patriotic Society (the *Patriotische Gesellschaft*) in 1724. Unlike most of the other *teutsch-übende Gesellschaften* of the day, its goals were not primarily literary and linguistic. Instead, it posed a self-consciously moral and patriotic reply to problems of communal governing.[19] *Der Patriot*,[20] the publication of the circle of friends who formed the society, ranks as Germany's premier "moral weekly." Like its English model, Addison and Steele's

Spectator, it sought to amuse and entertain, but it also endeavored to forge a new kind of public morality, seeking to cast citizens in the mold of patriot described in an early issue: "a being for whom the welfare of his fatherland is a weighty concern, who acknowledges his God, who honors the ministry, [who] cherishes truth and order, [who] obeys the authorities, and who genuinely strives to advance the common good, . . ."[21]

Patriotism in the context of the eighteenth century has generally been identified as a social and not a political trait.[22] An eighteenth-century patriot was, therefore, "a man who had done something to promote the common good, such as . . . written a book on agriculture, or education, or ethics, or who had performed a signal act of beneficence." Nonetheless, Hamburg's patriots never renounced politics, nor did they reject traditional political pathways. Rather, they expanded the realm of politics by alloying private initiative to public benefit. They mapped out for each patriot extensive duties in the social, economic, moral, and intellectual spheres, but simultaneously reinforced the traditional stature of the voluntary exercise of political office. Patriotism encapsulated a strong inner drive that had as its goal the improvement of state and society; patriots, therefore, sought all possible ways to further the welfare of the community in which they lived.[23] Later in the century, another patriot, Johann Albert Heinrich Reimarus, would extol Hamburg's "free constitution" while settling the responsibility for sustaining this "true liberty" squarely on the shoulders of Hamburg's citizens.

> [In Hamburg] no arbitrary power thwarts the exercise of our rights, the utilization of our energies, and the enjoyment of our property. The common consent of citizens determines our laws and our taxes. Public expenditures are made only for the common good. . . . We recognize no inherited family privileges. . . . Positions of authority are honorary, . . . the arrangements [guiding our] electoral process prevents [both] tyranny and factionalism.
>
> Most government offices are administered voluntarily; a method especially fitting for republics, so that citizens are [constantly] reminded that they should view public affairs as their own affairs. [This is] without doubt [a situation] which . . . produces more honesty and diligence in administration than is found in [other] places among paid bureaucrats.[24]

In the 1720s, the authors of *Der Patriot* wanted to reawaken men to their duties as citizens and revive languishing civic virtues, while instilling new ones suitable to Hamburg's place in the modern world. At the same time, it hoped to wean Hamburg's elites away from aristocratic pretensions and teach them the value of commitment to an older republicanism. A program of reform integrated within the boundaries of existing government and based on rational Christianity was an inseparable part of this vision. The patriot described here was a Christian, and patriotism admitted no contradiction between faith and rationality. *Der Patriot* could not imagine of "any state in which Christianity has decayed because some of its subjects rely on natural laws and rational principles, [and] work to guide their fellow citizens away from follies in those things which relate to everyday social relationships, domestic life, education, and so on." *Der Patriot* reasoned that the "Republick" lacked not more pious but "cleverer and more prudent citizens," and thus the patriot should bend his energies toward eliminating those "thousand things . . . which harm the soul, . . . impair [our] health, retard our prosperity, and damage our property."[25] Of the "thousand things" this Patriotic Society, as well as its more famous successor, the Patriotic Society of 1765, singled out for its attention was societal indifference to poverty and government inertia in providing for the poor.

The discussion of poor relief, however, never appeared in isolation: It was always locked within a larger framework of ways "to serve the republic." During the eighteenth century, the conviction grew among many that the condition of the poor reliably and accurately indicated the strength of a state as a whole. Such opposites as Samuel Johnson and Voltaire could agree that a decent provision for the poor was the truest test of civilization. A broad segment of public opinion—enlightened or not—came to share this belief, which perhaps accounts for the relative ease with which poor relief reform was achieved; however, such similarly enlightened objectives as the introduction of educational reforms or the securement of religious toleration simultaneously ran aground on the continued hostility of those same powerful interests—chief among them the pastors and merchants—who accepted poor relief reform as a necessary and exigent task of governing. Those who contributed to *Der Patriot,* of course, fostered such sentiment by pointing to the immense practicality of such programs for securing the blessings of economic prosperity and political stability. In expressing a sincere and deep admiration for the Netherlands, the authors of *Der Patriot* pointed out that Dutch freedom and *Kultur* derived as much from its laudable concern for the poor and for widows and orphans as from its evenhanded taxation policies, its plentitude of employment opportunities, and its invaluable—if intangible— "acquisitive drive." The last was panegyrized as the very "soul of the state." The United Provinces represented a polity (significantly like Hamburg a republic) where excellent social policies not merely underwrote, but indeed actuated true freedom.[26] This article argued that a well-constructed constitution alone could never guarantee freedom and wealth. It was worthless without the patriotic engagement of citizens to safeguard the liberty and affluence that begot the true happiness (*Glückseligkeit*) of a state for "a free republic is most fortunate when not only on the lips of flatterers but also in facts and deeds, the authorities act like fathers [and] the citizens like dutiful sons of the fatherland. Their concern for their own self-preservation binds them together like parents and children, and this mutual love generates a pact that once struck is forever indissoluble. . . ."[27]

Issue 37 of *Der Patriot* initiated the discussion of poor relief. Herein the hypothetical patriot evaluated the existing methods of poor relief in Hamburg, appending his own thoughts on their improvement. The author of this particular issue, Barthold Heinrich Brockes—the highly respected Bürgermeister and widely admired poet—listed all the various institutions existing for the poor in Hamburg, singling out parish relief as "that excellent arrangement" that maintained thousands in the city on a weekly basis. Yet while distributing praise, he also bared many inadequacies. He defined the central problem that plagued all forms of poor relief in early modern Europe: Despite the work of such "splendid institutions," the number of "brazen beggars" continued to rise and impoverishment increase. Both past observers and modern historians are inclined to agree that the eighteenth century was "the begging century," with more people than ever before going needy. The problems associated with mendicancy appeared to spread with sinister speed, hatching begging clans from which sprang ever new generations of social parasites.[28]

Brockes, like many of his contemporaries, linked the common good with suitable care for the poor. These men based their own theory and practice of welfare on the unquestioned necessity of supporting the deserving poor and adamantly opposed wasting charity on the undeserving. Brockes expressed a widely held sentiment when he declared himself "as great a friend of the poor man as the declared enemy of the beggar." No one in the eighteenth century thought otherwise. No one in the eighteenth century or since has seriously advocated aiding the "undeserving poor," regardless of how the latter are defined. The difficulty was and still is in deciding on the worthiness of the applicant. How did one measure, weigh, evaluate, and test such an ephemeral quality as "worth"? In small communities, where each person knew his neighbors fairly well, the decision took place informally, almost unconsciously, if not necessarily judiciously; however, in a large, anonymous city, the task became more arduous and uncertain. That was the dilemma the city had faced (albeit in smaller dimensions) since the criterion of worth had been introduced into charity. Brockes granted the dilemma in pointing out that

> [every]one knows needy people who have skills, capacity, and desire; however, in spite of their best efforts, they find nothing, simply because they have no connections. These suffer the most extreme afflictions and direst poverty, and if they do not resort to forbidden activities are cast into utter despair. Is there anything more reprehensible than by denying them work to degrade such persons, our neighbors, our fellow-Christians, and our brothers, who wish nothing more than to expend every mortal energy that human and Christian duty demands of them, into thieves, highwaymen, or even suicides? Nothing is easier for many people [acting together] than to find work for a needy person. Where this does not occur, there is a lack of love, a lack of proper order, or a deficit of both.

The ideal test of merit was to offer the supplicant work, but the individual citizen—especially in a metropolitan setting like that of Hamburg—was only seldom in a position to do so and thus the state or rather public institutions must deal with the problem in more expedient if less personal ways.[29]

It was then a question of how best to organize public institutions to handle the dual tasks of providing employment and testing worth. The supporters of *Der Patriot* accepted Becher's idea for a general workhouse as the most expeditious way to halt mendicancy and to discourage "foreign idlers" from entering the city; however, they saw beyond Becher's vision, suggesting that the real benefit of a workhouse was not that it prevented begging by frightening off beggars. Far more valuable was its pedagogical significance; that is, its ability to educate beggars to an honest livelihood. These goals could not be achieved by distributing alms. A generous and uncritical scattering of largess only had the undesirable and unwanted effect of turning laborers into laggards. Erecting houses of industry on the other hand, or establishing in them useful manufactories, promised to eliminate mendicancy, stimulate commerce, enrich the state, and underwrite its freedom.[30]

Der Patriot thus elevated poor relief to the level of other political affairs, such as foreign policy or finances. In stressing communal responsibility for the poor, *Der Patriot* preached nothing revolutionary. Poor relief in Hamburg had never been relegated to private initiative or left to ecclesiastical control. Nor did the principle of state action in this form in any way threaten the position of Hamburg's elites. Patriotism called on the same communal energy that had animated sixteenth-century parish relief. Just as the reform of poor relief in the sixteenth century had been expected to seal the rifts opened in Hamburg's society by religious turmoil, *Der Patriot,* in the midst of another crisis, called for reform to fortify political freedom and to cultivate republicanism.

We must briefly assess the influence that this circle of patriots exerted in order to understand and measure their ability to implement their ideas from abstract cogitation into concrete political action. Prominent political figures were among the small number of contributors to *Der Patriot:* Johann Julius Surland was a syndic to the Rat; Conrad Widow was a doctor of law, senator, Bürgermeister from 1742 until 1754, and a correspondent of Leibniz; Brockes, also a doctor of law, was elected to the Rat in 1720, and later became Bürgermeister; Johann Klefeker, another doctor of law, was syndic in the Rat, and the author of a twelve-volume compendium of Hamburg's government, as well as "one of the most important Hamburg politicians of his time"; finally, Johann Julius Anckelmann served in the influential role of secretary to the Oberalten. These patriots, then, wielded political clout and could act as a powerful pressure group. In addition, within their ranks shone some of the brightest lights in Hamburg's intellectual firmament; Johann Albert Fabricius, a doctor of theology and professor of morals and rhetoric at Hamburg's Academic Gymnasium; Johann Adolf Hoffmann, almost a Renaissance man (philosopher, philologist, merchant, and author); Christian Friedrich Weichmann state councillor to the prince of Braunschweig-Blankenberg and a member of the London Royal Society; and finally, John Thomas, pastor of the Anglican community in Hamburg from 1719 to 1737, who ended his days as bishop of Salisbury.[31]

To be sure, one should not overestimate the extent or overvalue the impact of the early Enlightenment in Hamburg. Before mid-century the advocates of Enlightenment were few, numbering no more than two or three dozen literati, intellectuals, and jurists. Furthermore, in the chilly Lutheran climate of Hamburg, the Enlightenment's sphere of action remained narrowly circumscribed and its proponents an embattled minority. Neither can one ignore the accumulated testimony of contemporaries on the "philistinism" of most Hamburg merchants, who bothered with little more than a fastidious balancing of their account books. Only later—toward the end of the century as the ideas of Enlightenment changed—did it gather supporters among the merchants and win over an increasing number of pastors. The Enlightenment thus became a sort of "Protestant lay theology."[32] Still, even the early patriots wielded more than a modest ability to sway public opinion. And one should not ignore the fact that as early as the 1720s the Enlightenment had drawn to its banner many citizens who were deeply engaged in the formulation of municipal policy at the highest level.

Poor Relief Reform in the 1720s

Almost 250 years had elapsed since poor relief had last occupied the time and energies of the Rat and Bürgerschaft. Only once, in 1711–14, had the city seriously reworked, and then only temporarily, the parish system by centralizing and streamlining relief efforts. That endeavor, as we have seen, quickly withered and died once the imminent threat of plague receded over the horizon. In the 1720s, a wave of intellectual ferment, a cooling of the economy, and political uncertainties revived interest in poor relief reform. In 1725, the city embarked on a major revision of poor relief policy following the lines first established by the board of health in 1711–14 and theoretically extended and embellished by the patriotic circle. Brockes probably raised the issue in the Rat and, with the probable assistance of other patriots who were influential in government, shepherded the plan through the Rat and Bürgerschaft.[33] Though not embracing all the ideals of *Der Patriot,* the proposal the Rat placed before the Bürgerschaft for budgetary approval in October 1725 did outline similar goals and suggest interrelated and equally desirable objectives. First, the new system would eliminate from the city all "dangerous beggars," who were depicted here as a source of especially grave concern when placed against a backdrop of "the overwhelming throng [of people] in Hamburg." Second, it would offer the poor an "opportunity to earn their bread" and thus "fashion out of these useless folk valued members of society." Finally, these revisions in poor relief promised to expand economic opportunities for the city by sustaining a broad spectrum of commercial activities.[34] The Rat stood firm in rejecting "the mere extension of alms" as an effective way to combat poverty, even if enough money could be raised because "such would . . . be fruitless for the Republic, merely allowing our state to be overrun with that many more idlers and bootless folk, who would eventually deprive the deserving poor and the truly needy of their rightful alms and exhaust [the goodwill and the funds] of their benefactors." Only through the "assignment of work" could the existence of the poor be rendered tolerable in a city and perhaps even be made to turn a profit.[35]

The founding purpose of the Zuchthaus had been identical; however, the principle reason why the Zuchthaus failed to fulfill its original "salutary intention" was that the size of the task vastly exceeded the available space in the

building. Moreover, the Zuchthaus imparted a stigma of dishonor, which frightened away the respectable poor. The Rat briefly debated the possibility of
adding an annex to the existing facilities, but quickly rejected it as too expensive. Even more tellingly, the Rat judged confinement in the Zuchthaus as
counterproductive in dealing with poverty because it isolated laborers from the
workaday world rather than reintegrating them. In lieu of confinement, the Rat
advanced the idea of "an auxiliary form of support," defined as "free work"
done outside the spatial confines of the Zuchthaus. The Rat believed that
"many people [will] be able to obtain a living through the orderly distribution
of . . . the wages which they draw in compensation for their labor."[36] Already
in the 1720s, therefore, Hamburg's elites had developed a healthy skepticism
about the efficacy of confinement as a panacea for all social problems.

The Rat then consulted several local manufacturers for expert assistance in
selecting the best form of work for the poor. They soon agreed on the knitting of
woolen hosiery as "convenient, easily, and quickly learned." It necessitated no
expensive equipment, little skill, virtually no strength (although some dexterity), making it fitting employment for women and children. Almost as an
afterthought, they included the more difficult if somewhat more profitable task
of spinning. Knitting would fulfill the labor requirements of local stocking
manufacturers without damaging the economic well-being of other trades. The
manufacturers with whom the Rat conferred promised that they could employ
some thirty to fifty thousand persons "effortlessly." For the Rat these broader
commercial advantages seemed as attractive as the short-range objective of
simply employing the poor. The hope in the Rat was to draw into the city the
work that manufacturers had previously farmed out to villages surrounding
Hamburg "so that the money spent [by knitters] in wages will remain within our
walls and circulate here, with the result that, as knitting grows in popularity . . . the woolen trade will vastly increase and . . . other related manufactures such as dyeing and stocking-pressing will prosper. . . ."[37]

A new era in Hamburg's social policies dawned in 1726. The Rat and
Bürgerschaft had effected—at least on paper—a centrally administered outdoor system of relief. The Relief Ordinance[38] published in February 1726 bade
all those who wanted work and who either had been born in Hamburg or had
resided there several years to report to their militia captain. The Rat charged
the captains with compiling accurate lists of all such persons in their regiments.
These lists were forwarded to the board of governors of the Zuchthaus because
they now coordinated all phases of the "new" poor relief. In 1725–26, the
registered poor (eingeschriebene Arme) numbered 2850, or about 3.2 percent
of a population of almost 90,000 (figures for 1710).[39] Minor Zuchthaus officials
distributed yarn or wool to the registered poor for spinning or knitting in their
homes and, if necessary, arranged for instruction in these skills. For the finished
yarn or stockings the workers received a weekly wage and a premium "because
it is so difficult for a single person, let alone those with young children, to earn
enough from knitting to feed himself in a city where all goods are so dear."
Indeed, those who first had to learn knitting were promised support during
their instruction. The ordinances led to the creation of a special office (Armen-

Comptoir) inside the Zuchthaus to coordinate the activities of the relief, to register the poor, to distribute raw materials and wages.[40]

Central to the success of the entire venture was the strict prohibition of all begging and all almsgiving. Apprehended beggars were sentenced to hard labor in the Zuchthaus, or banished if they were not natives of Hamburg. Almsgivers were threatened with a stiff fine of five Reichsthaler.[41] The job of controlling beggars remained in the hands of the church runners (*Kirchen-Vögte*) as it had ever since the Reformation. These runners were among the lowliest of salaried municipal officials and usually came from the very milieu that they were supposed to police. The common people despised them and their successors—the beggar chasers (*Armen-Vögte*) employed by the General Poor Relief—taunting them with slurs of "swine" and "scum" and frequently molesting them as they moved about the city. Almost no one wasted a good word on them, and loathing for them extended up and down the social ladder. Everyone suspected the chasers of misusing their office, of favoritism, of collusion, and even of outright cruelty. When these suspicions were verified, which was distressingly often, the Rat punished chasers for abusing their powers, principally for assailing innocent persons and wrongfully accusing them of mendicancy. Throughout the century, the Rat tried to increase the probity but also the security and prestige of the chasers as municipal officials—first by admonishing the garrison soldiers and night watchmen to assist the chasers (and not interfere with them as they often did!), then, by threatening to punish anyone who hindered chasers in the execution of their proper duties, and finally, by giving them their own special clothing and badge of office. All this proved futile, because the badges and special clothing only made it easier for their tormenters to identify them.[42]

Certain restrictions and limitations pertained to all those on the relief rolls. Anyone who "embezzled" charitable funds—that is, sold or pawned the yarn or equipment entrusted to them—ran the risk of severe punishment, including incarceration and, with further misbehavior, corporal chastisement. Furthermore, the 1726 relief ordinance denied the enrolled poor permission to move freely from one parish to another without notifying their respective militia captain in advance. This restriction was imposed to prevent anyone from obtaining support in two parishes simultaneously and was an administrative measure to impede the mobility of the poor. Those incapable of working—the old, the infirm, or the very young—had claim to assistance as long as they did not already benefit from parish relief or from private bequests.[43] Paupers enrolled in parish relief had always forfeited some of their inheritance rights and this same stricture also applied to those supported by the Zuchthaus. These conditions, as well as the dishonor of the pauper's funeral, functioned to some extent as a deterrent that discouraged all but the most destitute from appealing for aid. But it was also simply a method of replenishing funds. The seeming harshness of this rule was substantially mitigated by provisions that allowed surviving minor children to inherit the moneys due them from burial funds as well as any possessions or property—minus the sum required to defray the costs of the pauper's funeral.[44]

The governors of the Zuchthaus, or, as was increasingly the case, the two senior governors (*Jahresverwalter*) decided on who was eligible for support. The board of governors met weekly to amend the lists of the poor, striking the names of those who had died in the intervening eight days, or of those who, because of invalidism or illness, had been transferred to one of the hospitals. They also deleted those "who either do not need or are not deserving" of support, and "as circumstances allow" registered in their places those regarded as worthy replacements. The governors themselves never conducted the initial inspection of the poor as required in the relief ordinance of 1726; that job fell to five salaried inspectors (in 1771 the number was reduced to four). An inspector interviewed each pauper about his "circumstances and life-style," queried about burial funds and about alms received from other sources, ascertained the names and ages of family members, the amount of rent he paid, and the family's occupations and earnings. Working from this information, the governors then calculated on an individual basis how much each pauper would receive. The 1726 relief ordinance set no guidelines.[45]

The initial hearing was by far the most thorough. Follow-up interviews were ever less frequently performed, except in the most perfunctory manner. Each Thursday in the Zuchthaus chapel, one of the governors was to conduct an examination of all those wishing to register for relief. A ceremonious general visitation of all the registered poor by the governors was to take place annually. In fact, by the middle of the century, as the number of dependents reached 2,400, this sort of personal contact and supervision by the governors had long since fallen into abeyance. The overworked inspectors assumed an increasing amount of responsibility for the daily administration of poor relief. It was the inspectors who paid wages and ensured that rules were observed.[46]

The first reviews of the new relief resonated with promise. In July 1728, for example, the Rat boasted to the Bürgerschaft that "the city and its adjacent territories have been cleansed of all dissolute beggars, the idlers have been employed, and the needy given fair chance to earn their bread and keep."[47] Apparently reality proved less rosy. Despite forethought and care, the new poor relief never fulfilled these early great expectations. The board of governors had struck a bargain with local stocking manufacturers in 1727, but it was a short-lived and rocky relationship that satisfied neither party. The merchants continually complained about shabby workmanship, which they attributed to improper supervision, and refused to renew the agreement when it expired. The board of governors discovered to its dismay that the merchants could by no means employ 30,000–50,000 people (in 1732 only *142* paupers were working for them) and municipal subsidies rose staggeringly in a desperate effort to prop up the edifice.[48] The "new" poor relief soon degenerated into exactly what its proponents had wished to correct: It was an alms institution, capable of merely satisfying the immediate and most basic wants of its dependents with outlays of money, bread, clothing, and fuel, while demanding no useful work in return. The Zuchthaus was seen not as a house of industry but as a bower of idleness, which rewarded, and, far worse, encouraged indolence.[49]

The actual reasons for the collapse of the reform of 1725–26 became important for the lessons they taught those who would turn again to poor relief reform more than four decades later. According to Johann Georg Büsch, the faults of the plan were many, yet none stemmed from inadequate planning or even from insufficient funding alone. On the contrary, he had only praise for the 1726 measures as "more painstakingly prepared than anything which had gone before." The principles followed were sound: "for the industrious, not the indolent were to be helped." The premium paid in addition to wages was necessary because the public would always have to underwrite a relief predicated on employing the poor as wage earners. According to Büsch, the imperfections lay not in purpose but in execution, particularly in regard to the policy against beggars, the selection of work, and, perhaps most critically, in respect to staffing.[50]

Büsch argued that begging had not been sufficiently prohibited but only made somewhat riskier, and that the influx of foreign beggars had not been deflected. Because the Zuchthaus could accommodate only a limited number of persons and the governors quite understandably preferred expending their limited funds on the destitute (and were legally bound to allot certain sums to the care of prisoners incarcerated in the Zuchthaus for misdemeanors other than begging), the sentencing of a beggar to four or eight weeks in the Zuchthaus usually meant that he or she was shunted in one door and out the other, often within twenty-four hours.[51] Repeatedly in the 1740s and 1750s, the city tried other ways of handling "sturdy beggars." For example, in the 1740s, as the city rebuilt its crumbling fortifications, healthy beggars were routinely set to work with pick and shovel. In 1752, the governors hit upon the idea of transporting inmates to Nova Scotia as colonists.[52] None of these solutions was anything more than a palliative, temporarily siphoning off excess bodies, rather than providing a viable, long-term alternative to locking up beggars. Everyone seemed to acknowledge that this last solution was grossly inefficient as well as costly.

The selection of knitting as the principal occupation (few of the poor were able to spin) had turned out to be a critical miscalculation. Poor relief officials had foreseen that no one could nourish himself from knitting alone; however, they had not fully grasped how precipitously subsidies would rise. Then, when Danish and Mecklenburg competition undercut Hamburg's market in stockings, the administration of the relief vacillated, and seemed unable to shift gears and adopt another form of work. Its hesitation revealed either a lamentable lack of flexibility and marketing expertise, or, perhaps more fundamentally to Büsch, an inadequate grasp of the principles upon which Hamburg's economy was based.[53]

The final inadequacy that Büsch identified concerned personnel. The major reason the 1726 poor relief fell short of its goals was due in his estimation to a prevailing deficiency in civic spirit. This shortcoming led people to believe that salaried officials could somehow replace men who served voluntarily and that taxes, rather than contributions, would suffice to support the poor. The militia captains (themselves citizens), who were originally selected to carry out the regular inspection of the poor in their parishes, now no longer did so. In effect this duty had devolved on the shoulders of the five paid inspectors. "How did one come to suppose this possible!" mused Büsch. "In 1529 our forefathers chose forty-eight citizens who *out of a sense of duty* served their less fortunate fellows, . . . and now five hirelings are enough. . . ?"[54]

Furthermore, the rapid turnover among governors made the formulation— to say nothing of the execution—of consistent policies virtually impossible. In 1781, the Rat noted this problem and brought it to the attention of the board of governors. The Rat suggested that better results might be obtained by appointing governors for life, exempting them from their other communal duties, and augmenting their numbers while eliminating the expensive and time-consuming ceremonies—such as the seasonal banquets (*Mahlzeiten*)— required of them ex officio. Even though these admittedly modest improvements never took effect, the concerns voiced in 1781 signaled the awareness in the Rat of the gravity of the situation. New problems of governing now weighed heavily on public officers and institutions, and the concern of the Rat testified to the escalation of time and effort invested in administering social policies.[55] As in so many other branches of communal government, the obligations of the governors had become so multifarious and complex that no individual could satisfy them. As Caspar Voght observed, "Even the most zealous man in this position could never really know what he should be doing . . . or found himself in his turn [as senior governor] suddenly overwhelmed, [and thus] reduced to a slavish reliance on assistants who knew the routine. Finally he came to entrust the whole business to them."[56] Moreover, the existence of a sort of poor tax levied in the form of property taxes[57] to finance poor relief had, in Büsch's estimation, further reduced the sources of philanthropy. It became easier to hand out alms than struggle with the thornier problems of creating useful employment for the poor. At the same time, a poor tax opened a psychologically undesirable chasm between the richer citizen and his needier fellows, further stifling civic concern and diminishing (rather than augmenting as poor relief was supposed to do) a sense of civic spirit and public pride. Using salaried officials to execute the most essential tasks of relief—those most eminently suited to be conducted by citizens and by citizens alone, including the exacting investigation of the individual circumstances of each and every pauper—only sped the decline of community involvement and impeded a process of social learning that personal contact alone nurtured.[58]

Despite the rapid breakdown of the 1726 relief, so apparent to late eighteenth-century commentators like Büsch, little was done in the next four decades either to get the system back on track or to alter radically its propositions and execution. Instead, poor relief drifted back into the realm of the parish while the punishment of beggars fell to the praetors and the Zuchthaus. Perhaps this lassitude derived from disillusionment. However, the direction the economy took in the 1730s, 1740s, and 1750s probably provides a more likely answer; decades later this time was admired as a period of solid property and good employment opportunities when many branches of the economy encountered labor shortages. Yet the signs of social disequilibrium persisted, most clearly in the unrelenting problem of beggary. While it is possible that the number of the indigent declined, the number of foreign beggars—like the number of newcomers to the city in general—certainly rose. While the War of the Polish Succession (1730–35) caused relatively little disruption in central Europe—except along the upper Rhine—the War of the Austrian Succession (1740–48) sent thousands cascading out of war-torn areas. A considerable number of these refugees found their way to Hamburg. After 1730, Hamburg passed a series of stiff measures to control mendicancy. In addition to the normal, periodic drives for contributions to support public asylums like the Zuchthaus and the Pesthof, disasters prompted extraordinary collections. The escalating number of public collections in the 1760s and 1770s reflected as well the worsening economic situation of these years, an emergency that was especially pronounced during the subsistence crisis of 1771–72. Especially frequent in these years were collections for "the suffering poor in the cold of winter" and those made homeless by fire and especially by flood, as the dearth of cheap housing drove an increasing number of people to live in miserable cellar-dwellings that flooded with each heavy rain.[59]

In the end, however, it was a perceived "increasing plague of beggars" and the utter inability of poor relief to deal with impoverishment that led to new departures in poor relief in the 1770s and 1780s. It was the economic crisis that began in 1763, following as it did on the heels of an era of economic buoyance, that offered a startlingly clear picture of how precarious the security of the laborer was when prosperity sifted away.

The Patriotic Society of 1765

As the members of the first Patriotic Society died or left Hamburg, the Enlightenment lost momentum. It did not perish but instead retreated into less public forums, finding quiet refuge in a network of sociable clubs (like the *Freitags-Collegium von Rechtsgelehrten* and the *Dienstagsgesellschaft Hamburgischer Juristen*) and in informal circles of friends surrounding the three major intellectual figures still residing in Hamburg: the poet Friederich von Hagedorn; the philologist Michael Richey; and Hermann Samuel Reimarus, professor of Oriental languages, biblical scholar, and author of the controversial *Wolfenbütteler Fragmente,* posthumously published by Lessing. Two events tranformed the Enlightenment in Hamburg from the dreams harbored by a coterie of learned men with limited (if by no means negligible) importance and scope into a powerful and effective reform movement. The first event was the great economic crisis that engulfed Hamburg in 1763; the second was the accelerated infusion of cameralist and national economic teachings that shaped the message of the Enlightenment into a more pragmatic mold that was more palatable and more immediately relevant to merchants and statesmen.

The Patriotic Society of 1765[60] was a product of this realignment, and its greatest success was the reconstitution of poor relief in 1788. The society drew on the intellectual traditions of the earlier patriots, but never escaped the formative influence of the economic crisis of 1763 in which it was conceived. Hamburg's economy, like that of almost every other major European port, had always profited as much from war booms as it suffered from postwar contractions. Throughout the Seven Years' War, an unprecedented stream of easy credit offered by banks in Amsterdam, Berlin, and Hamburg encouraged unbridled, often reckless speculation that depended on a vast expansion of Prussian trade after the war to compensate the overextension of credit. By the late 1750s, however, runaway inflation had depreciated Hamburg's banking currency—the mark courant—to a point that adversely affected the city's foreign exchange; this led to a major reorganization of banking marked by a radical constriction of credit. When Frederick II inflated the value of the Prussian currency in 1763, a panic in the European money market arose first in Amsterdam and then radiated outward, striking Hamburg, Berlin, and Stockholm in quick succession. The resulting run on private banks in Hamburg brought down ninety-seven banking houses in 1763 alone, initiating the worst economic depression for Hamburg since the 1720s. The mercantilist policies adopted by many of Hamburg's major trading partners—especially Austria and Prussia—soon thereafter, deepened the existing financial crisis and endangered the health of Hamburg's export industries.[61]

Eighteenth-century observers saw the end of the Seven Years' War as a milestone, marking the beginning of a long period of depression that lasted through the 1780s. More accurate is that by the end of the 1770s Hamburg had made good its losses in the financial debacle of 1763 and was entering a period of slow growth that would continue until the boom of the 1790s provided Hamburg with previously unknown wealth and power. Thus, only when delimited by two periods of especially great prosperity (before 1763 and after 1788), can the 1770s and 1780s be regarded as especially depressed. Contemporaries, however, did not benefit from this perspective. They were deeply troubled by Hamburg's apparent inability to rebound from the almost crippling wave of bankruptcies, and they were unnerved by the specter of new mercantilist restrictions that threatened to sever Hamburg's access to lucrative markets in the European interior. Deeper, more lasting perturbations—among them the massive population growth that had pulled so many "outsiders" to Hamburg that old burghers were rapidly becoming a minority in their own city—combined with the weakened state of the economy to bewilder them and set into motion an evaluation of what had happened, what the future might bring, and how to deal with both. The founding in 1765 of the Hamburg Society for the Encouragement of the Arts, Manufacturers, and Commerce—commonly known as the Patriotic Society—was the most organized and focused part of this response.[62]

As an agent of Enlightenment, the Patriotic Society of 1765 differed from its predecessor principally in the amount of influence that it exerted on Hamburg's government, in its character as a practical reform movement, and in its membership, which reversed the merchant/intellectual ratio of the Patriotic Society of 1724 strongly in the favor of merchants. Precisely because merchants and intellectuals joined together in the new Patriotic Society, its deliberations and actions reveal the attitudes of a group of men who were simultaneously prominent in business, in government, and in intellectual life.[63] These men explored, in turn, Hamburg's politics and economics, its educational facilities, and its social welfare organizations. Their debates disclose a sometimes sophisticated, sometimes overly enthusiastic and naively optimistic approach to problems of social policy as they probed Hamburg's economic substratum for answers to social problems they perceived as pressing.

In 1765, a member of the Reimarus circle, the jurist Johann Ulrich Pauli, had penned an appeal "To All True Hamburg Patriots,"[64] calling for the establishment in Hamburg of an "economic" society modeled on those already existing in England, France, Leipzig, and Haarlem. The society he envisioned would devote itself to strengthening Hamburg's place "in the vanguard of European commercial cities" and "to promoting the expansion and improvement of her manufactories and trades, to preserving and increasing the security, happiness, and freedom of the city's inhabitants, and, finally, to beautifying the environment." The foremost goal was to stimulate a flagging economy. Pauli, like his friends, viewed "our republic [as] nothing more than a commercial state, where each and every thing derives its politics, its livelihood, and its very essence from commerce." Furthermore, because "our state lives from commerce and manufacturing [alone] . . . we must, therefore, elevate these [branches of the economy] and make them as remunerative as humanly possible."[65] Pauli articulated the connections between economic success and public welfare that by 1765 had formed in the minds of these men. Another prominent member of the Reimarus circle, Johann Albert Heinrich Reimarus (old Samuel's son), pointed out "that when we offer assistance to those who have already demonstrated their industry and ingenuity, when we publicly applaud ability, nourish cleverness and skill, [and] when we work to throw down the obstacles hampering the success of our ventures, . . . we believe then that we have not built on unsound foundations, and have not labored in vain."[66]

The seven-volume *Deliberations* (*Verhandlungen und Schriften*)[67] of the Patriotic Society mirror better than any other single source the concerns of Hamburg's elites and elucidate how these concerns shaped the program of the society. The society foreswore all "Chimären" and "Projecten" directing its energies into practical channels, establishing over a period of years, schools for draftsmen, navigators, businessmen, and clerks, formulating plans for insurance companies and pension funds, and laying the groundwork for the revision of poor relief that took place in 1788. The *Deliberations* offer equally valuable information on the ideological underpinnings of the society. Herein the society spoke directly to most of the major social and economic issues of the day. Their discussions and interests transcended narrow municipal or group interests. The society, for example, sponsored a series of essay contests on the decline of manufacturing, on the advantages and disadvantages of guilds, and on the causes of impoverishment.[68] When combined with the writings of several individual members of the the society—especially Büsch, the younger Reimarus, the merchants Johannes and Nicolaus Schuback, the jurist and later senator

Johann Arnold Günther, and Peter Heinrich Brodhagen—the *Deliberations* reveal best how Hamburg's elites viewed their economic circumstances.

The Patriotic Society advocated an early laissez-faire philosophy, characteristically opposing monopolies, guild privileges, mercantilist high tariffs, and the protectionist mentalities that accompanied them. It was an economic credo shared by the Rat and the Chamber of Commerce, if not entirely subscribed to by the Bürgerschaft, the membership of which included a number of guildmasters for whom protectionism was a sacred economic privilege and whose economic positions had already been seriously weakened by the directions that Hamburg's economy had taken since the beginning of the eighteenth century.[69] In point of fact, free trade was not established in Hamburg until 1874, yet much ground was gained toward that goal during the War of the Austrian Succession. Over the initial objections of the Bürgerschaft, Hamburg's merchant-bankers achieved a significant reduction of export duties and the abolition of transit imposts on certain commodities.[70] Several members of the Patriotic Society— Büsch, the Schubacks, and the younger Reimarus—counted among the most outspoken advocates of free trade in eighteenth-century central Europe. They composed sternly worded critiques of mercantilism, while advancing strong defenses of Hamburg's utility to the rest of Europe as long as it retained its position as a free-trading emporium. They produced as well a rough-and-ready theory of economic liberalism that antedated that of Adam Smith by several years. Yet their liberalism differed from the classical nineteenth-century variety in that they consistently refused to affirm the individual's right to "absolute freedom and arbitrariness [of action] in business."[71] They retained an attitude of Christian charity and an extended paternalism that called for state intervention into some matters—most clearly poor relief and public health—whenever and wherever "disequilibriums" developed.[72] They stopped short of what became political liberalism in the nineteenth century by seeking to preserve the many republican features of Hamburg's government, waging a fierce war against bureaucratization, while maintaining an unshakable belief in the desirability of involving civic-spirited, patriotic-minded men in government, and, of course, in preserving a government hierarchy based on selection or co-option, rather than election. The breakdown and disappearance of just this mentality is an important part of the story of Hamburg's slow creep away from paternalism and toward social laissez-faire policy.

The patriots promoted their brand of economic liberalism as universally applicable, although it relied on Hamburg's specific conditions, which were replicated in few other places on the continent. Hamburg's economy counted among those that Helen Liebel has so aptly labeled "pace-makers," Hamburg, like Amsterdam, "could afford free trade . . . because it was there that capital had accumulated and commercial mechanisms were apt to be understood."[73] Men like Büsch and Reimarus constructed their theories on a recognition that the basis of Hamburg's prosperity had, during the course of the eighteenth century, become intermediate trade (*Zwischenhandel,* a term Büsch coined) and that extensive if not totally unrestricted free-trade policies would only maximize Hamburg's already substantial advantages in the world market.[74] Admittedly, within this context, their assurances that all Europe profited from the privileged position of the Hansa cities appear more than a little self-serving.

They allied to their free-trade ideas a general hostility to most forms of protectionism. The Patriotic Society denied the claim of the guilds for economic monopolies because "such would greatly impede the freedom of trade." However, they acknowledged that the forcible abolition of guilds was impractical. Although since the end of the seventeenth century the guilds in Hamburg had enjoyed only the most fleeting kinds of political influence—and their economic stature continued to shrink in the eighteenth century—the Bürgerschaft still contained a fair number of guildmasters whose wishes would not be easy to ignore totally. The Patriotic Society, typically, trod a middle path, as did the Rat, for example, in allowing and even encouraging the settling of the Freimeister while upholding the status of the guilds, and suggesting that the "abuses and disorders so prevalent in the guilds" could best be eliminated "with caution and moderation, through wise legislation." Thus, naturally and gradually, "the guilds will wither away, or shed all those characteristics which are detrimental to society [as a whole]"[75] As the trade boom of the 1790s continued to lessen the guilds' share in the economic life of the city and the demands of a swollen population outran the guilds' ability to satisfy them, de facto freedom of labor (*Gewerbefreiheit*) triumphed, although it was not introduced as law until 1865.[76]

The Redefinition of Poverty

Within the realm of these global economic issues, Hamburg's patriots grappled with the problems of labor supply and poverty. They struggled to unearth the roots of what they perceived as a significantly increased impoverishment, while seeking to unravel the hidden relationship between labor and capital that might be manipulated to prevent further destitution. Their own experiences and their analyses of what their experiences signified generated a new definition of poverty, or perhaps altered their understanding of the conditions of labor and poverty by linking them to the structural changes in the economy that had convulsed Hamburg in the preceeding decades. Hamburg's elites slowly came to the realization that new ways of dealing with the poor had to be attempted. It was hardly accidental that one of the eighteenth century's most committed advocates of the freedom of trade and the freedom of the seas, Johann Georg Büsch, was also Hamburg's foremost and most vociferous advocate of poor relief reform.

Johann Georg Büsch was the son of a pastor who had moved to Hamburg in 1731 when Büsch was little more than an infant. Büsch received an excellent education at Hamburg's Johanneum and at the Academic Gymnasium. His teachers at the Gymnasium were those two old patriots, Hermann Samuel Reimarus and Michael Richey. Büsch later studied theology at the University of Göttingen and then returned to Hamburg. After a brief and very unhappy career as a private tutor, the city bestowed on him in 1756 the post he held for the rest of his long life: professor of mathematics at the Academic Gymnasium. In this capacity, he exercised considerable control over the intellectual formation of a whole generation of young Hamburg students, men who later attained positions of power in the interlocking webs of personal and public connections that bound together Hamburg's economic, social, and political worlds. Besides mathematics, Büsch's interests included history and economics, and he produced major works on all three subjects; however, his fame in the eighteenth century derived from his reputation as a national economist.[77]

Perhaps more than any other scholar of his day, Büsch helped close the gap between the intellectual and mercantile communities, establishing the fruitful exchange of ideas that characterized the Patriotic Society, and that, at least in part, accounts for the practical-mindedness of the Enlightenment in Hamburg. Most of the generation born in the 1750s—who came to possess political power in the 1780s and 1790s—were his students and his friends, members of a group that surrounded him and that intersected with another circle revolving around the successful merchants, Casper Voght and Georg Heinrich Sieveking. Together these groups formed focal points of the late Enlightenment in Hamburg.[78] Büsch was indefatigable in his labors for all sorts of useful projects. Unfortunately, due to a quirk of Hamburg's constitution, Büsch, like all other municipal employees, was barred from political participation. Being denied the chance to work directly for Hamburg did not prevent him from exerting himself in other ways. These restrictions, of course, did not touch the vast majority of his friends and students, and it is through them that Büsch's ideas bore their richest fruit.

Büsch's reputation as an economist has all but disappeared. In the eighteenth century, however, he was regarded as a major political economist, as an economic historian of some consequence, and as one of the most canny observers of economic realities in Europe. He was, in addition, the central figure in poor relief reform in Hamburg in the 1770s and 1780s and widely respected for his social writings. It is hard to determine which—his long involvement with Hamburg's economy through his close personal associations with merchants or his thorough cameralist training—was decisive in leading him to the idea that adequate provision for the poor and the unemployed was "one of the primary concerns of the state." Both experiences were probably equally responsible. What is crucial is that his spirit suffused the Patriotic Society and guided the reevaluation of poverty in the 1760s and 1770s.

Büsch's sensitivity to the problem of poverty and the poor was awakened by the undeniable and disquieting increase in the number of beggars and perhaps, more portentously, by a growing awareness of the depth and extent of a "secret need" no longer hidden. Büsch refused to accept the facile explanation that the poor were responsible for their fate, and chided those who acquiesced in it. He sought deeper reasons for impoverishment, scrutinizing the history of Hamburg's economic development in the eighteenth century for clues that would unlock the riddle of poverty. His understanding of economics formed his perception of poverty and informed his interpretation of the causes of impoverishment. According to Büsch, real wealth depended on the proper movement of money and not on its mere possession.[79] A state might possess great sums of money and yet be impoverished and miserable. He illustrated this with the example of Augsburg where crushing poverty existed in the shadow of enormous wealth. The true value of money, therefore, depended on how rapidly and uninhibitedly it moved from hand to hand, that is, on its speed of circulation (*Geldumlauf*). Monopolies, serfdom, and tariffs all hindered the movement of money; the conjunction of commerce and manufacturing, especially as it occurred in cities, stimulated it. Büsch commended free trade because he believed it offered the greatest potential for accelerating the movement of money, allowing its "magical power" to take hold, speeding along a progress that would eventually benefit all. Since isolated and independent economic systems merely impeded this process, Büsch opposed all forms of mercantilism that aimed at erecting autarkic economies. Instead, he championed an idealistic "international division of labor," in which each state did what it was best able to do, while freely exchanging goods and services with its counterparts: cooperating, therefore, not competing. Like his close friend, the younger Reimarus, Büsch argued that some industries (e.g., sugar refining) could not be artificially "transplanted" and "forced" as Frederick II had attempted to do in Prussia by granting a sugar monopoly. It was, of course, just this monopoly that had injured Hamburg's trade in refined sugar with Prussia.[80]

Büsch's conviction that the accelerated movement of money formed the basis of true wealth in a state determined how he viewed the growing impoverishment in Hamburg. Simply stated, Büsch insisted that the sluggish turnover of money—or, in other terms, a hampered circulation of money—was the principal if not the sole cause of large-scale impoverishment after mid-century. Moreover, almsgiving further deranged the economy and decelerated the movement of money.[81]

Büsch pointed out that Hamburg depended on others not only for food but also for many manufactured products precisely because it was a city–state. Paying for these commodities drained money from the city. Hamburg's intermediate trade, however, soon recovered a goodly part of this loss in the form of profits that enriched merchants and those who labored for them. Thus, except in times of trade depressions (*Handelskrisen,* another term Büsch coined), these people and Hamburg did well. Büsch reckoned, however, that at least 15,000 people in Hamburg (about 15 percent of the population) could not capitalize on this trade at all. In a cruel twist of fate, they actually suffered from Hamburg's exceptionally favorable position as a commercial giant and a trade entrepôt. The economic viability of these 15,000 people had become exceedingly precarious and their marginal occupations—begging, working on the fortifications, serving as the lowliest of municipal officials, hauling water, and peddling—were less able than ever before to support them. The existing forms of poor relief proved inadequate not only because they were overwhelmed by the scale of the task but, more decidedly, because they were the wrong types of institutions, extending the wrong kinds of assistance. And thus the problems of poverty and mendicancy inevitably had to grow. Hamburg in 1788, on the eve of the introduction of a new poor relief, was, in Büsch's words, "a true beggars' metropolis." These people—the unemployed, the destitute, but also the marginally employed and underemployed—retarded the advance of the rest of the economy. Even those among them who worked did little to help retrieve the money spent by the residents of Hamburg outside of the city; that is, they were not consumers. Their fault was that they handicapped rather than stimulated the circulation of money. They were in a sense economic parasites, although Büsch did not use this term. Under the conditions then prevailing in Hamburg, they were a permanent liability—a permanent underclass—who could be sustained by the city only as long as their numbers remained stable and as long as the city continued to prosper. But, as Büsch was quick to point out, that was not the way commerce worked. Eventually, the fiscal burden on the economy would rob Hamburg of its affluence and mortgage its future.[82]

Two other economic realities worsened the impact of this structural problem on the laboring poor. First, the period of depression after 1763 and the continued ailing state of Hamburg's economy through the 1770s and 1780s forced many out of work. However, the real problems lay deeper and were embedded in the very nature of Hamburg's economy. Büsch was among the first to acknowledge the vicissitudes of life for the lower classes in an environment in which they owned only their labor. He wrote sympathetically of the problems that plagued the little people in trying to earn a living in a city like Hamburg, painting a painfully moving picture of the unique obstacles created by a northern commercial center. As a result of the cold, the erratic weather, the seasonal character of many forms of employment, the necessity of housing and fuel, the bursts of inflation that caused rents and food prices to soar, their daily existence became a living hell of uncertainty.[83]

Because commerce always employed fewer people and at lower wages than manufacturing the decline of manufacturing became a chronic problem; moreover, commerce also provided a less stable income in an environment of often radical economic fluctuations. Manufactures, especially those producing for the domestic market, would, if stimulated or reintroduced, blunt the effect of trade crises that seemed inevitable in their periodicity, for "manufactures are the most expedient way by which men generate employment and sustenance for one another" and were, according to Büsch, "the prime mainspring of the circulation of money." Furthermore, "the most important manufactures for any state are those which produce for many people."[84] This kind of manufacturing, like agriculture (although Büsch was no physiocrat), actuated the best and healthiest flow of money, wherein money moved "naturally" from the bottom up. In Hamburg, however, while intermediate and colonial trade had expanded enormously, manufacturing had stagnated to the particular disadvantage of the common folk.[85] Thus, while the decline in manufacturing had not so much injured Hamburg in general—because the rise in trade had offset the loss incurred and had indeed made Hamburg an exceedingly rich and powerful city—the two sets of circumstances had engendered novel socioeconomic problems: a growing sensitivity (perhaps even a hypersensitivity) to trade imbalances and contractions and an environment in which it was increasingly difficult for the laboring man to avoid slipping repeatedly into poverty. Büsch recalled that in his youth Hamburg was still a great manufacturing city, pointing out that "fewer men made their living here than now, but these fewer lived better."[86] Caspar Voght related how many trades (e.g., velvet-weaving, skilled work in gold and silver thread-drawing, shipbuilding) "in which the common man found the most constant employment" had gone under in his lifetime.[87] The absence of an economic structure in which money flowed upward had spawned a working class in Hamburg dependent in very real ways on the crumbs that tumbled unnoticed from the tables of the rich.

> In short, while in other countries and states the great machine of circulation works up from the bottom, where the wealth of the better classes depends on the industry and ability . . . of the lower [classes], so is the working of the machinery in our state and in other cities like ours, completely topsy-turvy. The internal circulation moves almost exclusively from the top down. The little man can count on almost nothing for his sustenance, except what is flung to him by his betters.

Lacking stable incomes and long-term employment, the common people depended on a series of insecure and poorly paid jobs, and were frequently driven to add begging to their other occupations. Such, according to Büsch, was the unhappy experience of every great and populous city, but it was "nowhere worse than here in Hamburg."[88]

Büsch concluded that the poverty of the 1760s, 1770s, and 1780s was not merited. Not indolence and turpitude, but the very structure of Hamburg's economy had bred poverty. Voght, too, regarded only a minority of the poor in Hamburg culpable of their poverty, that is, products of "incapacity, folly, and vice." As he pointed out to his English audience, "I am afraid that by far the greatest number of poor in Europe is of a very different description. . . . Through a concurrence of numerous circumstances, the price of labour and of the necessaries of life is in a very unfavorable proportion for the poor in most countries of Europe."[89] Büsch had actually reversed his previous opinion of the poor, admitting that "[f]or a long time, I believed that mendicancy was generally the result of sloth and love of idleness. But I can no longer believe so . . . [I now] realize that our economy works in [such a perverse] way that it is impossible for a man who has not found a place in it early [in life] to manage to make a living in bad times, or having once lost his [particular] livelihood is ever able to regain it."[90]

These economic realities could probably not be turned around, nor was it necessarily desirable to do so. As far as possible, however, poor relief should assist the poor man to grope his way out of the labyrinth of impoverishment and back into the productive cycle of monetary circulation. Büsch maintained that the economic conditions reigning in eighteenth-century Hamburg had produced two dramatically different kinds of poor people. First, there were the "hopeless poor," who were too degraded by years of begging, or too infirm, or too old, to be returned to the world of work. Second, however, were those who under the right conditions, within the framework of a "rationally organized" poor relief, could be reintegrated into the economy as productive laborers. For the first class, Büsch saw nothing wrong in "feeding them to death," that is, with satisfying their minimal physical needs—in institutions if necessary—offering them support in the form of natural products. However, Büsch and others argued that such a policy of feeding to death that had constituted Hamburg's poor relief in mid-century, simply would not do for the poor of the second group, for these people "must not lose the habit . . . of budgeting the money they receive, be it ever so little. Civic life among civilized peoples depends too fully on a money economy. Whoever loses the ability [to deal with money] never recovers it."[91] Supported by wages, even the poor could promote monetary circulation and would thereby quicken, albeit in small ways, the sluggish movement of money in Hamburg.[92] On the other hand, the mere extension of alms, or support in kind compounded the existing problem of a sluggish circulation of money, aggravating, not relieving the conditions that provoked so much need: "When [the poor man] lies on straw, when he clothes himself in donated rags, and fills all his wants without [spending] money," then society retrieved nothing of value from the funds it expended on poor relief.[93]

Although Büsch and his contemporaries advanced strong economic arguments for poor relief reform (and Büsch was not reluctant to orient his appeal to the economic self-interest of his audience), it is neither correct nor fair to deny the existence of other motives. Büsch noted that

> [i]t is not the fault of paupers that their numbers are so great and that because of their numbers they suffer. They came into the world in the same way as the family-son, as the prince's heir. They want to live next to us and with us and have as much right to do so as we do. God's earth gives nurture to them, as to us. However, we are city-dwellers [*Bürger*] and not farmers [*Bauer*] and thus we cannot point out to them a spot of earth that they can till for themselves. We must seek other ways to let them find their living, by earning wages. The means is not in their [own] power.[94]

The poor relief Büsch planned for Hamburg would exploit economic self-interest in the service of the community, and the community would come to appreciate good social policies as the guarantors of political and economic freedom.

Büsch was not, of course, the only advocate of poor relief reform. He was its most articulate spokesman and prolific publicist. Yet neither his relatively positive view of the poor in general, nor his ideas of just how poor relief should be organized, were unanimously accepted and put into practice when reform came in 1788. Despite the inevitable adaptations and modifications, the major principles Büsch outlined—providing work and not alms, encouraging industriousness, investigating the individual circumstances of impoverishment, and perhaps most important of all, engaging more citizens in the work of communal government, of which poor relief was an important part—served as the bedrock for the reforms of the 1770s and 1780s. Büsch's ideas were in no way original, but they did strike resonant chords. Far from being mere lovely dreams conjured up in the high and isolated rooms of an ivory tower, Büsch's plans were hypotheses debated in the meetings of the Patriotic Society, mulled over in smoke-filled coffeehouses, and discussed with animation in drawing rooms and gardens over cups of tea and saucers of coffee. They matured in an atmosphere of friendship and conviviality in that most sociable of centuries. They were tempered by the views of his confidants and associates, by the members of the Patriotic Society, by the future directors of the General Poor Relief, by senators, syndics, and merchants—those men who governed Hamburg.

5

The Reorganization
of Poor Relief, 1786–1788

During the 1770s and 1780s no social issue excited more debate than poverty, and no topic was more vigorously discussed in Hamburg than poor relief reform. If at first few people envisioned more than a belated tinkering with the existing system of poor relief, by the late 1780s most of those involved acknowledged the futility of stopgap measures and admitted, sometimes begrudgingly, the need for a total refurbishing.[1] The truly momentous expansion of commerce, the quickened economic tempo, the narrowing gap separating the working poor from indigence (and the speed with which that gap closed) a city swarming with strangers, a less familiar and larger population—all these dictated new departures in social policies and transformed poor relief into an effective tool of government in ways only imperfectly realized earlier. An older tradition was to be revived as well. Not only would poor relief help govern and order the city more efficiently, but it would also be constructed to reassert a disintegrating sense of community and to reanimate the civic virtues that had somehow faded in the bustle of money-making.

In the late 1760s and early 1770s, the Patriotic Society considered poor relief reform at great length. At first, the society only sought the means to improve the existing relief. The society sponsored a series of essay contests on topics analyzing the causes of impoverishment and exploring the best means of providing work for the poor; these were an important part of the process by which the society collected information.[2] The contests attracted more than local interest and familiarized Hamburg's elites with the wide range of ideas poor relief reform had evoked in the Germanies and throughout Europe. Still, the members of the Patriotic Society never lost track of their raison d'être, and they refined general precepts of poor relief reform to unique Hamburg conditions. In the formal deliberations of the society as well as informally in interlocking circles of friends, the basis for poor relief reform was gradually developed. Then, in the 1770s and 1780s, these men embarked on tentative experiments that centered on the three crucial spheres of reform they had identified: work, health, and education.

It was the cameralists who first recognized the connections between work, health, and education. Their equation was simple: Want of work produced poverty, the sick and the invalid could not work, and neither could those who lacked the necessary skills. There were, of course, serious moral judgments implicit in these assumptions. The first was that the masses were undisciplined, (or unpoliced in the jargon of the time) and lacked the requisite virtue of industriousness as much as a job. Even poor health was not held totally blameless. Many "caused" their own illnesses by ignorance and wantonness. The attempts of both cameralists and philosophes to remedy these failings—to educate, to discipline, to instruct, and, if all else failed, to coerce—has often been interpreted in terms of social disciplining or social control.[3]

There is surely little doubt that the state in the eighteenth century (in whatever form) tried to reach more deeply into the lives of its subjects than ever before. There is, however, much reason to question its successes. Most social control arguments suffer from a tendency to endow the state, especially the early modern state, with greater powers of coercion and supervision than it possessed, while undervaluing the resistance of the populace to such measures. Social control arguments, then, tend to judge all "reforms" and "improvements" as essentially repressive, as merely offering more subtle means of control (*violence douce*) rather than representing any sincere effort to ameliorate untenable conditions. However, the view presented here considers poor relief not merely as yet another tool for the oppression of the lower classes, but as an integral part of governing that responded intelligently to deep alterations in the kind of city Hamburg had become by the late eighteenth century. The intention is not to deny the validity of a social control explanation for *some* aspects of poor relief, nor to obscure the play of forces transforming all of Europe, not only Hamburg—an economic revolution, the dying of an old paternalist system of governing, the slow germination of nineteenth-century liberal beliefs, and the realities of population growth.

In Hamburg, it was the interplay of two attitudes toward poverty that determined the characteristics of poor relief reform. The economic explanation for impoverishment was tempered by a second view that continued to attribute much poverty to moral failings. Büsch usually pressed home to his contemporaries the primacy of the economic determinants of poverty, arguing that in Hamburg "indolence and poor household economy" were only secondary causes. Yet, while recognizing that Hamburg's economic system as it existed after mid-century contributed to mass poverty, he refused to accept structural interpretations entirely. Johann Arnold Günther and Caspar Voght, after Büsch the most important actors in poor relief reform, also balked at discarding a moralistically tinged stance, even while they too saw in the mechanism of Hamburg's economy a major contributor to poverty. Günther, for example, conceded that the laboring poor in Hamburg faced many difficulties not of their own making, yet also pointed out that *despite* these economic impediments workers could manage to subsist if only they possessed a proper sense of "good management" (*Wirthschaftlichkeit*). The poor lacked money and jobs, but also "simplicity, frugality, restraint, and orderliness." They "added to their misery by their own faults." Voght also accepted a whole range of nonculpable causes of impoverishment. He admonished the well-to-do that one should not be so ready to penalize the poor for their flaws "as if corruption did not always spread from the higher to the lower classes." Yet Voght warned against indiscriminate liberality in the distribution of relief so that alms would not become "premiums held out to vice." Even Büsch, whose view of the poor was on the whole gentle and benevolent, could not totally shake the conviction that the poor might indeed be in some way to blame for their own destitution. Writing in 1780, he commented that "a usual cause of poverty is not lack of work but lack of industry."[4]

This dichotomy in the evaluation of the causes of poverty existed almost everywhere. Reformers vacillated between regarding poverty as the result of such impersonal, unavoidable occurrences as unemployment and illness, and blaming it on personal imperfections, indolence, lack of foresight, and degeneracy; however, both positions could accommodate the idea that poverty was bred by ignorance or lack of education. Poor relief reforms enacted in the late eighteenth century thus blended repressive with supportive measures. They elevated the traditional hostility toward beggars to a fierce war against them, yet promoted constructive programs for the education of pauper children, mostly in the form of schools of industry (*Industrie Schulen*). They were equally willing to provide employment possibilities and training if necessary, to subsidize rents and advance money to artisans or laborers who had fallen on hard times, and to attend to the health of the laboring classes.

Medical Relief as the First Step

The earliest and eventually the most ambitious undertaking in Hamburg before the major reform of 1788 was an attempt to strike at illness, that pitiless destroyer of the poor man's greatest asset—his health. Until the end of the 1760s, there was little medical care available for the domiciled poor or, for that matter, for the laboring classes. The city magistrates and the Gotteskastenverwalter offered temporary assistance in emergencies, but no system existed for aiding the sick poor on a regular basis, other than condemning them to the ancient Pesthof. These unhappy circumstances were occasionally mitigated by the ministrations of individual physicians and surgeons who held special office hours for the poor (*Armensprechstunden*), or treated ophthalmic, dermatological, or gynecological complaints free of charge. Still, it seems safe to argue that the care available to the ordinary person was meager and bad without suggesting that even those who enjoyed excellent care by the standards of the day benefited much from it. The municipality, however, showed far more interest in separating the sick from the well. In the words of a 1714 edict, "the preservation of the city" not only demanded the "isolation of the poor, the sick, and the miserable" from the rest of human society, but—especially in the time of plague—dictated the "removal of beggars, begging-Jews, and vagabonds, or other persons suspected of carrying disease" from the city and its territories.[5]

The direct tie between poverty and disease, or rather between disease and *impoverishment* did not, however, escape comment in the eighteenth century. It was widely accepted that illness formed the most frequent cause of destitution among the working classes. A *Report on the Care of the Sick-Poor* from 1781 pointed out that "if one let all our paupers recite the stories of their misfortunes, at least half of them would name an illness as the direct cause [of their misery]." Illness alone was not the only problem, the report asserted. If one examined the history of their illnesses, it soon became apparent that the initial manifestation of the disease or injury had been mild and cure "certain [sic!] if this unhappy person had been able to obtain proper medical care promptly." Nipping disease in the bud was supposed to curb poverty because "all too often a complaint that appears trivial becomes deadly" without prompt attention. Experience seemed to demonstrate that most ailments could be successfully treated at the beginning if not allowed to worsen into incurability. Cruelly victimized by such sequences of events was the laborer, who thereby lost his ability to work, his health, and all too often his life.[6]

In 1768, several physicians pledged to supply free medical care and medicines to the sick poor for a period of two years. Büsch and a deacon from St. Michaelis parish, Johann Matthias Liebrecht, did the bookkeeping, collected subscriptions, and coordinated the activities of the medical relief. Despite an auspicious beginning, the enterprise folded after only eighteen months.[7] Yet the path had been blazed and ten years later, in 1778, many of the same people, including the apparently indefatigable Büsch (this time assisted by the pastor of St. Petri, Christoph Christian Sturm), assumed the reins and founded a second Medical Relief (*Institut für Kranke Hausarmen*), this time on a much larger scale. It remained active until 1788, when it was incorporated into the General Poor Relief as its Medical Deputation. All three forms of medical relief functioned on the principles enunciated in 1768: "to save the lives and [preserve] the health of thousands," "to return many upright and honest workers to the state," and "to reduce the distress of suffering humanity."[8] The ten-year existence of the Medical Relief proved a fertile period of experimentation, which provided a generation of patriots their first real opportunity to put their ideas into practice.

Ultimately, the goal of medical relief was the prevention of impoverishment. The plan drew clear links between disease, illness, accidents, and poverty. For example, a "typical" family history might unfold with the family father, the sole breadwinner for his wife and several children, falling ill. Initially he tries a home remedy to set himself right; however, when that fails, he turns to the "next, best" apothecary or, as a last resort, to someone who maintains "I can cure that." Instead of improving, however, he sinks deeper into illness and misery. Finally, his wife is a widow and his children are orphans. Then his wife must carry on alone as best she can, until she, too, worn out by drudgery and worry, follows her husband to the grave. Perhaps she has already buried some of her children—children who, under more propitious circumstances, "could have become useful members of the republic." A fate that was just as tragic and far more common awaited such families when the father did not die, but remained invalid and bedridden for the remainder of his life. His illness sapped the strength of an entire family.[9]

The Medical Relief had to accept the harsh winter climate of Hamburg as another reality. As in other northern commercial centers, the weather presented the laboring classes with almost insurmountable obstacles to good health. Medical care alone could achieve little and only the coordination of all parts of poor relief could be "*fully* successful" in alleviating the misery of those "ravished by hunger, cold, and nakedness."[10] The concerns reflected here were as political as they were humanitarian, for only healthy persons, not cripples and invalids, were valuable to the state. Medical care for the laboring poor seemed to be an attractive "quick fix" for many of the problems of impoverishment. The first published *Report* of the Medical Relief pointed out that through its efforts "so many people . . . have been cured, [people] we can return to the state as more useful and far healthier members [of society] than [they were] previously, and thereby [we have] stopped up many wellsprings of bitterest want." There was, of course, another issue stressed here: Medical Relief reduced the burden on other charitable institutions as well as cutting economic losses due to illness.[11]

The proponents of medical charity claimed that illness could not facilely be regarded as self-induced because "illness is an evil of the human condition." Yet the Medical Relief assured its subscribers that it did not treat diseases resulting from "criminal dissipations," imprudence, or lack of restraint; this implied not only venereal diseases but also the pregnancies of unwed mothers.[12] The Medical Relief also incorporated a sort of discipline into its program; the clearest statement of this is found in the relief's *Instructions*. Briefly summarized, the *Instructions* detailed the conduct of the sick poor vis-à-vis the relief, regulating the timing and frequency of visits to physicians, demanding of the patient a "modest demeanor," threatening termination of support to "recalcitrants," denying the patient recourse to "medicines not prescribed by the physician, whether home remedies or other quack-medicines," and stipulating that "no one may withdraw without formally thanking [the relief] for his recovery."[13] The language seems officious and unambiguous. However, despite the rhetoric, the disciplinary actions undertaken by the Medical Relief and by its successor, the Medical Deputation of the General Poor Relief, were scattered, mild, and few. For example, while the 1781 *Report* recounted that several patients who "because of their intemperance and wanton ruination of their bodies, their decided rebelliousness and coarse behavior toward their physicians, unmindful of all previous warnings" had been "abjured and surrendered to their fate," the actual number of these in the first six months was an insignificant 5 of the 321 treated. By 1787 the relief reported that, although it still released some patients because of "recalcitrance or unsatisfactory adherence to their physician's orders," such cases were becoming "ever less frequent."[14] This evidence suggests that either the need for disciplining the sick poor were few or that, more likely, the relief found it impossible to enforce its will. It was far less draconian and uncompromising in its use of power than it might have been. The volunteer physicians of the Medical Relief wished their instructions to be followed dutifully and expected to receive a proper degree of respect and deference from patients.[15] Yet the number of patients who were denied care because of insubordination was always tiny, and neither the Medical Relief nor the General Poor Relief can be seen as willing and eager collaborators in physicians' bid for a medical monopoly. Furthermore, doctors themselves were sometimes reprimanded for misbehavior. When one physician for the General Poor Relief refused to treat an "intractable" patient, a relief officer was sent to investigate the problem. In his report, he complained that the physician in question had apparently taken offense because "instead of greeting the doctor with 'Guten Morgen, Herr Doktor' he had said only 'Guten Morgen.' " The relief officer was furious and clearly appalled by such high-handed behavior; consequently, the council censured the physician's conduct.[16]

More important than any program of disciplining was the realization that one was now dealing with a "new" poor for whom the older forms of medical care were obsolete. The medical care offered by the relief was invariably outdoor or domiciliary, rather than institutional. Enlightened opinion generally regarded the hospitals or "spitals," as they existed in the eighteenth century, as "gateways to death." Hamburg's hospitals enjoyed no better reputation.[17] In the eighteenth century, the city's principal institution for the ill— the Pesthof—was an overcrowded and unhappy place; the very word filled sufferers with dread. Even at the end of the eighteenth century, the Pesthof was a name to reckon with, calling up specters of chaos, apathy, abandonment, and death.

> Most of the patients are incurables who either pass away soon [after their admission] or live out the rest of their days with no attempt being made to treat their afflictions, or [they] are released on the slightest show of improvement. . . . Not a small portion of the patients are insane. . . . The quiet ones are kept in the wards. One tries to isolate the more violent from the dangerously ill; idiots wander about as they please. . . . The raving are chained to their beds.[18]

The Pesthof housed between 850 and 1,000 persons. Most were incurables; a few suffered from acute ailments. Mortality was high and cures were seldom and serendipitous. The Pesthof presented the stereotype of a premodern hospital, which was characterized by intense overcrowding, stinking hospital air, hopelessness, long stays, and the very real danger of dying from illnesses contracted there. The time when hospitals became places for curing the sick— and not refuges for the old, the moribund, the insane, in short, for all of those people whom society had cast off—had not yet come.[19]

The new Medical Relief explicitly rejected institutional or hospital care for the new poor,[20] just as ten years later the General Poor Relief would decide against institutionalization as a rational vehicle for more general relief. Agreement on the serious insufficiencies of hospitals, almshouses, and indeed the charity of the eighteenth century did not automatically create consensus on how such failings might be remedied. Almost everyone admitted that institutions inherited from the Middle Ages or constructed in the sixteenth and seventeenth centuries could not meet the demands placed on them in the eighteenth century. The criticism of hospitals led to a series of innovations in hospital planning and to novel plans for institutions designed either to supplement hospital care or to supplant it.[21]

The discussion on health care for the laboring poor assumed lively proportions in several European countries. Physicians, bureaucrats, and philanthropists in France, Denmark, Russia, the Austrian empire, and almost all the German states vigorously debated the pros and cons of hospitals versus visiting care. Two of the most vociferous and well-published advocates of the superiority of visiting care, Günther and Dr. Daniel Nootnagel, were from Hamburg. They threw themselves into the fray with a conviction born of their experience with the "demonstrated" advantages of visiting care. The preference for domiciliary aid ultimately rested on the emerging perception of the poor as the laboring poor. The stress on outdoor relief underscored the belief that it was no longer merely desirable but actually imperative to reintegrate the pauper into the workaday world. As much as possible he or she was to be caught up again in the productive cycle of the economy and not alienated from it. The Medical Relief emphasized the value of a noninstitutional approach in achieving these goals. Obviously, home care circumvented the need for expensive hospital buildings, yet it purportedly offered other advantages as well: The family nursed its own, sick mothers could continue to watch over young children, and breadwinners—if not totally incapacitated—might still be able to work a bit. Although such charitable institutions as hospitals made undeniable contributions to society, "not every patient who is poor . . . is able to avail himself of these facilities," and, more decisively, "it is anyway impossible to admit all those who require assistance."[22] Besides these advantages, the authors of the Medical Relief's outdoor solution could also boast of greater economy. Mortality rates were strikingly lower than in hospitals, and costs were significantly less. During the first thirty months of its existence, the Medical Relief cared for about 3,500 patients at a total cost of 16,000 marks, or little more than 4 marks 9 shillings per patient, thus, according to one observer, "accomplishing as much as a hospital, which admits 500 patients yearly, . . ."[23]

The Lessons Learned

This debate highlights some major shifts in attitudes toward health care and poor relief. First, the supporters of large-scale visiting programs rejected existing hospitals as proper centers for the medical treatment of the laboring poor. Only if the poor were "dispensable" or "extraneous" could these outmoded institutions be appropriate. However, because the new poor were not expendable, the ancient hospitals, like archaic methods of poor relief, no longer supplied timely answers to the modern problem of illness (or poverty) among the laboring classes. Thus, the Pesthof, like indoor relief in general, won little backing from Hamburg's reformers. The outmoded early modern hospital, sheltering a hodgepodge mismatch of sick, aged, and insane, was seen as refuse-heap relief. It did little to restore the sick man to health or the impoverished worker to productivity. Like the Zuchthaus and all such primitive institutions, the hospital had become an unsuitable place for the new working classes; all posed equally "life-threatening" hazards to the physical, economic, social, and moral well-being of thousands.[24]

If we jump a bit ahead into our story, into the 1790s, we uncover further proofs of how decisive the notion of a laboring poor was to the General Poor Relief's determination to incorporate people who were not "genuine paupers" into its program of free medical care. These people of small means and limited resources often found themselves unable to pay for medical consultations or medications. Without timely medical intervention, only poverty could result from their illnesses. The 1788 *Instruction* to the relief officers specified that free medical care could also extend to "those persons who can secure their own living and require no assistance as long as they retain their health." However, they, too, required prompt attention to rescue them "from the perils of poverty when smitten with dangerous or persistent maladies." The council formally inaugurated a program of medical aid to the nonregistered poor in 1793.[25]

The General Poor Relief consciously built on the experiences of the Medical Relief. Its greater resources, however, permitted the Relief to venture beyond a relatively limited field of action. By the early 1790s, medical relief had developed into an ambitiously conceived, far-reaching program that sought to weed out one of the taproots of poverty: unforeseeable, capricious illness. Free medical care without question extricated some families from poverty and prevented others from becoming destitute through poor health. The policy implicitly (but never explicitly) acknowledged the "honest worker's" prerogative of health as well as his right to support and to employment. It reached beyond almsgiving and into the realm of social security. It also proved, as we shall later see, an extremely costly endeavor.

However, the concept of expense was always relative. The architects of this new departure in poor relief were never constrained in the breadth of their vision nor miserly in their charity. They measured returns on their investments in poor relief in the coin of social benefits as well as in a harder currency of marks and shillings. The idea of what might fruitfully be tagged "social cost accounting" dominated their calculations and, despite precise bookkeeping and meticulous auditing of accounts, all appreciated that the profits on social investments were intangible. The rudiments of social cost accounting were woven throughout the fabric of public relief in eighteenth-century Hamburg. Those absorbed in mapping out social policies—whether they saw themselves as tradition-oriented city fathers or rallied around the device of Enlightenment, and whether they applied their ingenuity and expertise to reforms in poor relief, education, agronomy or public health—ultimately vindicated expenditures of both time and money by measuring them against the social benefits to be reaped. This is, as we shall see, the same logic that sustained make-work schemes, initiated unprofitable enterprises for employing the poor, and stoked a host of other improvements in prisons, schools, hospitals, and workhouses.[26] The Relief appealed to their subscribers' sense of cost accounting, championing at the same time a new variety of charity with, however, very near attachments to the venerable axioms of Christian charity, brotherly love, and duty, and to the Protestant (or not so Protestant) ethics of hard work, temperance, and thrift. The men of the Relief admitted to feeling the same joy that touched all hearts with a spontaneous gift of alms, but challenged the meaningfulness of "such pleasures" when "compared to the greater exhilaration which flows from relieving the misery of a helpless sufferer, [and] without even knowing him, saving his life, or rescuing his home, restoring children to their parents, or parents to their children, and preserving for the state one of its members?"[27] In a like manner, the funneling of compassion for the needy into less personal and far more constructive channels was exalted as the truest form of Christian charity because it was completely anonymous and selfless. Traditional occasions for charitable giving—recovery from a serious illness, escape from some pressing danger, or even a business windfall—were bent to fresh purposes.

The principles of rational charity penetrated all aspects of poor relief reform, but they also interacted with the equally insistent demands for increased citizen participation in the tasks of relief. Both were to enhance a sense of community that seemed in danger of falling apart. Thus the character of the Relief was both private *and* public. Like many other institutions in Hamburg, the Medical Relief (later the General Poor Relief) always possessed paradoxical qualities of "publicness" and "privateness," which were expressed in its semipublic (*halb-öffentliche*) configuration. Numerous municipal institutions, such as the Zuchthaus and the various hospitals, were simultaneously public and private; they were *privately* operated institutions for the *public* benefit and existed as integral components of normal government. For example, while founded by private persons and managed by a college of citizens, the Zuchthaus served public objectives, acting as prison, almshouse, and hostel. It is this dualism permeating all branches of government in Hamburg that seems to the modern observer a curiously mingled arrangement of private initiative and public benefit. The men involved, therefore, cannot legitimately be deemed private persons who chose civic responsibilities that the state could not or perhaps should not execute, but rather as citizens *and* patriots who parceled out among themselves the obligations of directing a free republic.[28] The men who put together the Medical Relief and later the General Poor Relief did not view their endeavors as somehow independent of the business of government. The founders of the Medical Relief desired to have their creation transformed into a public institution on the lines of those other semiprivate, semipublic organizations that had, since the Middle Ages, been part of Hamburg's political landscape.[29]

Somewhat later in this chapter we will turn to an analysis of the men involved in the General Poor Relief; for the present it is enough to indicate the kinds of persons deemed appropriate or thought to be especially suitable for such positions of trust. The Medical Relief, of course, hinged on the gratis cooperation of physicians;[30] yet it is really the physician as citizen and not as Aesculapian practitioner that concerns us here. The private/public duality and the difficulty of assessing actions to be either exclusively "private" or "public" becomes even more acute when we consider the various benefactors of the Medical Relief and the General Poor Relief. Not surprisingly, the various subscription lists for the Medical Relief show that the Patriotic Society was well represented among its patrons.[31] Of these, many were at the time, or soon became, members of municipal government councils, often—like the syndic Matsen and the senators Volkmann and Kirchhoff—prominently placed among the ruling elite. For example, on examining the names of those who participated in the first subscription (1 July 1779 through 1 July 1781), one finds a total of 276 subscribers, among them 12 members of the Rat, 1 syndic, 4 Oberalten, and 18 pastors. The second subscription (1 July 1781 through 1 January 1785) listed 356 subscribers, among them 2 syndics, 13 members of the Rat, 4 Oberalten, and 15 pastors.[32] This overlap between organs of government and organs of poor relief is a theme that we will later explore in detail. Here at the very least one must stress the futility of any attempt to isolate private and public spheres in Hamburg or to identify any fresh source of private initiative detached from the more traditional roles of citizens or emanating from new social groups seeking political power or substitutes for it.

A citizen, or group of citizens, might fruitfully undertake experimentation on a limited scale to determine the feasibility of a proposed project and to test its premises. In this capacity private initiative could and did function, but *not*—it should be noted—with the intention of legitimizing a private sphere of action unique and distinct from a public one, nor with the desire to designate specific tasks (e.g., charity) as better implemented by private persons and best left alone by the state. That was, we shall see, a later development unwrapped by the flowering of political liberalism and social laissez-faire policies in the nineteenth century.

One private experiment in the 1780s was, of course, the Medical Relief; another was the Spinning Institute, which was organized in October 1785 by three of Hamburg's most energetic patriots—Caspar Voght, J. F. Behrens, and J. Daniel Klefeker. They specified its mission as "to unite our strength [in the search to discover] something by which the impoverished inhabitants of this city would gain a means to earn a basic living even when their regular form of employment disappears." The main beneficiaries of their efforts were to be the laboring poor who had lost their normal means of livelihood, either temporarily or permanently, although "it might also impel the beggar once again to seek work." This institution, like the Medical Relief, laid the groundwork for the analogous venture embarked on by the General Poor Relief, which deliberately and admittedly built on the experiences gained in 1785–86, precisely as the founders of the Spinning Institute intended. "One sees it as his duty," Voght wrote, "to publicize [the results of] these ventures. . . . Perhaps a public relief can turn to its own use this private attempt which has already mastered the profound obstacles [confronting] any new enterprise, and with greater resources run it more advantageously."[33]

The Spinning Institute settled on flax-spinning as suitable employment for the poor. The institute provided flax to impoverished spinners at a price of twelve shillings per pound. Each "length" of spun yarn was then purchased back for four shillings. Anywhere from six to nine such lengths of yarn could be spun from one pound of flax (the average was seven) so a spinner could earn twenty-eight shillings, which, after subtracting the twelve-shilling cost of the original pound of flax, left one mark in wages. The report published in 1786 reckoned that "an industrious and skilled spinner" might earn as much as five shillings daily, while a family of spinners, "who labored [together] by the same fire and light" could maintain itself, at least for a time, by diligent toil. The report admitted that single people, especially the elderly or infirm, could not support themselves by spinning alone, yet what they did earn would lighten the burden on public relief, while testifying to their own worthiness and their right to further assistance. The most innovative part of the plan was the instruction in spinning provided both to adults and, especially, to the children of the poor "whose industrial and moral education are shamefully ignored." About 500 persons, adults and children, received instruction in the three-year duration of the experiment.[34] Perhaps the greatest advantage of spinning was that it gave the working poor an alternative or supplementary form of employment. The report recognized that spinning was only a stopgap measure for most, at best sustaining them until more lucrative work became available. But that was the intent.[35]

This was an expensive and not completely successful undertaking. The Spinning Institute did not conceal its dissatisfaction with the results of some aspects of its program, especially with productivity that lagged far behind that of "free" workers in Hanover and Braunschweig. The 170 "home" workers of the institute produced only a "disappointingly few" (250) lengths each week, whereas the same number of workers in Braunschweig and Hanover spun more than 2,000. This served to convince the founders of the institute "how degenerate the lowest class [in Hamburg] is." When they wondered why, "thoughtless charity" was the first answer that came to mind. According to Voght, the poor in Hamburg were "so spoiled, even led astray by the munificence of our fellow-citizens," that they had lost the ability and the desire to work hard. Despite these frustrations and a clear loss of more than 3,000 marks in fifteen months, the exertions of the Spinning Institute were not regarded as futile nor were they viewed as a philanthropic misfire. Important goals had been attained: 200 people had been employed for a solid year and many of them had acquired a new source of income and a marketable skill. Moreover, the per capita cost was low—only fifteen marks. Voght suggested that "perhaps spinning might even eventually become a Hamburg manufactured product if our poor can be reeducated to industriousness through the beneficent influence of a public relief."[36]

Büsch, as usual, smiled on these endeavors, valuing in equal measure the spirit of enterprise and the civic commitment that inspired them. His praise also struck notes of republican pride, extolling the traditional values of community in managing the problems of the modern world. He asserted that the civic virtues thereby manifested were equally precious in perpetuating Hamburg's republican heritage. Fully as valuable to Büsch was that these experiences demonstrated not only to him and to others of similar views, but also to a wider public that such approaches could achieve meaningful results and that more ambitious ventures were not without a potential for success. Clearly Büsch, like many of his Hamburg contemporaries, reacted to what they viewed as the oppressive rule exercised in many German territories (especially Prussia) by defending the self-rule of citizens and by stressing that the efforts of "a free citizenry" could be as successful and expedient as the monarch's "force of will." Despotism was not necessary to run a modern state, they argued, despite doomsayers who predicted the downfall of antiquated republics and lauded the proficiency of enlightened absolutism. By 1785–86, then, new ideas had been tested—if in modest ways—and now Büsch, Voght, and their compatriots would dare to take bolder steps.[37]

An Ambitious Undertaking

The 1780s buzzed with discussion while experimentation with small-scale projects, like the Spinning Institute and the Medical Relief, went forward accumulating useful stores of information and expertise, all of which flowed into the the making of the General Poor Relief. Facts on other endeavors at poor relief reform in other areas of Europe poured in, to be pondered and assessed for their adaptability to Hamburg's distinctive circumstances. The debate on poor relief reform went on throughout Europe, and Hamburg's elites kept their eyes on innovations that might be profitably exploited for their city's benefit. No one advocated slavish imitation. Everyone involved appreciated the peculiarities of Hamburg's situation, in particular "the unendingly greater complexities" presented by a metropolis (*Großstadt*) and not found in smaller towns and villages. In the early and mid-1780s, while the Patriotic Society solicited information on relief efforts elsewhere, the editors of Hamburg's newspapers and journals filled their columns with accounts of the progress of poor relief reform in other cities. All this bustle testified to a keen interest in the topic and to the breadth of desire for poor relief reform in Hamburg by the mid-1780s. And there was plenty to be excited about. Augsburg in 1783 (or 1782), Berlin in 1774, Bremen in 1779, Hanover in 1785, Lübeck in 1784, Lüneburg in 1776, Mainz in 1786, Strasburg in 1767, and, most notably, Vienna in 1784, had all introduced new measures to cope with a rising wave of impoverishment. Many of the Hamburg reformers were closely connected to other pioneers in poor relief reform, striking up personal acquaintances and lively correspondences with such figures as August Wilhelm Alemann in Hanover, Johann Joachim Eschenberg and Johann Anton Leisewitz in Braunschweig, Christian Garve in Breslau, Benjamin Thompson (Graf von Rumford) in Munich, Friedrich Eberhard von Rochow in Rekan, Heinrich Balthasar Wagnitz, and the Wagemann brothers, August and Ludwig, in Göttingen. Undoubtedly they learned much (as did their correspondents) and the Hamburg reform of 1788 can hardly claim originality or even chronological precedence over all other reforms. Yet it by no means docilely followed any one model. Rather, it became the new standard for a whole generation of poor relief reformers and, by the turn of the century, the apotheosis of what a "rationally organized" relief should be and could accomplish.[38]

But what *was* it intended to do? In the debates and discussion immediately preceding the inauguration of the General Poor Relief, it was once again the influence of Büsch and the Patriotic Society that predominated. The same men who led the Patriotic Society organized and ran the new General Poor Relief. The faces changed, of course, over the decades, and transformations in the philosophy and aims of poor relief and in style of government in Hamburg are equally incomprehensible unless considered against the backdrop of these shifts in personnel and the alteration in generations. Those most deeply involved in the period before Büsch's two seminal pamphlets, "Historical Report on the Progress and Continued Decay of Hamburg's Poor Relief Since the Reformation" and "General Remarks on Improving Poor Relief,"[39] appeared in 1786 were Büsch himself and several members of the old guard of the Patriotic Society, including its spiritual father, Pauli, the architect Sonin, and Pastor Krohn. Those who continued to strive for reform *after* 1786 included a group of men, Nicolaus Matsen, Friedrich Tonnies, and Nicolaus Anton Johann Kirchhoff, especially active in the affairs of governing in their roles as syndic, Oberalte, and senator. A group of newcomers to the society, the younger Reimarus and the neophyte lawyer, Günther, contributed fresh energies and ideas. Four others sustained the enthusiasm for reform while lending their own peculiar strengths and disparate abilities: the extremely popular Oberalte Claes Bartels, Johann Daniel Klefeker (later senator), Senator Peter Dietrich Volkmann, who spoke for the Enlightenment in the Rat, and the wealthy merchant and bon vivant, Caspar Voght. After the actual founding of the General Poor Relief in 1788, Voght's partner, Georg Heinrich Sieveking, and the Canon Friedrich Johann Lorenz Meyer, while never directly involved in the General Poor Relief, added their support.[40] This was the group that guided the fortunes of the Relief through the 1780s and 1790s. Some determined almost single-handedly the character of specific branches of the General Poor Relief, as Günther did for the Medical Deputation and as Voght did for the School and Factory Deputations. Yet these men were not mere clones of one another. They all adopted some basic points of policy, but almost never unanimously approved the same course of action, although they certainly all can be counted in the front ranks of Hamburg's growing coterie of Enlightenment proselytizers. Some, like Sieveking, agonized over the possible trampling of the rights and freedoms of all human beings; others, like Voght, assumed the posture of a strict but well-meaning father, and still others, like Günther, were particularly concerned with the legalistic aspects of poor relief. If they occasionally quarreled among themselves, and even were not immune from personal animosities (Voght, for example, held a low opinion of Bartels), they all acknowledged their enormous debt to Büsch as the father of poor relief reform, even if they like most adult children less willingly followed his counsel in all things. Later, Büsch was driven to admit that he would have done some things differently had he been allowed to guide the Relief.[41] But, alas, he was not; like other city employees (he was professor of mathematics at the Academic Gymnasium), Büsch was ineligible for all government positions and for membership in the collegial bodies. Still, he was the theorist and, to some extent, the strategist of poor relief reform in the 1780s and thus it is to Büsch that we must first turn our attention.

From 1785 to 1787 Büsch consumed reams of paper with the subject of poor relief reform: analyzing the problems obstructing reform, proposing guidelines for a rationally organized poor relief, pondering the best ways to select personnel. We have already seen how Büsch and others had come to appreciate the condition of the new poor as not inevitably the outcome of a life of vice or indolence (even if dissenting opinions also played a role). If laziness and iniquity could not be marked out as the principal wellsprings of poverty, then neither, according to Büsch, was a deficiency of charity. Hamburg's social dilemma resulted from too much benevolence, not too little. What was wanting were proper outlets for an already copious generosity. "What good is charity," queried Büsch, "if it is badly ordered?" His answer: nothing more than a "mere treasury of alms" that fell far short of realizing the aspirations a modern poor relief should have. In a city of Hamburg's size and populousness, alms alone could never cope with the numbers of the needy. More germanely, alms were, as we have seen Büsch argue before, an ill-suited means of assistance for the working poor. Büsch divided the great undifferentiated mass of the poor into two basic classes: those who could not work (the sick, the invalid, the ancient, and the infant) and those who could. (Others, like Voght, preferred to speak of a "nonculpable" poor, that is, those who through no fault of their own could not work, and a "culpable poor," the idlers and beggars.) And, Büsch continued, "when the primary root of impoverishment is this, that the common man earns too little to live on, then the second class [will always be] the larger." Thus the second class was at once the real object of poor relief and the problem of greatest urgency for the public's attention.[42]

Because the number of the needy was so large, Büsch insisted that mere Christian charity, as laudable as it was as a personal attribute, would never again be able to contend with the real job of poor relief. This kind of charity was sloppy, perverse, counterproductive, and truly disastrous—a calamity that was an equal misfortune for the individual, his family, and the community. Even if individuals could not be blamed for an initial incidence of impoverishment, nothing was more destructive in the long run, according to Büsch, than to allow them, indeed force them for want of a better alternative, to persist in their indigence and to become dependent on alms for their existence. Such compassion proved far too expensive for any state to bear.

Büsch realized that a more purposefully constructed poor relief would also create more work for men like him. Someone must undertake the meticulous investigation of each individual case of poverty, diligently and repeatedly. To the question of who was accountable for this painstaking business, Büsch knew only one answer: citizens, and citizens alone. He elaborated that "[t]his cannot be a job for just a few people; [and] it must never become the work of paid officials. Many citizens must [be prepared] to take upon themselves the special investigation and continued observation of the poor. . . . But this is not a task which one masters in a day. The pauper has his dodges [*Winkelzüge*], and gladly eludes the hand that would succor him, [and prefers] to live in his own manner, as best he is able, but at the cost of others."[43] Büsch appreciated the wisdom of the precepts that had directed parish relief since the sixteenth century. He criticized their failures, which he attributed primarily to "altered times and circumstances." He meant, of course, the phenomenal economic and demographic development of the city. Writing in either 1785 or 1786, he pointed to the reforms that had been praised as excellent in Lübeck and Bremen, arguing that while he did not wish to denigrate their achievements (in fact, he sincerely admired them), these cities had from the outset faced a less complicated assignment: "an incomparably smaller mass of human beings to supervise." Moreover, the inhabitants of both cities were not so packed together as in Hamburg and therefore it was less easy to escape the scrutiny of relief officers. In such "moderately populated municipalities," Büsch continued, "one neighbor knows the other, one street the next, one parish the rest," and thus the whole city could be "more effortlessly controlled." Larger cities fostered anonymity. Lack of knowledge, lack of oversight, and lack of contact were the greatest obstacles to a good poor relief, inhibiting if not actually frustrating the essential chore of surveillance. The same anonymity that made almost impossible the city's attempts to keep track of its inhabitants nullified hopes of apportioning the pauper the "appropriately mild or harsh treatment he deserves, the advice and guidance he requires to forge him into an able and useful member [of society]." Only "the special, individual, vigilant personal supervision" of each pauper by citizens could lay a solid foundation for poor relief. Only the engagement of citizens and their sense of civic duty could unravel the knotty complications of poor relief administration in a metropolis. The benefits Büsch anticipated from such a system would, however, touch not only the poor; those who were better off would also learn from their experiences. Moreover, a revived and elaborated civic patriotism promised to sustain the body politic by generating deeper commitments to republican institutions.[44]

The combination of the increased size of the city and the cruciality of the participation of citizens dictated, in Büsch's mind, the creation of "finely subdivided stewardships," which moreover "should not be ambulatory," should not shift month by month, or even year by year, from one person to another. Continuity and experience in office, not professionalization or bureaucratization, were the keys. For purposes of administration, the city should be arranged into numerous relief districts, with each district supervised by a relief officer elected by his fellow citizens. Thus, the pauper, who, according to Büsch, never before had known his overseer and even less frequently discussed with him his way of life and his problems, would now have as his overseer a familiar face: a neighbor who would know of his troubles, whom he could trust, and who would care for him with the compassion and sensitivity only a neighbor or friend could extend. "And in this way," Büsch continued, "the aid afforded him would be more effective, the advice [given him] more pertinent, and the disciplining and educational means [applied] more opportune."[45]

Büsch's ideal poor relief would have merged the affluent and the penniless, citizens and inhabitants into a single communal unit without, however, obliterating status and class distinctions. Even if the broader sense of community that the city had once supposedly enjoyed as a whole had dissipated under the pressures of population growth and urban sprawl, a reaffirmation of community, of civic responsibility, of duty and obligation, might be retrieved in the familiar realm of one's own neighborhood. Obviously what Büsch yearned for was a deeper immersion of middling citizens, those who historically had rarely assumed civic posts higher than that of militia captain, and those who were not entitled to attend the sessions of the Bürgerschaft, in the business of government. Büsch saw value in each group. "Rich and esteemed [citizens] . . . should not be alloted the tasks of individual supervision, although they can be entrusted with the overall administration to good effect, as they can safely be relied on in monetary matters; thus, while they are without doubt the most trustworthy accountants for the poor, they are definitely not their most serviceable overseers." Here, too, Büsch drew distinctions between those who were later designated relief officers and charged with the daily implementation of poor relief policies, and the directors who devised policies.[46]

Contained in Büsch's proposals lay some degree of social criticism directed at the wealthy (or perhaps only at the parasitic rich) who for various reasons proved unsuitable candidates for the pedestrian side of poor relief. Because they filled their lives with "time-consuming pleasures, . . . obligations and liaisons," they had few moments free for other pursuits and were easily "fatigued" by the demands placed on them, thus performing their duty only dilatorily or, even worse, hiring others to do it for them. Moreover, "that wealthy fellow who wiles away the winter in his urban palace and the summer at his distant country estate" was too far removed from the poor man to appreciate his problems. One wonders whom Büsch had in mind when he chastised the "idle rich"—probably those burghers who aped the noble's *fainéantise*. He would have found it hard to characterize his colleagues in the Patriotic Society, who were often extremely wealthy, as either indolent or frivolous."[47] To some extent he was mouthing eighteenth-century platitudes, although his concern was real and there is little doubt that he wished to stimulate a greater show of patriotism among Hamburg's merchant class, which to his way of thinking still inexcusably distanced itself from the broader affairs of community. At the same time, he was earnest in his desire to involve the solid middle range of the citizenry in civic activities. He also tied into an older tradition of patriotic writings in Hamburg, which worried about the aristocratic pretensions of Hamburg's upper class and the resulting decline of burgher and republican virtues. At the same time, he censured the bureaucracy-laden governments of monarchs. In place of bureaucrats, Büsch wanted as many citizens as possible. He, and others like him, regarded participation in communal or parish affairs as fundamental tutelage in civic duty for those who would eventually rise to pilot the ship of state. Still poor relief was not only to be an ambitious young man's obligatory first step on the ladder to a civic career; it was to be an end in itself and a meritorious civic obligation for those who lacked the time, money, aptitude, or perhaps the inclination, to assert themselves more vigorously in government. Here, too, Büsch confronted the notoriously narrow-minded commercialism of many Hamburg burghers who troubled themselves little about anything that snatched them out of their dark counting houses or separated them from their beloved ledgers. Like Büsch, Voght implored merchants to arrange a more comprehensive education for their children, one that exceeded an ability to assess market values, balance their books, and recite their catechism.[48]

One cannot overlook Büsch's conception of a poor relief that responded to social issues broader than merely the relief of poverty, the suppression of mendicancy, or, for that matter, the disciplining of the laboring classes. Far more ambitious aims lay embedded in Büsch's design and in the program of the General Poor Relief. The laboring morale of workers was to be raised, but the charitable impulses of citizens were also to be recast and rendered more fit for the world of late eighteenth-century Hamburg. Traditional charity in the form of almsgiving was seen as counterproductive. Once begging was abolished in the city, which was, Büsch insisted, the essential first step in the entire process of poor relief reorganization, "so will every well-to-do citizen [be able to] rejoice . . . and with no disquietude [be able to] rely on the new poor relief. . . . And [yet] he will trouble himself less than before with each individual pauper." In point of fact, Büsch's notion of a well-organized poor relief rested as much on disciplining the better-off members of society to accept modifications in traditional standards of charity and to embrace newly defined civic roles as it rested on disciplining the poor.[49]

Preventing the *giving* of alms was the initial step taken to alter outmoded ideals of altruism. While the officials of the General Poor Relief hoped to banish mendicants from Hamburg's streets by proscribing almsgiving (and by stiffening penalties for begging), they also worked to inculcate a modern philanthropic ethos contingent on principles of rational charity derived from natural laws. The idea was not to eliminate charity, but to redirect it. Money alone was never seen as the appropriate answer. Hamburg was already celebrated for the amount of money spent on philanthropic works. Yet munificence alone could not resolve the quandaries of eighteenth-century poverty. England was seen as the classic example of a state where vast sums gleaned from taxes had been squandered. Voght pointed out that in England "mismanagement has employed [the moneys], with very few exceptions, as a reward for sloth, idleness, impudence, untruth, has reared new generations of poor wretches, brought up to a life of disgusting profligacy."[50] Hamburg's reformers concluded that taxation was not a reasonable alternative to unsupervised charity. The first stifled civic spirit, the second spoiled the working classes with unthinking pity [which] has rashly stopped that natural course of things, by which want leads to labour, labour to comfort, the knowledge of comfort to industry, and to all those virtures, by which the toiling multitude so incalculably adds to the strength and happiness of a country: And while it neglects that respectable poverty which shrinks from public sight, it encourages, by profuse and indiscriminate charities, all those abominable arts which make beggary a better trade than a workshop.[51]

Charity and generosity were, of course, indispensable social virtues that no rational person dreamed of eliminating. Yet "in repairing . . . those evils, which society did not, or could not prevent," one should exercise caution and "ought to be careful not to counteract the wise purposes of nature, not to do more than to give the poor a fair chance to work for themselves." The real task for those who wished to alleviate poverty was to learn to be unyielding, to learn

to shut their ears to the cries of misery, and leave those to their fate who will not comply with the conditions under which they are to be relieved. . . . If, in a single instance, indulgence is shown, where, according to the law, it ought not, then all is lost: abuse creeps in, and in a short time this weekly allowance becomes a pension, that supersedes the necessity of working; then it becomes a matter of favour and protection, and the whole a system of corruption. . . .[52]

The idea of a poor tax was, moreover, ideologically repugnant to free citizens. Most of them opposed an assessment to cover the expense of poor relief not only because such moneys tended to be spent prodigally and ineffectively but also because such imposts would diminish, not augment, citizen accountability for civic affairs and perhaps even beget a paid bureaucracy of relief workers. Charity was to remain a Christian and civic duty. The dilemma was how to retain the benefits of Christian charity yet purge it of its impulsive qualities. The General Poor Relief's solution was a weekly collection taken up throughout the city. The beauty of the system was that the offerings were not quite voluntary and yet were also clearly not a tax. Each week one citizen in the district solicited his neighbors' contributions to the Relief. Records were kept of the amount each person or household pledged. A citizen could not without a good excuse refuse to go around with the collection box. One could, of course, balk at contributing, but it was difficult to look a neighbor in the eye and deny his request. The coercion was subtle but hardly the less productive for its subtlety. The Relief eased the transition in other ways, by retaining the mechanisms of earlier collections. The Rat, for example, announced the Relief's special collections in the same ways they had always proclaimed the customary offertories for the orphanage or Pesthof, that is, from the pulpit.[53]

The desirability of such new forms of charity was not accepted by everyone. Some posited that this type of relief denied persons the legitimate Christian joy they derived from personal giving. Rationalizing charity carried with it the possibility of throttling compassion as well. Some voiced apprehension that eradicating poverty might also crush the charitable urge and dampen humanitarian ardor. The General Poor Relief acknowledged the legitimacy of such fears and worked to quiet them. Some of the solutions were perceptive: the members of the Relief argued with effect the economy of such rational methods over the wastefulness of unsupervised almsgiving. Some measures were more naively conceived and probably far less serviceable. Voght portrayed the disquietude of the Relief: "We had observed that our Relief might entirely eliminate poverty from the sight of children of the so-called better classes and help them grow up inured to misery—thus, these [children], too, shall take up a collection among themselves and discover early in their lives how to perform a civic duty. I wish that I could devise a way for them to see the poor in their dwellings [as well]. Now isn't that a fine idea?"[54]

Equally decisive in determining the success of the new poor relief would be its ability to eliminate the need for handouts altogether and to shift the emphasis of poor relief to that of furnishing work for the poor instead of doling out alms. The major component of Büsch's system—the piece that he regarded as absolutely fundamental—was the creation of "factories where the well-intentioned pauper can find occupation enough to support himself either wholly or to a great extent, and which [at the same time] will deny the malingerer the excuse of lacking work with which he previously misled his benefactors. . . ."[55] According to Büsch, the Zuchthaus was the *least* appropriate location for such establishments. Even in the eighteenth century, it remained in the eyes of the common people a dishonorable house that the "honorable" poor avoided unless driven there by the greatest extremes of hunger and deprivation.[56] Voght, who in his youth had escorted the celebrated reformer, John Howard, on an inspection tour of Hamburg's poorhouses, maintained "that the very place which ought to bring back the offender to industry and virtue, is the school of crimes! Who feels not for men whose only crime is poverty when he sees them crowded into the same workhouses with shameless profligates,—*and into such workhouses*!"[57]

A successful poor relief must secure the trust of the poor, a requirement that, in Büsch's mind, loomed far larger than that of chastisement or discipline. Such trust would never be won within the walls of a prison. The Zuchthaus crammed the "shamefaced poor" into close quarters with an unholy mix of the city's dregs, the brazen beggars and rogues, cutpurses and thieves. Büsch admitted the necessity of "order, discipline, and correction . . . [Must] we, however, condone intimidation, coercion, and captivity?" Büsch visualized a unique workhouse, a voluntary house of industry, where the unemployed could go and be assured of employment. "Until such a place exists," Büsch wrote, "every struggle to curb mendicancy will fail." While it is clear that Büsch meant his factory to be a voluntary alternative for those "who could work and wished to work," he conceded its additional utility as a healthy deterrent for foreign beggars and for "idle [and] reckless" fellows. Still, Büsch's purposes did not require a mammoth edifice. Again, he stressed the importance of community ties and wanted to scatter a few "not very large such institutions" throughout the city, with one or more in each relief district.[58]

Büsch suggested the types of work to be chosen for such a factory. Perhaps, he mused, cotton spinning and weaving might be fitting employment for the poor while satisfying the demands of local calico printers, allowing them to buy at home rather than forcing them to import finished cloth from Saxony. Cotton spinning and weaving offered the additional boon of not being guilded trades in Hamburg, so no one had to worry about undercutting or impoverishing other workers in the city, nor would one be pestered by the complaints of guildsmen. The introduction of cotton spinning and weaving could prove propitious in yet another way: by launching other manufactories in Hamburg to assist in alleviating some basic problems of insufficient work and low wages.[59]

Wages, too, were a thorny issue. Determining the appropriate earnings for the poor employed in a factory proved a ticklish matter. For example, if wages or alms were set too high, it would injure other laborers in the city while handicapping, even competing with, employers in their attempts to attract workers. "Our milliners complain," Büsch related, "that they have difficulties turning up people willing to work at preparing felt (an unskilled and therefore poorly paid trade) because once workers obtain alms or parish handouts, they no longer stoop to such tasks." The question of wages involved painstaking calculation to avoid labor shortages and to avert an artificial and unhealthy elevation of both wages and prices. The General Poor Relief developed a whole string of industry schools and factories without ever successfully solving this problem, or the equally labyrinthine ones of locating reliable markets for their products or assuring their quality.[60]

The final trait of a well-ordered poor relief, as defined by Büsch and the other reformers, was an "unconstrained accessibility of information." Good publicity not only elucidated a relief's policy resolutions and justified its outlays, but also swept up the public's attention, endowing citizens with a sense of inclusion, inviting them to revel in successes and share in disappointments. The frequent *Reports* also served the more prosaic purpose of stimulating a flow of contributions. Büsch saw beyond these immediate pragmatic benefits and valued such forms of publicity as essential for republics in distinctive ways. Once again the contrasts between free republics and monarchies resonate: "Measures that sovereigns deem reputable might well be regarded in a republic as unworthy," and therefore substantially more preparation and a greater openness of discussion had to occur in republics before striking out in new directions. The absolute minimum that Büsch expected of any poor relief was to circulate among its subscribers "Lists of the names of all the [registered] poor, and excerpts from their accounts, remarks, plans, and [data on] special cases, etc." With this remark, Büsch unveils a further virtue of regular reports, namely, the public would be drawn into a dialogue on poor relief. Only in this way could the enterprise prosper and the more ambitious goals of poor relief—those that ranged beyond a mere assuagement of misery—be attained. Voght, too, grasped the point, acknowledging "that the success of such an undertaking depends wholly on the degree in which the public at large is satisfied of its necessity."[61]

Büsch contemplated the restoration, or perhaps the construction, of small, closely knit communities nestled inside the densely populated and increasingly unfamiliar city. By dividing the city into districts that corresponded roughly to neighborhoods, and through the election of overseers from among the inhabitants of each district, Büsch hoped to nurture active communal microcosms inside the metropolitan carapace. The overseer was to be neighbor and friend, as well as father and disciplinarian. On the one hand, civic spirit should prod the good citizens of each district to shoulder the duties of overseer. On the other hand, however, exercising the office should itself promote social learning and form an indispensable part of a broader education in civic virtue. Büsch yearned for the extension of a civic brotherhood beyond the relatively tiny clique of those who ordinarily assumed civic offices—a brotherhood that would draw wider circles of citizens into the business of governing. This was hardly a revolutionary proposal, as Büsch contemplated no reformation of Hamburg's constitution nor even desired a loosening of the requirements for civic office to include more of Hamburg's noncitizen inhabitants. Yet for Büsch the "*citizens* of smaller means and social stature" promised to bring the most to poor relief because they lived closer, geographically and psychologically, to their impoverished neighbors. Moreover, they were not, and probably never would be, caught up in the burdensome chores of higher municipal office in Hamburg.[62]

The Founding of the General Poor Relief

Büsch's suggestions served as a blueprint for the General Poor Relief; not every goal to which he aspired was achieved or even attempted, but if we compare his plan with the relief that was actually implemented, then the differences were few. Büsch's "Excerpts from a Revised Plan for Improving Poor Relief in Hamburg" was, according to his own testimony, solicited by "a respected person of authority" in government.[63] It was not only Büsch, or a small band of patriots, who had poor relief reform on their agenda; it had been an interest of both the Rat and the Bürgerschaft long before the 1780s. The economic uncertainties of the 1760s and 1770s had awakened a desire for reform, even if few people saw much further than an intensification of the repressive measures previously implemented. For example, during the deliberations of the Sixty on the reshaping of nexus guidelines, particularly with regard to the eradication of abuses in the Schutzverwandten system, the issue of poor relief reform was also discussed. The observations and recommendations of the Sixty mingled the old and the new, but mostly reflected the conservative, even timorous nature of the body. The Sixty was most concerned about seeking ways to deal with a "wildly proliferating mendicancy." In their opinion, "nothing is more injurious to the republic than when healthy and sturdy idlers, having accustomed themselves to begging as a very comfortable way to earn their daily bread, avoid all toil and not only themselves become millstones around the necks of the industrious and hard-working segments of our population but also rear their children to the same parasitic life-style, so that the city is soon filled with a mob of beggars and begging-brats."[64] The Sixty, while supporting a continued necessity to punish "sturdy, indolent beggars," had also come to understand that repressive measures alone had repeatedly failed. They seemed to appreciate a need for sustaining the able-bodied poor in times of severe unemployment yet advanced no strategy for how this goal might be realized. If their counsel was not new, at least they were willing to concede that the older methods of repression and lavish almsgiving had outlived their usefulness. It was the widespread acceptance of this attitude that merged the more conservative (like the Oberalten and the Sixty) and the more enlightened elements of society (the reform party in the Rat and the Patriotic Society) in a concerted effort that vivified poor relief reform in the 1770s and 1780s.

In 1787 the Oberalten, as constitutional spokesmen for the Bürgerschaft, drafted a plan for the reform of poor relief. They circumscribed the responsibilities and articulated the aims of a poor relief that in spirit approximated very closely the ideas of Büsch and his compatriots. Büsch's publications of 1785 and 1786 may well have been their guides. The Oberalten identified the reasons for the swollen impoverishment in the city, singling out

> the decline and, in some cases, the total obliteration of several useful trades and manufactures, which previously had busied so many hands; the growing propensity among a large number of our inhabitants to indolence, folly, and improvidence; the lottery, whose unfortunate effects are perhaps nowhere so obvious as here; the shoddy quality of our schools where children learn with alacrity to be shiftless and slothful, but acquire nothing which could be serviceable to them in the future; and also a misdirected sense of charity, which not only confirms our own wanton beggars in their indolence but also (and especially since the [recent] improvements in the poor relief systems of our neighbors) entices outsiders here to us.
>
> To these [causes] can be added the duration and harshness of the previous winters, whereby so many productive trades suffered an unusually early and protracted standstill, and with them fell the living of so many of our older and younger inhabitants who depend on their daily toil to survive; and [finally] the exceedingly poor harvests of the last few years which have driven prices of the most essential foodstuffs to the highest levels.

The Oberalten concluded that they still found it difficult to fathom "how so much real poverty and particularly how so much hidden misery" could persist in Hamburg, when there was a panoply of charitable institutions, Hamburg's citizens were so magnanimous, a flourishing commerce existed, various trades and manufacturers thrived in the city, and "that even the excessive luxury, unwholesome though it may be in so many ways, sires ample opportunities for employment." "The onus must lie," they concluded, "on the [way in which] poor relief is dispensed." The outline they submitted incorporated all the features for which the General Poor Relief later became renowned: the creation of a central agency for overseeing all forms of poor relief in the city, the empaneling of a select group of citizens to manage poor relief, factories to employ the able-bodied poor and schools for the children of paupers, a more stringent control of mendicancy, an uncompromisingly stern prohibition of casual almsgiving and, finally, a more businesslike way of financing poor relief.[65]

The General Poor Relief established in 1788 embodied all these points as well as drawing into itself older traditions of governing in Hamburg. It had never been a private organization but instead followed in that long line of semipublic institutions, which smoothly balanced private initiative and public benefit so that it was often impossible to discern where one left off and the other began. The General Poor Relief was *not* private charity in any real sense of the word because it formulated and executed other municipal policies, particularly those pertaining to population control and the punishment of petty offenders. It carried the tradition of civic duty and trusteeship to its fullest expression, successfully—for a while—involving hundreds of citizens in the administration of public welfare and schooling them for weightier municipal responsibilities. These objectives, and the success with which they were fulfilled, did not escape the scrutiny of contemporaries. And the judgment was overwhelmingly positive. To the Weimar rector and author, Karl August Böttiger, "The spirit of order which inspires an institution [the General Poor Relief] encompassing several thousand persons is truly admirable and bears the stamp of a true republican communal spirit of which Hamburg displays more proof than any other city in Germany."[66]

The General Poor Relief set up in 1788 incorporated the principles of community deep within its very structure. The entire city was divided into five districts (*Armen-Bezirke*), with each under the direct administration of two directors (*Armen-Vorsteher*). Each district was then additionally subdivided into twelve quarters, with each quarter placed under the supervision of three relief officers (*Armenpfleger*). There were, therefore, 180 relief officers for a population of about 100,000 people. Each relief officer took charge of about twenty to thirty pauper families. Districts cut across old parish dividing lines. Their boundaries were drawn, in a sort of benevolent gerrymandering, so that each district contained approximately equal numbers of poverty-stricken residents. Districts and quarters therefore varied in physical size.[67]

The council (*Armen-Kollegium*) was the administrative heart of the Relief. Composed of five members of the Rat, two Oberalten, ten directors, five parish Gotteskastenverwalter, and the senior governors of the three poorhouses (the orphanage, the Zuchthaus, and the Pesthof), it formulated policies. The Rat named its representatives to the council. The Oberalten were selected by the Sixty. The choice of directors was most crucial because they were the real workhorses of the system. Chosen by the Sixty "from the entire citizenry, that is, from all those in the civic nexus and qualified for other civic offices," they assumed their office for life, unless excused for reasons of health or business, or unless elected to the Rat or Treasury.[68] These men usually left behind their duties as directors when they ascended to loftier communal posts. Johann Friedrich Behrens was the first to seek his release from his duties as director upon his election to the Treasury in 1789. For equally credible reasons, others were excused.[69] When deaths or resignations tore gaps in the ranks of the directors, the council drew up lists of acceptable replacements. Eventually almost all of the men put forward were selected as directors, with their names appearing repeatedly on the lists until chosen. Some had been relief officers, but acting as a relief officer was not deemed an indispensable or even an especially desirable prerequisite for appointment as a director. The offices seemed designed for two rather different groups of citizens. The directors rapidly assumed leading roles in the municipality as senators, syndics, or Oberalten, whereas the relief officers as a rule did so far less frequently, rarely rising further than the Treasury. This trend seems especially pronounced after the mid-1790s.[70]

The way in which council members were designated embodied the most venerable traditions of government in Hamburg: All positions of power and trust, all policy-making posts, continued to be delegated to the same citizens who, like their fathers and grandfathers before them, ran the city. A new common experience for many of them was membership in the Patriotic Society. Some historians have advanced the thesis that "clubs" like the Patriotic Society, or organizations like the General Poor Relief, drew together disenfranchised citizens. Their participation in societies and associations that were dedicated ostensibly to the promotion of the common good granted them an opportunity for recognition in their community, endowing them with a sense of belonging, while buying them off with a sop of social respect to compensate for their political emasculation. On the other hand, some discern in such societies an embryonic political consciousness; these societies were places where the politically dispossessed learned how to organize for future political action.[71] Neither thesis holds much validity for Hamburg. Almost all members of the Patriotic Society already enjoyed access or, at the very least, the prerequisites for access to all governmental posts in Hamburg. They were already politically enfranchised and intimately involved in municipal politics. While the Patriotic Society was certainly an association of reform-minded, even enlightened, citizens, it cannot be interpreted as a germinal opposition group seeking to overturn or at least drastically modify the conventions of governing in Hamburg. Like the General Poor Relief it labored happily within the existing structure of government; yet both were also new components of middle-class culture.[72]

On 27 March 1788 the council convened for the first time. Around the table sat twenty-five of the city's most prominent and respected citizens. Fifteen were present ex officio: five members of the Rat (the syndic Nicolaus Matsen and the senators Volkmann, Lienau, Kirchhoff, and Hudtwalcker), two Oberalten, five Gotteskastenverwalter, and three governors of the poorhouses.[73] The presence of the Gotteskastenverwalter, the governors, and the Oberalten symbolized the renewed attempt to centralize poor relief and to conserve an older heritage by folding it into a new structure.

The documents pertaining to the history of the General Poor Relief, particularly the *Reports,* indicate very strongly that it was a mere handful of enterprising men who molded poor relief in those years. They were, of course, helpless without the support of the relief officers, impotent without the blessings of the Rat and Bürgerschaft, paralyzed without ample financial support, and doomed to failure without at least the tacit sanction of a broad cross section of Hamburg's citizens; yet the driving force emanated from a small number of people.

Directors and Relief Officers

The directors composed this critical group. Especially in the early years, these men forged the new poor relief by guiding its daily activities. They developed general policy, determined the varieties and set the levels of support, instituted new programs or reworked old ones, and—perhaps most importantly— were responsible for the image the General Poor Relief projected to the rest of the community and to the world.[74] The chores that fell to each director were myriad and assorted. It is perhaps unrealistic to accept Caspar Voght's burden of assignments as typical, but it demonstrates the range of activities that could gobble up a director's time. Voght was called on to compile a general accounting distilled from the reports of each district on flax spinning, twine winding, weaving, and on the expenditures of the Factory Deputation, the first two classes of the Industry School, and the Elementary School. Moreover, he estimated future expenses and requested monthly advances, drafted lengthy comments on all arising incidents, and attended council meetings. In addition, each month he prepared a list of the newly registered poor and charted alterations in individual support levels for his half-district. Additional regular duties included the paying of premiums to children in the second class of the Industry School, recording changes from the summer to winter relief rates, reviewing the changes for the council, and writing up the protocols of the Factory, School, and Clothing Deputations, which he headed. Finally, Voght (along with Johann Heinrich Bartels and Johann Arnold Günther) edited the Relief's semiannual *Report*.[75] Not every director was as animated as Voght, although all were ultimately answerable for everything touching on poor relief in their half of the district, all participated on one or more of the special deputations, and all were laden with a host of bookkeeping chores.[76] If one wishes to follow the transformation in poor relief *policies* over time, then it is to the directors, rather than to the relief officers, that one must turn. Two of the original ten directors, Caspar Voght and Johann Arnold Günther, were major forces in the early and most successful years of the General Poor Relief.

Caspar Voght[77] was in some ways typical, in other ways atypical, of the men who piloted the Relief in these years. Older historiography has generally acknowledged him and Büsch as the fathers of poor relief reform in Hamburg. Certainly no one played a more pivotal role in the first years of the Relief's existence. But his control over the later destiny of the Relief has been overstated. For prolonged intervals, especially after 1793, he was rarely in Hamburg and exercised his office as director by correspondence.

Born in 1752 into the family of a successful merchant and senator, Voght belonged to the first generation of merchants who embraced the cause of enlightenment: individuals who worshiped beauty and truth more than mammon, sighed for the poetry of Klopstock, and quivered in the presence of unspoiled nature—at least while they were young. He was a pioneer in poor relief reform and maintained a keen, if sometimes distracted, interest in such projects until his death at age eighty-six in 1839. Far more than any of his Hamburg contemporaries, he was involved in poor relief throughout Europe. Early in the nineteenth century he orchestrated reforms for the Holy Roman Emperor in Vienna, for the king of Prussia, and later for Napoleon in France and Italy.[78] Voght was amiable and sincere, if sometimes immodest. At times he credited himself with perhaps more than his fair share of accolades. Writing in his autobiography, he sketched out his part in poor relief reform: "With an energy bolstered [only] by Günther's stamina and propelled by an iron will, I mastered all difficulties, founded manufactories and schools and relished the spectacle [of seeing] them serve not only as mere assistance for the poor but also . . . as conduits [which] deflected poverty." He uncharitably (and not quite fairly) characterized the other directors as "eight older, less vigorous citizens."[79] Even if he was arrogant, he was not a vain braggart. The portion of relief work Voght and Günther assumed was enormous; they took part in or chaired at some time nearly all of the special deputations, which administered medical care, schools, factories, and distributed clothing, fuel, and bread.

Yet Voght, despite his undeniable dynamism, was also unlike the other directors. He was an dilettante who chased after many dreams in his long life. From his memoirs and letters, and in the judgment of his contemporaries, Voght appears to be a man who required constant diversion and much stimulation to curb his innate restlessness. He was easily bored. Though a merchant, he had never developed much taste for the business world or for anything he labeled "soulless commercial toil."[80] When his father died in 1781, he and his friend Georg Heinrich Sieveking,[81] the son of a prosperous draper, took over the business, which they managed with uncommon success. Yet Voght never delighted in the life of a merchant: "When commerce once failed to busy my imagination, it disgusted me," he wrote, "[and] the craving for [a life of] public service consumed me."[82] Therefore, he retired in 1793, leaving his friend Sieveking to run the business. Voght took up the life of a leisured gentleman (eventually buying an estate), prompting the wife of the American consul in Hamburg to quip: "Mr. Voght is a happy man, lives quietly in the country and his clerk is making money as fast as he can."[83]

Voght's passions were many: He loved the theater, country life on the English model, travel, and applause. His frequent journeys—a long grand tour from 1772–75, a two-year trip to England in 1793–95, and innumerable shorter jaunts—brought him into contact with the nobles and notables of almost every western European country. During the French occupation of Hamburg, he spent most of his time in France, Italy, Austria, and in Switzerland for a while as the "ami allemand" of Madame de Staël. Unlike most of his Hamburg compatriots, he felt drawn to the nobility and valued them, seeking out aristocratic companionship on his travels and moving in émigré circles at home. Uncharacteristic of a Hamburg merchant was his admiration for Frederick the Great.[84] While engrossed in the reform of poor relief in Vienna in 1801, he extolled (perhaps somewhat tongue in cheek) the enviable speed with which things could be accomplished in a monarchy: "The sovereign's word, his wish is still revered by these honest folk like the will of God."[85] Voght sometimes cast himself in the role of a benevolent despot, albeit on a small scale. For example, in his own tiny kingdom, his estate at Klein Flottbek, he enjoyed the role of munificent reforming landlord, reveling in scenes of "happy peasant families, together with their children clad in picturesque peasant garb, sitting in front of the neat cottages I had built for them." He celebrated the "festivals of sowing and harvesting, of age and youth" and lounged during fair weather in a straw hat "under the shade of my oak tree."[86] It is easy from the perspective of the twentieth century to caricature Voght and to miss the genuine commitment he, and many others like him, felt toward improving society and the lives of those who depended on them. Voght perceived his civic mission in works of a practical nature, regarding "all knowledge that could not be turned to humanitarian purposes . . . vain and empty."[87]

Voght was a Hamburg citizen, bound by the old legacies of civic service, yet temperamentally unsuited to the solid or even staid life of a merchant, or to that of one who played his role in civic affairs without fanfare. Yet perhaps in other ways Voght, like Büsch and to a lesser extent Günther, broke new ground, opening up different types of civic participation. This was also indicative of the slow shift in the definition of burgher away from an older legal definition toward a newer meaning based on life-style or culture. In still another way, Voght struck out on a course not followed by most of the other directors. Whereas they assumed the responsibilities of communal government throughout their lives, Voght held back. Although he joined the citizen's militia (a duty incumbent on all able-bodied citizens under the age of sixty) and even filled some minor civic offices, he never shed his need for independence and avoided major civic office in his lifetime. In fact, it was probably to prevent his elevation to the Rat that he accepted the position and title of a Danish *Staatsrat* in 1796, making himself ineligible for further civic honors in Hamburg. Later, in 1801, as recognition for his services in reforming poor relief in Vienna, the Holy Roman Emperor named him Freiherr von Voght.[88]

Johann Arnold Günther,[89] the colleague Voght most esteemed, was never apathetic to politics. In fact he reached the pinnacle of government in Hamburg with his election to the Rat in 1792. Günther was born in 1755 and, like Voght, was the son of a wealthy merchant. Young Johann acquired a taste for literature and poetry that did not please his more practical-minded father. At age fourteen, Günther was removed from school and placed in a counting house that allowed him time to read only at night. The lucky purchase of a lottery ticket, however, won him the significant sum of 100 thaler, which his father, rather surprisingly, permitted him to spend as he chose. With the money he purchased the books that formed the basis of the extensive library that he accumulated during his lifetime.[90] After a while his father relented and allowed Günther to attend first Hamburg's famous Johanneum and then, in

1774, the Academic Gymnasium. It was at the Gymnasium that he had as teachers Büsch and the historian and propagandist of the Enlightenment, Christoph Daniel Ebeling. In 1775 Günther went to the University of Göttingen to study law. At that time, the teachings of the cameralists and national economists strongly influenced the Göttingen legal curriculum. Günther frequented the lectures of the cameralists Selchow, Schlözer, Pütter, Gatterer, and Beckmann on constitutional law, history, statistics, economic and administrative science.

In 1778 he ended his university career, taking the law degree of licentiate. Following a standard course for young men of his class and education, he embarked on a lengthy tour that carried him to numerous German states, going like Goethe to Wetzlar to add to his legal expertise by observing the Imperial Court in action. Two years later he returned to Hamburg. It was not the happiest of homecomings. According to his friend and biographer, Johann Friedrich Lorenz Meyer, Günther lapsed into a deep depression: "The narrow city that closed around him did not match the soaring ambitions of this youthful careerist."[91] However, he soon shook off his malaise and began to make his way. His first forays into public life were not successful. After his return to Hamburg, he started up practice as an attorney. Apparently, however, law did not suit him and he wasted little time on what he later characterized as "legal jog-trot." In the 1780s, he aspired to several legal posts in the municipality, but bids in 1781, 1785, 1788, and 1789 all miscarried, and, at least for a time, the usual course open to Hamburg lawyers remained blocked to him.[92]

He was not inactive, however, and, like Voght, quickly made his mark in the field of public service. In 1781, he joined the Patriotic Society and in 1782 became one of its directors and its executive secretary. He had inherited a fortune, which he increased further when he married. As a man of means, he was free to apply himself to a diverse array of communal activities. In the 1780s, he conducted single-handedly almost all the administrative work of the Patriotic Society. Aided by several members who had come to the society in the 1780s, he breathed new life into an organization that had in the preceding decades lost some of its original verve and drive. His scope of civic involvement was greater than just the Patriotic Society. Together with his old teacher, Büsch, he laid out the design for a "Mortgage Bank for Estates and Properties," and then directed the venture until 1781. In 1786 he joined the managing board of the "General Assistance Institute," (which included one of the first savings plans in the Germanies), and in 1796 composed a Medical Ordinance upon which public health reform in 1818 was based. In addition he broached plans to improve fire insurance, to reorganize Hamburg's police, and to establish a Life-Saving Society.[93] Like many of his contemporaries, among them Voght and Sieveking, he welcomed the French Revolution, and like them, persisted in his enthusiasm for the slogans of "liberté, égalité, fraternité" until the Terror. But also like them he worked these ideas into existing frameworks of government and society in Hamburg while misjudging or misunderstanding their truly revolutionary message.[94]

Even though his name is virtually forgotten today, Günther was a prolific propagandist and publicist, editing several volumes of the Patriotic Society's *Deliberations*. Numerous lengthy reports and innumerable shorter contributions flowed unceasingly from his pen. He contributed to almost all the major journals and periodicals in central Europe, including Schlözer's *Staatsanzeiger*, the *Journal von und für Deutschland*, the *Reichsanzeiger*, and the *Allgemeine Literatur-Zeitung*.[95] He kept up a massive correspondence with such prominent reformers and well-known German Enlightenment figures as Rudolf Zacharias Becker, Johann Joachim Eschenberg, Bernhard Christoph Faust, Christoph Wilhelm Hufeland, Johann Anton Leisewitz, Christian Gotthilf Salzmann, Johann Christian Friedrich Scherf, and the brothers Arnold and Ludwig Gerhard Wagemann, who were editors of the *Göttingen Magazine for Industry and Poor Relief* to which he subscribed.[96]

Writing in 1796, Günther explained the ideals by which he had tried to live: "[Promoting] the public good in the widest sense was the chief axiom and consuming passion of my life. I followed this axiom so that I would not have lived in vain; gave into this passion because the struggle to attain this goal, . . . and the approbation [with which] honest and wise men viewed this ambition and its achievements afforded me greater joy than anything else in the world."[97] He considered 1788, the year which gave birth to the General Poor Relief, as "the most wearying yet the most gratifying of my life" and the twenty-fourth of February 1792, according to an entry in his diary, "the most important day . . . that decided [the rest of] my life," the day he was named senator. He was thirty-six, "still young enough," he recorded, "to initiate many projects for the public good." And he greeted his selection for the Rat as yet another chance to expand his sphere of "usefulness."[98]

Because of his position, range of activities, and background, Günther is a valuable and articulate spokesman for the sense of communal duty that inspired him and others. He personifies the importance that poor relief had by then assumed in governing the city. At the same time, his example facilitates our understanding of how the elites of eighteenth-century Hamburg conceived of the ideal citizen. For example, upon his election to the Rat, he was called on to deliver the customary eulogy for his predecessor in office, Peter Dietrich Volkmann. He took advantage of the opportunity to comment on how the office might be used to open up more avenues for change and to instill greater enlightenment. First, he spoke in general terms, requesting more backing for public works. Then he isolated the General Poor Relief for special attention: "I should and must bid my fellow citizens, to retain their trust in [the Relief] and their esteem for it . . . [and] let me assure them that [we] hold no duty more sacred than that of scrupulous economy, but also [let me point out] that the needs of our poor are vast and innumerable [and therefore] I should and must ask you not to deny the Relief your wholehearted support, without which this good work will surely perish." Günther argued that Hamburg's good citizens could not allow the Relief to falter "nor want . . . [to see] that child now maturing into a useful citizen return to begging, [nor] the sick man who thanks the Relief for restoring his health, once again be left to die unnoticed!"[99]

Later, toward the end of his life, after six years in office as senator, and after his disillusionment with the French Revolution, Günther drew up a balance sheet listing the fruits of his labors and measuring the progress of enlightenment in Hamburg. He admitted that of "positive gains for human happiness" there was "wretchedly little" about which to boast. Amid the gloom there occasionally glimmered a modest success: that of rescuing a family from poverty or snatching a newborn from certain death. "And who knows," he reflected, "if not in these single incidents there is more truth than in all the beautiful air-castles of cosmopolitanism, philanthropism, and patriotism, whose effects we so gladly accept on faith, because they flatter our vanity more than our humanity?"[100]

If Voght and Günther spearheaded poor relief reform in the 1790s, they hardly labored alone. Claes Bartels, admittedly the least prominent of this triumvirate of movers and shakers, performed a valuable service as the Relief's treasurer. His life experiences, while they differed in some ways from those of Voght and Günther, were unexceptional for Hamburg's merchant governors. Bartels was born in 1728 (and thus a generation older than Voght and Günther) and was apprenticed as a youth to a sugar refiner. He set up his own refinery in 1752; it was from refining that he grew wealthy. He joined the Patriotic Society just two years after its inception. His civic career followed a normal trajectory and was crowned in 1797 by his selection as Oberalte for the parish of St. Nikolai. Perhaps his business skills particularly suited him for the job of treasurer. Certainly he remained more in the background than did either Günther or Voght, yet he was always there, and remained active in the work of the Relief until one year before his death in 1806. He authored nothing in his long life, but his distinguished presence and great popularity were as precious to the Relief as other members' prose.[101]

Nicolaus Matsen should also be mentioned among the founders of the Relief. Matsen, the scion of an old Hamburg family and the son of an Oberalte, was himself a power to be reckoned with in Hamburg's government during the 1770s and 1780s, first as secretary to the Rat and then as a syndic. He was probably that "person of authority" who had asked Büsch to draw up plans for a new poor relief in 1786. Voght valued him highly and Günther prized him as a "man of spirit, strength, will, and deeds, like few others in the world, a true benefactor of his fatherland. . . ." He represented the Enlightenment in government and, with a core of others, formed a reform contingent in the Rat in the 1780s. The position of syndic was crucial and Matsen smoothed the passage of the new Relief Ordinance in the highest council of government.[102]

It was precisely this mix of men—those temperamentally and intellectually inclined toward public service, impatient with the humdrum routine of government and business but by no means totally disengaged from civic affairs, and those influential in government but sympathetic to new ideas—that created the General Poor Relief and steered it through its early years. In a less flamboyant manner, this blend characterized the entire company of directors. Of the fifty-four directors selected between 1788 and 1809, thirty-five were members of the Patriotic Society and were, we can assume, sympathetic to the ideals of the Enlightenment as a practical reform movement. They were equally well represented in the councils of government. Of the same fifty-four directors, at least twenty-three (42.6 percent) assumed a *high* civic office, that is, senator, Bürgermeister, Oberalte, Treasury representative, syndic, or archivarius. One can multiply these examples almost by the number of directors. Most attained higher office or were otherwise, through their business connections or legal expertise, commanding figures in their community.[103]

If one surveys the other eight citizens who joined Voght and Günther as directors in 1788, it is not really possible to accept Voght's estimation of them as "less active." Bartels can hardly have been considered lethargic, and the others—even if perhaps they did not live up to Voght's rigorous criteria of "activity" in poor relief—were, unlike him, deeply involved in municipal politics. Almost all were merchants or came from merchant families. All but two were members of the Patriotic Society. Almost all held or would hold an important post in the government and had already passed through a series of lesser offices. For many, the position of director was just another of the many civic roles they donned in their lifetimes. Johann Friedrich Behrens became a member of the Treasury in 1789. The distant cousins, Franz and Johann Daniel Klefeker, descended from a family conspicuous for its service to the city. Johann Daniel, along with Behrens, had been instrumental in setting up the Spinning Institute in 1785. Franz became Oberalte in 1799 and Johann Daniel was co-opted into the Rat in 1791. Vincent Oldenburg, like Günther, had studied law at Göttingen. He became secretary to the Oberalten in 1789, and in 1807 syndic to the Rat. Joachim von den Steenhoff was selected as Oberalte in 1799. Johann Friedrich Tonnies, one of the original members of the Patriotic Society in 1765, was named Oberalte in 1795. Only Johannes Poppe could be classified as a lesser figure in this municipal pantheon, because the highest civic offices that he assumed were the modest ones of militia captain and colonel. Yet he moved in the best circles as well, marrying first the daugher of a Bürgermeister and then the daughter of a senator.[104] If one wonders what criteria counted for selection as director, then membership in the Patriotic Society appears to have been a desideratum as was familiarity with the workings of government in Hamburg. Furthermore, one should not disregard the weight prestige and popularity carried in Hamburg society, where power relationships were still largely based on status and deference. The directors were chosen as much for their personalities and the aura of propriety and respectability that clung to them as for their administrative skills. If one looks, for example, at the obituary written by Meyer for Tonnies, one can identify all these attributes. Obituaries are, of course, often formulaic and almost invariably laudatory, but the qualities singled out for praise furnish a good idea of what the ideal civic patriot was supposed to be like: "A clear and sharp vision, principles untouched by prejudice, a deep understanding of the constitution of our father city, exact knowledge of domestic and foreign commercial arrangements, . . . and an unflagging desire to advance the common good, these were the main traits of his manly character."[105]

Other directors, especially those who might expediently be classified as a second generation, will be discussed in greater detail later. By 1802, as Voght noted, the original ten directors had all been replaced, with the exception of himself and Claes Bartels. Many of those who had represented the Enlightenment in Hamburg had died by 1805: Volkmann in 1792, Matsen and Sonin in 1794, Sieveking in 1799, Kirchhoff and Büsch in 1800, and Tonnies and Günther in 1805. This change in personnel explains in part the new face poor relief assumed in the nineteenth century. By the time of the French occupation, none of the original directors were left in office (except Voght in absentia). Few had experienced the halcyon days of the 1790s when almost everything the Relief touched turned to gold.[106] Some of the directors elected then— Amandus Augustus Abendroth, Otto von Axen, Johann Heinrich Bartels, Jonas Ludwig von Heß, Christian Nicolaus Pehmöller, and Johann Ernst Friedrich Westphalen among them—would later guide Hamburg through the trying times of the early nineteeth century. In some ways they formed living links to the world of the past, seeking to shore up the edifice of traditional communal government in Hamburg after the French departed. In other ways they challenged the older traditions, seeking to recast Hamburg's government along newer lines to some extent employing the models introduced by the hated French. The differences between these men, and between them and their predecessors, illustrate the dangers of portraying any group—even one as small and as tightly knit in interests, values, and family ties as this one was—as monolithic in their ideas and aspirations.

If the directors were the brains of the operation, then the relief officers (*Armen-Pfleger*) were its sinews. While the directors acted as watchdogs standing guard over the Relief's capital and principles, the relief officers did the legwork and were viewed, to some extent at least, as the advocates of the poor. It was in the quarter, the relief officer's immediate domain, that community was to be recreated. In theory, relief officers were intimately acquainted with the minutiae of poor relief, knowledgeable about their quarter, and well advised as to their charges. They were to be the familiar faces to whom the poor could turn without hesitation for comfort and assistance, the near and friendly persons who spoke for them and shielded them from further harm. They also represented the Relief in other ways: as neighbors, relatives, and friends of the other citizens in the quarter, it was their own integrity and probity that offered the best surety for the actions of the Relief.

The duties of the relief officer usually ended at the line dividing his quarter from the next. Yet, in his quarter he and his two colleagues were vital to the Relief's accomplishments. The three relief officers acting together carried out the first interview of any pauper requesting assistance, implemented the initial home visitation, repeated this inspection on a semiannual basis, scheduled and supervised the health visitation, filled out questionnaires for each pauper or pauper family, updated the relief rolls, and compiled the semiannual statistical reports that the directors drew upon in making policy decisions. Officers were also responsible for dispensing emergency aid to persons *not* registered with the Relief. This initial assistance might consist of any one of a wide variety of services, such as arranging medical care, disbursing alms, redeeming pawned tools, settling debts (especially paying delinquent rents), or organizing temporary shelter. Moreover, each relief officer regularly referred registered paupers to the special deputations, paid rent subsidies to landlords, watched their charges closely to prevent them moving clandestinely from one quarter into another, handed out the vouchers that entitled paupers to receive cheap fuel and food from the Relief's depots, doled out weekly alms, arranged for the education of children and monitored parents to make sure that they dutifully sent their children to school, referred persons to the physicians, surgeons, apothecaries, and midwives of the Relief, choreographed the pauper's funeral, saw to the disposition of his estate, and cared for his orphaned children. Needless to add, he was directed to keep accurate records and accounts on all the myriad transactions that he conducted in the name of the Relief.[107]

And yet the relief officers were less conspicuous in the community as a group than were the directors. Consequently, they are slipperier individuals to fasten onto biographically. Relief districts and quarters, and the respective directors and relief officers, were listed in each year's *State Calendar,* making it simple to learn their names; however, it is not always possible to ascertain their position in Hamburg's society. Their motivation or their feelings about their work as relief officers remain, with scattered exceptions, shrouded in darkness.[108]

Despite Büsch's wish that relief officers be elected by the inhabitants of their quarters, the office was apportioned in a different manner. Each quarter's three relief officers were selected by the council from the members of the One Hundred Eighty. Ideally, each relief officer resided in the quarter that he administered. Unfortunately, in the election of the first 180 Relief officers, the council reported that it was not always possible to ensure that each lived in his quarter, although it sought to ensure that he dwelled nearby. Relief officers held office for three years. Each year the senior member retired after submitting a "selection list of two persons in the municipal nexus" from which his successor was named. The Relief Ordinance freed some citizens from the duty of serving as relief officer. These included the members of the Rat, the Oberalten, the members of the council, the deputies to the Treasury, and all those older than sixty. Reselection was permissible, if a relief officer volunteered "for humanitarian reasons" to accept another term. This kind of rollover was extremely common; by 1792, forty-two men had already embarked on their second three-year term.[109]

Few relief officers recorded their experiences. One who did was Ferdinand Beneke. His detailed diary entries provide much valuable information on society and politics in Hamburg after 1796. Beneke was, however, not the average relief officer, because he eventually became a director and was later an extremely important figure in Hamburg's government. He was born in Bremen and educated as a lawyer in Göttingen, but returned to his father's birthplace—Hamburg—in 1795. He became a citizen and established a legal practice. He quickly embarked on a career in communal politics: In 1798 he was chosen as a relief officer, from 1800 to 1804 he sat on the Niedergericht, and in 1816 he was appointed secretary to the Oberalten. Beneke's diaries document how very frequently he was involved in his duties as a relief officer. Few days went by when he did not note that some task of poor relief had been executed or make some observation on his role. Unfortunately, these entries are usually brief jottings and not thoughtful reflections. Still, he was often deeply and personally involved in individual cases, and he reported that his office always afforded him "great satisfaction." Certainly he regarded his role as relief officer as a normal element of his participation in civic life.[110]

There is only sketchy information available on the social and economic status of the other relief officers. Taking as a sample those who held office in 1790, it is possible to discover how 152 of these 180 men (84.4 percent) earned their living by checking their occupations in the *Hamburg Address Book*. Not surprisingly, sixty-three (35 percent) were merchants while fifteen (8.3 percent) were involved in retail trade; only seven (3.9 percent) could be classified as artisans (three bakers, one confectioner, one sailcloth maker, one goldsmith, and one tinsmith). Four scholars, one Oberalte, one surgeon, three apothecaries, as well as twenty-one (11.6 percent) "Fabricanten" served as relief officers. Most of the Fabricanten (seventeen) were affluent sugar refiners; two were tobacco processors, one a silk manufacturer, and one a producer of dyestuffs. In only one district were a majority of relief officers not merchants. In several quarters all officers shared an occupation, for example, were merchants or sugar refiners. Occasionally business associates divided their civic responsibilities as well, coserving as relief officers. For example, in one quarter, Ernst Friedrich Westphalen and Martin Albert Rücker—partners in the firm Rücker and Westphalen—carried out two terms as officers together.[111]

These men were crucial to the making of the General Poor Relief. Some of their aspirations sprang from the same sources as did the great ideas of the European Enlightenment. Their plans vibrated to the same chords of optimism that more than fifty years ago led Carl Becker to tar the philosophes as mere utopian dreamers incapable of transforming their fine-sounding schemes into concrete realities. Few historians today accept Becker's harsh judgment. The Enlightenment has gained a far better reputation for practicality and the "rococo reformers" have been at least partly rehabilitated, and deservedly so.[112] We have also come to recognize just how deeply the ideas of the Enlightenment had penetrated bureaucracies and had become an accepted part of mainstream and even establishment beliefs by the end of the eighteenth century. Yet the General Poor Relief in Hamburg is still an outstanding example of an eighteenth-century reform initiative in action. Although the ideas that guided the Relief were not unique, they were pursued with a truly uncommon vigor and with truly impressive success, at least until 1800. If we look for the reasons for this *succès fou*, we must look to the meticulous planning that went into the Relief and especially to the men who guided it. They were indispensable and not only in terms of their own, often enviable, abilities and determination. If optimistic, they were not foolishly so. Their paramount virtue, however, was that they understood how to build on the past, blending municipal traditions with the more modern ideas of the Enlightenment. They jettisoned much as superstitious and wrong, but much they retained as wholesome and wise. They let the old values of civic pride and republican virtues mingle in the new vessel of patriotism, but never doubted that the old qualities—if not necessarily the old forms—were as suitable for governing Hamburg in the late eighteenth century as they had ever been. The General Poor Relief was thus successfully grafted onto the older traditions of governing in Hamburg, causing the venerable arteries of civic pride and republican virtue to pulsate with new life. But there was also a serendipity here that fostered ebullience and optimism; in the 1790s Hamburg prospered as never before.

6

The General Poor Relief, 1788–1799:
Triumphs and Enthusiasms

The 1790s were the most exciting and the most disquieting years in Hamburg's history. If for some it was bliss to be alive, for others the decade brought with it an economic activity that opened doors to stunning successes and equally outstanding failures. Explosive political circumstances threatened to engulf the city and draw it into a European-wide conflagration. While the city prospered as never before, that prosperity was clouded by hovering specters of impending doom. While the economy undoubtedly thrived, it grew in a fevered and undirected manner that encouraged hasty investments and reckless speculation.

Economic life in Hamburg had always responded palpably to political shock waves, but the 1790s were rocked by political frictions and diplomatic confrontations on a hitherto unimagined scale. Hamburg's commercial and economic ascendancy rested on its ability to preserve its independence and neutrality. Though economically puissant, Hamburg was still a small state, wedged between mightier neighbors and often unwillingly sucked into the fury of European-wide conflicts. The city was not only a valuable ally, but also a rich prize. Often these attributes worked to its advantage, attracting defenders who sought the city's favor or desired to prevent such a trophy from falling into the hands of others. Hamburg's wealth was just as often a liability that made the city the envy of rapacious neighbors. For more than a century, the Danish crown had insisted that Hamburg bow to its sovereignty. Despite the Imperial Court finding in 1618 that Hamburg was a free imperial city, not until 1768 did Hamburg successfully detach itself from Danish claims. In that year, the city concluded the Gottrop Settlement in which Denmark acknowledged Hamburg's status as a free imperial city in return for the annulment of Danish and Holstein debts owed the city.[1] This settlement cost Hamburg dearly, but Hamburg's capacity to buy off enemies had frequently redeemed it from conquest. The city's economic prosperity as well as its autonomy hinged on its diplomatic prowess and on its ability to maintain good relations with the major European powers. Connections with the Holy Roman Empire were on the whole satisfactory, though sometimes strained by religious differences. In mid-century, new tensions arose from the mercantilist policies pursued by Maria-Theresa's government.[2] Prussia had often stood as a guarantor of Hamburg's autonomy, especially against Denmark, but the mercantilist stance of Frederick the Great disturbed a once untroubled diplomatic and economic climate. Economic exchanges with the infant American republic were profitable and harmonious, though in the 1790s not of great significance.[3] By far the most cordial diplomatic liaison and the most lucrative economic ties Hamburg had in Europe were those with Bourbon France. Even the coming of the French Revolution did not demolish this old friendship. Nevertheless, the upheaval ushered in an era of increasing strain and uncertainty in the dealings between the two states. Many in Hamburg greeted the Revolution with partisan enthusiasm; just as many others remained skeptical. Hamburg was not spared for very long the international tensions or the tough political decisions that came with the revolutionary wars and that eventually damaged its profitable friendship with France. In 1793, primarily under pressure from Prussia, Hamburg was constrained to expel the French Republic's emissary, Lehoc. In retaliation, the French laid an embargo on Hamburg that begot a brief yet alarming recession, graphically illustrating how vulnerable Hamburg was to the displeasure of greater powers. Fortunately, Hamburg managed to smooth over the rift quickly. The embargo was lifted and trade resumed. At the same time Hamburg's commercial traffic with England began to assume wider dimensions, as did its trade with neutral states (such as Portugal) and with points overseas. In 1797, Hamburg joined the Prussian-sponsored Neutrality Pact. By then, however, European events were moving far too rapidly for Hamburg's habitual policy of neutrality to operate. The city was inevitably caught up in the clash between France and Great Britain; Hamburg was too little to fight and too important to escape unnoticed.[4] There were trying times ahead, although for the moment Hamburg fed on the misfortunes of others. The fall of Amsterdam (1795) only pumped more capital into Hamburg, making it for a time the banking center of northern Europe. Literally hundreds of new businesses were founded. Each year more than two thousand ships docked in Hamburg's harbor. A new plutocracy sprang up. At the very beginning of the nineteenth century there were more than fifty millionaires in Hamburg and more than four hundred men with lesser yet quite substantial fortunes, each totaling more than 100,000 marks.[5]

The amount of business done and wealth generated in the 1790s was prodigious. Jobs in commerce and in the export manufactories were plentiful, though wages were lower than in older, more traditional manufacturing and artisanal work. The evidence suggests, however, that the standard of living for the lower classes actually deteriorated. They were hit hard by an inflation that tripled rents and doubled the price of essential foodstuffs. What all this meant for the General Poor Relief is the subject of this chapter. In one way the Relief benefited from the general optimism and expansionism of the 1790s as money rolled in and the ranks of the unemployed shrank. Whether that decline resulted from the wisdom, or from the stringency, of the Relief's policies, or whether it was simply a by-product of a massive economic upswing, we shall want to examine in more detail. First, however, it is necessary to explore the opportunities created for the Relief by the economic dynamism of the 1790s, as the Relief reaped the whirlwind of affluence.

Taking Stock: The Report of 1799

In 1799, a full decade after its founding, the Relief drew up a balance sheet comparing conditions in Hamburg before its existence with those of 1798–99.[6] This accounting serves as an apt indicator of what the Relief supposed had been achieved in ten years as well as providing an excellent synopsis of the Relief's understanding of the problems associated with poverty and its appraisal of the solutions that it had applied. According to the Relief, conditions in 1787 were deplorable: The streets teemed with rude or whining beggars who monopolized the largess of Hamburg's charitably minded citizens and swindled alms from the shamefaced poor. By 1799, however, the Relief related that Hamburg's streets had been swept clear of beggars. The first investigation into the lives of the lower classes in Hamburg, which had been carried out in 1787, uncovered not only the "rascally beggars" but also "a throng of less fortunate paupers . . . without shelter and clothing, whom no one noticed" and who lived a nocturnal, shadowy existence "fearful of leaving their hovels except cloaked by a merciful darkness which concealed their nakedness." Ten years later the Relief boasted that "no one must endure such privation," for the Relief furnished everyone the opportunity to earn thirty-six shillings weekly or dispensed alms to supplement their wages. That first investigation had also unearthed more than 600 people without beds and blankets. Ten years later, "everyone in Hamburg is clothed" and had beds and bedding. The plight of pauper children in 1788 greatly distressed the members of the Relief; 220 children were found "ragged and crawling with vermin," moreover, they "lie about idly" and were seldom gainfully employed. Worse still, it was believed that "so very many of them are trained to beg and are raised in the unconstrained immorality of their parents." Here, too, the Relief felt it had made its mark, schooling these children, dispensing religious instruction, clothing them, delousing them, even locating positions for them when they reached maturity.

Furthermore, before the Relief existed, both "the destitution of unhappy individuals from the lower classes and the depravity of the most degenerate among them" lay, with few exceptions, "completely obscured." There were places in the city "where no human being ventured" (except the rent-collector) and where "innumerable obstacles" of topography and ignorance frustrated the tasks of governing. "An impervious barrier" supposedly stood between the benefactor and "the worthy object of his munificence." All this, it was insisted, had changed with the inception of the Relief. The unknown corners had been penetrated and the 2,000 paupers who met weekly with their relief officers were described as "just so many middlemen," who called to the attention of the authorities every imbroglio and every case of need in the vicinity. In 1788, few paupers had access to medical care. By 1799, reputedly, every member of the lower classes could obtain inexpensive medical assistance. The Relief further argued that before 1788 families with several children who had to subsist on the father's wage alone were almost doomed to impoverishment and the children "inevitably" condemned to beggary. That, too, was a situation that had, in the opinion of Relief officials, been totally reversed. Children in 1799 were depicted as "boons to the industrious, honest laborer." They received an education, and actually helped nourish the family with their earnings. Moreover, the Relief maintained that before 1788 any man whose income had been lost through "a shift in fashions or dearth of work, or sickness, death, or other calamity" plummeted into debt. One by one he sold or pawned his tools and other possessions until he was left with nothing and no chance to begin again. Once the Relief established its Loan Institute to aid such people with timely, interest-free advances, then it was assumed that "no honest, skilled and active family father in such circumstances need despair." In 1788 illegitimate children either perished or grew up in crushing poverty to become burdens on the state. After the Relief opened its Lying-In Ward in 1796, such children and their mothers were purportedly rescued from almost certain destitution and ruin. Finally, in 1788–89 the Relief had uncovered a total of 7,391 poverty-stricken individuals (5,166 adults) in Hamburg, constituting about 7 percent of the population. Worse, according to the Relief, was the fact that the dimensions of need in Hamburg exceeded those "in most populous cities," while mendicancy was seen to spread "like plague," infecting honest workers and propagating "shamelessness" among the lower classes. Yet by 1798–99, the number of adult poor had been reduced to 2,689, offering, the Relief insisted, incontrovertible proof that its programs were not untested theories but effective measures for assailing poverty.

The balance struck in 1799 was overwhelmingly positive and the mood of the Relief on the eve of its tenth anniversary exuded confidence. Still, it should be remembered that this balance sheet was designed for public consumption and cast the Relief in a most favorable light. Although privately the Relief's officers expressed some qualms about its future, there is no reason to doubt that they were mightily pleased with their accomplishments and well disposed to congratulate themselves in 1799. Furthermore, the Relief *was* successful and not only in its own estimation. The General Poor Relief proved singularly efficacious in organizing and directing a broad array of imaginatively conceived and lavishly funded programs. However, there are other levels on which its achievements must be judged. To what extent had the Relief realized its own objectives? And to what extent did the Relief alleviate the suffering of the poor or actually lift their standard of living? The two questions are related, of course, but they are not the same. When one examines the objective validity of the Relief's assertions it becomes clear that there are many half-truths here, some bombast, and much posturing, but no outright mendacity. Tentatively, one might suggest that the Relief helped most effectively the most needy. Yet it also provided—admittedly often on its own terms—the less impoverished with a fairly attractive array of such social services as schools, some employment, interest-free loans, and medical care. These were not otherwise available and cannot only be seen as part of a more comprehensive program of repression and social control.

In scrutinizing the program of the General Poor Relief, we will traverse much familiar territory. Little will surprise those well acquainted with the history of poor relief in early modern Europe or cognizant of the Enlightenment's general outlook on social reform and its appraisal of "the people."[7] Still, there are critical elements of the theory and practice of poor relief that have remained largely unelucidated, especially in regard to how poor relief corresponded to the spirit and practice of municipal governing by solving or attempting to solve some of the knotty problems emanating from fundamental shifts in the municipality's economic and social composition, and it is these elements rather than the now more familiar (and simplistic) story of social control and social disciplining that ought to be stressed. How did the General Poor Relief augment, alter, perfect, or simply discharge the traditional ends of governing? There is another side to this story as well, one that appraises the mood of Hamburg's patriotic elites in the 1790s and illuminates how they viewed their city and contemplated their world. It was an age of optimism and exuberance, a belle epoque—if one with a worm in the bud. The General Poor Relief reflected the ebullience of the times, planning with liberality (even with abandon), taking immense pride in its accomplishments, expanding its programs with assurance, committing the Relief ever more fully to the higher purpose of preventing poverty rather than merely salving over its visible wounds. Élan, not restraint, was the motto of the day and with élan the Relief went to work constructing by the end of the century what one contemporary praised as "the finest monument to civic patriotism" in Europe.[8]

Basic Principles

In its inaugural *Report,* the General Poor Relief established basic guidelines:

> First, the Relief investigates how much each pauper requires for subsistence. Then the Relief ascertains how much he earns by his labor or is able to earn and how much he already receives in charity. Once these things have been determined, it becomes a simple matter to decide how much additional assistance he must receive in summer and in winter, in sickness and in health. As long as the Relief adheres to these elementary principles, it will never run the danger of neglecting the truly needy or of advancing alms to those who really do not require them or are not worthy of them or are wastrels.[9]

In short the Relief's contract with the poor reduced itself to three short, almost epigrammatic rules: Each person must labor to the best of his ability; what he cannot earn for his subsistence, but no more, will be given him in alms; finally, he will receive only what he is *unable* to acquire honestly and not what he is *unwilling* to earn by working.

The cornerstone of the Relief's program rested upon a sincere desire to rehabilitate the pauper, to return him to the world of work. It was never the intention of the General Poor Relief to remove or to isolate the worker from the normal circumstances of life; for this reason—if not for this reason alone—the Relief rejected confinement categorically as a solution to the problems of poverty. Even though it was never the policy of the Relief to separate the poor man from the rest of society, it was policy to shield good workers from the "noxious" influence of indolents and mendicants. Moreover, the magnitude of the problem, expressed in the sheer numbers of the new poor, made confinement infeasible.

As simple as the basic rules were, they were not easy to execute. First the Relief required reliable information on the extent of poverty in the city. In order to acquire that information, the Rat ordered the militia captains to carry out a preliminary investigation in 1787. Some sense had to be made of the jumble of streets and alleyways in Hamburg. Thus streets received official names and houses numbers in an attempt to reduce geographical Babel. This ordering served far broader purposes than merely poor relief in governing a city grown out of familiar proportions and perplexing in its intricacy. For example, the same identifying marks facilitated the recording of subscription pledges and their collection. And now, for the first time, taxpayers were linked to specific addresses. Compiling muster rolls for the citizen's militia was also expedited as were the duties of those charged with keeping the peace and controlling crime. It was a step dictated by the topographic realities of a city with dimensions and complexities far exceeding the ken of any single person.[10]

The investigations of the militia captains as to the number of "the poor" residing in Hamburg was in many ways an amateurish effort that failed to satisfy all of the exacting demands of the General Poor Relief. One observer went so far as to characterize the results as practically worthless. The mandate that charged the captains with noting the poor in their companies apparently supplied them with no precise guidelines for defining poverty or for identifying a pauper.[11] Still, despite its shortcomings, the information gathered served some of the Relief's objectives: It generated a statistical basis for evaluating the extent of destitution in the city, offered abundant material for publicity, and allowed a division of the city into sensibly sized relief districts and quarters apportioned as to the numbers of paupers in each. The old parish delineations proved too large and cumbersome, especially as some parishes contained far more paupers than others. The militia captains located 3,903 pauper families (5,166 adults and 2,225 children), a total of 7,391 individuals who required immediate assistance.[12]

This investigation is only a crude example of how the Relief turned to statistical methods for the purposes of governing, yet it continued to encase them in traditional modes, avoiding the "soulless mentality" of bureaucrats. Its *Reports* overflowed with tables and charts. Attempts were made not only to gather facts but also to employ that information in formulating policies and in grasping complex realities by evaluating them statistically. The Relief initiated the most sophisticated and varied use of statistical tools the city had seen, and its statistical compilations were often turned directly to the process of governing. Lütkens would have been pleased, one imagines, with the accomplishments of a Relief that built its policies around an infrastructure of statistics. Calculations for the purposes of poor relief rested, of course, uppermost in the minds of Relief officials, but other motives were never very distant. Repeatedly the Rat or other government agencies used the findings of the Relief as the basis for policy decisions. Often this occurred in the most informal ways. Günther, for instance, frequently relied on his experiences in poor relief when later called on in his capacities as senator and praetor.[13]

Administrative and statistical sophistication revealed itself in the fastidious records kept by the directors and relief officers, in painstaking bookkeeping, in the detailed surveys of those who applied for support (which, unfortunately with few exceptions, are no longer extant), in a flurry of forms, and in the more rigorous delineation of the jurisdictional competencies of each branch of the Relief. The cancellation protocol (*Tilgungs-Protocol*) demonstrates how the Relief dealt with problems arising from the simple necessity of keeping track of the thousands who received support. From the point of view of relief policy, it was imperative to know when and why support had been terminated in order to stop those once denied aid from "sneaking back onto" the relief rolls. The cancellation protocol, introduced in 1793, recorded the names of those struck from the relief rolls with the grounds for their deletion. This would, it was hoped, eventually produce a "tabular history" effective in both foiling abuses and mastering the still imperfectly comprehended phenomenon of urban poverty.[14]

For the basic rules to function properly, however, some calculations of subsistence levels were urgently needed. The survey of the militia captains in 1787 had probed the depths of destitution, but had in no way ascertained the minimum standard of living that would become the new, quantifiable basis for relief. Relief officials had to answer the all-important question of how much each individual required for survival. They reckoned very closely, and by no means generously, minimum daily expenditures for a subsistence existence: For a single person, this totaled five shillings nine pfennigs a day in winter, four shillings nine pfennigs in summer.[15] For families or for people not living alone, other minimums applied. The Relief maintained (rather self-righteously) that two could live as cheaply as one, but also (more realistically) that a child of twelve needed fully as much as an adult, that a child between the ages of five and twelve required three-quarters of an adult's minimum, and that younger children required proportionally less support. The Relief believed however, that even these minimums were not rock-bottom figures and "that most paupers, especially those who had not yet sunk to begging on the streets, can make do with somewhat less. Partly this ability derives from long years of learning to do without and of helping themselves; but also partly from small incidentals and increments that are hard to calculate exactly and that even the paupers themselves are not in a position to evaluate accurately."[16]

Even Büsch held to the idea that the poor could get by with less: "twelve shillings daily for a day-laborer . . . when he earns these regularly are sufficient to support himself and his children."[17] His twelve shillings daily compared favorably, however, to the actual wages workers received in Hamburg in the late 1780s. On the average, a common laborer earned ten shillings four pfennigs daily, the poorest paid calico worker six shillings three pfennigs and the best paid fourteen shillings nine pfennigs, the most skilled workers on the fortifications fourteen shillings, street cleaners twelve shillings, tailors between eight and twelve shillings, apprentice cabinetmakers twenty-three shillings six pfennigs, and apprentice carpenters twenty-seven shillings. Women who sewed brought in (besides free meals) four shillings a day, scrubwomen between eight and nine shillings, and seamstresses between eight and ten shillings. Laundering paid sixteen shillings and wringing laundry between eight and nine shillings. Spinning and knitting were starvation jobs for both men and women. Spinners earned between two and five shillings a day and knitters earned a paltry two to three shillings.[18] The maximum weekly support levels set by the Relief reflected, therefore, a *lower* daily rate than almost all of these wage earners and the Relief afforded these maximums only to those lacking all other income or capacity to work.[19] The principle was clear: Poor relief was to offer the pauper less money than most occupations so that the level of support would not dislodge workers from their jobs by seducing them to join the ranks of the idle. But the principle of less eligibility was hardly new. It had governed most organized forms of poor relief since the Middle Ages and was a concomitant of the obligation incumbent on every supplicant for relief to labor as much as he or she was able.

Similar precepts guided the decision to pay support in cash rather than in "naturalia" (food, fuel, clothing). Part of the weekly dole (usually four shillings) went directly to landlords. The remaining amount was handed to the pauper in cash.[20] Especially in the first two years, the Relief distributed much aid in the form of clothing, food, bedding, and fuel. Throughout the 1790s these expenditures continued to monopolize a large portion of the Relief's budget. Still, the vast majority of direct relief took the form of cash payments. Some doubted whether support was best provided in this way. Cash, it was argued, could all too quickly be wasted on drink or other vices, leaving the pauper and his family penniless and bereft of further resources. Alternatively, he could plead with his relief officer for "just a little bit more" to tide him over until the next payday. As the protocols of the Relief show, such petitions proved devilishly hard to resist. The council repeatedly admonished relief officers not to succumb to such "blackmail"—mostly in vain.[21] Those who advocated cash relief pointed out that the poor man could easily pawn or sell items entrusted to him if he could not obtain money in other ways. Maintaining depots of food, clothing, and fuel was fraught with difficulties. Buying up large quantities of grain, potatoes, or peat interfered with free market prices and angered retailers. Furthermore, the Relief officials insisted, a rush of people always tried to procure cheap commodities from the depots under the false pretense of poverty. Spoilage was another problem that required attention.[22] Moreover, as the proponents of cash support insisted, the pauper must not be sheltered from the realities of life. He must learn, or relearn, to handle money and budget his resources. Büsch had observed that "civic life among civilized nations is closely bound up with the management of money." Therefore, "the man who has forfeited this skill can no longer function in such societies."[23] Of course, an additional argument for cash support was that it benefited the economy and forestalled impoverishment in deeper ways. Money distributed as alms would quickly find its way into the general flow of cash and stimulate Hamburg's notoriously sluggish monetary circulation by priming the economic pump.[24] Falling behind in rent payments was probably the first debt incurred by working-class families whose principal breadwinner lost his job or fell ill.[25] Paying rents directly to landlords alleviated this problem and also prevented the pauper from frittering away his rent money. The Relief hoped that the pauper would learn to manage his own finances, although it also recognized that the task of saving up for a rent that fell due only semiannually might prove too formidable for those with low incomes and only rudimentary budgeting skills. In addition, by ensuring the regular payment of rents the Relief assisted owners of cheap rental property, who were at that time caught in a market of declining values, and helped halt the economic deterioration of another section of the population.[26]

The Relief recognized that a fastidious calibration of support levels alone was insufficient. The Relief also must have the power to enforce its will, must solve the riddle of unemployment, must educate the children of the poor in their duties as "Christians, human beings, and citizens" while occupying them with work "appropriate to their age," and must ensure that no worker's health was senselessly sacrificed.[27] These objectives formed the four major pillars of the Relief's program and it is against them that one can measure the extent of its ambitions, its zeal, its triumphs, and, ultimately, its failures. What follows is not an exhaustive study of the details of poor relief in Hamburg but an analysis of how the Relief wove its program into the larger concerns of the community and of the extent to which its policies were conditioned and its success determined not by the wisdom of its own program, nor even merely by a revival of civic patriotism, but by the greater historical forces buffeting or benefiting Hamburg in these decades.

It is perhaps a good idea to pause here and note that Hamburg's General Poor Relief deviated little in its principles from other contemporary reform efforts. Yet the entire historical development of Hamburg, especially in the eighteenth century, dictated that poor relief there would diverge from poor relief in other cities and territories in the Germanies. Historians have isolated several characteristics as "typical" of eighteenth-century initiatives in poor relief reform. First, they have traced a general decline in the role of the church and an augmentation in the role of the state in poor relief. However, this change was already well under way in the sixteenth century. Second, it has been argued that with the eighteenth century came the debut of private (versus public) charitable enterprises, reflected in the numbers of voluntary participants in poor relief, and prefiguring as well the separation of state and society that would come to characterize the nineteenth and twentieth centuries. It is easy on the surface to assume that this also happened in Hamburg. Yet that shift is only apparent. In Hamburg private and public were so thoroughly blended as to render any such clear distinctions nonsensical. A decided move to an increasing rationalization of charity has also been documented as occurring throughout Europe. Hamburg, too, followed some of these trends but never allowed rationalization to disrupt the older traditions of governing. Indeed, the city's elites retained what more objectively have been seen as obsolete practices. Finally, bureaucratization supposedly accompanied poor relief reform.[28] This, too, did not occur in Hamburg. For example, the number of "Officianten"—the Relief's word for its paid employees—while larger than the number of those employed by the "old" relief system in Hamburg, remained small. Many minor officials—the messengers and runners, the nurses and cooks, the instructresses in spinning and weaving, and the sewing mistresses—were drawn almost exclusively from the ranks of the poor and were those "who get one shilling per week, perhaps, more than what the Relief would be obliged to allow them" in support. They handled such unimportant tasks as that of bearing messages between the council, the directors, and the relief officers. The number of salaried officials was even fewer: five district runners, the beggar chasers (themselves often paupers), two teachers for the Elementary School, a bookkeeper, an accountant, and later a few runners for the School Deputation. The physicians and surgeons of the Relief were volunteers, although each received a modest honorarium. The Relief paid midwives' fees and after 1796 employed one midwife and her husband to manage the Lying-In Ward. Occasionally, situations required the employment of other persons temporarily. Yet generally the number of paid officials was small—insignificant actually when compared to the over two hundred volunteers who served as relief officers or directors. Their salaries formed only a miniscule part of the total expenditures of the Relief. These people were *never* involved in policy decisions, in setting levels of support, or even in distributing alms except under the direct supervision of a relief officer or director. Thus, one can hardly speak of a professionalization of relief work in the normal sense of the word. The Relief accepted more elaborate methods of administration, but rejected as antithetical to its purposes and spirit any attempt to wrest control away from voluntary administrators.

As we follow the program of poor relief in Hamburg, we are treading a path that cannot be understood by applying broad generalizations in a procrustean way, lopping off the facts that do not quite fit our neat categories. Poor relief in Hamburg must always be situated against a unique background. It was firmly rooted in venerable traditions and in deeply held beliefs about how the community should be managed, traditions that had in truth altered little since the sixteenth century.[29]

Registered Paupers

What did it mean to be a registered pauper? Each registered pauper received from his relief officer a printed copy of the "Instructions for the

Poor." It formed a sort of contract. Each pauper was "earnestly and emphatically" admonished to labor as much as his health and his abilities allowed and to see that his children attended the Relief's schools regularly. In return, the Relief promised that all those who faithfully upheld their end of the bargain would not be abandoned in illness, old age, or other emergencies. The Relief further pledged that it harbored no desire to confiscate "what you will have from the burial clubs, or your other possessions." These assets would pass undiminished to children or other near relatives. Furthermore, each pauper was guaranteed the right to arrange his funeral himself "as well as he wants and is able to afford." Those, however, who "out of pure malice and slothfulness" refused to work, to send their children to school, or who pawned or sold goods distributed to them by the Relief, who begged, drank excessively, played in the lottery, or otherwise squandered their alms, were threatened with loss of support or even, in more flagrant instances, with confinement in the Zuchthaus.[30]

The Relief's network of relationships with its charges brings us to the meaning of policing the poor in the context of the eighteenth century. The word *Armenpolicey* had a plurality of readings that frustrate any simple translation. It could encompass all the *policies* that touched on the poor, or, in a more restricted sense, refer only to the executive and judicial *powers* the Relief exercised over the poor. The Relief Ordinance promulgated on 3 September 1788 endowed the Relief with competency to act in all matters directly involving poor relief. Exactly what the composition and extent of these powers were to be and how they were to be executed took rather longer to determine. What the Relief wanted were extensive police powers. The idea of policing encompassed a many-faceted theory of punishment, which simultaneously acted as correction, reconciliation, and improvement. It was essentially paternalist as well, when applied in the spirit of what the cameralists named the patriarchal "correctoria et directoria." Policing, however, ended at the point where improvement could no longer be reasonably expected. Policing did not involve cases where "unimprovable members of society must suffer either civil or natural death." Such ultimate punishments belonged to the realm of criminal justice.[31]

Policing, therefore, generally applied to minor infringements of the law, although its range of competencies was far greater than this definition might suggest. Only toward the end of the eighteenth century did policing gradually come to approximate its modern definition: the control of crime. Police penalties were rarely severe, compensating for their lack of harshness by their inevitability and swiftness. Infringements of police laws were punished without clemency and almost always without appeal.[32] A large element of prevention always characterized police laws because policing was a community's attempt to forestall more serious offenses much like a father disciplined his children. Police strictures were communal standards and the whole idea of policing functioned on the basis of familiarity—the familiarity of the magistrate or other agent of police with the people they policed. It was also based on the idea of a unitary not a pluralistic society. Such familiarity and unity were rapidly disappearing in Hamburg. The intricacies of government and the complexities of society would eventually render outmoded the ideas of paternalism and personalized supervision, like the broader concept of policing.

The General Poor Relief, like Hamburg's government, was pinched between the dual desires of maintaining traditions while increasing efficiency. While it cast its aspirations within the context of an older language of policing, it at the same time innovated and furthered the transition to a new world of administrative expertise, unwittingly helping to unravel the web of traditional governing in Hamburg. What the Relief wanted in 1788 were the same powers enjoyed by other agents of police and other legal corporations such as the Zuchthaus and the Spinnhaus. The council sought from the Rat competence— or, to use its term, cognition—in six areas: in respect to all things specifically concerning poor relief, authority to penalize the officials of the Relief for any violations they committed, permission to imprison beggars seized on the streets, the right to discipline idle and intractable paupers through a system of forced labor, the liberty to fine almsgivers, and finally the ability to deal with "shiftless or furtive" aliens.[33]

The Relief framed its prohibition of begging in the strongest terms, asking for the right to proceed against beggars with severity and dispatch, "for most of them have sunk to such unbelievable degrees of laziness, indolence, and reluctance to work that we simply can find no other means [except force] to wean them away from these detestable habits."[34] The least controversial of the Relief's claims for police powers was the sentencing of beggars apprehended on the streets to the Zuchthaus merely on the testimony of the beggar chasers or night watchmen. "In these cases," the Relief insisted, "a full proof in legal form can never be required without disrupting the investigation with all sorts of chicanery, thereby undercutting the purpose of all prohibitions on begging." The Relief went further and argued that, even if one person was unjustly accused, it was still far better for such a "shiftless street-bum" to endure four weeks' hard labor in the Zuchthaus than to tie up the whole process in pettifogging complications.[35] This cognition over beggars was not a novelty. Prohibitions against begging had taken an increasingly draconian tone since the Middle Ages, and the praetors and the Zuchthaus had long exercised such summary justice over mendicants.

The desire of the General Poor Relief for police powers over the registered poor was a bit trickier from a legal standpoint, but here too there was ample precedent. In particular, the council wished authority to punish "lazy and disobedient" paupers with a four-week (or longer) Zuchthaus sentence. A special committee—the Corrections Deputation—composed of one of the members of the Rat who sat ex officio on the Relief's council, the district director involved, and the pauper's relief officer, decided whether punishment was warranted and if so, determined the sentence.[36] The Relief also requested greater prerogatives in investigating and taking action against "the forbidden transport of beggars into the city or concealing them here," as well as all "injurious or shady operations" such as illegal recruiting, procuring, keeping bawdy houses, selling lottery tickets, and loan-sharking. It requested as well the right to punish those who defrauded money from testamentary or charitable sources.[37]

By far the riskiest of the competencies the council wished was the right to reprove or penalize the *givers* of alms. The Relief Ordinance of 1788 specified a five-thaler fine for each incident of illegal almsgiving. After 1788, spontaneous almsgiving was punishable by law. In this case, the Relief would be interfering not with the poor and unprotected, but, conceivably, with members of the better classes in Hamburg—with their own equals. Caution was recommended. And the Relief trod gingerly, setting out alternative procedures for dealing with almsgivers from different classes. Wealthier persons, "distinguished or esteemed" persons accused of almsgiving received far more indulgent treatment than a "mere common artisan, day-laborer, or servant" likewise accused.[38] The whole issue of almsgiving caught the Relief in a dilemma. Its founders saw the ban on almsgiving, like the interdiction of begging, as a linchpin of effective poor relief. Casual almsgiving had to be suppressed, yet the Relief also wished to preserve "that so commendable feeling of charity." Even illegal almsgiving was almost virtuous and must not be punished in a way that caused painful embarrassment or worse, evoked resentment in the giver.[39]

The Relief's objectives were, in the context of the times, conservative and well bolstered by existing practices. Even so, some members of the Rat viewed these demands as too radical or perhaps merely too aggressive, as an instructive exchange of letters between the council and the Rat in fall of 1788 illustrates. Günther, with his legal training, was perhaps the best suited to argue the Relief's position. He built his case on the essential conservatism of the council's supplication. In a note to the syndic, Georg Anckelmann, Günther assured the Rat that the Relief's request for such prerogatives represented no "arrogance," no desire to usurp the position of the Rat. "We merely seek [to obtain] . . . a forceful and effective legal tool without which the entire intricate machine of poor relief would grind to a halt and be thrown out of gear." He went on to point out that if the pauper successfully evaded work without being punished for his sloth, or if his punishment involved the directors and relief officers in "irksome formalities," then all hope of a constructive poor relief was thwarted from the very beginning. Furthermore, he argued that what the Relief asked for conformed "in every way" to Hamburg's constitution and was analogous to the powers exerted by other branches of government. Moreover, they were "powers that in no way contradict our constitution, [which are] in fact not even singular."[40] Besides, the Relief did not petition for the ability to punish grievous offenses. Rather, it requested the authority to deal with less serious transgressions mostly by suspending alms. Before the existence of the Relief, the board of governors of the Zuchthaus could punish paupers working in the Zuchthaus. Such a right, the Relief maintained, was generally conceded as absolutely essential to the functioning of the Zuchthaus. It was even more imperative for a poor relief that did not operate within the confines of four walls. The praetors had previously executed numerous instances of policing, including the authority to punish beggars, transport aliens out of the city, and the like. Now, however, the Relief insisted that these matters should no longer be referred to them because "such trifling cases have become far too frequent" to burden the already overworked praetors. If the praetors were, however, forced to attend to these petty incidents, they would be overwhelmed and could deal with them only in the most superficial manner, or be forced to turn them over to their subordinates. The latter solution would only serve to undermine their position and eventually "to demean men clothed by the Rat with a public office." In addition, the praetors and their officials could not effectively investigate all the alien beggars or those practicing harmful trades and thus poor relief would soon be inundated by a flood of "foreign rabble" without having the ability to defend itself and its resources against them. The relief officers, however, could closely observe what occurred in their own quarters, and would unfailingly notice strangers or other suspicious persons. It was not, of course, merely the beggars and vagabonds who proved troublesome. The Relief clearly perceived how impediments to enforcing population policies waxed exponentially in a "populous city . . . whose human numbers constantly ebb and flood." The revolutionary wars exacerbated the simplest tasks of population control as waves of strangers rolled into Hamburg.[41]

What the Relief proposed in all these instances was really not new. It drew on existing paradigms. Council members envisioned the same kinds of men exercising the same sorts of powers that had run Hamburg for centuries. They merely recalibrated, noting the necessity to expand the number of citizens active in government and to introduce a hitherto absent administrative rigor to cope with the increased size of the city. If they suggested gathering the powers to deal with poor relief affairs into a new organization, it was still one that cherished and defended the principles of Hamburg's constitution as it existed. Still, despite the undeniable influence the council had with the Rat, and the sympathy and support the Rat gave the Relief, not all members of the Rat were willing to assent to the Relief's requests. Two members in particular, Senator Amsinck and Syndic Anckelmann, warned that the Rat should be wary of permitting too much authority to slip through its fingers. Anckelmann vigorously argued that such police powers should not be decentralized more than "utmost necessity dictates." Both felt it was desirable to preserve the older modality of allowing the praetor—a member of the Rat—to hold onto the right to punish beggars and paupers.[42]

The Rat eventually decided, not surprisingly, to follow a middle road, granting the Relief wide discretionary powers yet retaining some control, especially over the banishment of aliens. The Rat decided that the Relief could not be denied "cognition in matters that concern the registered poor." Yet the Relief only received the right to assign a four-week Zuchthaus sentence to paupers who proved lazy and disobedient. The Relief might banish from the city "unemployed or suspicious persons, insofar as they are also beggars." Other "suspicious persons who have not begged" could only be brought to the attention of the praetors. The Relief enjoyed a clear mandate to punish those who gave alms, those who refused or neglected to canvass with the collection boxes, and those who sheltered beggars.[43]

Far more interesting to know, of course, is how frequently and how rigorously the Relief applied the powers it possessed. An incomplete but indicative answer to this question comes from a survey of the activities of the Relief's Police Deputation. Information on the first years is sketchy. As we near the middle of the decade and as the officials became more adept at their bookkeeping, information becomes more plentiful. By far the most effective cudgel the Relief wielded was its unquestioned right to terminate support. The reasons why people forfeited aid varied greatly. For example, the *Report* from February 1797 recounted that in the previous year 234 persons had been removed from the relief rolls. Of these, 46 had been admitted to the Pesthof, 16 had vanished, 5 were struck from the rolls for "exposed deceit," 3 had been sent to the Zuchthaus for unspecified reasons (probably lack of housing), 8 refused to comply with regulations, 4 rebuffed the work offered them, 22 would not send their children to school, 36 had found more lucrative employment or received an inheritance, 2 had been accepted as pensioners in one of the city's charitable foundations, 28 had declared they no longer required assistance and withdrew voluntarily, 14 had improved their fortunes by remarrying, 10 had found positions as servants, 15 had left Hamburg, 14 failed to request further aid, and 4 were found unneedful of support. (For purposes of comparison, in the same period 183 families were added to the rolls.[44]) Even more revealing is the report of the Police Deputation for 1797. The number of beggars seized on the streets was 88, but the Relief disciplined only 20 paupers in the same period.[45] Reports for other years show strikingly similar tendencies. In other words, punishing beggars (in moderate numbers) rather than disciplining paupers remained the chief policing activity. This is only one indication of a theme that will be pursued in more detail later: While the social disciplining or social control objectives of the Relief figured prominently in its rhetoric, its actions differed far less from those of its predecessors than has often been asserted. In particular, it exercised a milder program of coercion than its insistence on extensive police powers has led some to believe.

Yet the Relief fully intended to act as guardian to the poor; it is nonsense to suggest that it did not expect to exert a formative and, in its own eyes, salutary influence on how the pauper lived. Little of his life was to remain undisturbed by the probings of the Relief. The pauper's possessions were, after 1791, no longer his at all. Despite the promises advanced in 1788, he forfeited many of his rights of inheritance and could not dispose of his estate freely. Moreover, he was no longer able to live where and with whom he pleased. Indeed, he lost the privilege of being buried as he desired. Even in this age of Enlightenment, in the dawning of the rights of man, few seriously questioned the license of the Relief to punish or correct. Where there was opposition, it usually came from a public unconvinced by the Relief's arguments and whose mentality was still shaped by older traditions of charity and linked to a more rigorous Christian or Protestant orthodoxy. Almost everyone, however, conceded society's right, even its duty, to bring the insane into safekeeping and to limit the freedom of children. Thus there was little opposition to the Relief's attempts to discipline the poor, at least as long as this disciplining coincided with traditional ideas of propriety and the just exercise of power.

Faced with the problems of administering an elaborate system of poor relief in a large urban community, the Relief tried to restrict the mobility of the poor. No one who enjoyed permanent or temporary support from the Relief was permitted "without the knowledge and consent of his relief officer . . . to leave his present dwelling. . . . If he is evicted by his landlord or if he for whatever reasons believes it is urgent to move then he must, *before he rents another place,* speak with his relief officer, who will investigate the matter and if he deems it necessary, grant him permission to change his place of residence."[46] Failure to comply with this rule could mean cessation of support. The Relief insisted that in most cases the desire to move was frivolous or duplicitous resulting from "simple ill will, squabbles with neighbors, hopes of covering up misconduct," or a ploy to see if perhaps a different relief officer might be more liberal with alms. Mobility offered a way, of course, to dodge the controls the Relief endeavored to apply, as well as to escape other city officials. It was easy enough to sink into Hamburg's teeming masses with little fear of being turned up again. The Relief also forbade single paupers to reside alone "as it is too expensive." Relief officers could arrange for a pauper to lodge with others or could compel him to take lodgers into his own home. How often either actually happened is unknown, but it must have been a hit-and-miss affair. While on the one hand the restrictions on mobility were to make it simpler for the Relief to account for its charges, on the other hand, by limiting mobility the Relief also desired to stabilize rents.[47]

Restricting the mobility of the poor was a formidable task. One of the major reasons the city had been so deliberately squared off into districts and quarters was to decrease or at least to expedite monitoring "the frequent roving" of the poor. Only a few months after its founding, the Relief confessed to a lack of success because "the number of those on the move grows with each half-year." Much of this mobility was due to the poor man's unending search for cheap housing, a search that became more desperate and less successful as the decade progressed and as more cheap housing was demolished to accommodate commercial expansion. By 1790, the Relief complained that some paupers had within the short span of two years switched relief officers six or eight times. All these unauthorized moves putatively handicapped the efficiency of the Relief, for "a rational system of poor relief demands that the situation, conduct, ability to work, and the needs of each and every pauper [be known] . . . down to the minutest details." Frequent relocations thwarted the Relief's attempts to obtain such knowledge, and from November 1788 through November 1793 the Relief canceled support to fifty-five persons who "clandestinely left their quarter" and to another fifty-six who "without permission have moved several times."[48]

The Relief Ordinance of 1788 also permitted the Relief to recover any property—beds, tools, clothing—given to the registered pauper or redeemed from pawn for him. An officer of the Relief marked all these items with an indelible stamp "A.O." (for *Armen-Ordnung*) to designate them as possessions of the Relief. Further sale or pawn was strictly forbidden, as was any effort to obliterate the mark. The purchase of marked goods amounted to receiving stolen property and was prosecuted as such. The Revised Ordinance of 1791 substantially augmented the recovery rights of the Relief, extending them to all the possessions of the registered poor and not just to those the Relief had given to or redeemed for them. Some directors—notably Voght, Günther, and Tonnies—proposed using the marking of possessions as a touchstone or test by which one discovered if a pauper truly required assistance. The Relief viewed such tests as legitimate ways of determining whether or not a pauper should be aided. They were not *solely* intended to discourage people from applying for aid. Rather, these tests functioned as substitutes for personal knowledge and as a way to render judgments more objective when dealing with thousands of cases. Those who declined the marking of their possessions were to be categorized as "not truly needy" and were to be refused all support. But opposition in the council killed this proposal, as other directors worried about sowing a "misapprehension" among the public. While even the opponents of marking admitted that the right of recovery was "a very beneficial tool for reducing the numbers of the supported poor," they feared the repercussions of such an act. The council finally voted to hold back because "such a procedure presents insurmountable difficulties."[49]

The Relief certainly did not hesitate to place other restrictions on how the pauper might live his life or even on how he might die. Practically no one, even those in the bloom of health and the freshness of youth, failed to think about provisions for his final earthly act: his entombment. A magnificent funeral attested to the superior social status of the deceased, but a shabby one indicated just the opposite. Men remained unequal even *devant le mort.* Funerals furnished "the last if by no means the least affirmation of the social status of the deceased."[50] Even for the rich this sometimes pinched. The less fortunate, however, were hard-pressed to finance even a modest funeral. Often buying into a burial club was the only way an ordinary man prepared for his demise and ensured a tiny pension for his widow and children.[51] The Relief frowned on the burial clubs, seeing in them vampirelike creatures that "suck the poor dry." According to the Relief, meeting fee deadlines robbed the poor of money better spent on necessities, literally snatching bread out of the mouths of their children. The Relief stressed that it had no desire to deny the poor man a decent funeral, but it only objected to "senseless" and "unseemly" pomp and expense. The Relief condemned the poor man's supposed "hunger for ostentation" as irrational, improvident, and superstitious. Everyone knew of, or thought they knew of, cases like that of an ordinary chambermaid who stashed away every penny of her earnings in order to finance a sumptuous funeral. Such stories are, of course, apocryphal or grossly exaggerated, but were evoked whenever the moral needed reinforcement.[52] From its inception the General Poor Relief arranged internment for the poor. The Gotteskasten had previously buried its parish poor, while the praetors occasionally managed free burials for the homeless, the unidentified, and those whose relatives could afford no funeral for them. The city buried prisoners and inmates of the various municipal institutions unless relatives claimed the bodies. All these received pauper funerals. Still, everyone hoped to avoid an ignominious end in the potter's field. As late as the second quarter of the nineteenth century, the Relief related that the majority of the poor continued to regard the pauper's funeral as vile.[53]

The pauper's funeral presented another way to measure need and test merit. When a person applied for assistance, the Relief assumed responsibility for the premium payments of the burial clubs "to which almost all of our poor subscribe." Later, the Relief collected the proceeds and had the pauper interred "in a plain, yet fully respectable manner." Some members of the council viewed the "completely simple pauper's funeral" as an excellent way to "get off our necks . . . those who have relatives or others to whom they can turn and who do not want to be buried as paupers."[54] Almost without exception the Relief had its dependents buried in one of the new cemeteries outside the city. Yet the Relief was hardly the first to employ the threat of a "shameful" or merely less attractive funeral to discourage undesirable behavior. The *sepultura asinina,* or burial in unhallowed ground without a religious ceremony, had at one time awaited all criminals as well as the untouchables of Western civilization: parricides, executioners, vagabonds, and the like. The fear of the *sepultura asinina* had often been deliberately applied to introduce new standards of civic behavior. By the late seventeenth century in Hamburg, the Rat threatened duelists with a dishonoring burial to discourage vigilantism and to restrict the lawful use of force to the government. In a similar way the Relief applied the pauper's funeral as a form of deterrence. But public opinion was sensitive on this subject and would not sanction treating a Christian pauper like a criminal. Thus, the Relief had to tread gingerly and scrupulously maintain at least the facade of respectability in staging its paupers' funerals.[55]

Death raised another testy issue: inheritance rights. The Relief Ordinance of 1788 defined the right of inheritance in a way calculated to reassure the pauper and to avoid agitating the Relief's subscribers. The Relief pledged to "all paupers who conduct themselves properly" that it would "neither arrogate to itself what they might expect to receive from their burial funds nor anything else from their estate," and would allow their children or other near relatives to inherit everything "undiminished." In its early days the Relief was particularly circumspect in its pronouncements, downplaying its rights of inheritance and recovery, stressing that both aimed at nothing more than the replacement of "that which the deceased had accepted from the Relief." While this was a fiction, there is no indication that either greed or a sense of punition alone impelled the Relief.[56]

The Revised Ordinance of 1791, however, considerably augmented the recovery rights of the Relief. In the same year the Relief upped its claims to paupers' estates. A circular to relief officers distributed in the summer of 1791 announced a new policy concerning inheritance. Beginning at that point, all of those who enjoyed permanent support were to be apprised "that upon their deaths their entire estate will fall to the Relief." If the person did not voluntarily decline the support guaranteed under these terms, consent was taken for granted and his possessions were stamped. This was, of course, clearly another test. The second specification, however, was intentionally *not* precisely defined in the revised ordinance, where the formula read more innocuously. Similarly in the *Report* for that year, the Relief carefully explained its objectives to the public as "merely a wish to divert the flood of those many persons who truly do not require our assistance and to prevent the total disintegration of familial charity toward near relatives among our lower and middle classes. It is in no way designed to generate more income for the Relief at the expense of the less fortunate."[57]

Upon the death of a registered pauper, his property was sealed and inventoried. Once these preliminaries were completed and, "after notifying the clothing-sellers and Jewish peddlers," the Relief auctioned off the estate. After covering outstanding debts and funeral expenses, the remainder of the proceeds flowed into the coffers of the Relief. Surviving spouses, "if he or she actually cohabited," enjoyed the rest of the estate during their lifetimes. Thereafter, what was left reverted to the Relief. Dependent children became wards of the Relief, which administered the proceeds of their estates, placed them with foster parents (or had them admitted to the orphanage), deducting these expenses, when feasible, from their inheritances. Only extraordinary circumstances impelled the Relief to relinquish its rights in favor of grown children or more distant relatives.[58]

One might wonder why the Relief regulated the rights of inheritance so strictly. Surely most paupers' estates could not have been worth the trouble. In the vast majority of cases the assets barely defrayed the costs of the funeral.[59] In the end, however, despite all humanitarian and by no means insincere talk about aiding suffering humanity and assisting the less fortunate, the Relief fully intended the status of the registered pauper to be disadvantageous. The severity of the 1791 inheritance regulations specifically aimed at diverting what was referred to as "the overwhelming press of persons whose relatives are perfectly capable of supporting them" or who could work for themselves. The Relief felt its position on inheritance rights and funerals would discourage applicants, and regarded it as a perfectly defensible—not even a particularly cruel or harsh—method of protecting resources. A 1792 report highlighted the decline of the numbers receiving support in the winter of that year, pinpointing the reason as "the rights exercised by the Relief over the estates of the poor." Even though a person might no longer be held completely responsible for his penury, neither was there any reason why he should be allowed to live "comfortably pampered" by the free bread of the Relief.[60]

These basic precepts would have been just as readily acclaimed by poor relief reformers two centuries or more earlier. Humanity and Christian duty dictated that society assume accountability for the pauper's continued existence. He should not be allowed to perish miserably. He also could not be permitted to exist in more comfort than the humblest free worker. The disadvantages of being a registered pauper were to be real, but that did not deflect the Relief from its other great purpose of preventing poverty. In all these instances, the Relief wielded a double-edged sword and ran the risk of offending many. Assuredly those people existing just above poverty could themselves empathize (if not necessarily sympathize) with the fate of their only slightly poorer or less lucky brethern. There is also substantial evidence to suggest that such tactics bothered potential or actual contributors who remained somewhat skeptical of the changes in philanthropic behavior the Relief tried to foist on them. Relief officers resented having to exercise severity, and in almost every instance of the council chastising a relief officer, or of a relief officer coming into conflict with his district director, it was almost invariably because the relief officer balked at reducing support or had handed out support "too indulgently." And the Relief was well aware that it steered between Scylla and Charybdis. A 1791 meeting of the council was called specifically to discuss how to publicize the revised ordinance. At that meeting, it was decided best to keep silent about the new policy on inheritance to avoid fomenting a "sensation" among the public, especially in view of the approaching special collection for the Relief.[61]

Of course, there was another hitch: In trying to discourage shirkers and ne'er-do-wells, the Relief unnerved perfectly worthy persons who retained perhaps "old-fashionedly delicate" ideas. Those unfortunate people who were too proud to submit to the indignity of registering as a pauper had to suffer in silence unless they found private benefactors. Although the Relief had originally protected the anonymity of those who were déclassé, these provisions were deleted from the 1791 ordinance. This indicates further how the older ideas of the poor and of poverty were slowly being transformed. The poor were no longer the depressed individuals of a better class beset by hard times nor for that matter a small segment of the permanently destitute; they were the working class. Poverty ceased to be an individual's fate and the object of personal altruism, but became a feature describing a whole class and a matter for broad community action.[62]

The Duty of Work

A study of poverty in early modern Europe published not too long ago characterized the change in attitudes toward the poor in the eighteenth century as a shift to patronage and surveillance on a large scale, arguing that "during the 1770s and 1780s the bourgeoisie did everything in its power to turn the poor into a docile labour force." Accustoming paupers to work and instilling in them a work ethic were undeniably two of the fundamental goals of the General Poor Relief. But apart from the indistinctness of "the bourgeoisie" as a category describing the multiplicity of persons, and the vagueness of "bourgeois" as a label encompassing the assortment of ideas involved in formulating poor relief policy in the late eighteenth century, it should also be remembered that if this disciplining existed, it marched hand in hand with broader municipal policies and can never be understood separate from them.[63] Furthermore, at this stage in Hamburg's development it seems apparent that, although the shapers of poor relief believed that work was the root of all good, especially for the poor man, this faith derived from an older tradition integral to Western civilization at least since the Middle Ages. Work-disciplining has often been regarded as a critical step in the development of an industrial labor force. In describing *The Making of the English Working Class*, E. P. Thompson illustrated how the working man was drilled until his "working paroxysms" were "methodised . . . [and] the man adapted to the discipline of the machine."[64]

In eighteenth-century Hamburg, of course, there was little need to synchronize men to the rhythms of machines. Far more important was securing a plentiful supply of not particularly skilled laborers. That these men placed uppermost in their minds the creation of a docile work force is questionable. What they did understand was that unemployment and underemployment were the danger signs of economic disequilibrium. They were astute enough to recognize that in some obscure way (which they pondered but never more than imperfectly grasped) the very wealth of the city had generated an immense poverty. Likewise, it is unnecessarily Machiavellian to twist their attempts at poor relief into an orchestrated effort to depress wages artificially (one cannot, for example, identify among the framers of poor relief those who would directly benefit) or to grind workers into a slavish tractability. This is not to suggest that no one was interested in flattening out the wage curve. Everyone appreciated the value of low wages to employers, but they were equally alert to the attendant necessity of low prices and an availability of cheap housing if Hamburg was to prosper. Few involved in government would blindly accept the idea of sacrificing workers to destitution merely to further the interests of the wealthier classes in society. Their view of social justice, while at times blinkered, ran deeper than that. They recognized that cities must attract workers as well as wealthier settlers by such varied tactics as tax incentives, religious toleration, moderate living costs, plentiful and cheap housing, and even beautifying the city's environment. The intention here is hardly to suggest that no one desired to hold workers in thrall. For example, the rich calico printer, Nicolaus Burmester, after experiencing some disturbing bouts of worker unrest in the 1790s, looked to uncomplaining machines as substitutes for troublesome humans.[65] Among most of Hamburg's governing elites, however, an older mentality prevailed that still drew strongly on the venerable paternal traditions of the muncipality and that was still anchored in the world of the "whole house economy" in which ties of obligations ran vertically through the layers of society. It was a mentality that was slowly losing its potency, yet for all its flaws of self-righteousness and intolerance of diversity, its social rigidity, and its still smoldering religious intolerance, did offer a deep sense of social and civil responsibility based on preserving (an already dying) social unity. This world of community was dissolving and would eventually vanish, to be replaced by the devil-take-the-hindmost individualism of the early nineteenth century—a century that did not find its social conscience easily or quickly.

The Relief promised the pauper much: medical care for himself and his family, weekly alms, rent subsidies, food, shelter, clothing, and, most importantly, employment. "For each person who lacks employment," the Relief obliged itself to find or create work for him. Like its predecessors, the Relief warned the applicant that "we cannot nourish idlers, [therefore] each person must agree to work according to the measure of his strength and ability."[66] The cameralists had seen in the poor a group of workers whose productive capacities had long lain fallow. Central Europe's enlightened reformers took up the cause of instilling the virtues of diligence and thrift into the working classes. In a real sense, therefore, work was its own reward; profit was not a major inducement for the Relief.[67]

All the expectations the Relief entertained of preventing poverty were predicated on offering work to the unemployed. The pauper must not be permitted to remain idle and prey to all the vices suckled by indolence, even if he was not responsible for that idleness. This was why everyone regarded begging as such an insidious menace. The numbers of recidivist beggars and registered paupers who supposedly preferred to beg rather than accept work on the Relief's terms seemed to demonstrate how difficult it was "to turn lazy, shiftless, and burdensome creatures into active and serviceable ones." Begging was thought equally pernicious because it infected willing workers with the germ of laziness and subverted industriousness. The evil influence the beggar exerted on the rest of the working class population made him a treacherous figure in the minds of eighteenth-century reformers. While it was conceded that many honest persons struggled heroically "even in the most harrowing circumstances" to avoid mendicancy, it seemed just as axiomatic that beggar's bread worked a maleficent miracle on anyone who tasted it. The beggar's life-style and its "easy pickings" (*sic!*) soon eroded the last remnants of self-esteem, turning once productive and respectable families into nothing more than the spawning-grounds of new generations of beggars.[68]

After several years' experience in providing work for the poor, however, the Relief concluded that locating work for the poor proved much simpler than inducing them to accept the available jobs. Except in times of severe depression, the Relief argued (not unjustifiably) that jobs in Hamburg abounded. It chose to believe that the lack of a desire to work, not the lack of work, caused unemployment in many cases. Only in the worst months of winter, the Relief reported, were employers able to locate all the "steady and robust" workers they needed. The Relief tried to act as a broker, for a time operating an informal labor exchange whereby relief officers mediated between employers and employees. The response, however, proved disheartening for both sides. Directors kept lists of people hunting for jobs, but apparently almost no one applied to them for workers. It was more probable that as employment opportunities multiplied in the 1790s workers preferred to be their own agents. The Relief also hesitated to recommend most of its charges without reservation.[69]

The duty of work (*Pflichtarbeit*) applied to all supplicants for aid. The question remained, however, of how and what kind of work would be most fitting. A long history of endeavors to locate a suitable occupation for the poor in Hamburg had yielded poor results. The Zuchthaus in 1726 had initiated a putting-out industry in stocking knitting that soon collapsed. The cloth that inmates wove for the garrison was so inferior that the contract was canceled. The Private Spinning Institute (1785) had experimented somewhat successfully with flax spinning, but only on a small scale. Throughout central Europe, reformers devoted much attention to make-work projects, focusing their efforts on nurturing or stimulating infant industries. Frequently, they lauded a confinement solution, in the form of workhouses for the poor, as ideal.[70] The measures recommended for economically backward areas, territorial states, and monarchies did not easily transfer to economically dynamic, republican Hamburg. The Relief, for example, explicitly rejected confinement solutions. Confinement was regarded as expensive, artificial, and even injurious. Too often, it was pointed out, the environment of confinement only infected paupers with scabies, or left them tainted by the corruption of fellow inmates.

The make-work plan that the Relief settled on, therefore, replicated the actual world of work. The task chosen was to fulfill four criteria. First, the product must find a convenient, stable, and elastic market. Second, the work must demand only moderate strength to suit it for women, young children, the elderly, and the infirm. It must, moreover, be a rapidly acquired skill so that even the very young and those of ordinary intelligence and dexterity could quickly master it. Furthermore, the work ought not to damage local manufacturers or impair their ability to procure workers. Finally, and most important, it should test in a reliable fashion the individual's industriousness. According to this prescription, an average laborer should be able to fabricate a standard product of quality or quantity deriving not so much from his skill as from his assiduity.[71]

The Private Spinning Institute had afforded proof of how well flax spinning tallied with these specifications. The Relief selected the same occupation as the principal employment of the poor. The Relief assigned administration of this pivotal program to a special commission—the Factory Deputation—headed by Caspar Voght. The deputation purchased hackled flax and marketed the finished yarn. Paupers proficient in spinning could request a "spinning card" from their relief officer. They then presented this card to the overseer of the flax depot, who distributed to each spinner a pound of dressed flax and, if necessary, loaned out a spinning wheel and spindle. Depending on the spinner's skill, the yield from each pound of flax ranged between seven and twelve lengths of yarn. At the very least, the Relief estimated that each worker could be expected to produce six lengths. Most individuals, however, would probably be more adroit and able to spin eight lengths. The Relief paid five shillings for each length of evenly spun yarn so that those who spun eight lengths weekly earned forty shillings, from which one subtracted sixteen shillings' deposit on the next pound of flax. This generated a weekly income of twenty-four shillings. Workers who spun more than eight lengths weekly received correspondingly higher wages. According to the Relief's calculations, twenty-four shillings covered the barest necessities of life, if the Relief provided for rent, fuel, and clothing. What paupers could not earn by spinning, the Relief extended to them in alms up to a maximum of twenty-four shillings weekly. They got more if their family was large or children ailing. Later the Relief introduced other types of work to complement spinning; twine making was introduced in 1790, linen weaving in 1791, and in the same year arrangements were made with local manufacturers to employ some of the poor with stocking knitting and wool spinning. The Relief resisted unrestricted expansion: The consensus was that flax spinning served its purposes as well as any other task. There was a fear as well that expansion might incur the wrath of other producers who felt impeded in their search for workers or subjected to unfair competition from an organization that did not depend for its existence on turning a profit. Also, with the introduction of more forms of work, the Relief would be burdened with more extensive administrative responsibilities.[72]

Spinning was to serve the Relief as a valuable and objective measure of diligence and integrity in that it supposedly tested whether a healthy worker really required assistance. Anyone given a spinning card who subsequently used it satisfied the Relief as to need and meritoriousness. A refusal to spin for any reason, however, justified the Relief's decision to withhold aid. It also helped the Relief gauge quite handily the amount of additional support a pauper might require by assuming that each holder of a spinning card automatically possessed a weekly income of at least twenty-four shillings. Moreover, those who failed to fabricate the minimum of six lengths a week had shown themselves, in the eyes of the Relief, to be shirkers who were entitled to no further consideration and even liable to punishment.[73]

The Relief acknowledged that such make-work schemes could not be concerned merely with production and sales. It attached higher value to the less tangible goals of habituating workers to diligence, weaning them away from indolence, and developing self-reliance. These traits were expected to prevent impoverishment. Although the Relief in an initial burst of enthusiasm had entertained the notion that spinning would pay for itself, it explicitly sought no profits and never shied away from losses. However, when the gamble failed and losses became a haunting reality, the Relief comforted itself and its public with the knowledge that the loss was always less than it might have been (cold comfort!), and that the good done for the morality of the poor far outweighed monetary setbacks. In fact, the Relief retained spinning even when it proved *extremely* unprofitable, insisting that social gains more than offset financial deficits, and persisted in this stance when expenditures alarmingly overbalanced incomes. From 1791 through 1808 the Relief sacrificed almost 80,000 marks. Only in two years were very modest profits recorded. Voght defended flax spinning despite its notorious unprofitability because only thus did he believe it possible "to weave alms into wages."[74] One major cause of this loss was an impropitious decline in the market for flax. Another, the Relief argued, lay with the high wages the Relief paid. Manufacturers in the surrounding countryside and further afield—in Lüneburg, Braunschweig, and Hildesheim—where flax spinning was a well-entrenched cottage industry, retained workers at much lower wages. The Relief appreciated the higher costs of living in a city like Hamburg and bowed to this necessity, as well as to the one "of overcoming the pauper's antipathy toward work in general and toward spinning in particular." Only thus, it was insisted, could paupers learn that, with exertion, they could support themselves by spinning.[75]

Flax spinning had never employed large numbers of workers in Hamburg. One reason that the poor had little stomach for spinning was that it paid next to nothing for quite hard work. It was admitted even in the Relief that to earn a meager existence a spinner had to be very diligent and must "rise at 4 A.M. and then work through until 8 P.M. If he has no family, it is very useful to arrange with his relief officer to lodge him with others who can prepare his food for him so that he does not lose time." This was hardly an alluring prospect! Eventually the Relief came to regard flax spinning as merely stopgap employment that could be picked up in moments of economic strain or crisis, as well as a test of worthiness. The old, the infirm, women with children at home, could all spin to supplement family income. Precisely because flax spinning had never taken hold in Hamburg as it had in other areas of central Europe, few adults could spin. Some had perhaps learned as children growing up in villages where such cottage industries flourished, but just as many others required instruction. The Relief thus founded a school for adults and for children offering training in spinning. Each applicant for relief who could not spin, and "whether he desires to or not," had to present himself and his children at school for a course of instruction that ran six weeks. Upon graduation the trained spinner received wheels and spindles on loan; these could eventually be purchased on time. Strong warnings forbade the sale or pawn of tools or flax, threatening offenders with the Zuchthaus.[76]

By these means the Relief sought to return at least some of the unemployed poor to profitable employment. Its optimism, however, was not unbounded and the Relief expected little from those who previously had "only eked out the barest existence from knitting and parish handouts." Almost nothing, the Relief sighed, could turn these people into productive workers. One could only sustain them with a minimum of alms until they died out as a group. The Relief harbored brighter dreams for the future when "the entirely useless part" of the present generation would have passed away, to be replaced by a new and better prepared one. Then and only then would the cost of poor relief diminish with the shrinking numbers of the helpless poor.[77]

Despite painstaking preparation, no enthusiastic rush of applicants greeted the inauguration of the program. Apparently the poor regarded the whole project with great misgiving. As early as March 1789, Caspar Voght reported on an immediate response so meager that the Spinning School could easily accommodate more spinners, including persons who were not destitute. Yet the first reports on flax spinning were glowing. The Relief pointed with satisfaction to the 500 women, "creatures once totally dependent on charity" who now earned at least a little money. More cheering was how "even the worst children . . . the laziest, dirtiest, and most spoiled little brats are soon converted into obedient, busy youngsters with scrubbed faces who respond politely and modestly to questions."[78]

By 1791, however, the rosy hue glimmered less brightly. Several problems had arisen. Too much badly spun yarn, combined with the untimely decline in demand, created a backlog of unsold and for the most part unsalable yarn. The collusion of several instructresses and supervisors aggravated the fraudulent practices of some workers. Chronically declining productivity made the Relief despair of a quick metamorphosis of laggards into laborers. Even while baffled by the difficulties of remedying these problems, the Relief retained its faith in work as the basis of all rational poor relief. The monetary losses suffered—often quite substantial—did not restrain the spokesmen of the Relief from a spirited defense of the overall utility of its schools and make-work projects. Proposals to discontinue either one were met with staunch resistance, and the mere suggestion of reducing wages was firmly squelched because such would "decidedly inhibit the will to work among good and active laborers; [and] it would completely wipe out what little income our weaker and less capable spinners have." More ominously, cutting wages would "cast a pall of despondency" over workers.[79]

The Relief did not totally resist the pressure to revise and economize, however. By 1791 the Relief had convinced itself that "healthy and honest workers, who are willing to exert themselves" could always find work without relying on spinning. Revisions carried out in that year relegated spinning to children under ten, to old, infirm, or rheumatic persons, and to young and strong women who might spin occasionally. The Relief believed that "swaggering beer-bellies" or those "riddled with vice" would never discover employers willing to deal with them, and could also spin. Despite belt-tightening and attempts to deal more severely with shirkers and cheats by applying rules more stringently, the Relief continued to lose money. Only in especially prosperous years, when other work was plentiful, did negative balances shrink. For example, in 1795, the Relief registered smaller deficits than in previous years but instead of crediting its austerity program, the Relief conceded that "the advantages of Hamburg's present economic efflorescence have touched almost all workers." Manufacturers reported wages up from twenty-four or twenty-eight to forty-four shillings a day.[80]

If the Relief accepted monetary losses with resigned equanimity, it was more distressed by the failure of spinning to have a beneficial pedagogical impact on paupers. Dwindling productivity signaled the program's vain attempt to adapt the poor smoothly and quickly to honest labor. From early 1789 through February 1792, 1,665 persons enrolled to spin for the Relief: 934 enrollees (56.1 percent) satisfactorily completed the course in spinning; the remaining 731 appeared at the school only once or a few times. Many never returned after pocketing their first wages. The Relief reckoned that 934 active workers should be spinning at the very least 1,000 lengths of yarn monthly. Actual production rates, however, totaled less than one-third of that amount. Even worse, the corps of spinners in 1792 fabricated less salable yarn than *fewer* spinners had in 1789. This was a maddening and puzzling drop in productivity. Appalled by these results, the Relief initiated an "uncommonly vigorous" investigation to ascertain how many people still actually worked for the Relief. Those people who had abandoned spinning because they had found more lucrative employment should no longer be eligible for alms. Closer surveillance was introduced along these lines first in 1793 and then, in a milder form, in 1796. Both initiatives only reduced losses temporarily. The change of seasons from winter to summer also adversely affected productivity. There were always fewer spinners in summer. Even short-term fluctuations in the weather had an impact. Unusually good weather in September 1795 had, for example, meant that fewer people applied for either work or alms.[81]

By the end of the century, the problem still rankled. An inquiry conducted by the Relief in 1801 disclosed just how few of the registered alms-receiving poor in fact worked for the Relief. Günther conducted an impromptu survey in his half-district; he wanted to verify how many of the aid recipients who had borrowed spinning wheels and spindles still used them. In the nine years from 1792 through 1800, 137 persons had signed up to spin and a total of 124 spinning wheels and 103 spindles had been dispensed. By 1800 only 16 persons spun even occasionally. Yet only 10 wheels and 7 spindles had been returned to the Relief. If these results were multiplied by the total number of half-districts, then well over a thousand pieces of equipment had gone astray in less than a decade. Of course, we have no way of knowing if this half-district was typical. At any rate, the outcome of this personal survey dispirited Günter so markedly that he urged the council to suppress his findings in order to prevent despair among the Relief's friends and glee among its critics.[82]

The duty of work pertained to all petitioners for support; however, work might also be turned to the different purpose of punishment.[83] The members of both the Relief and the Patriotic Society had long mulled over the issue of what specifically might be done with those who "wantonly" shunned employment. In 1790 the Patriotic Society sponsored an essay contest on "how to employ lazy and recalcitrant paupers of both sexes" with some form of compulsory labor. The terms of the contest defined a "lazy worker" as "any pauper, be it man, woman, or child, who does not by his own application earn enough to support himself, nor can by means of gentle persuasion, by strict supervision, or threat of castigation be induced to produce what his strength and his skills should allow him to produce." A fractious worker was one "who stubbornly refused to work or who labors with little animation." The purpose of compulsory labor lay in "rousing an indolent nature, familiarizing first hands then hearts" to a life of constant industry. Compulsory labor was never intended for all the poor. It was best employed as a way to dig out firmly rooted habits of indolence and implant in their stead an enterprising spirit. The idea was common. The prison reformer Friedrich Benedict Weber, in reviewing the many common types of poor relief, described a special kind of workhouse "in which merely the dissolute, slothful, bad-tempered, and recalcitrant poor, who cannot be brought round to reason in normal workhouses, are to be sequestered and forced to labor without recompense, partly to reaccustom them to the habits of work and partly to control vagabondage and beggary."

Another penal reformer, August Rulffs, carefully distinguished between houses of correction (*Zuchthäuser*) and workhouses (*Arbeitshäuser*). He conceded that common usage sloppily confused the two, but he insisted on a strict differentiation. In the former "work was correction or punishment," while in the latter it was charity. Force was justifiable only when milder methods had miscarried. The Relief, which looked askance at all forms of indoor relief, believed that implementing a system of compulsory labor would "empty out the prisons" by effectively preventing the idleness that led to mischief or crime. In addition, a form of compulsory work would place the Relief's officers "in a stronger position to be the educators of the poor rather than merely their taskmasters." The Relief in the 1790s thus plainly distinguished between the duty of work (*Pflichtarbeit*) and compulsory labor (*Zwangsarbeit*): the first an obligation incumbent on all the poor, the second a weapon to be used judiciously and sparingly against the obstreperous. It was a subtle distinction that reflected a mentality rooted in a historical paternalism, which rather abruptly disappeared in Hamburg after 1815.[84]

Although much discussion centered on the work suitable for compulsory labor, more critical was "the form of supervision, the exertion necessary, and the living conditions." The work was to be toilsome and performed in an atmosphere of "restraint, seclusion, monotony, and deprivation." When these conditions alone fell short of achieving the desired result, then "decreasing the amount and palatability of diet" and even mild corporal punishments might be indicated. However, the work was never to be unhealthy or to debilitate the physical strength of the subject. Compulsion was therapeutic under the best of circumstances, because it contrived to accustom loafers to diligence and to force them to acquire that virtue or at least assume it. In the Zuchthaus imparting a marketable skill—important to the Relief in other ways—or extracting profits was of negligible concern. The simple four-week Zuchthaus sentence as meted out to beggars was appraised as worse than useless, for not even a man of "goodwill" could acquire the indispensable habits of perseverance within the short span of a month and far less improvement could be expected of an ill-tempered rowdy or a practiced cheat. Unhappily, a month of associating with the "rotten fellows" in the Zuchthaus exposed the novice to "evil practices." To be effective, therefore, a program of compulsory labor had to be soundly conceived and not merely left to the caprice of the Zuchthaus.[85] In this case, the Relief relinquished at least in part its antipathy to confinement. Because the Relief's aid was outdoor assistance, it lacked crisp and immediate control over its charges. Idlers, for example, could not be punished "with the pangs of hunger." Corporal punishments could be dodged.

Lacking a house of correction of its own, the Relief in the early 1790s arranged with the Zuchthaus to organize a separate form of compulsory labor there. The detainees of the Relief were to be kept isolated from the other inmates. The Relief clothed them and compensated the Zuchthaus for their expenses. The program of compulsion merged confinement with hard labor, uncomfortable and somber surroundings, and even—though very infrequently—with blows. Stronger disciplinary measures included a diet of bread and water, solitary confinement, and wearing heavy wooden blocks around their ankles while at work. Furthermore, the work was carefully considered. It must be adaptable to the differing strengths of individuals, yet it could not interfere or compete with local manufacturers. And the work adopted must clearly be "less agreeable than any other the Relief offers to its charges." Weaving hair rugs was disqualified as unhealthy; wool spinning was thought to demand too much skill; flax and cotton spinning were rejected as not distasteful enough. The shredding of dyewoods such as sassafras, rosewood, and quassia, as well as the sawing of hartshorn, had long been done in the Zuchthaus by men of robust constitution. It was heavy labor that taxed the strength of "the most strapping knaves" who could not shred or saw for more than six hours daily "without the bracing benefit of spirits." It was, however, healthy and arduous and eminently suitable for strong men. For women and less hardy males, nothing more felicitous suggested itself than spinning; the amount to be spun each day was simply doubled. The agreement stipulated that first offenders would be confined for four weeks. Those who failed to attain their daily quotas had time tacked onto their sentences. Those who exceeded their quotas had the time of their sentences reduced.[86]

It is exceedingly difficult to come to any conclusion regarding the practical results of compulsory labor. The Relief seldom resorted to it. The threat and actuality of compulsion seem not to have been very useful in mastering the continued problem of mendicancy. Economic and political upheavals and inclement weather sent the numbers of the unemployed and of beggars spiraling upward just as much after 1788 as before. Even more exacting is the task of deciding how effective duress was in combating indolence among the poor and in raising their industriousness quotient. The existing evidence is not terribly conclusive, but the impression is that results were pretty wretched.[87] We have seen how productivity declined without ceasing, and yet those subjected to compulsory labor were few. Perhaps because the Relief viewed the Zuchthaus as an inappropriate venue for a program of constructive compulsion, it was infrequently applied. The chronic overcrowding of the Zuchthaus left little room for a separate and closely monitored program of compulsory labor along the lines envisioned by the Relief officials. In the first few years of the nineteenth century, the Relief repeatedly raised the idea of constructing its own house of improvement as a more promising alternative to the Zuchthaus, but the plans got lost in a rush of events that made the Relief fearful of its own existence—let alone willing to contemplate further expansions.

The Hope for the Future

If work was the sole—and by no means certain—prospect for redeeming the current generation of paupers, education was the hope for the future. Within the Enlightenment a fierce debate raged about what education could accomplish. While some, like Helvetius, believed education to be omnipotent, others were less optimistically inclined. Still, few people denied that the present generation fell far short of its potential. If education could not cure all the evils of society or right the wayward nature of man, it nonetheless seemed the best chance of alleviating ignorance and reducing poverty in the next generation. Eighteenth-century pedagogical reformers all labored to improve educational methods, but often held divergent beliefs about the blessings that education might bestow. Educational theory and practice were strongly class oriented. For the working classes, most agreed it was enough for children to receive training for their future place in life.[88] Reformers cautioned teachers: "do not aim for the stars; set modest goals." Elementary schools should teach all children to value virtue and industry. Reformers groomed citizens "to care about the welfare of their families, to be interested in the well-being of society, to render obedience to the state, and to be warmly patriotic." These goals easily meshed with the aims of most eighteenth-century governments. In France, Fleury spoke of a state education designed to cultivate "good sons, good husbands, good fathers, good friends, in a word, zealous defenders of the state and its laws."[89]

Poor relief reform and educational reform overlapped. Both identified ignorance as a prime evil. When the Oberalten presented their six-point plan for the improvement of poor relief to the Rat in 1787, they focused on "the inferior quality of our schools where children quickly learn to be idle and profligate and are taught nothing that could be of utility to them in the future" as one of the leading causes of impoverishment.[90] A principal goal of the Relief was to educate the children of the poor as useful members of society. Children who grew up in the Zuchthaus, ran wild, or begged were already *mauvais sujets,* incapable of being shaped into honest laborers.[91]

The problem of educating the children of the lower classes lay not only in coercing or cajoling their parents to send them to school; the first requirement was to elevate the quality of the schools themselves. Enlightened opinion in Hamburg severely criticized most of the existing "Ragged Schools" for teaching children nothing more beneficent than prayer, if that, and for neglecting to educate their bodies. As early as age four, it was claimed, children were "pressed together in tiny airless rooms, and for five or six hours a day hunch on stools from which they are not allowed to budge except to stand for a few moments and recite by rote their ABCs."[92] As a corrective to such "institutions of learning," school reformers recommended new curricula that would stimulate minds and bodies. In their elementary schools (*Volksschulen*) and their industry schools (*Industrie-Schulen*), the program of instruction drilled judgment more than memory, hands as well as hearts. Not only would children learn the alphabet and addition tables, but they would also acquire such skills as sewing, knitting, spinning, and weaving. The teaching plan could be endlessly modified. In rural areas, for example, gardening and viticulture could be introduced.[93]

The industry schools developed by Friedrich Eberhard von Rochow on his estate at Rekan, by Heinrich Sextroh in Braunschweig, and by the Wagemann brothers in Göttingen were the Relief's models. The directors had read the great educational reformers—Rochow, Pestalozzi, Campe, and Basedow—and knew many of them personally. The Relief saw in the concept of the industry school a splendid tool with which to combat poverty.[94] It was in this concept that the General Poor Relief placed its fondest hopes for the future and planned with the greatest assurance, or even—as its critics later charged—with reckless abandon. Most active in setting up the schools of the Relief were Voght and Günther, who were ably supported by Joachim Christoph Bracke, pastor for the parish of St. Nikolai and a moderate reformer.[95] Once again it was the Patriotic Society that had laid the footing for educational reform. An essay contest announced in 1787 set the topic: "What is the proper preparation of the lower classes for their future vocations?" This contest produced results that Günther later acclaimed as "the almost indispensable groundwork" for the Relief's schools. The prize winner in 1787 was J. C. E. Buchmann, a theology student, who later served as the first schoolmaster of the Relief's Elementary School. His essay envisioned an intimate reciprocation between work and learning in schools. He foresaw the major role of elementary schools as the "transmission of moral education." His goals for the lower classes centered on training them to be "useful beings, good household managers, conscientious housefathers, [and] faithful laborers." These ideas and these goals—unaltered—shaped the schools of the Relief.[96]

In return for alms, the Relief expected parents "to bring up their children as Christians and as God-fearing persons, to keep them clean and orderly, and to instruct them in proper behavior." Concretely speaking, this meant that parents must send their children to the Relief's schools in order to continue receiving support. It was there that youngsters would learn reading, writing, reckoning, and receive a moral education. At the same time, they would be instructed in spinning and in other kinds of work "whereby they can eventually earn their own living and assist their parents."[97] These schools intended that each child master a skill along with his three R's, although he was much more likely to acquire the first than the second. The Relief's schools combined hours of work with classes in reading, writing, and religion. The great Swiss pedagogue Pestalozzi desired "to bind together learning and working, to fuse one with the other." Günther wanted to instruct children while they spun, suggesting that instructors could read aloud from one of the many popular didactic volumes available.[98]

As central as work was to a proper education of the lower classes, perhaps just as crucial was moral instruction. This was now, however, simply religious catechization. The goal was to impart to children the virtues and habits that would serve them well in later life. Religious instruction, if not paramount, was not neglected. In this regard, the preceptor was Pastor Bracke who endeavored to awaken in his students moral feelings and who refused to use the Hamburg Catechism because he considered it too involved for children and too doctrinaire. He replaced it with Luther's Small Catechism and the enlightened Hanover Catechism. Educators like Pestalozzi and Rochow, whose works Günther found eminently suited for pauper schools, mapped out syllabi in a simple and practical morality equally valuable for workers, servants, parents, and farmers. This moral code stressed thrift, obedience, cleanliness, and foresightedness. Günther donated to the Relief's schools numerous copies of Rochow's popular primer, *The Child's Companion*. Its short parables and stories ended on properly moralistic tones: "The Day-Laborer" concluded that "poverty is the partner of sloth"; the selection on "Happiness" versified the joys of satisfaction with one's lot in life, no matter how meager; "The Clever Housekeeper in Times of Scarcity" showed how thrift could preserve a family in hard times.[99]

Relief believed that for young children—between the ages of six and twelve—the instruction in morals was best unadorned. Examples were drawn from everyday life and dealt with incidents familiar to youngsters. In addition, these virtues must be simple ones (e.g., cleanliness) that even a small child could rehearse. Instruction for older children—in the twelve to fifteen age group—prepared them for their approaching confirmation and instilled in them a sense of "the proper relationship of adults to masters, employers, neighbors, and the authorities." They also acquired a basic knowledge of laws pertaining to their lives as servants, employees, subjects, and citizens. While all children learned budgeting and the basic rules of good husbandry, women were specially instructed in the skills of housekeeping, diet, and expenditure that supposedly helped them live better for less. The education of girls, of course, aimed at "teaching them to cherish and hold sacred the roles of wife and mother." Children remained in school until a position could be found for them. Strong girls seemed excellent material for farmers' families; others were found places as servants or seamstresses in well-to-do households. Most boys were apprenticed. Some went to sea. Less desirable, from the Relief's point of view, were positions in the manufactories, as valets, or as unskilled laborers.[100]

The history of the Relief's endeavors in the field of education can be succinctly summarized: modest beginnings, great expectations, disappointing results. The first of the Relief's schools—the Spinning School—opened in August 1789 with 210 pupils. The Relief hired instructors and instructresses from the working classes to direct the children in knitting and spinning. Each day began at the stroke of dawn, when all children had to be at their places. After a short prayer and the singing of a verse or two from a well-known hymn, the children labored until eight, when they ate a breakfast consisting of beer and bread. Then it was back to work until noon. School resumed at two, again with prayer and song; another meal of bread and beer was served at five, and at eight school was out. At the end of each week, children were given their wages. For each child dutifully sent on to school, parents obtained a modest increment of alms. The course of spinning lasted twelve weeks, after which children were released to spin at home.[101] A system of rewards and punishments (pieces of clothing or shaming penalties) offered added incentives to the children to be productive and pliant. Corporal punishment was banned. Since the Relief was convinced that "many children once freed from instruction in spinning [would] soon sink back into their idle ways," it set aside heated and supervised workrooms in the old orphanage building. This was intended to prevent children from reverting to bad habits and to protect them from being led astray by the deleterious examples supposedly set by their parents. Besides, the Relief reasoned, the children could thus more conveniently attend classes in reading and writing.[102]

The Relief in these first years set unpretentious goals as to what their schools were to accomplish. The Spinning School, for example, aimed at nothing more than inculcating cleanliness and attentiveness. The entry class accepted six-year-olds who had to learn "still-sitting" before they could be expected to absorb anything else.[103] Later, in 1790, the School Deputation found the children "improved enough" to profit from more advanced schooling and more diversified vocational training. It began to broaden its program by adding first a second class to the Industry School where boys worked at making canvas and girls also learned to weave and sew. By 1793, 354 children attended the various classes of the Industry School; in 1796 the number was 441. It was acknowledged by Relief officials that every augmentation in schooling precipitated greater outlays of money, but the Relief put off its critics with the argument that "there can be no doubt that this is the most pragmatic way to apply our resources and that . . . education is precisely the field that must be the most thoroughly tilled to prevent future impoverishment."[104]

In February 1789 the Elementary School began with the mere handful of students who had already finished twelve weeks of instruction in spinning. But gradually, and then more rapidly, the Elementary School grew, eventually exceeding the Spinning School in its dimensions. By 1793, 647 children were enrolled in the Elementary School; by 1796 it was 842. The enrollment peaked for all schools in 1803 with a total of 1,358 pupils. All the children of registered paupers between the ages of six and eighteen, if neither physically or mentally handicapped, nor already in other schools, nor gainfully employed, had to attend school. Relief policy preferred compulsory education for all able-bodied pauper children, yet willingly comprised with the reality of child labor in Hamburg. The Relief's administrators admitted how important, even vital, a child's wages could be to a struggling family; nor did they deny manufacturers their "legitimate need" for laboring hands, even small ones. The Relief tried to convince employers to permit these youngsters to go to school part-time or at least to participate in the classes in reading and religion. The Relief inaugurated its Evening and Sunday Schools in 1791 and in 1792 especially for these young laborers, although all children had to attend Sunday School. In 1795 the Relief opened its schools to the children of the nonregistered poor. In fact, even before the Relief developed a stated policy of accepting children who were not paupers, they sometimes did so, as in the case of Frau Rieckmann who earned her living by knitting and who petitioned to have her twelve-year-old daughter admitted to school. The School Deputation agreed, arguing that it retained the right to extend free schooling to such families at its discretion "as an inestimable measure" for curbing future impoverishment. By 1800 almost 85 percent of all pupils in the Elementary School were children of the nonregistered poor, and in 1801 an average of fifty-eight such children a month were admitted. Frau Sander even promised to place one mark quarterly in the poor box if the Relief allowed her son to attend its school simply because she believed the instruction there to be "so much superior" to that available elsewhere.[105]

As schools increased in size and diversity, there was a constant pressure to reorganize and reapportion tasks. By the end of the century, for example, the School Deputation was assuming full responsibility for all children who in any way came into contact with the Relief, as well as for many children of the nonregistered poor. As early as 1791–92, the School Deputation had virtually taken over all the duties of supervising pauper children directly. By the end of 1792, it was finding jobs or positions for children who were almost ready to leave school. By the late 1790s, this inflation of tasks led to the recognition that child welfare ought to be more distinctly segregated from poor relief proper. Voght first suggested the desirability of such a division of duties, and in 1797–98 the School Deputation was reorganized. Special school districts were created and school directors were named who, over the protests of many relief officers, assumed full responsibility for all children touched by the Relief—school-aged or not, registered poor or not—throughout the city.[106]

While the workshops struggled with declining productivity and sloppy workmanship, truancy afflicted the schools. Particularly at first, parents agreed to send their children to school only reluctantly and many preferred, whenever possible, to find work for them. How much of parents' aversion stemmed from a distrust of new fangled schooling and resentment over the Relief's interference in their lives, and how much from sheer economic necessity, we will probably never know. We do know, however, that only when employment opportunities dried up did pauper parents regularly pack their children off to school to earn their "sitting money." Schools, which were jammed in winter, emptied out again in the summery days of easy employment. It was a ubiquitous complaint. Ferdinand Kindermann encountered similar problems in Bohemia. Parents, he groused, often kept children at the hearthside or in the fields instead of sending them to their desks or workbenches.[107] Confronted with growing truancy, the council responded with an investigation in early 1791. By October the results showed that of the 660 school-aged children in thirty-nine quarters, fully 405 (61.4 percent) did not attend schools; 186 children went to other schools, were physically incapacitated, or were required at home. The parents of 219 others assured their relief officers that they would send their children to school "directly." Other reports identified the seasonal variations in school attendance. For example, for the year 1791–92, more than 700 children attended in winter but fewer than 500 in summer. The Relief combated truancy by threatening to cancel support and by raising the premiums paid children for diligent attendance.[108]

The protocol of the School Deputation illustrates how tenaciously it fought truancy and also demonstrates how closely school directors monitored their charges. The evidence speaks of the close contact and familiarity that each director had with the intimate details of family life—knowledge based on personal contact, not on hearsay. The directors conversed regularly with the family members themselves and with employers and landlords, either to arrange apprenticeships or to mediate in housing disputes. In 1797, for example, the school director for the fourth district, Johann Hinrich Oberdörffer, reported on his relationship with the Bussau family over a number of years. Frau Bussau, a widow with seven children, cut corks for a living. Her eldest daughter, already confirmed, was a domestic servant. The next child, a girl of fourteen, lived at home and worked halfdays for a family nearby, for which she received meals in addition to wages. This girl, whom Oberdörffer described rather uncharitably as "somewhat stupid," attended the Evening and Sunday Schools sporadically. He refused to advance her any clothing because "I would prefer to see her in our Industry School than work as a servant sometimes here and sometimes there." Earlier the Relief had arranged for a fifteen-year-old brother to be apprenticed to a wheelwright. However, his mother soon "snatched" him away from his master, "an upright and gentle man" according to Oberdörffer, and found him work with a calico printer. This boy and a younger brother, aged ten, earned good wages there. They attended the Sunday School "infrequently and lackadaisically." The three youngest children were not yet school-aged. Oberdörffer hoped to get the eldest of the three into school soon; however, he remarked pessimistically that "most probably force will have to be applied to achieve this." The real problem, in Oberdörffer's estimation, was the mother. He regarded her with great aversion and felt she alone would deserve no assistance if not for the children. He charged that she allowed her children to go hungry, even though they dutifully handed over their earnings to her, while she "lives it up with her lover." He applied the carrot and the stick similarly to other cases. A girl who often played truant had been brought around to regular school attendance by intermittently denying her mother support. Using the same techniques, he "cured" the Holtzmann family of truancy and slovenliness. The two children, boys of nine and twelve, were enrolled in the Industry School. The twelve-year-old, though literally lousy, behaved himself passably well. The younger was much worse. Not only did he appear at school clad in filthy rags, but was very disinclined to apply himself. Once again Oberdörffer's tactics seemed to win the day. After two years of working on this family, he boasted (in words that ring with odious self-satisfaction): "at least I have transformed these surly recalcitrants into obedient human beings, who accept good advice with humility." There is no doubt here that Oberdörffer, like so many others among his colleagues, spent long hours carrying out the duties of reestablishing at least some sort of communal responsibility for the poor. Ferdinand Beneke's comments in his diary testify to a more kindhearted and less self-righteous approach, even if he occasionally referred to his relief quarter as "my kingdom!"[109]

The Nonregistered Poor

Like education, the program of medical care was also vigorously enlarged in the 1790s. The Relief's Medical Deputation was, like its predecessor, a domiciliary program. Its scale of operations, however, was more impressive, reaching out to handle almost 50,000 cases from 1788 through 1801.[110] Most interesting is the extension of medical care to the nonregistered poor, under which many members of the working classes became eligible for free medical care. The 1788 *Instructions* to relief officers specified that free medical assistance applied not only to paupers but also to a wider group of persons able to earn their own living only while they remained healthy. Their circumstances, however, deteriorated rapidly once confronted with sudden, severe, or crippling illnesses. Anyone thus struck down whose reserves were slim or nonexistent could receive free medical care from the Relief. It was the identical medical assistance that the registered pauper enjoyed with, however, none of the disadvantages of being a registered pauper.[111] The numbers of the nonregistered poor who applied for free medical care grew rapidly. In 1788–89 there were only 516, about 12 percent of all patients. By 1792 there were 1,135, or about 30 percent (see Table 6.1). In some ways, this was cause for jubilation. Voght, for example, postulated that "the increase of the nonregistered poor treated among the sick shows how much this procedure contributes to the attainment of our goals of preventing destitution through timely assistance." Still, it swallowed great sums of money and the members of the council began to feel that perhaps they were being deceived into advancing free medical care to people who could well afford to pay. A period of more rigorous control from 1793 to 1795 (a period that, as we have seen, coincided with a brief economic recession and was

Table 6.1 Medical Deputation: Patients Treated, 1788–1809

Year	Total Patients	Registered Poor	Percentage	Nonregistered	Percentage
1788–89	4,226	3,710	87.79	516	12.21
1789–90	4,269	3,713	86.98	556	13.02
1790–91	4,474	3,232	72.24	1,242	27.76
1791–92	4,018	2,883	71.75	1,135	28.25
1792–93	3,264	2,695	82.57	569	17.43
1793–94	3,424	3,402	99.36	22	.64
1794–95	3,569	3,562	99.80	7	.20
1795–96	3,339	3,332	99.79	7	.21
1796–97	3,045	2,463	80.89	582	19.11
1797–98	3,175	2,014	63.43	1,161	36.57
1798–99	3,379	2,028	60.02	1,351	39.98
1799–0	3,545	2,012	56.76	1,583	44.65
1800–1	4,156	2,290	55.10	1,866	44.90
1801–2	4,738	2,661	56.16	2,077	43.84
1802–3	3,956	1,981	50.08	1,975	49.92
1803–4	5,150	2,405	46.70	2,745	53.30
1804–5	4,445	2,050	46.12	2,395	53.88
1805–6	6,249	2,750	44.01	3,499	55.99
1806–7	9,297	4,717	50.74	4,580	49.26
1807–8	7,938	3,659	46.09	4,279	53.91
1808–9	9,599	4,484	46.71	5,115	53.29

Source: 36ste Nachricht (May 1810): 206–7.

marked by a general austerity program in the Relief) drastically cut the numbers of the nonregistered poor who could obtain medical care. To reduce expenses, the Relief in 1793 instituted a program of "half-free" medical care for those poor people who could not cover a physician's fees but could purchase medicines if provided at the low rates set in the Relief's *Pauper's Pharmacopia.* It was a short-lived experiment and the restrictions were quickly abolished (by early 1796) because the Relief feared that it prevented people who truly required care from seeking it. After 1796 the numbers of the nonregistered poor shot up so steeply that by 1797–98 a full 36.57 percent of those receiving medical care were not registered paupers, and the numbers continued to climb. Costs, of course, ascended as well—especially after the Relief established a Lying-In Ward for poverty-stricken and unwed mothers in 1796. Yet even when financially strained, the Relief was extremely unwilling to cut back on medical care for the nonregistered poor.[112]

The Relief's Loan or Assistance Program (*Vorschuß-Anstalt*) was perhaps the clearest example of how the Relief dedicated itself increasingly in the 1790s to a spiritedly pursued program of preventive social welfare, although in this area there was a long list of precedents as well. For example, redeeming pawned tools and household items to aid "honest but impoverished" artisans, like dowering marriageable, impoverished young women, had long constituted parts of Christian and private charity. In its January 1798 *Report,* the Relief explained the loan program as an attempt to do more to forestall impoverishment. The Relief found that despite the excellent provisions then existing for paupers there was still "a numerous class," especially in every great city, "whose existence hangs solely on the fruits of their daily labor." The Relief painted a moving picture of the "lucky few" among these people who could budget their family income to cover the expenses of the coming week. Most, however, were barely able to repay the debts of the previous seven days. The prosperity of this class was both "the most sensitive barometer of the inner strength of a state" and a "never failing source of power."[113] The Factory Deputation offered assistance to these hardworking families in the form of loans or advances. The Relief sought to halt the "heartrending slide" into destitution of a once independent family because of such uncontrollable circumstances as an illness or a death in the family. Prompt assistance for these people also diminished the numbers of "parasitic poor" in the future. Advances were not always paid in cash. The Relief redeemed pawn tools or other items, repaid debts directly, and distributed clothing. Sometimes the Relief disbursed small sums to start up a shop again or cover some other immediate requirement. These were interest-free loans that the recipient paid back in small installments and that, in fact, were mostly recovered. About 54 percent of the Relief's debtors were good risks, and from 1798 through 1804 the Relief had already recovered more than two thirds (67 percent) of its advances. The Relief estimated that this program would cost about 30,000 marks annually, but reckoned it was money well spent if it rescued hundreds of people from destitution and handed them a chance to fight their way back to self-reliance. It proved almost as expensive as Relief administrators had anticipated. From 1798 to 1802, 103,085 marks were advanced, about 25,000 marks a year. By 1800, the General Poor Relief had furnished at least 2,875 persons with this kind of assistance.[114]

The Measures of Success

But how successful was the Relief? There is no solid evidence to suggest that the living standard of the working classes was higher in the 1790s than it had been in the 1780s. In fact, the opposite appears to be the case: despite higher wages and more jobs, real wages apparently declined. Still, the plight of the most desperate among the poor probably improved. Success, however, must be judged by many measures. Surely one such measure was the Relief's ability to expand programs almost constantly and always ambitiously and to advance beyond the limited goal of distributing immediate assistance to the totally destitute. The Relief went much further, committing itself to the prevention of poverty, reaching out to those whom they called the nonregistered poor, those whom we recognize as the laboring classes. The schools of the Relief came to function as a public school system, albeit an incomplete one. The School Deputation cared for children practically from cradle to adulthood, even into their wage-earning years. Medical care reached a wider section of the population than ever before. Short-term loans became available to the distressed members of the working classes in greater profusion than earlier. Moreover, and most gratifyingly to the Relief, relief rolls shrank from a high of 3,903 families in 1789 to 2,326 in 1799, more than a 40 percent decline. One should, of course, point out that perhaps some of this decline was due to stricter supervision and control, and a greater part of it was surely the result of the favorable economic climate of the 1790s. Yet every indicator seemed to testify that Hamburg's philanthropic reserves had been tried and not found wanting. During this decade, few doubted that the truly splendid achievements of the Relief might be attributable to anything but its superb organization, its officers' dedication, and its well-managed finances. Traditional paternalism, traditional republican values—the same old vintages poured into new bottles—had, their supporters claimed, triumphed and proved their ability to cope as swiftly and as effectively with the problems of a modern world as any monarch aided by legions of bureaucrats. Hamburg's poor relief system became the envy of all Europe.

But how solid were these successes? Clearly the Relief's inculcation of a work ethic was less than a resounding triumph, since flax spinning (as well as other occupations) and the schools continually lost money. If one analyzes the expenditures of the Relief, it quickly becomes apparent that the largest sums went for aid to the domiciled poor in the form of alms, clothing, fuel, and bread—the least innovative and most traditionally oriented of the Relief's efforts. From 1789 through 1799, these amounted to between 63.55 and 79.90 percent of total expenditures, far outweighing costs for such highly touted programs as medical care (which ranged between 6.01 and 8.65 per-

Table 6.2. Expenditures: Workshops and Schools, 1789–1815

Year	Total Expenditures in Thaler	To Workshops and Schools in Thaler	Percentage
1789	88,501	8,499	9.60
1790	92,722	9,922	10.70
1791	100,925	8,098	8.02
1792	99,922	7,619	7.62
1793	87,410	4,524	5.18
1794	94,551	6,050	6.40
1795	100,664	6,517	6.47
1796	101,676	3,643	3.58
1797	109,317	5,091	4.66
1798	119,251	7,441	6.42
1799	164,160	8,581	5.23
1800	203,162	9,652	4.75
1801	164,131	13,387	8.16
1802	151,533	15,737	10.39
1803	143,912	13,691	9.51
1804	155,834	18,648	11.70
1805	161,542	19,560	12.11
1806	158,406	22,470	14.19
1807	167,003	23,380	14.00
1808	181,150	25,845	14.27
1809	187,673	27,379	14.59
1810	180,823	19,745	10.92
1811	165,357	27,571	16.67
1812	120,606	—	—
1813	66,728	—	—
1814	18,932	—	—
1815	57,655	1,252[a]	2.17

Source: Kollmann, "Ueberblick," pp. 132–3.

[a]The entire amount went only into schools.

cent) and schools and workshops combined (between 3.58 and 10.50 percent). Similarly, most recipients of alms were the "old" poor: widows and children. Thus the most innovative parts of poor relief, and especially those parts usually most intimately linked to social control or social disciplining theories—schools and make-work projects—formed only a small portion of the Relief's total expenditures when compared to the far more traditional rubric of alms (see Tables 6.2–6.4).

Another sign of the Relief's success, on another plane, was the continued trust placed in it by the general public in the form of contributions. Contributions were so bounteous that the Relief could plan handsomely and feel secure enough to swallow even substantial losses without fear of seriously endangering its financial integrity. Three forms of income were important: voluntary contributions and subscriptions, as well as bequests, direct government subventions, and the interest on accumulated capital. In the period from 1789 to 1799, voluntary contributions clearly overshadowed the rest, forming more

Table 6.3. Expenditures: Medical Relief, 1789–1815

Year	Total Expenditures in Thaler	Medical Relief	Percentage
1789	88,510	6,881	7.78
1790	92,722	8,021	8.65
1791	100,925	7,958	7.89
1792	99,922	6,617	6.62
1793	87,410	6,371	7.29
1794	94,551	6,917	7.32
1795	100,664	7,743	7.69
1796	101,676	7,606	7.48
1797	109,317	8,614	7.88
1798	119,251	9,366	7.85
1799	164,160	9,867	6.01
1800	203,162	10,213	5.03
1801	164,131	11,579	7.05
1802	151,533	11,493	7.58
1803	143,912	11,892	8.26
1804	155,834	13,685	8.78
1805	161,542	18,216	11.28
1806	158,406	16,036	10.12
1807	167,003	18,431	11.04
1808	181,150	18,369	10.14
1809	187,673	21,531	11.47
1810	180,823	22,769	12.59
1811	165,357	18,386	11.12
1812	120,606	12,069	10.01
1813	66,728	6,186	9.27
1814	18,932	1,397	7.38
1815	57,655	15,091	26.17

Source: Kollman, "Ueberblick," pp. 132–33.

than two thirds (67.59 percent) of total income. In this period, the leaders of Hamburg never contemplated introducing a direct tax to cover poor relief. State subsidies included transfers from the municipal treasury, proceeds from some irregular taxes, and from a percentage of all goods sold at auction. The annual income from contributions and testamentary moneys ranged from a low of 63,523 thaler in 1789 to a high of 139,540 thaler in 1797; the average was more than 75,000 thaler a year. Not until the second decade of the nineteenth century did voluntary contributions seriously decline. The quite substantial sums collected suggest to some degree the amount of public trust the institution enjoyed. By the end of 1792, the Relief had spent 23,854 thaler more than it had received. Some of this deficit resulted from the initial costs of setting up the Relief: Blankets, beds, and shirts had to be purchased for hundreds of people, and pawned tools and households items had to be redeemed. From 1793 to 1795 the Relief tightened its belt for a while as expenses rose, although contributions remained steadily high despite the recession of 1793. And yet, the financial signs for the first decade, if not totally auspicious, were at the very least extremely satisfactory. The huge public responses of

Table 6.4. Expenditures: Aid to Domiciled Poor, 1789–1815

Year	Total Expenditures in Thaler	To Domiciled	Percentage
1789	88,501	64,125	72.46
1790	92,722	68,860	74.27
1791	100,925	78,065	77.35
1792	99,922	77,858	77.92
1793	87,410	69,837	79.90
1794	94,551	72,792	76.99
1795	100,664	77,234	76.72
1796	101,676	80,565	79.24
1797	109,317	86,737	79.34
1798	119,251	92,425	77.50
1799	164,160	104,320	63.55
1800	203,162	107,089	52.71
1801	164,131	112,067	68.28
1802	151,533	107,298	70.81
1803	143,912	103,526	71.94
1804	155,834	110,087	70.64
1805	161,542	110,016	68.10
1806	158,406	104,604	66.03
1807	167,003	111,965	67.04
1808	181,150	123,033	67.92
1809	187,673	122,718	65.39
1810	180,823	118,945	65.78
1811	165,357	105,893	64.04
1812	120,606	98,765	81.89
1813	66,728	57,564	86.27
1814	18,932	15,869	83.82
1815	57,655	37,905	65.74

Source: Kollmann, "Ueberblick," pp. 132–3

1796 and 1797 produced a surplus of almost 90,000 thaler on the Relief's ledgers.[115] By the end of the decade the Relief was busily engaged in plans for building its own schoolhouse. Optimism ran high and finances were sound. The Relief had rapidly offset its first losses and the restraint practiced from 1793 to 1795 was soon superfluous.[116] At the end of the decade income exceeded expenditures by 122,945 thaler. Furthermore, this excess can in no way simply be seen as a result of harsh cutbacks in aid to the poor. Although the Relief in 1798 refused to distribute further alms to "sturdy paupers," especially to able-bodied adult males, it did continue to provide them with work.[117] And we must remember that jobs *were* more plentiful, if not necessarily better paying, in the late 1790s. The amounts spent in relief work continued to rise. The average level of support went up, although it is doubtful whether the increase more than merely compensated for the inflation of the 1790s. If, however, one considers a larger chronological period, the situation appears in a less favorable light. Over a twenty-seven-year period, from 1789 to 1815, expenditures exceeded income by 105,288 thaler. Thus, one suspects (a suspicion we will explore in more detail in the next chapter) that much of the Relief's success depended directly on the good times of the 1790s when contributions flowed freely and the number of the destitute declined. Still, this does not obscure the principle of civic-spirited participation of citizens on which the Relief was predicated and functioned, so that it had no difficulty in recruiting relief officers or directors in this decade. At its most sanguine, the Relief intended much more than a mere mean-spirited doling out of pitiful alms. The Relief was sincere in its promise about preventing poverty and justifiably boasted about its achievements in drawing large numbers of citizens into the often laborious and the always time-consuming business of poor relief.

Some, it is true, worried about the increasing deficits (especially in flax spinning) and about the imbalance in the schools' budgets, about overtaxing the Relief's resources, about the advisability of so ambitious a program of social welfare, and about the continued commitment of the citizens who manned the Relief. Few people thought, however, that the "disappearance" of poverty might be illusory, an epiphenomenon that was attributable more to the economic prosperity of the 1790s than to the efforts of the Relief per se. And there were signs that these fortunate times would not linger long. Inflation persisted, forcing the Relief to raise its levels of support.[118] Housing, too, had become a serious problem. Rents had increased threefold during the decade and the number of affordable dwellings for the working class had dropped significantly. The number of the homeless grew. The Relief was not unaware of the problem. In the latter half of the decade, it began to plan inexpensive housing for the poor and lamented the real difficulties the working man had in finding a home he could afford. The increase in population—the numbers drawn to Hamburg by its prospering economy, or driven from their homelands—only aggravated the pressure on a limited housing market.[119]

The Relief recognized that the prosperity of the 1790s presented a not quite unadulterated blessing. Commenting on employment possibilities in Hamburg in the 1790s, the Relief pointed out that the "sudden and unexpected" proliferation of jobs had not brought with it "true prosperity." Unfortunately, it had all too often merely encouraged indolence, profligacy, immorality, and an unhealthy desire to get rich quickly. The Relief cautioned that this could only lead to tragedy because this "unprecedented escalation" in earnings was also fragile, "the result of a unique chain of circumstances that cannot endure, and that will not reappear." Such false prosperity would be abruptly, catastrophically ended by "the so desired return of peace."[120] The Relief, quite unknowingly, was writing its own obituary, although foreign occupation and not peace spelled the end. Yet the Relief hardly took its own counsel to heart. Buoyed by the two largest collections in its history, the Relief lost itself in dreams of newer, ever more splendid ventures.[121] Poised on the brink of the next century, the Relief radiated enthusiasm and optimism. Alert to, but by no means fearful of the changes that might come, the Relief's administrators felt confident that the patriotism and civic-spiritedness that had carried them so far would not fail them in the future. They were to be disappointed.

7

The General Poor Relief, 1799–1830:
Decline and Rebirth?

As the eighteenth century drew to a close, Hamburg stood at the very zenith of its power. The harbor was jammed with ships, warehouses bulged with the goods of five continents, and merchants coolly calculated the profits to be reaped from a war-torn Europe. Not all the signs were auspicious, of course. The conflict between republican France and Great Britain threatened to disrupt or even break the cycle of European and world trade that had so richly rewarded Hamburg. Some men, perhaps more prescient than the rest, worried that the widening European conflict would eventually sweep northward and feared that Hamburg might suffer the same terrible fate as Antwerp and Amsterdam. But, on the whole, the mood on the eve of the nineteenth century was one of optimism. Few people suspected that within less than a decade economic growth would give way to stagnation, and even decay, and proud independence to the fawning servility of a client state. Yet this was the fate that awaited the city.

Even the 1790s, for all their grandeur, had not been a decade of unbroken good fortune. Economic euphoria had led to rash speculation and bill-discounting, activities that harbored the seeds of financial disaster. Merchants, anticipating a continued rise in already unprecedented prices, stock-piled goods, gauging the appropriate moment to attempt one last coup. The hundreds of undercapitalized and poorly managed businesses that had shot up in the 1790s lay ripe for ruin once the tempo of economic growth slowed. In 1799 the crash came. First the weather turned foul; the winter of 1798–99 was one of the harshest on record. Ice choked the harbor, immobilizing ships and hampering the transfer of goods from holds to warehouses. Sales fell off, prices plummeted, and the whole edifice of bill-discounting tumbled down like the house of cards it was. In 1799, 152 firms declared their insolvency, although most older, more established companies emerged intact if not unshaken. Yet the results of the crisis of 1799, shocking though they were in the short run, caused few lasting problems. These economic wounds soon healed. But political events were fast overtaking Hamburg. The city prospered throughout the 1790s, benefiting, if incidentally, from the pitiful plight of commercial rivals. Now Hamburg's turn, too, had come. The squalls of war moved ever closer and Hamburg soon became the object of the political

177

ambitions of other states. During the 1790s, Hamburg repeatedly bribed the French Republic, using its riches to disentangle itself from sticky diplomatic predicaments. In 1801, however, as a result of the clash between Russia, Sweden, Denmark, and Prussia on one side, and Great Britain on the other, Danish troops briefly occupied Hamburg. This was Hamburg's first real taste of a war that had ravaged so many other states and cities. With the failure of the Peace of Amiens and the resumption of hostilities in 1803, the English blockaded the Elbe. The blockade, which lasted from July 1803 through mid October 1805, accelerated the slide of a once lofty banking and commercial center "to the level of a mere country town." In 1804, several major firms collapsed and in the ensuing period an average of thirteen businesses filed bankruptcy each month. Some companies with large capital reserves weathered the storm or even exploited the generally dismal circumstances to their own advantage. But this would not last long.[1]

The economic crashes of 1799 and 1803—severe though they were—only marked the beginning of Hamburg's anguish. In August 1806, the Holy Roman Emperor laid down his crown and the empire dissolved. The neutrality and autonomy of the six remaining imperial free cities, ensured by the *Reichsdeputationhauptschluß* of 1803, became extremely precarious. Bavaria soon swallowed up Nuremberg and Augsburg, while Frankfurt became part of the newly created Federation of the Rhine. Only the three Hansa cities—Hamburg, Bremen, and Lübeck—retained a fragile hold on sovereignty. The hope for Hamburg's survival as a free-trading, cosmopolitan center in a war-torn world proved illusory. Historically Hamburg had played a pivotal role as a transshipment port for British goods—a role that Napoleon surely would no longer tolerate. On 19 November 1806, the French marched into Hamburg and the city was soon amalgamated into the Continental System.[2] Soon thereafter, Great Britain renewed the blockade of the Elbe, effectively severing Hamburg's overseas trade lines. An enormous smuggling traffic quickly sprang up, running through Helgoland and still neutral Altona. The continental blockade had slashed the arteries of Hamburg's commerce and—deprived of raw materials and markets—the major manufacturing branches of the economy withered.[3] The sugar refiners lost access to sugarcane from the French colonies and to coal from England. In 1813 an Englishman observed that only 28 of some 600 refiners were still in business, with their workers "reduced to inactivity and ruin."[4] Calico printing declined as precipitously. Whereas in 1797 there were 1,392 printing tables employing about 3,100 workers, by 1811 there was virtually no printing industry remaining.[5] And the situation worsened with each year. By 1811, firms respected throughout the commercial world declared bankruptcy while those that survived were crippled.[6]

The crises that paralyzed commerce and lamed the manufacturing branches of Hamburg's economy struck the laboring classes hardest. Thousands of workers were idled, unemployment was chronic, and smuggling became a way of life for many. Even when the Elbe blockade was only three months old, its "inevitably tragic results" were everywhere unmistakable. The virtual cessation of trade necessitated the release of thousands of workers. One eyewitness won-dered "how many dorymen, jollyboatmen, ship's carpenters, coopers, day-laborers . . . and all varieties of other workers have been partly or completely robbed of their livelihood since this commercial disaster [began]. And what about those thousands whose existence depends indirectly on trade and com-merce?"[7] If approximately seven to eight thousand men labored in the harbor, then about twenty-one to twenty-four thousand persons depended on com-merce for their daily bread. Of the twelve thousand people once employed in the various manufactories, most had lost their jobs by 1809–10. For example, of the five to eight thousand men and boys who once earned a living in the sugar refineries, in 1809 only a small number remained at work. We cannot gauge the total number of those the blockade crushed economically, but an estimate of fifty thousand or more must be close to accurate.[8] For the laboring poor, the blockade meant more than a loss of livelihood; it also meant the end of charity. The lives of once respectable laborers were shattered. Unable to find work and deprived of relief, they became ragged and hungry. And, to some, they now became vermin.

To add to the misery, the inflation of prices and the shortage of housing, which had haunted the 1790s, now escalated. In the 1790s food prices in northern Germany doubled and tripled as estate owners and grain merchants found eager purchasers among the armies of the belligerent powers, selling at especially advantageous rates to the Prussians and Austrians bivouacked in southern Germany. The General Poor Relief calculated that rents, which before 1798 had averaged about 8 thaler (3 marks to a thaler) a year, had by late 1800 reached 22.5 thaler; fuel for a family, once 25 marks, now cost 40–45 marks; the essential foodstuffs for an individual, which had totaled 112 marks a year, now amounted to 150 marks. Thus, whereas a family of four in 1795 spent, according to computations by the Relief, an average of 468 marks annually for necessities in 1800 the same family needed about 30 percent more than that amount, or 625 marks. After Napoleon's victories at Jena and Auerstadt, prices climbed ever more steeply. For example, in 1798 a *Pfund* of barley cost 2.5 shillings, but eight months later it cost 6.5 shillings. During preparations for siege in 1813–14, the same Pfund was only to be purchased for 12 shillings. A loaf of bread, which in 1798 bakers sold for 1 mark, cost 3 in 1800, and 16 in 1813–14. Selling at 3 marks in 1798, 10 Pfund of potatoes sold for 7 marks in 1800, and for 36 in 1813–14. And it must be remembered that the prices of 1798—offered here as a base index—were already inflated com-pared to those of the previous decade.[9]

Rents within the city tripled in the 1790s as new warehouses replaced many cheap residential buildings. This inflationary spiral abruptly accelerated in the early 1800s. Property values quickly appreciated, as did rents. The approximately seventeen thousand small dwellings (the *Sähle, Häuslein, Buden,* and *Keller*) occupied by the lower classes now cost an average of 144 marks a year, *eight* or ten times higher than in 1790. As the population in-creased and émigrés and emigrants streamed into the city, the fight for even these not particularly desirable (yet expensive) dwellings became fiercer. The

Relief correctly perceived that the source of much impoverishment lay in this unnatural inflation of rents. Its questionnaires revealed that rents, which ran little more than about 35–36 marks in 1796–98, had more than doubled—almost tripled—by 1806.[10]

Worse times were yet to come during the French occupation. The prices of foodstuffs and other essentials skyrocketed, troops were billeted with the populace, and Hamburg's finances were ravaged by wave after wave of extortionist demands.[11] Chroniclers depicted 1812 as a year that "reaped victims by the thousands," but by comparison with 1813 it was almost pleasant. By mid December, the military government under Marshal Davout initiated preparations for siege by ordering "the expulsion [from the city] within forty-eight hours of all those who are unable to provision themselves for [a minimum of] six months." The next day those people without provisions began to leave. Later the French drove them out. At the same time, the French demolished Hamburg's suburbs in order to create a free field of fire. In the next days, the French corps of engineers tore down or burned houses, while a steady stream of humanity passed through the city's gates. Some of these refugees eventually found shelter in Lübeck and Bremen. On Christmas eve the French ordered the evacuation of all the charitable institutions, and on the coldest days of the year several hundred people were transported in open wagons out of the city. Many died from exposure. During 1813 and 1814 probably about fifty-five thousand or more people fled Hamburg. The total cost of the occupation to Hamburg is, of course, impossible to tally, but contemporaries estimated figures anywhere from about thirty million marks to more than five times that figure.[12]

The General Poor Relief in Decline

What all this meant for the General Poor Relief is almost self-evident. And we do not lack for eyewitnesses. Caspar Voght's observations at four points in this period (in 1802, 1806, 1812, and 1813) reflect well the fading fortunes of the Relief. In 1802, Voght portrayed the Relief as "blooming." By 1806 his optimism had appreciably waned:

> [T]he blockade of the Elbe, the occupation of the city by the French, and those other, even more disastrous events, which I had [correctly] foreseen, threatened to destroy the work of my life and the object of my zeal at the very moment when one could expect that the achievements of the last fifteen years, which had cost millions, would bear fruit and spread eternal prosperity and morality among Hamburg's lower classes.

In 1812 he saw a "city barren and uninhabited, the benefactors of the poor impoverished, the needy abandoned, my life's work smashed." By 1813, all appeared lost. Voght could only rue the chances lost and lament the "deep suffering of the lower classes," "the degeneration of morals," and "the unspeakable horrors of the prisons." Voght's opinions were personal and for the most part private, revealed only in letters to his friends or held secret in his memoirs, but they were nonetheless astute.[13]

Perhaps the clearest indicator of the Relief's distress was the rapid deterioration of its finances. Deficits for 1799 and 1800 totaled more than 70,000 thaler, and from 1799 to 1814 the Relief incurred a total debt of 260,000 thaler.[14] These monetary woes, grave though they were, convey only half the story of the anguish of the Relief. Beginning in 1799, the General Poor Relief fought desperately against increasingly difficult circumstances, first to maintain its programs intact, later to assist the neediest, and finally for its very life. These fifteen years show an almost unbroken chain of misfortunes, despite the century's promising beginning. In its *28th Report,* which appeared in January 1801, the Relief proudly announced the completion of its schoolhouse (*Schul- und Arbeitshaus*), characterizing this imposing edifice as the culminating point of all its pedagogy and philanthropy. It was, in the Relief's own words, its "proudest monument." The building contained classrooms, storerooms for finished products and raw materials, and housing for some of the Relief's few paid employees. It represented at once the Relief's most costly venture and, at the same time, its last truly ambitious undertaking. For already by 1801, the Relief had fallen on hard times. In the ensuing years, the Relief's leaders reexamined its founding precepts and found them deficient. The policies of restraint and retrenchment that followed after 1800 culminated by 1816 in the almost total abandonment of the principles of 1788.[15]

The posture of the Relief toward the poor changed in these years as well. Even in early 1801, attitudes had perceptibly hardened. A harsher note crept into the language of the Relief in the form of a greater inclination to blame the poor themselves for their misfortunes. At first the rhetoric altered little and, taken out of context or read in isolation, many of the pronouncements barely deviate from the mixed language that had always characterized the Relief's judgments on the poor. Yet the balance had shifted. And soon the idea emerged that economic incapability was itself somehow culpable. Yet these tendencies should not be overestimated because the Relief in these years never totally forsook the position that poverty, at least to some extent, arose from economic structures and events that individuals could not direct. However, even in 1801, the tone is more relentless, less forgiving. For example, the Loan Institute already suffered financial embarrassment. And while the Relief acknowledged that individuals, through no fault of their own, were often victimized by economic change, it also pointed out that "part of this impoverishment stems . . . from physical and moral impairments; in highly competitive circumstances the person who is less industrious, less skilled, less honest, less sober, and less frugal will, of course, lose out." By 1803 the council felt it necessary to stress that the Relief was not obliged to nourish the poor or provide them employment.[16]

New ways of disbursing aid signaled this portentous transformation of perspective. In 1788, the Relief had deliberately chosen to distribute most of its assistance in the form of cash payments in order to reintegrate the pauper most expeditiously into a cash economy. By 1801, the Relief was turning to means of support that seemed more easily supervised, less easily abused, and, ultimately, cheaper. For example, in 1800 the Relief introduced the famous (or infamous!) Rumford soup as an integral part of normal assistance. Thus, instead of obtaining support entirely (or almost entirely) in cash, registered paupers received a number of soup coupons that had no cash value and that could only be redeemed for portions of soup cooked in communal kitchens.[17]

Several factors—most clearly the financial distress of the Relief and the swollen dimensions of the problem of poverty in these years, but also economic stagnation, inflation, and war—cultivated a less sympathetic impression of the poor among Hamburg's elites. One result was an increasing concern in the relief administration with cost-cutting measures. Another was the decision to eliminate programs now widely regarded as superfluous or indulgent. Equally important in these years was the growing swell of criticism *within the council itself* of the principles upon which the Relief had been founded.

In the late 1790s, some directors had worried about the deficit problem that was already apparent if not yet grave. The council, however, despite expressing some alarm at these trends, never felt obliged to recommend major cutbacks in programs during the first years of the new century. The council refused to panic, justifying their decision to preserve existing levels of support because of "the continuing inflation [in the prices] of all comestibles" and in anticipation of a "more propitious moment." Prosperity, however, continued to play truant and, by 1802, when expenditures vastly exceeded income the Relief's willingness (and perhaps its ability) to wait and see slowly oozed away. In 1803, for the very first time in its history, the Relief tapped its capital reserves to offset its operating expenses. By 1804, deficits exceeded 67,000 thaler. A year later the council communicated to the Rat its trepidations for the future: "For a long time, the council has watched uneasily as the time approached when the needs of the poor would exceed the regular income of the Relief. We are now at this point." The Relief appealed for assistance from the Rat; this it received in the form of a tax levy that was repeated for the next year as well. At the same time, the Relief began to study in earnest the possibility of reducing deficits. Yet no vigorous measures, certainly no major cutbacks, were inaugurated in 1806 or 1807. Perhaps everyone was preoccupied by the arrival of the French. By 1808, however, the Relief again appealed to the Rat for further subsidies. The Relief now reported that decreases in income and necessary increases in expenditures made its current programs "unstable" and its future "most uncertain." The Rat once more came to the Relief's aid, granting it the proceeds of two special tax levies. Beginning at this point, state funds regularly exceeded private donations. And thus crumbled one of the pillars on which the Relief had been built: voluntary contributions. The Rat stipulated that if the Relief had to rely on its support, the Relief must attempt to restore order to its finances. Consequently, the Rat asked the council to pare down its programs, a step that the council was by then clearly willing to take.[18]

The next years were painful for the Relief, highlighted as they were by

Table 7.1 General Poor Relief: Income and Expenditures

Year	Income in Thaler	Expenditures	Deficits/Surpluses
1789	77,928	88,501	−10,573
1790	89,387	92,722	−3,335
1791	95,640	100,925	−5,285
1792	95,261	99,922	−4,661
1793	92,311	87,410	+4,901
1794	105,169	94,551	+10,618
1795	115,422	100,664	+14,758
1796	122,912	101,676	+21,236
1797	197,069	109,317	+87,752
1798	133,212	119,251	+13,961
1799	140,059	164,160	−24,101
1800	156,244	203,162	−46,918
1801	139,744	164,131	−24,387
1802	146,668	151,533	−4,865
1803	149,451	143,912	+5,539
1804	129,010	155,834	−26,824
1805	126,128	161,542	−35,414
1806	154,806	158,406	−3,600
1807	160,715	167,003	−6,288
1808	146,363	181,105	−34,742
1809	157,909	187,673	−29,764
1810	190,545	180,823	+9,722
1811	134,245	165,357	−31,112
1812	114,535	120,606	−6,071
1813	66,278	66,728	−450
1814	17,713	18,932	−1,219
1815	65,860	57,655	+8,205

Source: Kollmann, "Ueberblick," pp. 132–33.

uncontrollable deficits and the enervation of its programs. Still, nothing checked the onrushing financial disaster. In 1812, after the Relief had reduced itself to a mere skeleton, deficits for that year totaled more than 6,000 thaler (see Table 7.1). By then, a tone of profound embitterment and deepest despair issued from the council, with the comment that "this balance reveals the General Poor Relief in its decline; the various rubrics of income demonstrate only too clearly the demise of affluence, the loss of civic spirit, and the absence of the warm participation of the state and the public, without which the Relief can accomplish nothing."[19] By 1814 the Relief was virtually bankrupt.[20]

The sharp downward plunge of the Relief's finance offers unambiguous evidence as to the severity of the Relief's distress in these long years of war and occupation, but it imparts only some of the tale. The Relief's records mirror equally the utter misery endured by the lower classes during these years. The general decline in living standards and the frightening increase in the numbers of the absolutely destitute can be measured in the avalanche of requests for assistance. The records disclose that at the moment of greatest privation the Relief found itself unable (and perhaps later unwilling) to help.

One telltale sign of this desperation was the revival of widespread mendicancy. Whereas in 1799 the Relief had boasted, somewhat untruthfully, that the streets had been swept clean of beggars, no one dared to assert such a thing just a few years later. As early as 1800 the increase was evident and noted, but the number of beggars apprehended on the streets soared after 1807. Inevitably, city government, acting on specific requests of the Relief, passed stronger measures against begging and beggars. The number of beggars was only the tip of the iceberg, of course: For every beggar there were many paupers.[21] The grim reports of the Loan Institute trace out the slow economic destruction of the laboring poor in these years. Inflation wrecked the meager fortunes of many. More people solicited advances to combat high rents as well as a general and unprecedented escalation of all prices. During the brief Peace of Amiens, some workers momentarily regained their financial equanimity as the harbor opened and they were reemployed. The inflation of food prices and the shortage of housing did not abate, while the outbreak of an "epidemic fever"—probably typhus—made 1803 the first year that more nonregistered than registered poor received medical care. The total number of relief applicants, which had declined each year since 1788, now rose. During the first ten months of 1802, 165 families applied; during the same period in 1803 about one third more (217) applied. In the first eight months of 1802, the Loan Institute lent 9,000 marks; in the first eight months of 1803 it lent 15,000 marks (about a 40 percent increase). Furthermore, the demand for the low-paying, normally unattractive jobs on the city's fortifications mounted rapidly. Throughout the 1790s the Relief had sought in vain for such workers. Now, however, supply and demand had reversed themselves. Whereas in December of 1802 the Relief had paid only 6 fortification workers, in December of 1803 there were 202 on the payroll and a total of 561 persons had applied. In 1804, the Relief supported in one capacity or another 15,400 persons, 3,000 more than in the previous year.[22]

Little doubt existed among the council members (or elsewhere) as to the causes of the tidal wave of impoverishment that now washed over Hamburg.

> Ten years ago, our population grew apace with an unprecedented increase in commerce . . . which elevated wages for a day's labor to two or three times the normal level [and] every branch of industry lacked workers.
>
> As a result, thousands of new families sprang up. Thoughtless journeymen deserted their masters, imprudent workers left their employers, [and] joined in foolish marriages, believing that the good times would never end. Each took advantage of the economic upswing. . . .
>
> Everyone enjoyed the luxury and frivolity produced by the unusually easy earnings of the moment. After four or five years, [however], the tempo slackened, while [at the same time] rents rose by threefold and food became expensive. . . . The blockade of our estuary threw thousands of families into misery.
>
> Those unhappy creatures, who had married during the halcyon years, were now burdened with four or five children, [and] came to us starving. Very often the father had already fled, leaving behind his wife and pauper brood.

The healthy worker, who up to that point had almost never requested assistance from us, now became an object of relief, as the number of those hunting jobs doubled and the demand for workers fell off by more than half.[23]

One would have had to be blind not to have recognized the disaster that touched all levels of Hamburg's economy. The Relief continued to acknowledge the impact of economic events on poverty, yet stressed more emphatically than ever before *self-responsibility* for one's fate. Thus economic disaster alone could not be held accountable for the indigence of thousands of workers, rather it was their own improvidence, their own irresponsibility, and their own prodigality that had just as surely ruined them. Of course, these themes had been sounded before. Now, however, they rang with new insistence. Moralists quickly catalogued faults that had gnawed away Hamburg's prosperity: lack of patriotism, disobedience, extravagance and fashion, the neglected education of children, gluttony, the reading of novels, the theater, and the inopportune founding of families. All these "failings" were trotted out to account for Hamburg's decline. These flaws were seen to be those of the rich as well as of the poor, but the moral censure fell heaviest on the less fortunate, as did the physical consequences. And, indeed, the rich might be excused their vices, for

> if we accept that the rich and well-to-do injure the lower classes in one way or another, do they not rectify these little injustices in other ways? How many suffering and needy persons are sustained by their selfless sacrifice? Who founds and maintains charities? Who created and furthers our General Poor Relief? Who builds the factories . . . and thereby generates new jobs? Who promotes the arts and industry? Who clothes and comforts the poor . . . ?[24]

The rich, of course. Still, one did not yet suggest that vice was the most important determinant of impoverishment or even *the* fount of destitution. Despair and desperation drove people to drink and to seek in gin and debauchery momentary surcease of their woes. Admittedly, these were wrong and foolish responses, but not the roots of all poverty. The poor became drunkards and prostitutes. So, if the poor were found guilty of a lack of judgment, they were not accused of deep-seated immorality and vice, nor were they yet relegated to a different species: homo improvidens.

Little the Relief did, however, slowed its disintegration. Despite deep cuts in programs, deficits climbed. Between 1800 and 1814 the Relief gradually deteriorated into exactly what its founders had so ardently wished to avoid: a mere almsgiving institution. The council jettisoned one program after another in frantic attempts to keep afloat. Like a victim of gangrene, however, the Relief's limbs first had to be shortened, then amputated. Through the early years of the century, despite the massive financial burdens wrought by economic stagnation, the Relief managed to maintain almost intact the integrity of its programs. Cutbacks introduced in 1805 soon endangered this integrity, however. After 1809, programs vanished one by one: In 1809 the Relief closed the Industry School; in 1810 the French confiscated the schoolhouse for use as a barracks, and by 1811 the Relief did little more than dole out alms to the worst victims of poverty, while trying to preserve the remnants of a once extensive medical relief. Gone were the schools, the work programs, the Loan Institute, and almost every other initiative the Relief had so confidently launched in the 1790s. By 1813, the council admitted that begging should once more be permitted: It is hard to imagine a clearer statement of the defeat of everything for which the Relief had once stood. The years 1813 and 1814 were terrible ones for the poor and the working classes in Hamburg, as food, fuel, and even shelter became scarce. Macabre scenes of the unprovisioned, the orphans, the inmates of the hospitals being carried out of the city in the snow and ice of December add painful details to this portrait of suffering.[25]

In these years, the Relief confronted its inability to deal with the immensity of the task it faced. Every cut in assistance and every retrenchment moved the Relief further away from the principles of 1788. The crippling of its body sapped the Relief's once vibrant spirit. At first each proposed reduction in its program excited passionate debates among council members and, for a while, drew determined opposition. Yet gradually a policy of parsimony won out and a whole new mentality came to prevail in the council. To be fair, things could clearly not go on as they had before. But now not only did a majority of council members justify restrictions in terms of necessity, they also doubted and even censured the very ideals upon which the Relief had been built. This conflict between proponents of reform and advocates of continuity is difficult to trace except where it flared into public view or aroused uncommonly acrimonious exchanges between individuals or groups in council meetings. Moreover, the shift did not occur overnight. As late as 1805, the council agreed to carry out its agenda almost undiminished. Particularly sacrosanct were the educational programs. The council quickly jumped to the defense of its policy on schooling whenever it encountered public criticism and repeatedly championed its resolution to extend schooling to children of the nonregistered poor.[26] By 1807, however, the council wavered in its opposition to retrenchment. And this new willingness to eliminate the procedures instituted in the 1790s reflected the attitudes held by many of the more assertive and younger (in terms of holding office) members of the council. The older generation of patriots— the founders of the Relief as well as those who had experienced its greatest triumphs in the 1790s—had now mostly withdrawn from public life. Perhaps Voght's departure from the School Deputation in 1806 and from the council in 1813 marked the turning points. Still, it is too simple to attribute these crucial modifications of policy solely to the growing influence of a less sympathetic generation. The Relief experienced concrete problems of almost overpowering dimensions, and it is hard to see how any group—regardless of its dedication to the principles of 1788—could have successfully withstood the pressure to reevaluate what had been done in the 1790s. A significant rearrangement of personnel occurred, however, and those who piloted the Relief in the early 1800s were the same men who rebuilt it after 1815 and who in doing so totally transformed its character.

By 1809 a spirit of frugality had permeated the council. Measures for restraint and spending cuts were introduced and enacted in rapid succession. Underlying these revisions "in all branches of the General Poor Relief" was the conviction that "as the state exacts inordinate sacrifices from everyone, we owe it to our fellow citizens to reduce their burden by cutting back [in poor relief] . . . [and] by countenancing no special outlays for the poor."[27] The *Report* issued in May 1810 narrated the sad decline of the Relief in the years from 1807 to 1809 when it was forced to exercise "the greatest possible economy in spending." Thereafter, the *Reports* fall silent until 1816, testifying as well as anything to the almost complete torpor of the council. The 1816 *Report* recapitulated in some detail the events of 1810–1815. In 1811 the council further reduced the levels of support and closed the Spinning Institute: "We [continue to] provide bread, even if we can no longer offer instruction or employment." The Relief forfeited its police powers, leaving the disciplining of the poor and the apprehending of beggars to the new *police correctionelle* established by the French.[28]

One of the most sensitive indicators of the slow rot of the Relief is the fragmentary record left for the period after 1809. The council met sporadically and attended to only the absolute "necessities." The years took their toll on personnel as well. Some of the attrition was the normal loss due to age and death. Voluntary resignations tore even more gaps in the directors' ranks. In 1807 von Heß resigned (for reasons we will discuss later), in 1811 Schütze and Plath left, in 1812 Senator Westphalen, and in 1813 Voght, along with Jürgensen and Nohr, withdrew from the council. By 1814, therefore, none of the original founders of the Relief still actively participated. Few of those who had lived through the productive years of the 1790s remained.[29] The council was virtually new in composition; its senior members were those who had steered the Relief through the harrowing times since 1800. It is, therefore, perhaps understandable that their perceptions of what poor relief could—and should—accomplish, like their view of the proper limits of state action, differed from that of their predecessors: Their goals were more narrowly circumscribed; they were more circumspect. In many ways an entire generation of Hamburg's elite had passed from the scene in those years, and "with the death and dispersion of the men and women in whose middle stood Klopstock, Georg Heinrich Sieveking, Caspar Voght, and Büsch, closed forever an epoch for Hamburg. . . . Men of the stature of Voght and Sieveking, who understood how to blend mercantile practicality and love of culture into a harmonious whole, were rarely seen in Hamburg again."[30]

This is not to suggest that the principles of 1788 died easily, or ever disappeared wholly. Some directors fought to uphold the programs they believed in and many relief officers clung fast to the brighter visions of the late eighteenth century. These usually were the relief officers who had held office through the 1790s. This historical connection plus the ultimate burden of implementing harsher policies made them unreceptive to cuts in programs and assistance. They were also vocal in their discontent with the direction the Relief was taking in these years. In 1806, the director Jonas von Heß energetically protested the ways in which the Relief had "slashed" aid. The restrictions in assistance, "these shackles on humanitarianism," so flagrantly offended his patriotism and sense of duty that he resigned from the council in 1807. Many relief officers, too, objected to the council's waxing "callousness." They did not envision their role as that of denying assistance.[31] The debate that fed on the problems of the early 1800s reexamined the whole mission of poor relief. A new disposition that now dominated had been forged in the crucible of economic decay and political emasculation. It was an attitude that reflected a significant transformation in the position of the poor in society and an alteration in the understanding of the role the state or the community should assume in social welfare policies. However, it was also more than that, and nothing less than a debate on how Hamburg's government and society should be reconstituted once freed from the French yoke. The two themes of the debate intertwined as did the participants. And it was here that triumphant liberalism overturned the principles of 1788 by rejecting the patriotism of the eighteenth century.

Voght was the most articulate witness to these events. His observations intrigue us because he represented the generation gone by. Yet, despite his retirement from all Relief affairs by 1813, he continued to be a keen and by no means dispassionate observer of events. He also in many ways embraced both sides of the argument: He deplored the weakening of the principles of 1788, but in the 1790s he had been the most vociferous critic of the Relief's "irresponsible" spending. Voght's opinion cannot be taken as average or typical, as he often held idiosyncratic and even eccentric ideas. Furthermore, he tended to judge others harshly, regarding his compatriots in poor relief (with the significant exception of Günther) as far less competent and prescient than he. These factors dictate some caution when evaluating Voght's comments, yet by no means discredit him as a knowledgeable onlooker. As early as 1802, Voght was upset by the material conditions of the Relief and even more by the direction in which the Relief was moving. "Greater demands, greater immorality and indolence among the poor, reduced resources for their assistance, and more important than all these, the increasing deviation from the principles [upon which the Relief had been founded], in particular, by neglecting the need to police the poor, threaten the Relief with ruin at that very instant when it might have become a model for all Europe." The Relief's "propensity" for spending more than it received troubled him. But he was considerably more perturbed by a situation in which "every attention to [inculcating] a work ethic in the poor and to enhancing their ability to labor has been practically abandoned, while the alms distributed to the poor are far too generous." He bemoaned the demise of paternalistic interest in the moral education of the working classes and scolded the Relief for its inattention to controlling mendicancy. He advised a return to the principles of 1788; in particular, he sought the restitution of the test to determine the ability to work. He held tenaciously to this precept as the sine qua non of all "rationally organized" relief and for the rest of his long life remained unshakably persuaded that only thus could the moral improvement of the poor be achieved. Yet he also welcomed new ideas. He enthusiastically supported introducing Rumford soup as an integral part of weekly support. He acknowledged the necessity for the Relief to devise its own form of forced labor because the Zuchthaus had all too clearly failed in this task. In private his censure of the Relief sounded a shriller note, and he also attacked the personnel of the Relief and the personalities of its directors. In 1802, in a letter to a friend, he wrote:

> I am still disquieted by the Relief's troubles. . . . Here we observe the results of slighting the education of our children and of allowing a mere business-oriented mentality to prevail. In fifteen years the council has, except for Bartels and myself, completely renewed itself. [And Bartels] has in many ways harmed the Relief as much as his great popularity has benefited it. The axioms that fifteen years ago everyone accepted and believed in have now been renounced. Cranks and know-nothings (at least in this field), men who are incapable of putting two ideas together, desire to guide the enterprise, but they have failed to catch its spirit.[32]

By the early 1800s Voght was physically distant from the events in Hamburg. Still, because of the longevity of his association with poor relief in Hamburg and throughout Europe (he was still writing on the subject in 1838), and because of the pivotal role he played in poor relief in the 1780s and 1790s, his observations are telling. Undoubtedly of greater immediate impact, however, on the Relief's policies were the opinions and actions of the council members still living in Hamburg.

The debate in the council on the present dilemmas and future course of the Relief did not merely touch on matters of marks and shillings; it also contained the seeds of a deeper conflict over the very purposes of poor relief and the role of government. Two factions and two sets of opinion slowly coalesced during these years. Although the contours of these two positions are fairly distinct, it is a laborious task to identify all the proponents of each viewpoint or even to pursue methodically the controversies as they matured. Meetings of the council tended to occur less frequently in this period and were, moreover, less fully documented. Commissions or deputations of a few members, for which we have only fragmentary records, did most of the work. In any case, the protocols of the council rarely gave any details of discussions. As in Hamburg's government at all levels, many decisions were concluded in private, disagreements were concealed behind closed doors, and often no evidence of these struggles appears in the written record. This was characteristic of a reign of fathers and uncles. Still, it is possible to describe both positions in some detail, even if gaps are inevitable and coverage rather more exiguous than one might desire. First, there were those who wished to adhere resolutely to the principles of 1788 and who regarded the financial embarrassment of the Relief as temporary and, in any case, less perilous than the proposed modifications. Rollbacks in programs would, they conceded, substantially reduce expenses, but would also undermine the whole edifice of poor relief. The other position, which eventually prevailed, was held by those who had come to believe that the doctrines of 1788 had not only failed to avert the disasters of the early 1800s but had actually provoked them. Most of the younger, more aggressive and vigorous directors—like Christian Nicolas Pehmöller and Amandus Augustus Abendroth, who climbed to power in the nineteenth century—believed this. These men seemed to make up the majority by 1809, and judging by the actions of the council in reviving poor relief in 1815, their point of view had by then won the upper hand. One should not draw these lines too definitively, however, because directors and relief officers vacillated; they were pressured by the seeming inevitability of bankruptcy but also tormented by thoughts of shirking the duties incumbent upon them as patriots and humanitarians and of breaking an almost sacred trust with their fellow citizens.

Two Adversaries

Two members of the council embodied the two opposing opinions. Their personal and theoretical differences stirred up uncommon turmoil in the council throughout 1806 and 1807. Both eventually defended their positions in print. Jonas Ludwig von Heß opposed reductions in programs. Even more adamantly he deprecated the dominance of a harsher mentality that he termed "repugnant" within the council. Although von Heß did not become a director until 1805, he had previously served both as relief officer and as a member of the School Deputation. Moreover, in the 1790s he had been an intimate of the Sieveking–Reimarus circle. He authored an influential three-volume topographic study of Hamburg that explored all aspects of life in the city and did not hesitate to expose its flaws.[33]

In a pamphlet, which appeared in 1806, simply titled "To The Council," he sketched the dichotomy in the vision of poor relief that he had observed developing: "In respect to the fundamental tenets of poor relief, two thoroughly contradictory ideas are now current. One group asserts that assistance to the poor . . . should be tied to the 'momentary' state of the treasury. Others believe that everything that poor relief offers should be gauged to the true need [of the poor]. I am totally convinced that only this latter position is just."[34] In this case, von Heß referred to the principles of 1788, arguing that little attention should be given to the "momentary" or "accidental" level of funds. For von Heß, the Relief could only achieve its goals (which he, like the founders of 1788, defined far more generously than a "mere relief of the most pressing needs") when it refused to be guided by a "bookkeeper's mentality." Von Heß accepted the necessity of spending liberally, even "profligately" in poor relief. To him, such extravagance did not signal grave or indefensible "fiscal whimsy," but demonstrated a laudable compassion for humanity. In poor relief one could not, according to von Heß, appraise accounts on the footing of marks and shillings, and on zero deficits alone. Charity necessitated a more flexible ledger: the social cost accounting hitherto practiced by the Relief. Von Heß went further, arguing that some relief programs, for example, the Loan Institute, could *only* succeed when they showed negative balances. Surpluses, not deficits, were to be distrusted. Poor relief should never become what von Heß accused the General Poor Relief of having become: "merely an instrument of punishment." In the early 1800s, according to von Heß, the Relief penalized the poor, chastised but did not succor the impoverished, and damned pauper children to socioeconomic perdition for the "sins" of their parents. He sternly rebuked the "pettymindedness" and the "bureaucratic spirit" he now saw ruling the Relief. He found efficiency alone an inappropriate yardstick, for "what is charity without humanity?"[35]

Although it is also true that there had always been a tension between fiscal integrity and humanity, the stance taken by von Heß largely reflected the beliefs of 1788. If von Heß worried little about balancing budgets, he struck at the munificence of Hamburg residents from another angle. He argued that the Relief had in reality *always* been undercapitalized: "Our entire relief system— as paradoxical as this may sound—costs little, very little, and considering how expensive it is [for the lower classes] to live in Hamburg, *far too little.*" Thus, instead of being prodigal in its spending, the Relief was and always had been miserly. Von Heß even dared assail the vaunted charity of his fellow citizens as less than that of many other cities and, in light of Hamburg's great wealth, shamefully deficient. As von Heß saw it, the problem did not derive from any promiscuous squandering of resources; quite to the contrary, funds had always been insufficient. To remedy this shortage, he proposed a general tax. With this proposal, obviously, he departed from the principles of free charity upon which the Relief had been founded. Yet he continued to believe that voluntary charity was preferable, if not practical.[36]

Von Heß, like all of his contemporaries as well as his opponents, drew wider political implications from the path poor relief followed in the 1800s. The kind of poor relief Hamburg possessed in the early nineteenth century he pronounced incompatible with a "free republican constitution" and, for that matter, at odds with economic reality. With this position von Heß echoed the concerns of the eighteenth-century patriots. But he added a new twist, endowing Hamburg's constitution with connotations that most patriots would not have totally accepted. He opposed, for example, the restrictions on attaining citizenship and on settling in Hamburg that the Relief had sponsored in the first decade of the nineteenth century. He found these constraints "incompatible with the history and future of our . . . free state." "The time may come," he predicted, "when these encumbrances on our political existence and our commerce . . . will prove extremely disadvantageous." Von Heß insisted that the natural rights of man could only be maintained and "the political freedoms which are woven throughout our constitution" could only be upheld when the "interaction" of Hamburg's governing bodies "is undisturbed and the essentially unfettered stream of people into our city remains unrestricted." He vigorously protested the three-year residency rule that had recently been introduced, lambasted the "unconditionally stiff" penalties for paupers who transgressed against even the most trifling of the Relief's "pettifogging" rules, objected to the long hours children were expected to work (as long as twelve hours daily), and argued against the "inhuman" stipulation that only the curably ill received free medical care. Von Heß was no anarchist. He acknowledged the necessity of guidelines but felt they should only be provisional, because in distributing relief, he believed it was always better to err on the side of humanity, even at the expense of solvency. Von Heß went further than all his contemporaries in his defense of the political rights of the common man. Certainly he worried less about the problem of aliens, recognizing that almost all the laborers and servants in the city—all these "so indispensable folk"—were once migrants. He branded it immoral to use these people and then cast them off. Von Heß granted the pauper a *right* to relief: a positive right, guaranteed by law. He argued that the state must deal fairly with all its inhabitants and not just those who were privileged.[37] In his championship of these principles, however, von Heß represented only himself. It is doubtful that the founders of 1788 would have endorsed the *right* of the poor to assistance. And yet in their readiness to help the nonregistered poor, and even aliens, they were perhaps closer to von Heß than to those who reshaped the Relief after 1815 on quite different premises.

Representing the position opposite to that of von Heß was Christian Nicolas Pehmöller, a governor of the Zuchthaus and ex officio member of the council in 1806. Pehmöller was a rising political star in the early 1800s: his career was capped in 1816 by his selection as senator.[38] Significantly, he replaced von Heß as director when the latter resigned in 1806. In a pamphlet published in 1808,[39] Pehmöller contested the charges of von Heß and refuted his arguments. He isolated two periods responsible for the crisis in poor relief: the economic distress of the early 1800s and the Relief's actions during the 1790s. In other words, Pehmöller located the roots of the problem in the glory years of the 1790s. The first and most grievous of these mistakes was the failure to attend to the "inviolable rule of thumb for every house-father": to adjust expenditures to income. Pehmöller insisted that each expansion of the Relief in the 1790s had disregarded this canon, and that this failing had created the enormous deficits in the Relief's treasury by 1808.

Yet Pehmöller identified the mismanagement of funds and ill-conceived expansion of the 1790s as only component parts of a larger problem. He and others criticized, really for the first time, the *very founding principles* of the General Poor Relief as naively optimistic and recklessly lavish. The Relief's distress derived not from a good idea gone awry, but flowed inevitably from the erroneous presuppositions of 1788: "All previous reports unmistakably demonstrate that the Relief from the very beginning assumed greater obligations and set for itself more ambitious objectives than any such organization should."[40] Such goals, Pehmöller continued, could only be attained in a perfect world where funds were virtually limitless. He argued that the prosperity of the 1790s had brought with it "a general decline in morals" that had assumed "worrisome dimensions." Most of all, Pehmöller ranked as the most urgent priority a thorough reorganization of finances. His answer—the institution of a tax to support poor relief—paralleled that of von Heß if his reasoning differed. The voluntary contributions that had once sustained the Relief were no longer abundant nor, even in their previous extent, adequate. A poor tax appeared unavoidable to both von Heß and Pehmöller.[41]

For Pehmöller the introduction of such a tax dictated as well a contraction in the limits of poor relief. Once subsidized by tax moneys the Relief must also, he insisted, respond more responsibly to public wishes. He would only favor tax-supported relief if it were fused with significant reductions in the cost of assistance. However, in 1808 Pehmöller's advocacy of a poor tax found few supporters. The council failed to act on his suggestion, which it held "inappropriate to the spirit of our institution."[42] Pehmöller proposed discarding the principles of 1788 and establishing an entirely new foundation for poor relief calibrated to the realities of the nineteenth century as he perceived them. It was time, Pehmöller exhorted his fellow citizens, to acknowledge failures, repudiate faltering precepts, and march on.

> Twenty years' experience has taught us that despite all our pains and exertions, despite all the dreams engendered by humanitarianism, despite so many sacrifices of time and energy, the goals which the Relief strove to attain—to educate and improve the middle and lower classes and thus beget a general and widespread prosperity . . .—these goals remain unfulfilled and are never to be realized.[43]

Pehmöller endorsed restricting aid to the "truly needy." The broadly conceived programs of the "old" relief, which touched so many of the nonregistered poor, Pehmöller viewed as the quaint artifacts of a dead age. And Pehmöller's aspirations for poor relief, which diverged substantially from those of 1788, apparently directed the reform of poor relief in Hamburg after 1815.

Pehmöller looked especially askance at the Relief's program of education for pauper children. First, such schooling was expensive, consuming almost half of each year's entire income. Second, and far worse, in Pehmöller's opinion, was that it was counterproductive. Pehmöller did not wish to deny the lower classes educational opportunities, but he deemed the Relief's program of education, and the extent to which the Relief had also become caught up in the education of nonpauper children, misguided. "If we take into account the lessons of the past," he mused, "it is now the moment to reflect and decide if the youth of the lower classes are best served by the existing system of schooling or whether they do not run more danger of being miseducated by it?" He regarded the typical course of instruction that, according to him, encompassed reading, writing, reckoning, moral direction, natural history, health and hygiene, German, religious history, religion, geography, mathematics, music, and "the Socratic method," as highly inappropriate for the lower classes. (It did not matter, of course, that the Relief actually dispensed a far less elaborate education to the vast majority of its pupils.) Rhetorically, he asked: "Can anyone still believe that this kind of teaching contributes to the happiness of the lower classes?"[44]

Equally idealistic, but ill-advised, Pehmöller maintained, was the Relief's devotion to the prevention of poverty. This goal had entangled the Relief in the ruinous expense of creating work for the unemployed. Pehmöller believed that the unchangeable geographic realities of Hamburg's location would always combine to frustrate the success of such programs.

> Territorial states have both the space and the varied means available to employ the poor, so that when one branch of earning lags, unemployed hands can be directed to another, be it industry or agriculture, [and] such states will find these programs useful. But if we survey Hamburg's tiny land mass, and if we recognize that the well-being of this small state depends almost entirely on the florescence of commerce, . . . then how far can we, and should we, pursue a program of preventing poverty [in this way]?

Providing employment for the poor in the form of a putting-out industry had, Pehmöller argued, financially ravaged the Relief. The chosen task of flax spinning was unprofitable because there was little or no market for the yarn. As a result, the Relief had accumulated a mountain of unsalable yarn that Pehmöller characterized as a "boring cancer" in the Relief's finances. The only way Pehmöller felt that the Relief could reduce this particular deficit was to introduce new industries. Of course, in the dark times of the early 1800s, such innovations seemed ridiculously visionary. Pehmöller concluded that for the moment "it is surely wiser to think of ways to reduce the numbers dependent on us for work, rather than to add to them."[45]

For similar reasons, Pehmöller endorsed stronger prohibitions against aliens settling in Hamburg. He also pushed for an extension of the residency requirement from three to ten years. Pehmöller conceded that this rule would do little or nothing to damn the flow of migrants into the city—indeed, it was not supposed to—but it would serve "to alleviate the liability of the state" for them.[46] Equally bankrupt in Pehmöller's view was the Loan Institute. He saw no proof that the loan program had succeeded in averting impoverishment; in this case the council followed much the same line. A lengthy report on the Loan Institute presented to the council in 1806 listed the problems of delinquent payments as well as admitting how difficult it was to assess the benefits of such loans. In light of this report, the council suspended the loan program, except in the special cases in which benefactors earmarked their contributions for such purposes.[47] Pehmöller responded more positively to the idea of medical relief and, even though "the costs . . . have risen immoderately in the past years," he regarded medical care as one of the most beneficial branches of the Relief that "has done much good" and "has forestalled greater misery." Yet here, too, abuses had crept in, especially in respect to care for the nonregistered poor. Pehmöller, however, only suggested that one should keep a sharper eye on the medical relief, but not abolish or even severely restrict it.[48]

In his attitude toward the policing activities combined with poor relief, Pehmöller articulated the rising call for thorough administrative reform. This wish for improvement touched all parts of government, but sounded most unrelentingly in respect to Hamburg's fragmented police. In short, Pehmöller felt that policing the poor should no longer be a function of poor relief. Poor relief should at the same time shed all hopes of improving paupers. The other role that the police assumed, controlling beggars and foreigners, would be more effectively executed by a centralized police bureau. Moreover, the Relief itself would benefit from such an amalgamation of policing functions, which would, Pehmöller insisted, slice through red tape and streamline tortuous and time-consuming administrative pathways.[49]

In conclusion, Pehmöller claimed that the Relief had been deeply compromised in its finances by a fiscal improvidence that left it tottering on the brink of disaster. To survive, the Relief must secure an adequate and reliable source of income by inaugurating a poor tax, and then it could bend itself once more to its proper task of gratifying "every true need." Pehmöller contended that such modest goals were the only ones appropriate for poor relief and "all the extravagances which occurred in the last years must be purposefully restrained . . . [because] they have not produced the desired result, nor ever could have. It is now time to introduce new measures fitting for a new environment. The Relief should be reconstructed on the most unadorned foundations." Specifically, Pehmöller advocated the elimination of the Loan Institute, asked for a temporary suspension of new school admissions, and prescribed the immediate introduction of the ten-year residency rule.[50] The acceptance of Pehmöller's suggestions would (and, to the extent that they and similar initiatives were accepted, did) totally alter the character of the General Poor Relief.

Pehmöller only represented most visibly a position others supported or to which they acquiesced. Apparently one of his backers was Amandus Augustus Abendroth.[51] Abendroth had been a director between 1795 and 1800, when he was elected into the Rat. He also served as Hamburg's first mayor under the French. Although Abendroth did not address these issues in print at the time that Pehmöller did, his later publications indicate that he too was moving in the same direction and almost certainly supported the changes Pehmöller urged. Writing in 1831, Abendroth evaluated the activities of the Relief in the opening years of the nineteenth century.[52] He reproached the founders of the Relief in the same ways and in much the same language Pehmöller used. In practice, according to Abendroth, the pretty goals that the Relief had set itself were never attained *precisely* because they were unrealistically conceived:

> [O]ne entertained the completely humane, clever, but totally impractical idea of stopping up the very sources of impoverishment, while simultaneously working for the betterment of humankind so that eventually only the elderly and invalid poor would require assistance; all other need having been abolished, . . . and so independently of aid to the adult poor the Relief disbursed money (in the form of school premiums) to pauper children. The result was that the parents who did not receive aid from the Relief suffered more than those whose children the Relief was educating. We erected a superb school system, built spinning rooms and workshops, set up soup kitchens, and provided low-interest loans . . . [and] ran the entire operation in a way that honored the noble minds and warm hearts of the Relief's founders. Money flowed freely at a time when the Relief's incomes were large and poverty itself not very widespread. Who would not have been content to see this continue, but it could not.[53]

He was, of course, disturbed by the financial problems of such a generous relief. Still, his disapproval, like that of Pehmöller, reached deeper. When he weighed the desirability of a return to the principles of 1788—not in 1831, but even earlier, in 1815—he reacted negatively. Poor relief, Abendroth asserted, "cannot give itself over to enthusiasm." By doing so in the 1790s, he claimed, the Relief itself had perniciously affected the morality of the poor. Poverty had lost its sting; it was no longer disadvantageous enough, and so it happened that "those supported by the Relief lived better than those whose sense of honor restrained them from asking for handouts. There developed in the minds of this class no good reason to resist applying for charity. In short, soon there was no honor left in self-help." Abendroth's understanding of the legitimate boundaries of poor relief coincided with that of Pehmöller:

> [T]he pauper must never live as well or better than the industrious, honest worker who relies on his own resources. The sick must be attended to, helpless children raised and educated, invalid paupers sustained, but one must go no further than this, one cannot go further than this without greatly endangering the whole enterprise. One must not establish the principle that the state or poor relief has a duty to provide work for the poor. Into what labyrinth would that lead us? Which state has the means to discharge that task? Such a principle would overturn all proper order. . . .

Abendroth even saw a dark side to the "abounding charity" of Hamburg's inhabitants in the 1790s. Hamburg's very magnanimity had been destructive, nurturing what Abendroth diagnosed as a malaise among the lower classes: a pandemic inability to help oneself.[54] Abendroth's position demonstrates how far poor relief had moved from 1788 by the 1830s. The shift, however, had been accomplished far earlier. In 1805, for example, when the Relief requested assistance from the Rat in employing the unemployed, the Rat refused. It was argued that such would "wound the self-respect" of the poor and, even worse, would perhaps lead them to the erroneous conclusion that the state "owed them" a living.[55]

But not everyone involved in poor relief accepted the logic of Pehmöller and Abendroth. The series of proposed cuts introduced in the council in 1808 and 1809 provoked a quick riposte from Johann Ernst Friedrich Westphalen. Westphalen had served as director since 1797; in 1809 he was elected to the Rat. In 1809, he lashed out at the "mean-spiritedness" of the Rat in respect to poor relief. He specifically deplored the thinking of men like Pehmöller. Perhaps he was unaware that he lamented an age gone by: "How can I not grieve when I read in an extract from the Rat's protocol that the present extension of the Relief exceeds all the *proper* limits of poor relief." He regretted that the members of the Rat thought only in terms of savings measures. "Are we now willing at one stroke to brand the standards of the Relief, once universally praised as sagacious and humane, as no longer so merely because we lack money?" Although his objections did not prevent the Rat from demanding and the council from initiating major cuts, neither did the council endorse Pehmöller's plans.[56]

This battle, which had been waged on the two fronts of fiscal integrity and humanity, was fought a second time in the even more desperate circumstances of 1813. In that year, thirty-six relief officers, who identified themselves as longtime participants in poor relief, protested the extreme reductions that the council had inaugurated the previous year. In October, the council had mandated "for the present" to issue neither clothing nor rent subsidies to the poor. Weekly alms were "to be disbursed only in accordance with the actual state of the Relief's finances." To these steps the relief officers replied, "dare one call this *assisting* the poor?" Such precepts, they maintained, completely travestied the principles for which the Relief had always stood and soured the sense of satisfaction they had always derived from their duties: "[W]hat remains to us now, except the unsavory task of informing the poor that [from now on], 'you will receive no clothing, no straw mattress, no rent, not even the *certainty* of meager alms.' " They felt as if the Relief had broken trust with them and with the poor by rescinding all "its publicly sworn promises." And now, "we appear like nurses in a hospital with no roof, no blankets, no heat, neither medicine nor nourishment, not even straw to bed its patients, where the dying find no comfort and the ill no refreshment, [we are like] a crowd of helpers who, however, have nothing to offer." The relief officers argued that these new constraints weighed especially cruelly on the poor, who were at that time even less guilty of their poverty than ever before. The dwindling of many once lucrative branches of manufacturing and the almost complete extinction of commerce had "ground thousands down into a misery from which they [could not] escape." Tellingly, even the "very best" of the poor were now thrown into the most appalling circumstances. "How can we ignore our obligations to them," the relief officers protested, "when it concerns the morality, the health, the very life of several thousands of fellow inhabitants of our ancient home." "We would be extremely ungrateful," they asserted, "if we overlook how much good, how much enjoyment, how much civic peace and happiness we owe to their presence. How can we forget what these people mean to us and what they meant to our forefathers?" These men did not minimize the gravity of the Relief's financial predicament. They by no means denied the urgency of the issues raised by Pehmöller and others, but their own experiences with the poor, and in their quarters, convinced them that the solutions the council had proposed and implemented were simply "not right." If the circumstances were actually so desperate, then would not it be far better, the relief officers suggested disingenuously, to terminate the old General Poor Relief and establish a new one that would be more fitted to the times? Such a decision would cause them inexpressible pain. The dissolution of the "old" Relief, in which they still fervently believed, and that "we have helped shape and watched improve, and whose benevolence has worked its magic on the morality, health, and life of thousands in our city," would be a bitter pill to swallow.[57] It would also toll the death knell for an older sense of civic duty and seal the fate of eighteenth-century patriotism.

A Harsher World

The induration of a harsher attitude toward the poor revealed itself as well in the intensely punitive measures directed against aliens and beggars during these same years. Punishments for mendicancy were increased, while the city similtaneously toughened prohibitions against the "covert in-migration of aliens." Both, but especially the first, embodied the more rigorous definitions of insiders and outsiders that now pertained, reflecting as well a less tolerant attitude toward immigrants. At the same time, and in the same ways, the residency requirements for poor relief were institutionalized to correspond to firmer, less fluid, and ultimately more restrictive definitions of citizenship. Such a mind set also impelled the Relief to render the conditions of poverty less advantageous and to restrict, often drastically, the varieties and amounts of support available. To some extent, of course, these changes grew naturally out of the concerns for population control and supervision that had already surfaced in the middle of the eighteenth century and that were intensified by the years of war, depression, and occupation. They became, however, in the nineteenth century more rigid and unyielding.[58]

It was not, of course, startling that the General Poor Relief desired heavier penalties for begging in order to dissuade the indigenous poor from illicit forms of self-help. In presenting its case to the Rat in 1806, the Relief referred to the provisions activated in 1801 that had stipulated a six-month Zuchthaus penalty for beggars (and as long as a year for recidivists): "The Relief then believed that aliens would desist [from begging] for fear of this long sentence, while it would force local paupers to turn to the Relief for aid." Unfortunately, "both hopes were in vain." Thus the Relief appealed for intensification of the already strict prohibitions on begging. The petition led to the ordinance of 12 March 1806, which laid down more severe penalties for mendicancy. It threatened beggars not only with incarceration, but with incarceration on a diet of bread and water, in darkness, while subjecting them to corporal chastisement and shaming.[59]

The Relief also urged tighter restrictions governing citizenship. As early as the summer of 1804, the Relief confronted several problems that emanated from its decision to implement a three-year residency rule. Unfortunately, this statute had in no way diverted the flow of "impecunious family fathers" and their dependents into the city. Once there, they frequently joined the city's garrison, or found work as night watchmen or on the fortifications. According to the Relief, stories like the one related by the school director, Schuback, had become commonplace.

> On 8 June a family named Lemmermann appeared before me [in my quarter] seeking support from the School Deputation. [The family consists of] a thirty-four-year-old sickly father, a thirty-two-year-old mother, and four small, ailing children, of whom the eldest is just seven, the youngest only one. This family comes from Kloster Zeven near Bremen, where the father could no longer scrape together a living as a cobbler. Therefore, and [he admits] principally with the thought in mind of applying to the Relief for assistance in raising and educating his children, he moved to Hamburg in April of this year. I understand that he was promptly enrolled in the city's soldiery, Captain Behrens' company. They have already pawned their few possessions for eighteen shillings. The children are half-naked. Immediate help is necessary.

For this problem there was no easy solution. The Relief petitioned the Rat to forbid the "all-too-rapid employment" of "those impoverished in other places" as members of the garrison, as night watchmen, or on the fortifications. In 1805, the Rat acceded to this request and simultaneously augmented the requirements for citizenship, de facto, though not de jure, terminating the status of quasi citizenship. The Rat specified in this mandate that the purpose of the new regulation was primarily to thwart the settling of "already impoverished persons who journey here with their large families and quickly become charges of the city." "Already impoverished persons" were to be denied access to the city entirely. The municipality ringed its population controls with greater stringency than even before. In particular, the city sought—fruitlessly, one assumes—to amass more concrete information on the backgrounds of those looking to make their homes in Hamburg. One might wonder whether the political anxieties of the early 1800s dictated this new caution. That is, to what extent was Hamburg's government far more worried about dangerous rather than impoverished strangers? There is, of course, no unambiguous answer. One plainly cannot overlook the possibility of a hidden agenda of political priorities. Yet the mandates, as well as the discussions that preceded their publication, appear at least on the surface, to be almost exclusively concerned with problems of population control and poverty not with the threat of provocateurs and spies.[60]

Confronted with a flood of aliens at a time when its own resources were almost depleted, the Relief accepted the exigency of fundamental changes in the theory and practice of policing. The reorganization in police that took place during these years slowly distanced the Relief from the realm of policing. The Relief, for its part, readily abdicated its position as a policing agent, surrendering with remarkably little fuss a role seen in 1788 as paramount to the realization of its objectives. Policing in the 1780s and 1790s retained all the older connotations of correction, guidance, and instruction, and in respect to the poor, the additional ones of educating pauper children and morally bettering both adults and children. The Relief in the 1800s had gradually detached itself from these goals as it devoted more attention to avoiding "suffocation under an avalanche of alien paupers." Thus, the council willingly participated in the redefinition of the role of police. "Police" lost its policy-making functions and was left only the more narrowly circumscribed field of the execution of policy: control and punishment remained, while guidance and improvement fell away. The Relief had cast off its paternalistic mantle, thrusting the poor out of a sheltered position and into the crueler world of social laissez-faire now being created.

Admittedly, that world was not only, or even principally, of Hamburg's making. During the occupation, the French had significantly refashioned Hamburg's administration and its social policies. When the French first entered the city in 1806, they allowed charitable institutions to continue on their previous path, at least provisionally. This provisional state of affairs lasted until 1 January 1811, when Napoleon incorporated Hamburg into the French empire as "une bonne ville." This was quickly followed by major changes in government: The old constitution was abrogated, a mayor was appointed, a unitary citizenship and the French Civil Code were introduced. The French replaced Hamburg's archaic, sprawling, decentralized administrative structure with Gallic centralization and rigor. The French erased the multiplicity of older policing agents and created a single police bureau (*police correctionelle*), which assumed competency over all civil and criminal affairs.[61]

Unfortunately for poor relief, the French also declined to pay some of the subventions and honor some of the financial arrangements the old government had assumed. This meant that the new government stopped interest on state loans, and appropriations for various charitable organizations virtually ceased. The effect on the poorhouses and on institutions like the Zuchthaus and the orphanage, was immediate and calamitous. At least since 1805, serious financial difficulties had plagued their every step. They relied increasingly on state subventions, or like the orphanage, tried to survive by appealing for assistance to the better funded General Poor Relief. But that particular cornucopia was soon emptied. By 1812, the hospital (the old Pesthof) notified the mayor of a deficit of almost 45,000 marks, pointing out that without prompt aid it would soon be unable to attend to its patients. The plight of the orphanage was hardly better; its director documented how a series of events had drained a once well-endowed treasury: an increase in the numbers of orphans (the orphanage took care of about 1,000 children, of which about 450–500 actually lived in the building), the growing number of youngsters abandoned by desperate parents, the sheer impossibility of arranging suitable apprenticeships for older children, and a "crippling" burden of illegitimate children. The Relief had always reimbursed the orphanage for the care of illegitimate children and for many others as well, but now the Relief—itself reduced to penury—was no longer able to do so. The Zuchthaus, if in less dire circumstances because an earlier administrative reorganization had removed some of its inmates to other institutions, still experienced major financial problems.[62]

The French, besides reshaping the police in Hamburg, also separated the administration of prisons from that of poorhouses. In 1811 the French empaneled two commissions: the "Commission administrative des hospices" (with J. H. Bartels at its head) for charities (the competence of which, however, excluded the General Poor Relief), and the "Conseil gratuit et charitable des prisons" for all correctional facilities. The French renamed most of these institutions to match more closely their new tasks. The Spinnhaus, now the "maison de réclusion," remained a prison for felons. The Zuchthaus was converted into the "maison de correction" for petty offenders, and the poor were transferred to a special "hospice de charité."[63]

Thus, although the French did not tamper directly with the General Poor Relief, these changes affected it nonetheless powerfully for their obliquity. The French apparently viewed the Relief as a private association that fell outside municipal jurisdiction. It was an instructive misreading of the Hamburg system based on a more technocratic mentality toward administration that defined far more precisely the lines between the private and public spheres. This formal distinction between public and private affairs, forced into being by the French, had always been resisted by the Hamburg elite in the eighteenth century. It would gain enhanced respectability and favor in the next century, though slowly. In truth, while the French activated these administrative innovations, many native residents of Hamburg had long been entertaining similar notions. Günther, for example, in the late 1790s had called for a reform in the office of praetor.[64] Still it was the French fait accompli that swept aside the tangle of policing agents, while reuniting some of them under the umbrella of a single *police correctionelle*. Sieveking, as senior governor of the Zuchthaus in 1799, had tried unsuccessfully to abolish the magisterial prerogatives of the governors that licensed them to imprison persons at their own discretion. (J. A. von Beseler's similar proposal was finally accepted by the governing council of the Zuchthaus in 1805.[65]) Christian Pehmöller, while still governor of the Zuchthaus, put forward proposals for the establishment of a reformatory. He emphasized the desirability of removing children from the Zuchthaus environment. The Zuchthaus, he argued, mixed ideas and objectives that were incompatible, even contradictory, and that were especially dangerous for the young. Pehmöller wished

> to improve that institution so that it will fulfill the potentiality of its name and be recreated as a house of industry or workhouse. Neither has truly existed here [in Hamburg]. . . . The existing house rules reveal a place where an undetermined number of human beings from all classes and representing greatly differing degrees of moral degeneracy are housed together . . . and associate freely with one another. One might better have named the place a school of vice and crime. . . .

Pehmöller sought to dismember the Zuchthaus into three separate institutions: a prison, a workhouse–poorhouse, and a reformatory. Pehmöller diagrammed a plan very similar to the one proposed by Jeremy Bentham in his *Panopticon*, which also advocated strict isolation and uncompromising supervision. These ideas proved extremely influential in prison reform in Europe and America in the early nineteenth century. Not everyone, of course, was thrilled by Pehmöller's scheme. And, interestingly enough, his most penetrating critics were old *Aufklärer* like Ernst Christian Trapp and Johann Jakob Rambach.[66] At any rate, larger political events stalled these initiatives (if indeed there might have been enough support to activate them), delaying change until after 1815.

During the French occupation, a wave of criticism and a thirst for reform surfaced in several forums. It is not coincidental that many of the same people involved in reevaluating the role of poor relief were also drawn into the debate about how to rebuild Hamburg's government after the French withdrew. By 1813 it was obvious that the French would leave sooner rather than later, and the debate burned with new intensity and fervor. While many people longed to return to Hamburg's "good old" constitution, "neither completely aristocratic, nor completely representative, but both together," even these seemed resigned to the inevitability of some break with the past. A few, like von Heß, envisioned widesweeping reforms that would usher in representative government. But most abhorred such radicalism. And these men belonged overwhelmingly to that coterie which had always governed Hamburg and would continue to do so. The most outspoken was Amandus Abendroth, whose *Wishes for Hamburg's Resurrection*—published while he was in exile in Kiel—provoked lively discussion. Abendroth sketched plans for a series of reforms in government. Despite his status as a reformer, however, he refused to doubt many of the older governing traditions. In particular Abendroth stood for the complete detachment of justice from administration, the establishment of a comprehensive police system (that is, to retain what the French had already neatly accomplished), the reworking of municipal finances and taxes, and the introduction of a unitary type of citizenship. He agreed, albeit cautiously, to granting greater civic and political liberties to the non-Lutheran and Jewish members of Hamburg's community. The desire for many of these reforms had sprung from the experiences of the eighteenth century and were spurred onward by the increasing size of the city and the baffling complexities of governing. Other innovations had demonstrated their worth under the French. Yet Abendroth, while he exemplified the reform elements in the restored Rat, favored no major innovations that would challenge the existing social and political structures at their apexes. He denied the hubris of 1793, and entertained no hopes of "giving birth to a perfect state." Somewhat like Edmund Burke, he believed "we can most safely near our goals by improving our good and beneficent constitution, whose minor faults we know." He did not seek to experiment for the sake of experimentation, or to substitute for the old anything startlingly new "about which experience can teach us neither what is good nor what is evil." Perhaps he was only being politic, but there is no reason to doubt the sincerity of his conclusion that Hamburg's constitution, "this matchless gift of our forefathers," should remain inviolate.[67]

Reaction, Rebirth, or New Beginning?

What was restored in 1815 was very like what Hamburg had known before the French occupation. Old practices and old traditions persevered, unruffled by the hurricane winds blown up by the French Revolution. The Revolution had found numerous adherents, even enthusiasts, among the elite in Hamburg. But the ideas that flowed from Paris northward were not used to call up the specter of revolution. Instead, they only added impetus to reform initiatives already in motion. Men like Sieveking, Voght, and Günther, among others, tended to interpret events in France as yet another proof of what "bloodthirsty despotism" could lead to, rather than as a model to be emulated. Most agreed with the émigré Charles de Villers that Hamburg's constitution was "a masterpiece of political organization for a small state."[68] Yet change was not completely foiled. In 1814, the Rat and Bürgerschaft jointly appointed a Reorganization Deputation to weigh reform proposals and to suggest improvements in Hamburg's constitution. The twenty members (and therefore the name, the Twenty) were drawn from existing government organs: the Rat, the

Treasury, the Chamber of Commerce, and the various collegial bodies. Christian Pehmöller was one of them.[69] Thus, even the men who sat on the commission (one cannot really call them representatives of a reform party) were intimately tied into Hamburg's traditional governing structure. The Twenty drafted a thirty-six-point plan that proposed modifications in Hamburg's government. None were even faintly tinged with radicalism. Of these, the most important points involved the disconnection of justice from administration in the Rat (previously melded in the persons of the praetors and the Weddeherren), the election of Oberalten (a step toward the separation of church and state), easement of restrictions on settling in Hamburg (especially for wealthy immigrants), citizenship rights for Jews, a thorough revision of the guilds and of guild regulations, and a revamping of municipal finances (especially in the management of the public debt).[70] Even these modest initiatives won few backers and the number of alterations in Hamburg's government at this time (and, for that matter, at least until 1848 or even later) were few. True representative government never received serious study. Most members of the Rat, like the conservative Bürgermeister and "stalwart champion of an enlightened, paternalistic municipal regime," Johann Heinrich Bartels, tended to regard representative government as "demeaning to Hamburg's burghers and incompatible with the freedom and equality of all citizens." An older worldview guided Bartels and a majority of those in government: "Everything for the people, yet nothing by the masses. The first fosters freedom and order, the second breeds revolution and anarchy."[71] It would be ahistorical and shortsighted to dismiss such ideals as mere self-serving duplicity.

In sum, historians generally agree that reforms in Hamburg's government during the Vormärz were meager. The few momentous innovations that took place were in finances, including taxes, in the admission of non-Lutheran Christians to the Bürgerschaft (Jews remained excluded from citizenship until 1848), in some long-desired improvements in commercial laws, harbor regulations, and shipping, in the simplification of Hamburg's territorial administration, and in the separation of judiciary and administrative functions, which, as we have seen, meant the perpetuation of the separate police bureau first set up by the French. It is not presumptuous to assume that the government's first and overriding concern in these years was the restoration of a shattered economy. Certainly it would be unrealistic to anticipate total metamorphosis when the men involved were overwhelmingly holdovers from the old regime: thirteen Bürgermeister and senators (of twenty-four), as well as three of the four syndics, who assumed office again in 1814 had first taken up their (lifelong) offices in the eighteenth century. Indicative of this continuity, the Rat dominated Hamburg's politics as much after 1814 as before.[72] Yet the failure to introduce liberal *political* institutions should not obscure the way other salient developments in the daily governing of the city heralded a future triumph of liberal principles. Not surprisingly, a top-to-bottom restructuring of poor relief after 1814 was among these changes, although one needs to look as well at the separation of justice from administration, and the genesis of a unified police force. Thus much changed while much stayed the same. Hamburg's

elites in the first half of the nineteenth century would be political conserva-
tives *and* yet deny the need for more collective controls on the economy and
on social welfare.[73]

The introduction of new tax laws abetted the demise of an older style of
governing and undermined the older comprehension of what citizenship
meant. For example, in 1815, a series of direct taxes replaced the traditional
indirect ones. The *Schoß,* a property tax that had always been determined "on
the citizen's sworn oath," that is, on the unquestioned testimony of each
individual as to the value of his property, was succeeded by a direct tax
calculated by tax officials. The Schoß had been for centuries "an inseparable
part of the republican self-perception of each Hanseatic burgher." It was fine
perhaps for the fifteenth or even sixteenth centuries, but it was impossible to
administer in a city of thousands of anonymous faces. Yet many bemoaned its
passing. Johann Michael Hudtwalcker, in response to Abendroth's proposal
for direct taxes in his *Wishes,* disparaged "a new statecraft" that mandated
"provable" taxes because "it ridicules the principle that each man is honest
unless he proves himself the contrary."[74] Clearly Hudtwalcker failed to comprehend the essential point that the world in which each man's honesty
quickly demonstrated itself to his neighbors no longer existed.

The ancient role of the praetor also vanished. The praetorship had always
combined administrative tasks, particularly in the realm of social policy, with
the distribution of justice. Now the city established the position of police
senator, which Abendroth, significantly, was the first to fill. Hamburg therefore opted to preserve the French model of an independent police charged
merely with the execution of policy but no longer empowered to formulate it.
For poor relief, this reform had the notable consequence of fixing the Relief's
retreat from policing.[75]

In respect to almshouses and prisons, the municipality also accepted many
French innovations. In 1814–15, a Commission of Prisons superseded the
"Conseil gratuit et charitable des prisons." In 1823, the Commission of Prisons was slightly reshuffled and, at the same time, the government separated
the Werk- und Armenhaus from the Zuchthaus—thus achieving at long last a
complete partition of charitable and correctional facilities. The same commission acquired other responsibilities, some of which the General Poor Relief
had previously borne. For example, the city built an annex to the Zuchthaus
in 1816 to accommodate and treat venereal diseases and scabies. This annex
assumed tasks once filled by the old St. Hiob's Hospital. In 1821, the municipality placed the Lying-In Ward, which the General Poor Relief had founded
in 1796, under the direction of the Bureau of Police.[76] In 1818–19, the city
embarked on a campaign to erect a general hospital to replace the Pesthof,
which had been destroyed during siege preparations. In 1825 the city dedicated the new building, located in the suburb of St. Georg, and it became one
of the first of a growing number of new general hospitals constructed in the
nineteenth century. The revision and codification of the scandalously outdated laws relating to medical practice in Hamburg, which resulted in the
passing of a comprehensive Medical Ordinance in 1818 and the establishment

of a permanent Board of Health, complemented the completion of a modern hospital. But the new medical ordinance differed in no substantial way from the recommendations first advanced by Johann Arnold Günther more than twenty years earlier.[77]

The spirit that impelled these reforms could superficially be termed one of rationalization. The older unity of policing that encompassed, often inadequately and defectively, all sorts of institutions—public welfare, judicial, and corrective tasks—broke apart and was never rejoined. So, too, crumbled time-worn ideals of community. It is easy, of course, to attribute these novelties to the forcible intrusion of French administrative science into an antiquated governing system. The French did propel events along, but it was not the French who first stirred up the winds of change. Everything the French did after 1806, or after 1811, had an indigenous origin in Hamburg and had earlier been contemplated by the patriots of the late eighteenth century, if, however—and this is crucial—within a different setting. Men like Günther, Büsch, Bartels, Voght, and von Heß had all desired to make Hamburg's government more proficient, even more businesslike. Yet they continued to embed their innovations in a matrix of patriotism. Thus, while accepting, even welcoming rationalization and improvement, they always disavowed bureaucracy and disapproved of any attempts to dislodge government from the hands of the patriots, of citizens like themselves. Their projects, especially the General Poor Relief, aspired to retain and tighten the bonds of community, even in the greatly changed and swiftly changing environment of the last half of the eighteenth century. Paternalism was to be preserved as a good in itself and as a measure of social responsibility. The multifunctionality of the General Poor Relief fostered the unity of policing, of social welfare concerns, of education, correction, relief, and assistance that were so dear to Hamburg's patriots. The Relief acted not only as caretaker, educator, and disciplinarian of the poor but also as a school of civic virtue for their social superiors. In the years after 1815, this unity dissipated and came to be deemed "inefficient," "idealistic," and "old-fashioned" by a new generation of men like Pehmöller and Abendroth, whose devotion to improvement and impatience with the adversities of the early 1800s led them to break the older bonds of community and deny—implicitly if never explicitly—the patriotism that had inspired their predecessors. In was not necessary for them to abandon their inherited political conservatism; the new social policies not only fit right in, but they actually also sustained the political inertia of early nineteenth-century liberalism in Hamburg. And poor relief in Hamburg now took a road the patriots of the 1780s and 1790s had undeniably (if unconsciously) opened but never traveled.

The General Poor Relief that emerged after 1815 was very different from its precursor. Historians of social policy have sometimes described the rebirth of the Relief in 1815 as a "new beginning."[78] The desperate financial and economic plight of the city in 1815 seemed to many a far less favorable climate for charitable endeavors than the 1790s. The population had shrunk drastically (according to one observer to about 58,000), the wealthy struggled to regain lost ground, the middling classes fought off impoverishment, and the poor wallowed in misery. The council complained, on the one hand, "of the reduced charity . . . of benefactors as well as of their readiness to ignore the misery of their neighbors, acquaintances, and even relatives," and "shamelessly" referred them to the Relief for assistance. On the other hand, deep-seated immorality and unbelievable viciousness were seen to distinguish those who appealed to the Relief.[79] The numbers requesting assistance, especially in the confused weeks and months following the liberation, shot up steeply. The number of newly admitted families rose from 883 in July 1814 to 1,304 in July 1815; by December 1815, 1,389 families were receiving an average weekly alms of about sixteen shillings.[80] Confronted with these statistical realities, the council felt it had no option but to prune the programs of the Relief even further. This is exactly what was done:

> Where would it have led had we given too much and too indiscriminately? Would not the demand for assistance have become even greater and would we not have run the peril of having to deny help precisely where it was most needed? . . . Our sacred duty is to ensure that no one suffers *real* deprivation; [but] nonetheless sacred is our duty to demonstrate to the pauper how to marshal his own resources and to reawaken his often only slumbering strength. Many of those who chide us and censure [our parsimony] would be astonished to see young couples with a pair of children by the hand appealing for aid when they really should be helping themselves. Our critics would quickly be silenced if they were expected to support those in whom . . . one could clearly discern the marks of their degeneracy and depravity. . . . It is sad but true that the morality of the lower classes has declined enormously [in the past years] and it will take time to restore their old honesty. Admittedly it would be desirable to offer the poor some sort of employment. Still, unhappy experiences [in the past] . . . preclude such endeavors at the present; such [hopes] best remain reserved for the future. We trust that as prosperity slowly returns, more sources of employment will open up and enlarge the existing demand for labor, so that the costs of the Relief will diminish. . . . Even more importantly, this will cultivate the sense of self-respect among the poor and thus [add to] their morality.[81]

Caspar Voght, writing in 1838, commented, "Who can think evil of these men, that they did not restore the Relief to its previous footing?"[82] Just as clearly he viewed these cuts as temporary measures and not as ideals.

Deliberations about the future of the Relief began in the summer of 1814 and dragged on for several months. Not until 1817 did the council issue a new set of guidelines to relief officers.[83] The new Relief offered six forms of assistance: weekly alms for the registered poor (in practice though, restricted almost exclusively to the elderly and to invalids), free schooling, recommendations for admission to other charitable institutions, the foster care of orphaned or abandoned illegitimate children, a onetime allotment of clothing or a onetime loan to distressed workers, and medical care. Despite the seeming range of programs delineated here, this was a far less ambitious approach than that of the 1790s. Visibly missing were provisions for the nonregistered poor.

When rebuked for its penny-pinching methods, the Relief took the offensive in terms that Samuel Smiles would have approved:

> Must we not fear the opposite extreme, that we may support too many unworthy people and that too much assistance may undermine feelings of self-confidence and sap an ability to rely on one's own strength, qualities which are the proper means of self-preservation for *each* human being? It is a tragic state of affairs when we lose our independence. [But] this occurs to a greater or lesser extent whenever we accept charity. Thus only those whose own strength is totally exhausted should receive alms. We believe therefore that we have not acted harshly, only prudently.

The Relief abandoned the position that economic structures or dislocations in the economy—over which individuals had little influence and even less control—*principally* determined both poverty and prosperity among the lower classes. The Relief accepted that temporary economic shifts, and especially the inflation that plagued the early decades of the nineteenth century, immiserated the lower classes. Yet most poverty, the Relief insisted, sprang directly from the flaws of the poor themselves, for

> commerce and business once again [1818] present rich sources of employment for the working classes. New construction and the repair of older buildings offer frequent opportunities for good earnings. Thus the number of those seeking help would not be as great [as it is], our expenditures would not be as enormous [as they are], if only the lower classes would keep their own households in order, and not create so much of their own misery by [concluding] early and frivolous marriages and by [living] thoughtlessly. If the pauper who has arrived at the door of despair would not give up so quickly, but would strain to mobilize his own strength, and learn to regard self-help as honorable, he would not fail [to survive].

After 1815, the Relief predicated its program on the alleviation of existing distress. The prevention of poverty became a repudiated dream. The 1814 commission rejected the older precepts of poor relief as "faulty" and "misconceived," and dished up a far leaner diet of assistance for the poor.[84]

Each branch of the Relief that was not actually erased, was pared back, often drastically. For example, the Relief moved away from disbursing cash and instead distributed soup coupons as a way to prevent fraud. The Relief now granted rent subsidies only in "extremely uncommon" circumstances, whereas previously such subsidies had been perhaps the *most* frequent form of relief. The Relief handed out little in the form of "naturalia," that is, food, fuel, or clothing; medical care was also reduced in scope. From 1816 through 1824, the number of people, especially among the nonregistered poor, who turned to the Relief for medical assistance, skyrocketed as did expenses for their care. In 1817, of the 9,089 persons who obtained medical care, 5,454 (about 60 percent) were nonregistered poor; in 1821, of 16,442, it was 11,301 (almost 70 percent). These statistics shocked the council, which quickly attributed this "paralyzing" assault on its resources to excessive generosity and lack of sufficient rigor on its part and, in particular, on the part of relief officers. Perhaps more realistically, one should seek the causes for this drastic increase of expenditures for medical care in the harshness with which the Relief now greeted supplicants for support: A little medical care was *all* the Relief now promised.[85] Even earlier, in 1814, the council had begun to regard medical care as a creator of poverty, not as a preventive.

> It became customary for any family which did not exactly live in comfort to request free medical care each time a family member felt the least bit un-well . . . [and] so the number of the "ill" multiplied enormously. Soon these same people asked for monetary support [during their illness]. Thus many family fathers whom previously shame had deterred from turning to the Relief, and who, despite a large family, really did not require aid, began to plead for assistance. A child fell sick, and the father realized that it only cost him a trip to the relief officer to obtain free medical care. Otherwise he would never have thought to seek medical advice for such a malady. Now he saw it as his *duty*. A second illness occurred and he [immediately] requested mone-tary support. Once he has come to know the relief officer, he approaches him once each winter for a bit of support for just a few months, "because he has so many children." Then he seeks a prolongation, and thus we finally have a man as a registered pauper who perhaps never would have become one if he had had to request alms [instead of medical care] initially.[86]

The Relief now claimed that the Medical Deputation was frequently called upon to treat illnesses that sprang directly from immorality: to care for those whose dropsy had resulted from furious drinking bouts in taverns and whose consumption had been contracted in dance halls. Consequently, between 1824 and 1829, the Relief introduced several restrictions on medical care. In 1824, the Relief stipulated that those who benefited only from medical care must submit to the embossing of their possessions with the sigil of the Relief, as the registered poor long had to do; they also had to cede their estates to the Relief. In the revised instructions for relief officers circulated in 1829, the Relief decreed: "the nonregistered poor are ineligible for monetary sup-port during illness."[87]

Education was similarly restructured. During the French occupation, a privately organized school convent had intervened and placed pauper children in existing schools when the Relief was forced to close its schools. In 1815, in the decisions surrounding the resurrection of the Relief, the council decided that henceforth it would educate only the children of the registered poor. In 1817, when the Relief considered it once again financially feasible to offer free schooling to some nonpauper children, the Rat, which now provided most of the Relief's income, objected and would not sanction the plan. Moreover, the Relief no longer maintained its own schools, although the Relief paid for tuition and at times hired teachers. And yet, even then, some nonpauper children, though many fewer than before, continued to be educated at the Relief's expense. At the same time, the Relief envisioned education less comprehensively than before. That old combination of basic schooling and vocational training, which Voght had seen as "laying the groundwork for the future," vanished. With its disappearance much of the buoyant optimism of the 1790s dissipated as well. One observer noted that schools after 1815 distributed only "facts" and "skills," no longer providing either "education" or "moral direction."[88]

The Relief similarly denied any obligation to create work for the poor. The economic environment of the 1800s seemed to militate against make-work schemes. Besides, the Relief insisted, it was more imperative

> to impress upon the pauper that he must [first] seek assistance from the circle of his acquaintances; [must] gather his own abilities and apply his own strength, and . . . determine if he cannot nourish himself and his family *honorably* and thus escape the oppressive alms of the Relief. . . . For when the pauper will do nothing to improve his own lot in life, he will sink ever deeper into misery, whereas . . . honest effort will certainly be rewarded.[89]

And in other ways the new regime of poor relief was both harsher in its methods and narrower in its objectives. The three-year residency rule was more rigorously enforced. The Relief no longer exercised the police powers that an earlier generation had regarded as "absolutely indispensable." It wasted little thought and less time on the corrective functions of policing. The new Police Bureau dealt with recalcitrants and mendicants. And the Relief relied less on the free charity of Hamburg's citizens, less on the efforts of patriots, and more on state support. During the period 1800 to 1815, state subventions had come to outweigh voluntary contributions and the trend continued throughout the nineteenth century (see Table 7.2). As the state shouldered the direct responsibilty for the relief of destitution, citizens turned their attentions ever more to private charity and poor relief per se became increasingly punitive and neglected.[90]

One can interpret retrenchment of this kind as simply the inevitable and hardly unreasonable response of an organization with limited resources and massive problems. But one should also see it as part of a wider process in government whereby the older avuncular style of governing, which was bolstered and sustained beyond its capacities by a revived patriotism and the extremely favorable economic situation of the 1790s, finally collapsed under the pressures of population aggregation and the inevitable consequences of massive urbanization and convulsive economic and social changes. The collapse was, of course, hastened by the political debacles of the Napoleonic era. Under all these pressures, Hamburg's communal government and the delicate mixture of private and public roles slowly disappeared. They changed almost imperceptibly in the 1780s and 1790s, and then with a rush in the 1800s. The city's muddled administration went first, soon followed by the apparatus of poor relief erected in the 1790s. Later, the rest of liberalism would develop: separation of church and state, a comprehensive type of citizenship, and finally, belatedly, representative government. State and society had moved apart. Charity became increasingly privatized and compartmentalized as well. As the Relief shed its globality and reduced its tasks, the number of private charities grew immensely, helping to push ever further apart the private and

Table 7.2 General Poor Relief: Sources of Income

Year	Contributions in Thaler	Percentage of Total	State Subventions	Percentage of Total
1789	63,523	81.51	14,405	18.49
1790	68,198	76.29	20,425	22.85
1791	66,311	69.33	28,262	29.55
1792	67,713	71.08	26,637	27.96
1793	68,401	74.10	22,930	24.84
1794	68,160	64.81	35,888	34.12
1795	67,847	58.78	46,666	40.43
1796	84,002	68.34	36,749	29.90
1797	139,540	70.81	53,031	26.91
1798	67,295	50.52	61,191	45.93
1799	68,559	48.95	65,536	46.79
1800	63,894	40.89	82,852	53.03
1801	70,020	50.11	67,554	48.34
1802	67,822	46.24	76,735	52.32
1803	67,098	44.90	80,355	53.77
1804	66,164	51.29	60,224	46.68
1805	64,487	51.13	59,235	46.96
1806	71,997	46.51	81,640	52.74
1807	66,108	41.13	93,439	58.14
1808	67,003	45.78	78,489	53.63
1809	61,531	38.97	94,646	59.94
1810	57,311	30.08	133,234	69.92
1811	54,681	40.73	78,611	58.56
1812	51,741	45.17	61,361	53.57
1813	29,956	45.20	36,107	54.48
1814	10,616	59.93	6,804	38.41
1815	30,111	45.72	33,200	50.41

Source: Kollmann, "Ueberblick," pp. 132–33

Note: Total income also included capital revenues, so percentages here do not necessarily add up to 100 percent.

public spheres.[91] Perhaps this was a necessary corollary to the development of liberalism, of representative government, and, eventually, of democracy, but in the short run at least, it closed the poor and the working classes more completely than ever before out of the community and left them with no champions and no guardians—in the best senses of those often misused words. And if one would hardly wish to argue that the paternalism of eighteenth-century patriots was a perfect and perfectly compassionate or equitable system, it is impossible to believe that the early nineteenth-century liberals in Hamburg did more or succeeded better in succoring the poor.

CONCLUSION

One always hesitates before writing "the end" to an era. Was 1815 a watershed in Hamburg's history, or was there more continuity than change? I argue that there were critical shifts in the mind-set of Hamburg's elites and how the city was governed. Most historians, however, have made the case for continuity, insisting that Hamburg retained its older style of governing at least through the 1840s and 1850s and that the power of its premodern elites persisted well into the machine age almost undiminished.[1] Others have argued that a crassly self-serving regime dominated by "fractions of capital"[2] bore the blame for such disasters as the government's almost total inability to come to grips with the cholera epidemic of 1830, for the Great Fire of 1842 (which devastated half the city), and for the renewed outbreak of cholera in 1892 at a time when the disease had been banished from western Europe by sanitary reform. Part of this argument is acceptable, but the idea that the government of Hamburg *after* 1815 was merely a holdover of a system that existed *before* 1815 is not as credible. There is, of course, no disputing that merchants and lawyers were just as firmly in control. However, the generation that arose after 1815—those men who began to wield power during the French occupation—took a view of city government and social responsibility that was quite different from the generation of Büsch, Voght, Günther, von Heß, Sieveking, and Bartels. This change was particularly marked in social policies. After 1815, quite simply, the city's governors lost their social conscience when they rejected the older sense of community, patriotism, and civic pride that had previously motivated them.

The question that remains to be answered is why. My thesis has been that to a large extent it was the very growth of the city combined with the multiplying complexities of government that engineered the shift. Avuncular government simply failed to keep pace with the demands placed on it by a city of 100,000 and more residents. The patriots of 1765 and 1788 first recognized the problem. They sought its solution in the new tools of administrative expertise (in statistics but not in bureaucracy) and, even more importantly, in an ambitious attempt to regenerate community and revive patriotic commitment. And they were successful, albeit temporarily. Their achievements were at least partly due to their own uncommon vigor, ingenuity, and dedication, but even more to the highly favorable economic milieu of the late eighteenth century. Their nineteenth-century successors followed the far easier path of social laissez-faire, simply ignoring some of the intricacies of governing the metropolis that faced them as they sank deeper into a rush of money making. The extent of this retreat from civic responsibility was well indicated by the way in which the General Poor Relief was reconstituted after 1815. The cholera epidemics and the Great Fire dramatically underscored the deficiencies of government and social policy in the nineteenth century. In contrast, the patriots of 1765 and 1788 were never mere businessmen, despite their conviction that commerce had made Hamburg great, despite their defense of free trade, and despite their own—often fabulous—wealth. As we have seen, the younger Reimarus was perhaps the strongest advocate of free trade and yet, like his compatriots, never affirmed the individual's right to "absolute freedom and arbitrariness [of action] in business," and he accepted the necessity of government intervention whenever and wherever disequilibriums occurred.[3] Considering the expansion of the city as well as the troubles and strains of the early 1800s, it seems almost inevitable that this paternalism and this patriotism declined. But the liberalism that grew from it and replaced it offered no better idea of how to govern and had less sense of social accountability. Liberalism was, therefore, only a partial heir to the patriotism of the eighteenth century. It accepted free trade and valued the individual, but denied the equally important tenet of patriotism: collective responsibility for the common good.

It is hard to laud the virtues of paternalistic government today. No one would want to defend Hamburg's government in the eighteenth century as either democratic or particularly benevolent. For example, no one accepts Curio's curious claim that Hamburg had only a single class, that of citizens. That was patently false. The restrictions on civil and political rights were severe, whether drawn because of religion, wealth, or social class. Yet, when compared to the nineteenth century in Hamburg, there remains much to admire. One should point out that social calcification and political disenfranchisement were possibly *less* pronounced in the eighteenth than in the early nineteenth century. Hamburg's circle of governing elites appears to have been at least slightly more permeable to newcomers in the seventeenth and eighteenth centuries (especially if one adjusts for the numbers who were restricted from access to government by religion) than in the nineteenth century. Moreover, apparently the percentage of citizens actually *declined* during the course of the nineteenth century: In 1875 only 8.7 percent of Hamburg's population (34,000 of 390,000) were citizens.[4] In 1759, about 80 percent of Hamburg's inhabitants were not citizens,[5] but then 20 percent were. (However, it should not be forgotten that the older system of Large Burghers, Small Burghers, and Schutzverwandten had disappeared in the nineteenth century, thus probably reducing the total number of citizens.) And one could also claim that political representation might well have been wider in the eighteenth century at least at the level of deputations and the parishes. There is a rather Tawneyesque ring to all this. Tawney viewed Puritanism as demonstrating an uncomfortable tendency to deny collective social obligations. Yet he admitted that its greatest contribution was a new valuation of the individual.

Early liberalism in Hamburg surely had a darker side: its laissez-faire attitude toward social policies.[6]

Under the reign of social laissez-faire, the program of poor relief in Hamburg was far less comprehensive and far more punitive than it had been.[7] Similarly, poor relief became increasingly a matter for private initiative and decreasingly a concern of the state. Previously, however, poor relief in Hamburg had never been isolated from the more global concerns of governing. Poor relief *was* government. This was reflected in the almost sacrosanct tradition of voluntarism. The existence of close personal contacts between men who faced each other daily in a variety of private and public circumstances was presumed an expedient and desirable way to reach consensus and remedy problems. Since the Reformation, governmental practices and poor relief methods had settled into similar patterns that functioned adequately in a city still knowable, and therefore, governable, by a handful of civic-spirited individuals. Based as it was on a more or less immediate relationship between ruler and ruled, this traditional paternalism held on tenaciously but was slowly losing its grip. The patriotism of the late 1700s rekindled this older paternalism, yet both proved increasingly unable to deal with the problems prevalent in the city Hamburg had become by 1800. A new synthesis was needed, but not forthcoming. The very changes in Hamburg's social and economic structure doomed the older style of government as they had earlier doomed the older forms of poor relief. The transformation of the economy, the growth of the population, the numbers of the laboring poor, the sheer size of the city itself, threw ever heavier burdens on municipal government and its welfare organizations, burdens under which they eventually foundered. Throughout the eighteenth century, Hamburg's voluntarist government still operated, although it moved ever more slowly through tortuously twisted administrative channels. The breakdown of both poor relief and government at the end of the eighteenth century created a consensus of opinion in favor of change. First to be amended were the guidelines defining the social duties of citizens; these were followed much later by more delicate and potentially more volatile shifts in the political identity each citizen assumed. By 1860 the old custom of voluntarism in government was dying (if not yet dead), and so was the citizen's responsibility for active participation in public affairs. Hamburg's growth through the centuries had dissipated civic pride, destroyed the city's unity as a community, and rendered forever obsolete the paternalistic conscience that had once so surely guided city fathers.

NOTES

ABBREVIATIONS

ACN	*Adreß-Comptoir Nachrichten*
ADB	*Allgemeine Deutsche Biographie*
AESC	*Annales. Economies, Sociétés, Civilisations*
AHR	*American Historical Review*
ARG	*Archiv für Reformationsgeschichte*
AZ	*Altonaische Zeitschrift*
BJ	*Braunschweigisches Journal*
CEH	*Central European History*
CSH	*Comparative Studies in Society and History*
EHR	*Economic History Review*
EM	*Ephemeriden der Menschheit*
GG	*Geschichte und Gesellschaft*
GM	*Göttingisches Magazin für Industrie und Armenpflege*
HA	*Hamburg und Altona*
HGB	*Hansische Geschichtsblätter*
HGH	*Hamburgische Geschichts- und Heimatsblätter*
HJ	*The Historical Journal*
HJWG	*Hamburgisches Jahrbuch für Wirtschafts- und Gesellschaftspolitik*
HM	*Hanseatisches Magazin*
HP	*Historische Portefeuille*
IRSH	*International Review of Social History*
JFH	*Journal of Family History*
JHI	*Journal of the History of Ideas*
JFW	*Jahrbuch für Wirtschaftsgeschichte*
JIH	*Journal of Interdisciplinary History*
JMH	*Journal of Modern History*
JSH	*Journal of Social History*
JVGW	*Jahrbuch des Vereins der Geschichte Wiens*
LS	*Leipziger Sammlung von Wirthschaftlichen, Policey-, Cammer- und Finanzsachen*
MVHG	*Mitteilungen des Vereins für Hamburgische Geschichte*
NDB	*Neue Deutsche Biographie*
PP	*Past and Present*

PS	*Population Studies*
RH	*Revue Historique*
RHMC	*Revue d'histoire moderne et contemporaine*
SEHR	*Scandinavian Economic History Review*
SH	*Social History*
SHPB	*Schleswig-Holsteinische Provinzialberichte*
TVG	*Tijdschrift voor Geschiedenis*
TVSG	*Tijdschrift voor Sociale Geschiedenis*
VS	*Verhandlungen und Schriften der Hamburgischen Gesellschaft zur Beförderung der Künste und nützlichen Gewerbe (Patriotische Gesellschaft)*
VSWG	*Vierteljahresschrift für Wirtschafts- und Sozialgeschichte*
ZNF	*Zeitschrift für Niederdeutsche Familienkunde*
ZVHG	*Zeitschrift des Vereins für Hamburgische Geschichte*
ZVLG	*Zeitschrift des Vereins für Lübeckische Geschichte*

Introduction

1. "Bericht über eine im Auftrag der Mährischen Lehensbank durchgeführte Kommerzialreise—Eine zeitgenössische Bestandsaufnahme zur Wirtschaftslage mittel-europäischer Städte um die Mitte des 18. Jahrhunderts (Teil III)," ed. Gustav Otruba, *JFW* (1976/II): 258. Unless otherwise noted, all translations are the author's.

2. Vienna's population in 1750 was about 150,000, in 1800 circa 200,000. Berlin in 1770 had a population of about 130,000, and by 1797 it had grown to 180,000 inhabitants. Helga Schultz (with Jürgen Wilke), *Berlin, 1650–1800: Sozialgeschichte einer Residenz* (Berlin [G.D.R.], 1987), p. 296; and Hans-Ulrich Wehler, *Deutsche Gesellschaftsgeschichte*. Vol. 1: *Vom Feudalismus des Alten Reiches bis zur Defensiven Modernisierung der Reformära, 1700–1815* (Munich, 1987), pp. 69–70.

3. J[ohann] U[lrich] Pauli, *An alle wahre Patrioten Hamburgs gerichtete Ermahnung, zur Aufrichtung einer ähnlichen Patriotischen Gesellschaft, zur Aufnahme der Handlung, der Künste, der Manufacturen und des Ackerbaues, wie die zu London und Paris ist; nebst einer Beylage: Auszug aus der Handlungszeitung von Paris genannt, den gegenwärtigen Zustand beyder Gesellschaften betreffend* (Hamburg, 1765).

4. Johann Arnold Günther, "Versuch einer Geschichte der patriotischen Gesellschaft," *VS* 2 (1792): 87.

5. Pauli, *An alle wahre Patrioten Hamburgs,* p. 15, quoted in Franklin Kopitzsch, *Grundzüge einer Sozialgeschichte der Aufklärung in Hamburg und Altona* (Hamburg, 1982), p. 332.

6. Harvey Chisick, *The Limits of Reform in the Enlightenment: Attitudes Toward the Education of the Lower Classes in Eighteenth-Century France* (Princeton, N.J., 1981), pp. 223–24.

7. Jonathan Knudsen (*Justus Möser and the German Enlightenment* [Cambridge, Eng., 1986], pp. 11–12) points out that the German Enlightenment "retained its special character" because its advocacy of Enlightenment ideals "remained confined within the institutions of the old regime. . . ." Knudsen describes this form of Enlightenment as follows:

> The first component of corporatist or estatist Enlightenment is political paternalism accompanied by an allegiance to the political institutions of the old regime. . . . [T]he

model of the family remained primary, shaping all political arguments. . . . Though certain of these ideas were current elsewhere in Europe, paternalism was central to German enlightened thought. Politically, such paternalism entailed a defense either of the corporate bodies as a form of aristocratic republicanism or of absolute government; socially, it called for the primacy of paternal power in the family and defended the legitimacy of the master-servant relationship; culturally, it raised the ideal of an aristocracy of letters with "naturally" superior corporate rights and privileges.

With some caveats, Knudsen's observations also pertain to the Enlightenment in Hamburg. The best and by far the most complete treatment of the Enlightenment in Hamburg to date is Kopitzsch, *Grundzüge.*

8. This type of paternalism was common in early modern cities. Christopher R. Friedrichs, in his study of Nördlingen (*Urban Society in an Age of War: Nördlingen, 1580–1720* [Princeton, N.J., 1979], pp. 199, 204) describes the paternalism of its city council in this way:

> Nothing is more striking about the council of Nördlingen than the breadth of its concerns. Everything came within its purview, from the weightiest issues of state to the smallest cases of individual misbehavior. For all significant decision making in the community was vested in these fifteen men alone, and they enjoyed a broad conception of their mandate. On one level, the council of Nördlingen, like virtually all governments, was concerned with the maintenance of order, the protection of property, and the preservation of its own authority and resources. Yet at the same time, the councillors attributed to themselves a God-given duty to supervise in close detail the moral conduct of the thousands of souls under their charge. . . . And even beyond this, it is clear that— at least in the sixteenth and seventeenth centuries—the councillors took their obligations to uphold the public welfare seriously and felt a real sense of paternal obligations toward their fellow citizens.

See, generally, chapter 7 of Friedrichs' study.

9. Quote from David Blackbourn and Geoff Eley, *The Peculiarities of German History: Bourgeois Society and Politics in Nineteenth-Century Germany* (Oxford, 1984), p. 154. On the directions historical writing on Germany have taken since World War II, and especially in the 1970s and 1980s, see David Blackbourn's introduction to his *Populists and Patricians: Essays in Modern German History* (London, 1987), pp. 1–29; Richard J. Evans' introduction to *Rethinking German History: Nineteenth-Century Germany and the Origins of the Third Reich* (London, 1987), pp. 1–20; Blackbourn and Eley's introduction to *Peculiarities of German History,* pp. 1–35; R. G. Moeller, "The Kaiserreich Recast? Continuity and Change in Modern German Historiography," *JSH* 17 (1985): 655–83; and Konrad Jarausch, "German Social History— American Style," *JSH* 17 (1985): 349–59.

Among the books that defined the German Sonderweg are the following: Ralf Dahrendorf, *Society and Democracy in Germany* (London, 1967); Barrington Moore, Jr., *Social Origins of Dictatorship and Democracy* (Boston, 1966); Leonard Krieger, *The German Idea of Freedom: History of a Political Tradition* (Boston, 1957); Ernst Fraenkel, *Deutschland und die westlichen Demokratien* (Stuttgart, 1964); Theodor Eschenberg, ed., *The Road to Dictatorship: Germany 1918–1933* (London, 1964); Helmuth Plessner, *Der verspätete Nation: Über die politische Verführbarkeit bürgerlichen Geistes* (Stuttgart, 1959); Gerhard A. Ritter, *Deutscher und britischer Parlamentarismus: Ein verfassungsgeschichtlicher Vergleich* (Tübingen, 1962); Fritz Stern, *The Politics of Cultural Despair: A Study in the Rise of the German Ideology* (Berkeley, Calif., 1961); Kurt Sontheimer, *Antidemokratisches Denken in der Weimarer Republik* (Munich, 1962); Hans-Jürgen Puhle, *Politische Agrarbewegungen in kapitalistischen*

Industriegesellschaften Deutschland, USA und Frankreich im 20. Jahrhundert (Göttingen, 1975); and Klaus Bergmann, *Agrarromantik und Großstadtfeindschaft* (Miesenheim a. Glan, 1970).

Critiques of the Sonderweg thesis include the following: Blackbourn and Eley, *Peculiarities of German History;* Karl Dietrich Bracher et al., eds., *Deutscher Sonderweg: Mythos oder Realität? Kolloquien des Instituts für Zeitgeschichte* (Munich, 1982); Jürgen Kocka, "Der 'deutsche Sonderweg,' " *German Studies Review* 5 (1982): 365–79; Dieter Groh, "Le 'Sonderweg' de l'histoire allemand: mythe ou réalité?" *AESC* 38 (1983): 1166–87; and Helga Grebing, *Der "deutsche Sonderweg" in Europa, 1806–1945: Eine Kritik* (Stuttgart, 1986).

10. See James Sheehan, *German Liberalism in the Nineteenth Century* (Chicago, 1978), pp. 1–48; Rudolf Vierhaus, "Der Aufstieg des Bürgertums vom späten 18. Jahrhundert bis 1848/49," in Jürgen Kocka, ed., *Bürger und Bürgerlichkeit im 19. Jahrhundert* (Göttingen, 1987), pp. 64–78; and Jürgen Kocka, "Bürgertum and Bürgerlichkeit als Probleme der deutschen Geschichte vom späten 18. zum frühen 20. Jahrhundert," in *Bürger und Bürgerlichkeit*, pp. 21–63.

11. See, especially, Jürgen Kocka's introduction to *Bürger und Bürgerlichkeit*, pp. 7–20 and his "Bürgertum und Bürgerlichkeit als Probleme," in *Bürger und Bürgerlichkeit*, pp. 21–63. See also Jürgen Kocka, ed., *Bürgertum im 19. Jahrhundert: Deutschland im europäischen Vergleich*, 3 vols. (Munich, 1988), which contains the papers presented at a symposium held from 12 to 14 December 1985 on "Bürgerlichkeit" as part of the project on the middle classes at the Zentrum für interdisziplinäre Forschung (Zif) at the University of Bielefeld; and Heinz Schilling and Hermann Diedriks, eds., *Bürgerliche Eliten in den Niederlanden und in Nordwestdeutschland: Studien zur Sozialgeschichte des europäischen Bürgertums im Mittelalter und in der Neuzeit* (Cologne and Vienna, 1985).

12. See Percy Ernst Schramm, *Hamburg, ein Sonderfall in der Geschichte Deutschlands* (Hamburg, 1964); see also the chapter on the rise of the middle classes in his *Hamburg, Deutschland und die Welt: Leistung und Grenzen hanseatischen Bürgertums in der Zeit zwischen Napoleon I. und Bismarck: Ein Kapitel deutscher Geschichte* (Munich, 1943), pp. 35–38. Compare Kopitzsch, *Grundzüge*, p. 138.

13. Gerald L. Soliday, *A Community in Conflict: Frankfurt Society in the Seventeenth and Early Eighteenth Centuries* (Hanover, N.H., 1974). See also Christopher R. Friedrichs, "Citizens or Subjects? Urban Conflict in Early Modern Germany," in Miriam U. Chrisman and Otto Gründler, eds., *Social Groups and Religious Ideas in the Sixteenth Century* (Kalamazoo, Mich., 1978), pp. 46–58.

14. Peter Gay referred to Hamburg as a "great port city" that "avoided the decay of most of the others [free cities] by welcoming foreigners of all nationalities and giving them a share in civic and commercial affairs. The Hamburg Constitution of 1712, perhaps the least oligarchical urban charter of the age, reflected this liberal spirit and promoted it." *The Enlightenment: An Interpretation.* Vol. 2: *The Science of Freedom* (New York, 1969), pp. 47–48. Hamburg is also favorably mentioned by Etienne François in "De l'uniformité à la tolérance: Confession et société urbaine en Allemagne, 1650–1800," *Social History—Histoire Sociale* 16 (1983): 7–33. Joachim Whaley points out the problematic nature of this religious toleration in his *Religious Toleration and Social Change in Hamburg, 1529–1819* (Cambridge, Eng., 1985). The image of social peace is challenged in several essays in Jörg Berlin, ed., *Das andere Hamburg: Freiheitliche und demokratische Bestrebungen in der Hansestadt seit dem Spätmittelalter* (Hamburg, 1981). Richard Evans (*Death in Hamburg: Society and Politics in the Cholera Years, 1830–1910* [Oxford, 1987]) is also skeptical of the myth.

15. On the relationship between workers and middle classes, see Jürgen Kocka,

ed., *Arbeiter und Bürger im 19. Jahrhundert: Varianten ihres Verhältnisses im europäischen Vergleich* (Munich, 1986); Jean Gutton, *La Société et les pauvres: L'Exemple de la généralité de Lyon, 1534–1789* (Paris, 1970). My point that a laboring poor emerged in the eighteenth century may be weak. Michel Mollat discovered both "la pauvreté laborieuse" and "pauvres des villes" in the Middle Ages; see his book *Les Pauvres au Moyen Age: Étude Sociale* (Paris, 1979), esp. pp. 192–202. Natalie Z. Davis also describes what is basically a "laboring poor" in "Poor Relief, Humanism, and Heresy," in her *Society and Culture in Early Modern France: Eight Essays* (Stanford, Calif., 1975), pp. 16–64. These are just two studies that suggest the existence of a laboring poor before the eighteenth century. But I think that the assertion is still valid. It is not until the eighteenth century (perhaps earlier in some great commercial centers) that a *mass* class of laboring poor existed whose survival was very closely tied to changes in European- or world-wide markets.

16. Michel Foucault, *Madness and Civilization: A History of Insanity in the Age of Reason* (New York, 1965), *The Birth of the Clinic: An Archaeology of Medical Perception* (New York, 1973), and *Discipline and Punish: The Birth of the Prison* (New York, 1977). Randall McGowen, among others, has pointed out that historians have been far too reductionist in their reading and application of Foucault's arguments ("Foucault Among the Historians," unpublished paper presented at the American Historical Association annual meeting, Cincinnati, 1988). Two important articles on the development of the idea of "social disciplining" are the following: Gerhard Oestreich, "Strukturprobleme des europäischen Absolutismus," *VSWG* 55 (1969): 329–47; and Stefan Breuer, "Die Evolution der Disziplin zum Verhältnis von Rationalität und Herrschaft in Max Webers Theorie der vorrationalen Welt," *Kölner Zeitschrift für Soziologie und Sozialpsychologie* 30 (1978): 409–37. See also Christoph Sachße and Florian Tennstedt, eds., *Soziale Sicherheit und soziale Disziplinierung: Beiträge zu einer historischen Theorie der Sozialpolitik* (Frankfurt, 1986). For examples of works on poor relief that depend, explicitly or implicitly, on social control and social disciplining models, see Sachße and Tennstedt, *Geschichte der Armenfürsorge in Deutschland,* 2 vols. (Stuttgart, 1980, 1988); Robert Jütte, *Obrigkeitliche Armenfürsorge in deutschen Reichsstädten der frühen Neuzeit: Städtisches Armenwesen in Frankfurt am Main und Köln* (Cologne and Vienna, 1984); Nicole Haesenne-Peremans, *Les Pauvres et le pouvoir: Assistance et répression aux pays de Liège (1685–1830)* (Liège, Belgium, 1983); Catharina Lis, *Social Change and the Labouring Poor: Antwerp, 1770–1860* (New Haven, Conn., and London, 1986); Catharina Lis and Hugo Soly, *Poverty and Capitalism in Pre-Industrial Europe* (Brighton, Eng., 1979); Hannes Stekl, *Österreichs Zucht- und Arbeitshäuser, 1671–1920: Institutionen zwischen Fürsorge und Strafvollzug* (Vienna, 1978); idem, "Soziale Sicherung und soziale Kontrolle: Zur österreichischen Armengesetzgebung des 18. und 19. Jahrhunderts," *Bericht über den 14. österreichischen Historikertag in Wien* (1979): 136–51; Bernd Weisbrod, "Wohltätigkeit und 'symbolische Gewalt' in der Frühindustrialisierung: Städtische Armut und Armenpolitik in Wuppertal," in Hans Mommsen and Winfried Schulze, eds. *Vom Elend der Handarbeit: Probleme historischer Unterschichtenforschung* (Stuttgart, 1981), pp. 334–57; Ernst Köhler, *Arme und Irre: Die liberale Fürsorgepolitik des Bürgertums* (Berlin, 1977); and Pierre Bourdieu, "Sur le pouvoir symbolique," *AESC* 23 (1977): 405–11.

17. On the Elberfelder System, see Emil Münsterberg, *Das Elberfelder System: Festbericht aus Anlaß des fünfzigjährigen Bestehens der Elberfelder Armenordnung* (Leipzig, 1903), esp. pp. 4–16; and Sachße and Tennstedt, *Geschichte der Armenfürsorge,* vol. 1, pp. 214–22, 283–89. On the condition of early industrialization in Barmen, see Wolfgang Köllmann, *Sozialgeschichte der Stadt Barmen im 19. Jahrhundert* (Tübingen, 1960).

Chapter 1

1. There are numerous older works that treat the history of poor relief in Hamburg: Werner von Melle, *Die Entwicklung des öffentlichen Armenwesens in Hamburg* (Hamburg, 1883); Kurt Erichson, *Die Fürsorge in Hamburg: Ein Überblick über ihre Entwicklung, ihren gegenwärtigen Stand und dessen gesetzliche Grundlagen* (Hamburg, 1930); Hermann Joachim, "Die Entwicklung von Armenpflege und Wohltätigkeit in Hamburg bis ins 19. Jahrhundert," in his *Historische Arbeiten aus seinem Nachlaß* (Hamburg, 1936), pp. 100–33 and Hermann Joachim, ed., *Handbuch für Wohltätigkeit in Hamburg* (Hamburg, 1901; 2nd ed., 1909); Gustav Schönfeld, "Die Armen in Hamburg während des 16., 17. und 18. Jahrhunderts," *Die Neue Zeit* 14 (1895–96): 316–20, 348–52, 378–84, 411–16; idem, *Beiträge zur Geschichte des Pauperismus und der Prostitution in Hamburg* (Weimar, 1897); Walther Möring, *Die Wohlfahrtspolitik des Hamburger Rates im Mittelalter* (Berlin and Leipzig, 1913); J. C. F. Neßmann, "Hamburg," pp. 262–82 in C. B. Arwed Emminghaus, ed., *Das Armenwesen und die Armengesetzgebung in europäischen Staaten* (Berlin, 1870); Adolf Streng, *Geschichte der Gefängnisverwaltung in Hamburg von 1622–1872* (Hamburg, 1890); Hermann Baumeister, *Die halb-öffentlichen milden Stiftungen in Hamburg* (Hamburg, 1869). Invaluable is the section on poor relief and charitable institutions ("Armen-Verfassungen") in Klefeker, vol. 1, pp. 225–447.

For more recent works, see Renate Hauschild-Thiessen, *Die Niederländische Armen-Casse: "Hamburgs stille wohlthäterin." Ihre Geschichte von 1585 bis zur Gegenwart* (Hamburg, 1974). A few recent publications focus on poor relief in Hamburg in the eighteenth and nineteenth centuries: Detlev Duda, *Die Hamburger Armenfürsorge im 18. und 19. Jahrhundert: Eine soziologisch-historische Untersuchung* (Weinheim and Basel, 1982); Bernhard Mehnke, *Armut und Elend in Hamburg: Eine Untersuchung über das öffentliche Armenwesen in der ersten Hälfte des 19. Jahrhunderts* (Hamburg, 1982). Antje Kraus, *Die Unterschichten Hamburgs in der ersten Hälfte des 19. Jahrhunderts: Entstehung, Struktur und Lebensverhältnisse—Eine historisch-statistische Untersuchung* (Stuttgart, 1965) includes a discussion on poor relief in Hamburg at some length and is far more reliable than the work by Duda. Also useful is Rita Bake, *Vorindustrielle Frauenerwerbsarbeit: Arbeits- und Lebensweise von Manufakturarbeiterinnen im Deutschland des 18. Jahrhunderts unter besonderer Berücksichtigung Hamburgs* (Cologne, 1984). On the development of hospitals in Hamburg, see Heinz [Heinrich] Rodegra, *Vom Pesthof zum Allgemeinen Krankenhaus: Die Entwicklung des Krankenhauswesens in Hamburg zu Beginn des 19. Jahrhunderts* (Münster, 1977).

An excellent short introduction to Hamburg's political life is Jürgen Bolland, *Senat und Bürgerschaft: Über das Verhältnis zwischen Bürger und Stadtregiment im alten Hamburg* (Hamburg, 1954).

2. Christoph Sachße and Florian Tennstedt, *Geschichte der Armenfürsorge in Deutschland* (Stuttgart, 1980), vol. 1, pp. 25–84; Hans Scherpner, *Theorie der Fürsorge* (2nd ed.), ed. Hanna Scherpner (Göttingen, 1974), pp. 42–109; Catharina Lis and Hugo Soly, *Poverty and Capitalism in Pre-Industrial Europe*, trans. James Coonan (Brighton, Eng., 1979), esp. pp. 54–96; Gerhard Uhlhorn, *Die christliche Liebestätigkeit*, 2nd ed. (Stuttgart, 1882–90; reprint ed., Darmstadt, 1959), pp. 495–512; Ludwig Feuchtwanger, "Geschichte der sozialen Politik und des Armenwesens im Zeitalter der Reformation," *Jahrbuch für Gesetzgebung* 32 (1908): 1423–60; ibid., 33 (1909): 191–228; Thomas Fischer, *Städtische Armut und Armenfürsorge im 15. und 16. Jahrhundert: Sozialgeschichtliche Untersuchungen am Beispiel der Städte Basel, Freiburg i. Brsg. und Straßburg* (Göttingen, 1979); and Natalie Zemon Davis, "Poor

Relief, Humanism, and Heresy," in idem, *Society and Culture in Early Modern France: Eight Essays* (Stanford, Calif., 1965), pp. 17–64.

3. See Harold Grimm, "Luther's Contribution to Sixteenth-Century Organization of Poor Relief," *ARG* 61 (1970): 222–34; Georg Ratzinger, *Geschichte der kirchlichen Armenpflege* (Freiburg im Breisgau, 1868), pp. 432–62. This may not be a generous evaluation of sixteenth-century poor relief. In Lyon, at least for a while, a far more ambitious program prevailed. See Davis, "Poor Relief, Humanism, and Heresy."

4. Early in the twentieth century, Feuchtwanger dispelled the myth of any sudden reformation of poor relief policy ("Geschichte der sozialen Politik," pp. 1427, 1430). See also Sachße and Tennstedt, *Geschichte der Armenfürsorge* vol. 1., pp. 30–35, 63–80.

5. von Melle, *Entwicklung,* pp. 3–6; Möring, *Wohlfahrtspolitik,* pp. 100–113; Baumeister, *Stiftungen;* and Klefeker, vol. 1, pp. 227–309.

6. Klefeker points out that "the foundation of [parish] poor relief was at the same time the beginning and basis of [Hamburg's] constitution" (vol. 1, p. 227).

7. These included the eight-membered *Kirchengeschworene* (or *Juraten*), the four *Beeden* (beadles), and the *Leichnamgeschworene.* Collectively they were known as the *Geschworene* and were responsible for church and parish matters including education and poor relief as well as the maintenance of church buildings and the beautification of the altar. The Geschworene occasionally consulted with the Rat on constitutional or political matters. *Hamburg: Geschichte der Stadt und ihrer Bewohner,* vol. 1, *Von den Anfängen bis zur Reichsgründung,* Hans-Dieter Loose and Werner Jochmann, eds. (Hamburg, 1982), pp. 194–95; Klefeker, vol. 1, pp. 232n–34n.

8. My discussion of the Reformation in Hamburg draws heavily on the work of Rainer Postel, *Die Reformation in Hamburg, 1517–1528* (Gütersloh, 1986); his contribution on the Reformation and Counter-Reformation in Loose and Jochmann, eds., *Hamburg: Geschichte der Stadt,* vol. 1, pp. 191–258; and his articles: "Reformation und bürgerliche Mitsprache in Hamburg," *ZVHG* 65 (1979): 1–20; "Obrigkeitsdenken und Reformation in Hamburg," *ARG* 70 (1979): 169–201; "Sozialgeschichtliche Folgewirkungen der Reformation in Hamburg," in Wenzel Lohff, ed., *450 Jahre Reformation in Hamburg: Eine Festschrift* (Hamburg, 1980), pp. 63–84. See also Joachim Whaley, *Religious Toleration and Social Change in Hamburg, 1529–1819* (Cambridge, Eng., 1985), pp. 13–22.

9. Loose and Jochmann, eds., *Hamburg: Geschichte der Stadt,* vol. 1, pp. 211–15; Georg Daur, *Von Predigern und Bürgern: Eine hamburgische Kirchengeschichte von der Reformation bis zur Gegenwart* (Hamburg, 1970), pp. 13–80.

10. "Gottes-Kasten Ordnung. Anfang der Kisten/ so tho Underholdinghe der Armen in Sunte Nicolaus Kercken binnen Hamborch gestellet is," 16 August 1527, in Nicolaus Staphorst, *Historia Ecclesiae Hamburgensis diplomatica, das ist: Hamburgische Kirchen-Geschichte, aus Glaubwürdigen und mehrentheils noch ungedruckten Urkunden . . . Gesammlet beschrieben und in Ordnung gebracht,* pt. 2, vol. 1, pp. 112–23. See also Klefeker, vol. 1, p. 228.

11. The same men simultaneously filled parish and government positions. They bore the titles "deacons" and "subdeacons" in communal government; in the parish they were called Leichnam- and Kirchengeschworene. The office of Oberalte, however, was unknown in the parish and functioned only in secular government. "Articuli, von den Oberalten und Vorstehern uffgerichtet dannach sie sich zu ihren Ampte richten und verhalten sollen. Ao 1568," StAHbg, Senat Cl. VII Lit. Ba, no. 2, vol. 2; Staphorst, *Historia Ecclesiae Hamburgensis,* pt. 2, vol. 1, p. 156; Klefeker, vol. 1, pp. 232n–34n; F.[riedrich] Georg Buek, *Die hamburgischen Oberalten, ihre bürgerliche Wirksamkeit und ihre Familien* (Hamburg, 1857), p. 2; Ursula Rotzoll, "Kastenordnungen der Refor-

mationszeit: Von der mittelalterlichen zur neuzeitlichen Armenpflege," typescript, StAHbg, *Handschriftensammlung* 695.

12. Hamburg's *cursus honorum* usually began with selection as a member of the One Hundred Eighty. Almost all officeholders were chosen directly from that body. New subdeacons were appointed to various government deputations, usually to one of those in charge of collecting the tax on beer or on cattle for slaughter (*Bieraccise* or *Viehaccise*). From this deputation, his career might go in several directions. Martin Reißmann, *Die hamburgische Kaufmannschaft des 17. Jahrhunderts in sozialgeschichtlicher Sicht* (Hamburg, 1975), pp. 364–65; Buek, *Oberalten*, p. 494; and Nicolaus A. Westphalen, *Hamburgs Verfassung und Verwaltung in ihrer allmähligen Entwickelung bis auf die neueste Zeit* (Hamburg, 1841), vol. 1, pp. 216–19.

Normally, officeholders worked on several deputations of lesser importance, often holding many positions concurrently, before being chosen for the more important posts of Treasury representative (*Kammerdeputierte*), bank representative (*Banco-Bürger*), Oberalte, or even senator. The path David Doormann (1715–81) took to the post of Oberalte was similar to that followed by many: at age 30 in 1745, Bieraccise, Mehlkauf, Bürgerzoll; 1747, Admiralitätszoll; 1748, Matten; 1750, Adjunct, Kriegskommissar; 1752, Niedergericht, Gasthaus, Schoß, Feuercasse; 1753, Fortifikation; 1754, Kalkhof; 1757, Artillerie, Admiralität; 1758, Bauhof; 1762, St. Hiob; 1764, Diakonus, Bancobürger; 1765, Regulierung der Ämter, Jurat, Gotteskastenverwalter; 1771, Deputation zur Austiefung des Herrengrabens; 1774, at age fifty-nine, Oberalte; 1775, Börsenalter; 1777, Leichnamgeschworene. Buek, *Oberalten*, pp. 256–57. Buek (p. 302) considers it "very unusual" that two sons of the merchant Johann Hinrich Droop held civic offices in the 1600s without ever being members of the One Hundred Forty-Four.

13. On the Oberalte, see Buek, *Oberalten;* Rudolf Kayser, *Die Oberalten: Festschrift zum vierhundertjährigen Gedächtnis der Einsetzung des Kollegiums* (Hamburg, 1928); Walther Peter Möller, *Chronologische Verzeichnisse der Mitglieder des Rathes, der Oberalten und der Kämmerei-Verordneten* (Hamburg, 1820); and Daur, *Von Predigern und Bürgern*, pp. 330–36.

14. Loose and Jochmann, eds., *Hamburg: Geschichte der Stadt*, vol. 1, p. 196; Postel, "Reformation und bürgerliche Mitsprache in Hamburg," p. 6; Buek, *Oberalten*, p. 144; "Kämmerei-Ordnung 5 April 1563," StAHbg, Senat Cl. VII Lit. La, no. 1, vol. 2b; and no. 9, vol. 3d. The Long Recess is reprinted in *Supplementband zu dem neuen Abdruck der Grundgesetze der Hamburgischen Verfassung und deren Nachträge* (Hamburg, 1825), pp. 47–107.

15. Basil Hall, "The Reformation City," *Bulletin of the John Rylands Library* 54 (1971): 112.

16. "Vollmacht der Bürger den 12. Vorsthendern der Armen und sonst den 24. Verordneten Bürgern aus jedem Kirchspiel gegeven Anno 1528. ante Petri & Pauli," in Staphorst, *Historia Ecclesiae Hamburgensis*, pt. 2, vol. 1, p. 156. On the revival of civic spirit, see Postel, "Reformation und bürgerliche Mitsprache in Hamburg," pp. 16–17, and Bernd Moeller, *Imperial Cities and the Reformation: Three Essays,* ed. and trans. H. C. Erik Midelfort and Mark U. Edwards (Philadelphia, 1972), p. 25.

17. "Gottes-Kasten Ordnung [1527]," in Staphorst, *Historia Ecclesiae Hamburgensis,* pt. 2, vol. 1, pp. 112–23.; [Johannes Bugenhagen], "Der Erbaren Stadt Hamborg Christliche Ordeninge, tho denste dem Evanglio Christi, Christliker heve, Tucht, Frede und Einickeit. 1529," in Aemilius Ludwig Richter, ed., *Die evangelischen Kirchenordnungen des sechszehnten Jahrhunderts: Urkunden und Regesten zur Geschichte des Rechts und der Verfassung der evangelischen Kirche in Deutschland,* vol. 1, *Vom Anfange der Reformation bis zur Begründung der Consistorialverfassung im J. 1542* (Weimar,

1846), pp. 132–34; Karl Bertheau, ed., *Johannes Bugenhagen's Kirchenordnung für die Stadt Hamburg vom Jahre 1529* (Hamburg, 1885), pp. xiii–xiv; "Armenordnung von 1550," and "Armen- und Gottes-Kasten-Ordnung, aufgerichtet Anno 1622," in Klefeker, vol. 1, pp. 310–15.

18. von Melle, *Entwicklung,* pp. 13–23; Johann Georg Büsch, "Historischer Bericht von dem Gange und fortdauernden Verfall des Hamburgischen Armenwesens seit der Zeit der Reformation," in Büsch, *Zwei kleine Schriften die im Werk begriffene Verbesserung des Armenwesens in dieser Stadt Hamburg betreffend* (Hamburg, 1786), unpag., pars. 5–9; and Caspar Voght, *Gesammeltes aus der Geschichte der Hamburgischen Armen-Anstalt während ihrer fünfzigjährigen Dauer* (Hamburg, 1838), p. 6.

19. Büsch, "Historischer Bericht," pars. 5–9.

20. Klefeker, vol. 1, pp. 378–79.

21. A "Rath- und Bürgerschluß" of 7 February 1695 provided for the "Salarirung" of the Oberalte. The Principal Recess of 1712 (*Haupt-Recess*), Art. XIX, canceled the honorarium, but it was quickly restored by a "Rath- und Bürgerschluß" of 22 September 1712, which granted the Oberalte tax exemptions and a "doceur" of 1,000 "Marck Lübisch Species." In 1767, the honorarium was increased to 1,250 marks, in 1806, to 2,000 marks, "Rath- und Bürgerschluß" of 17 February 1767 and 13 November 1806. Westphalen, *Verfassung und Verwaltung,* vol. 1, p. 219.

The Principal Recess of 1712 also required that anyone selected for the office of subdeacon, deacon, Oberalte, senator, Bürgermeister, or any other "Ehrenamt" could not refuse the honor. Refusal to accept the office could result in loss of citizenship and banishment. Only age and illness freed a man once chosen. Westphalen, *Verfassung und Verwaltung,* vol. 1, p. 218. Dispensations were rare, as were requests for them; see "Varia, verschiedene gewährte und abgeschlagene Gesuche um Dispensation von bürgerlichen (und kirchlich-bürgerlichen) Offizien betreffend. 1727–1807," StAHbg, Senat Cl. VII Lit. Bc, no. 13, fasc. 1. See also the short list of resignations from the Rat in StAHbg, Senat Cl. VII Lit. Ab, no. 3, vol. 5.

In 1684, in order to save money, the city decided to sell outright or lease certain, lesser, government positions. Two years later a special permanent deputation (*Deputation zur Regulirung der Aemter*) was set up to manage the sale and lease of offices. Article IX of the Principal Recess divided all municipal offices into three groups: (1) those filled by (s)election and for which there was no payment promised or security demanded (these were the *Ehrenämter*), (2) positions open only to candidates judged capable by the Rat of filling a particular office and who were required to post bond for their actions with the Treasury, and (3) those jobs sold or leased to the highest bidder and that required a fee to be paid to the Treasury. Apparently the sale or lease of office never functioned satisfactorily and, after 1814, all these fees and charges were abolished. Third-category municipal officials were thereafter paid a fixed salary thereby creating for the first time in Hamburg a paid civil service, though a small one. Buek, *Oberalten,* pp. 406–8; Friedrich Voigt, *Beiträge zur hamburgischen Verwaltungsgeschichte:* vol. 1, *Bericht von 1644 mit Vorschlägen für die städtische Verwaltung, insbesondere durch Ersparen an den Besoldungen der Beamten und Angestellten;* vol. 2, *Der Verkauf, später das Verpachten städtischer Dienststellen in Hamburg, 1684–1810* (Hamburg, 1917, 1918); Westphalen, *Verfassung und Verwaltung,* vol. 1, pp. 27–32, 95–96. A list of purchasable offices is found in Jonas Ludwig von Heß, *Hamburg, topographisch, politisch und historisch beschrieben,* 2nd ed., 3 vols. (Hamburg, 1810–11), vol. 3, pp. 431–32.

22. In 1809, Charles de Villars commented on the fine "balance" of Hamburg's government. He praised Hamburg's constitution as a "masterpiece of legislation" that "perhaps deserves to be valued above the most famous laws of the ancient and contem-

porary worlds." Quoted in Loose and Jochmann, eds., *Hamburg: Geschichte der Stadt,* vol. 1., p. 434.

23. Buek, *Oberalten,* pp. 4, 144, 494; Kayser, *Oberalten,* p. 20; Loose and Jochmann, eds., *Hamburg: Geschichte der Stadt,* vol. 1, pp. 217–18, 269–70, 358.

24. Klefeker, vol. 1, p. 230; von Melle, *Entwicklung,* pp. 7–18; Buek, *Oberalten,* pp. 8–9, 412–13, 418–20, 451–55, 476–77; and Rotzoll, "Kastenordnungen," pp. 61–62, 76–79.

25. Kayser, *Oberalten,* p. 52; "E. Oberalten Aemter-Rollen von 1715–1766," StAHbg, Senat Cl. VII Lit. Ba, no. 2, vol. 2; Reißmann, *Kaufmannschaft,* pp. 340–68.

In the late eighteenth century, the Oberalte raised objections to the "revolutionary" *société littéraire* founded by the Klopstock-Sieveking circle. The Oberalten were also poorly represented in Hamburg's leading enlightened society—the Patriotic Society of 1765. Only five Oberalten were members: Rudolf Amsinck (1789–1809), Johann Phillip Tietjens (1786–87), Johann Friedrich Tonnies (1795–1805), Claes Bartels (1797–1806), and Peter Friedrich Röding (1837–46). It must be noted, however, that Tonnies and Bartels were very active in forming and then administering the new General Poor Relief of 1788. Kayser, *Oberalten,* p. 56; and *Mitglieder und Associirte der Hamburgischen Gesellschaft zur Beförderung der Künste und nützlichen Gewerbe von ihrer Stiftung im Jahr 1765 an bis in die Mitte des Jahres 1803* (Hamburg, 1803).

26. Loose and Jochmann, eds., *Hamburg: Geschichte der Stadt,* vol. 1, p. 358.

27. Reißmann, *Kaufmannschaft,* pp. 340–68; Geert Seelig, *Die geschichtliche Entwicklung der hamburgischen Bürgerschaft und die hamburgischen Notabeln* (Hamburg, 1900), pp. 148–49. See also Wilhelm Bleek, *Von der Kameralausbildung zur Juristenprivileg: Studium, Prüfung und Ausbildung der höhern Beamten des allgemeinen Verwaltungsdienstes in Deutschland im 18. und 19. Jahrhundert* (Berlin, 1972), and Percy Ernst Schramm, *Hamburg, ein Sonderfall in der Geschichte Deutschlands* (Hamburg, 1964). J. K. Curio did not merely flatter his adopted city when he said: "We have no nobles [here], no patricians, no slaves, no, not even subjects. All true Hamburgers belong to and acknowledge only one class, that of burgher. We are all burghers, nothing more and nothing less!" *HA* 1, no. 3 (1803): 78, quoted in Schramm, *Hamburg, ein Sonderfall,* p. 16.

The following table (assembled from figures presented by Reißmann, *Kaufmannschaft,* p. 236) demonstrates the relative permeability of Hamburg's major communal offices to immigrants:

Office	Immigrants	Percentage	Natives	Percentage	Total
Commerce Deputy	10	14.08	56	78.87	71
Juraten					
St. Petri	30	30.30	65	65.65	99
St. Nikolai	34	35.05	58	59.79	97
Leichnamgeschworene					
St. Petri	6	25	18	75	24
St. Nikolai	6	28.57	15	71.43	21
Treasury Deputy	43	25.6	119	70.83	168
Bank Deputy	14	15.91	70	79.55	88
Oberalte	52	32.1	101	62.35	162
Ratsherrn (merchants)	22	25	63	71.59	88
Bürgermeister (merchants)	1	16.66	4	66.66	6
Totals	218	26.46	569	69.05	824

Percentages do not total 100 because background information is missing on some officeholders. Between 1713 and 1815, 20 percent of Oberalten were emigrants to Hamburg. Franklin Kopitzsch, *Grundzüge einer Sozialgeschichte der Aufklärung in Hamburg und Altona* (Hamburg, 1982), pp. 158, 200–3.

28. Reißmann, *Kaufmannschaft,* pp. 340–64, esp. pp. 353–55, 366–68.

29. For example, three or more members of the following families were all Oberalten: von Spreckelsen (7), Sillem (6), Schröttingk (5), von Eitzen (4), Jacobson (4), Rentzler (4), Moller (4), Rentzel (4), von der Fechte (4), Amsinck (3), Beckmann (3), Doormann (3), Heisterbach (3), Kellinghusen (3), Langenbeck (3), Langermann (3), Schroeder (3), Stampel (3), von Kampe (3), Wetken (3), Wichmann (3), and Witte (3). This list covers the period 1528–1860. Kayser, *Oberalten,* p. 20.

30. There are numerous family histories available. The collective biographies I found most useful are the following: Percy Ernst Schramm, *Hamburg, Deutschland und die Welt: Leistung und Grenzen hanseatischen Bürgertums in der Zeit zwischen Napoleon I. und Bismarck. Ein Kapitel deutscher Geschichte* (Munich, 1943; 2nd ed. Hamburg, 1952), pp. 29–30; idem, *Neun Generationen: Dreihundert Jahre deutscher "Kulturgeschichte" im Lichte der Schicksale einer Hamburger Bürgerfamilie, 1648–1948,* 2 vols. (Göttingen, 1963–64); idem, *Gewinn und Verlust: Die Geschichte der Hamburger Senatorenfamilien Jencquel und Luis (16. bis 19. Jahrhundert): Zwei Beispiele für den wirtschaftlichen- und sozialen Wandel in Norddeutschland* (Hamburg, 1969); Hildegard von Marchthaler, *Aus Alt-Hamburger-Senatorenhäuser: Familienschicksale im 18. und 19. Jahrhundert* (Hamburg, 1966). See also Reißmann, *Kaufmannschaft.* Cf. Ruth Prange, *Die bremische Kaufmannschaft in sozialgeschichtlicher Betrachtung* (Bremen, 1963).

On individual families, Hans Kellinghusen, *Geschichte der Familie Kellinghusen:* vol. 1, *Die Stammfolge der Familie in Hamburg von Hans bis Jürgen Kellinghusen, 1507–1686 (1757)* (Hamburg, 1919); vol. 2, mss. in StAHbg, Bibliothek; "Amsinck, führende Hamburger Kaufmanns- , Reeder- und Juristengeschlecht niederländischer Herkunft," *NDB;* "Hermann Doormann, Hamburger Diplomat und Syndicus (1752–1820)," *NDB;* and G. Heinrich Sieveking, "Vom Leben auf dem Hammerhofe vor 100 Jahren," *HGH* 14, no. 3 (1853): 191–98.

31. Buek, *Oberalten,* pp. 17–21, 112, 163, 384; Reißmann, *Kaufmannschaft,* pp. 40, 289, 363, 372, 375, 377; "Anckelmann," in *Lexikon der Schriftsteller;* Wilhelm Heyden, "Die Familie Anckelmann in Hamburg," *ZNF* 7 (1925): 273–79.

32. Percy Ernst Schramm, "Die von den Hamburgern bevorzugten Universitäten (Ende des 17. bis Anfang des 18. Jahrhunderts," *ZVHG* 52 (1966): 83–90; Hans Bruhn, "Hamburger Studenten auf der Universität Göttingen 1734 bis 1837," *ZNF* 30 (1955): 117–29, 168–70; Marc Raeff, *The Well-Ordered Police State: Social and Institutional Change Through Law in the Germanies and Russia, 1600–1800* (New Haven, Conn. and London, 1983), pp. 45, 129; and Keith Tribe, "Cameralism and the Science of Government," *JMH* 56 (1984): 263–84.

33. Buek, *Oberalten,* pp. 81–84, 99, 109–10, 463; "Rentzel," *Lexikon der Schriftsteller;* and Reißmann, *Kaufmannschaft,* pp. 117, 120, 140, 337, 177, 380.

34. Michel Foucault, *Discipline and Punish: The Birth of the Prison* (New York, 1977).

35. On Hamburg's "poorhouses," see Klefeker, vol. 1, pp. 227–447; von Melle, *Entwicklung,* pp. 24–63; Adolf Streng, *Geschichte der Gefängnisverwaltung in Hamburg von 1622–1872* (Hamburg, 1890), pp. 7–70 (Werk- und Zuchthaus), pp. 71–101 (Spinnhaus); Anton Hagedorn, "Das Werk- und Zuchthaus in seiner historischen

Entwicklung," archival report, StAHbg, Bibliothek; Andreas Ehrenfried Martens, *Das Hamburgische Criminal-Gefängniss genannt: Das Spinnhaus und die übrigen Gefängnisse der Stadt Hamburg nach ihrer innern Beschaffenheit und Einrichtung beschrieben, nebst einigen Ansichten und Ideen über Verbesserung ähnlicher Anstalten überhaupt* (Hamburg, 1823); and Heinrich Sieveking, "Hamburger Gefängnisfürsorge im 18. Jahrhundert," *AZ* 3 (1933–34): 94–106.

36. Klefeker, vol. 1, pp. 243–45; "Von der Stiftung des Waisen-Hauses. Ordnung des Waisen-Hauses, von Anno 1604 den 27 September," Klefeker, vol. 1, pp. 322–51; Meno Günter Kiehn, *Das hamburgische Waisenhaus: Geschichtlich und beschreibend dargestellt* (Hamburg, 1821), pp. 1–29.

37. "Von der Stiftung des Waisen-Hauses," Klefeker, vol. 1, pp. 325–26, 329.

38. Foucault, *Discipline and Punish;* Lis and Soly, *Poverty and Capitalism,* pp. 116–29; Sachße and Tennstedt, *Geschichte der Armenfürsorge,* vol. 1, pp. 112–25, 159–73; Hannes Stekl, *Östereichs Zucht- und Arbeitshäuser, 1671–1920: Institutionen zwischen Fürsorge und Strafvollzug* (Vienna, 1978); Volker Hunecker, "Überlegungen zur Geschichte der Armut im vorindustriellen Europa," *GG* 9 (1983): 498.

39. Lis and Soly, *Poverty and Capitalism,* p. 120. Sachße and Tennstedt give somewhat different dates, for Bremen 1609, for Lübeck 1613, and for Hamburg (incorrectly) 1620 (*Geschichte der Armenfürsorge,* vol. 1, p. 113).

40. "Florrentissimum Emporium totius Germaniae" was how the City Physician, Johannes Böckel, described Hamburg in his *Pestordnung in der Stadt Hamburg* (Hamburg, 1597), unpag.

On the Dutch influence, see Loose and Jochmann, eds., *Hamburg: Geschichte der Stadt,* vol. 1, pp. 240, 250, 265–66; Hauschild-Thiessen, *Die Niederländische Armen-Casse;* A. Hallema, *Geschiedenis van het gevangeniswezen hoofdzakelijk in Nederland* (The Hague, 1958); and Thorsten Sellin, *Pioneering in Penology: The Amsterdam Houses of Correction in the 16th and 17th Centuries* (London, 1944).

41. "Ordnung des Zuchthauses, vom 8. März 1622," Klefeker, vol. 1, pp. 283–88, 373–407. On the history of the Zuchthaus, von Melle, *Entwicklung,* pp. 39–43; Streng, *Gefängnisverwaltung,* pp. 7–70; Hagedorn, "Werk- und Zuchthaus"; Christian Ludewig von Griesheim, *Verbesserte und vermehrte Auflage des Tractats: die Stadt Hamburg in ihrem politischen, öconomischen und sittlichen Zustande; nebst Nachträgen zu diesem Tractate; und Beyträgen zu der Abhandlung: Anmerckungen und Zugaben* (Hamburg, 1760), pp. 58–62; von Heß, *Hamburg* (2nd ed.), vol. 2, pp. 106–60; "Beschreibung der Gebäude [Zuchthaus]," n.d. (beginning of seventeenth century), in StAHbg, Gefängnisverwaltung, A25; and "Der Zustandt unndt Gelegenheidt des Werck und Zuchthauses zu Hamburgk, auch die Disciplin unndt Zucht so darin gehalten wirdt," n.d. (beginning of seventeenth century), StAWf 2 Alt 14609, pp. 31–32.

42. Hagedorn, "Werk- und Zuchthaus," p. 3; Klefeker, vol. 1, pp. 384–85, 394, 405; Streng, *Gefängnisverwaltung,* pp. 28–29; Gerhard Comminchau, "Zur Geschichte der hamburgischen Jugendfürsorge im 18. Jahrhundert," (Ph.D. diss., Hamburg, 1961), pp. 55–58, 150–62.

43. von Melle, *Entwicklung,* pp. 24–63.

44. Streng, *Gefängnisverwaltung,* pp. 31–36, 39; von Heß (2nd ed.) vol. 2, pp. 106–59. The "Bettel-Ordnungen" were numerous. The "Mandate gegen die Betteley," promulgated on 11 March 1692, was typical in its provisions and served as a model for later ordinances, Blank, vol. 1, pp. 421–24.

45. Klefeker, vol. 1, pp. 389–90; Streng, *Gefängnisverwaltung,* pp. 58–66; von Heß, *Hamburg* (2nd ed.), vol. 2, pp. 119–31, esp. the long footnote on pp. 122–26.

46. Klefeker, vol. 1, pp. 378–400; Streng, *Gefängnisverwaltung,* pp. 26–70; von Heß, *Hamburg* (2nd. ed.), vol. 2, pp. 132, 141, 144–46; and "Verzeichniss der Provisoren, 1615–1811," StAHbg, Gefängnisverwaltung, A19.

47. Loose and Jochmann, eds., *Hamburg: Geschichte der Stadt,* vol. 1, pp. 269–81; Hans-Dieter Loose, "Die Jastram-Snitgerschen Wirren in der zeitgenössischen Geschichtsschreibung," *ZVHG* 53 (1967): 1–20; C.[hristian] F.[riedrich] Wurm, *Der europäische Hintergrund der Snitger-Jastram'schen Wirren in Hamburg 1686* (Hamburg, 1855); and Hermann Rückleben, *Die Niederwerfung der hamburgischen Ratsgewalt: Kirchliche Bewegungen und bürgerliche Unruhen im ausgehenden 17. Jahrhundert* (Hamburg, 1970), p. 359.

48. Loose and Jochmann, eds., *Hamburg: Geschichte der Stadt,* vol. 1, pp. 281–87; Whaley, *Religious Toleration,* pp. 17–19; Daur, *Von Predigern und Bürgern,* pp. 108–24; Gerd Augner, *Die kaiserliche Kommission der Jahre 1708–1712: Hamburgs Beziehung zu Kaiser und Reich zu Anfang des 18. Jahrhunderts* (Hamburg, 1983).

49. Ludwig von Heß, *Unwiederrufliches Fundamental-Gesetz, Regimentsform, oder Haupt-Receß der Stadt Hamburg* (Hamburg, 1781), pp. 3–4; Heinrich Hübbe, *Die kaiserliche Commission in Hamburg* (Hamburg, 1856), pp. 272–318; Loose and Jochmann, eds., *Hamburg: Geschichte der Stadt,* vol. 1, pp. 358–59; Whaley, *Religious Toleration,* pp. 20–22; and "Vereinigung zwischen Oberalten, Sechszigern und Hundertachtzigern in 1712. Mai 25," StAHbg, Senat Cl. VII Lit. Bb, no. 6. More generally on these conflicts over sovereignty in the imperial free cities, see Otto Brunner, "Souveränitätsproblem und Sozialstruktur in den deutschen Reichsstädten der frühen Neuzeit," *VSWG* 50 (1973): 329–60.

50. By far the most complete discussion of the 1712–14 epidemic in Hamburg is Adolf Wohlwill, *Hamburg während der Pestjahre, 1712–1714* (Hamburg, 1893). Most of the documents available to Wohlwill were destroyed in World War II. See also Hermann Gustav Gernet, *Mittheilungen aus der älteren Medicinalgeschichte Hamburgs: Kulturhistorische Skizze auf urkundlichem und geschichtlichem Grunde* (Hamburg, 1869), pp. 273–84; for contemporary observations on the plague, see Johann Franz Beerwinckel, *Excerpta quaedam ex observatis in nupera peste Hamburgensi* (Jena, 1714) and Wolfgang Matthias Brunner, *Observationes bei der sogenannten Contagion, welche sich Anno 1712 in Hamburg angefangen und 1714 geendigt* (Regensburg, 1715). On earlier plague epidemics and municipal ordinances passed to deal with them, see Gernet, *Mittheilungen,* pp. 101–7 and "Erinnerung daß ein jeder dem Pest- und Kranken-Hause vor dem Millern-Thore mildiglich unter die Arme greifen soll," 4 September 1664 (Blank, vol. 1, p. 220) and 25 March 1666 (Blank, vol. 1, p. 229).

51. Wohlwill, *Pestjahre,* pp. 42–44, 50–52, 67; Gernet, *Mittheilungen,* pp. 264, 287; a mandate of 30 December 1707 forbade all Polish Jews admission to the city (Wohlwill, *Pestjahre,* p. 4); it was repeated in 1710, "Mandat, zur Abweisung der Pohlnischen und andern Bettel-Juden bey den Contagieusen Läuften," 29 January 1710 (Blank, vol. 2, pp. 648–50). See also other mandates relevant to plague control in 1710 and 1711 in Blank, vol. 2. For later mandates relevant to plague control, see notes 53 and 54 below.

52. Wohlwill, *Pestjahre,* pp. 54, 64–70, 70n, 109, 112–13; Brunner (*Observationes*) advanced an anticontagionist viewpoint and argued that the "political institutions" established to prevent or combat the plague "not only are futile" but were "even more painful and harmful [to the community] than the plague itself." A report from October 1713 ("Rationes gegen die Abschleissung des Ochsen- und Billwerders von der Stadt Hamburg"), pointed out that "Hamburg is burdened with more than 30,000 people

who, because of the decline in commerce, have no way to earn their living." Two other reports, from 12 and 19 September 1713, mentioned that the number of needy inhabitants was almost 40,000 in the city (Wohlwill, *Pestjahre,* p. 67n).

53. Wohlwill, *Pestjahre,* p. 67; von Melle, *Entwicklung,* pp. 54–56; Klefeker, vol. 1, p. 295; "Zur Zeit der contagieusen Läufte beliebte Armen-Ordnung," 24 August 1711 (Blank, vol. 2, pp. 724–29). The "Armen-Ordnung" was also published separately as *E.E. Rahts der Stadt Hamburg, Armen-Ordnung de Anno 1711.* Further references are to this form of the Armen-Ordnung [Cited as *Armen-Ordnung 1711*].

54. *Armen-Ordnung 1711,* pp. 2–4, 8–11. Numerous other plague-related ordinances were passed in these years of which the most important were the "Mandate wider die Gassen-Betteley, nach eingeführter neuer Armen-Ordnung, und in Absicht auf die Contagion," 11 September 1711 (Blank, vol. 2, pp. 739–42); "Verordnung zur Abwendung der Contagion, nach errichtetem Collegio Sanitatis," 18 September 1711 (Blank, vol. 2, pp. 742–46); "Mandat wegen der Contagion," 7 September 1712 (Blank, vol. 2, pp. 783–89); "Contagions-Verordnung, besonders wegen des Collegii Sanitatis und dessen Bedienten," 8 September 1713 (Blank, vol. 2, pp. 814–24); "Mandat gegen die abermals eingerissene Gassen-Betteley," 30 November 1714 (Blank, vol. 2, p. 857), and the similar mandate from 10 September 1717 (Blank, vol. 2, pp. 902–3); "Conl. & Commis. der löbl. Colonell, zu veranstalten, daß ein jeder Capitain in seiner Compagnie eine accurate Liste aller darin befindliche Personen verfertigen, auch die Schor[n]steine aufzeichnen soll," 6 March 1709 (Blank, vol. 2, pp. 602–4); "Warnung, bey der contagieusen Läuften niemand ohne Paß in die Häuser auf- und anzunehmen," 22 August 1710 (Blank, vol. 2, pp. 662–64).

55. *Armen-Ordnung 1711,* pp. 11–12 and "Praesation der zum Behuf der Armen Ordnung destinirten Einzeichnungs-Bücher," 10 March 1712 (Blank, vol. 2, pp. 756–59).

56. Wohlwill, *Pestjahre,* pp. 116–18. On Garlieb Sillem, see Buek, *Oberalten,* pp. 48, 107–8 and *ADB.*

57. The praetors, *Präturen* or *Gerichtsverwalter,* were members of the Rat appointed to the lower court in Hamburg, the *Niedergericht.* They were also empowered to decide petty claims of less than 40 marks and certain minor offenses. In Hamburg, the two praetors closely approximated what were in other cities often referred to as police magistrates. They exercised their police powers summarily, that is, at their own discretion and in absence of a formal process. In particular, they were charged with punishing beggars, vagrants, vagabonds, prostitutes, ship thieves, and brawlers. These cases—like domestic, matrimonial, and paternity disputes—were conducted "auf den Dielen," that is, summarily, and originally as the phrase suggests, in the entry hall of the praetor's home. Klaus Bramst, *Das hamburgische Strafrecht im 17. Jahrhundert: Der Übergang vom städtischen zum gemeinen Strafrecht* (Hamburg, 1958), p. 140; Klefeker, vol. 3, pp. 478–79; The best descriptions of the office and its tasks are those "handbooks" compiled by praetors for their successors in office. See Nicolas Schuback, "Versuch einer systematischen Abhandlung von richterlichen Ampte in Hamburg," StAHbg, Senat Cl. VII Lit. Ma, no. 5, vol. 3d3, section I, p. 11; Matthias Schülter, "Von den Rechten und Pflichten der Gerichtsverwalter in Hamburg," ca. 1715, StAHbg, Senat Cl. VII Lit. Ma, no. 5, vol. 3dl; Johann Schulte, "Aufzeichnungen über die Zweite und Erste Praetur, 1796–1798, fortgesetzt von Johann Arnold Günther, 1798–1800," StAHbg, Senat Cl. VII Lit. Ma, no. 5, vol. 3d6, pp. 93–95. See also "Drey Extract. Prot. extraj. Senatus, die Bestrafung der Unzucht betreffend," 27 June 1732 (Blank, vol. 3, pp. 1176–80).

58. As is well illustrated by the "Em[p]fang und Ausgabeabrechnungen der Prätoren," StAHbg, Kämmerei I, no. 196 (by years). For a specific example of the

competencies of praetors, see Mary Lindemann, "Maternal Politics: The Principles and Practice of Maternity Care in Eighteenth-Century Hamburg," *JFH* 9, no. 1 (Spring 1984): 47–51.

59. [Moses Pitt] and William Nicolson, *The English Atlas*, vol. 2, *Containing the Description of Part of the Empire of Germany viz. The Upper and Lower Saxony* (Oxford and London, 1681), p. 55.

Chapter 2

1. Johannes Böckel, *Pestordnung in der Stadt Hamburg* (Hamburg, 1597), unpag.

2. Loose and Jochmann, eds., *Hamburg: Geschichte der Stadt,* vol. 1, pp. 247–51, and Richard Ehrenberg, "Hamburger Handel und Handelspolitik im 16. Jahrhundert," pp. 281–321 in Karl Koppmann, *Aus Hamburgs Vergangenheit: Kulturhistorische Bilder aus verschiedenen Jahrhunderten,* 2 vols. (Hamburg, 1885–86), vol. 1. On the Dutch influence in Hamburg, see Robert van Roosbroeck, "Die Niederlassung von Flamen und Wallonen in Hamburg (1567–1605): Ein Überblick," *ZVHG* 49/50 (1964): 53–76; C. H. Wilhelm Sillem, "Zur Geschichte der Niederländer in Hamburg von ihrer Ankunft bis zum Abschluß des niederländischen Contracts 1605," *ZVHG* 1 (1841): 241–48; *Hamburg und Holland: Kulturelle und wirtschaftliche Beziehungen* (Berlin, 1940); Ludwig Beutin, "Aus der Wirtschaftsgeschichte der Hansestädte und der Niederlande [rev. art.]," *VSWG* 38 (1949): 69–78; and Renate Hauschild-Thiessen, *Die Niederländische Armen-Casse: "Hamburgs stille Wohlthäterin." Ihre Geschichte von 1585 bis zur Gegenwart* (Hamburg, 1974). On the establishment of the stock exchange (*Börse*) in Hamburg, see Gottfried Klein, *400 Jahre Hamburger Börse: Eine geschichtliche Darstellung* (Hamburg, 1958) and Gustav Heinrich Kirchenpauer, *Die alte Börse, ihre Gründer und ihre Vorsteher: Ein Beitrag zur hamburgischen Handelsgeschichte* (Hamburg, 1841).

3. On the Bank, see Heinrich Sieveking, "Die Hamburger Bank 1619–1875," in *Festschrift der Hamburgischen Universität ihrem ehrenrektor Herrn Bürgermeister Werner Melle . . . zum 80. Geburtstag am 18. Oktober 1933 dargebracht* (Gluckstadt and Hamburg, 1933), pp. 21–110. On the Commerz-Deputation, see Klefeker, vol. 6, pp. 406–11; Ernst Baasch, *Die Handelskammer zu Hamburg, 1665–1913,* 3 vols. (Hamburg, 1915), vol. 1; and *Dokumente zur Geschichte der Handelskammer Hamburg* (Hamburg, 1965), pp. 13–72.

4. Loose and Hochmann, eds., *Hamburg: Geschichte der Stadt,* vol. 1, pp. 288, 328–34; Martin Reißmann, *Die hamburgische Kaufmannschaft des 17. Jahrhunderts in sozialgeschichtlicher Sicht* (Hamburg, 1975), pp. 48–53, 61–62; Ernst Baasch, ed., *Quellen zur Geschichte von Hamburgs Handel und Schiffahrt im 17., 18. und 19. Jahrhundert* (Hamburg, 1910), pp. 108–70; Percy Ernst Schramm, *Deutschland und Übersee. Der deutsche Handel mit den anderen Kontinenten, insbesondere Afrika, von Karl V. bis zum Bismarck: Geschichte der Rivalität im Wirtschaftsleben* (Braunschweig, Berlin, Hamburg, and Kiel, 1950), pp. 18–50; Ernst Baasch, "Hamburgs Seeschiffahrt und Waarenhandel vom Ende des 16. bis zur Mitte des 17. Jahrhunderts," *ZVHG* 9 (1894): 295–420, and his *Handelskammer,* vol. 1, pp. 16–117; Wilhelm Schmidt, "Die wirtschaftlichen Folgen des 30-jährigen Krieges für Hamburg," (Ph.D. diss., Hamburg, 1921); Hermann Kellenbenz, *Unternehmerkräften Hamburger Portugal- und Spanienhandel, 1590–1625* (Hamburg, 1954), pp. 105–6; Hans Pohl, *Die Beziehungen Hamburgs zu Spanien und dem spanischen Amerika in der Zeit von 1740 bis 1806* (Wiesbaden, 1963); Sune Dalgård, "Hamburg-Iberian Trade, 1590–1625," *SEHR* 9,

no. 2 (1962): 195–204; Fred-Conrad Huhn, "Die Handelsbeziehungen zwischen Frankreich und Hamburg im 18. Jahrhundert unter besonderer Berücksichtigung der Handelsverträge von 1716 und 1769" (Ph.D. diss., Hamburg, 1952); Christoph Friedrich Menke, "Die wirtschaftlichen und politischen Beziehungen der Hansestädte zu Rußland im 18. und frühen 19. Jahrhundert" (Ph.D. diss., Göttingen, 1959); Eike Eberhard Unger, "Nürnbergs Handel mit Hamburg im 16. und beginnenden 17. Jahrhundert," *Mitteilungen des Vereins für Geschichte der Stadt Nürnberg* 54 (1966): 1–85; and Herbert Koch, "Handelsbeziehungen zwischen Hamburg und Jena 1768 bis 1786," *HGH* 17 (1959): 1–9. In 1793 a senator commented that "the commerce with France is the most substantial and for us the most advantageous branch [of trade]." Quoted in Walter Grab, *Demokratische Strömungen in Hamburg und Schleswig-Holstein zur Zeit der ersten französischen Republik* (Hamburg, 1966), p. 23.

5. Loose and Jochmann, eds., *Hamburg: Geschichte der Stadt,* vol. 1, pp. 374–77; Erwin Wiskemann, *Hamburg und die Welthandelspolitik von den Anfängen bis zur Gegenwart* (Hamburg, 1929), pp. 110–42; Erich von Lehe, Heinz Ramm, and Dietrich Kausche, *Heimatchronik der Freien und Hansestadt Hamburg,* 2nd. ed. (Cologne, 1967), pp. 117–27; Pierre Jeannin, "Die Hansestädte im europäischen Handel des 18. Jahrhunderts," *HGH* 89 (1972): 41–73; Walther Vogel, "Handelskonjunkturen und Wirtschaftskrisen in ihrer Auswirkung auf den Seehandel der Hansestädte," *HGH* 74 (1956): 63–64; Sieveking, "Hamburger Bank," p. 70.

6. Loose and Jochmann, eds., *Hamburg: Geschichte der Stadt,* vol. 1, pp. 374–77; Franklin Kopitzsch, *Grundzüge einer Sozialgeschichte der Aufklärung in Hamburg und Altona* (Hamburg, 1982), pp. 178–85; Vogel, "Handelskonjunkturen," pp. 50–64; Helen Liebel, "Laissez-faire vs. Mercantilism: The Rise of Hamburg and the Hamburg Bourgeoisie vs. Frederick the Great in the Crisis of 1763," *VSWG* 52 (1965): 224; Franklin Kopitzsch, "Die Hamburgische Gesellschaft zur Beförderung der Künste und nützlichen Gewerbe (Patriotische Gesellschaft von 1765) im Zeitalter der Aufklärung: Ein Überblick," in Rudolf Vierhaus, ed., *Deutsche patriotische und gemeinnützige Gesellschaften* (Munich, 1980), p. 71.

7. An investigation conducted by the General Poor Relief in 1800 revealed that the price of bread had increased by almost 190 percent, the price of potatoes more than 260 percent, the price of butter more than 150 percent, and the price of milk 200 percent. *28ste Nachricht* (January 1801), p. 287. See also J. F. Voigt, "Die Steigerung des Preises der Lebensbedürfnisse und die Wohnungsnoth in Hamburg im letzten Jahrzehnten des 18. Jahrhunderts," address presented to Verein für Hamburgische Geschichte, 12 March 1883, typescript, StAHbg, Bibliothek; Rolf Engelsing, "Hanseatische Lebenshaltungskosten im 18. und 19. Jahrhundert," in Engelsing *Zur Sozialgeschichte deutscher Mittel- Und Unterschichten* (Göttingen, 1978) pp. 26–50; Wilhelm Abel, *Massenarmut und Hungerkrisen im vorindustriellen Europa: Versuch einer Synopsis,* 2nd ed. (Göttingen, 1977); Johann Georg Büsch, *Ueber die der Stadt Hamburg in jezigen Zeitumständen nothwendig werdende Erweiterung* (Hamburg, 1792); Georg E. Bieber, *Ueber den nachtheiligen Einfluss der hohen Miethe, und der Belastung unentbehrlicher Bedürfnisse auf Hamburgs Wohl, nebst einigen Vorschlägen dagegen* (Hamburg, 1803); and "Lebensmittelpreise in Hamburg während der Belagerung durch die Franzosen," *MVHG* 7 (1900): 405–6. Moritz J. Elsas demonstrates similar if not quite as spectacular rises in prices for Frankfurt am Main and Leipzig, *Umriß einer Geschichte der Löhne und Preise in Deutschland von ausgehenden Mittelalter bis zum Beginn des 19. Jahrhunderts,* 3 vols. (Leiden, 1936, 1940, 1949), here vol. 3.

8. Huhn, "Handelsbeziehungen," pp. 132–47, 178–83; Loose and Jochmann, eds., *Hamburg: Geschichte der Stadt,* vol. 1, pp. 374–77.

9. The harbor was the largest single employer in Hamburg, although it is impossible to estimate exactly how many people were working there at any one time. Heinrich Laufenberg's estimate of at least forty- to forty-five thousand seems plausible: *Hamburg und sein Proletariat im achtzehnten Jahrhundert: Eine wirtschaftshistorische Vorstudie zur Geschichte der modernen Arbeiterbewegung im niederelbischen Städtegebiet* (Hamburg, 1910), p. 105; Wiskemann, *Hamburg und die Welthandelspolitik,* pp. 132–35; Sieveking, "Hamburger Bank," p. 86; Johann Georg Büsch, *Geschichtliche Beurtheilung der in der Handlung Hamburgs im Nachjahr 1799 entstandenen großen Verwirrung* (Hamburg, 1799); and Johann Ernst Westphalen, "Der Zustand des Handels in Hamburg wärend der letzten Fünfzig Jahre," mss., StAHbg, *HS* 381b, pp. 16–20.

Several firms transferred their headquarters farther east. For example, the Hamburg tobacco merchant and processing firm of F. Justus established a branch in Leipzig in 1811. Ernst Baasch, "Zur Geschichte einer hamburgischen Groß-Tabaksfirma im 18. und 19. Jahrhundert," *ZVHG* 29 (1928): 30–31. In the same year the Hamburg merchant, Johann Georg Kirchenpauer, moved his business to St. Petersburg. Hildegard von Marchtaler, *Aus Alt-Hamburger Senatorenhäusern: Familienschicksale im 18. und 19. Jahrhundert* (Hamburg, 1959) pp. 112–13. See also Erik Amburger, "Aus dem Leben und Wirken von Hamburgern in Rußland," in Peter Classen and Peter Scheibert, eds., *Festschrift Percy Ernst Schramm zu seinem 70. Geburtstag von Schülern und Freunden zugeeignet,* 2 vols. (Wiesbaden, 1964), vol. 1, pp. 3–25.

10. Hans Mauersberg, *Wirtschafts- und Sozialgeschichte zentraleuropäischer Städte in neuerer Zeit: Dargestellt an den Beispielen von Basel, Frankfurt a.M., Hamburg, Hannover und München* (Göttingen, 1960), pp. 141–43, 336–37; Liebel, "Laissez-faire vs. Mercantilism." [Johann Albert Heinrich Reimarus], *Handlungs-Grundsätze zur wahren Aufnahme der Länder und zur Beförderung der Glückseligkeit ihrer Einwohner aus der Natur und Geschichte untersucht* ("Cosmopolis" [Frankfurt am Main and Leipzig], 1768) articulated the free-trade position of the Patriotic Society. The Chamber of Commerce declared itself "an enemy of protectionism in any form." Quoted in Baasch, *Handelskammer,* vol. 1, p. 118.

11. Jonas Ludwig von Heß, *Hamburg, topographisch, politisch und historisch beschrieben,* 3 vols. (Hamburg, 1787–92), vol. 2, pp. 278–79.

12. von Heß, *Hamburg* (2nd ed.), vol. 3, p. 377; Klefeker, vol. 1, pp. 146–224; and Otto Rüdiger, *Die ältesten Hamburgischen Zunftrollen und Brüderschaftsstatuten* (Hamburg, 1874).

13. von Heß, *Hamburg* (2nd ed.), vol. 3, pp. 382–408.

14. "Das von Ihro Römis.[chen] Kaiserl.[ichen] Majestät Allergnädigst confirmirte und von Dero Hohen Commißion publicirte neue Reglement der Hamburgischen Aemter und Brüderschaften. De Dato 7. Sept. Anno 1710," in Klefeker, vol. 1, pp. 155–224.

15. "Protocol des Amt[es] der Schmiede. Worinn sich die unzünftigen verschreiben, so wohl Grob als Kleinschmiede, welche die Profession mit ihren eigenen Hände ohne die geringste neben Hülfe betreiben," StAHbg, Amt der Schmiede, VI. 1. a.

16. For *Bönhasen,* I have borrowed Mack Walker's translation, "ground rabbits," *German Home-Towns: Community, State, and General Estate, 1648–1871* (Ithaca, N.Y., 1971), p. 86. The term apparently derives from the response of the unguilded, illegally working artisans, who, when hunted by guildsmen, ran like rabbits or hares (*Hasen*), scurrying across the garrets and rooms where they worked. Grimm gives two definitions of *Boden* or *Bohn,* "garret" and "ground." See Otto Rüdiger, "Böhnhasen und Handwerksgesellen," in Theodor Schrader, ed., *Hamburg vor 200 Jahren:*

Gesammelte Vorträge (Hamburg, 1892), pp. 217–59, esp. pp. 225–30; von Heß, *Hamburg* (1st ed.), vol. 2, pp. 285–88; and Antje Kraus, *Die Unterschichten Hamburgs in der ersten Hälfte des 19. Jahrhunderts: Entstehung, Struktur und Lebensverhältnisse-Eine historisch-statistische Untersuchung* (Stuttgart, 1965), p. 21.

17. Rüdiger, "Böhnhasen."

18. von Heß, *Hamburg* (2nd ed.), vol. 3, pp. 314, 338–39; P. H. C. Brodhagen, "Auszug aus den Verhandlungen der Gesellschaft über einen ihr eingeschickten Vorschlag zur Anlegung einer Manufactur halbseidener Zeuge [1790]," *VS* 1 (1792): 307–9.

19. von Heß, *Hamburg* (2nd ed.), vol. 3, pp. 392–408.

20. Ibid.

21. Laufenberg (*Proletariat,* p. 105) suggested that these three industries employed as many as twelve thousand workers and supported at least an additional eighteen thousand people. The eighteenth century referred to the types of industries described here as either *Manufakturen* or *Fabriken. Krünitzs Encyklopädie,* S.v. "Fabrik," defines a *Fabrik* as "a workplace where articles are produced in large numbers by non-guilded workers. . . . [Examples are] ribbon, leather, stocking, sugar, tobacco 'Fabriken.' " See Rudolf Forberger, "Zu den Begriffen 'Manufactur' und 'Fabrik' in technischer und technologischer Sicht," in Ulrich Troitzsch, ed., *Technologischer Wandel im 18. Jahrhundert* (Wolfenbüttel, 1981), pp. 175–87.

22. S. D. Chapman, "The Role of Calico Printing in the Eighteenth Century Economy," in Troitzsch, *Technologischer Wandel,* pp. 53–72, esp. pp. 53–55; S.v. "Kattun" in *Krünitzs Encyklopädie; Cambridge Economic History,* vol. 5, pp. 250–53; Ruth Schillinger, *Die wirtschaftliche Entwicklung des Stoffdrucks: Langfristige Tendenzen und kurzfristige Einflüsse* (Cologne, 1964).

23. Chapman, "Role of Calico Printing," p. 54; Loose and Jochmann, eds., *Hamburg: Geschichte der Stadt,* vol. 1, p. 334.

24. Johann Georg Büsch, *Versuch einer Geschichte der Hamburgischen Handlung, nebst zwei kleineren Schriften eines verwandten Inhalts* (Hamburg, 1797), p. 66.

25. A "piece" of calico varied from "28–40 Brabanten Ellen" long, that is, between about 27 and about 36 inches (69–92 cm): Martin Knorr, "Mit Druckform, Krapp und Indigo: Die Geschichte der Hamburger Zitzkattun- und Blaudruckerei vom Ende des 17. bis zur Mitte des 19. Jahrhunderts," vol. 1, pp. 101–2, StAHbg, *HS* 987a; and Gustav Otruba, ed., "Bericht über eine im Auftrag der Mährischen Lehensbank durchgeführte Kommerzialreise-Eine zeitgenössische Bestandsaufnahme zur Wirtschaftslage mitteleuropäischer Städte um die Mitte des 18. Jahrhunderts (Teil III)," *JFW* (1976/II), p. 259.

26. von Heß, *Hamburg* (2nd ed.), vol. 3, pp. 333–34; Knorr, "Mit Druckform," vol. 1, p. 175; quote from Chamber of Commerce in Knorr, "Mit Drückform," vol. 1, p. 175. On the technical aspects of calico-printing, see Knorr, "Mit Druckform," p. 3, in vol. 3; Chapman, "Role of Calico Printing," pp. 61–64; S.v. "Kattun" in *Krünitzs Encyklopädie.*

27. On families of calico printers, see Knorr, "Mit Druckform," vol. 1, pp. 182, 205; Peter Gabrielsson, "Klopstocks Schwager Hartmann Rahn als Entrepreneur der Hamburger Kattundruckerei, 1763–1770," *ZVHG* 70 (1984): 37–72. Another calico printer, Nicolas Burmester (1762–1843), was active in many communal offices and a member of the Patriotic Society since 1795. He was appointed a deputy to the Versorgungs-Anstalt in 1811 and became an Oberalte in 1838. *Mitglieder und Associirte* of the Patriotic Society, and Friedrich Georg Buek, *Die hamburgischen Oberalten, ihre bürgerliche Wirksamkeit und ihre Familien* (Hamburg, 1857), pp. 346–47.

28. The van Rahusens owned printeries in Hamburg and Altona, which were active for more than a hundred years. Their in-laws, the von Roosens, were important printers in Altona: Knorr, "Mit Druckform," vol. 1, pp. 48–56; vol. 3, pp. 3–11; Berend Karl Roosen, *Geschichte unseres Hauses* (Hamburg, 1905).

29. von Heß, *Hamburg* (2nd ed.), vol. 3, pp. 334–35; "Zustand der Manufakturen und Fabriken in Altona: Am Schlusse des Jahres 1786," StAHbg, Senat Cl. XI Generalia no. 1, vol. 12.

30. "Penciling" produced the most elaborate and expensive prints. Indigo was ground to a fine powder, then made into a paste by mixing it with a solvent (ferrous sulfate or orpiment). This mixture was then penciled onto the cloth. Chapman, "Role of Calico Printing," p. 61. On the *Schildermädchen*, see von Heß, *Hamburg* (1st ed.), vol. 2, p. 247, and Rita Bake, *Vorindustrielle Frauenerwerbsarbeit: Arbeits- und Lebensweise von Manufakturarbeiterinnen im Deutschland des 18. Jahrhunderts unter besonderer Berücksichtigung Hamburgs* (Cologne, 1984), pp. 144–45. The number of workers is calculated from information given in von Heß, *Hamburg* (2nd. ed.), vol. 3, pp. 329–35. This corresponds closely to the total of 3,200 workers employed in twenty-one printeries estimated by Schillinger, *Entwicklung des Stoffdrucks,* pp. 117–18. Laufenberg (*Proletariat,* p. 105) says that about 4,000 worked in calico printing, while Knorr ("Mit Druckform," vol. 1, p. 102) gives the considerably higher figures of between 5,500 and 5,600.

31. On the importance of sugar refining to Hamburg, see von Heß, *Hamburg* (2nd ed.), vol. 3, p. 326; Otruba, ed., "Bericht über eine Kommerzialreise," pp. 258–59; and Koppmann, *Aus Hamburgs Vergangenheit,* vol. 1, pp. 209–31. On sugar refining as an European-wide industry, see *Cambridge Economic History,* vol. 5, pp. 539–41; Noel Deerr, *The History of Sugar* (2 vols; London, 1949–50); Sidney Mintz, *Sweetness and Power: The Place of Sugar in Modern History* (New York, 1985); Immanuel Wallerstein, *The Modern World-System,* 2 vols. (Chicago, 1974, 1980), vol. 2, pp. 44, 102–3; and Elizabeth Fox-Genovese and Eugene D. Genovese, *Fruits of Merchant Capital: Slavery and Bourgeois Property in the Rise and Expansion of Capitalism* (New York, 1983), pp. 45–46.

In 1750 there were 365 sugar refineries in Hamburg; in 1791 there were 330, and in 1807, 428. By 1826 there were only 200. Ludwig Becker, *Die Geschichte des Hamburger Zuckerhandels (Von den Anfängen bis zum Weltkrieg)* (Rostock, 1933), p. 27. See also the list of "Zuckerfabrikanten in Hamburg 1799," StAHbg, Senat Cl. VII Lit. Kb, no. 20, vol. 1. Of the 298 refineries active in 1790, 217 produced loaf and lump sugar, 78 made candies, and 3 boiled syrup. Johann Georg Büsch, *Ueber die Hamburgischen Zucker-Fabriken und den vergeblichen Wetteifer der Nordischen Staaten mit denselben, auf Veranlassung der Fragmente des Herrn Ritters von Zimmermann über Friedrich den Grossen* (Hamburg, 1790), p. 18.

32. von Heß, *Hamburg* (2nd ed.), vol. 3, pp. 326–27n.

33. "Verzeichnis desienigen, was warscheinlich iährlich in Hamburg durch die Zucker Fabriquen umgesetzt und erworben wird," n.d., apparently 1789, StAHbg, Senat Cl. VII Lit. Kb, no. 20, vol. 1, repr. in Becker, *Zuckerhandels,* pp. 36–37.

34. Laufenberg, *Proletariat,* p. 105; Becker, *Zuckerhandels,* p. 70. von Heß, *Hamburg* (2nd ed.), vol. 3, pp. 328–29, gives a figure of about 5,000 directly involved in refining and a total of 8,000 who thus directly or indirectly lived from refining. These figures pertain to either 1807 or 1810–1811 when the refining industry had already experienced a decline from its former prosperity.

35. Büsch, *Zucker-Fabriken,* p. 18; Becker, *Zuckerhandels,* pp. 24–35; C.[aesar] Amsinck, *Die niederländische und hamburgische Familie Amsinck: Ein Versuch einer*

Familiengeschichte (Hamburg, 1886); "Namen derer Zuckerbecker welche Anno 1730 in Hamburg wohnhaft gewesen," StAHbg, Senat Cl. VII Lit. Kb, no. 20, vol. 1; and "Zuckerfabricanten in Hamburg 1799," in ibid.

36. *Cambridge Economic History,* vol. 5, p. 539. See the petition of Johann Heinrich Ebert, who in June 1717 requested a "Privilegium" from the Rat to protect his secret process—"arcana"—for refining sugar. Although we find nothing more indicating the response of the Rat, his request was almost certainly not granted. StAHbg, Senat Cl. VII Lit. Kb, no. 20, vol. 1.

37. Prices for refined sugar are found in Becker, *Zuckerhandels,* pp. 68–69, and in Johann Theodor Graff, *Jährliche Uebersicht des Hamburger Zuckerhandels seit Ende der Belagerung bis Ende des Jahrs 1823 unter Beifügung sämmtlicher Preise von Monat zu Monat und Bemerkung der Haupt-Beweggründe zu deren Veränderung, nebst einer specificirten Aufstellung der jährlichen Zufuhren &c* (Hamburg, 1823).

38. Becker, *Zuckerhandels,* pp. 40–43, 45–47.

39. Ibid., pp. 72–73; and Rainer Ramcke, *Die Beziehungen zwischen Hamburg und Österreich im 18. Jahrhundert: Kaiserlich-reichsstädtisches Verhältnis im Zeichen von Handels- und Finanzinteressen* (Hamburg, 1969), Table II, "Hamburg's Zuckerhandel nach Österreich, 1749–1795."

40. von Heß, *Hamburg* (2nd ed.), vol. 3, pp. 335–36; Baasch, "Zur Geschichte einer Groß-Tabaksfirma"; "Gedächtnisschrift zum 175-jährigen Jubiläum der Firma Joh. Wilh. von Eicken, Hamburg 1770–1. Januar 1945," mss., StAHbg, Bibliothek; Laufenberg, *Proletariat,* p. 105.

41. von Heß, *Hamburg* (2nd ed.), vol. 3, pp. 316–21; "Verhandlungen der Gesellschaft, über die Ursachen des Verfalls der hiesigen Manufacturen, Fabriken und Gewerbe, und über Mittel zur Herstellung derselben [1792]," *VS* 3 (1795): 97–166, here p. 139; Michael Richey, "Anmerckungen über die bey Rengern in Halle herausgekommene Nachricht von Hamburg nebst einer Anleitung zur Hamburgischen Histoire," ([Hamburg], 1758), StAHbg, *HS* 273, comments to p. 308; Wolf Bing, "Hamburgs Bierbrauerei vom 14. bis zum 18. Jahrhundert," *ZVHG* 14 (1909): 209–332; Laufenberg, *Proletariat,* p. 54.

42. von Heß, *Hamburg* (2nd ed.), vol. 3, pp. 321–25; "Verhandlungen der Gesellschaft, über die Ursachen des Verfalls," *VS* 3 (1795): 145; Richey, "Anmerckungen," comments to p. 308; Laufenberg, *Proletariat,* p. 54.

43. von Heß, *Hamburg* (2nd ed.), vol. 3, p. 339; "Verhandlungen der Gesellschaft, über die Ursachen des Verfalls," *VS* 3 (1795): 134–35; on the stocking manufactory of one Altona entrepreneur, a Johann Wilhelm Paap, see *SHPB* 6 (1792): 253–57; and on one (rather halfhearted) effort of the Chamber of Commerce to assist the struggling stocking manufacturers, see *Protocollum Commercii,* 19 and 28 December 1791, Commerzbibliothek, Protocollum Commercii, LLL 1791/92, pp. 257–59, 272–74. On the "new" experiment in poor relief in 1725/26, "Proposition E. E. Raths an die Erbgesessene Bürgerschaft vom 4 Oct. 1725," Klefeker, vol. 1, pp. 408–22, esp. pp. 412–15; and Werner von Melle, *Die Entwicklung des öffentlichen Armenwesens in Hamburg* (Hamburg, 1883), pp. 56–59.

44. von Heß, *Hamburg* (2nd. ed.), vol. 3, pp. 314–15, 321, 340–42; "Verhandlungen der Gesellschaft, über die Ursachen des Verfalls," *VS* 3 (1795): 131–32, 137–38, 144.

45. *6te Nachricht* (June 1790), p. 52. On women wage earners in Hamburg, see Bake, *Vorindustrielle Frauenerwerbsarbeit.*

46. von Heß, *Hamburg* (2nd ed.), vol. 3, p. 246.

47. von Heß, *Hamburg* (1st ed.), vol. 2, pp. 285–88; Johann Georg Büsch,

Erfahrungen (Hamburg, 1792), vol. 3, p. 11; Reißmann, *Kaufmannschaft,* pp. 17–28; Loose and Jochmann, eds., *Hamburg: Geschichte der Stadt,* vol. 1, p. 334; Kopitzsch, *Grundzüge,* pp. 184–85. The balance had tipped even further by the middle of the nineteenth century. In 1856, 15 percent of the production totals were artisanal and 85 percent manufactured products. C[arl] W[ilhelm] Ascher, *Bericht der von der technischen Section der Hamburgischen Gesellschaft zur Beförderung der Künste und nützlichen Gewerbe ernannten Commission zur Untersuchung der Gewerbeverhältnisse in Hamburg* (Hamburg, 1861), pp. 19–20.

48. Laufenberg, *Proletariat,* pp. 80–100; Willi Bredel, *Unter Türmen und Masten: Geschichte einer Stadt in Geschichten* (Berlin, G.D.R., 1968), pp. 63–64; Rüdiger, "Böhnhasen," pp. 239–51. This "strike" in 1791 fits more closely the model of a preindustrial revolt than that an early form of general strike, despite Susanne Petersen's contention in " 'Heck ock dahl legt' August 1791: 'Generalstreik' in Hamburg," pp. 36–47 in Jörg Berlin, ed., *Das andere Hamburg: Freiheitliche und demokratische Bestrebungen in der Hansestadt seit dem Spätmittelalter* (Hamburg, 1981). On the uprising of the cabinetmakers in 1750, see "Protocollmässige Geschichte Erzehlung die zwischen den Meistern und Gesellen des hiesigen Tischler-Ampts unlängst vorgefallene Händel, und den von letztern darüber erregten Aufstand betreffend . . . publiciret d. 26. Junii 1750," in StAHbg, Senat Cl. XI Generalia, no. 1, vol. 11. For the reaction of the government to the troubles of 1753, see the "Befehl" from 6 April 1753 and the "Maaßregeln, nach welchen, bey etwanigem Aufstande der Handwerks-Gesellen es hinkünftig soll gehalten werden . . . publiciret den 21. December 1752," both in Senat Cl. XI Generalia, no. 1, vol. 11. On the 1770 disturbances, see "Protocollmäßige Geschichtes-Erzehlung des hier entstandenen Aufstandes der Tischler-Gesellen," in ibid. The troubles in 1791 are the most fully documented and have received the most historical attention. See StAHbg, Senat Cl. XI Generalia, no. 1, vol. 14, and Petersen, " 'Heck ock dahl legt,' " for a Marxist account. Contemporaries wrote voluminously on the subject as well. The most complete account, and one of the most interesting here because its author, Johann Arnold Günther, was a very influential figure in the General Poor Relief, is *Ueber den Aufstand der Handwerksgesellen zu Hamburg im August 1791; nebst einigen Reflexionen über Zunftgeist und Zunfterziehung: Aus dem Journal von und für Deutschland [8, no. 7]* (Frankfurt a. M. and Leipzig, 1792), available in StAHbg, Bibliothek, and also see Senat Cl. XI Generalia, no. 1, vol. 15 (1792). This event was also the subject of innumerable pamphlets and articles in various newspapers and journals, for example, *Möglichst spezielles und richtiges Tagebuch vor allem, was in den unruhigen Tagen in Hamburg im Monat August 1791 bei dem Aufstand der Handwerksgesellen Tag vor Tag vorging* (Hamburg, 1791) and *Unparteiische und deutliche Beschreibung der in Hamburg entstandenen Handwerksunruhen, die den 19. August 1791 ihren Anfang nahmen und erst ab den 26. August beendigt wurden* (n.p., n.d., [Hamburg, 1791]). The incident revived the debate about the value of guilds. See Günther, *Ueber den Aufstand;* and *Müssen die Zünfte abgeschafft werden, nebst einer wahren Darstellung der neuen Unruhen in Hamburg* (Hamburg, September 1791).

Chapter 3

1. See Raymond Williams, *The Country and the City* (London, 1973).

2. Josiah Tucker in his *A Treatise Concerning Civil Government, in Three Parts* (1781), quoted in Charles Mullett, "Community and Communication," in Paul Fritz

and David Williams, eds., *City and Society in the 18th Century* (Toronto, 1973), p. 77; Rousseau and Johnson quote in Arthur J. Weitzman, "Eighteenth-Century London: Urban Paradise or Fallen City?" *JHI* 36 (1975): 469–70, 473.

3. Johann Jakob Rambach, *Versuch einer physisch-medizinischen Beschreibung von Hamburg* (Hamburg, 1801), p. 291. See also "Erinnerung an das Medicinal-Policeywesen, wegen der zum öftern in ganzen Ländern unsers Vaterlandes grassierenden Krankheiten," *LS* 14 (1760): 213.

4. Roger Emerson, "Enlightenment and Social Structure," in Fritz and Williams, eds., *City and Society,* pp. 99–100; Otto Laufer, "Hamburg als Vorort deutscher Kultur im 18. Jahrhundert," idem, *Hamburg,* (Leipzig, 1912), pp. 104–13; and Franklin Kopitzsch, *Grundzüge einer Sozialgeschichte der Aufklärung in Hamburg und Altona* (Hamburg, 1982), pp. 328–451.

5. "Vorzüglichsten Quellen der Verarmung," *VS* 1 (1790): 359n–60n.

6. Johann Georg Büsch, *Zum Andencken Alemanns des Menschenfreundes* (Hamburg, 1784), pp. 8–9; Williams, *Country and City,* p. 90.

7. On Polizei, see Georg-Christoph Unruh, "Polizei, Polizeiwissenschaft und Kameralistik," pp. 388–427 in Kurt G. A. Jeserich, Hans Pohl, and Georg-Christoph Unruh, *Deutsche Verwaltungsgeschichte,* vol. 1, *Vom Spätmittelalter bis zum Ende des Reiches* (Stuttgart, 1983); Marc Raeff, *The Well-Ordered Police State: Social and Institutional Change Through Law in the Germanies and Russia, 1600–1800* (New Haven, Conn. and London, 1983), p. 5; "Polizeistaat," in Paul Heere, ed., *Politisches Handbuch* (Leipzig, 1923); S.v. "Polizei" in *Krünitzs Encyklopädie.*

8. Marc Raeff, "The Well-Ordered Police State and the Development of Modernity in Seventeenth- and Eighteenth-Century Europe: An Attempt at a Comparative Approach," *AHR* 80 (1975): 1222, 1227. In his book on the subject that appeared later, Raeff explained in more detail what he meant by modernity:

> There are many ways of defining modernity, of course. The most simple-minded is to equate modernity with the present, in contrast to the past, the old, but such a definition lacks analytical and heuristic value. As some have suggested, it may be a sigh of arrogance and sociocentrism to claim for the culture of the Western world—that is, the culture that emerged in central and Western Europe in the course of the seventeenth and eighteenth centuries and then spread to North America and to most of the world—the distinction of being peculiarly modern. Yet there is no denying that from about the dawn of the sixteenth century (with origins going farther back, of course), Europe embarked on an extraordinary departure from the traditional cultural patterns that one observes in its own past and in most of the world prior to its contact with the West. The most outstanding and characteristic feature of the pattern that makes Western Europe exceptional and that eventually subjected to its sway most societies the world over is an extraordinary dynamism, an entrepreneurial spirit, and the willingness to take risks for results in the distant future. The creative energy and dynamism (some would call it arrogance and aggressiveness) were predicated on an essential assumption: that the resources at man's disposal are greater than perceived, that they may be unlimited, and that it is the task of man's rational and purposeful action to discover, develop, and make use of these resources that lie more or less fallow in the natural state.

The Well-Ordered Police State, pp. 2–3.

9. Klefeker, vol. 12, pp. 555–57, 405.

10. Hamburg's three fundamental law codes were the *Redaction* of 1497, the *Gerichtsordnung* of 1570, and the *Stadtrecht* of 1605. Otto Stobbe, *Geschichte der deutschen Rechtsquellen* (Braunschweig, 1864; repr. ed., Aalen, 1966), vol. 2, pp. 309–15 and Klefeker, vol. 12, pp. 412–16. See the collection of "Conclusa et Commissoria

perpetua, welche das Officum der Herren Praetorum betreffend, so viel sich deren auffinden lassen, in chronologische Ordnung, 1699–1800," StAHbg, Präturen, I, 1, vol. 1; "Jurisdiktion der Hr. Bürgermeistern u. Präturen. Formulare u. conclusa perpetua," StAHbg, Senat Cl. VII, Lit. Ma, no. 5, vol. 3b2; Johann Schulte, "Aufzeichnungen über die Zweite und Erste Praetur 1796–1798, fortgesetzt von Senator Lic. Johann Arnold Günther 1798–1800 mit wenigen späteren Nachträgen u. a. von Senator Lic. J. J. Jänisch (1800/01) und Senator Dr. J. H. Bartels (1805)," mss., StAHbg, Senat Cl. VII, Lit. Ma, no. 5, vol. 3d6; Matthias Schülter, "Von den Rechten und Pflichten der Gerichtsverwalter in Hamburg," ca. 1715, mss., StAHbg, Senat Cl. VII, Lit. Ma, no. 5, vol. 3d1; and Nicolai Schuback, "Versuch einer systematischen Abhandlung von richterlichen Ampte in Hamburg," ca. 1750, mss., StAHbg, Senat Cl. VII, Lit. Ma, no. 5, vol. 3d3.

11. See, for example, "Verbindung der Wedde- und übrigen Policey-Verfassungen," in Klefeker, vol. 12, pp. 399–584, and also "Project einer allgemeinen Policey-Ordnung in einem gewissen Lande, 1739, entworffen," *LS* 2 (1745): 916–33. The variety, extent, and interaction of police powers is well illustrated by the range and complexity of senators' duties, especially of those senators who were charged with the administration of one of Hamburg's rural satellites. See *Aufzeichnungen des Senator und Landherrn Lict. Wilhelm Amsinck über seine Verwaltung der Landherrschaften von Bill- und Ochsenwärder 1800/1801* (Hamburg, 1911).

12. As is explained in a letter from Amandus Augustus Abendroth to Caspar Voght, 26 June 1832. StAHbg, Familienarchiv Voght, V. 2.

13. Duties of the Wedde are described by Klefeker, vol. 12, pp. 399–575. The Deputation for the Admission of Aliens (*Deputation zur ietzigen Annehmung der fremden Einwohner*) made decisions on which people to admit to the so-called *Fremden-Kontract,* which applied in particular to affluent immigrants and immigrants of different religions, such as the Dutch Calvinists. It was composed of the four members of the Wedde, two other members of the Rat, two members of the Treasury, and two members from the Sixty. The Senior Wedde-Herr alone handled the far more informal admission to Schutzverwandschaft. Klefeker, vol. 12, p. 443; Nicolaus A. Westphalen, *Hamburgs Verfassung und Verwaltung in ihrer allmähligen Entwickelung bis auf die neueste Zeit,* 2nd ed., 2 vols. (Hamburg, 1841), vol. 1, pp. 380–90.

14. Klefeker, vol. 3, pp. 478–79. The diverse powers executed *in publicis* are well indicated by the expenditures of the praetor's discretionary funds; see "Empfang und Ausgabeabrechnungen der Prätoren," StAHbg, Kämmerei I, no. 96. Quote from *Der Stadt Hamburgt Gerichts-Ordnung und Statuta (1605)* (Hamburg, 1605), Tit. III, Art. I. 3.

15. Claus Bramst, *Das hamburgische Strafrecht im 17. Jahrhundert: Der Übergang vom Städtischen zum gemeinen Strafrecht* (Hamburg, 1958), p. 40; StAHbg, Senat Cl. VII, Lit. Ma, no. 5, vol. 3d3, § I, p. 11; Senat Cl. VII, Lit. Ma, no. 5, vol. 3d6, pp. 93, 95; Senat Cl. VII, Lit. Ma, no. 5, vol. 3d1, unpag.; and "Drey Extract. Prot. extraj. Senatus, die Bestrafung der Unzucht durch die Herren Gerichtsverwalter betreffend," 27 June 1732, Blank, vol. 3, pp. 1176–80. See also Mary Lindemann, "Armen- und Eselbegräbnis in der europäischen Frühneuzeit, eine Methode sozialer Kontrolle?" in Richard Toellner and Paul R. Blum, eds., *Studien zur Thematik des Todes im 16. Jahrhundert,* (Wolfenbüttel, 1983), pp. 125–40; idem, "Maternal Politics: The Principles and Practice of Maternity Care in Eighteenth-Century Hamburg," *JFH* 9, no. 1 (Spring 1984): 44–63.

16. Ferdinand Beneke in his diary, StAHbg, Familiearchive Beneke, C2 Tagebuch Ferdinand Beneke 1792–1848, entry for 26 September 1799. Another praetor, Johann

Arnold Günther, referred to the job as requiring "more strength than the most indefatigable can muster," quoted in Friedrich Johann Lorenz Meyer, *Johann Arnold Günther: Ein Lebensgemälde* (Hamburg, 1810), p. 118. On the Wedde, StAHbg, Senat Cl. VII, Lit. Cc, no. 13, vol. 6.

17. Georg Heinrich Zincke, *Cameralisten-Bibliothek, worinne nebst der Anleitung die Cameral-Wissenschaft zu lehren und zu lernen, ein vollständiges Verzeichniss der Bücher und Schriften von der Land- und Stadt-Oeconomie, dem Policey- Finanz- und Cammerwesen zu finden, so theils kurz beurtheilet, theils umständlich vorgestellt worden,* 2 vols. (Leipzig, 1751, 1752; repr. ed., Glashütten im Taunus, 1973), vol. 2, p. 343.

18. Büsch, *Ueber die Ursachen der Verarmung in Nordischen Handelsstädten und die wirksamsten Mittel denselben zu begegnen* (Hamburg, 1785), pp. 10–11. Another reformer, Ludwig Gerhard Wagemann, editor of the *Göttingisches Magazin für Industrie und Armenpflege,* agreed that differences in wealth and the coexistence of rich and poor together in a state were two of "those great imponderables whose elimination is as impossible as it is undesirable." "Über einige vorzügliche Ursachen des Verarmens und Bettelns," *GM* 1 (1788): 82.

19. Population statistics in Hamburg before the nineteenth century are not very reliable. Apparently the growth of population was more rapid in the late seventeenth century than in the period from 1715 through the late 1770s or early 1780s. But then beginning with about the middle of the 1780s, and throughout the 1790s, population growth accelerated dramatically. The rate of increase was linked to economic fluctuations and to conditions prevailing in neighboring states. Kopitzsch, *Grundzüge*, pp. 140–41; Heinrich Reincke, "Hamburgs Bevölkerung," in idem, *Forschungen und Skizzen zur hamburgischen Geschichte* (Hamburg, 1951). In the eighteenth century, many came from the eastern parts of Holstein, from Mecklenburg, and from Hanover. Ernst Finder, *Hamburgisches Bürgertum in der Vergangenheit* (Hamburg, 1930), p. 441. This quickened rate of growth in population was not unique to Hamburg. Several other German cities—Berlin, Breslau, Dresden, Frankfurt, Koblenz, Leipzig, Mainz, Munich, Schwerin, Vienna—exceeded Hamburg's rate of growth in the seventeenth and eighteenth centuries, but only Vienna and Berlin grew larger. Schultz, *Berlin, 1650–1800*, pp. 296, 323.

20. Jonas Ludwig von Heß, *Hamburg, topographisch, politisch und historisch beschrieben,* 2nd ed., 3 vols., (Hamburg, 1810–11), vol. 3, p. 444.

21. Reincke, "Hamburgs Bevölkerung," p. 174; Werner Matti, "Bevölkerungsvorgänge in den Hansestädten Hamburg und Bremen vom Anfang des 19. Jahrhunderts bis zum Ersten Weltkrieg," *ZVHG* 69 (1983): 106; and Hans Mauersberg, *Wirtschafts- und Sozialgeschichte zentraleuropäischer Städte in neuerer Zeit: Dargestellt an den Beispielen von Basel, Frankfurt a.M., Hamburg, Hannover und München* (Göttingen, 1960), p. 73. von Heß calculated that 96,365 persons lived in the city. *Hamburg* (1st ed.), vol. 2, pp. 353–78. Hamburg's population, according to the 1811 census, was distributed as follows: 108,735 people lived in "greater" Hamburg, 96,735 in Hamburg proper (the five municipal parishes), 5,200 in St. Georg, 6,800 in St. Pauli. Of the 96,735 who resided within the walls of the city, there were 24,680 adult females (25.51 percent), 22,297 adult males (23.05 percent), and 37,874 children (39.15 percent). In addition, 11,884 servants (12.29 percent of total population) worked in the city: 6,768 were female and 3,451 male. Furthermore, 1,665 persons (1.72 percent) were listed as aliens. The census probably underreported, missing about 13 percent of the population; see Barbara Winkler, "Die Bevölkerungsentwicklung der Stadt Hamburg in der letzten hundert Jahren unter besonderer Berücksichtigung der Stadtteile,"

100 Jahre Statistisches Amt Hamburg 1866–1966 (Hamburg, 1966), p. 64. If we include the 13 percent not reported (i.e., 14,131 persons), we arrive at a total of 122,831 for the area of Hamburg, St. Georg, and St. Pauli. Cf. Matti, "Bevölkerungsvorgänge," pp. 108–9. Mauersberg (*Wirtschafts- und Sozialgeschichte,* pp. 43, 47–48) presents the following population estimates, which he calculated from the number of baptisms, using a multiplier of twenty-five.

Year	Population
1710	76,200
1715	71,950
1764	82,358
1766	74,575
1788	69,650
1800	105,225
1810	105,675
1811	106,983

The figures for 1710, 1764, 1800, 1810, and 1811 are based on baptisms in Hamburg's five metropolitan parishes (and these, of course, list only Lutherans), including St. Georg and St. Pauli (except for 1788, list also only Lutherans), and for the Mennonites, Catholics, members of the English Court, but not the Jews. The figures for 1715, 1766, and 1788 do not include Catholics and the Mennonites. In addition, it must be remembered that aliens in the city, or those who made the city their home without legal status, that is, without joining the civic nexus, were generally not found in these baptismal records.

22. *25ste Nachricht* (July 1799), p. 177.

23. Figures for 1764 are calculated from the *Kopfgeldverzeichnis,* that is, from the lists of those who paid Hamburg's most inclusive tax, including all those who did not live from alms. See *Classification des von E. E. Rath und der Erbgesessenen Bürgerschaft am 26. April 1759 beliebten Kopf-Geldes* (Hamburg, 1759); *Reglement wegen des Kopf-Geldes. Auf Befehl Eines Hochedlen Raths der Stadt Hamburg publicirt den 7. May 1770* (Hamburg, 1770); and Ludwig Behrends, *Die Entwicklung der direkten Steuern in Hamburg und die Errichtung der Steuerdeputation am 9. März 1815* (Hamburg, 1915), pp. 6–9. Figures for 1764 are taken from Mauersberg, *Wirtschafts- und Sozialgeschichte,* p. 43; figures for 1811 are taken from census data, von Heß, *Hamburg* (2nd ed.), vol. 3, Appendix—Table I.

1764

Parish	Number Listed	Percentage
St. Michaelis	11,388	25.54
St. Petri	9,169	20.57
St. Jakobi	8,390	18.82
St. Nikolai	8,373	18.78
St. Katharinen	7,264	16.29
Totals	44,584	

1811

Parish	Number Listed	Percentage
St. Michaelis	28,659	31.49
St. Petri	15,105	16.60
St. Jakobi	19,590	21.53
St. Nikolai	13,820	15.19
St. Katharinen	13,826	15.19
Totals	91,000	

24. On housing in Hamburg and the development of the housing shortage in the 1790s, see Jürgen Ellermeyer, "Zu Handel, Hafen und Grundeigentum Hamburgs im 17. und 18. Jahrhundert," in Ellermeyer and Rainer Postel, eds., *Stadt und Hafen: Hamburger Beiträge zur Geschichte von Handel und Schiffahrt* (Hamburg, 1986), pp. 58–79; Wilhelm Melhop, *Alt-Hamburgische Bauweise: Kurze geschichtliche Entwicklung der Baustile in Hamburg, dargestellt am Profanbau bis zum Wiedererstehen der Stadt nach dem großen Brand von 1842 nebst chronistisch-biographischen Notizen* (Hamburg, 1908); C. A. Stuhlmann, "Erläuterungen zu den Tabellen über die Bevölkerungszustände Hamburgs und seiner Vorstädte," *Beiträge zur Statistik Hamburgs* (1854): 11–12; Friedrich Winkelmann, *Wohnhaus und Bude in Alt-Hamburg: Die Entwicklung der Wohnverhältnisse von 1250 bis 1830* (Berlin, 1937); Georg Bieber, E., *Ueber den nachtheiligen Einfluss der hohen Miethe, und der Belastung unentbehrlicher Bedürfnisse auf Hamburgs Wohl, nebst einigen Vorschlägen dagegen* (Hamburg, 1803); and F. Voigt, "Die Steigerung des Preises der Lebensbedürfnisse und die Wohnungsnoth in Hamburg im letzten Jahrzehnt des 18. Jahrhunderts," typescript, Vereinsnachrichten, Verein für Hamburgische Geschichte, 12 March 1883, StAHbg, Bibliothek. Apparently it was not unknown for heavy rainfall to produce flash floods in which people living in low-lying cellars actually drowned. Franz Heinrich Ziegenhagen, *Lehre vom richtigen Verhältnisse zu den Schöpfungswerken, und die durch öffentliche Einfürung derselben allein zu bewürkende algemeine Menschenbeglückung* (Hamburg, 1792), pp. 26n–27n.

The following table, comparing the types of dwellings in Hamburg in 1811, is taken from von Heß, *Hamburg* (2nd ed.), vol. 3, Appendix—Table II. If one uses Matti's figures ("Bevölkerungsvorgänge," p. 110), one comes up with slightly different percentages of *Sählen*: St. Nikolai, 25.7 percent, St. Petri, 37.3 percent, St. Katharinen, 56.9 percent, for St. Jakobi, 46.8 percent, and St. Michaelis, 51.7 percent. Matti also calculated that 34.3 percent of the population—those he terms the "well-to-do"—lived in houses; 20.4 percent—the lower middle classes—lived in *Buden* or cellars; the rest, 45.3 percent—the "poor"—lived in *Sählen*.

Parish	Dwellings	Cellars	Percentage	Sählen	Percentage
St. Nikolai	2,683	312	11.63	670	24.97
St. Petri	4,733	369	7.8	1,715	36.23
St. Katharinen	3,488	230	6.59	1,941	55.65
St. Jakobi	4,991	267	5.35	2,335	46.78
St. Michaelis	7,577	450	5.94	3,907	51.56
Totals	23,472	1,628	(6.94)	10,568	(45.02)

25. See the article "Census," in the *Encyclopedia Britannica* (1959 ed.), which defines a modern periodic census as "primarily an official enumeration . . . of all the people either physically present or regularly residing [in a state]." Usually acknowledged as the first modern censuses were those taken in 1665 and 1754 in Quebec and Nova Scotia. Beginning in the middle of the eighteenth century, numerous other governments followed suit.

26. Article "Berechnung des Volkes im Lande," *Krünitzs Encyclopädie*.

27. T. H. Hollingsworth, *Historical Demography* (London, 1969), pp. 70–77. When city officials in Rheims called for an enumeration in 1482 and again in 1500, they specifically omitted the poor. Jean-Noel Biraben, "La population de Reims et de son arrondisement, et la vérification statisque des recensement numériques anciens," *Population* 16 (1961): 722–30. Quote from article "Census" in *Encyclopedia Britannica* (1959 ed.).

28. James H. Cassedy, *Demography in Early America: Beginnings of the Statistical Mind* (Cambridge, Mass., 1969), p. 164. See also Eberhard Reichmann, *Die Herrschaft der Zahl: Quantitatives Denken in der deutschen Aufklärung* (Stuttgart, 1968), pp. 7–15, and Gustav Seibt, "Statistik," pp. 1–43 in S.P. Altmann et. al., eds., *Die Entwicklung der deutschen Volkswirtschaftslehre im neunzehnten Jahrhundert,* 2 vols. (Leipzig, 1908), vol. 1.

29. See "Über die verschiedenen Meinungen von der Anzahl der Menschen in alten und neuen Zeiten," *ACN* (24 May 1769); "Was für einen Werth kann der Staat auf jeden einzelnen Menschen setzen?" ibid. (31 October 1771); "Von der Bevölkerung des deutschen Reiches," ibid. (21 October 1776); "Über die Bevölkerung einiger vorzüglichen Städte Europas," ibid. (21 and 31 May 1798); "Über die göttliche Ordnung in der Erhaltung des menschlichen Geschlechts," *Wöchentlich gemeinnützige Nachrichten von und für Hamburg* (9, 12, 23, 26, 30 September and 3 October); "Ursachen der grossen Sterblichkeit der neugebornen Kinder," ibid. (1 February 1797); and "Benedict Franklyns, Esqu. in Philadelphia, Betrachtungen über das Wachstum der Menschen, die Bevölkerung der Länder, u.s.w.," *Hamburgisches Magazin oder gesammelte Schriften aus der Naturforschung und der angenehmen Wissenschaften überhaupt* 17 (1756): 3–13.

30. *Hamburgisches Diarium von Anno . . . Die . . . Woche/ von . . . bis . . . Enthaltend die Zahl derjenigen Persohnen/ so Wochentlich in jeden Kirchspiel sind gebohren/ proclamiert, als auch Copuliert, und gestorben* (Hamburg, 1711–15).

31. Mandates from 3 January 1749 and 5 December 1749, Blank, vol. 3, pp. 1673, 1701.

32. Joachim Ehlers, *Die Wehrverfassung der Stadt Hamburg im 17. und 18. Jahrhundert* (Boppard am Rhein, 1966), pp. 108–12. See the many mandates concerning the activities of the militia captains in gathering information for the government for various purposes in Blank and Anderson. Especially important is the "Mandat die gute Begegnung der Bürgercapitaine bey der zum Behuf einer bessern Einrichtung des Armenwesens vorzunehmenden Aufzeichnung der Armen betreffend," 30 April 1787, Anderson, vol. 2, pp. 180–2. On the investigation of the militia captains in 1787, see "Extr. Prot. Sen. Hamb," 2 April 1787, StAHbg, Senat Cl. VII, Lit. Qa, no. 3, vol. 12, fasc. 1, and "Listen der Bürger-Kapitaine über die in ihren Kompaniebezirken wohnenden Arme, 1787," in StAHbg, AAI, 58. At the same time, similar lists were required from the Zuchthaus, Pesthof, Kloster St. Johannis, Hospital St. Georg, and of those receiving alms from the Gotteskasten. Administrators of these institutions and the Gotteskastenverwalter were to include with the lists a personal evaluation of whether these people could still work, should be kept in the poorhouses, or were aliens

who could be removed from the city, see "Extr. Prot. Sen. Ham.," 3 January 1787, StAHbg, Senat Cl. VII, Lit. Qa, no. 3, vol. 12, fasc. 1; "Extr. Prot. Sen. Ham." 11 April 1787, and "Extr. Prot. Sen. Ham.," 17 August 1787, in ibid.

33. Franz Lütkens, "Versuch einer Berechnung von der Zahl der Einwohner dieser Stadt," in his "Cammer-Meditationes, zur Instruction antretender Kämmerey-Bürger abgefasst, 1768," mss., StAHbg, Senat Cl. VII, Lit. Dd, no. 4, vol. 3, p. 108.

34. Preface to Lütkens, "Cammer-Meditationes."

35. Allen Sharlin argues that it was precisely the immigrants, not the permanent residents of the towns, who experienced the highest mortality rates; it was the immigrant presence that caused the excess of deaths over births. This argument seems persuasive, but it is also necessary to remember that Sharlin is speaking about reality. The *perception* of contemporaries was, in most cases, very different. "Natural Decrease in Early Modern Cities: A Reconsideration," *PP* no. 79 (1978): 126–38.

36. Johann Peter Süssmilch, *Die göttliche Ordnung in den Veränderungen des menschlichen Geschlechts, aus der Geburt, dem Tode und der Fortpflanzung desselben,* 2 vols., 2nd ed. (Berlin, 1765), vol. 2, pp. 103–9. See also the comments of Christian Baumann, who edited the fourth edition of Süssmilch's *Göttliche Ordnung,* 3 vols. (Berlin, 1775–76), vol. 3, p. 52; "Listen der in 1782. in den vornehmsten Städten von Europa Gebohrenen und Gestorbenen," *HP* 2, no. 1 (1783): 396–97; and Frederick S. Crum, "The Statistical Work of Süssmilch," *American Statistical Association,* n.s., 55 (September 1901): 22–25.

37. An article in *HP,* 2, no. 1 (1783): 396–97 gives the following figures, which suggest that Hamburg's record compared favorably with those of other major European cities, "Listen der in 1782. Gebohrenen."

Births and Deaths in Selected European Cities, 1782

City	Born	Died	Gain/Loss
Hamburg	2,687	2,691	−4
Altona	639	694	−55
Amsterdam	4,318	8,445	−4,127
Berlin	4,875	4,704	+171
Frankfurt/Main	876	1,253	−377
Copenhagen	2,822	4,244	−1,422
Leipzig	902	1,485	−583
London	17,101	17,918	−817
Munich	1,329	1,683	−354
Paris	19,387	18,953	+434
Strasburg	1,691	1,817	−126
Vienna	9,392	10,974	−1582

38. Reincke, "Hamburgs Bevölkerung," pp. 184–85; Rambach, *Versuch,* p. 252; Lütkens, "Cammer-Meditationes," p. 108.

39. Rambach, *Versuch,* p. iii, and sessions of Council of General Poor Relief, 14 January, 11 March, and 9 December 1802, in StAHbg, AAI, 9, vol. 8.

40. Rambach, *Versuch,* p. 252. von Heß reported that over the course of the eighteenth century the number of *reported* illegitimate births had doubled. *Hamburg* (2nd. ed.), vol. 3, p. 460.

41. Many cities seemed to have higher illegitimacy rates than Hamburg.

An earlier issue of the *HP* reported the following illegitimacy rates for Hamburg: in 1777, 10.56 percent (278 illegitimate/2,633 births) and in 1779, 10.48 percent (286/2,729).

Illegitimacy Rates in 1782

City	Illegitimate Births	All Births	Percentage Illegitimate
Munich	287	1,329	21.6
Leipzig	180	902	19.96
Dresden	204	1,655	12.33
Weimar	17	149	11.41
Hamburg	227	2,460	9.23

Source: "Nachtrag zum Etwas über uneheliche Geburten," *HP* 2, no. 2 (1783): 90–96.

42. "Von den Gesetzen, in dem Verhältnisse welches sie mit der Anzahl der Einwohner haben," *Neues gemeinnütziges Magazin für die Freunde der nützlichen und schönen Wissenschaften und Künste* (Hamburg, 1761), pp. 135–36.

43. Süssmilch, *Göttliche Ordnung* (2nd ed.), vol. 1, Appendix, Table A59; "Warum sind neue Ehen, vorzüglich unter den höhen Ständen, jetzt so seltene Erscheinungen," *ACN* (8 and 12 May 1794); Rambach, *Versuch,* p. 254; idem, "Ueber die Bevölkerung und Sterblichkeit in Hamburg," *ACN* (8 May 1800): 282; von Heß, *Hamburg* (1st ed.), vol. 2, p. 360; "Ueber Ehelösigkeit," *ACN* (5 and 9 May 1803); and Lütkens, "Cammer-Meditationes," p. 107.

44. Rambach, *Versuch,* pp. 251, 253; von Heß, *Hamburg* (2nd ed.), vol. 3, pp. 451–52; and Lütkens, "Cammer-Meditationes," pp. 106, 105.

45. "Jurisdiktion Herren Bürgermeister und Pratoren," StAHbg, Senat Cl. VII, Lit. Ma, no. 5, vol. 3d6, p. 87.

46. Article "Bürger" in Otto Brunner, Werner Conze, and Reinhart Koselleck, eds., *Geschichtliche Grundbegriffe: Historisches Lexikon zur politisch-sozialen Sprache in Deutschland* (Stuttgart, 1972–), vol. 1, pp. 704–5, 710; Jürgen Kocka, "Bürgertum und Bürgerlichkeit als Probleme der deutschen Geschichte vom späten 18. bis zum frühen 20. Jahrhundert," in idem, ed., *Bürger und Bürgerlichkeit im 19. Jahrhundert* (Göttingen, 1987), pp. 21–30, here esp. p. 29. In 1794, the *Allgemeine Landrecht für die Preußischen Staaten* (II, 8, §1) defined "Bürgerstand" negatively in regard to all those born neither nobles nor peasants.

47. Kocka, "Bürgertum und Bürgerlichkeit," pp. 30–41. For Hamburg, see StAHbg, Senat Cl. VII, Lit. Bc, no. 7b, fasc. 12, 20, and 27a; and Westphalen, *Verfassung und Verwaltung,* vol. 1, pp. 390–400.

48. The German word is *Bürger.* I have been inconsistent in translating this term as either citizen or burgher and use these two terms pretty much interchangeably.

49. Mack Walker, *German Home-Towns: Community, State, and General Estate, 1648–1871* (Ithaca, N.Y., 1971), pp. 29–30; Adolph Laufs, *Die Verfassung und Verwaltung der Stadt Rottweil, 1650–1806* (Stuttgart, 1963), p. 222; and article "Bürger" in *Geschichtliche Grundbegriffe*. On the differences between citizens and various types of quasi citizens in Hamburg, see Klefeker, vol. 2, pp. 239–53.

50. "Anmerckungen über das System der Policeyfreiheit in Absicht auf die freyen Städte," *EM* 12 (1777): 256.

51. Curio quoted in Schramm, *Hamburg, ein Sonderfall,* pp. 15–16. On the patriciate in Lübeck und Bremen, see G. Fink, "Die Frage des Lübecker Patriziats im Lichte der Forschung," *ZVLG* 29 (1938): 257–80, and Werner Henning, "Die

Rathsgeschlechter Bremens im Mittelalter: Ein Beitrag zur hansischen Sozialge-schichte" (Ph.D. diss., Göttingen, 1957). On the general topic of patriciates in the Germanies, see Karl Heinrich Roth von Schreckenstein, *Das Patriziat in den deutschen Städten besonders Reichsstädten, als Beitrag zur Geschichte der deutschen und des deutschen Adels* (Tübingen, 1885; repr. ed., Aalen, 1970). Helen Liebel, "Laissez-faire vs. Mercantilism: The Rise of Hamburg & the Hamburg Bourgeoisie vs. Frederick the Great in the Crisis of 1763," *VSWG* 52 (1965): 207–38, speaks of Hamburg's "patriciate" but apparently she means a "circle of kinsmen and friends," or those who maintained a certain, similar life-style, rather than the closed and legally defined patriciates that existed in many cities. On the "noblelike" fraternities, see Gerald L. Soliday, *A Community in Conflict: Frankfurt Society in the Seventeenth and Early Eighteenth Centuries* (Hanover, N.H., 1974), pp. 71–95; Laufs, *Verfassung und Verwaltung der Stadt Rottweils,* pp. 42–46; Franklin L. Ford, *Strasbourg in Transition, 1648–1789* (Cambridge, Mass., 1958), pp. 16–17; and Gerald Strauss, *Nuremberg in the Sixteenth Century: City Politics and Life Between Middle Ages and Modern Times,* 2nd ed. (Bloomington, Ind., and London, 1976), pp. 67–69, 80–81.

52. For Hamburg, see esp. Percy Ernst Schramm, *Hamburg, ein Sonderfall in der Geschichte Deutschlands* (Hamburg, 1964); idem, *Neun Generationen: Dreihundert Jahre deutscher "Kulturgeschichte" im Lichte der Schicksale einer Hamburger Bürger-familie, 1648–1948,* 2 vols. (Göttingen, 1963–64); idem, *Gewinn und Verlust: Die Geschichte der Hamburger Senatorenfamilien Jencquel und Luis (16. bis 19. Jahr-hundert): Zwei Beispiele für den wirtschaftlichen und sozialen Wandel in Norddeut-schland* (Hamburg, 1970); idem, *Hamburg, Deutschland und die Welt: Leistung und Grenzen hanseatischen Bürgertums in der Zeit zwischen Napoleon I. and Bismarck: Ein Kapitel deutscher Geschichte* (Munich, 1943); Hildegard von Marchtaler, *Aus Alt-Hamburger Senatorenhäusern: Familienschicksale im 18. und 19. Jahrhundert* (Hamburg, 1959); Martin Reißmann, *Die hamburgische Kaufmannschaft des 17. Jahrhun-derts in sozialgeschichtlicher Sicht* (Hamburg, 1975); Kopitzsch, *Grundzüge,* esp. pp. 195–97.

53. "Conclusum E. O. [beralten]," 23 April 1756. StAHbg, Senat Cl. VII, Lit. Db, no. 21, vol. 1, p. 82. Late in the century, Georg Heinrich Sieveking expressed virtually the same point of view. *Fragmente über Luxus, Bürger-Tugend und Bürger-Wohl für hamburgische Bürger, die das Gute wollen und können; am 17ten November 1791 in der Gesellschaft zu Beförderung der Künste und nützlichen Gewerbe gelesen. Mit Beiträgen und Bemerkungen von zweien seiner Freunde [J. M. Hudtwalcker, J. A. Günther].* (Hamburg, 1797), pp. 14–15.

54. Protocollum Commercii from 3 August 1745 and 13 September 1745. Commerzbibliothek, Protocollum Commercii, AA 1745/49, pp. 64, 79–80.

55. On the concept of *bürgerliche Nahrung,* see "Nahrung" in Johann Christoph Adelung, *Grammatisch-kritisches Wörterbuch der Hochdeutschen Mundart, mit beständiger Vergleichung der übrigen Mundarten, besonders aber der Oberdeutschen,* 2nd rev. ed. (Leipzig, 1793–1801); *Krünitzs Encyklopädie;* and Walker, *German Home-Towns,* p. 101. On the exercise of the burgher's livelihood in Hamburg, see Klefeker, vol. 12, pp. 439, 442, and Christian Ludwig von Griesheim, *Verbesserte und vermehrte Auflage des Tractats: Die Stadt Hamburg in ihrem politischen, öconomischen und sittlichen Zustande, nebst Nachträgen zu diesem Tractate und Beyträgen zu der Abhandlung: Anmerckungen und Zugaben über den Tractat: Die Stadt Hamburg, welche selbigen ebenfalls verbessern und gewisser machen* (Hamburg, 1760), pp. 110–25.

56. Klefeker, vol. 3, pp. 288–92; Hans Walther Lehr, *Das Bürgerrecht im hamburgischen Staate* (Hamburg, 1919), pp. 11, 16–17; Johann Heinrich Bartels, ed.,

Neuer Abdruck der Vier Haupt-Grundgesetze der Hamburgischen Verfassung (Hamburg, 1823), pp. 57–109; Geert Seelig, *Die geschichtliche Entwicklung der hamburgischen Bürgerschaft und der hamburgischen Notabeln* (Hamburg, 1900), p. 95; Westphalen, *Verfassung und Verwaltung*, vol. 1, pp. 99–100; Jürgen Bolland, *Die hamburgische Bürgerschaft in Alter und Neuer Zeit* (Hamburg, 1959), p. 20; and Kopitzsch, *Grundzüge*, pp. 152–54.

57. Klefeker, vol. 2, pp. 292–93, 303–12; "Rath- und Bürger-Schlüsse," from 7 and 15 September 1799 (Blank, vol. 1, p. 455). Furthermore, on civic regulations, see "Articuli Darauff Von E. E. Hochw: Raht der Stadt Hamburg die Einwohnere daselbsten angenommen werden," 1653, StAHbg, Senat Cl. VII, Lit. Cc, no. 2, vol. 1, fasc. 2; "Articuli, Darauff Von E. E. Hochw. Rath der Stadt Hamburg die Einwohnere daselbsten angenommen werden," 1 September 1697, Commerzbibliothek, S599, *Verschiedenes*, vol. 4, no. 180; "Revidirte Articuli, darauf von E. Hochedl. Hochw. Rath der Stadt Hamburg die Einwohner daselbst angenommen werden," 1765, StAHbg, Senat Cl. VII, Lit. Cc, no. 2, vol. 1, fasc. 5; "Revidirte Articuli, darauf von Hochedl. Hochw. Rath der Stadt Hamburg die Einwohner daselbst angenommen werden," 1796, StAHbg, Senat Cl. VII, Lit. Cc, no. 2, vol. 1, fasc. 5; and "Vorschrift für diejenigen die das Bürgerrecht nachsuchen," 20 November 1805 (Anderson, vol. 7, pp. 56–58).

58. The "Fremder Kontrakt" was specially designed for "wealthy aliens" ("begüterte Fremde"). Lehr, *Bürgerrecht*, pp. 16–17. Copy of "Niederländischer Contract," 1605 in StAHbg, Senat Cl. VII, Lit. Cc, no. 2, vol. 1, fasc. 2; see also Klefeker, vol. 2, pp. 302–16; Hermann Kellenbenz, *Sephardim an der unteren Elbe: Ihre wirtschaftliche und politische Bedeutung vom Ende des 16. Jahrhunderts bis zum Beginn des 18. Jahrhunderts* (Wiesbaden, 1958), pp. 54–57; Ernst W. Shepansky, "Ein Beispiel zur Sozialgeschichte der Fremden: Mennoniten in Hamburg und Altona zur Zeit des Merkantilismus," *HJWG* 24 (1979): 219–34; Maria Möring, "Die Englische Kirche in Hamburg und die Merchant Adventurers," *HGH* 20 (1963): 93–112; and Joachim Whaley, *Religious Toleration and Social Change in Hamburg, 1529–1819* (Cambridge, Eng., 1985).

59. Klefeker, vol. 12, p. 442.

60. The basis for the regulation of *Schutzverwandschaft* was laid down in the Hauptrezess, Cap. 1 Par. 4, reprinted in Bartels, *Neuer Abdruck*. See also StAHbg, Senat Cl. VII, Lit. Db, no. 8, vol. 6, and "Extract. Prot. extrajud. Senat die Designation der Schutzverwandschaften betreffend," 5 January 1720 (Blank, vol. 2, p. 925). The ceremony of entering Schutzverwandschaft is described by Westphalen, *Verfassung und Verwaltung*, vol. 1, p. 384.

61. Westphalen, *Verfassung und Verwaltung*, vol. 1, p. 384.

62. See "Gedancken über eine neue Einrichtung des Schutzwesens," 8 October 1772, StAHbg, Senat Cl. VII, Lit. Db, no. 8, vol. 6. There is an enormous volume of documentation on the activities of the several Treasury commissions established during the eighteenth century to deal with fiscal crises. See material on "Verbesserung des Kammerwesens," StAHbg, Senat Cl. VII, Lit. De, no. 2 (1700–32), No. 3 (1752–1800), and no. 4 (1794–1800). Hans Mauersberg's treatment of Hamburg in his *Wirtschafts- und Sozialgeschichte* (Göttingen, 1960) first suggested to me the possibility of using Treasury documents to investigate the formation of social policies. The following files were especially valuable in establishing the linkage between population control, fiscal crisis, nexus policies, and poor relief: "Cammer-Meditationes"; "Copia des am 14 Jan. 1754 im Senatus vorlesenen Cämmerey Antrages, insoweit er die Verbesserung des Einnahme der Cammer in

Ansehung der Bürger-Gelder, und Schutz-Thaler etc. betrifft," StAHbg, Senat Cl. VII, Lit. Db, no. 21, vol. 1; "Conclusum Collegii 60er," 19 September 1759, in ibid.; "betref. die neue Regulierung des Graben-, Schutz- und Bürger Geldes," 1767–73, StAHbg, Senat Cl. VII, Lit. Db, no. 8, vol. 6; and "Geheime Nachricht von dem Zustand der Cammerey," 1771–78, StAHbg, Senat Cl. VII, Lit. Da, no. 1, vol. 4, fasc. 5.

63. StAHbg, Senat Cl. VII, Lit. Db, no. 8, vol. 6 (1769).

64. Ibid.; "Conclusum Collegii der Sechsziger," 9 September 1759, in StAHbg, Senat Cl. VII, Lit. Db, no. 21, vol. 1.

65. StAHbg, Senat Cl. VII, Lit. Bc, no. 7b, fasc. 1 (1730); Ibid., fasc. 4b (1769).

66. Johann Peter Willibrand, *Grundriß einer schönen Stadt, in Absicht ihrer Anlage und Einrichtung zur Bequemlichkeit, zum Vergnügen, zum Anwachs und zur Erhaltung ihrer Einwohner, nach bekannten Mustern Entworfen. Nebst einer Vorrede von der Wirkung des Clima auf die Gesinnung und Gesetzgebung der Völker,* 2 vols. (Hamburg and Leipzig, 1775–76), vol. 2, pp. 117, 125–26.

67. Memorandum of H. Graffen to Rat, 16 April 1805, StAHbg, Senat Cl. VII, Lit. Bc, no. 7, fasc. 6a.

68. Mandate from 21 July 1727, Blank, vol. 2, p. 1080; prohibition repeated in "Erneuertes Mandat gegen die heimliche Verkuppel- und Verlobung, auch Copulirung von andern, als der Stadt ordinirten Predigern," 2 January 1769, Blank, vol. 6, p. 267; similar ruling in 1789, StAHbg, Senat Cl. VII, Lit. Db, no. 8, vol. 6, and Cl. VII, Lit. Bc, no. 7b, fasc. 4b.

69. The Oberalten remarked in 1752 that "the *Schutzthaler* does the Treasury more harm than good." "Extractus Conclusii Ehrb. Oberalten," 19 April 1752, StAHbg, Senat Cl. VII, Lit. Db, no. 21, vol. 1.

70. "P.P." to Rat, 23 August 1796, StAHbg, Senat Cl. VII, Lit. Db, no. 21, vol. 1.

71. Lütkens, "Cammer-Meditationes," p. 2.

72. "Befehl, daß ein ieder den umschreibenden Bürger-Captains oder ihren Officieren bescheiden begegnen, und richtige Antwort geben soll," Blank, vol. 4, pp. 2130–31; "Conclusum Collegii der Sechsziger," 19 September 1759, StAHbg, Senat Cl. VII, Lit. Db, no. 21, vol. 1; earlier list (1732) of those found not "in nexi," in StAHbg, Wedde I, no. 21–23.

73. Mauersberg, *Wirtschafts- und Sozialgeschichte,* pp. 38, 145.

74. See "Introduction" to "Register der von der Wedde in Hamburg von 1698 bis 1750 angenommenen Schutzverwandten," StAHbg, Wedde I, no. 19. Of course, all the numbers here pertain only to *adult males.* Thus, if, for example, we take the numbers given here for 1759—9,000 citizens, 4,000 Schutzverwandten, and 3,300 "others"— they sum to a total of 16,300. If we then use a crude multiplier of four, we reach a population total of about 48,900, to which we must add about 10,000–12,000 Jews. Thus, we arrive with a rough estimate of about 70,900 for 1759, which compares fairly well with the size of the population, 74,575 (excluding Catholics, members of the Dutch Reformed Church, and residents of the parishes of St. Pauli and St. Georg) Mauersberg computed for 1766. Mauersberg, *Wirtschafts- und Sozialgeschichte,* p. 47.

75. "P.P." presented to Rat on 23 August 1796, StAHbg, Senat Cl. VII, Lit. Db, no. 21, vol. 1.

76. "Relation" presented by Johann Daniel Klefeker to the Treasury commission, n.d., StAHbg, Senat Cl. VII, Lit. Db, no. 8, vol. 6.

77. StAHbg, AAI, 58. Locating a specific dwelling in such circumstances was next to impossible. See Finder, *Hamburgisches Bürgertum,* pp. 239–42, 415–16.

78. 30 September 1754, StAHbg, Senat Cl. VII, Lit. Db., no. 21, vol. 1.

79. "Register der von der Wedde in Hamburg von 1698 bis 1750 angenommenen Schutzverwandten," compiled by Arnim Classen in 1963, StAHbg, Wedde I, no. 19; StAHbg, Senat Cl. VII, Lit. De, no. 3, vol. 6 (1741), details here from the company of Captain Lorenz Poppe, St. Jakobi Regiment.

80. Details here from St. Petri parish, 1 February 1732, StAHbg, Senat Cl. VII, Lit. Ga, pars. 2, no. 13, vol. 2.

81. StAHbg, Senat Cl. VII, Lit. Db, no. 8, vol. 6 (1789).

82. According to an untitled lead article on *Polizei* in *ACN* (27 June 1770).

83. Klefeker, vol. 12, pp. 449–55. There were numerous ordinances pertaining to marriage policies passed in the seventeenth and eighteenth centuries. The most important of these, and the model for those following it, was the Wedde mandate of 30 April 1732, Blank, vol. 3, p. 1169.

84. From 30 September 1754, StAHbg, Senat Cl. VII, Lit. Db, no. 21, vol. 1; "Conclusum et Commission," 27 October 1756 in ibid.

85. "Conclusum et Commission," 27 October 1756, StAHbg, Senat Cl. VII, Lit. Db, no. 21, vol. 1; "Conclusum Collegio 60er," September 1759, in ibid.; StAHbg, Senat Cl. VII, Lit. Db, no. 8, vol. 6.

86. "Rückblick auf die Hamburgische Geschichte des Jahres 1803," *HA* 3, no. 1 (1804): 14.

87. *ACN* (27 June 1770).

88. See StAHbg, Senat Cl. VII, Lit. Db, no. 8, vol. 6, and mandate from 2 January 1769 (Blank, vol. 6, pp. 263–64).

89. StAHbg, Senat Cl. VII, Lit. Db, no. 21, vol. 1. See also "Relation cum Voto sowohl über die künftige Regulierung des Schutzgeldes als die damit zu verbindender Gewinnung des Bürgerrechts vom 28. Jun. 1769," StAHbg, Senat Cl. VII, Lit. Db, no. 8, vol. 6.

90. Lütkens, "Cammer-Meditationes," p. 2.

91. "Relation cum Voto . . . ," 28 June 1769, StAHbg, Senat Cl. VII, Lit. Db, no. 8, vol. 6.

92. See StAHbg, Senat Cl. VII, Lit. Db, no. 8, vol. 6, for deliberations from 1770–72; proposal advanced by Senator Volckmann in 1786, "Vorschlag zu einem Commissiorio für die Wohlweisen Wedde Herren die Gewinnung der grossen oder kleinen Bürgerschaft betreffend," 1786, StAHbg, Senat Cl. VII, Lit. Bc, no. 7b, vol. 20, fasc. 4b; deliberations from 1796, StAHbg, Senat Cl. VII, Lit. Db, no. 21, vol. 1; and "Acta die neue Einrichtung der Aufnahme zum Bürger betreffend," 1802–5, StAHbg, Senat Cl. VII, Lit. Bc, no. 7b, vol. 20, fasc. 6c.

93. "Jahresbericht der Wedde über die zum Bürgerrechte als sowie zur Proclamation Zugelassenen, 1790–1817," StAHbg, Senat Cl. VII, Lit. Cc, no. 13, vol. 16a; "Bürgerrecht, varia von der Notwendigkeit Bürger zu werden, oder in Schutz- oder in Fremden-Contrakt zu treten. 1565–1753, 1759–1810," StAHbg, Senat Cl. VII, Lit. Bc, no. 7b, vol. 20, fasc. 1; "Bürgerbuch," StAHbg, Senat Cl. VII, no. XI, vol. 1, fasc. 1a; Mauersberg, *Wirtschafts- und Sozialgeschichte*, p. 34; and the report compiled by Otto Beneke in 1849, "In den bürgerlichen Nexus der Stadt getretene von 1800 an." StAHbg, Senat Cl. VII, Lit. Nc, no. 12, vol. 5a.

94. See mandates from 6 October 1743 and 9 June 1758 in StAHbg, Senat Cl. VII, Lit. Ga, Pars. 2, no. 7. Lists from 1637, 1708, 1710, 1713, 1715, 1734, 1757, 1758, 1771, and 1772 in StAHbg, Senat Cl. VII, Lit. Ga Pars. 2, no. 134, vol. 1; list for 1732, ibid., vol. 2; list for 1734, Senat Cl. VII, Lit. Ga, Pars. 2, no. 7; lists of soldiers, "Englanders," persons lodging aliens, dance halls, and wine taverns from 1807, in StAHbg, Wedde I, 25.

95. From 26 April 1643, in StAHbg, Senat Cl. VII, Lit. Lb, no. 15, fasc. 1; 9 July 1655, Blank, vol. 1, pp. 140–41; 17 December 1671, ibid., pp. 295–96; 31 May 1682, ibid., p. 361; 1 February 1686, ibid., p. 370; 23 February 1686, ibid., p. 371; 12 July 1693, ibid., pp. 429–31; 22 August 1710 [plague], ibid., vol. 2, pp. 662–64; 1 December 1710 [plague], ibid., pp. 693–94; 27 January 1713 [plague], ibid., pp. 794–95 and StAHbg, Senat Cl. VII, Lit. Lb, no. 15, fasc. 1; 21 February 1713, Senat Cl. VII, Lit. Lb, no. 15, fasc. 1; 7 May 1742, Blank, vol. 3, pp. 1401–2; 15 January 1753, ibid., vol. 4, pp. 1886–87; 19 September 1757, ibid., pp. 2103–4; 12 July 1765, ibid., vol. 6, pp. 54–63; 8 April 1768 [esp. sailors], ibid., p. 227; 26 May 1769 [again sailors], ibid., pp. 275–76; 11 March 1772 and 16 September [forbidding innkeepers to advance credit to sailors], ibid., 468–71, 508–9; 28 December 1791 [General Poor Relief], Anderson, vol. 3, pp. 261–62; 9 November 1792 [émigrés], ibid., pp. 344–47 and StAHbg, Senat Cl. VII, Lit. Lb, no. 15, fasc. 2; 9 February 1795 [émigrés], Anderson, vol. 4, pp. 71–75, and StAHbg, Senat Cl. VII, Lit. Lb., no. 15, fasc. 3; 11 November 1795, ibid., fasc. 4; 22 September 1797 [émigrés], Anderson, vol. 5, p. 14; 6 June 1803, ibid., vol. 6, pp. 143–44; 20 November 1805, ibid., vol. 7, pp. 51–55; 10 January 1806 [citizens and *Schutzverwandten* in St. Pauli], ibid., pp. 67–72; 22 January 1807, ibid., pp. 135–36; see also "Verordnungen in Betreff der Fremden," from 1713–1816, StAHbg, Senat Cl. VII, Lit. Lb, no. 15, fasc. 1–3.

96. For examples, see mandates from 19 September 1757, Blank, vol. 4, pp. 2103–4; 12 July 1765, ibid., vol. 6, pp. 54–63; and 11 March 1772, ibid., 468–71.

97. Among others, those from 22 August 1710, Blank, vol. 2, pp. 662–64; 1 December 1710, ibid., pp. 693–94; and 27 January 1713, ibid., pp. 794–95. See also StAHbg, Senat Cl. VII, Lit. Lb, no. 15, fasc. 1.

Chapter 4

1. Karl Biedermann, *Deutschland im achtzehnten Jahrhundert,* 4 vols. (Leipzig, 1867–80), vol. 1, pp. 395–418; Gerhard Uhlhorn, *Die christliche Liebestätigkeit,* 3 vols. (Stuttgart, 1882–90), vol. 3, p. 272; Lotte Koch, *Wandlungen der Wohlfahrtspflege im Zeitalter der Aufklärung* (Erlangen, 1933); Werner von Melle, *Die Entwicklung des öffentlichen Armenwesens in Hamburg* (Hamburg, 1883); Hildegard Urlaub, *Die Förderung der Armenpflege durch die Hamburgische Patriotische Gesellschaft bis zum Beginn des neunzehnten Jahrhunderts* (Berlin, 1932), pp. 1–16; Martin Brandt, *Die Bestrebungen der Hamburgischen Armenanstalt von 1788 zur Erziehung der Armenbevölkerung: Ein Beitrag zur Geschichte der Industrieschule* (Hamburg, 1937), pp. 7–41; Hans Scherpner, *Die Kinderfürsorge in der Hamburgischen Armenreform vom Jahre 1788* (Berlin, 1927); Carl Schultheiss, "Die philanthropische Pädogogik in Hamburg," *MVHG* 14 (1826): 197–200; Adolf Streng, *Geschichte der Gefängnisverwaltung in Hamburg von 1622–1872* (Hamburg, 1890); Wilhelm Traphagen, *Die ersten Arbeitshäuser und ihre pädagogische Funktion* (Berlin, 1935); Heinrich Sieveking, "Hamburgische Gefängnisfürsorge im 18. Jahrhundert," *AZ* 3 (1933–34): 94–106.

2. Marc Raeff, *The Well-Ordered Police State: Social and Institutional Change Through Law in the Germanies and Russia, 1600–1800* (New Haven, Conn. and London, 1983), esp. introduction and pt. 1: "Intellectual Background to Change"; Mack Walker, "Rights and Functions: The Social Categories of Eighteenth-Century German Jurists and Cameralists," *JMH* 50 (1978): 234–51; and Joachim Heinrich Peter, *Die Probleme der Armut in den Lehren der Kameralisten: (Eine dogmengeschichtliche Studie)* (Berlin, 1934).

3. On the importance of statistics to the cameralists, see Raeff, *Well-Ordered Police State*, p. 158; Franz Eulenberg, "Zur historischen Bevölkerungsstatistik in Deutschland," *Jahrbücher für Nationalökonomie*, 3rd ser. 29 (1905): 519–27; Ferdinand Felsing, *Die Statistik als Methode der politischen Ökonomie im 17. und 18. Jahrhundert* (Borna-Leipzig, 1930); Erich Frohneberg, *Bevölkerungslehre und Bevölkerungspolitik des Merkantilismus unter besondere Berücksichtigung des 17. und 18. Jahrhunderts und der Länder Deutschland, England, Frankreich und Italien* (Gelnhausen, 1930); and Oskar Jolles, *Die Ansichten der deutschen nationalökonomischen Schriftsteller des 16. und 17. Jahrhunderts über Bevölkerungswesen* (Jena, 1886).

4. Peter, *Probleme der Armut*, pp. 112–34, 151–74; Christoph Sachße and Florian Tennstedt, *Geschichte der Armenfürsorge in Deutschland* (Stuttgart, 1980), vol. 1, pp. 99–113.

5. Sachße and Tennstedt, *Geschichte der Armenfürsorge*, vol. 1, pp. 113–25.

6. As did Johann Joachim Becher in his *Politischer discurs, von den eigentlichen ursachen des auff- und abnehmens der städt länder und republiken in specie, Wie ein Land Volckreich und Nahrhafft zu machen/ und in eine recht Societatem civilem zu bringen. Auch wird von dem Bauern- Handwercks- und Kauffmanns- Standt/ derer Handel und Wandel/ Item, Von dem Monopolio, Polypolio und Propolio von allgemeinen Land-Magazinen, Niederlagen/ Kauffhäusern/ Montibus Pietatis/ Zucht- und Werck-Häusern/ Wechselbäncken und dergleichen ausführlich gehandelt*, 3rd ed. (Frankfurt, 1688), here quoted in Peter, *Probleme der Armut*, p. 203.

7. Peter, *Probleme der Armut*, p. 218; Sachße and Tennstedt, *Geschichte der Armenfürsorge*, vol. 1, pp. 113–25.

8. Johann Heinrich Gottlob von Justi, *Grundsätze der Policeywissenschaften, in einem Vernünftigen, auf den Endzweck der Policey gegründeten, Zusammenhänge und zum Gebrauch Akademischer Vorlesungen, abgefasset*, 3rd rev. ed. (Göttingen, 1782; repr. ed., Frankfurt, 1969), vol. 2, pp. 432, 218.

9. Peter, *Probleme der Armut*, pp. 70–174.

10. Peter identified in cameralism—in this case represented by Seckendorff—"the articulation of a drive toward economic progress" (*Probleme der Armut*, pp. 195–96). See also Raeff, *Well-Ordered Police State*, pp. 89–91. Cf. bibliography in Georg Heinrich Zincke, *Cameralisten-Bibliothek, worinne nebst der Anleitung die Cameral-Wissenschaft zu lehren und zu lernen, ein vollständiges Verzeichniss der Bücher und Schriften von der Land- und Stadt-Öconomie, dem Policey- Finanz- und Cammerwesen zu finden, so theils kurz beurtheilet, theils umständlich vorgestellt worden*, 2 vols. (Leipzig, 1751–1752; reprint ed., 1973), vol. 1, pp. 215–28, 282–96.

11. Becher, *Politischer discurs*, p. 78. Cf. Joachim Georg Darjes, *Erste Gründe der Cameralwissenschaften* (Jena, 1756), p. 454.

12. Zincke favored a tax, while Justi didn't. Peter, *Probleme der Armut*, pp. 217, 222.

13. Ibid., p. 226.

14. Ibid.; Sachße and Tennstedt, *Geschichte der Armenfürsorge*, vol. 1, pp. 125–30.

15. This "conscious drive [of society] to maximize all its resources and to use this new potential dynamically for the enlargement and improvement of its way of life," Marc Raeff defined as modernity. Specifically, the state assumed "the active, dynamic task of fostering the productive energies of society" as well as providing "the appropriate institutional framework." "The Well-Ordered Police State and the Development of Modernity in Seventeenth- and Eighteenth-Century Europe: An Attempt at a Comparative Approach," *AHR* 80 (1975): 1222, 1227.

16. Paul Billerbeck, "Sozialpolitische Ideen in der deutschen kameralistischen und

pädagogischen Literatur des 18. Jahrhunderts" (Ph.D. diss., Cologne, 1938); Wilhelm Bleek, *Von der Kameralausbildung zur Juristenprivileg: Studium, Prüfung und Ausbildung der höhern Beamten des allgemeinen Verwaltungsdienstes in Deutschland im 18. und 19. Jahrhundert* (Berlin, 1972); Walther Merk, *Der Gedanke des gemeinen Besten in der deutschen Staats- und Rechtsentwicklung* (Weimar, 1934); Hans Jürgen Puhle, "Vom Wohlfahrtsausschuss zum Wohlfahrtsstaat: Entwicklungstendenzen staatlicher Aufgabenstellung und Verwaltungsprobleme im Zeichen von Industrialisierung und Demokratisierung," in Gerhard A. Ritter, ed., *Vom Wohlfahrtsausschuss zum Wohlfahrtsstaat: Der Staat in der modernen Industriegesellschaft* (Cologne, 1973), pp. 29–68; Albion W. Small, *The Cameralists: Pioneers of German Social Polity* (New York, 1909).

17. There was, for example, an association of former Göttingen students in Hamburg who met regularly on Saturday evenings. Franklin Kopitzsch, *Grundzüge einer Sozialgeschichte der Aufklärung in Hamburg und Altona* (Hamburg, 1982), p. 531. Their records are preserved in Sonnabendgesellschaft Hamburgischer Studenten in StAHbg, 614–1, Gelehrte Gesellschaften. See also Percy Ernst Schramm, "Die von den Hamburgern bevorzugten Universitäten (Ende des 17. bis Anfang des 18. Jahrhunderts)," *ZVHG* 52 (1965): 83–90. On the reform program of the Enlightenment, see Franco Venturi, *Utopia and Reform in the Enlightenment* (Cambridge, Eng. 1971); Rudolf Vierhaus, *Deutschland im Zeitalter des Absolutismus (1648–1763)* (Göttingen, 1978); Helen Liebel, *Enlightened Bureaucracy versus Enlightened Despotism in Baden, 1750–1792* (Philadelphia, 1965); Eberhard Weis, "Absolute Monarchie und Reform in Deutschland des späten 18. und frühen 19. Jahrhunderts," in Franklin Kopitzsch, ed., *Aufklärung, Absolutismus und Bürgertum in Deutschland: Zwölf Aufsätze* (Munich, 1976), pp. 192–219; and Charles Ingrao, "The Problem of 'Enlightened Absolutism' and the German States," *JMH* 58, suppl. (1986): S161–S180.

18. On the various "patriotic societies" in Germany, see the articles in Rudolf Vierhaus, ed., *Deutsche patriotische und gemeinnützige Gesellschaften* (Munich, 1980).

19. Kopitzsch, *Grundzüge*, pp. 269–96; Hans Hubrig, *Die patriotischen Gesellschaften des 18. Jahrhunderts* (Weinheim, 1957); Wolfgang Martens, *Die Botschaft der Tugend: Die Aufklärung im Spiegel der deutschen moralischen Wochenschriften* (Stuttgart, 1968). In the very last issue of *Der Patriot* to appear, no. 156 (28 December 1726), the editor indicated that its purpose had been primarily "to improve the morals of my fellow-citizens," to polish the German language, and to call attention to social and moral problems "that otherwise would not be discussed or would be ignored."

20. *Der Patriot* appeared weekly from 1724 through 1726. Wolfgang Martens has brought out a modern edition, *Der Patriot nach der Originalausgabe Hamburg 1724–1726 in drei Textbänden und einem Kommentarband kritisch herausgegeben von Wolfgang Martens*, 4 vols. (Berlin and New York, 1972, 1984); Jürgen Rathje, " 'Der Patriot,' eine hamburgische Zeitschrift der ersten Hälfte des 18. Jahrhunderts," *ZVHG* 65 (1979): 123–43, and idem, "Geschichte, Wesen und Öffentlichkeitswirkung der Patriotischen Gesellschaft von 1724 in Hamburg," in Vierhaus, *Deutsche patriotische und gemeinnützige Gesellschaften*, pp. 51–69; and Jörg Scheibe, *Der "Patriot" (1724–1726) und sein Publikum: Untersuchungen über die Verfasserschaft und die Leserschaft einer Zeitschrift der frühen Aufklärung* (Göppingen, 1973).

21. No. 4 (27 January 1724). Compare the very similar definitions of patriot and patriotism advanced by Johann Moritz Gericke, *Versuch einer allgemeinen Abhandlung vom Patriotismus* (Hamburg, 1792), p. 13, and by J.A.H. Reimarus, "Anrede an die den 10ten October 1765 zum erstenmal von den Vorstehern zusammenberufenen Mitglieder der Gesellschaft," *VS* 1 (1792): 9–17. See also the definition of "Patriot" in

Johann Heinrich Zedler, *Grosses vollständiges Universal-Lexikon, aller Wissenschaften und Künste, welche bishero durch menschlichen Verstand und Witz erfunden und verbessert worden . . .,* 64 vols. (Leipzig and Halle, 1732–50), cf. the article "Patriot" in *Krünitzs Encyklopädie* (1808), which reflects the change toward the nineteenth-century meaning of patriot.

22. As Harvey Chisick has quite correctly indicated, in the eighteenth century "patriotism was primarily a social, and not, as it was in antiquity and was again to become, a political concept." Enlightenment patriotism was "positively oriented towards assuring the well-being of the whole community." *The Limits of Reform in the Enlightenment: Attitudes Toward the Education of the Lower Classes in Eighteenth-Century France* (Princeton, N.J., 1981), p. 223. The most complete treatment of civic patriotism in Hamburg is Steven D. Uhalde, "Citizen and World-Citizen: Civic Patriotism and Cosmopolitanism in Eighteenth Century Hamburg" (Ph.D. diss., University of California, Berkeley, 1984).

23. Quote from Chisick, *Limits of Reform,* p. 223; see also Kopitzsch, *Grundzüge,* pp. 344–48.

24. Johann A. H. Reimarus, and his *Entwurf eines allgemeinen Staats-Unterrichts für künftige Bürger* (Hamburg, 1803), in which he defined service to the fatherland as working to achieve the common good and of educating children to be upright, active, and skilled citizens. Here, pp. iv–v.

25. *Der Patriot,* no. 4 (27 January 1724).

26. *Der Patriot,* no. 113 (28 February 1726).

27. Ibid.; see also Wolfgang Martens, ed., *Der Patriot nach dem Originalausgabe Hamburg 1724–1726 in drei Textbänden und einem Kommentarband kritisch herausgegeben,* 4 vols. (Berlin, 1969–84), vol. 4, pp. 366–69.

28. *Derr Patriot,* no. 37 (13 September 1724); comments in Martens, *Patriot nach der Originalausgabe,* vol. 1, pp. 311–12, 315, and vol. 2, pp. 199–200.

29. *Der Patriot,* no. 37 (13 September 1724).

30. *Der Patriot,* no. 17 (14 June 1725).

31. On the circle of "patriots," see Kopitzsch, *Grundzüge,* pp. 260–72, and Christian Petersen, "Die Teutsch-übende Gesellschaft in Hamburg," *ZVHG* 2 (1847): 533–64; on individual members, see Johann Otto Thiessen, *Versuch einer Gelehrtengeschichte von Hamburg nach alphabetischer Ordnung mit kritischen und pragmatischen Bemerkungen,* 2 vols. (Hamburg, 1780), vol. 1, pp. 67–69 [Brockes], p. 349 [Klefeker], p. 15 [Anckelmann], p. 174 [Fabricius], and pp. 315–16 [Hoffmann]; Karl Jacoby, "Litterarisches Leben um die Wende des 17. Jahrhunderts," in Theodor Schrader, ed., *Hamburg vor 200 Jahren: Gesammelte Vorträge* (Hamburg, 1892), pp. 49–142, esp. pp. 107–14 [Richey] and pp. 114–42 [Brockes]; the relevant articles in *NDB, ADB,* and *Lexikon der Schriftsteller;* Kurt Detlev Möller, "Johann Albert Fabricius, 1668–1736," *ZVHG* 36 (1937): 1–64; Friedrich Brachmann, *Johann Hübner. Johannei Rector 1711–1731: Ein Beitrag zur Geschichte der deutschen Literatur* (Hamburg, 1899); Hans-Dieter Loose, ed., *Barthold Heinrich Brockes (1680–1747). Dichter und Ratsherr in Hamburg: Neue Forschungen zu Persönlichkeit und Wirkung* (Hamburg, 1980); and Elger Blühm, "Christoph Friederich Weichmann: Redakteur des Schiffbeker 'Correspondenten,' " *ZVHG* 53 (1967): 69–78.

32. Joachim Whaley, "The Protestant Enlightenment" in Roy Porter and Mikuláš Teich, eds., *The Enlightenment in National Context* (Cambridge, 1981), p. 108.

33. Franklin Kopitzsch, "Die Hamburger Aufklärung und das Armenproblem," in Arno Herzig, Dieter Langewiesche, and Arnold Swottek, eds., *Arbeiter in Hamburg* (Hamburg, 1983), pp. 51–60; von Melle, *Entwicklung,* pp. 54–61.

34. "Proposition E. E. Raths an die Erbgesessene Bürgerschaft, vom 4 Oct. 1725," Klefeker, vol. 1, pp. 408–22; see also Klefeker, vol. 1, pp. 298–99.

35. Klefeker, vol. 1, p. 410.

36. Ibid., pp. 411–12.

37. Ibid., pp. 413–15.

38. "Neue Armen-Ordnung, und Anweisung zur Abschaffung der Gassen-Betteley, daß nemlich die nothleidenden Armen sich bey den Provisoren des Werk- und Zucht-Hauses zum Wollen-Spinnen und Strumpf-Stricken melden sollen," Blank, vol. 2, pp. 1062–69; see also Klefeker, vol. 1, pp. 300–4.

39. In the years after 1726, the number of supported poor ranged between 1,200 and 2,500. Streng, *Gefängnisverwaltung,* p. 65.

40. "Neue Armen-Ordnung," Blank, vol. 2, pp. 1064–65; "Notifikation wegen der Strumpf-Strickerey beym Werk- und Zuchthause," Blank, vol. 2, p. 1075.

41. Blank, vol. 2, pp. 1064–67.

42. "Mandat gegen das Hereindringen der Bettler, und die Bettler Herbergen," 23 March 1650, Blank, vol. 1, pp. 82–83; "Renovirtes- Mandat vom 1663. 13 Dec. für die Bettel-Voigte," Blank, vol. 1, pp. 223–24 (cf. Klefeker, vol. 1, p. 292); "Mandate gegen die Bettley," from 11 March 1692, Blank, vol. 1, pp. 421–24; "Mandat, daß die Vöigte alle Bettler wegnehmen . . ." 21 March 1701, Blank, vol. 2, pp. 543–46 (cf. Klefeker, vol. 1, p. 293); and "Verhaltungs-Orden für die Substituten der Kirchen- und Bettelvögte," 6 April 1735, Blank, vol. 3, pp. 1245–47 (cf. Klefeker, vol. 1, p. 304).

Records of punishment of beggar-chasers who abused their office are found in the "Decretenbücher des Zuchthauses," StAHbg, Gefängnisverwaltung, A15a, vol. 1 (1776–89). For example, acting on the complaint of one Johann Carl Riebling, the magistrates ordered the imprisonment of two beggar chasers who had falsely accused him of (indeed, arrested him for) begging on the streets. "Extr. Prot. Senat. Hamb." from 8 January 1777 in Decretenbücher, vol. 1. The governors of the Zuchthaus recognized that "die strengste Disciplin" was necessary to keep the Vögte in hand according to "Compendium," StAHbg, Gefängnisverwaltung, A16, pp. 68–69. Yet the abuses continued, even under the new regime of the General Poor Relief. See Jonas Ludwig von Heß, *Hamburg, topographisch, politisch und historisch beschrieben,* 2nd ed. 3 vols. (Hamburg, 1810–11), vol. 2, pp. 112n–15n.

Numerous mandates were passed to try to provide more security and more respect for the beggar chasers, apparently to no avail. See, for example, mandates from 15 October 1742, Blank, vol. 3, p. 1409 (cf. Klefeker, vol. 1, p. 305) and from 17 March 1745, Blank, vol. 3, pp. 1497–99 (cf. Klefeker, vol. 1, p. 305).

43. Blank, vol. 2, pp. 1066–68.

44. "Compendium," StAHbg, Gefängnisverwaltung, A16, pp. 66–67.

45. Ibid., pp. 65–69.

46. Ibid., pp. 67–69.

47. Quoted in Klefeker, vol. 1, pp. 302–3.

48. "Notifikation wegen der Strumpf-Strickerey beym Werk- und Zuchthause," from 29 May 1727, Blank, vol. 2, p. 1075 (cf. Klefeker, vol. 1, pp. 302–3). On the number of people engaged in knitting stockings in 1732, see Streng, *Gefängnis-verwaltung,* p. 64.

49. Johann Georg Büsch, "Historischer Bericht von dem Gange und fortdau-erndem Verfall des Hamburgischen Armenwesens seit der Zeit der Reformation," in his *Zwei kleine Schriften die im Werk begriffene Verbesserung des Armenwesens in dieser Stadt Hamburg betreffend* (Hamburg, 1786), §§36–38, and his *Erfahrungen,* 4 vols. (Hamburg, 1792–94), vol. 3, pp. 22–24.

50. Büsch, "Historischer Bericht," §34.

51. Büsch, *Erfahrungen,* vol. 3, pp. 22–23; von Heß, *Hamburg* (1st ed.), vol. 1, p. 349.

52. "Wurden die gesunden Bettler im Jahre 1741 zum damaligen Vestungs-Bau an der Stern-Schanze auf eine Zeitlang gewidmet, . . . ," Blank, vol. 3, p. 1375; Klefeker, vol. 1, p. 305; "Verordnung, dass die frevelnden muthwilligen Bettler zuerst ins Werk- und Zuchthaus gebracht, demnächst aber als Colonisten nach Neu-Schottland ausgeschifft werden sollen," Blank, vol. 4, pp. 1880–81 (cf. Klefeker, vol. 1, p. 305).

53. Büsch, *Erfahrungen,* vol. 3, pp. 22–23; Streng, *Gefängnisverwaltung,* pp. 30–36.

54. Büsch, "Historischer Bericht," §35.

55. "Extr. Prot. Sen. Ham.," September 1781 in Decretenbücher des Zuchthauses, vol. 1 (1776–89), StAHbg, Gefängnisverwaltung, A15a.

56. Caspar Voght, *Gesammeltes aus der Geschichte der Hamburgischen Armen-Anstalt während ihrer fünfzigjährigen Dauer* (Hamburg, 1838), p. 7.

57. The Rat and Bürgerschaft financed the new Relief, at least in part, through a property tax (*Grabengeld*). Later they added other sources of revenue. The Relief regularly received one third of the semiannual collection taken up for the Zuchthaus, and a further sum from the moneys raised by the *Gotteskasten*. After 1740, the proceeds of a 0.5 percent tax on all goods sold at auction flowed into the coffers of the Relief and later, in 1774, the Relief shared in the revenues from yet another property tax (*Dreckkarrengeld*). von Heß, *Hamburg* (1st ed.), vol. 1, p. 359; "Extract. Prot. extraj. Senatus, für den Ausrufer, wegen des halben Procents von Kaufmanns-Waaren, so der Armen-Ordnung gewidmet," 9 March 1740, Blank, vol. 3, pp. 1359–61; "Notification wegen des von der Makler-Courtage zu zahlenden Quarts, zum Behuf der Armen-Ordnung," 12 May 1730, Blank, vol. 2, p. 1105 (cf. Klefeker, vol. 1, p. 303).

58. Büsch, "Historischer Bericht," §35.

59. These periodic collections occurred at least once or twice each year, most regularly in December, January, and February—see Blank and Anderson for examples. Collections were taken up to deal with special circumstances; two collections were taken to help the flood victims in Finkenwärder, 22 October 1777 (Anderson, vol. 1, pp. 241–44) and 18 November 1778 (Anderson, vol. 1, pp. 290–92), and "durch den diesjährigen Eisgang und darauf erfolgte Wasser-Noth . . ." 2 June 1784 Anderson, vol. 2, pp. 40–42. Another collection aided the "abgebrannte," 18 November 1778 (Anderson, vol. 1, pp. 290–92). The inflation of 1771–72 required additional collections, for example, "Notification einer am Neujahrs-Tage des bevorstehenden 1772sten Jahres, zur Versorgung der hiesigen Armen mit Brodt, bey gegenwärtiger Theuerung, öffentlich anzustellenden Sammlung milder Gaben, welche am ersten heil. Weihnachts-Tage vor den Kanzeln abzulesen verordnet worden," 20 December 1771, Blank, vol. 6, pp. 462–64.

60. The archive of the Patriotic Society was partially destroyed in the Great Fire of 1842 and ravaged by fire several more times over the years. Only two or three manuscripts survive. The library burned in the bombings during World War II. The literature on the Patriotic Society of 1765 is voluminous—almost overwhelming! The most recent and best works, from the standpoint of modern historical research, are those written by Franklin Kopitzsch, especially his "Die Hamburgische Gesellschaft zur Beförderung der Künste und nützlichen Gewerbe (Patriotische Gesellschaft von 1765) im Zeitalter der Aufklärung: Ein Überblick," in Vierhaus, ed., *Deutsche patriotische und gemeinnützige Gesellschaften,* pp. 71–118, and Kopitzsch, *Grundzüge,* pp. 328–56; Uhalde, "Citizen and World-Citizen," esp. pp. 259–334. Several somewhat older

works are still valuable, especially Gustav Kowalewski, *Geschichte der Hamburgischen Gesellschaft zur Beförderung der Künste und nützlichen Gewerbe* (*Patriotische Gesellschaft*), 3 pts. in 7 vols. (Hamburg, 1897–1913). The first volume (*Geschichte der Hamburgischen Gesellschaft zur Beförderung der Künste und nützlichen Gewerbe*) is an invaluable introduction to the history of the Patriotic Society. See also *165 Jahre Patriotische Gesellschaft: Ein hamburgisches Jahrbuch 1930* (Hamburg, 1930); Ernst Baasch, "Der Einfluß des Handels auf das Geistesleben Hamburgs," *Pfingstblätter des hansischen Geschichtsvereins*, vol. 5 (Leipzig, 1909); Gustav Kowalewski, "Die Gründung der Patriotischen Gesellschaft im Urteile der Zeitgenossen," in *Jahrbuch der Hamburgischen Gesellschaft zur Beförderung der Künste und nützlichen Gewerbe* (*Patriotische Gesellschaft, gestiftet 1765*) (1907–9), pp. 1–5, and "Die Hamburgische Patriotische Gesellschaft und die Wirtschaftssysteme des 18. Jahrhunderts," in ibid., pp. 6–33; Otto Brunner, "Die Patriotische Gesellschaft in Hamburg im Wandel von Staat und Gesellschaft (1965)," in his *Neue Wege der Verfassungs- und Sozialgeschichte*, 2nd enl., ed. (Göttingen, 1968), pp. 335–44; *Die Patriotische Gesellschaft zu Hamburg, 1765–1965; Festschrift der Hamburgischen Gesellschaft zur Beförderung der Künste und nützlichen Gewerbe* (Hamburg, 1965); Helen Liebel, "Laissez-faire vs. Mercantilism: The Rise of Hamburg & the Hamburg Bourgeoisie vs. Frederick the Great in the Crisis of 1763," *VSWG* 52 (1965): 207–38. Important contemporary accounts are the *Nachricht von der Hamburgischen Gesellschaft zur Beförderung der Künste und nützlichen Gewerbe* (Hamburg, 1770); Johann A. H. Reimarus, "Anrede an die den 10ten October 1765 zum erstenmal von den Vorstehern zusammenberufenen Mitglieder der Gesellschaft [1765]," *VS* 1 (1792): 9–17; and Johann Arnold Günther, "Versuch einer Geschichte der Gesellschaft in den ersten 25 Jahren nach ihrer Einrichtung: Vorlesung am 15. April 1790," ibid., pp. 52–95.

61. Baasch, "Einfluß des Handels"; Liebel, "Laissez-faire vs. Mercantilism," pp. 222–24. On the crisis of 1763, see Liebel, "Laissez-faire vs. Mercantilism"; Stephen Skalweit, *Die Berliner Wirtschaftskrise von 1763 und ihre Hintergründe* (Stuttgart and Berlin, 1937); W. O. Henderson, "The Berlin Commercial Crisis of 1763," *EHR* 15 (1962–63): 89–102; and Elizabeth E. de Jong-Keesing, *De economische crisis van 1763 te Amsterdam* (Amsterdam, 1939).

62. I have drawn on the following contemporary accounts, which present a picture of severe depression from 1763 through at least the middle of the 1780s: Johann Georg Büsch, *Kleine Schriften über die Handlung* (Hamburg and Kiel, 1784); idem, *Schriften über Staatswirthschaft und Handlung*, 3 vols. (Hamburg, 1780–84); idem, *Versuch einer Geschichte der Hamburgischen Handlung, nebst zwei kleineren Schriften eines verwandten Inhalts* (Hamburg, 1797); P.H.C. Brodhagen, "Allgemeine Bemerkungen über die ehemalige Verfassung des hamburgischen Manufaktur- und Fabrikwesens, über die damit bis auf unsere Zeit vorgegangenen Veränderungen und über den Zustand der gegenwärtig [1792] hieselbst existierenden Manufakturen, Fabriken und Gewerbe," *VS* 3 (1795): 97–168; idem, "Auszug aus den Verhandlungen der Gesellschaft über einen ihr eingeschickten Vorschlag zur Anlegung einer Manufactur halbseidenener Zeuge [1790]," *VS* 1 (1792): 305–12; von Heß, *Hamburg* (2nd ed.), vol. 3, pp. 233–437; "Des Herrn Michäl Richey der Geschichte und griechischen Sprache öffentlichen Lehrers und dies Jahr des Gymnasii zu Hamburg Rectors Anmerckungen über die bey Rengern in Halle herausgekommene Nachricht von Hamburg nebst einer Anleitung zur Hamburgischen Histoire: Im Jahre 1758," StAHbg, *HS* 272. Compare the modern historical works that basically corroborate this view: Henning Matthaei, *Untersuchungen zur Frühgeschichte der deutschen Berufsschule dargestellt am Wirken der Patriotischen Gesellschaft zu Hamburg im 18. Jahrhundert* (Ham-

burg, 1967), pp. 37–39; Walther Vogel, "Handelskonjuncturen und Wirtschaftskrisen in ihrer Auswirkung auf der Seehandel der Hansestädte 1560 bis 1806," *HGB* 74 (1956): 57–64; Heinrich Laufenberg, *Hamburg und sein Proletariat im achtzehnten Jahrhundert: Eine wirtschaftshistorische Vorstudie zur Geschichte der modernen Arbeiterbewegung im niederelbischen Städtegebiet* (Hamburg, 1910); Hans Mauersberg, *Wirtschafts- und Sozialgeschichte zentraleuropäischer Städte in neuerer Zeit: Dargestellt an den Beispielen von Basel, Frankfurt a.M., Hamburg, Hannover und München* (Göttingen, 1960), pp. 335–37, 343–47, 350–52, 364, 369–72. A dissenting view is expressed by J.E.F. Westphalen. Writing in 1806, he gave an account of sustained and even accelerated growth beginning soon after the "momentary crisis" of 1763. "Der Zustand des Handels," StAHbg, *HS,* 381b.

63. August von Hennings, "Hamburg im vorigen Jahrhundert. (Aus den Nachrichten eines Engländers über Holstein, Hamburg, Altona, etwa 1785, mit Bemerkungen von 1884, von Hennings' Handschriften, 17, 49)," *Mittheilungen aus der Stadtbibliothek Hamburg* 3 (1886): 5–8.

64. J[ohann] U[lrich] Pauli, *An alle wahre Patrioten Hamburgs gerichtete Ermahnung, zur Aufrichtung einer ähnlichen Patriotischen Gesellschaft, zur Aufnahme der Handlung, der Künste, der Manufacturen und des Ackerbaues, wie die zu London und Paris ist; nebst einer Beylage: Auszug aus der Handlungszeitung von Paris genannt, den gegenwärtigen Zustand beyder Gesellschaften betreffend* (Hamburg, 1765).

65. Ibid., quoted in Kopitzsch, *Grundzüge,* p. 333.

66. Reimarus, "Anrede."

67. *Verhandlungen und Schriften der Hamburgischen Gesellschaft zur Beförderung der Künste und nützlichen Gewerbe,* 7 vols. (Hamburg, 1792–1807).

68. Brodhagen, "Auszug über Anlegung einer Manufaktur halbseidener Zeuge [1790]"; idem, "Allgemeine Bemerkungen über den Zustand der gegenwärtig hieselbst existierenden Manufakturen, Fabriken und Gewerbe [1792]," pp. 101–22; "Verhandlungen der Gesellschaft, über die Vortheile und Nachtheile der Zünfte und Gilden, und über Verbesserung oder gänzliche Aufhebung derselben [1792]," *VS* 3 (1795): 169–324; "Verhandlungen über die anwendbarsten Vorschläge zu zweckmäßigen Arten von Zwangs-Arbeiten für faule und widerspenstige Arme beiderlei Geschlechts [1790]," ibid., vol. 1, pp. 175–212; "Verhandlungen der Gesellschaft über die Untersuchung der vorzüglichsten Quellen der Verarmung in den niedern Ständen, in besonderer Rücksicht auf Hamburg, und der würksamsten und anwendbarsten Mittel dieser Verarmung zu wehren [1790]," ibid., pp. 333–96.

69. The following were some important statements on free trade and the advantages offered by free commercial cities: Büsch, "Allgemeine Anmerkungen über den Zustand der Handlung, vornehmlich in den Europäischen Staaten, und über einige Vorurtheile in der neuern Handlungspolitik," in his *Kleine Schriften von der Handlung und anderem gemeinnützigen Inhalte* (Leipzig 1772), pp. 35–170; idem, *Versuch einer Geschichte der hamburgischen Handlung, nebst zwei kleineren Schriften eines verwandten Inhalts* (Hamburg, 1797); idem, *Grundriss einer Geschichte der merkwürdigsten Welthandel neuerer Zeit in einem erzählenden Vortrage,* 3rd rev. and enl. ed. (Hamburg, 1796); Johann A. H. Reimarus, *Handlungs-Grundsätze zur wahren Aufnahme der Länder und zur Beförderung der Glückseligkeit ihrer Einwohner aus der Natur und Geschichte untersucht* ("Cosmopolis" [Frankfurt am Main and Leipzig], 1768); *Die wichtigen Fragen von der freyen Aus- und Einfuhre des Getraides, nach der Natur und Geschichte untersucht* (Hamburg, 1771); idem, "Verhandlung der Gesellschaft über die Preisaufgabe über den Einfluss der Handels-Städte auf benachbarte Staaten [1795–96]," *VS* 5 (1799): 97–196; [Johannes Schuback], "Vorstellung welche

an den kön.[iglichen] preuss.[ischen] geheimen Etats Minister Herrn von Horst ist eingesandt worden, enthaltend ein Gutachten wie die Handlung in und nach den Preuss.[ischen] Staaten in besseren Flor zu bringen ist, Oct. 13, 1769," repr. in Ernst Baasch, ed., *Quellen zur Geschichte von Hamburgs Handel und Schiffahrt im 17., 18. und 19. Jahrhundert.*, (Hamburg, 1910), pp. 172–89.

70. In 1721 Hamburg became a *porto transito,* abolishing transit duties on many goods, but retaining it on others, in particular, on grain. This freedom was, however, only enjoyed by the large burghers. In 1748 a *transito* for grain was granted. In a series of decisions [in 1764 ("Extract. Protocolli Senatus Hamb. wegen der den Leinewandten, auch dem Garn, Kupfer und Blech beygelegten Zoll-Freyheit," 27 June, Blank, vol. 5, pp. 2442–43), in 1765 ("Extractus Protocolli Senatus Hamb. wegen Extendirung der Zoll-Freyheit von Leinen, Garn, Kupfer und Blech," 20 February, Blank, vol. 6, pp. 23–24), in 1768 ("Abdruck des Rat- und Bürger-Schlusses vom 24. November 1768, einige Zol-Artikel betreffend," 30 November, Blank, vol. 6, pp. 244–46), in 1770 ("Extractus Protocolli Senatus Hamb. wegen Verzollung des Reißes," from 28 May, Blank, vol. 6, p. 345), in 1775, in 1777, and in 1786], the Rat abolished other export and transit duties on linen, yarn, tin, copper, wine, brandy, vinegar, and wood. Klefeker, vol. 12, pp. 585–618; Erwin Wiskemann, *Hamburg und die Welthandelspolitik von den Anfängen bis zur Gegenwart* (Hamburg, 1939), p. 112.

71. Ernst Baasch, *Die Handelskammer zu Hamburg, 1665–1913,* 3 vols. (Hamburg, 1915), vol. 1, p. 119.

72. Reimarus, for example, saw the need for state intervention to remedy many sorts of "social disequilibriums": Liebel, "Laissez-faire vs. Mercantilism," p. 232; Reimarus, "Bedenken über die Frage—ob der Staat Gesetze für die Erziehung und den Unterricht der Kinder verschreiben soll?" *BJ* 1 (1790): 71–83, and his *Entwurf eines allgemeinen Staats-Unterrichts für künftige Bürger* (Hamburg, 1803). Yet he refused to accept state regulation of the professions. See his *Untersuchung der vermeinten Nothwendigkeit eines autorisirten Kollegii medizi und einer medizinischen Zwangs-Ordnung* (Hamburg, 1781).

73. Liebel, "Laissez-faire vs. Mercantilism," p. 238.

74. Baasch, *Handelskammer,* vol. 1, p. 118.

75. "Verhandlungen der Gesellschaft, über die Vortheile und Nachtheile der Zünfte und Gilden," *VS* 3 (1795): 169–324, here p. 176.

76. *Gewerbefreiheit* was proclaimed into law on 7 November 1864 ("Gewerbegesetz. Auf Befehl E. H. Senats der freien und Hansestadt Hamburg publicirt den 7. November 1864," Anderson/Lappenberg, vol. 32, pp. 161–79) and went into effect on 1 February 1865. Hans-Dieter Loose and Werner Jochmann, eds., *Hamburg: Geschichte der Stadt und ihrer Bewohner,* 2 vols. (Hamburg, 1982–86), vol. 1, pp. 531–32; Hermann Kwiet, "Die Einführung der Gewerbefreiheit in Hamburg 1861 bis 1865," (Ph.D. diss., Hamburg, 1947).

77. There is no full-length biography available for Büsch. Thus, his autobiography is still the most important source on his life, esp. his *Erfahrungen,* vol. 4, *Ueber den Gang meines Geistes und meiner Thätigkeit.* See also Büsch in *ADB; Lexikon der Schriftsteller; Meusels Lexikon,* vol. 1, pp. 693–700; obituaries in *ACN* (9 October 1800) by von Ebeling and by Günther (probably) in the *HM,* respectively, vol. 4, pp. 337–45, and vol. 5, p. 165; and J. Joachim Eschenberg, *Dem Andenken des Prof. J. G. Büsch* (Braunschweig, 1800). See also J. H. B. Nolting, *Johann Georg Büsch: Professor der Mathematik an dem Gymnasium in Hamburg* (Hamburg, 1801); Hans Nirrnheim, "Johann Georg Büsch, (Mitbegründer und der erste Vorsteher der Patriotischen Gesellschaft.) Vortrag, gehalten im Verein für Hamburgische Geschichte am 3. Decem-

ber 1900 . . ."; and Franklin Kopitzsch, "Johann Georg Büsch oder von hamburgischen Tradition der Sozialarbeit," in *Jahresbericht der Hamburgischen Gesellschaft zur Beförderung der Künste und nützlichen Gewerbe (Patriotische Gesellschaft von 1765) für das Geschäftsjahr 1981/82* (Hamburg, 1982), pp. 35–40.

78. Kopitzsch, *Grundzüge,* pp. 539–41.

79. Johann Georg Büsch, *Theoretisch-praktische Darstellung der Handlung in ihren mannichfaltigen Geschäften,* 2 vols. (Hamburg, 1792, 1799), vol. 1, p. 34.

80. Ibid., vol. 2, p. 237; Büsch and Christoph Daniel Ebeling, eds., *Handlungsbibliothek,* 3 vols. (Hamburg, 1785, 1789, 1797), vol. 3, pp. 104–10. Mack Walker points out the influence of Büsch's idea of circulation (Walker translates *Geldumlauf* as "velocity") in *Johann Jakob Moser and the Holy Roman Empire of the German Nation* (Chapel Hill, N.C., 1981), p. 203.

81. Büsch, "Abhandlung von dem Geldumlauf in anhaltender Rücksicht auf die Staatswirthschaft und Handlung," in his *Schriften über Staatswirthschaft und Handlung,* vol. 2, pp. 489–514.

82. Johann Georg Büsch, "Allgemeine Winke zur Verbesserung des Armenwesens," in idem, *Zwei kleine Schriften,* unpag.

83. *Ueber die Ursachen der Verarmung in Nordischen Handelsstädten und die wirksamsten Mittel denselben zu begegnen* (Hamburg, 1785).

84. Büsch, *Darstellung der Handlung,* vol. 1, pp. 41, 54; vol. 2, pp. 212, 226.

85. Ibid., vol. 1, p. 88; Johann Georg Büsch, *Ueber die in den jetzigen Zeiten nothwendig werdende Erweiterung der Stadt Hamburg* (Hamburg, 1792), pp. 6–8.

86. Büsch, *Erfahrungen,* vol. 3, p. 11.

87. Voght, *Gesammeltes,* pp. 7–8.

88. "Allgemeine Winke," unpag.

89. *Account of the Management of the Poor in Hamburgh Since the Year 1788 in a Letter to Some Friends of the Poor in Great Britain* (Edinburgh, 1798), p. 5.

90. "Allgemeine Winke," unpag.

91. Ibid.

92. Büsch, *Versuch einer Geschichte der hamburgischen Handlung,* p. 140; idem, "Abhandlung von dem Geldumlauf," in Büsch, *Schriften über Staatswirthschaft und Handlung,* vol. 2, pp. 92–95.

93. Büsch, "Abhandlung von dem Geldumlauf," in Büsch, *Schriften über Staatswirthschaft und Handlung,* vol. 2, p. 94.

94. Quoted in Kopitzsch, "Johann Georg Büsch," p. 37.

Chapter 5

1. Several older works are invaluable because their authors had access to the no longer extant records and archives of the Patriotic Society: See especially Hildegard Urlaub, *Die Förderung der Armenpflege durch die Hamburgische Patriotische Gesellschaft bis zum Beginn des neunzehnten Jahrhunderts* (Berlin, 1932); Hermann Joachim, *Historische Arbeiten aus seinem Nachlaß* (Hamburg, 1936); Gustav Kowalewski, *Geschichte der Hamburgischen Gesellschaft zur Beförderung der Künste und nützlichen Gewerbe (Patriotische Gesellschaft),* 3 pts. in 7 vols. (Hamburg, 1897–1913); Werner von Melle, *Die Entwicklung des öffentlichen Armenwesens in Hamburg* (Hamburg, 1883). Only in these older works can we get some glimpses of the discussions on poor relief that took place within the Patriotic Society before 1780. See Urlaub, *Förderung,* p. 45.

2. For example, "Welche Arbeiten könnte man einführen, um die Armen bequemer zu unterhalten und dem Publico doch nichts beschwerlich zu fallen? Und wie müsste eine so wichtige Reform angefangen werden?" in March 1768; "Auf die beste Abhandlung über die Frage: Welche Arbeiten für Waisen- Zucht- und Werk-Häuser und überhaupt für Beschäftigung des geringen Manns am zuträglichsten und unserm Staat, besonders angemessen seyn mögten und wie solche am besten zu befördern wären ein Preis von 50 Spec. Ducaten," on 15 November 1770 and repeated in 1772.

3. See Michel Foucault, *Discipline and Punish: The Birth of the Prison* (New York, 1977); Marc Raeff, *The Well-Ordered Police State: Social and Institutional Change Through Law in the Germanies and Russia, 1600–1800* (New Haven, Conn. and London, 1983); Gerhard Oestreich, "Strukturprobleme des europäischen Absolutismus," *VSWG* 55 (1969): 329–47; Catharina Lis and Hugo Soly, *Poverty and Capitalism in Pre-Industrial Europe,* trans. by James Coonan (Brighton, England, 1979); Catharina Lis, "Sociale politiek te Antwerpen, 1779. Het controleren van de relatieve overbevolking en het reguleren van de arbeidsmarkt," *TVSG* 5 (1979): 146–66, and her *Social Change and the Labouring Poor: Antwerp, 1770–1860* (New Haven, Conn. and London, 1986); Christoph Sachße and Florian Tennstedt, eds., *Soziale Sicherheit und soziale Disziplinierung: Beiträge zu einer historischen Theorie der Sozialpolitik* (Frankfurt a.M., 1986); and Ute Frevert, *Krankheit als politisches Problem, 1770–1880: Soziale Unterschichten in Preußen zwischen medizinischer Polizei und staatlicher Sozialversicherung* (Göttingen, 1984).

4. Büsch in *ACN* (1785), p. 19; Johann Arnold Günther, *Versuch einer Vollständigen Untersuchung über Wucher und Wucher-Gesetze, und über die Mittel, dem Wucher ohne Straf-Gesetze Einhalt zu thun; in politischer, justizmässiger und mercantilistischer Rücksicht* (Hamburg, 1790), p. 167; Caspar Voght, *Account of the Management of the Poor in Hamburgh Since the Year 1788 in a Letter to Some Friends of the Poor in Great Britain* (London, 1796), pp. 11, 5, 8–9; and Johann Georg Büsch, *Schriften über Staatswirthschaft und Handlung,* 3 vols. (Hamburg, 1780–84), vol. 2, p. 498. See also Urlaub, *Förderung,* pp. 38–39.

5. Quoted from Klefeker, vol. 12, pp. 63–69. See "Etwas über die hamburgische Gesundheitspolizei aus einem Brief eines reisenden Arztes an seinen Freund L. in Thüringen. Hamburg, den 18. Juni 1805," *HA* 4, no. 2 (1805): 355–56.

6. The classic statement of the advantages of a good medical police to a polity is, of course, Johann Peter Frank, *System einer vollständigen medicinischen Polizey,* 4 vols. (Mannheim, 1779–88). For a more complete discussion of medical police, see Alfons Fischer, *Geschichte des deutschen Gesundheitswesens,* 2 vols. (Berlin 1933), vol. 2, pp. 52–160; and George Rosen, *From Medical Police to Social Medicine: Essays on the History of Health Care* (New York, 1974). For Hamburg, see the contemporary evidence given in "Schreiben eines Arztes an die Herausgeber der Hamburgischen Adress-Nachrichten, über die Zustand der Medicin in Hamburg, bey Gelegenheit des 25sten Stücks der Adress-Blätter von diesem Jahre," [1781] in StAHbg, Bibliothek. Jonas Ludwig von Heß, *Hamburg, topographisch, politisch und historisch beschrieben,* 3 vols. (Hamburg, 1787–92), vol. 2, p. 146, commented that, although the number of physicians in Hamburg was "extremely high," all sorts of irregularities in medical practice continued to undermine the health of Hamburg's inhabitants.

On the history of medical licensing and regulation in Hamburg, see Heinrich Rodegra, *Das Gesundheitswesen der Stadt Hamburg im 19. Jahrhundert unter Berücksichtigung der Medizinalgesetzgebung (1586–1818–1900)* (Wiesbaden, 1979); and Johann Julius Reincke, *Das Medizinalwesen des Hamburgischen Staats: Eine Sammlung der gesetzlichen Bestimmungen für das Medizinalwesen in Hamburg,* 3rd rev. enl. ed. (Hamburg, 1900). More specifically on the care of the sick poor, see "Nachrichten von der Verfassung des medicinischen Armen-Instituts in dem ersten zweyjährigen Zeitraume vom 1sten Jul. 1779 bis zum 1sten Jul. 1781," pp. 19–20; an undated report signed by Directors von Axen, Prösch, and Oberdorffer in StAHbg, AAI, 106; and Georg Merkel, *Briefe über einige der merkwürdigsten Städte im nördlichen Deutschland* (Leipzig, 1801), p. 300.

The point was not that the poor lacked medical care but that they lacked a proper attitude toward illness and demonstrated an unwillingness to recognize the early manifestations of illness with an even greater reluctance to consult a physician. Implicit in this viewpoint was another, that the average man preferred quacks to Aesculpian respectability, choosing to consult irregular practitioners until the illness advanced to such a stage that God alone could cure it. And Hamburg had, in the eighteenth century, a quite lurid reputation as the "quacksalvers' paradise," partly because there were no medical licensing laws until 1818. Johann Jakob Rambach, one of Hamburg's City-Physicians and the author of an exemplary medical topography, agreed, vividly depicting what he considered the unhappy medical chaos in the city. "It is not to be believed," he pointed out, "just how many ply the trade of quacksalver. Executioners, out-of-work schoolmasters, discharged field surgeons, ships' surgeons, a host of almost a thousand barber-surgeons and old wives. . . ." In prose viscous with sarcasm, he laid bare how "this most praiseworthy art" produced great profits by attracting the common man "with glib promises of certain cures." Thus, when critics pointed out that "the weakest side of government in Hamburg is its medical police . . . [an idea] of which we still [1801] have no good conception," they were usually referring to the lack of medical ordinances, the absence of licensing for practitioners, the flourishing charlatanry, but also the inadequate provisions of medical care for the great masses of the population. The harm done by those circumstances to the health of the people was considered tragic. Johann Jakob Rambach, *Versuch einer physisch-medizinischen Beschreibung von Hamburg* (Hamburg, 1801), pp. 374–75, 359.

7. See the announcement in *ACN* (14 May 1768) and in *Gemeinnützige Nachrichten aus dem Reiche der Wissenschaften und Künste* (15 January 1768); and also "Vereinigungs-Plan verschiedener Aerzte und Wundärzte zum Vortheil der hamburgischen kranken Hausarmen," in *Berlinische Sammlungen zur Beförderung der Arzneywissenschaft, der Naturgeschichte, der Haushaltungskunst, Cameralwissenschaft und der dahin einschlagenden Litteratur* 1 (1768): 162–73. StAHbg, Senat Cl. VIII (1768), pp. 110b, 162b, 443; ibid. (1769), p. 819b. In his "Cammer-Meditationes," StAHbg, Senat Cl. VII, Lit. Dd, no. 4, vol. 3, p. 175, Lütkens refers to this "new enterprise" in reference to the desire to preserve the population.

8. "Nachricht an das Publikum," *ACN* (14 May 1768).

9. *Plan zum Vortheil der hiesigen kranken Haus-Armen* (Hamburg, 1779), par. 2. Also in *ACN* (20 and 27 May 1779).

10. J. C. Bracke and J. G. Büsch, "Nachricht von dem Fortgang des medicinischen Armen-Instituts in der lezten Hälfte des Jahrs 1781," *ACN* (4 February 1788); idem, "Ueber das medicinische Armen-Institut," *ACN* (9 August 1787).

11. *Nachricht von der neuerrichteten medicinischen Anstalt für kranke Haus-Arme in Hamburg* [hereafter cited as *Nachricht 1781*] (Hamburg, 1781), pp. 16, 20; and *Zweite Sammlung von der Nachrichten vom medicinischen Armen-Institut in Hamburg: Vom 1sten Juli 1781 bis Januar 1784* [hereafter cited as *Nachricht 1784*] (Hamburg, 1784), p. 40.

12. *Nachricht 1781*, p. 20.

13. "Verhaltungs-Regeln für diejenigen, welche vom Armen-Institut curirt seyn wollen," May 1779, in *Nachricht 1781,* pp. 10–12. The Medical Deputation of the General Poor Relief applied similar injunctions, even strengthening the control and disciplinary power they could exercise over disobedient and ungrateful patients. For example, recalcitrant and/or insubordinate patients, those who allowed their relatives to insult or interfere with visiting physicians, and "those who stop taking their medicines before the physician gives them permission," could lose not only their right to medical care but also their weekly support money. If the offense proved egregious enough, such patients (or their relatives!) could theoretically be punished by a short incarceration in the Zuchthaus. Pars. 16–17, 4, 6–7, 14 of "Verhaltungs-Regeln für die auf Kosten der Armen-Anstalt zu verpflegenden Kranken und deren Angehörige," reprinted in Johann Arnold Günther, *Ueber die Einrichtungen der mit der Hamburgischen Allgemeinen Armenanstalt verbundenen Kranken-Besuch-Anstalt* (Leipzig, 1793), pp. 3–13.

14. The *Nachricht 1781* (reporting on the period 1 July 1779 through 1 January 1780) and *Nachricht von dem Fortgang des medicinischen Armen-Instituts in der lezten Hälfte des Jahrs 1787* (Hamburg, 1788).

15. Pars. 5 and 7 of the "Verhaltungs-Regeln für diejenigen, welche vom Armen-Institut curirt seyn wollen."

16. Letter from Johann Hinrich Plass, Relief Officer in the 8th Quarter, 3rd District, 27 March 1792. StAHbg, AAI, 99.

17. The city had inherited from the previous centuries five institutions that served the city as hospitals in the eighteenth century. On the general development of hospitals, see Dieter Jetter, *Geschichte des Hospitals,* vol. 1, *Westdeutschland von den Anfängen bis 1850* (Wiesbaden, 1966); Arthur Imhof, "Die Funktionen des Krankenhauses in der Stadt des 18. Jahrhunderts," *Zeitschrift für Stadtgeschichte, Stadtsoziologie und Denkmalpflege* 4, no. 2 (1977): 215–42. On hospital development in Hamburg, see Klefeker, vol. 1, pp. 245–47, 250–61; Artur Kressin, "Vom alten Hamburger 'Krankenhof' zum neuen 'Allgemeinen Krankenhaus' in der Vorstadt St. Georg," typescript, Hamburg, 1961, in StAHbg, Bibliothek; Heinz [Heinrich] Rodegra, *Vom Pesthof zum Allgemeinen Krankenhaus: Die Entwicklung des Krankenhauswesens in Hamburg zu Beginn des 19. Jahrhunderts* (Münster, 1977); *Krankenhauswesen,* omnibus volume, in StAHbg, Bibliothek; and J. J. Menuret, *Essai sur la ville d'Hambourg considéreé dans ses rapports avec la santé au lettres sur l'histoire médico-topographique de cette ville* (Hamburg, 1797).

18. On the history of the Pesthof, see Rodegra, *Vom Pesthof zum Allgemeinen Krankenhaus.* Quoted from Rambach, *Versuch,* pp. 411–12, 416–17.

19. Jetter, *Geschichte des Hospitals: Westdeutschland;* and Jean Imbert, *Les Hôpitaux en France* (Paris, 1974), pp. 22–59. Arthur Imhof has pointed out that "regarded from a therapeutical standpoint, the hospital in the eighteenth century failed to show any significant successes." "Die Funktionen des Krankenhauses," p. 241.

20. "Nachricht an das Publikum," *ACN* (14 May 1768); "Plan zum Vortheil der hiesigen kranken Haus-Armen" (Hamburg, 1779); and Günther, *Ueber die Einrichtungen.*

21. Physicians and lay reformers, for example, usually advocated a whole series of improvements for hospitals: changes in sickroom and ward design, novel if not particularly efficacious ventilation technologies designed to banish the noxious "spital air," dismemberment of mammoth institutions, erection of more compact, more specialized, more easily managed units, a tighter financial administration, and better training for the

nursing and surgical staffs. See "Krankenhaus" in Georg Gottfried Strelin, *Realwörterbuch für Kameralisten und Oekonomen,* 8 vols. (Nördlingen, 1783–96); "Kranken-Haus" and "Medicinal-Anstalt" in Johann Georg Krünitz, *D. Johann Krünitz's ökonomisch-technologische Encyklopädie oder allgemeines System der Staats-, Stadt-, Haus-, und Landwirthschaft und der Kunstgeschichte in alphabetischer Ordnung,* 242 vols. (Berlin, 1782–1858); Fischer, *Geschichte des deutschen Gesundheitswesens,* vol. 2, pp. 120–39; Franz Xaver von Haeberl, *Abhandlung über öffentliche Armen- und Krankenpflege mit einer umständlichen Geschichte der in dem ehemaligen Krankenhause zum heil. Max bey der barmherzigen Brüdern gemachten Erweiterungs- und Verbesserungs-Versuchen und den hiervon in neuen allgemeinen Krankenhause zu München gemachten Anwendungen* (Munich, 1820); Jetter, *Geschichte des Hospitals: Westdeutschland,* pp. 74–130; and Imhof, "Die Funktionen des Krankenhauses."

The question of how dangerous hospitals in the eighteenth and early nineteenth century really were is not yet settled. See Thomas McKeown and R. G. Brown, "Medical Evidence Related to English Population Changes in the Eighteenth Century," *PS* 9 (1955): 119–41; E. M. Sigsworth, "Gateways to Death? Medicine, Hospitals and Mortality, 1700–1850," in Peter Mathias, ed., *Science and Society, 1600–1900* (Cambridge, Eng., 1972), pp. 97–110; and John Woodward, *To Do the Sick No Harm: A Study of the British Voluntary Hospital System to 1875* (London and Boston, 1974). Woodward concludes (p. 146) that "the thesis that the voluntary hospitals may well have contributed to an increase in mortality, based as it is on extremely unreliable or irrelevant data, does not appear to be substantiated when the records of the individual hospitals are examined."

22. "Hamburgischer Medicinische Anstalt für kranke Haus-Arme," p. 288.

23. *Nachricht 1781,* p. 29; *Nachricht 1784,* p. 44. The debate over which system offered more advantages—hospitals or domiciliary care—went on throughout Europe. It was the subject of an essay contest sponsored by the Royal Academy of Sciences in Göttingen: August Friedrich Hecker, "Beantwortung der von der Königlichen Societät der Wissenschaften in Göttingen auf dem Monat Julius aufgegebenen Preisfrage: Welches sind die bequemsten und wohlfeilsten Mittel, kranken Armen in den Städten die nöthige Hülfe zu verschaffen? Gekrönte Preisschrift . . ." *Neues Hannoverisches Magazin* (1793): nos. 83–85. See the summary on the course of the debate in *Krünitzs Encyklopädie,* the articles on "Kranken-Haus" and "Medicinal-Anstalten"; and Fischer, *Geschichte des deutschen Gesundheitswesens,* vol. 2, pp. 83–85. The most important writings in the debate, besides those by Günther, include: Johann Georg Reyher, *Ueber die Einrichtung kleiner Hospitäler in mittlern und kleinern Städten* (Hamburg and Kiel, 1784); Philipp Gabriel Hensler, *Ueber Kranken-Anstalten* (Hamburg, 1785); idem, "Vortheile der Krankenhäuser verglichen mit Krankenbesuchanstalten," *Staatsanzeiger* 7 (1785): 272–83; Daniel Nootnagel, "Über Krankenbesuchanstalten: Vortheile der Kranken Besuch Anstalt," ibid., pp. 284–95; vol. 4, no. 2 of *Scherfs Archiv;* Adalbert Friedrich Markus, *Von den Vortheilen der Krankenhäuser für den Staat* (Bamberg and Würzburg, 1790); and "Krankenbesuchanstalten in kleinen Städten und Marktflecken," *Gruners Almanach für Aerzte und Nichtärzte* (1796): 1–52.

24. The stress on the laboring poor also resulted in the greatest efforts being directed toward healing those who could be helped and not toward the more expensive and long-term care the invalid or incurable required. In principle, both the Medical Relief and the Medical Deputation refused to accept invalids and incurables for treatment. In practice, however, the better funded Medical Deputation made some provisions for supportive care. "Antrag der Medicinal Deputation, 1789," StAHbg, AAI, 106; *Nachricht 1781,* pp. 20–22; "Convention zwischen der Armen-Anstalt und dem

Pesthof. Vom Jahr 1789"; "Extractus Protocolli der Medicinal-Deputation," 14 January 1789, StAHbg, AAI, 105; Günther, *Ueber die Einrichtung*, pp. 64–67; and "Übersichten und die Beschlüsse der Medizinaldeputation betr. die Behandlung langwieriger Kranken, 1789–1792," StAHbg, AAI, 107.

25. Par. 60 of "Des Großen Armen Collegii nähere Erläuterung für die Herrn Armen-Pfleger. Im August 1788. Nebst vollständigem Register," in *Vollständige Einrichtungen*, pp. 98–100; and StAHbg, AAI, 94.

26. *ACN* (23 February 1769). Cf. August C. H. Niemann, *Uebersicht der neuen Armenpflege in der Stadt Kiel Sr. Königl. Hoheit des Kronprinzen Befehl vorgelegt von der Gesellschaft freiwilliger Armenfreunde in Auftrag derselben abgefasset von ihrem Wortführer, Prof. Niemann* (Altona, 1798), p. 61.

27. "Plan zum Vortheil der hiesigen kranken Haus-Armen," par. 7; *Nachricht 1781*, pp. 20, 30.

28. Hermann Baumeister, *Die halb-öffentlichen milden Stiftungen in Hamburg* (Hamburg, 1869), pp. 1–23; "Plan zum Vortheil," par. 11.

29. "Hamburgischer Medicinische Anstalt für kranke Haus-Arme. Hamburg, 16 Dec. 1782," *Staatsanzeiger* 2 (1782): 295.

30. Lists of personnel in StAHbg, AAI, 110.

31. "Verzeichniss der Wohlthäter," *ACN* (1 November 1779): 673–76; ibid. (30 January 1783): 65–69; ibid. (13 June 1785): 353–57; ibid. (17 September 1787): 577–80; *Nachricht 1784*, pp. 40–41. The lists included (among many others) the following people who play an important part in this book: Claes Bartels, Büsch, Günther, J. H. and Michael Hudtwalcker, Kirchoff, Nicolas Matsen, C. C. Pehmöller, Georg Heinrich Sieveking, Voght, and Volkmann.

32. *Nachricht 1781* and *Nachricht 1784*.

33. *Privat-Anstalt zum Unterricht im Kaufgarn-Spinnen*. Sources are rather sketchy and include two reports: "Etwas über eine in Hamburg im Oktober 1785 gestiftete Anstalt zum Unterricht im Kaufgarn-Spinnen und zur Ausbreitung dieses Gewerbes," *ACN* (29 March 1787) and *1ste Nachricht* (October 1788), pp. 4–5.

34. *1ste Nachricht* (October 1788), p. 5n.

35. "Etwas über eine gestiftete Anstalt," *ACN* (29 March 1787).

36. Ibid.

37. J. C. Bracke and J. G. Büsch, "Lezte Rechenschaft von dem Fortgange des medicinischen Armen-Instituts bis zu dessen Uebergang unter die Vorsorge der preiswürdigen allgemeinen Armen-Anstalt," *ACN* (11 June 1789).

38. See Urlaub, *Förderung*, pp. 54–60. On Augsburg, see "Die neue Polizeianstalt der Armen zu Augsburg," *ACN* (2 January 1783); on Berlin, see [Friedrich Nicolai], *Beschreibung der Königl. Residenzstädte Berlin und Potsdam*, 3rd ed. (Berlin, 1786), pp. 626–47, and Karl Biedermann, *Deutschland im achtzehnten Jahrhundert*, 4 vols. (Leipzig, 1867–80), vol. 1, p. 412; on Bremen, see W. von Bippen, "Die Ausbildung der bürgerlichen Armenpflege in Bremen," *Bremisches Jahrbuch* 11 (1880): 143–61; on Braunschweig, see Peter Albrecht, "Die Reform der Braunschweigischen Armenanstalt nach Hamburger Vorbild, 1796–1805," in Rudolf Vierhaus, ed., *Kultur und Gesellschaft in Nordwestdeutschland im 18. Jahrhundert*, forthcoming; on Hanover, see Büsch, *Zum Andencken Alemanns des Menschenfreundes* (Hamburg, 1784), and Ursula Brügmann, "Die öffentliche Armenpflege der Stadt Hannover in den Jahren 1700–1824," *Hannoversche Geschichtsblätter*, n.s., 24 (1970): 89–146; on Lüneburg, see "Nachricht von der Armenanstalt für die Stadt Lüneburg und ihrem jetzigen Zustande," *ACN* (11 and 14 September 1780); on Mainz, see Friedrich Rösch, *Die Mainzer Armenreform von Jahre 1786* (Berlin, 1929), and StAHbg, AAI, 1; on

Strasburg, see "Nachricht von der zu Strassburg publicirten Verordnung, das Betteln betreffend," *ACN* (24 December 1767); and on Vienna, "Nachricht von der Einrichtung des Armeninstituts in Wien," *ACN* (10 June 1784, 14 June 1784). See also Sachße and Tennstedt, *Geschichte der Armenfürsorge,* vol. 1, pp. 112–32.

For minibiographies on some of the men involved, see Christoph Sachße and Florian Tennstedt, eds., *Bettler, Gauner und Proleten: Armut und Armenfürsorge in der deutschen Geschichte, ein Bild-Lesebuch* (Reinbek bei Hamburg, 1983), pp. 275–77, 279. On Alemann, see the testimony of his friend and admirer, Johann Georg Büsch, *Zum Andencken Alemanns;* Friedrich Eberhard von Rochow, *Versuch über Armenanstalten und Abschaffung aller Betteley* (Berlin, 1789); Christian Garve, *Anhang einiger Betrachtungen über Johann Macfarlan's Untersuchungen die Armut betreffend* (Leipzig, 1785). (In 1785, Garve also translated into German John MacFarlan, *Inquiries Concerning the Poor* [Edinburgh, 1782]); and Theodor Philipp von der Hagen, *Plan zur besseren Einrichtung der Armenkasse und Verteilung der Almosen in Berlin* (Berlin, 1787). According to Büsch, "All of Germany and . . . all of the German reading and speaking part of Europe are keenly interested in the poor relief system in Hamburg." Johann Georg Büsch, *Erfahrungen,* 4 vols. (Hamburg, 1792–94), vol. 3, p. 5.

39. "Historischer Bericht von dem Gange und fortdauernden Verfall des Hamburgischen Armenwesens seit der Zeit der Reformation" and "Allgemeine Winke zur Verbesserung des Armenwesens."

40. Urlaub, *Förderung,* pp. 66–67, 71. Monika Zachau briefly reviews the ideas of the members of the Patriotic Society in respect to poor relief in *Zwangsläufig oder Abwendbar? Auffassungen von Armut in Hamburg innerhalb und außerhalb der "Hamburgischen Gesellschaft zur Beförderung der Künste und nützlichen Gewerbe" zwischen 1788 und 1840* (Hamburg [1988]).

41. Johann Georg Büsch, *Versuch einer Geschichte der Hamburgischen Handlung, nebst zwei kleineren Schriften eines verwandten Inhalts* (Hamburg, 1797), pp. 137–38; Urlaub, *Förderung,* p. 70, nn. 80, 81.

42. Büsch, "Allgemeine Winke," unpag.; Voght, *Account.*

43. Büsch, "Allgemeine Winke," unpag.

44. Büsch, "Vorschläge zur Verbesserung des Hamburgischen Armenwesens 1786," in StAHbg, AAI, 1; idem, "Allgemeine Winke," unpag. Büsch's plans were strongly influenced by MacFarlan, *Inquiries Concerning the Poor.*

45. Büsch, "Vorschläge zur Verbesserung."

46. Ibid.

47. Ibid. On the great, indeed almost furious, activity of men like Sieveking, see Heinrich Sieveking, *Georg Heinrich Sieveking: Lebensbild eines hamburgischen Kaufmanns aus dem Zeitalter der französischen Revolution* (Berlin, 1913), p. 40.

48. Büsch in "Vorschläge zur Verbesserung" and *Ein Wort an die Bürger Hamburgs über die Nichtachtung brauchbarer Gelehrsamkeit in der Erziehung ihrer Söhne und den daher rührenden Verfall unserer beiden öffentlichen Lehrinstitute* (Hamburg, 1800); and Voght, for example, in a letter from 11 July 1794, in Kurt Detlev Möller and Annelise Tecke, eds., *Caspar Voght und sein Hamburger Freundeskreis: Briefe aus einem tätigen Leben,* 3 vols. (Hamburg, 1959, 1964, 1967), here vol. 2, pp. 24–26; and again in a letter to Madame Sieveking, 29 November 1794, in Möller and Tecke, eds., *Freundeskreis,* vol. 2, pp. 36–40. This was, however, apparently less true after mid-century. See Ernst Finder, *Hamburgisches Bürgertum in der Vergangenheit* (Hamburg, 1930), pp. 82–83. Indeed, one might well argue that the better and broader education of merchants' sons, especially after about 1750, despite the complaints of Büsch and

Voght, was what ensured the triumph of the practical, reform-minded Enlightenment in Hamburg.

49. Büsch, "Vorschläge zur Verbesserung" and "Allgemeine Winke," unpag.

50. Voght, *Account,* pp. 8–9. The General Poor Relief forbade almsgiving (*Armen-Ordnung 1788,* par. 28) and this prohibition was seen as the "cornerstone" of the entire relief (StAHbg, AAI, 2, July 1788).

51. Voght, *Account,* p. 9.

52. Ibid., pp. 8, 45–46.

53. "Mandat, die Einzeichnung einer wöchentlichen milden Gabe zur Unter-stützung der neuen Armen-Anstalt, und die vorzunehmende Untersuchung der Armen betreffend," 4 June 1788 (Anderson, vol. 2, pp. 288–91); "Mandat wegen der zu St. Georg, im Neuenwerk und auf dem Stadtdeich vorzunehmenden Einzeichnung milder Gaben zur Unterstützung der neuen Armen-Anstalt," 11 October 1788 (Anderson, vol. 2, pp. 387–88); and "Ankündigung einer am Neujahrs-Tage 1788 anzustellenden Sammlung milder Gaben," 17 December 1787 (Anderson, vol. 2, p. 197).

54. The General Poor Relief struggled with the problem of prohibiting almsgiving without damaging "so honorable a feeling as free charity" (StAHbg, AAI, 2, July 1788); letter from Voght to Madame Sieveking, September 1790, Möller and Tecke, eds., *Freundeskreis,* vol. 2, p. 13.

55. Büsch, "Vorschläge zur Verbesserung."

56. On popular concepts of dishonor, see Otto Beneke, *Von unehrlichen Leute: Culturhistorische Studien und Geschichte aus vergangenen Tagen deutscher Gewerbe und Dienste,* 2nd ed. (Berlin, 1886); Werner Dankert, *Unehrliche Leute: Die verfemten Berufe* (Bern and Munich, 1963).

57. Voght, *Account,* p. 61.

58. Büsch, "Vorschläge zur Verbesserung."

59. Ibid.

60. Ibid.

61. Ibid.; and Voght, *Account,* p. 13.

62. Büsch, "Vorschläge zur Verbesserung"; and Mary Lindemann, "Bürgerliche Karriere und patriotische Philanthropie: Armenpolitik in Hamburg vor und nach der Reform von 1788," in Christoph Sachße and Florian Tennstedt, eds., *Jahrbuch der Sozialarbeit* 4 (1981): 157–180.

63. *Erfahrungen,* vol. 3, p. 205.

64. "Conclusum Collegii 60er," 19 September 1759, StAHbg, Senat Cl. VII, Lit. Db, no. 21, vol. 1, pp. 137–44. Members of other branches of government—especially, of course, those involved in the administration of the poorhouses—were also active in suggesting ways to improve poor relief. See, for just one example, the Promemoria presented by the Governor of the Zuchthaus in 1787, Hinrich Middeldorf, on methods to reduce the number of beggars in the city. Adolf Streng, *Geschichte der Gefäng-nisverwaltung in Hamburg von 1622–1872* (Hamburg, 1890), p. 35.

65. StAHbg, Senat Cl. VII, Lit. Qd, no. 3, vol. 12, fasc. 1.

66. Karl August Böttiger, *Literarische Zustände und Zeitgenossen,* in K. W. Böttiger, ed., *Schilderungen aus Karl Aug. Böttiger's handschriftlichen Nachlasse,* 2 vols. (Leipzig, 1838), vol. 2, p. 43.

67. Established by the "Neue Armen-Ordnung," 3 September 1788 (Anderson, vol. 2, pp. 341–76); "Mandat die am ersten November zu eröffende neue Armen-Anstalt betreffend," 20 October 1788" (Anderson, vol. 2, pp. 398–403); Caspar Voght, *Gesammeltes aus der Geschichte der Hamburgischen Armen-Anstalt während*

ihrer fünfzigjährigen Dauer (Hamburg, 1838), p. 9; and von Melle, *Entwicklung,* pp. 64–93.

68. Actually there were two councils. Besides a Large Council (described here) there was a Small Council composed of the members of the Rat, the Oberalten, and the directors—in all seventeen *permanent* members—which acted as a smaller executive body and did the real work of poor relief. I have simplified this and refer merely to the council as the chief executive body. "Neue Armen-Ordnung," pp. 342–43).

69. Council Session, 4 March 1789, StAHbg, AAI, 9, vol. 3. For instance, on 9 June 1789 Franz Klefeker submitted a petition to the council asking to be freed from his duties as director, citing reasons of age and the press of private affairs. Yet this was hardly the end of Klefeker's civic involvement; in 1799, he became Oberalte. Council session, 9 June 1791, StAHbg, AAI, 9, vol. 4, and *Chronologisches Verzeichniß.*

70. StAHbg, AAI, 15; and StAHbg, AAI, 9. Detailed description of the selection of two new directors, in this case Johann Hinrich Christian Oberdörffer and Conrad Johann Matthiessen, in council session, 22 June 1791, StAHbg, AAI, 9, vol. 4. In this case all three of the "also rans," Johann Georg Lotz, Johann Nicolaus Bulle, and Peter Daniel Prale, later became directors: Lotz in 1793, Bulle in 1796, Prale in 1795. But Prale resigned almost immediately following his election to the Treasury in the same year (and to the Oberalten in 1816). On Prale's election and subsequent resignation, see Council session, 20 October 1795, StAHbg, AAI, 9, vol. 4; and Friedrich Georg Buek, *Die hamburgischen Oberalten, ihre bürgerliche Wirksamkeit und ihre Familien* (Hamburg, 1857), pp. 312–13.

71. See Thomas Nipperdey, "Verein als soziale Struktur in Deutschland im späten 18. und frühen 19. Jahrhundert," in Harmut Boockmann et al., eds., *Geschichtswissenschaft und Vereinswesen im 19. Jahrhundert: Beiträge zur Geschichte historischer Forschung in Deutschland* (Göttingen, 1972), pp. 1–44.

72. For a more complete analysis of the membership of the Patriotic Society and its representation in Hamburg's government, society, and economy, see Franklin Kopitzsch, *Grundzüge einer Sozialgeschichte der Aufklärung in Hamburg und Altona* (Hamburg, 1982), pp. 340–43; and Lindemann, "Patriotische Philanthropie." On defining middle-class culture, see Jürgen Kocka, "Bürgertum und Bürgerlichkeit als Probleme der deutschen Geschichte vom späten 18. bis zum frühen 20. Jahrhundert," in idem, ed., *Bürger und Bürgerlichkeit im 19. Jahrhundert* (Göttingen, 1987), pp. 42–48; "The Discrete Charm of the Bourgeoisie," David Blackbourn's contribution to Blackbourn and Geoff Eley, *The Peculiarities of German History: Bourgeois Society and Politics in Nineteenth-Century Germany* (Oxford and New York, 1984), pp. 259–92; and Hans H. Gerth, *Bürgerliche Intelligenz um 1800: Zur Soziologie des deutschen Frühliberalismus,* ed. by Ulrich Hermann (Göttingen, 1976).

73. "Neue Armen-Ordnung," pp. 342–54; *Vollständige Einrichtungen der neuen Hamburgischen Armenanstalt, zum Besten dieser Anstalt herausgegeben vom Hamburgischen Armen Collegio* (Hamburg, 1788); Voght, *Gesammeltes,* pp. 9–10; and council session, 27 March 1788, StAHbg, AAI, 9, vol. 3.

74. *Vorläufige Nachricht von der einzuführenden Neuen Hamburgischen Armen-Ordnung* (Hamburg, 1788), unpag.; "Neue Armen-Ordnung."

75. Letter of Voght to the council, 1 October 1793, StAHbg, AAI, 15.

76. Besides the duties apportioned to the directors by the terms of the new Relief Ordinance of 1788, see StAHbg, AAI, 9; and AAI, 13.

77. Biographical information on Voght, *ADB; Lexikon der Schriftsteller;* Nicolaus Heinrich Julius, *Dem Andenken des Königl. dänischen Etatsrath und Ritters Caspar*

Freiherrn von Voght (Hamburg, 1839); Voght's brief autobiography, *Lebensgeschichte* (Hamburg, 1917); Möller and Tecke, eds., *Freundeskreis;* Kurt D. Möller, "Caspar von Voght. Bürger und Edelmann 1752–1839," *ZVHG* 43 (1956): 166–93; Otto Rüdiger, *Caspar von Voght: Ein hamburgisches Lebensbild* (Hamburg, 1901); Otto Rüdiger and Georg Hermann Sieveking, "Kleine Studien über Caspar Voght," *MVHG* 7 (1902): 147–48, 161–64, 339–44, 356–65, 394–97; several works by Heinrich Sieveking, "Das Handlungshaus Voght und Sieveking," *ZVHG* 17 (1912): 54–128; idem, "Der Hamburger Armenfreund Caspar v. Voght in seiner internationalen Wirksamkeit," in *Festgabe für Erich Zürcher* (Bern, 1920), pp. 73–108; idem, "Caspar Voght, der Schöpfer des Jenisch-Parks, ein Vermittler zwischen deutscher und französischer Literatur," *ZVHG* 40 (1949): 89–123; Gerhard Ahrens, *Caspar Voght und sein Mustergut Flottbek: Englische Landwirtschaft in Deutschland am Ende des 18. Jahrhunderts* (Hamburg, 1969). Good short sketches of Voght's life and activities are found in Kopitzsch, *Grundzüge,* pp. 388–98, and Steven D. Uhalde, "Citizen and World-Citizen: Civic Patriotism and Cosmopolitanism in Eighteenth-Century Hamburg," (Ph.D. diss., University of California, Berkeley, 1984), pp. 346–49.

See Voght's numerous contributions to the *Reports* on many instances of the Relief. *Nachrichten,* passim; his *Ueber die vortheilhafteste Art, Kochöfen in kleinen Wohnungen einzurichten* (Hamburg, 1800); and his *Auszug aus dem der patriotischen Gesellschaft abgelegten und dem Armen-Kollegium mitgetheilten Bericht über Flachsgarn-Spinnerey und Weberey* (Hamburg, 1834). An almost complete list of his writings on poor relief is found in *Lexikon der Schriftsteller.* On his library and his collection of works on poor relief, *Verzeichniß der Bibliothek Voght* ([Hamburg], 1839), pp. 14–18.

78. [Voght], "Was ich zum Behuf der Armenanstalten außer Hamburg getan habe," StAHbg, Familienarchiv Caspar von Voght, VIII, 4; Joseph Karl Mayr, "Zwei Reformatoren der Wiener Armenfürsorge: Eine sozialgeschichtliche Studie," *Jahrbuch des Vereins der Geschichte Wien* (1951): 151–86; Sieveking, "Der Hamburger Armenfreund in seiner internationalen Wirksamkeit."

79. Voght, *Lebensgeschichte,* p. 49.

80. Ibid., p. 19.

81. Sieveking has been characterized as "one of the best educated, best informed, and most successful" of Hamburg's merchants in the second half of the eighteenth century. Kopitzsch, *Grundzüge,* pp. 393–94.

82. Quoted in Rüdiger and Sieveking, "Kleine Studien," *MVHG* 7 (1902): 396.

83. Sieveking, "Handlungshaus," p. 87. Sieveking was apprenticed to Voght's father in 1766. When Voght's father died in 1781, Voght and Sieveking took over the business, forming the partnership of Voght and Sieveking in 1788. After Voght's "retirement" in 1793, Sieveking ran the business successfully for a number of years. The high watermark of the company was 1795. The firm did less well in the following years; one observer attributed the decline to a poor selection of personnel and to some personal flaws of both partners. Gustav Poel, *Bilder aus vergangener Zeit: Nach Mittheilungen aus großentheils ungedruckten Familienpapieren* (Hamburg, 1884), vol. 1, p. 76. Then Sieveking died suddenly in 1799. The firm, however, survived his loss and the economic crisis of 1799, but was reduced from its former importance. In April 1811 the firm finally folded (H. Sieveking, "Handlungshaus"). Mrs. Parish's remark, quoted in H. Sieveking, "Handlungshaus," p. 62.

84. See Voght's comments on England in his letter to Magdalena Pauli, 11 May 1794, in Möller and Tecke, eds., *Freundeskreis,* vol. 1, pp. 2–7. In his autobiography he described the English as "das Exemplar der Menschheit in der höchsten Potenz" (*Lebensgeschichte,* pp. 23, 42–44, and passim); on his friendship with Madame de

Staël, see Otto Kluth, "Un ami allemand de Mme de Staël," *Alma Mater* 15 (December 1945): 489–98; Alfred Aust, *Mir ward ein schönes Loos: Liebe und Freundschaft im Leben des Reichsfreiherrn Caspar von Voght* (Hamburg, 1972), esp. pp. 39–64; and Kopitzsch, *Grundzüge*, p. 205.

85. In a letter to Madame Sieveking from Vienna, 25 March 1802, in Möller and Tecke, eds., *Freundeskreis*, vol. 2, p. 82.

86. Voght, *Lebensgeschichte*, p. 50. See also Ahrens, *Caspar Voght und sein Mustergut.*

87. Voght, *Lebensgeschichte*, p. 14.

88. Ibid., p. 44; *ADB; Lexikon der Schriftsteller*

89. Biographical information on Günther is drawn from the following sources: *Lexikon der Schriftsteller; ADB;* Friedrich Johann Lorenz Meyer, *Johann Arnold Günther: Ein biographischer Umriß.* (Hamburg, 1806); idem, *Johann Arnold Günther: Ein Lebensgemälde* (Hamburg, 1810); Hildegard von Marchtaler, *Aus Alt-Hamburger Senatorenhäusern: Familienschicksale im 18. und 19. Jahrhundert* (Hamburg, 1959), pp. 1–57, 83–87; obituary by Meyer in *ACN* (1806) and in *HA* 4 (1806): 215–27; other obituaries appearing in *HA* 3 (1805): 253–55 and in *Tübingisches Morgenblatt*, 1807, nos. 114–15; and also Kopitzsch, *Grundzüge*, pp. 434–39.

90. He left his library to the Patriotic Society and it formed a large part of the society's extensive collection. See *Verzeichniß der Bibliothek welche der hamburgischen Gesellschaft zur Beförderung der Künste und nützlichen Gewerbe von ihrem verdienten Mitgliede Herrn Senator Johann Arnold Günther Lt. d. R. im Jahr 1805 hinterlassen ist* (Hamburg, 1806).

91. Meyer, *Lebensgemälde*, pp. 18–19.

92. In 1781 and 1788 he stood for a position on the Niedergericht, which he failed to attain. In 1785, he lost the chance to become Archivarat to the Senat. Four years later he received not a single vote as candidate for secretary to the Oberalten. Ibid., pp. 20, 27–28.

93. See Johann Arnold Günther, "Geschichte der Entstehung, Fundation und Ausbreitung, der von der Gesellschaft im Jahre 1778 errichteten Hamburgischen Allgemeinen Versorgungs-Anstalt bis zum Jahr 1793, . . . nebst einer Fortsetzung der Geschichte dieses Instituts bis zum Jahre 1806," *VS* 7 (1807): 337–96; Kopitzsch, "Sparkassenrealität und Sozietätsbewegung im Zeitalter der Aufklärung," in *Historische Marktanalyse, Frühe Sparkassenideen: Utopie und Realität* (Neustadt a.d. Aisch, 1984), pp. 123–56; William Boehart, ". . . *nicht brothlos und nothleidend zu hinterlassen: Untersuchungen zur Entwicklung des Versicherungsgedankens in Hamburg, insbesondere zur Entstehung der Hamburgischen Allgemeinen Versorgungsanstalt von 1778* (Hamburg, 1985); Günther, "Vorarbeiten zur Revision der hamburgischen Medizinal-Polizei, auf Veranlassung des im Jahr 1796. erledigten Physikats und Subphysikats, vom Senator Günther in Hamburg," *Scherffs Archiv-Beyträge* 7, no. 2 (1798): 1–22; and Heinrich Rodegra, *Das Gesundheitswesen der Stadt Hamburg im 19. Jahrhundert unter Berücksichtigung der Medizinalgesetzgebung (1586–1818–1900)* (Wiesbaden, 1979).

94. For all of them the Terror proved a shock. According to Voght, in a letter written from England in 1794 about his experiences in France, "I have received a rude awakening!" Letter to Magdalena Pauli, 11 May 1794, in Möller and Tecke, eds., *Freundeskreis*, vol. 1, p. 4. See Walter Grab, *Demokratische Strömungen in Hamburg und Schleswig-Holstein zur Zeit der ersten französischen Republik* (Hamburg, 1966), pp. 239–55; and Kopitzsch, *Grundzüge*, pp. 610–23. Joachim Whaley, *Religious Toleration and Social Change in Hamburg, 1529–1819* (Cambridge, England, 1985), p. 43,

points out that "the debate over reform was enriched but not fundamentally redirected by the new political currents."

95. Complete list in *Lexikon der Schriftsteller.*

96. See *VS,* 7 vols. (1792–1807); Meyer, *Lebensgemälde,* p. 88; and the subscription list in Ludwig G. Wagemann, ed., *Göttingisches Magazin für Industrie und Armenpflege* 1 (1789).

97. Günther, *Erinnerungen aus den deutschen Kriegs-Gegenden, aus der Schweiz und aus den angrenzenden Ländern in vorzüglicher Hinsicht auf Natur-Schönheit und auf Völker-Glück Aufgesammelt im Sommer 1796 von J. A. Günther, Senator der Reichstadt Hamburg. Nach dessen Tode hg. von F[riedrich] J[ohann] L[orenz] Meyer, präsidirendem Capitalur des Hamburgischen Domstiftes* (Hamburg, 1806), pp. vii–viii.

98. Diary entry for 24 February 1792, printed in Meyer, *Lebensgemälde,* p. 114. While he was senator, Günther worked on a full range of deputations, served as a praetor, was involved in the reorganization of the Life-Savings Institute, participated in the improvement of street lighting and fire fighting. He continued his work for the General Poor Relief and became its advocate in the Rat. Meyer, *Lebensgemälde,* pp. 59–60.

99. "[des Herrn Senator Günther] Anrede an die erbgesessene Bürgerschaft den 26. April 1792. / Tibi erit providendum, ne a bonis desideretur./ Tacitus," in StAHbg, Senat Cl. VII, Lit. Ab, no. 3, vol. 7. Part of this address, the paean to Peter Dietrich Volkmann, was later printed as *Andenken an Volkmann* (Hamburg, 1794).

100. Diary entry for 31 December 1798, printed in Meyer, *Lebensgemälde,* p. 120.

101. Bartels held the full range of civic offices, beginning with his appointment to the Beer-Accise Deputation in 1753 and culminating with his selection as Oberalte in 1797. Biographical information from Buek, *Hamburgische Oberalten,* pp. 285–86; and "Einige Mittheilungen aus dem Leben und Wirken des weiland Oberalten Class Bartels zu Hamburg," *Hamburgische Nachrichten* (5 July 1851).

102. Günther writing in *Hanseatisches Magazin,* vol. 153, quoted in Buek, *Hamburgische Oberalten,* p. 325; see also the appreciation of Matsen by Johann Friedrich Lorenz Meyer in *VS* 4 (1797): 27; and Kopitzsch, *Grundzüge,* pp. 468, 484, 498–99. Matsen played an important role in the extension of religious toleration to Catholics and Calvinists; see Joachim Whaley, "Patriotism versus Orthodoxy: The Struggle for Limited Religious Freedom," chap. 5 in Whaley, *Religious Toleration,* esp. pp. 150, 157–58. On the powerful position of syndic in Hamburg's government, see Martin Ewald, *Der hamburgische Senatssyndicus: Eine verwaltungsgeschichtliche Studie* (Hamburg, 1954).

103. In analyzing the membership and activities of the directors, I have used the following sources: *Mitglieder und Associirte der Hamburgischen Gesellschaft zur Beförderung der Künste und nützlichen Gewerbe* (Hamburg, 1796, 1803, 1815) [hereafter cited as *Mitglieder und Associirte*]; protocols of council, StAHbg, AAI, 9; "Alphabetisches Personalverzeichnis der AA, 1788–1792," [hereafter cited as "Alphabetisches Personalverzeichnis"], StAHbg, AAI, 13; "Die Armenvorsteher; Wahl, Rücktritt, Beschwerden, Aufgaben, 1793–1846," StAHbg, AAI, 15; "Personale der Hamburgischen allgemeinen Armen-Anstalt für das Jahr, . . . mit beigefügter Eintheilung sämtlicher Armen-Quartiere und einem topographischen Register," printed each year in *Staatskalender Hamburg* [hereafter cited as "Personale der Armenanstalt (year)"]; *Lexikon der Schriftsteller; Chronologisches Verzeichniß;* and Buek, *Hamburgische Oberalten.*

104. Information on office held is taken from *Chronologisches Verzeichniß.* Beh-

rens (17?–?) served as director from 1788 to 1790; Franz Klefeker (1731–1802) served as director from 1788 to 1799 (Buek, *Hamburgische Oberalten,* pp. 287–88). Johann Daniel Klefeker (1733–1806) served as director from 1788 to 1791 (Buek, ibid., p. 245); Oldenburg (1759–1833) served as director from 1788 to 1790, (Buek, ibid., pp. 592, 269, 387); Poppe (1737–93) served as director from 1788 to 1792 (Buek, ibid., pp. 232–33); von den Steenhof (1734–1823) served as director from 1788 to 1800 (Buek, ibid., p. 288); Tonnies (1734?–1805) served as director from 1788 to 1795 (Buek, ibid., pp. 281–84); obituary by Johann Friedrich Lorenz Meyer in *VS* 7 (1807): 114; and Kopitzsch, *Grundzüge,* pp. 330, 340, 548.

105. In *VS* 7 (1807): 114.

106. Voght in a letter from Vienna to Madame Sieveking, 25 March 1802, in Möller and Tecke, eds., *Freundeskreis,* vol. 2, p. 81. Biographical information from *Nachrichten,* passim; *Staatskalender Hamburg;* and *Personalverzeichnis.*

107. See "Neue Armen-Ordnung," Anderson, vol. 2, pp. 341–76. For a complete description of the duties of the Armen-Pfleger, see *Des großen Armen-Collegii vorläufige Nachricht an die Herren Armen-Pfleger, über die Absicht der neuen Armen-Ordnung, und die von ihnen in Gemäsheit derselben gleich zu Anfang zu übernehmenden Geschäfte* (Hamburg, April 1788); *Des großen Armen-Collegii nähere Erläuterung für die Herren Armen-Pfleger, über die nach Massgabe der neuen Armen-Ordnung von ihnen zu übernehmenden Geschäfte* (Hamburg, August 1788); *Versprochener Nachtrag zu der den Herren Armen-Pflegern mitgetheilten näheren Erläuterung, welcher die vorbehaltene nähere Bestimmung des 16ten Abschnittes dieser Erläuterung enthält* (Hamburg, October 1788); *Des großen Armen-Collegii näherer Bericht an die Herren Armen-Pfleger, über die zur Beschäftigung der Armen angelegte Spinn-Anstalt, und über die im vormaligen Waisenhause eingerichteten Spinnschulen für Erwachsene und für Kinder* (Hamburg, December 1788); and "Instruction und Mittheilungen für die Armen-Pfleger, 1788–1802," StAHbg, AAI, 19.

108. One important exception was Ferdinand Beneke (who later occupied the important post of secretary to the Oberalten). Beneke's diary records numerous instances of his activities as relief officer. *Tagebuch Ferdinand Benekes, 1792–1848,* StAHbg, Familienarchiv Beneke, C2. Selections from his diary have been published by Renate Hauschild-Thiessen, "Hamburg um die Wende vom 18. zum 19. Jahrhundert. Tagebuchaufzeichnungen Ferdinand Benekes," *HGH* 9, no. 8 (December 1974): 181–208. Steven Uhalde made extensive use of Beneke's diary in his dissertation, "Citizen and World-Citizen." Another Relief Officer who recorded his observations (if far less regularly) was the apothecary, Theodor Hasche (1799–1876), but his experiences reflect the conditions of poor relief in the nineteenth century. Renate Hauschild-Thiessen, *Theodor Hasche: Das Leben eines Hamburger Apothekers. Erinnerungen aus der ersten Hälfte des 19. Jahrhunderts* (Hamburg, 1981), esp. pp. 78–79.

109. "Neue Armen-Ordnung," pp. 348–49; council session, 10 April 1788, StAHbg, AAI, 9, vol. 3; and *Staatskalender Hamburg,* 1788–92.

110. Biographical information on Beneke: Kopitzsch, *Grundzüge,* pp. 92, 99, 155, 161, 171, 197, 226, 325, 399–400, 416, 418, 420–21, 443, 490–91, 494–95, 517–18, 522, 527, 532, 539, 546, 556, 564–68, 574–75, 578, 583, 588, 597, 603, 613, 643–44, 663, 689–90, 694, 698, 707; Rudolf Kayser, *Die Oberalten: Festschrift zum vierhundertjährigen Gedächtnis der Einsetzung des Kollegiums* (Hamburg, 1928), pp. 97–100; Hauschild-Thiessen, "Hamburg um die Wende vom 18. zum 19. Jahrhundert," pp. 187–88; and *Tagebuch Ferdinand Benekes.* I systematically surveyed two years of the diary, 1799–1800. Steven Uhalde generously called my attention to some useful passages in Beneke's diary, and I thank him for this.

111. *Staatskalender Hamburg* 1790; and *Neues hamburgisches Addreßbuch,* 1787–92.

112. Carl L. Becker, *The Heavenly City of the Eighteenth-Century Philosophers* (New Haven, Conn., 1932).

Chapter 6

1. Adolf Wohlwill, "Zur Geschichte des Gottorper Vergleichs vom 27. Mai 1768," *Jahrbuch der Hamburgischen Wissenschaftlichen Anstalten* 13 (1895): 1–42.

2. Rainer Ramcke, *Die Beziehungen zwischen Hamburg und Österreich im 18. Jahrhundert: Kaiserlich-reichsstädtisches Verhältnis im Zeichen von Handels- und Finanzinteressen* (Hamburg, 1969). On the religious troubles between Lutheran and Catholic communities in Hamburg, see Joachim Whaley, *Religious Toleration and Social Change in Hamburg, 1529–1819* (Cambridge, Eng., 1985), pp. 45–69.

3. Heinrich Franz Köppen, *Die Handelsbeziehungen Hamburgs zu den Vereinigten Staaten von Nordamerika bis zur Mitte des 19. Jahrhunderts* (Cologne, 1973); Walter Kresse, "Die Auswirkungen der Handelsverträge der Hansestädte mit den amerikanischen Staaten auf die Hamburger Schiffahrt," *ZVHG* 60 (1974): 139–46.

4. On trade patterns, see Walter Kresse, *Materialien zur Entwicklungsgeschichte der Hamburger Handelsflotte, 1765–1823* (Hamburg, 1966), pp. 32–33; on the general history of the period, see Adolf Wohlwill, *Neuere Geschichte der Freien und Hansestadt Hamburg insbesondere von 1789 bis 1815* (Gotha, 1914); Hans-Dieter Loose and Werner Jochmann, eds., *Hamburg: Geschichte der Stadt und ihrer Bewohner,* 2 vols. (Hamburg, 1982–86), vol. 1, pp. 351–414.

5. Heinrich Sieveking, "Die Hamburger Bank 1619 bis 1875," in *Festschrift der Hamburger Universität ihrem Ehrenrektor Herrn Bürgermeister Werner von Melle . . . zum 80. Geburtstag am 18. Oktober 1933 dargebracht* (Gluckstadt and Hamburg, 1933), p. 82 and Percy Ernst Schramm, *Hamburg, Deutschland und die Welt: Leistung und Grenzen hanseatischen Bürgertums in der Zeit zwischen Napoleon I. und Bismarck: Ein Kapitel deutscher Geschichte* (Munich, 1934), p. 659. Between 1742 and 1748 there were 4,200 to 5,000 business accounts (*Bankfolien*) in Hamburg; in 1765 9,000, in 1788 10,925, and in 1796 20,067. At the very beginning of the nineteenth century, the fortunes of 222 Hamburg residents amounted to 100,000 marks, 65 between 100,000 and 150,000 marks, 83 between 200,000 and 400,000 marks, 33 between 500,000 and 1 million marks, 41 more than 1 million, and 12 more than 2 million marks. Regarding the importance of the Revolutionary Wars to the increase in Hamburg's commerce, see Adolph Soetbeer, *Ueber Hamburgs Handel* (Hamburg, 1840), pp. 16–17; Erwin Wiskemann, *Hamburg und die Welthandelspolitik von den Anfängen bis zur Gegenwart* (Hamburg, 1939), pp. 132–33 and Heinrich Hitzigrath, *Hamburg und die Kontinentalsperre* (Hamburg, 1900), pp. 4–7.

6. *25ste Nachricht* (July 1799), pp. 172–77.

7. General works on the reform program of the Enlightenment: Franco Venturi, *Utopia and Reform in the Enlightenment* (Cambridge, Eng., 1971); and Eberhard Weis, "Absolute Monarchie und Reform in Deutschland," in Kopitzsch, ed., *Aufklärung, Absolutismus und Bürgertum,* pp. 192–219. On poverty and poor relief in the age of Enlightenment, see Rudolf Endres, "Das Armenproblem im Zeitalter des Absolutismus," in Kopitzsch, ed., *Aufklärung, Absolutismus und Bürgertum,* pp. 220–41; Olwen Hufton, *The Poor of Eighteenth-Century France 1750–1789* (Oxford, 1974); Lotte Koch, *Wandlungen der Wohlfahrtspflege im Zeitalter der Aufklärung* (Erlangen,

1933); Catharina Lis and Hugo Soly, *Poverty and Capitalism in Pre-Industrial Europe,* trans. by James Coonan (Brighton, Eng., 1979), esp. pp. 130–214; Christoph Sachße and Florian Tennstedt, *Geschichte der Armenfürsorge in Deutschland* (Stuttgart, 1980), vol. 1, pp. 85–178; Hans Scherpner, *Theorie der Fürsorge,* 2nd. ed. (Göttingen, 1974), pp. 109–18; Ernst Schubert, *Arme Leute Bettler und Gauner im Franken des 18. Jahrhunderts* (Neustadt a.d. Aisch, 1983), pp. 92–234; and Kai Detlev Sievers, *Volkskultur und Aufklärung im Spiegel der Schleswig-Holsteinischen Provinzialberichte* (Neumünster, 1970), esp. pp. 200–34. On education and "work-education," see Harvey Chisick, *The Limits of Reform in the Enlightenment: Attitudes Toward the Education of the Lower Classes in Eighteenth-Century France* (Princeton, N.J., 1981); Kurt Iven, *Die Industrie-Pädagogik des 18. Jahrhunderts: Eine Untersuchung über die Bedeutung des wirtschaftlichen Verhaltens für die Erziehung* (Berlin and Leipzig, 1929); Wilhelm Traphagen, *Die ersten Arbeitshäuser und ihre pädagogische Funktion* (Berlin, 1935). On the general attitude of the Enlightenment toward the "people," see Harry Payne, *The Philosophes and the People* (New Haven, Conn., 1976).

8. The purpose of preventing poverty appears in every issue of the *Nachricht* in the 1790s. See, for example, *23ste Nachricht* ([January 1798], esp. pp. 107–12), but also the earlier progress report on the accomplishments of the Relief through 1796 (*20ste Nachricht* [June 1796], pp. 53–60) and the end-of-the-decade balance (*25ste Nachricht* [July 1799], pp. 172–82).

9. *1ste Nachricht* (October 1788), p. 2. See also *7te Nachricht* (March 1791), pp. 62–63.

10. "Notification wegen Bezeichnung und Numerirung der Gassen, Häuser, u.s.w.," 7 April 1788 (Anderson, vol. 2, pp. 286–87); on the use of this system for population control and taxes, see "Extract. Protoc. Senatus Hamb.," 10 June 1789 (Anderson, vol. 2, pp. 69–71); "Mandat die Umschreibung der Bürger-Capitaine, und Anzeige der Nummer der Häuser, etc. bey den Schoß-Tafeln betreffend," 12 June 1789 (Anderson, vol. 3, pp. 72–74); also similar mandates from 8 June 1790, 2 August 1793, and 16 July 1794 (Anderson, vol. 3, p. 239; vol. 4, pp. 47, 62). The system of numbering houses was cumbersome and hardly perfect, but was not changed or significantly altered until 1833–34. Ernst Finder, *Hamburgisches Bürgertum in der Vergangenheit* (Hamburg, 1930), p. 242.

11. *1ste Nachricht* (October 1788), pp. 1–8; Werner von Melle, *Die Entwicklung des öffentlichen Armenwesens in Hamburg* (Hamburg, 1883), pp. 70, 95; and StAHbg, AAI, 58 contains the paperwork. The vast majority simply list "a poor family," a widow "with many children," "an impoverished woman," and so on. The syndic Matsen, in a note to Johann Arnold Günther, pointed out that the lists could only be used to determine, if crudely, the number of poor families, but that the lists failed "to fulfill their intended purpose" (5 April 1788, in StAHbg, AAI, 58).

12. *25ste Nachricht* (July 1799), pp. 172–73; von Melle, *Entwicklung,* p. 61; and *2te Nachricht* (April 1789), pp. 9–16, esp. p. 11.

13. Especially in his work on the revision of public health laws and fire insurance in the city. See "Vorarbeiten zur Revision der hamburgischen Medizinal-Polizei, auf Veranlassung des im Jahr 1796. erledigten Physikats und Subphysikats, . . ." *Scherfs Archiv-Beyträge* 7, no. 2 (1798): 1–22; and *Versuch zu einem Entwurf einer revidirten Ordnung für die General-Feuercasse der Reich-Stadt Hamburg* (Hamburg, 1802).

14. *15te Nachricht* (February 1794), pp. 225–27. For more on such cancellations, see *21ste Nachricht* (February 1797), pp. 68–69, and *23ste Nachricht* (January 1798), pp. 112–14.

15. The Relief calculated the existence minimums in this way (summer figures in

parentheses): rent, at a yearly rate of seven to eight Reichsthaler, one shilling (1 shilling) daily; clothing, at nine to ten marks a year, five pfennigs (5 pfennigs) daily; fuel for heating and cooking, one shilling (four pfennigs); light, four shillings (0); bread, one shilling, (one shilling); other food and drink, two shillings (two shillings), for a total of five shillings nine pfennigs in winter, four shillings nine pfennigs in summer, the difference resulting from the need for less fuel and light in summer. *Versprochener Nachtrag zu der den Herren Armen-Pflegern mitgetheilten näheren Erläuterung, welcher die vorbehaltene nähere Bestimmungen des 16ten Abschnittes dieser Erläuterung enthält* (Hamburg, October 1788), p. 24.

16. Ibid., p. 27–28.

17. Johann Georg Büsch, *Ueber die Ursachen der Verarmung in Nordischen Handelsstädten und die wirksamsten Mittel denselben zu begegnen* (Hamburg, 1785), p. 17.

18. *Verspochener Nachtrag*, pp. 32–33.

19. Calculated from information given in *Nähere Erläuterung*, p. 174. The specifics were that each adult received in weekly support one mark eight shillings in winter, and one mark four shillings in summer; each child over the age of twelve (and after taking into consideration how many other children were involved), received between one mark and one mark eight shillings in winter, and between fourteen shillings and one mark four shillings in summer; each child between the age of five and twelve received thirteen shillings in winter and twelve shillings in summer; each child between the ages of one and five received nine shillings in winter and eight shillings in summer; and each child under the age of one received five shillings in winter and five shillings in summer.

20. During the first decade of its existence, the Relief paid about 20 percent of its support moneys in the form of rent subsidies. Calculated from the statistics given in *HA* 1, no. 3 (1802): 47; see also Paul Kollmann, "Ueberblick über die Wirksamkeit der 'Allgemeinen Armenanstalt' der Stadt Hamburg von 1788 bis 1870," *Statistik des Hamburgischen Staats* 3 (1871): 126, 132–33.

21. StAHbg, AAI, 9, vols. 3–6.

22. *2te Nachricht* (April 1789), pp. 12–13. In February 1789 the Relief distributed 4,686 shirts, 875 beds, and 811 blankets. See the announcements for two collections for this purpose, 17 December 1787 and 13 October 1788 (Anderson, vol. 2, pp. 197–98, 389–92). Providing clothing for the poor became part of the Relief's general program; see *Nachrichten*, passim, and for the period 1792–1800, StAHbg, AAI, 77.

23. Büsch, "Allgemeine Winke," unpag. For more on budgeting and the "economy of necessity" see Georg Heinrich Zincke, "Abhandlung von der Wirtschaftskunst der Armen und Dürftigen, sammt denen allgemeinen Regeln ihrer Wirtschaft," *Der Duisbergischen gelehrten Gesellschaft Deutsche Schriften* (Duisberg and Düsseldorf, 1759); J. E. von Koch Sternfeld, *Versuch über Nährung und Unterhalt in zivilisierten Staaten: insbesondere über Wohlfeilheit und Teuerung. Gekrönte Preisschrift* (Munich, 1805); Günther, *Versuch über Wucher*, especially the section entitled "Die Erziehung des Bürgers zur Geldwirtschaft und zur Frugalität," pp. 160–76; "Doktor Franklins freundschaftlicher Rath für erwerbsame Arme, oder Anweisung, zur Zeit der Theurung viel aus wenigem zu machen," *ACN* (29 April 1799).

24. Büsch, *Ueber die Ursachen der Verarmung*, p. 3.

25. *14te Nachricht* (May 1793), p. 179.

26. Jürgen Ellermeyer, "Zu Handel, Hafen und Grundeigentum Hamburgs im 17. und 18. Jahrhundert," in idem and Rainer Postel, eds., *Stadt und Hafen: Hamburger Beiträge zur Geschichte von Handel und Schiffahrt* (Hamburg, 1986), p. 71;. On the efforts of the Patriotic Society to prop up or secure the income of property owners, see C. A. Stuhlmann, *Die Hamburgische Credit-Casse für Erben und Grundstücke, nach*

ihrer Entstehung, Natur und Wirksamkeit und ihrer Umformung durch die revidirten Artikel von 1846 (Hamburg, n.d.); William Boehart, ". . . *nicht brothlos und nothleidend zu hinterlassen: Untersuchungen zur Entwicklung des Versicherungs-gedankens in Hamburg, insbesondere zur Entstehung der Hamburgischen Allgemeinen Versorgungsanstalt von 1778* (Hamburg, 1985), pp. 45–47.

27. *1ste Nachricht* (October 1788), pp. 2–5.

28. See Sachße and Tennstedt, *Geschichte der Armenfürsorge*, vol. 1, pp. 85–131.

29. Caspar Voght, *Account of the Management of the Poor in Hamburgh Since the Year 1788 in a Letter to Some Friends of the Poor in Great Britain* (London, 1796), pp. 54–55. See the Haupt-Bilanzen published annually by the Relief in the *Nachrichten*. On the duties, obligations, and salaries of officials, see StAHbg, AAI, 14, 16, 20; for physicians, AAI, 99, 102; on the forms used in Relief work, see the instructions for Relief Officers, AAI, 19 and 25; for runners, AAI, 20; instructions for use in medical relief, AAI, 100 and 101; and forms used in medical relief, AAI, 108.

30. *Nähere Erläuterung*, pp. 125–27 and "Neue Armen-Ordnung," 3 September 1788 (Anderson, vol. 2, pp. 341–76).

31. Klefeker, vol. 12, pp. 405, 555–57; Johann Heinrich Zedler, *Grosses vollstän-diges Universal-Lexikon, aller Wissenschaften und Künste, welche bishero durch mensch-lichen Verstand und Witz erfunden und verbessert worden . . .*, 64 vols. (Leipzig and Halle, 1732–50); s. v. "Polizey"; Georg Heinrich Zincke, *Cameralisten-Bibliothek, worinne nebst der Anleitung die Cameral-Wissenschaft zu lehren und zu lernen, ein vollständiges Verzeichniss der Bücher und Schriften von der Land- und Stadt-Oeconomie, dem Policey- Finanz- und Cammerwesen zu finden, so theils kurz beurtheilet, theils umständlich vorgestellt worden*, 2 vols. (Leipzig, 1751–52), vol. 2, pp. 364–65; and Marc Raeff, *The Well-Ordered Police State: Social and Institutional Change Through Law in the Germanies and Russia, 1600–1800* (New Haven, Conn. and London, 1983), p. 5.

32. To this day the execution of summary justice is an extremely poorly researched area, partly because written records were often not kept. What Geoffrey Elton wrote more than a decade ago is still true today: "For offenses outside the strictly criminal machinery, the dark areas of the unknown are larger. . . . [And when] it comes to summary procedure and arbitration, we have just about everything still to learn" (Introduction to J. S. Cockburn, ed., *Crime in England, 1550–1800* [Princeton, N.J., 1977], p. 8).

33. "Ueber die Competenz des großen Armen-Collegii in Armen-Sachen und deren Ausübung," July 1788, and "Nähere Vorschläge über das Verfahren in Armen-Sachen," 4 September 1788, both in StAHbg, AAI, 2.

34. "Ueber die Competenz des großen Armen-Collegii," July 1788, StAHbg, AAI, 2.

35. Ibid. The exact modalities to be observed were complicated and differed de-pending on whether the person caught begging was an inhabitant of Hamburg, a stranger, or a registered pauper. See prohibition against begging in "Neue Armen-Ordnung," pars. 26–27; and "Des großen Armen-Collegii näherer Entwurf über die Ausübung der denselben in der neuen Armen-Ordnung beigelegten Cognition in Armen-Sachen," 16 and 20 September 1788, StAHbg, AAI, 2.

36. The Relief established two different committees to deal with two separate instances: The Corrections Deputation handled cases involving registered paupers while a Police Deputation executed "the general supervision over all matters relevant to poor relief." The Police Deputation was responsible for the care of the poor who had been sent to the Zuchthaus for correction, for aliens and strangers of all kinds, and for those who had once been convicted of begging. "Des großen Armen-Collegii

näherer Entwurf," section on "Von der Zuerkennung und Execution der Zuchthaus-strafe über unfleißige und widerspenstige Arme," n.d., and "Haupt-Inhalt. Die nähere Vorschläge des großen Armen-Collegii über die Cognition in Armen-Sachen" (probably September 1788), StAHbg, AAI, 2.

37. "Des großen Armen-Collegii näherer Entwurf," StAHbg, AAI, 2.

38. Ibid., see "Vierter Punkt von dem Erkenntniß über die in der Armen-Ordnung verfügte Strafen." For example, if the Council received "credible" notification that someone had given alms, the procedure to be followed differed depending on his status. If he was "of a low class, such as a common artisan, day laborer, or servant, or the like," he would be summoned to the next meeting of the Police Deputation and, after hearing his defense, be sentenced to pay a fine, or, if he could not afford it, "would be sharply warned." If, however, the offender was "from a higher position, or [was] a respectable, prominent man," he was not summoned like a common thief to the meeting of the Deputation. Instead the Deputation sent him a polite note, signed by all its members, asking him if he had indeed given alms, explaining to him why such almsgiving was counterproductive, and then allowing him to make a contribution to the Relief. If he denied the charge, nothing more was done.

39. Almsgiving was prohibited in par. 28 of the "Neue Armen-Ordnung." Here, see "Ueber die Competenz des großen Armen-Collegii" and "Pro-Memoria des großen Armen-Collegii an Ampl. Senat," 4 October 1788, StAHbg, AAI, 2.

40. Letter of Günther to Syndic Georg Anckelmann, 11 October 1788, StAHbg, AAI, 2.

41. The Relief was quick to point out that it had no desire to disturb aliens "in the peaceful pursuit of their business." "Pro-Memoria des großen Armen-Collegii an Ampl. Senat," presented in Senat on 4 October 1788, StAHbg, AAI, 2. The quote comes from *10te Nachricht* (July 1791), p. 114. The Relief noted the increasing difficulties of the times in "Anzeige und Ersuchen an die sämmtlichen Herren Armen-Pfleger. Hamburg, im März 1795," *18te Nachricht* (June 1795), pp. 51–52. See also "Notification wegen Arretirung der Bettler," 19 February 1796 (Anderson, vol. 4, p. 107); "Notification wider das Herumtragen von Collecten-Büchern und Bettel-Briefen von verarmten Personen aus der Fremde," 3 February 1797 (Anderson, vol. 5, pp. 1–2); "Notification zu mehrer Bekanntmachung des art. 8 der A. O. von 1791," concerning "obviously pregnant women" who entered the city, 5 May 1797 (Anderson, vol. 5, p. 12); "Notification wider das Betteln und Herumtragen von Collectenbüchern und Bettelbriefen," 1 July 1801 (Anderson, vol. 6, pp. 57–59); and "Mandat wegen Bestrafung der auswärtigen und hiesigen Bettler," Anderson, vol. 7, pp. 75–76); *18te Nachricht* (June 1795), p. 30; *22ste Nachricht* (June 1797), p. 92; and Mary Lindemann, "Maternal Politics: The Principles and Practice of Maternity Care in Eighteenth-Century Hamburg," *JFH* 9, no. 1 (Spring 1984): pp. 54–56.

42. "Pro Memoria" from Amsinck to the Rat (n.d., probably late September or early October) and two "Pro Memoria" to Rat from Anckelmann (n.d. probably also late September or early October), StAHbg, AAI, 2.

43. Thus most of the power the Relief wanted for the Correction Deputation it got. In respect to the Police Deputation, the Rat made some restrictions and changes in the plans the Relief had submitted. The Rat saw no reason to deny the Relief the right to punish beggars seized by the beggar chasers on the streets with the Zuchthaus. Yet, those beggars seized, especially if they were members of the city's garrison or of the night watchmen corps, were to continue to remain under the praetors' jurisdiction. The Relief quickly concluded arrangements with the Zuchthaus to that effect. "Extractus Protocolli Senatus Hamburg [ensis]," 17 October 1788, and agreement between

the council and the Zuchthaus concerning penalties for "paupers needing correction" and beggars, from 23 October 1788, StAHbg, AAI, 2.

44. *21ste Nachricht* (February 1797), p. 69.

45. *23ste Nachricht* (January 1798), p. 113. Compare the statistics for 1800 on the numbers of inmates of the Zuchthaus on the account of the Relief. There was a total of 251. Of these, 107 (42.6 percent) had been arrested for begging; 106 (42.2 percent) were described as homeless (including 33 "homeless Negroes"); only *1* was a "strafälliger Arme" and 16 persons (disobedient children or parents?) had been sent there by the School Deputation; 20 were there for the cure of scabies and 1 for treatment of mange. Of the 107 beggars, only 2 were registered paupers, 18 were locals, and the rest (87 or 81.3 percent) were aliens (*28ste Nachricht* [January 1801], pp. 269–72). The number of beggars apprehended continued to grow after 1800. In 1807, for example, 534 were netted. "Extractus Protocolli des großen Armen-Collegii," 14 May 1807, StAHbg, AAI, 86. See also "Berichte über die als Arme eingetragenen und unterstützten Cath. D. Heyer und Zacharias W. Keck wegen ihres böswilligen, die Armut verursachenden Verhaltens, 1789 u[nd] 1802," StAHbg, AAI, 62.

46. "Allgemeine Regeln für alle diejenigen, welche von der neuen Armen-Anstalt unterstützt werden wollen," n.d. (1789), copy available in StAHbg, AAI, 82.

47. Ibid.; "Wiederholte Resolution des Armen-Collegii, die Verhütung des Umziehens der Armen betreffend," 9 December 1790. On rent subsidies, see von Melle, *Entwicklung,* pp. 83–93 and *HA* 1, no. 3 (1802): 47.

48. "Ersuchen an die Herren Armen-Pfleger die möglichste Verhütung des Umziehens der Armen betreffend," 10 December 1789; "Wiederholtes Resolution," 9 December 1790; and "Tilgungs-Protocoll," *15te Nachricht* (February 1794), pp. 226–27. On the housing situation in eighteenth-century Hamburg, see Ellermeyer, "Zur Handel, Hafen und Grundeigentum."

49. "Neue Armen-Ordnung," pp. 355–57; *1ste Nachricht* (October 1788), p. 8; "Revidirte Armen-Ordnung des Kaiserl.[ichen] freyen Reichsstadt Hamburg. Beliebt durch Rat und Bürger-Schluß den 19 May 1791. Auf Befehl E. H. Raths publicirt den 20 May 1791" [hereafter cited as "Revirdirte Armen-Ordnung 1791"], Anderson, vol. 3, p. 211; "Mandat daß die mit dem Zeichen der hiesigen Armen-Anstalt A. O. bemerkten Kleidungs-Stücke, Betten, Geräthschaften und andre Sachen, weder auf Pfänder angenommen noch gekauft werden dürfen," 20 June 1791 (Anderson, vol. 3, pp. 240–41); *10te Nachricht* (July 1791), p. 122; and Council session, 12 April 1792, StAHbg, AAI, 9, vol. 4.

50. François Lebrun, *Les hommes et la mort en Anjou aux XVIIe et XVIII siècles: Essai de démographie et de psychologie historiques* (Paris, 1975), p. 345.

51. The simplest of the *Sterbecaße* merely insured a proper burial and at best offered small sums to widows and orphans to allow them time to adjust to the loss of a breadwinner. Apparently in Hamburg it was fairly common for unscrupulous administrators to abscond with funds. Georg Heinrich Sieveking, *Fragmente über Luxus, Bürger-Tugend und Bürger-Wohl für hamburgische Bürger, die das Gute wollen und können; am 17ten November 1791 in der Gesellschaft zur Beförderung der Künste und nützlichen Gewerbe gelesen. Mit Beiträgen und Bemerkungen von zweien seiner Freunde [J. M. Hudtwalcker, J. A. Günther]* (Hamburg, 1797), p. 33. See C. Neumann, "Die deutsche Versicherungsliteratur des XVIII. Jahrhunderts," *Zeitschrift für die gesamte Versicherungswissenschaft* 12 (1912): 317–34; and for Hamburg's experiences, see Boehart, ". . . *nicht brothlos und nothleidend.*" Several of those involved in shaping poor relief in Hamburg, including Büsch and Günther, were also interested in savings banks, insurance, and similar social security projects including fire insurance: see, for

example, Büsch, *Allgemeine Uebersicht des Assecuranz-Wesens, als Grundlage zu einer unbefangenen Beurtheilung von G. E. Biebers Plan zur Einrichtung einer für Hamburg möglichst vortheilhaften Versicherungs-Compagnie gegen Feuers-Gefahr* (Hamburg, 1795); Günther, *Ueber Leibrenten, Witwen-Cassen, und ähnliche Anstalten, und besonders über die im Jahre 1778 zu Hamburg errichtete allgemeine Versorgungs-Anstalt* (Hamburg, 1788); idem, "Ueber die Entstehung, Fundation und zeitherige Ausbreitung der im Jahre 1778 von der Gesellschaft zur Beförderung der Künste und nützlichen Gewerbe errichteten Hamburgischen Allgemeinen Versorgungs-Anstalt," *VS* 7 (1807): 341–70.

52. "Hamburgs alte und neue Zeit. Eine Parallel," *HA* 2, no. 2 (1803): 269–85; "Ueber Luxus, besonders in Beziehung auf Hamburg," *HA* 5, no. 2 (1806): 320–21.

53. von Melle, *Entwicklung,* p. 139. The Relief had always been concerned with how to arrange free burial for the poor "in a simple way." The original provisions for a pauper's funeral left much to the discretion of the district director. By 1795, the Relief had worked out a complete plan "for a more respectable internment of the poor." The entire funeral cost less than six marks. Council sessions, 30 October 1788, 18 April 1789, 14 January 1790, and 12 November 1795, StAHbg, AAI, 9, vols. 3 and 4; and "Anzeige an die Herren Armen-Pfleger, die Beerdigung der Armen betreffend" [February 1796], *19te Nachricht* (April 1796), pp. 51–52. This was considerably cheaper than some other pauper funerals. For example, the city's Gast- und Krankenhaus paid fifteen marks for an adult's funeral and the parish of St. Katherin paid three marks twelve shillings just for a coffin (StAHbg, Gast- und Krankenhaus, D3, and StAHbg, St. Katherinen Kirche, B. VII. b. 5).

54. Caspar Voght, *Gesammeltes aus der Geschichte der Hamburgischen Armen-Anstalt während ihrer fünfzigjährigen Dauer* (Hamburg, 1838), pp. 15–16; and council session, 12 April 1792, StAHbg, AAI, 9. The pauper's funeral also mirrored how attitudes toward funerary exhibitionism were altering among Hamburg's elites. While the superstitions connected to the cult of death slowly died out among more enlightened groups, the veneration of necrophilic relics and the reverence for a respectable, even a magnificent funeral, still retained a firm grasp on the minds of most people. The stigma attending the pauper's funeral and the value attached to the resplendent one were slowly losing their potency among the upper classes. The tendency toward greater simplicity in funeral corteges and death rites was probably a European-wide phenomenon even if, as LeRoy Ladurie remarks, "it was not always sincere." See Emmanual LeRoy Ladurie, "Chanu, Lebrun, Vovelle: la nouvelle histoire de la mort," in his *Le territoire de l'historien* (Paris, 1973), p. 398; and John McManners, *Death and the Enlightenment: Changing Attitudes Toward Death Among Christians and Unbelievers in Eighteenth-Century France* (New York, 1981). For a discussion of changes in funeral practices in Hamburg in the seventeenth and eighteenth centuries, see Joachim Whaley, "Symbolism for the Survivors: The Disposal of the Dead in Hamburg in the late Seventeenth and Eighteenth Centuries," in Whaley, ed., *Mirrors of Mortality: Studies in the Social History of Death* (New York, 1981), pp. 80–105.

55. Otto Beneke, *Von unehrlichen Leuten: Culturhistorische Studien und Geschichte aus vergangenen Tagen deutscher Gewerbe und Dienste,* 2nd. rev. ed. (Berlin, 1889); Werner Danckert, *Unehrliche Leute: Die verfemten Berufe* (Bern and Munich, 1963); on dueling, see "Mandat, daß niemand zu Duellen ausfordern, noch ausfordern lassen soll," 29 February 1660 (Blank, vol. 1, p. 170); "Mandat gegen die Duelle," 4 June 1687 (Blank, vol. 1, p. 373); "E. E. Raths erneuertes und extendirtes Edictum vom 10 Febr. wider die Duelle," 9 December 1720 (Blank, vol. 2, pp. 974–75); and Otto Beneke, *Hamburgische Geschichte und Denkwürdigkeiten,* 2nd rev. ed. (Berlin,

1886), p. 295. St. Jakobi designated part of its cemetery a "paupers' plot," which also received the deceased inmates of the Spinnhaus, "Extractus Protocolli Senatus Hamburgensis," 14 September 1753, in "Protocoll des Spinnhauses," vol. 2, 1752–80, StAHbg, Gefängnisverwaltung, A29.

56. "Allgemeine Regeln," and council session, 4 December 1788, StAHbg, AAI, 9, vol. 3.

57. "Anzeige an die Herren Armen-Pfleger, einige auf Veranlassung der revidirten Armen-Ordnung in Absicht des Nachlaßes der Armen und über einige andre Gegenstände festgesetzte Bestimmungen betreffend" (Hamburg, July 1791); "Revidirte Armen-Ordnung 1791," pp. 217–18; and *10te Nachricht* (July 1791), p. 123.

58. Unsuspected heirs often surfaced quickly whenever a sizable inheritance was involved. This is, however, no reason to suspect that most of them were frauds. Surely many persons did not advertise that they lived as dependents on poor relief; in fact, they probably did all they could to keep it concealed. Some registered under assumed names to mask an irregular or even a criminal past. Others feared that if they listed relatives the Relief would either deny them support altogether or coerce their relatives to provide for them. People sometimes assumed that their relations no longer cared about them or were dead. Others had simply lost track of their families. Two stories illustrate the problems. Frau Schneider, a widow and registered pauper, died in 1794, presumably without heirs. Soon thereafter, two unsuspected grandchildren turned up: one in the orphanage and the other as the illegitimate child of a second son. The Relief reluctantly agreed to divide the inheritance between the two but emphasized that this case was an exception and not to be considered as a precedent. A second case involved a woman—a nonregistered pauper—who died in 1791 leaving a young son, about 100 marks in cash, and no other heirs. The Relief deposited the money in the boy's name with the Assistance Bank and found him foster parents. Some months later a Prussian grenadier appeared claiming to be the boy's father, and demanded both his son and the money. The officials of the Relief were understandably skeptical, but an investigation verified his claim. He legitimized the child and returned with the boy to his regimental headquarters in Magdeburg, but without the money. Some months later, on the petition of the Prussian charge d'affaires in Hamburg, and now convinced that the grenadier was sincere, the Relief released the money to him. Council sessions, 13 February 1794 and 10 September 1795, StAHbg, AAI, 9, vol. 4.

59. We do not know the extent of the estates involved because the inventories, with scattered exceptions, have not survived. Sometimes, however, paupers managed to amass money and property without the knowledge of officials. A widow named Hagen had received support from the Relief since 1788. When she died in 1796, she left an estate of about 250 marks in cash plus linen weaving equipment and other possessions worth more than 100 marks. Moreover, other people owed her money. Even after deducting 400 marks 13 shillings to reimburse the Relief for eight years of support, there still remained a tidy sum of almost 250 marks (council sessions, 12 September and 10 October 1796, StAHbg, AAI, 9, vol. 5).

60. Council sessions, 16 June 1791 and 9 February 1792, StAHbg, AAI, 9, vol. 4.

61. Council session, 7 July 1791, StAHbg, AAI, 9, vol. 4.

62. Compare the "Neue Armen-Ordnung," Anderson, vol. 2, pp. 360–61, and "Revidirte Armen-Ordnung 1791," Anderson, vol. 3, p. 215. See also von Melle, *Entwicklung,* p. 75.

63. Lis and Soly, *Poverty and Capitalism,* pp. 195, 205. Both Catharina Lis and Hugo Soly have emphasized in other places the close connections between poor relief and a regulation of the labor market. See Lis, "Sociale politiek te Antwerpen, 1779.

Het controleren van de relatieve overbevolking en het reguleren van de arbeids-markt," *TVSG* 5 (1979): 146–66; idem, *Social Change and the Labouring Poor: Antwerp, 1770–1860* (New Haven, Conn. and London, 1986); and Soly, "Economische ontwikkeling en sociale politiek in Europa tijdens de overgang van middeleeuwen naar nieuwe tijden," *TVG* 88 (1975): 584–97.

64. E. P. Thompson, *The Making of the English Working Class* (London, 1963), p. 363. See also Sidney Pollard, "Factory Discipline in the Industrial Revolution," *EHR,* 2nd ser. 16 (1963–64): 254–71; Keith Thomas, "Work and Leisure in Pre-Industrial Societies: Conference Paper," *PP* 29 (1964): 50–62; and E. P. Thompson, "Time, Work-Discipline, and Industrial Capitalism," *PP* 38 (1967): 56–97. For a discussion of the rise of "leisure" time in Hamburg, see Wolfgang Nahrstedt, *Die Entstehung der Freizeit: Dargestellt am Beispiel Hamburgs: Ein Beitrag zur Strukturgeschichte und zur strukturgeschichtlichen Grundlegung der Freizeitpädagogik.* (Göttingen, 1972).

65. "Beschreibung einer von dem Kattunfabrikanten Nicolaus Heinrich Burmester, Mitglied der Gesellschaft, erfundenen Kattunklopfer-Maschine," *VS* 5 (1799): 515–18.

66. "Allgemeine Regeln" (1789). Later editions of these rules: "An die Einwohner Hamburgs, die sich ihrer Hände Arbeit nähren, über die Hülfe, die sie von der Armen-Anstalt erhalten können, wenn sie durch Krankheit oder andere *unverschuldete* Vorfälle in Verlegenheit gerathen," *24ste Nachricht* (September 1798), pp. 146–50; "Dargebotene Hülfe, für solche, die in Verlegenheit gerathen," *28ste Nachricht* (January 1801), pp. 318–21; "Über die bestehenden Grundsätze der Armen-Anstalt und deren Verwendung," *35ste Nachricht* (June 1809), pp. 149–56; and "Ueber den Fortgang der Flachsgarnspinnerei in Hamburg," *ACN* (29 March and 1 April 1790).

67. Joachim Heinrich Peter, *Die Probleme der Armut in den Lehren der Kameralisten: (Eine dogmengeschichtliche Studie)* (Berlin, 1934); Rudolf Vierhaus, *Deutschland im Zeitalter des Absolutismus (1648–1763)* (Göttingen, 1978), p. 45; F.-W. Henning, *Das vorindustrielle Deutschland 800 bis 1800,* 3rd ed. (Paderborn, 1977), pp. 259–63; and see also *Der Patriot,* no. 122 (2 May 1726).

68. Voght, *Gesammeltes,* p. 8; "Gedanken von dem moralischen Einfluß der Betteley auf die, so nicht betteln," *ACN* (18 February 1771); and "Etwas von Betteln," *ACN* (28 May 1768).

69. On the Relief's attempts to run a labor exchange, see scattered reports in the *Nachrichten* (through 1792); "Verhandlungen über die anwendbarsten Vorschläge zu zweckmäßigen Arten von Zwangs-Arbeiten für faule und widerspenstige Armen beiderlei Geschlechts," *VS* 1 (1790): 202–4.

70. Peter, *Probleme der Armut,* esp. pp. 198–239; Focko Eulen, "Vom Gewerbefleiß zur Industrie: Ein Beitrag zur Wirtschaftsgeschichte des 18. Jahrhunderts" (Ph.D. diss., Hamburg, 1966); Iven *Industrie-Pädagogik des 18. Jahrhunderts;* August F. Rulffs, *Von der vortheilhaftesten Einrichtung der Werk- und Zuchthäuser* (Göttingen, 1783), p. 12.

71. *5te Nachricht,* (March 1791), pp. 45–48.

72. "Etwas über eine in Hamburg im Oktober 1785 gestiftete Anstalt zum Unterricht im Kaufgarn-Spinnen und zur Ausbreitung dieses Gewerbes," *ACN* (29 March 1787); *1ste Nachricht* (October 1788), pp. 3–6; "Des großen Armen-Collegii näherer Bericht an die Herren Armen-Pfleger, über die zur Beschäftigung der Armen angelegte Spinn-Anstalt, und über die im vormaligen Waisenhause eingerichteten Spinnschulen für Erwachsene und für Kinder. Hamburg, im December 1788," pp. 2–5; *3te Nachricht* (June 1789), p. 29; and *5te Nachricht* (March 1790), pp. 45–48. On the

introduction of twine making for boys and men, *6te Nachricht* (June 1790), p. 55, and *7te Nachricht* (March 1791), pp. 68–69. On wool spinning and stocking knitting, see Caspar Voght's reports, "Vorschläge der Fabrik-Deputation über die Beschäftigung der Armen mit Strumpf-Stricken und Wolle-Spinnen" and "Vorschläge und Bericht der Fabrik-Deputation über die bisher in der Spinn-Anstalt ausgetheilten Almosen . . ." both in *8te Nachricht* (March 1791), pp. 73–76, 77–82.

73. *6te Nachricht* (June 1790), p. 55, and "Näherer Bericht über die Spinn-Anstalt," pp. 2–5.

74. Voght, "Bericht der versammelten Vorsteher über die Revision sämtlicher Anstalten in Rücksicht auf mögliche Ersparung. . . . im Februar und März 1793," supplement to *14te Nachricht* (May 1793), pp. 195–96. See also *1ste Nachricht* (October 1788), p. 3. Losses were already obvious by 1791, as is made clear in Voght's report on warehousing and selling of flax yarn in *8te Nachricht* (March 1791), pp. 77–82. The total loss on the selling price of the yarn was 79,642 marks 9 shillings. 7.5 pfennigs. Only in two years—1793 and 1796—were profits recorded, and then only 356 marks and 796 marks. And, yet, even more than a quarter century later, Voght was convinced of the necessity and benefit of such projects. See Voght, *Ueber die ersten Fortschritte der Anstalt, deren Zweck es ist, zu untersuchen, inwiefern es möglich sei, durch angemessene Verausgabung die Spinnerei zu einem dauernden Erwerb für die arbeitslosen Armen Hamburgs zu machen* (Hamburg, 1835), unpag., appendix. Expenditures on schools and workshops were large throughout the 1790s, although they did not rival the amounts spent on medical care or alms to the domiciled poor; cf. Karl Wilhelm Ascher, *Die Hamburgische Armenanstalt im Jahre 1830* (Hamburg, 1830), p. 5; and Kollmann, "Ueberblick," pp. 132–33.

75. "Ueber den Fortgang der Flachsgarnspinnerei in Hamburg," *ACN* (29 March and 1 April 1790).

76. Ibid.; *8te Nachricht* (January 1791), p. 79; "Nachricht an die Armen, über die Spinn-Anstalt" (1789); see also *1ste Nachricht* (October 1788), pp. 3–4; *3te Nachricht* (June 1789), p. 28; *5te Nachricht* (March 1790), pp. 45–48; and *6te Nachricht* (June 1790), pp. 54–55.

77. *1ste Nachricht* (October 1788), p. 3, and *3te Nachricht* (June 1789), p. 28.

78. *5te Nachricht* (March 1790), pp. 45–48, and *8te Nachricht* (January 1791), pp. 77–82.

79. *8te Nachricht* (January 1791), p. 79.

80. Ibid.; and Voght, "Bericht der versammelten Vorsteher über die Revision sämtlicher Anstalten in Rücksicht auf mögliche Ersparung. . . . im Februar und März 1793," supplement to *14te Nachricht* (May 1793), pp. 189–99. Voght argued that the vigorous application of the rules or work as a test in 1792 had produced a rise in productivity and a decline in truancy. "During that year, 3,000 bundles of yarn more were spun, 300 children more went to school, and the institution saved £1,250, which would have fallen to the share of idleness, and which is nearly the amount of the greater earnings of the poor in that year" (Voght, *Account*, p. 45). And see also "Die Haupt-Bilanz des zu Ausgang Junius 1792 abgeschlossenen vierten Jahres der Armen-Anstalt, und die Aussichten über den Bestand derselben, betreffend. Nebst einer Beilage, das Resultat der Revision sämtlicher Anstalten, in Rücksicht auf möglichste Ersparung, enthaltend. Hamburg, im May 1793," in *14te Nachricht* (May 1793), pp. 173–84. In this report Voght made the "sad confession" that the loss of 15,000 marks reported in the previous *Report* was "the last money the Relief is able to lose." Nothing remained from the excess created from the liquidation of the older relief and from that

point onward the "existence of the new General Poor Relief depends entirely on the contributions of our good citizens" (ibid., p. 176). Monthly report for May 1795 in StAHbg, AAI, 86.

81. Council sessions, 8 March 1792 and 29 February 1792, StAHbg, AAI, 9, vol. 4; and report of the Factory Deputation for September 1795 in StAHbg, AAI, 86.

82. Günther's report (1801) to the council, StAHbg, AAI, 81.

83. "Allgemeine Regeln," and "Grudsätze nach welchen die Vorsteher der Fabrik-Deputation in Absicht der zur Zwangs-Arbeit zu übergebenden Armen zu verfahren haben," n.d. [1789] StAHbg, AAI, 82.

84. "Verhandlungen über Zwangsarbeiten," *VS* 1 (1790): 177–212, two quotes taken from pp. 177–79. About six essays were submitted. One suggested a nitrates factory. Another wanted to establish a tobacco manufactory, which was to be combined with cultivating tobacco plants. Other projects called for temporarily "colonizing" workers in the countryside, housing them in cottages right in the fields, and setting them to work building roads, planting and caring for mulberry trees, raising silkworms, and spinning silk. Another proposal advanced the idea of a house of correction to serve as a middle point between a prison and a "voluntary workhouse." There men would labor making canvas and the women would assist them by turning the reels, hackling, pounding, and rolling up the finished cloth. Weber, *Staatswissenschaftlicher Versuch über das Armenwesen und die Armenpolizey mit vorzüglicher Hinsicht auf die dahin einschlagende Literatur* (Göttingen, 1807), pp. 141–42; and Rulffs, *Von der vorteilhaftesten Einrichtung*, pp. 7, 12.

85. "Verhandlungen über Zwangsarbeiten," pp. 177–79, 204, and J. D. Klefeker, "Vorschlag zur Verbesserung der Armen-Polizey," StAHbg, AAI, 82.

86. Klefeker, "Vorschlag zur Verbesserung der Armen-Policey"; "Grundsätze nach welchen die Vorsteher der Fabrik-Deputation in Absicht der zur Zwangs-Arbeit zu übergebenden Armen zu verfahren haben," and "Vorläufige Gedanken über die Anordnung zweckmäßiger Zwangs-Arbeiten für faule und widerspenstige Armen," 31 August 1789, all in StAHbg, AAI, 82; "Verhandlungen über Zwangsarbeiten," pp. 196, 199; "Convention zwischen der Armen-Anstalt und dem Zuchthaus," 24 April 1790, and "Vergleich des Zuchthauses mit der Armen-Ordnung über die Aufnahme solcher Arme, die keine Wohnung haben" [1790], in StaHbg, AAI, 82; and "Vergleich des Zuchthauses mit der Armen-Ordnung zur Errichtung einer Zwangsarbeit im Zuchthaus" and "Instruction für den Jahresverwaltenden Provisor des Zuchthauses wegen der Zwangs-Arbeit," 26 December 1790, reprinted in *VS* 1 (1790): 209–12 as "Einrichtung der im hamburgischen Zuchthause anzuordnenden Zwangs-Arbeiten für die von der Armen-Anstalt dem Zuchthaus übergebenden faulen und widerspenstigen Armen." In 1793, the conventions concerning compulsory labor were repeated and slightly modified. "Zwischen dem großen Armen-Collegio und dem großen Collegio des Zuchthauses ist am heutigen Tage folgende *Renovation* und resp: Abänderung der vorstehenden vorhie zwischen der Armen-Anstalt und dem Zuchthaus verabredeten *Convention* geschlossen worden," StAHbg, AAI, 82.

87. *25ste Nachricht* (July 1799), p. 172; *28ste Nachricht* (January 1801), pp. 269–72; and "Extractus Protocolli des großen Armen Collegii," 14 May 1807, StAHbg, AAI, 86. For detailed information on two cases that illustrate just how far the Relief had to be pushed before resorting to compulsory labor, see "Berichte über die als Arme eingetragenen und unterstützten Cath. D. Heyer und Zacharias W. Keck wegen ihrer böswilligen, die Armut verursachenden Verhaltens, 1789 und 1802," StAHbg, AAI, 62.

88. Helvetius quoted in James Leith, "The Hope for Moral Regeneration in French

Educational Thought, 1750–1789," in *City and Society,* p. 128. On the Enlightenment and education, see also Norman Hampson, *The Enlightenment* (Harmondsworth, Eng., 1968), p. 110; Chisick, *Limits of Reform,* pp. 128–82; and Payne, *Philosophes and People,* esp. pp. 94–116. On the Enlightenment and school reform in the Germanies, see Anthony J. LaVopa, *Prussian Schoolteachers: Profession and Office, 1763–1848* (Chapel Hill, N.C., 1980), pp. 25–37; James Van Horn Melton, *Absolutism and the Eighteenth-Century Origins of Compulsory Schooling in Prussia and Austria* (Cambridge and New York, 1988); and Ulrich Herrmann, ed., *"Das pädagogische Jahrhundert": Volksaufklärung und Erziehung zur Armut im 18. Jahrhundert in Deutschland* (Weinheim, 1981); specifically on Hamburg, Martin Brandt, *Die Bestrebungen der Hamburgischen Armenanstalt von 1788 zur Erziehung der Armenbevölkerung: Ein Beitrag zur Geschichte der Industrieschule* (Hamburg, 1937); Hartwig Fiege, *Geschichte der Hamburgischen Volksschule* (Hamburg, 1970); Hans Scherpner, *Die Kinderfürsorge in der Hamburgischen Armenreform vom Jahre 1788* (Berlin, 1927); Hildegard Urlaub, *Die Förderung der Armenpflege durch die Hamburgische Patriotische Gesellschaft bis zum Beginn des neunzehnten Jahrhunderts* (Berlin, 1932), pp. 84–92; and "Gedanken über die Erziehung des Menschen zum brauchbaren Bürger," *ACN* (28 March 1791).

89. Quoted in Sievers, *Volkskultur und Aufklärung,* pp. 273, 282, 304, and Fleury quoted in Leith, "Hope for Moral Regeneration," p. 222.

90. "Proposition Senatus in Conventu senatus et Civium," 12 July 1787, StAHbg, Senat Cl. VII, Lit. Qd, no. 3, vol. 12, fasc. 1.

91. *11/12te Nachricht* (December 1791), p. 149.

92. *VS* 2 (1793): 488.

93. *11/12te Nachricht* (December 1791), p. 140. Johann Heinrich Pestalozzi contributed much to the theory of industry schools. See his "Skizze eines Memoire über die Verbindung der Berufsbildung mit den Volksschulen, 1790," *Sämtliche Werke,* ed. Artur Buchenau, Eduard Spranger, and Hans Stettbacher (Berlin, 1927–), vol. 10, pp. 53–64; "Zweck und Plan einer Armen-Erziehungs-Anstalt. Oktober 1805," ibid., vol. 18, pp. 53–76; and "Über Volksbildung und Industrie," ibid., pp. 139–70.

For more on the industry school movement in central Europe, see Heinrich Philip Sextroh, *Über die Bildung der Jugend zur Industrie: Ein Fragment* (Göttingen, 1785); Friedrich Eberhard von Rochow, *Materialien zum frühen Unterricht in Bürger- und Industrieschulen* (Berlin and Stetten, 1797) (for a discussion of Rochow's methods by one of his disciples and admirers, see Johann Friedrich Reimann, *Beschreibung der Rekanschen Schule* [Berlin and Stettin, 1781; 2nd ed., 1792]); Ludwig Erhard Wagemann, "Ueber Industrieschule im allgemeinen und über die Göttingische insbesondere," *Göttingisches Magazin für Industrie und Armenpflege* 1, no. 1 (1789): 1–34, 127–36, and 2, no. 3 (1790): 1–32; and Fritz Trost, *Die Göttingische Industrie-Schule* (Berlin, 1930). Josef Aigner, *Der Volks- und Industrieschulen-Reformator Bischof Ferdinand Kindermann* (Vienna, 1867), demonstrates that the enthusiasm for schools of industry was not exclusively Protestant.

94. *11/12te Nachricht* (December 1791), pp. 145, 147–49. Claes Bartels, J. A. Günther, J. D. and Franz Klefeker, Nicolas Matsen, Vincent Oldenberg, Johannes Poppe, Joachim van den Steenhof, J. F. Tonnies, and Caspar Voght all subscribed to the *Göttingisches Magazin für Industrie und Armenpflege;* see subscription list in vol. 1 (1789). On Voght, see Olga Essig, "Caspar Voght über Pestalozzi. Ein Brief aus Yverdun an die Patriotische Gesellschaft," *HGH* 8 (1935): 177–80.

95. Scherpner, *Kinderfürsorge,* p. 14. Johann Arnold Minder characterized Bracke as a man who trod a middle path, steering between "over zealous enthusiasm for

reform" and a "stubborn clinging to traditional opinions" (*Briefe über Hamburg*, [Leipzig, 1794], p. 165).

96. Urlaub, *Förderung*, p. 85; Günther, "Versuch einer Geschichte," p. 85; on Buchmann, see *Lexikon der Schriftsteller* and Urlaub, *Förderung*, pp. 87–91; selection from Buchmann's essay quoted in Urlaub, *Förderung*, p. 87. Buchmann was one of the two teachers sent to Rekan by the General Poor Relief to learn Rochow's method. The Patriotic Society paid for most of the expenses and for a trip to all the leading centers of educational reform in the Germanies: Berlin, Halle, Magdeburg, Halberstadt, Göttingen, and Hanover. Urlaub, *Förderung*, p. 91; Scherpner, *Kinderfürsorge*, p. 42, n. 3; and *3te Nachricht* (June 1789), pp. 22, 28; and *11/12te Nachricht* (December 1791), pp. 144–45. Voght felt that "[a] careful education of *all* children, would undoubtedly be the most effectual way of promoting the happiness of the rising generation" (*Account*, pp. 59–60).

97. *1ste Nachricht* (October 1788), pp. 2, 6.

98. Pestalozzi in *Sämtliche Werke*, vol. 8, p. 418; and Günther quoted in Scherpner, *Kinderfürsorge*, p. 38, n. 1.

99. Joachim Christoph Bracke, *Ermähnungsrede bei Eröffnung der Sonntagsschule für die Armenkinder im vormaligen Waisenhaus am 3. Weihnachtsfeiertag 1791 gehalten* (Hamburg, 1792); Scherpner, *Theorie der Fürsorge*, pp. 43–44; Brandt, *Bestrebungen*, p. 60; *11/12te Nachricht* (December 1791), pp. 142–43; *6te Nachricht* (June 1790), p. 54; and von Rochow, *Der Kinderfreund, ein Lesebuch zum Gebrauch für Landschulen*, 2 vols. (Berlin and Leipzig, 1776, 1780).

100. See the protocols of the School Deputation, StAHbg, AAI, 145; also *1ste Nachricht* (October 1788), p. 6; *7te Nachricht* (March 1791), p. 69; *10te Nachricht* (July 1791), p. 122; and esp. *11/12te Nachricht* (December 1791), pp. 136–60.

101. Fiege, *Geschichte der Hamburgischen Volksschule*, p. 26.

102. "Näherer Bericht über die angelegte Spinnschule," pp. 9–10, and *11/12te Nachricht* (December 1791), pp. 155–65.

103. *3te Nachricht* (July 1789), pp. 19–22; *6te Nachricht* (June 1790), p. 56; *11/12te Nachricht* (December 1791), pp. 137, 142–43; and "Näherer Bericht über die angelegte Spinnschule," p. 8.

104. *11/12te Nachricht* (December 1791), p. 137. The Relief adopted the plan proposed earlier (May 1791) by Voght, "Vorschläge und Bericht der Fabrik- und Schul-Deputation über die bisher in den Schul-Einrichtungen bemerkten Mängel; über die Nothwendigkeit der besondern Aufsicht des Bezirks-Vorsteher auf die Kinder der Armen; und über die Art, wie diese geführt und die bisherigen Schulen in eine Erziehungs-Anstalt für die Armen verwandelt werden können," printed as supplement to *11/12te Nachricht* (December 1791), pp. 147–60. Statistics on children attending schools for 1793, *15te Nachricht* (February 1794), p. 221; and for 1796, *22ste Nachricht* (June 1797), pp. 83–84.

105. *15te Nachricht* (February 1794), p. 221; *22ste Nachricht* (June 1797), p. 83; *28ste Nachricht* (January 1801), pp. 248–49; and *31ste Nachricht* (May 1804), pp. 8–10. On the evening and Sunday schools, see Caspar Voght, "Vorschlag der Schul-Deputation über die Erziehung der Kinder unsrer Armen, und über die Einrichtung der Sontags-Schulen," supplement to *11/12te Nachricht* (December 1791), pp. 140–46; "Anzeige an die Herren Armen-Pfleger, die Anordnung einer Abends- und Sontags-Schule für solche Armen-Kinder betreffend, die wegen anderen Brod-Erwerbs die Spinnanstalt nicht besuchen können" (Hamburg, 9 December 1790); Brandt, *Bestrebungen*, pp. 48–51; and Scherpner, *Theorie der Fürsorge*, pp. 48–49. On the Elementary School, see esp. *11/12te Nachricht* (December 1791), pp. 142–44. The Rieckmann

decision was made in a session of the School Deputation, 9 February 1793, StAHbg, AAI, 145, vol. 1; appeal of the mother of Christian Wilhelm Sander, session of School Deputation, 28 May 1796, ibid., vol. 2; other petitions of a similar nature can be found in the protocols of the School Deputation, vols. 1–6.

106. Scherpner, *Theorie der Fürsorge,* pp. 47–48, 54, 57–62; *11/12te Nachricht* (December 1791), pp. 147–60; *24ste Nachricht* (September 1798), pp. 129–31; and "Tabelle zur Vergleichung der Haupt-Bezirke und der Schul-Distrikte," in ibid., pp. 141–45; discussion on revision of elementary schools in these years in StAHbg, AAI, 124. Allotment of children to school directors, session of School Deputation, 18 November 1797, StAHbg, AAI, 145, vol.; 2; on the protest of Relief Officers, session of School Deputation, 15 March 1798 in ibid., vol. 3.

107. Sessions of the School Deputation, StAHbg, AAI, 145; AAI, 83. Ferdinand Kindermann, "Nachricht von der Landschule in Koplitz," published as an unpaginated appendix to Josef Aigner, *Der Volks- und Industrieschulen-Reformator Bischof Ferdinand Kindermann,* (Vienna, 1867).

108. Council sessions, 7 July 1791, 20 October 1791, 9 February 1792, and 14 June 1792, StAHbg, AAI, 9, vol. 4, and "Anzeige an die Herren Armen-Pfleger," December 1795, supplement to *19te Nachricht* (April 1796), pp. 49–50.

109. Report on 4th District, Quarters 7–12 in session of the School Deputation, 12 August 1797, StAHbg, AAI, 145, vol. 3; Beneke, *Tagebücher.*

110. On program and goals, see *6te Nachricht* (June 1790), p. 56; *9te Nachricht* (March 1791), pp. 85–108; on types of care offered, see especially *15te Nachricht* (February 1794), pp. 222–23, and *24ste Nachricht* (September 1798), p. 131. See also the deliberations of the Medical Deputation from 1788 to 1793 in StAHbg, AAI, 94, and the material covering the period 1789–1806 in StAHbg, AAI, 109. Total number of patients treated in this time span: 48,465. Sources: *21ste Nachricht* (February 1797), p. 67; *23ste Nachricht* (January 1798), p. 112; *25ste Nachricht* (July 1799), p. 170; *27ste Nachricht* (February 1800), p. 234; *28ste Nachricht* (January 1801), p. 273; and *30ste Nachricht* (May 1803), pp. 352–53; and Kollmann, "Ueberblick," p. 128.

111. "Nähere Erläuterung," pp. 98–100.

112. Deliberations on how to save money and how to introduce the system of "half-free" care in StAHbg, AAI, 106; see also "Anzeige und Ersuchen an die Herren Armen-Pfleger, die Ausgebung der Kranken-Zettel für solche Nicht-Eingezeichnete Arme betreffend, die zwar nicht die ganze Cur, aber doch die Arznei bezahlen können [March 1793]," supplement to *14te Nachricht* (May 1793), pp. 207–8; and *22ste Nachricht* (June 1797), pp. 85–86. See also deliberations of Medical Deputation from 1793 and 1796 in StAHbg, AAI, 94.

113. *23ste Nachricht* (January 1798), pp. 107–12, quote from p. 107.

114. Ibid., pp. 107–9; Voght's report on the Vorschuß-Anstalt, *28ste Nachricht* (January 1801), pp. 281–90; and *24ste Nachricht* (September 1798), pp. 127, 129. See also "Nähere Anzeige des Armen-Collegii an die Herren Armen-Pfleger überhaupt, über . . . die, der Fabrik-Deputation aufgetragenen Hülfsleistung, durch welche die Verarmung guter und nützlicher Einwohner dieser Stadt vorgebeugt werden kann," and "Extractus Protocolli des großen Armen-Collegii. Donnerstag den 13sten September 1798. Die Ausrichtung der Beschlüsse der Fabrik-Deputation, und die Einlieferung des wöchentliche Abtrags derer die Vorschuß erhalten haben betreffend," *24ste Nachricht,* pp. 159–60. From 1798 through 1804, 2,243 persons received advances; 1,203 of these were, according to the Relief, "gute Zahler." In the same period, the Relief recovered 84,400 marks of the 148,000 marks it had advanced (*32ste Nachricht* [June 1805], p. 46).

115. Calculated on the basis of data in Kollmann, "Ueberblick," pp. 132–33.

116. See "Bericht der versammelten Vorsteher über die Revision sämtlicher Anstalten in Rücksicht auf mögliche Ersparung [March 1793]" supplement to *14te Nachricht* (May 1793), pp. 185–211; council sessions throughout 1792–93, StAHbg, AAI, 9, vol. 4; and on measures taken in medical care, see StAHbg, AAI, 106.

117. *24ste Nachricht* (September 1798), p. 126.

118. *21ste Nachricht* (February 1797), p. 64; in 1798, the Relief raised weekly rates from 24 to 36 shillings (*23ste Nachricht* [January 1798], p. 94, and *24ste Nachricht* [September 1798], p. 126).

119. *21ste Nachricht* (February 1797), pp. 71–72; *22ste Nachricht* (June 1797), pp. 84–85, 92, 94; *24ste Nachricht* (September 1798), pp. 133–35; and StAHbg, AAI, 78 and 79. See also C. E. Bieber, *Ueber den nachtheiligen Einfluss der hohen Miethe, und der Belastung unentbehrlicher Bedürfnisse auf Hamburgs Wohl, nebst einigen Vorschlägen dagegen* (Hamburg, 1803); Büsch, *Ueber die der Stadt Hamburg nothwendig werdende Erweiterung;* and Ellermeyer, "Zu Handel, Hafen und Grundeigentum."

120. *23ste Nachricht* (January 1798), pp. 94–95.

121. See *24ste Nachricht* (September 1798). Another statement, this time to the poor themselves, of the extent of the program of the Relief at the end of the century is "An die Einwohner Hamburgs, die sich ihrer Hände Arbeit nähren, über die Hülfe, die sie von der Armen-Anstalt erhalten können, wenn sie durch Krankheit oder andere unverschuldete Vorfälle in Verlegenheit gerathen" (*24ste Nachricht*, pp. 146–50).

Chapter 7

1. Heinrich Hitzigrath, *Hamburg und die Kontinentalsperre* (Hamburg, 1900), p. 8; Adolf Wohlwill, *Neuere Geschichte der Freien und Hansestadt Hamburg insbesondere von 1789 bis 1815* (Gotha, 1914), pp. 230–67.

2. On the French in Hamburg: Carl Mönckeberg, *Hamburg unter dem Druck der Franzosen, 1806–1814* (Hamburg, 1864); Karl Henke, *Davout und die Festung Hamburg-Harburg, 1813–1814* (Berlin, 1911); Wohlwill, *Neuere Geschichte*, pp. 335–514; J. Hahn, *Aus Hamburgs Schreckentagen* (Hamburg, 1909); [Marianne Prell], *Erinnerungen aus der Franzosenzeit in Hamburg* (Hamburg, 1863); Anton Hagedorn, "Bedrückung Hamburgs durch die Franzosen, 1806–1814," archival report, 8 March 1917, StAHbg, Bibliothek; and *Ein treues Bild der französischen Militär-Herrschaft in Hamburg: Die wichtigsten Mandaten und Verordnungen der Jahre 1806 bis 1813, nach ihrem Wortlaute mitgetheilet* (Hamburg, 1863).

3. Adolph Soetbeer, *Ueber Hamburgs Handel* (Hamburg, 1840), pp. 3, 19; Percy Ernst Schramm, *Kaufleute zu Haus und über See.* (Hamburg, 1949), pp. 4, 10, 16; and Hitzigrath, *Hamburg und die Kontinentalsperre*, p. 24. This is the generally accepted opinion of how seriously disadvantaged Hamburg's trade was. Walter Kresse, however, suggests that the situation was not quite as desperate as it is usually portrayed; see his *Materialien zur Entwicklungsgeschichte der Hamburger Handelsflotte, 1765–1823* (Hamburg, 1966), p. 35.

4. Hannibal Evans Lloyd, *Hamburgh; or, a particular Account of the Conduct of the French in that City* (London, 1813), p. 26.

5. *Ohnmasgeblicher Vorschlag eines Volksfreundes um einer durch die Sperrung der Elbe ausser Arbeit gesetzten Menge Menschen in Hamburg baldigst Arbeit zu verschaffen, und sie vor Mangel und gänzlichen Verarmung, noch vor Eintritt des nahen Winters, zu schützen* (Hamburg, [1803]), p. 3.

6. Schramm, *Kaufleute*, pp. 10, 16.

7. *Ohnmasgeblicher Vorschlag*, p. 3.

8. Friedrich W. C. Menck, *Synchronistisches Handbuch der neuesten Zeitgeschichte* (Hamburg and Leipzig, 1826), vol. 1, pp. 315–16.

9. *28ste Nachricht* (January 1801), p. 287. Data compiled from the questionnaires documents a sharp increase in rents. Before 1795 the average rent was 8 thaler (24 marks); in 1798 12.20 thaler (more than 36 marks); in 1799 21.63 thaler (almost 66 marks); in 1800 24.50 thaler (73 marks, 8 shillings); 1802 27.50 thaler (82 marks, 8 shillings); and in 1804 32.50 thaler (97 marks, 8 shillings). *32ste Nachricht* (June 1805), p. 49. See also Jürgen Ellermeyer, "Zu Handel, Hafen und Grundeigentum Hamburgs im 17. und 18. Jahrhundert," in idem and Rainer Postel, eds., *Stadt und Hafen: Hamburger Beiträge zur Geschichte von Handel und Schiffahrt* (Hamburg, 1986), pp. 70–73. Food prices rose similarly. A comparison of prices from 1800 to 1805 shows a doubling of the price of rye flour (from 40 shillings for a *Himpten* to 80 shillings); a fourfold rise in the price of potatoes (from 2–2.5 shillings for ten *Pfund* to 8–10 shillings), Joseph Heckscher, "Lebensmittelpreise in Hamburg während der Belagerung durch die Franzosen," *MVHG* 7 (1900): 405–6. In 1806, von Heß reported that "only a few years ago" the average rent for a poor married couple was 40–50 marks yearly, bread cost 40 shillings, and potatoes 2–3 shillings weekly. At that time, he calculated the lowest wage to be about 5 shillings per week. In the winter of 1805–6, rents had climbed to 72 marks, bread to 80 shillings, potatoes to 8–10 shillings. That is, everything had at least doubled in price while the lowest wage in the city, which was paid to fortification workers by the Relief, was 30 shillings per week (von Heß, *An das Große Armen-Collegium* (Hamburg, 1806), pp. 7–8).

10. Hitzigrath, *Hamburg und die Kontinentalsperre*, pp. 18–19; *32ste Nachricht* (June 1805), p. 49; and *34ste Nachricht* (May 1807), p. 148.

11. The first order for the billeting of French troops was promulgated on 21 November 1806. Hamburg paid all costs of billeting. For conditions, see "Wozu verpflichtet, wozu berichtigt das neu revidierte Einquart. Regl. vom 21 Octob. 1808," (Hamburg, 1808). See also Jacob Schleiden, *Bemerkungen über die jetzige Einrichtung der Einquartierung in Hamburg nebst Vorschlägen zur Verbesserung derselben in einem Schreiben an ein Mitglied des Collegii der Herren Sechziger* (Hamburg, 1808); and "Reglement für die Einquartierung, 1808–1812," in StAHbg, Mairie Hamburg, 78. Conscription began in 1811; see *Rathgeber für Conscribirte und deren Verwandte. Enthalten: das Verfahren bei der Conscription: die Gesetze und besondern Vorschriften darüber, nebst Angabe derjenigen Fälle, in welchen die Befreiung statt hat. Aus dem Französischen übersetzt* (Hamburg, 1811); Wohlwill, *Neuere Geschichte*, pp. 386–420.

12. The provisioning was declared on 12 November 1813, see *Ein treues Bild, p. 5; Menck, Synchronistisches Handbuch*, vol. 2, p. 15; *Allgemeiner Bericht über den Zustand der, während der Belagerung aus Hamburg Vertriebenen, und über die, zur Milderung ihres Schicksals, angewandten Mittel. Erster Bericht bis Ende März 1814* (Altona, [1814]); *Letzter allgemeiner Bericht über die im Winter 1813 und 1814 den vertriebenen und ausgewanderten so wie den wieder heimgekehrten Hamburger bewilligten Summen. Fortsetzung des im März 1814 an die Wohlthäter dieser Unglücklichen abgestatteten Berichts* (Hamburg, 1815); J[ohann] H[einrich] Bartels, *Actenmäßige Darstellung des Verfahrens der Franzosen bei dem durch den Marschall Davoust befohlenen Verbrennen des Krankenhofs zwischen Hamburg und Altona, im Jahre 1813 und 1814* (Hamburg, 1815); and [Heinrich Wilhelm Gravenhorst], *Das Hamburgische Allgemeine Krankenhaus*, 2nd enl. ed. (Hamburg, 1848), p. 3. See also the records of the "Hamburgische (und Centrale) Unterstützungs-Kommission," from 1814–1815 in

StAHbg, Senat Cl. VII, Lit. Qd, no. 3, vol. 13. Johann Westphalen estimated that between 1809 and 1814 the occupation cost Hamburg about 75 million francs (*Hamburgs tieffste Erniedrigung* [Hamburg, 1814], p. 25); Wilhelm Amsinck estimated that the total cost of war and occupation to Hamburg was about 80 million Courantmark ("Promemoria über die finanzielle Lage Hamburgs [1814]," StAHbg, Senat Cl. VII, Lit. Da, No. 2, vol. 6a, fasc. 1, p. 4. Heinrich Laufenberg pointed out that estimates ranged from 70 to 150 million marks (*Hamburg und sein Proletariat im achtzehnten Jahrhundert: Eine wirtschaftshistorische Vorstudie zur Geschichte der modernen Arbeiterbewegung im niederelbischen Städtegebiet* (Hamburg, 1910), p. 35, while J. F. Voigt meticulously calculated the total debt (rather than the *cost*) to have been 31,286,787 marks 4 shillings ("Der Schuldenbestand der Stadt Hamburg im Jahre 1814," *MVHG* 12 [1914]: 57–63).

13. Caspar Voght, *Lebensgeschichte* (Hamburg, 1917), pp. 62–63; letter to Magdalena Pauli, from 2 September 1812 in Kurt Detlev Möller and Annelise Tecke, eds., *Caspar Voght und sein Hamburger Freundeskreis: Briefe aus einem tätigen Leben,* 3 vols. (Hamburg, 1959, 1964, 1967), vol. 1, pp. 63–67, here p. 64; and letter to same, from 11 February 1813, in *Freundeskreis,* pp. 67–72, here p. 70.

14. Paul Kollmann, "Ueberblick über die Wirksamkeit der 'Allgemeinen Armenanstalt' der Stadt Hamburg von 1788 bis 1870," *Statistik des Hamburgischen Staats* 3 (1871), pp. 120–21, 132–33; Werner von Melle, *Die Entwicklung des öffentlichen Armenwesens in Hamburg* (Hamburg, 1883), p. 114.

15. Total cost of the schoolhouse was 262,755 marks 3 shillings (*28ste Nachricht* [January 1801], p. 260; see also pp. 311–13. Bernhard Menke exploits printed materials in a similar discussion of the policies of restraint and retrenchment in these years (although his conclusions and interpretations are rather different from mine) in *Armut und Elend in Hamburg: Eine Untersuchung über das öffentliche Armenwesen in der ersten Hälfte des 19. Jahrhunderts* (Hamburg, 1982), esp. pp. 97–127.

16. "Beilage No. 11. Bericht des Herrn Vorstehers Voght, über die Vorschuß-Anstalt," *28ste Nachricht* (January 1801), pp. 281–90, here p. 287; and council session, 8 September 1803, StAHbg, AAI, 9, vol. 9.

17. See a series of supplements to the *28ste Nachricht* (January 1801), pp. 294–309.

18. "Anzeige an die Herren Armen-Pfleger," November 1800, *28ste Nachricht* (January 1801), pp. 308–9; *29ste Nachricht* (May 1802), p. 334; *31ste Nachricht* (May 1804), p. 21; "Nähere Beleuchtung des Deficits des 16ten Jahres der Anstalt und seiner Ursachen," presented to the Rat on 6 May 1805, StAHbg, Senat Cl. VII, Lit. Qa, no. 3, vol. 12, fasc. 38c; "Bericht der vom Armen-Collegium zur Untersuchung, wie der jetzigen Verlegenheit der Armen-Anstalt abzuhelfen und ihre künftige Dauer zu sichern sey, niedergesetzten Commission; abgestattet im großen Armen-Collegium, den 25sten April 1805," *32ste Nachricht* (June 1805), pp. 60–80; deliberations in council from March through May 1808, StAHbg, AAI, 9, vol. 14, and StAHbg, Senat Cl. VII, Lit. Qa, no. 3, vol. 12, fasc. 39a; "Aufsuche der Allgemeinen Armen-Anstalt um eine Aushülfe an Betrag 127,000 Mark Banco und Bewilligung zweyer außerordentlicher Grabengelder für selbige durch R. und B. Schluß vom 9 July," in April and May 1808, StAHbg, Senat Cl. VII, Lit. Qa, no. 3, vol. 12, fasc. 39a; "Beliebung eines außerordentlichen Grabengeldes, . . . [1808]," in StAHbg, Senat Cl. VII, Lit. Qa, no. 3, vol. 12, fasc. 39b; "Beliebung eines einfachen Kopfgeldes zur außerordentlichen Unterstützung der A. A. durch R. und B. Schluß vom Augt. 1809," ibid.; and "Dominierung zweier Mitglieder Senatus zum Behuf der Einleitungen Wege zu treffende Ersparung und Einschränkungen bei der A. A. mit Mitglieder des Armen Collegii zusammen zu treten und deshalbige Verhandlungen," ibid; and relevant mandates from 31 October 1805 when the Rat approved the release of approximately 60,000

marks over a five-year period from the state-run Fire Insurance Company (Anderson, vol. 7, p. 48); other mandates granting the Relief state subsidies, all in Anderson, vol. 7: 18 December 1805 (pp. 63–64); 31 March 1806 (pp. 77–78); 13 November 1806 (p. 85); 19 December 1806 (pp. 115–16); 23 March 1807 (pp. 151–52); 15 October 1807 (p. 186); 23 December 1807 (pp. 230–31); 30 March 1808 (pp. 283–84); 19 December 1808 (pp. 375–76); and 23 November 1809 (Anderson, vol. 8, p. 61).

19. *37ste Nachricht* (October 1816), p. 230.

20. Kollmann, "Ueberblick," pp. 120–21.

21. In 1808, 1,059 beggars were apprehended; in 1809, 1,287. Jonas Ludwig von Heß, *Hamburg, topographisch, politisch und historisch beschrieben,* 2nd ed. 3 vols. (Hamburg, 1810–11), vol. 2, pp. 114n–15n. On increased penalties for begging, see "Mandat wegen Bestrafung der auswärtigen und hiesigen Bettler," 12 March 1806 (Anderson, vol. 7, pp. 75–76); *33ste Nachricht* (May 1806), pp. 114–16; debate in the Rat over these measures (StAHbg, Senat Cl. VII, Lit. Qa, no. 3, vol. 12, fasc. 38d); see also the stronger measures enacted against aliens in the following *Verordnungen* from Anderson, vol. 7: "Verordnung über die gegen das Einschleichen der Fremden erlassene Verfügung und bei der Annahme zum Bürger beliebte Einrichtung," 20 November 1805" (pp. 51–55); "Vorschrift für diejenigen, die das Bürgerrecht nachsuchen," 20 November 1805 (pp. 56–58); "Extract. Protoc. Senatus Hamb. Merc. d. 20 Nov. 1805. betreffend die Umschreibung durch die Bürger Capitaine" (pp. 58–65); "Verordnung über die gegen das Einschleichen der Fremden erlassene Verfügung und bei der Annahme zum Bürger oder Schutzbürger beliebte Einrichtung; zur Publication in der Jurisdiction des Wohlw. Landherren des Hamburgerberges," 10 January 1806 (pp. 67–72). Another mandate concerns the "Umschreibung," 28 May 1806, (Anderson, vol. 7, p. 80); "Notification wegen der von den ankommenden Fremden vorzuzeigenden Pässen und Befehl an die Wirthe, alle zu beherbergende Fremde anzuzeigen," 22 January 1807 (Anderson, vol. 7, pp. 135–36); and further mandates on "Umschreibung," 13 May 1807 and 24 February 1808 (Anderson, vol. 7, pp. 155 and 279).

22. *31ste Nachricht* (May 1804), pp. 1–5, 17, 19; Hitzigrath, *Hamburg und die Kontinentalsperre,* p. 19.

23. *33ste Nachricht* (May 1806), pp. 102–3; and see also deliberations of the council in 1805 and 1806, StAHbg, AAI, 9, vols. 11 and 12.

24. Joseph Listert, *Ursachen des Verfalls des Wohlstandes der Hanse-Städte und Mittel diesen Uebeln auf die zweckmäßigste Weise abzuhelfen* (Hamburg, Bremen, and Lübeck, 1808), pp. 16–17, 99.

25. Hans Scherpner, *Die Kinderfürsorge in der Hamburgischen Armenreform vom Jahre 1788* (Berlin, 1927), p. 74; Caspar Voght, *Gesammeltes aus der Geschichte der Hamburgischen Armen-Anstalt während ihrer fünfzigjährigen Dauer* (Hamburg, 1838), pp. 95, 98–100. After the closing of the industry schools and the sacrifice of the schoolhouse, Voght commented that "no one spoke any more of an educational institution," (*Gesammeltes,* p. 105).

26. *32ste Nachricht* (June 1805), pp. 66–67.

27. *35ste Nachricht* (June 1809), p. 151. See also StAHbg, AAI, 64.

28. *36ste Nachricht* (May 1810), esp. p. 157; *37ste Nachricht* (October 1816), pp. 233, 240–41.

29. *34ste Nachricht* (May 1807), p. 140; *36ste Nachricht* (May 1810), p. 226; and *37ste Nachricht* (October 1816), pp. 233, 240–41.

30. Theodor Friedrich Böttiger, *Hamburgs Patrioten, 1800–1814* (Berlin and Leipzig, 1926), pp. 13, 17.

31. von Heß, *An das Große Armen-Collegium,* here esp. p. 86; *37ste Nachricht* (October 1816), p. 240; and council sessions, 8 January 1813 and, especially, 15 February 1813, StAHbg, AAI, 9, vol. 17.

32. "Schreiben des Armenvorstehers Caspar Voght aus Wien betr. die Revision der Armenordnung 1802," StAHbg, AAI, 5. In his autobiography Voght paints a different picture, preferring to linger on the accomplishments of the relief, describing the year 1802 as a zenith (*Lebensgeschichte,* p. 62). Still, a year earlier Voght had expressed his concern about the current state of the Relief in letters to his friend Madame Sieveking. At the time, he was in Vienna engaged in the reform of that city's poor relief. To some extent his testimony here might well be seen as reflecting his own feeling that everything was deteriorating now that his influence was no longer dominant. But his distress seemed real. Letters to Madame Sieveking, 16 December 1801 and 25 March 1802, Möller and Tecke, eds., *Freundeskreis,* vol. 2, pp. 77–79, 79–85.

33. *Lexikon der Schriftsteller; ADB.*

34. von Heß, *An das Große Armen-Collegium,* p. 40.

35. Ibid., pp. 18–31, 67, 42.

36. Ibid., pp. 51–52, 56.

37. Ibid., pp. 12–14, 15–26, 31, 75.

38. Christian Nicolas Pehmöller (1769–1845) was the son of a wealthy sugar refiner and himself a merchant. As a young man he traveled widely on business. He spent three years in the emerging United States and was acquainted with many prominent American statesmen, including George Washington. In 1799 he returned to Hamburg and went into business with a friend, Heinrich Droop. Despite the economic depression, the firm flourished. Pehmöller became active in communal government, filling in rapid succession the normal sequence of offices. In 1803 he became a director of the Zuchthaus (in 1806 ex officio, a member of the Relief council), in 1805 a member of the One Hundred Eighty, in 1807 a Relief Director to replace von Heß, and from 1812 to 1814, he served on the Bank Deputation and tried to defend its resources from confiscation by the French. In 1814 he was elected a deputy to the Treasury and served as a member of the Twenty (the committee called to discuss government reform after the French departed). In 1816 he was elected senator (*Lexikon der Schriftsteller; ADB;* and *Neuer Nekrolog der Deutschen* [1847].

39. [Christian Nicolaus Pehmöller], *Über den gegenwärtigen Zustand der Armen-Anstalt. Eine Untersuchung, in den Sitzungen des großen Armen-Collegii vom 15ten und 22sten September 1808 vorgetragen von einem Mitgliede desselben* (Hamburg, n.d. [1808]).

40. Ibid., pp. 5–6.

41. Ibid., pp. 5–6, 27, 32–33, 36–40.

42. Ibid., p. 41. Besides von Heß, Abendroth, and Pehmöller, some others, like the Relief Officer F. G. Schuback, also supported the idea of a tax: F. G. Schuback, "Wünsche, die Armen Anstalt betreffend," December 1808, StAHbg, AAI, 15. Opinion of council, "Extractus Protocolli des großen Armen-Collegii, Donnerstag, den 15ten Sept. 1808," StAHbg, Senat Cl. VII, Lit. Qa, no. 3, vol. 12, fasc. 39b.

43. Pehmöller, *Zustand,* pp. 41–43.

44. Ibid., p. 50. Discussion of the Relief's schools, pp. 47–54.

45. Ibid.

46. Ibid., pp. 56–57.

47. Ibid., pp. 57–58; and council session, 13 December 1806, StAHbg, AAI, 9, vol. 12.

48. Pehmöller, *Zustand,* pp. 59–60.

49. Ibid., p. 64.

50. Ibid., pp. 65–66.

51. *Lexikon der Schriftsteller; ADB; NDB.*

52. *Bemerkungen über die Armen-Anstalt von 1791 und 1830* (Hamburg, 1832).

53. Ibid., pp. 5–6.

54. Ibid., pp. 7–8, 10, 22.

55. StAHbg, Senat Cl. VII, Lit. Cc, no. 1, vol. 4g, fasc. 8[1].

56. Westphalen was referring to the 29 November 1808 session of the Rat, StAHbg, Senat Protocol, Senat Cl. VIII. Westphalen's comments in a "Pro Memoria" to the Rat, n.d. [1809], StAHbg, Senat Cl. VII, Lit. Qa, no. 3, vol. 12, fasc. 39b.

57. Dated 1 January 1813, in StAHbg, AAI, 64.

58. On the harsher penalties for begging, see especially "Mandate wegen Bestrafung der auswärtigen und hiesigen Bettler," 12 March 1806 (Anderson, vol. 7, pp. 75–76) and discussions on measures to be taken against beggars in StAHbg, Senat Cl. VII, Lit. Qa, no. 3, vol. 12, fasc. 38d. See the various mandates concerning the "Umschreibung" by militia captains; all in Anderson: 4 May 1804 (vol. 6, p. 239); 16 November 1804 (vol. 6, p. 271); esp. 20 November 1805 (vol. 7, pp. 58–61); 28 May 1806 (vol. 7, p. 80); 13 May 1807 (vol. 7, p. 155); 24 February 1808 (vol. 7, p. 279); 26 May 1809 (vol. 8, p. 28); and 20 November 1805 (vol. 7, pp. 58–61). On citizenship requirements, see "Verordnung über die gegen das Einschleichen der Fremden erlassene Verfügung und bei der Annahme zum Bürger beliebte Einrichtung," 20 November 1805 (Anderson, vol. 7, pp. 51–55); "Vorschriften für diejenigen, die das Bürgerrecht nachsuchen" (Anderson vol. 7, pp. 56–58). Later mandates and regulations can be found in Anderson/Lappenberg: 13 June 1814 (vol. 1, pp. 97–98); 18 November 1814 (vol. 1, pp. 305–7); 12 July 1830, (vol. 11, pp. 193–94; especially "Rath- und Bürger Schluß betreffend die Norm der Legitimation der Erbgesessenheit," 11 October 1832 (vol. 12, pp. 117–20) and "Verordnung über die Gewinnung, die Kosten und die Aufgebung des Bürgerrechts," 30 December 1833 (vol. 11, pp. 488–97).

The French abolished the category of Schutzverwandten. It was not restored in 1814–15. At the end of the 1820s, there was a renewed debate about whether citizenship was too easy or too difficult to obtain, and whether there should be a second-class citizenship. No decision was reached but it became rather more difficult to become a citizen. In 1837 it became necessary to introduce a Heimatsrecht to distinguish members of one state from another for purposes of assigning responsibility for social welfare, and so a new category of Schutzbürger was introduced. It lasted only about twenty years before being made obsolete by the constitutional changes of the 1850s. See "Acta betr. die Reassumirung der Verhandlungen zur Regulirung der hiesigen bürgerrechtlichen Verhältnisse, Fremden- u. Gesinde-Polizei, und daraus resultirende neue Verordnung, 1829–1837," StAHbg, Senat Cl. VII, Lit. Bc, no. 7b, fasc. 20; and Hans Walter Lehr, *Das Bürgerrecht im hamburgischen Staate* (Hamburg, 1919). pp. 15–16, 26–29. I would like to thank John Breuilly for helping clarify this for me.

59. "Mandate wegen Bestrafung der auswärtigen und hiesigen Bettler" (Anderson, vol. 7, pp. 75–76).

60. See the petition presented to the Rat by the Relief, 5 March 1806, StAHbg, Senat Cl. VII, Lit. Qa, no. 3, vol. 12, fasc. 38d; "Mandate wegen Bestrafung der auswärtigen und hiesigen Bettler," 12 March 1806 (Anderson, vol. 7, pp. 75–76); petition presented to the Rat by the Relief on 20 June 1804, StAHbg, Senat Cl. VII, Lit. Qa, no. 3, vol. 12, fasc. 38a; "Verordnung über die gegen das Einschleichen der

Fremden erlassene Verfügung und bei der Annahme zum Bürger beliebte Einrichtung," 20 November 1805 (Anderson, vol. 7, pp. 51–55, here p. 51); and "Vorschriften für diejenigen, die das Bürgerrecht nachsuchen," 20 November 1805 (Anderson, vol. 7, pp. 56–58). These mandates only spoke of "Bürgerrecht" and mentioned no lesser form of citizenship, or state of quasi citizenship.

61. On the reorganization and creation of the "Hanseatic Department," see *Bulletin des Arrêtés de la Commission de Gouvernement établie par le décret impérial du 18 Décembre 1810* (Hamburg, 1811); Antoinette Joulia, "Les institutions administratives des départements Hanséatiques," *RHMC* (July–September 1970): 880–92; Hans-Dieter Loose and Werner Jochmann, eds., *Hamburg: Geschichte der Stadt und ihrer Bewohner,* 2 vols. (Hamburg, 1982–86), vol. 1, pp. 415–29; Ernst Baasch, *Geschichte Hamburgs, 1814–1914,* 2 vols. (Gotha, 1924–25), vol. 1, pp. 1–2; Wohlwill, *Neuere Geschichte,* pp. 364–85; Heinrich Redeker, *Die Reorganization der hamburgischen Polizei im 19. Jahrhundert* (Saalfeld, 1932), p. 3; Erich von Lehe, "Überblick über die Geschichte der hamburgischen Verwaltung vom Mittelalter zur Neuzeit," typescript, (Hamburg, 1950), pp. 139–42; and Nicolaus A. Westphalen, *Hamburgs Verfassung und Verwaltung in ihrer allmähligen Entwickelung bis auf die neueste Zeit,* 2nd ed., 2 vols. (Hamburg, 1841). For discussions of policing during the eighteenth and early nineteenth century, see *Über das Prinzip, die Gränzen und den Umfang der Polizei* (Leipzig, 1808); and *Krünitzs Encyklopädie,* s.v. "Polizei." On the shift in the meaning and functions of police: F. X. Funk, "Die Auffassung des Begriffs der Polizei im vorigen Jahrhundert," *Zeitschrift für gesamte Staatswissenschaft* 19 (1863): 489–555; Dionys Zobst, "Der Polizeibegriff in Deutschland," (Ph.D. diss., Munich, 1933); Charles Reith, *The Police Idea, Its History and Evolution in the Eighteenth Century and After* (Oxford, 1938); Kurt Wolzendorff, *Der Polizeigedanke des modernen Staats: Ein Versuch zur allgemeinen Verwaltungslehre unter besonder Berücksichtigung der Entwicklung in Preußen* (Breslau, 1918; repr. ed., Aalen, 1964); Karolina Zobel, "Polizei. Geschichte und Bedeutungswandel des Wortes und seiner Zusammensetzungen," (Ph.D. diss., Munich, 1952); *Dictionary of the History of Ideas; Encyclopedia of the Social Sciences; Handwörterbuch der Sozialwissenschaften; Handwörterbuch der Staatswissenschaften; Politisches Handwörterbuch;* and Carl von Rotteck and Carl Welcker, eds. *Staatslexicon, oder Encyklopädie der Staatswissenschaften im Verbindung mit vielen der angesehensten Publicisten Deutschlands* (Altona, 1834–43)—s.v. "police" and "Polizei."

62. Hagedorn, "Bedrückung Hamburgs," p. 2; conditions in Heilige Geist Hospital from 1812 to 1813, StAHbg, Senat Cl. VII, Lit. Qb, No. 3, vol. 3a; on Pesthof (*Krankenhof*), see reports of 10 and 22 August 1812, StAHbg, Senat Cl. VII, Lit. Qb, no. 8, vol. 20; on conditions in the orphanage, StAHbg, Senat Cl. VII, Lit. Qc, no. 3, vol. 21; concerning illegitimate children, StAHbg, Senat Cl. VII, Lit. Qa, no. 3, vol. 12, fasc. 38b; on Zuchthaus, StAHbg, Senat Cl. VII, Lit. Qd, no. 1, vols. 14d and 18a; on conditions in the Zuchthaus in 1809, see report of the Board of Governors to the Rat, 19 June 1809, StAHbg, Senat Cl. VII, Lit. Qa, no. 3, vol. 12, fasc. 39b; and on the Spinnhaus, Andreas Ehrenfried Martens, *Das Hamburgische Criminal-Gefängnis genannt: Das Spinnhaus und die übrigen Gefängnisse der Stadt Hamburg nach ihrer innern Beschaffenheit und Einrichtung beschrieben, nebst einigen Ansichten und Ideen über Verbesserung ähnlicher Anstalten überhaupt* (Hamburg, 1823).

63. Anton Hagedorn, "Das Werk- und Armenhaus in seiner historischen Entwicklung," archival report, December 1902, p. 7, in StAHbg, Bibliothek; Adolf Streng, *Geschichte der Gefängnisverwaltung in Hamburg von 1622–1872* (Hamburg, 1890), pp. 702–79; and Westphalen, *Verfassung und Verwaltung,* vol. 1, pp. 466–68.

64. Friedrich Johann Lorenz Meyer, *Johann Arnold Günther: Ein Lebensgemälde* (Hamburg, 1810), p. 118.

65. Streng, *Gefängnisverwaltung*, pp. 49–51.

66. "Vortrag im großen A[rmen]-C[ollegium] abseiten des Zuchthauses wegen Entfernung der Kinder," 12 March 1807, StAHbg, AAI, 124a. See also protocol of the School Deputation, session of 21 April 1807, StAHbg, AAI, 145, vol. 6; [Pehmöller], "Ueber die Corrections-Anstalt für Minderjährige; Vortrag bey der Schuldeputation 1807 d. 24. Nov.—im großen A[rmen]-C[ollegium] d. 17 Dec.," StAHbg, AAI, 124a. Pehmöller apparently had been influenced by American examples and referred to several works that dealt with similar institutions in the United States. Broader implications of such plans are explored by, among others, Michel Foucault, *Discipline and Punish: The Birth of the Prison* (New York, 1977); David J. Rothman, *The Discovery of the Asylum: Social Order and Disorder in the New Republic* (Boston and Toronto, 1971); and Michael Katz, *The Irony of Early School Reform* (Cambridge, Mass., 1968).

67. Amandus Augustus Abendroth, *Wünsche bei Hamburgs Wiedergeburt im Jahre 1814* (Kiel, 1814); and see Johann Michael Westphalen's response *Bemerkungen über die Schrift* on reception of *Wünsche*, F. Voight, "Wünsche für Hamburg um Frühjahr 1814, als die Kapitulation der Hamburg besetzt haltenden Franzosen bevorstand," *MVHG* 12 (1914): 66–77. And these men were not the first to suggest improvements in Hamburg's administration and police. See, for example, *Freimüthige und bescheidene Rügen einer hamburgischen Polizei-Mängel, nebst unmassgeblichen Vorschlägen zu ihrer Abstellung: Eine patriotische Schrift zur Beherzigung für Gesetz-Geber und Gesetz-Pflichtige* (Hamburg, 1810).

68. Quoted in Karl-Joachim Dreyer, "Hamburg als Mitglied des Deutschen Bundes," (Ph.D. diss., Hamburg, 1976), p. 73. Cf. Günther's positive valuation of Hamburg's constitution, which he praised along with the Bern and Zurich systems, as best able to avoid "bloodthirsty despotism" and "mob violence" (*Erinnerungen aus den deutschen Kriegs-Gegenden, aus der Schweiz und aus den angrenzenden Ländern in vorzüglicher Hinsicht auf Natur-Schönheit und auf Völker-Glück. Aufgesammelt im Sommer 1796 von J. A. Günther, Senator der Reichsstadt Hamburg. Nach dessen Tode hg. von F[riedrich] J[ohann] L[orenz] Meyer, präsidirendem Capitular des Hamburgischen Domstiftes* [Hamburg, 1806], pp. xvi–xviii).

69. Members of the Twenty: Franz Detlof Bieber, member of the Commerce Deputation; Georg Elert Bieber, member of the Treasury; Johann Caspar Gläser, Oberalte; Jacob Hinrich Jencquel, senator; Herman Friederich Justus, member of the Treasury; Georg Knorre, member of the Treasury; Christian Hinrich Lohmann, Oberalte; Johann Diedrich Luis, member of the Commerce Deputation; Heinrich Johann Merck, later (1820) senator; Johann Georg Mönckeberg, protocollist of the Commerce Deputation and chairman of the Twenty; Johannes Moller, member of the Treasury; Christian Nicolas Pehmöller, member of the Treasury and later senator (1816); Siegmund Diedrich Rücker, Oberalte; Johann Meinhard Schmidt; Peter Philipp Schmidt, member of the Treasury; August Schwalb, bank director and later Oberalte; Gabriel Gerhard Schwartze, member of the Chamber of Commerce; Johann Friedrich Voigt, member of the Treasury; and Georg Wortmann, member of the Treasury and Commerce Deputation. Johann Friedrich Voigt, *Beiträge zur Hamburgischen Verwaltungsgeschichte*, vol. 3, *Die Protokolle der am 27. Mai 1814 erwählten Reorganisationsdeputation von zwanzig Bürgern* (Hamburg, 1918), pp. 168–70.

70. Helmut Böhme, *Frankfurt und Hamburg: Des deutschen Reiches Silber- und Goldloch und die allerenglischste Stadt des Kontinents* (Frankfurt a.M., 1968), pp.

116(n. 13), 116–18; Loose and Jochmann, eds., *Hamburg: Geschichte der Stadt,* vol. 1, pp. 435–36; and Baasch, *Geschichte,* vol. 1, pp. 3–31.

71. Quoted in *NBD* and in [Otto Beneke], *Der Hamburgische Bürgermeister Johann Heinrich Bartels: Ein Arbriß seines Lebens und Wirkens, nebst Fragmenten aus seinen Schriften* (Hamburg, 1850), pp. 87, 360.

72. See, for example, Böhme, *Frankfurt und Hamburg,* pp. 116–18; Loose and Jochmann, eds., *Hamburg: Geschichte der Stadt,* vol. 1, pp. 433–41; Baasch (*Geschichte,* vol. 1, p. 1) remarks that "much which now [1924] appears new to us, was only a more or less modernized version of older ideas and practices"; see also pp. 1(n.1), 3–31; W. Luhrs, "Der Hamburgischer Senat vom 1815 in englischer Sicht," *ZVHG* 48 (1962): 103–10; and on financial distress, see Wilhelm Amsinck, "Promemoria über die finanzielle Lage Hamburgs [1814]," StAHbg, Senat Cl. VII, Lit. Da, no. 2, vol. 6a, fasc. 1.

73. This argument coincides with the one that has early liberals in cities like Hamburg willing to accept social laissez-faire policies and to reject more collective controls on social welfare while at the same time accepting and using older political mechanisms, such as a very limited franchise, to prop up and protect existing sociopolitical structures.

74. Johann Michael Hudtwalcker, *Bemerkungen über die Schrift: Wünsche bey Hamburgs Wiedergeburt* (Hamburg, 1814), p. 41; on taxes, Ludwig Behrends, *Die Entwicklung der direkten Steuern in Hamburg und die Errichtung der Steuerdeputation am 9. März 1815* (Hamburg, 1915), pp. 3–6, 19.

75. See the mandate promulgated on 15 February 1821 concerning police, among other matters (Anderson/Lappenberg, vol. 8, pp. 16–17).

76. Rath- und Bürgerschluß, 23 October 1823 (Anderson/Lappenberg, vol. 8, pp. 94–96); Streng, *Gefängnisverwaltung,* pp. 120–25; Karl Eduard Abendroth, *Betrachtungen über die gegenwärtigen Verhältniße des Werk- und Armenhauses* (Hamburg, 1846); C. W. Ascher, *Ueber das Gefängniswesen in Hamburg* (Hamburg, 1839); C. Grapengiesser, *Werk- Armenhaus und Gefängnisse: Ein Wort zur Verständigung* (Hamburg, 1866); Hagedorn, "Das Werk- und Armenhaus"; and A. E. Martens, *Spinnhaus.*

77. Rath- und Bürgerschlusse, 1 October 1818, 9 September 1819, and 23 October 1823 (Anderson/Lappenberg, vol. 5, p. 303; vol. 6, p. 73; vol. 8, pp. 95–96); Dieter Jetter, *Geschichte des Hospitals,* vol. 1, *Westdeutschland von den Anfängen bis 1850* (Wiesbaden, 1966); Arthur Kressin, "Vom alten Hamburger 'Krankenhof' zum neuen 'Allgemeinen Krankenhaus' in der Vorstadt St. Georg," typescript, 1961, StAHbg, Bibliothek; Rodegra, *Vom Pesthof;* "Medizinal-Ordnung für die freye Hansestadt Hamburg und deren Gebiet durch Rath- und Bürgerschluß von 19. Februar 1818 beliebt" (Anderson/Lappenberg, vol. 6, pp. 44–143); *Entwurf zu einer Medizinal-Ordnung für die freie Hanse-Stadt Hamburg und deren Gebiet, großentheils nach Günther und Rambach redigirt und zum Behuf der Erleichterung der Deliberation darüber, als Manuscript herausgegeben* (Hamburg, 1816); [J. A. Günther], "Vorarbeiten zur Revision der hamburgischen Medizinal-Polizei, auf Veranlassung des im Jahr 1796. erledigten Physikats und Subphysikats, vom Senator Günther in Hamburg," *Scherffs Archiv-Beyträge* 7, no. 2 (1798): 1–22; and Heinrich Rodegra, *Das Gesundheitswesen der Stadt Hamburg im 19. Jahrhundert unter Berücksichtigung der Medizinalgesetzgebung (1586–1818–1900)* (Wiesbaden, 1979), pp. 44–72, 111–25.

78. von Melle, *Entwicklung,* p. 134.

79. *37ste Nachricht* (October 1816), pp. 248–49. Similarly in *38ste Nachricht* (July 1818), p. 257, the Relief spoke of the "reduced charity" among the affluent and,

among the lower classes, of the "increased demand for support . . . caused by a lack of pride and ambition."

80. *37ste Nachricht* (October 1816), p. 248; "Receptions-Protocoll für die erwachsenen Armen," StAHbg, AAI, 66, vol. 1: 1815 March through 1815 June; vol. 2: 1815 June through 1816 April.

81. *37ste Nachricht* (October 1816), p. 249.

82. Quoted in von Melle, *Entwicklung,* p. 135.

83. "Bericht der von dem großen Armen-Collegio, um Vorschläge über die Wiederherstellung der Armen-Anstalt und die Modalität ihres künftigen Bestandes zumachen, Niedergesetzten Commission, abgestattet in dem Collegio den 27sten Juny 1814," and "Nachricht an die Herren Armenpfleger über den Geschaftsgang bey der Armenfürsorge. Nach dem Wünsche der Pfleger, und auf Veranstaltung des großen Armen-Collegii zusammengetragen [1817]" (Anderson/Lappenberg, vol. 4, pp. 265–330).

84. On general conditions of assistance, see "Nachricht an die Herren Armenpfleger [1817]," pp. 269–301; and *37ste Nachricht* (October 1816), pp. 254–55; on retreat from the belief that economic conditions triggered most poverty, see *38ste Nachricht* (July 1818), p. 258, and Voght, *Gesammeltes,* p. 114; and on the Relief's response to criticisms that its program of assistance had become "mean-spirited" and "stingy" *37ste Nachricht* (October 1816), p. 254.

85. In 1816 the Relief treated 2,096 patients at a cost of 4,711 thaler; in 1817, 9,089 at cost of 16,066 thaler; in 1818, 10,529 at cost of 17,284 thaler; in 1819, 11,533 at cost of 18,027 thaler; and in 1820, 15,800 at cost of 20,583 thaler. Kollmann, "Ueberblick," p. 128. On Relief Officers and their role in medical care, see "Nachricht an die Herren Armenpfleger [1817]," pp. 310–27; in 1816 the medical relief was reorganized as a semi-independent organ, "The Institute for the Care of the Sick-Poor"; see "Rat-und Bürger-Schluß, das Institut für die Heilung kranker Armen betreffend," 22 August 1816 (Anderson/Lappenberg, vol. 3, pp. 137–52); "Verordnung des Instituts für die Heilung kranker Armen" (Anderson/Lappenberg, vol. 3, pp. 152–87); von Melle, *Entwicklung,* p. 141; and Kollmann, "Ueberblick," p. 122.

86. Council session, 1814, StAHbg, AAI, 9, vol. 17. Here quoted in von Melle, *Entwicklung,* pp. 141–42.

87. *38ste Nachricht* (July 1818), p. 270; and *Nachricht an die Herren Armenpfleger über den Geschaftsgang bei der Armenfürsorge* (Hamburg, 1829), here p. 64.

88. On schools and provisions for children, see "Nachricht an die Herren Armenpfleger [1817]," pp. 302–10; Hartwig Fiege, *Geschichte der Hamburgischen Volksschule* (Hamburg, 1970), pp. 30–32; Westphalen, *Verfassung und Verwaltung,* vol. 2, pp. 292–94; "Auszüge aus den Protocollen des großen Armen-Collegii das Schulwesen betreffend," council session, 10 July 1817, StAHbg, AAI, 9, vol. 18, excerpted in AAI, 125; "Die vom Senat versagte Unterstützung der vom Schulverein übernommenen Unterrichtung der Kinder der nicht eingetragenen Armen, seine Aufklärung und die Übertragung der Mittel auf der Allgemeine Armenanstalt, 1816–1817," StAHbg, AAI, 126; on schools after 1815, Scherpner, *Kinderfürsorge,* p. 75; on the council's position on schools in 1816, *37ste Nachricht* (October 1816), pp. 251–54; and on School Convent, ibid., p. 227.

89. On the Relief's decision not to reinstitute work programs, *38ste Nachricht* (July 1818), pp. 275–76, quote from p. 276.

90. On restricted police powers of the Relief, see "Nachricht an die Herren Armenpfleger [1817]," pp. 326–30; on financial status of Relief, Kollmann, "Ueberblick," pp. 134–35, 121–25.

91. For listings of all charities founded in Hamburg in the nineteenth century, see Hermann Joachim, *Handbuch für Wohltätigkeit in Hamburg* (Hamburg, 1901; 2nd ed., 1909); and *Die milden Privatstiftungen zu Hamburg* (Hamburg, 1845).

Conclusion

1. Ernst Baasch, *Geschichte Hamburgs, 1814–1914*, 2 vols. (Gotha, 1924–25), vol. 1, p. 2.

2. See Richard J. Evans, *Death in Hamburg, Society and Politics in the Cholera Years 1830–1910* (Oxford, 1987), pp. 1–49 and Loose and Jochmann, eds., *Hamburg, Geschichte der Stadt*, vol. 1, pp. 415–90.

3. See chap. 4, p. 92.

4. Evans, *Death in Hamburg*, p. 48.

5. Hans Mauersberg, *Wirtschafts- und Sozialgeschichte zentraleuropäischer Städte in neuerer Zeit: Dargestellt an den Beispielen von Basel, Frankfurt a.M., Hamburg, Hannover und München* (Gottingen, 1960), p. 38.

6. Donald Rohr, *The Origins of Social Liberalism in Germany* (Chicago and London, 1963). Rohr may very well be right that liberalism in Germany in the early nineteenth century was more sympathetic to government intervention in social and economic affairs than is generally believed, although that does not seem to have been true for Hamburg's leaders. See Evans, *Death in Hamburg*, pp. 1–49.

7. Evans, *Death in Hamburg*, pp. 74–78; Antje Kraus, *Die Unterschichten Hamburgs in der ersten Hälfte des 19. Jahrhunderts: Entstehung, Struktur und Lebensverhältnisse-Eine historisch-statistische Untersuchung* (Stuttgart, 1965), pp. 48–51; and Werner von Melle, *Die Entwicklung des öffentlichen Armenwesens in Hamburg* (Hamburg, 1883), pp. 127–51.

BIBLIOGRAPHY

Archives and Newspapers

The two most important archival collections for this book were Senat and Allgemeine Armenanstalt I (Staatsarchiv Hamburg). Pages in these files are either not numbered or numbered in a nonuniform manner. I consequently either refer to documents by date or use some descriptive term (e.g., Pro Memoria to, letter to). The *Nachrichten* published by the General Poor Relief are cited by number (date), page(s) (e.g., *1ste Nachricht* [October 1788], p. 2). The *Nachrichten* were collected into volumes and numbered consecutively. I have omitted the volume numbers since they can be confusing. Newspaper articles from the period are generally cited by date or by date and page/column numbers.

Staatsarchiv Hamburg (StAHbg)

Senat
   Cl. VII Innere Angelegenheiten
      Lit. A: Rat, Ratsbedienstete; Senat, Senatämter
      Lit. B: Bürgerschaft und Verwaltung; bürgerliche Rechte und Pflichten
      Lit. C: Einzelne Verwaltungszweige und Verwaltung überhaupt
      Lit. D: Kämmerei, Finanz- und Steuerverwaltung
      Lit. G: Militärwesen
      Lit. K: Handel- und Schiffahrt
      Lit. L: Stadtrecht, Rezesse; Gesetzgebung und einzelne Gesetzgebungsmaterien
      Lit. M: Justizangelegenheiten
      Lit. N: Chronistik, Ortsbeschreibung und Genealogisches; Statistik
      Lit. Q: Armen- und Krankenfürsorge; Sozialfürsorge; Gemeinnützige Anstalten
      Lit. T: Seuchen- und Ungezieferbekämpfung
   Cl. VIII Stadtbücher und Protokolle (Senat, 1742–)
   Cl. XI Handwerke, Gewerbe und Industrie
Präturen
Gefängnisverwaltung
Kämmerei I (1563–1811)
Wedde I (1600–1811)
Werk- und Armenhaus
Allgemeine Armenanstalt I [AAI]
   1. Material zur Neuen Armenordnung. 1786–88.
   2. Der Übergang der verwaltungsmässigen Zuständigkeiten in Armensachen auf die Allgemeine Armenanstalt 1788.
   3. Revision der revidierten Armenordnung von 1791. 1792–97.

4. Protokoll und Beilagen betr. die Revisions-Versammlung zur Verbesserung des Armenwesens. 1800–1801.

5. Schreiben des Armenvorstehers Caspar Voght aus Wien betr. die Revision der Armenordnung. 1802.

6. Revision der Armenordnung. 1832–34.

7. Erörterungen Caspar Voghts aus Anlass der Revision der Armenanstalt. 1832–34.

8. Protokoll und Beilagen betr. die Revisions-Kommission zur Verbesserung des Armenwesens. 1854–58.

9. Armenkollegium (Protokolle) 20 vols. 1788–1809.

11. Material zu Beschlüssen in den Armen Kollegien. 1788–1897.

12. Personalverzeichnis der Allgemeine Armenanstalt. Gedruckt. (Teil des Staats-Kalenders) 1788–98, 1833–79.

13. Alphabetisches Personalverzeichnis der A.A. 1788–1892.

14. Gesüche von Offizianten, Bezirksboten etc. im eigenen Angelegenheiten. 1791–1855.

15. Die Armenvorsteher; Wahl, Rücktritt, Beschwerden, Aufgaben. 1793–1846.

16. Übersicht über die im Dienst der Allgemeinen Armenanstalt Beschäftigen und über ihre Bezahlung. 1801.

19. Instruction und Mittheilungen für die Armen-Pfleger. 1788–1802.

20. Instruction für die Bezirks- und Quartiersboten. 1788–1844.

25. Instruction für die Verwaltung der in der Armenpflege benutzten Vordrücke. 1791, 1838.

29. Massnahmen und Vorschläge zur Vermehrung der Einnahmen der Allgemeinen Armenanstalt. 1789–98.

31. Rat- und Bürgerschaftsbeschlüsse betr. die Erhebung von Grabengeldern für die Allgemeine Armenanstalt. 1791–93.

33. Genehmigung und Bekanntmachung der kirchlichen Kollekten für die Allgemeine Armenanstalt; Tabellarische Übersicht über die Ergebnisse der Kollekten. 1796–1852.

38. Vorschläge zur Senkung der Haushaltungsausgaben für die Allgemeine Armenanstalt. 1804, 1829, 1844.

46. Bilanzen der Allgemeinen Armenanstalt. 1793–1808.

58. Listen der Bürger-Kapitäne über die in ihren Kompaniebezirken wohnenden Arme. 1787.

59. Zusammenarbeit der Allgemeinen Armenanstalt mit dem Geistlichen Ministerium zur Durchführung fürsorgerischen Massnahmen. 1788–90.

60. Entwurf einer Vereinbarung der Allgemeinen Armenanstalt und das Waisenhauses betr. die Leistung des Unterhalts an Waisenkinder und andere unterstützungsbedürftige Kinder. 1789–90.

61. Verzeichnis der von der katholischen Gemeinde unterstützten Personen und die Einstellung der Zahlungen nach der Einführung der Allgemeinen Armenordnung. 1789.

62. Berichte über die als Arme eingetragenen und unterstützten Cath. D. Heyer und Zacharias W. Keck wegen ihres böswilligen, die Armut verursachenden Verhaltens. 1789, 1802.

63. Zuständigkeit der Allgemeinen Armenanstalt betr. die Versorgung der Invaliden der Garnison und der Angehörigen der Nachtwache. 1792–93.

64. Gewährung der Unterstützungssätze im Verhältnis der jeweiligen Kassenlage. 1813.

65. Unterstützungsgesuche und -entscheidungen (Muster)-fälle. 1792, 1840–60.
66. Aufnahmebücher—Erwachsene. 1815–69.
67. Register A–K, L–Z.
68. Aufnahmebücher—Kinder. 1817–43.
69. Register, A–L, M–Z.
70. Die Angabe warmer Mahlzeiten, insbesondere die Einführung der Rumford-schen Suppe. 1800–1807.
71. Protokoll der Suppendeputation (Deputation zur Verbreitung ökonomischer Speiseanstalten). 2 vols. 1802–27.
76. Vereinbarung der Allgemeinen Armenanstalt mit dem Zuchthaus betr. die Unterbringung der obdachlosen Armen und die Zuweisung von Arbeit im Zuchthaus. Regelung der Vermögensverhältnisse und der Einkünfte der Eingewiesenen. 1789–91.
77. Statistik und Verfahren betr. die Versorgung mit Bekleidung. 1792–1808.
78. Massnahmen zur Behebung der Wohnungsnot, insbesondere der Bau von Baracken bei der Ollmühle auf dem Hamburger Berg, die Planung im Kirchspiel St. Michaelis und in der Vorstadt St. Georg und die Hausordnung für die Bewohner des Drillhauses. 1797–98.
79. Die Kapitalverwaltung betr. die Armenordnungen "Hinter dem Strohhause" in St. Georg, unter anderen Bau- und Grundstückskontrakte von 1798–99, 1830–47, 1859–70.
81. Die Heranziehung der von der Armenanstalt unterhaltenen Erwachsenen und Kinder zur Pflichtarbeit in der Spinnanstalt, die Unterweisung in Spinnschulen und die Instruktionen für das Aufsichtspersonal. 1788–1805.
82. Die Einrichtung der Armen-Polizei und die Ausführung von Zwangsarbeit im Zuchthaus. 1789–96, 1807.
83. Berichte und Rechnungsabschlüsse betr. die Spinnschule (Industrieschule). 1789–90, 1800.
84. Massnahmen zur Verbesserung des Betriebes der Spinnanstalt. 1789–92.
85. Gemeinsame Angelegenheiten der Lehr- und Industrieschulen. 1792–1808.
86. Monatsberichte betr. die Arbeitsleistungen in den Arbeitsanstalten. 1793–98, 1836.
89. Quartelsberichte und Rechnungslegung betr. die medizinische Versorgung. 1788–89, 1793–98.
91a. Jährliche Übersichten über die Leistungen und Ausgaben zur Heilung kranker Arme. 1819–33.
94. Konzept-Protokoll der Medizinal-Deputation der Allgemeinen Armenanstalt. 1788–93.
95. Protokoll der Medizinal-Deputation mit Register. 1816–30.
99. Die Armenärzte—Anstellung, Beschwerden—. 1784–92, 1823–44.
100. Instruktion betr. die Armenkrankenpflege, insbesondere Ärzte, Wundärzte, Apotheker, Speisewirte, Wehmütter, Krankenwärterinnen. 1788–96, 1816–49.
101. Sammlung der Instruktionen für die im Medizinalwesen der Armenanstalt beschäftigten Personen. 1788–1871.
102. Erhöhung der Gehälter der Armenärzte. 1791.
104. Die Zusammenarbeit mit den Armen- und Krankenhäusern betr. die Aufnahme und Entlassung unterstützter Armen. 1788.
105. Vereinbarung der Armenanstalt mit dem Pesthof betr. die Überweisung der unterstützten Armen in Krankheitsfälle an den Pesthof. 1789–92.

106. Ersparungs- und Verbesserungsvorschläge betr. die Armenkrankenpflege und die Bekanntmachung über die Aufnahme halbfreier Kranken. 1789–93.
107. Übersichten und die Beschlüsse der Medizinaldeputation betr. die Behandlung langwieriger Kranken. 1789–92.
108. Sammlung der Formulare betr. die Armenkrankenpflege, c. 1790.
109. Die medizinische Versorgung der eingezeichneten Armen—Organisation und Einzelfälle. 1789–1806, 1826, 1837.
110. Bericht des Armenvorstehers Günther über die medizinische Versorgung auf Grund der Rechnungsabschlüsse. 1788–90.
112. Monatliche Berichte über die Behandlung grindköpfiger Kinder. 1789.
113. Monatliche Krankentabellen der Armenärzte, untergliedert nach Hauptbezirken und Quartieren. 2 vols. 1789–92.
114. Die Abgabe pharmazeutischer Mittel und die Feststellung der Taxe. Preisliste der Medikamente, *Pharmacopoea Pauperum* (1785). 1788–90.
115. Die Einrichtung eines Ammen-Comtoirs. Formularmässige Berichte der Bezirkärzte über die Eignung der auf Kosten der Armenanstalt Entbundenen zu Ammendiensten. 1789–91.
117. Jahresberichte und Material betr. die Verwaltung der Entbindungsanstalt. 1796–97, 1853–56.
117a. Erörterung der freien Kur und Krankenpflege für nicht eingezeichnete Arme. 1808.
118. Einrichtung, Verwaltung und Schliessung der Fütterungsanstalt (später Kostkinderinstitut). 1798–1802; Einrichtung von Warteschulen. 1832–45.
124. Die Revision der Lehrschulen der Armenanstalt. 1798–1801.
124a. Geplante Einrichtung einer Korrektionsanstalt für Minderjährige. 1807–8.
125. Die Revision des Schulwesens. 1815–20.
126. Die vom Senat versagte Unterstützung der vom Schulverein übernommenen Unterrichtung der Kinder der nicht eingetragenen Armen. 1816–17.
145. Protokoll der Schuldeputation der Allgemeinen Armenanstalt. 6 vols. 1792–1811.
146. Protokoll des Schulkonvents. 1815–30.

Waisenhaus   St. Katerinen Kirche
Gast- und Krankenhaus   Familienarchive
Amt der Schmiede   Handschriftensammlung [HS]

Commerzbibliothek

Protocollum Commercii
S599 Verschiedenes

Staats- und Universitätsbibliothek-Hamburg

Handschriftensammlung

Newspapers

Hamburg und Altona [HA]
Hamburger Relations-Courier
Hamburgischer Correspondent
Hamburgische Neue Zeitung

Hamburgische Adreß-Comptoir Nachrichten [*ACN*]
Wöchentlicher Gemeinnützige Nachrichten von und für Hamburg [*Hamburger Nachrichten*]

Published Sources

Adelung, Johann Christoph. *Grammatisch-kritisches Wörterbuch der Hochdeutschen Mundart, mit beständiger Vergleichung der übrigen Mundarten, besonders aber der Oberdeutschen.* 2nd rev. and enl. ed. Leipzig, 1793–1801.

Allgemeine Armenanstalt. "Allgemeine Regeln für alle diejenigen, welche von der neuen Armen-Anstalt unterstützt werden wollen." October 1788.

————. "Des grossen Armen-Collegii näherer Bericht an die Herren Armen-Pfleger, über die zur Beschäftigung der Armen angelegte Spinn-Anstalt, und über die im vormaligen Waisenhause eingerichteten Spinnschulen für Erwachsene und für Kinder." Hamburg, December 1788.

————. "Nachricht an die Armen, über die Spinn-Anstalt." [Hamburg], 1788.

————. "Nachricht an die Herren Armenpfleger über den Geschäftsgang bei der Armenfürsorge." 2nd ed. Hamburg, 1829.

————. "Nachricht an die Herren Armenpfleger über den Geschäftsgang bey der Armenfürsorge." In Anderson, *Verordnungen,* vol. 4, pp. 265–330.

Allgemeiner Bericht über den Zustand der, während der Belagerung aus Hamburg Vertriebenen, und über die, zur Milderung ihres Schicksals, angewandten Mittel. Erster Bericht bis Ende März 1814. Altona, [1814].

Anderson, Christian Daniel, ed. *Sammlung hamburgischer Verordnungen: Eine Fortsetzung sowol der Sammlung hamburgischer Gesetze und Verfassungen, als der Sammlung hamburgischer Mandate.* 8 vols. Hamburg, 1783–1820. (Cited as Anderson.)

Anderson, Christian Daniel and Johann Martin Lappenberg, eds. *Sammlung der Verordnungen der freien Hanse-Stadt Hamburg seit deren Widerbefreiung im Jahre 1814.* 33 vols. Hamburg, 1814–65. (Cited as Anderson/Lappenberg.)

Baasch, Ernst, ed., *Quellen zur Geschichte von Hamburgs Handel und Schiffahrt im 17., 18. und 19. Jahrhundert.* Hamburg, 1910.

Bartels, Johann Heinrich, ed., *Neuer Abdruck der Vier Haupt-Grundgesetze der Hamburgischen Verfassung.* Hamburg, 1823.

Bericht der von dem großen Armen-Collegio, um Vorschläge über die Wiederherstellung der Armen-Anstalt und die Modalität ihres künftigen Bestandes zu machen, niedergesetzten Commission. Hamburg, 1814.

Bertheau, Karl, ed. *Johannes Bugenhagens Kirchenordnung für die Stadt Hamburg vom Jahre 1529.* Hamburg, 1885.

Blank, Johann Friedrich, ed. *Sammlung der von E. Hochedlen Rathe der Stadt Hamburg so wol zur Handhabung der Gesetze und Verfassungen als bey besonderen Eräugnissen in Bürger- und Kirchlichen, auch Cammer- , Handlungs- und übrigen Policey-Angelegenheiten und Geschäften vom Anfange des siebenzehnten Jahr-Hunderts bis auf die itzige Zeit ausgegangenen allgemeinen Mandate, bestimmten Befehle und Bescheide, auch beliebten Aufträge und verkündigten Anordnungen.* 6 vols. Hamburg, 1763–74 (Cited as Blank.)

Ein treues Bild der französischen Militär-Herrschaft in Hamburg: Die wichtigsten Mandate und Verordnungen der Jahre 1806 bis 1813, nach ihrem Wortlaute mitgetheilt. Hamburg, 1863.

Bulletin des Arrêtés de la Commission de Gouvernement établie par le décret impérial du 18 Decembre 1810. Hamburg, 1811.

Classification des von E. E. Rath und der Erbgesessenen Bürgerschaft am 26. April 1759 beliebten Kopf-Geldes. Hamburg, 1759.

Dokumente zur Geschichte der Handelskammer Hamburg. Hamburg, 1965.

Entwurf zu einer Medizinal-Ordnung für die freie Hanse-Stadt Hamburg und deren Gebiet, grossentheils nach Günther und Rambach redigirt und zum Behuf der Erleichterung der Deliberation darüber, als Manuscript herausgegeben.

Hamburger, Georg Christoph, and Johann George Meusel, eds. *Das gelehrte Deutschland: oder, Lexikon der jetzt lebenden teustchen Schriftsteller.* 5th ed. Lemgo, 1796–1834.

Hamburgisches Diarium von Anno . . . Die . . . Woche/von . . . bis . . . Enthaltend die Zahl derjenigen Persohnen/so Wochentlich in jeden Kirchspiel sind gebohren/ proclamiert, als auch Copuliert, und gestorben. Hamburg, 1711–15.

Heß, Ludwig von. *Unwiederrufliches Fundamental-Gesetz, Regimentsform, odor Haupt-Receß der Stadt Hamburg.* Hamburg, 1781.

Klefeker, Johann. *Sammlung der Hamburgischen Gesetze und Verfassung in Bürger- und Kirchlichen, auch Cammer- Handlungs- und übrigen Policey-Angelegenheiten und Geschäften samt historischen Einleitungen.* 12 vols. Hamburg, 1765–73. Index, 1774. (Cited as Klefeker.)

Krünitz, Johann Georg. *D. Johann Georg Krünitz's ökonomisch-technologische Encyklopädie oder allgemeines System der Staats-, Stadt-, Haus-, und Landwirthschaft und der Kunstgeschichte in alphabetischer Ordnung.* 242 vols. Berlin, 1782–1858.

Kühl, Heinrich. *Hamburgische Raths- und Bürgerschlüsse vom Jahre 1700 bis zum Ende des Jahres 1800.* Hamburg, 1803.

Letzter allgemeiner Bericht über die im Winter 1813 und 1814 den vertriebenen und ausgewanderten so wie den wieder heimgekehrten Hamburger bewilligten Summen. Fortsetzung des im März 1814 an die Wohlthäter dieser Unglücklichen abgestatteten Berichts. Hamburg, 1815.

Lexikon der hamburgischen Schriftsteller bis zur Gegenwart. Edited by Hans Schröder, F. A. Cropp, C. R. W. Klose, and A. H. Kellinghusen. 8 vols. Hamburg, 1851–83. (Cited as *Lexikon der Schriftsteller.*)

Lohmann, Peter Daniel. *Hamburgische Rath- und Bürgerschlüsse vom Jahr 1801 bis zum Ende des Jahres 1815 mit getreuen Auszüge aller den Rath-Propositionen hinzugefügten Beylagen.* 5 vols. Hamburg, 1828–41.

Die milden Privatstiftungen zu Hamburg. Hamburg, 1845.

Mitglieder und Associirte der Hamburgischen Gesellschaft zur Beförderung der Künste und nützlichen Gewerbe von ihrer Stiftung im Jahr 1765 an bis in die Mitte des Jahres 1803. Hamburg, 1803.

Möller, Walther Peter. *Chronologische Verzeichnisse der Mitglieder des Rathes, der Oberalten und der Kämmerei-Verordneten.* Hamburg, 1820.

Nachricht an die Herren Armenpfleger über den Geschaftsgang bei der Armenfürsorge. Hamburg, 1829.

Nachricht von der neuerrichteten medicinischen Anstalt für kranke Haus-Arme in Hamburg. Hamburg, 1781.

Nachrichten von der Einrichtung und dem Fortgang der Hamburgischen Armen-Anstalt. Nos. 1–54 in 2 vols. 1788–1840.

Nachricht von dem Fortgang des medicinischen Armen-Instituts in der lezten Hälfte des Jahrs 1787. Hamburg, 1788.

Neues hamburgisches Addreßbuch. Hamburg, 1787–98.

Nucleus Recessum et Conventuum Hamburgensium oder: Kurtzer/ doch gründlich und ausführlicher Kern-Auszug aller von Anno 1410. bis Anno 1704. in Hamburg ergangener und gehaltener Raht und Bürgerlichen Recesse und Versammlungen; Aus welchem der geneigte Lesser und Liebhaber nicht nur den wahren Grund aller Bürgerlichen und Gemeine Stadt Frey-Hoheit und Gerechtigkeiten erlernen und sehen/ sonder auch alles/ was in Bürgerlichen Versammlungen vorgefallen/ ausgesprochen und geschlossen worden/ gleichsam im Spiegel und nach dem Wörtlichen Einhalt vorfinden kan. Altona, 1705.

Der Patriot. Nos. 1–156. 5 January 1724–28 December 1726.

Der Patriot nach dem Originalausgabe Hamburg 1724–1726 in drei Textbänden und einem Kommentarband kritisch herausgegeben von Wolfgang Martens. 4 vols. Berlin, 1969–84.

[Pitt, Moses] and William Nicolson, *The English Atlas.* Vol. 2, *Containing the Description of Part of the Empire of Germany viz. The Upper and Lower Saxony.* Oxford and London, 1681.

Plan zum Vortheil der hiesigen kranken Haus-Armen. Hamburg, 1779.

Praefaction der zum Behuff der Armen-Ordnung destinierten Einzeichnungs-Bücher (10 März 1712). Hamburg, 1712.

Reglement wegen des Kopf-Geldes. Auf Befehl Eines Hochedlen Raths der Stadt Hamburg publicirt den 7. May 1770. Hamburg, 1770.

Richter, Aemilius Ludwig, ed. *Die evangelischen Kirchenordnungen des sechszehnten Jahrhunderts: Urkunden und Regesten zur Geschichte des Rechts und der Verfassung der evangelischen Kirche in Deutschland.* Vol. 1, *Vom Anfange der Reformation bis zur Begründung der Consistorialverfassung im J. 1542.* Weimar, 1846.

[Schuback, Arnold]. *Chronologisches, bis auf die neuesten Zeiten fortgesetztes Verzeichniss der bisherigen Mitglieder Eines Hochedlen und Hochweisen Raths, der Ehrbaren Oberalten und der Verordneten löblicher Cämmerey der freyen Stadt Hamburg.* Hamburg, 1820.

Der Stadt Hamburgt Gerichts-Ordnung und Statuta (1605). Hamburg, 1605.

Staphorst, Nicolaus. *Historia Ecclesiae Hamburgensis diplomatica, das ist: Hamburgische Kirchen-Geschichte, aus Glaubwürdigen und mehrentheils noch ungedruckten Urkunden, so wol Kaiserlichen/ Königlichen/ Fürstlichen/ Gräflichen/ etc. als auch Päbstliche/ Erz-Bischöflichen und andrer beider Geistlicher als Weltlicher Personen respectiv Gnaden Freiheits- und Bestätigungs-Briefen, Concessionen, Indulten, Stifftungen, Vermächnüssen, Verordnungen, Statuten, Verträgen, Contracten, Vergleichungen und andern dergleichen vielfältigen Schrifften, Gesammelt/ beschrieben und in Ordnung gebracht.* 2 pts., 5 vols. Hamburg, 1723–29.

Strelin, Georg Gottfried. *Realwörterbuch für Kameralisten und Oekonomen.* 8 vols. Nördlingen, 1783–96.

Supplementband zu dem neuen Abdruck der Grundgesetze der Hamburgischen Verfassung und deren Nachträge. Hamburg, 1825.

Über den gegenwärtigen Zustand der Armen-Anstalt. Hamburg, 1808.

Verhandlungen und Schriften der Hamburgischen Gesellschaft zur Beförderung der Künste und nützlichen Gewerbe. 7 vols. Hamburg, 1792–1807.

Versprochener Nachtrag zu der den Herren Armen-Pflegern mitgetheilten näheren Erläuterung, welcher die vorbehaltene nähere Bestimmungen des 16ten Abschnittes dieser Erläuterung enthält. Hamburg, October 1788.

Versuch zu einem Entwurf einer revidirten Ordnung für die General-Feuercasse der Reich-Stadt Hamburg. Hamburg, 1802.

Verzeichniß der Bibliothek welche der hamburgischen Gesellschaft zur Beförderung der Künste und nützlichen Gewerbe von ihrem verdienten Mitgliede Herrn Senator Johann Arnold Günther Lt. d. R. im Jahr 1805 hinterlassen ist. Hamburg, 1806.

Vollständige Einrichtungen der neuen Hamburgischen Armenanstalt, zum Besten dieser Anstalt herausgegeben vom Hamburgischen Armen Collegio. Hamburg, 1788.
    1. "Neue Hamburgische Armen-Ordnung, beliebt durch Rath- und Bürger-Schluss den 18. Februar und 7. Juli 1788."
    2. "Verzeichniss der zu einem jeden Armen-Quartier Gassen, Plätze, Twieten und Gängen, nebst Register."
    3. "Des grossen Armen-Collegii vorläufige Nachricht an die Herren Armen-Pfleger. Im April 1788. Mit beigefügten Fragestücken zur Abhörung der Armen, und der Tabelle zur Armen-Liste."
    4. "Des grossen Armen-Collegii nähere Erläuterung für die Herren Armen-Pfleger. Im Jahre 1788. Nebst vollständigem Register."

Zedler, Johann Heinrich. *Grosses vollständiges Universal-Lexikon, aller Wissenschaften und Künste, welche bishero durch menschlichen Verstand und Witz erfunden und verbessert worden . . .* 64 vols. Leipzig and Halle, 1732–50.

Zincke, Georg Heinrich. *Cameralisten-Bibliothek, worinne nebst der Anleitung die Cameral-Wissenschaft zu lehren und zu lernen, ein vollständiges Verzeichniss der Bücher und Schriften von der Land- und Stadt-Oeconomie, dem Policey-Finanz- und Cammerwesen zu finden, so theils kurz beurtheilet, theils umständlich vorgestellt worden.* 2 vols. Leipzig, 1751, 1752; repr. ed., Glashütten im Taunus, 1973.

Zweite Sammlung von der Nachrichten vom medicinischen Armen-Institut in Hamburg. Vom 1sten Juli 1781 bis Januar 1784. Hamburg, 1784.

Contemporary Works

Abendroth, Amandus Augustus. *Bemerkungen über die Armen-Anstalt von 1791 und 1830.* Hamburg, 1831.

[————]. *Was kann das Publikum von der Allgemeinen Armenanstalt in der jetzigen Zeit erwarten?* Hamburg, [1831].

————. *Wünsche bei Hamburgs Wiedergeburt im Jahre 1814.* Kiel, 1814.

Abendroth, Eduard. *Betrachtungen über die gegenwärtigen Verhältniße des Werk- und Armenhauses.* Hamburg, 1846.

[Amsinck, Wilhelm]. *Aufzeichnungen des Senator und Landherrn Lict. Wilhelm Amsinck über seine Verwaltung der Landherrschaften von Bill- und Ochsenwärder 1800/1801.* Edited by J. W. Voigt. Hamburg, 1911.

Ascher, C[arl] W[ilhem]. *Bericht der von der technischen Section der Hamburgischen Gesellschaft zur Beförderung der Künste und nützlichen Gewerbe ernannten Commission zur Untersuchung der Gewerbeverhältnisse in Hamburg.* Hamburg, 1861.

Ascher, C. W. *Die Hamburgische Armenanstalt im Jahre 1830.* Hamburg, 1830.

————. *Über die Hamburgische Armenanstalt 1831.* Hamburg, 1831.

————. *Ueber das Gefängniswesen in Hamburg.* Hamburg, 1839.

Baldrian, Johann. *Kleine Characteristik von Hamburg, von einem Kosmopoliten, zwei Treppen hoch.* [Hamburg], 1782.

Bartels, Johann Heinrich. *Actenmäßige Darstellung des Verfahrens der Franzosen bei dem durch Marschall Davoust befohlenen Verbrennen des Krankenhofs zwischen Hamburg und Altona, im Jahre 1813 und 1814.* Hamburg, 1815.

[———.] *Bericht über das was im Jahr 1813 vom 12ten März bis den 30sten May unter meinen Augen und unter meiner Mitwirkung in Hamburg vorging wie auch Actenmäßige Berichtigung verschiedener irriger Angaben in der von Herrn von Hess herausgegebenen Schrift unter dem Titel Agonieen der Republik Hamburg im Frühjahr 1813.* Hamburg, 1815.

[———]. *Einige Abhandlungen über Gegenstände der Hamburgischen Verfassung von dem Verfassesr der dem Abdruck der Hamburgischen Grundgesetze hinzugefügten erläuternden Uebersicht.* Hamburg, 1835.

Becher, Johann Joachim. *Politischer discurs, von den eigentlichen ursachen/ des auff- und abnehmens der städt/ länder und republiken/ in specie, Wie ein Land Volckreich und Nahrhafft zu machen/ und in eine recht Societatem civilem zu bringen. Auch wird von dem Bauern- Handwercks- und Kauffmanns-Standt/ derer Handel und Wandel/ Item, Von dem Monopolio, Polypolio und Propolio von allgemeinen Land-Magazinen, Niederlagen/ Kauffhäusern/ Montibus Pietatis/ Zucht- und Werck-Häusern/ Wechselbäncken und dergleichen aussführlich gehandelt.* 3rd rev. and enl. ed. Frankfurt, 1688; repr. ed., Glasshütten im Taunus, 1972.

Beerwinckel, Johann Franz. *Excerpta quaedam ex observatis in nupera peste Hamburgensi.* Jena, 1714.

Bianchi, von, C. *Historische Darstellung der Hamburgischen Anstalt zur Unterstützung der Dürftigen, Verhütung des Verarmens und Abstellung der Betteley.* Vienna, 1802; Hamburg, 1802.

Bieber, C. E. *Ueber den nachtheiligen Einfluß der hohen Miethe, und der Belastung unentbehrlicher Bedürfnisse auf Hamburgs Wohl, nebst einigen Vorschlägen dagegen.* Hamburg, 1803.

Böckel, Johannes. *Pestordnung in der Stadt Hamburg.* Hamburg, 1597.

Bracke, Joachim Christoph. *Ermahnungsrede bei Eröffnung der Sontagsschule für die Armenkinder im vormaligen Waisenhaus am 3. Weihnachtsfeiertag 1791 gehalten.* Hamburg, 1792.

Brodhagen, P. H. C. "Allgemeine Bemerkungen über die ehemalige Verfassung des hamburgischen Manufaktur- und Fabrikwesens, über die damit bis auf unsere Zeit vorgegangenen Veränderungen und über den Zustand der gegenwärtig [1792] hieselbst existierenden Manufakturen, Fabriken und Gewerbe." *VS* 3 (1795): 97–168.

———. "Auszug aus den Verhandlungen der Gesellschaft über einen ihr eingeschickten Vorschlag zur Anlegung einer Manufactur halbseidener Zeuge." *VS* 1 (1792): 307–9.

Brunner, Wolfgang Matthias. *Observationes bei der sogenannten Contagion, welche sich Anno 1712 in Hamburg angefangen und 1714 geendigt.* Regensburg, 1715.

Büsch, Johann Georg. *Allgemeine Uebersicht des Assecuranz-Wesens, als Grundlage zu einer unbefangenen Beurtheilung von G.E. Biebers Plan zur Einrichtung einer für Hamburg möglichst vortheilhaften Versicherungs-Compagnie gegen Feuers-Gefahr.* Hamburg, 1795.

———. *Erfahrungen.* 4 vols. Hamburg, 1792–94.

———. *Geschichtliche Beurtheilung der in der Handlung Hamburgs im Nachjahr 1799 entstandenen grossen Verwirrung.* Hamburg, 1799.

———. *Grundriss einer Geschichte der merkwürdigsten Welthandel neuerer Zeit in einem erzählenden Vortrage.* 3rd. rev. and enl. ed. Hamburg, 1796.

————. *Kleine Schriften über die Handlung.* Hamburg and Kiel, 1784.

————. *Kleine Schriften von der Handlung und anderem gemeinnützigen Inhalte.* Leipzig, 1772.

————. *Die politische Wichtigkeit der Freiheit Hamburgs und ihrer Schwesterstädte Lübeck und Bremen für das ganze handelnde Europa in ein neues Licht gestellt.* Hamburg, 1797.

————. *Schriften über Staatswirthschaft und Handlung.* 3 vols. Hamburg, 1780–84.

————. *Theoretisch-praktische Darstellung der Handlung in ihren mannichfaltigen Geschäften.* 2 vols. Hamburg, 1792, 1799.

————. *Ueber die Ursachen der Verarmung in Nordischen Handelsstädten und die wirksamsten Mittel denselben zu begegnen.* Hamburg, 1785.

————. *Ueber die Hamburgischen Zucker-Fabriken und den vergeblichen Wetteifer der Nordischen Staaten mit denselben, auf Veranlassung der Fragmente des Herrn Ritters von Zimmermann über Friedrich den Grossen.* Hamburg, 1790.

————. *Ueber die in den jetzigen Zeiten nothwendig werdende Erweiterung der Stadt Hamburg.* Hamburg, 1792.

————. *Versuch einer Geschichte der Hamburgischen Handlung, nebst zwei kleineren Schriften eines verwandten Inhalts.* Hamburg, 1797.

————. *Ein Wort an die Bürger Hamburgs über die Nichtachtung brauchbarer Gelehrsamkeit in der Erziehung ihrer Söhne und den daher rührenden Verfall unserer beiden öffentlichen Lehrinstitute.* Hamburg, 1800.

————. *Zum Andencken Alemanns des Menschenfreundes.* Hamburg, 1784.

————. *Zwei kleine Schriften die im Werk begriffene Verbesserung des Armenwesens in dieser Stadt Hamburg betreffend.* Hamburg, 1786. (1) "Historischer Bericht von dem Gange und fortdauernden Verfall des Hamburgischen Armenwesens seit der Zeit der Reformation." (2) "Allgemeine Winke zur Verbesserung des Armenwesens."

Darjes, Joachim Georg. *Erste Gründe der Cameralwissenschaften.* Jena, 1756.

Entwurf zu einer Medizinal-Ordnung für die freie Hanse-Stadt Hamburg und deren Gebiet, großentheils nach Günther und Rambach redigirt und zum Behuf der Erleichterung der Deliberation darüber, als Manuscript herausgegeben. Hamburg, 1816.

Eschenberg, J. Joachim. *Dem Andenken des Prof. J. G. Büsch.* Braunschweig, 1800.

Frank, Johann Peter. *System einer vollständigen medicinischen Polizey.* 4 vols. Mannheim, 1779–88.

Freimüthige und bescheidene Rügen einer hamburgischen Polizei-Mängel, nebst unmassgeblichen Vorschlägen zu ihrer Abstellung: Eine patriotische Schrift zur Beherzigung für Gesetz-Geber und Gesetz-Pflichtige. Hamburg, 1810.

Garve, Christian. *Anhang einiger Betrachtungen über Johann Macfarlan's Untersuchungen die Armut betreffend.* Leipzig, 1785.

Gericke, Johann Moritz. *Versuch einer allgemeinen Abhandlung vom Patriotismus.* Hamburg, 1792.

Godeffroy, Carl. *Theorie der Armuth: Ein Versuch.* Hamburg, 1834.

Graff, Johann Theodor. *Jährliche Uebersicht des Hamburger Zuckerhandels seit Ende der Belagerung bis Ende des Jahrs 1823 unter Beifügung sämmtlicher Preise von Monat zu Monat und Bemerkung der Haupt-Beweggründe zu deren Veränderung, nebst einer specificirten Aufstellung der jährlichen Zufuhren &c.* Hamburg, 1823.

Grapengiesser, C. *Werk-, Armenhaus und Gefängnisse: Ein Wort zur Verständigung.* Hamburg, 1866.

Griesheim, Christian Ludwig von. *Verbesserte und vermehrte Auflage des Tractats: Die*

Stadt Hamburg in ihrem politischen, öconomischen und sittlichen Zustande, nebst Nachträgen zu diesem Tractate und Beyträge zu der Abhandlung: Anmerckungen und Zugaben über den Tractat: Die Stadt Hamburg, welche selbigen ebenfalls verbessern und gewisser machen. Hamburg, 1760.

Günther, Johann Arnold. *Andenken an Volkmann.* Hamburg, 1794.

———. *Argumente und Erfahrungen über Kranken-Besuch-Anstalten aus den 2jährigen Rechnungs-Abschlüssen des Medicinal Departments der Hamburgischen Armenanstalt.* Hamburg, 1791.

———. *Erinnerungen aus den deutschen Kriegs-Gegenden, aus der Schweiz und aus den angrenzenden Ländern in vorzüglicher Hinsicht auf Natur-Schönheit und auf Völker-Glück. Aufgesammelt im Sommer 1796 von J. A. Günther, Senator der Reichsstadt Hamburg. Nach dessen Tode hg. von F[riedrich] J[ohann] L[orenz] Meyer, präsidirendem Capitular des Hamburgischen Domstiftes.* Hamburg, 1806.

———. "Geschichte der Entstehung, Fundation und Ausbreitung, der von der Gesellschaft im Jahre 1778 errichteten Hamburgischen Allgemeinen Versorgungs-Anstalt bis zum Jahre 1793, . . . nebst einer Fortsetzung der Geschichte dieses Instituts bis zum Jahre 1806." *VS* 7 (1807): 337–96.

———. *Müssen die Zünfte abgeschafft werden, nebst einer wahren Darstellung der neuen Unruhen in Hamburg.* Hamburg, September 1791.

———. *Ueber den Aufstand der Handwerksgesellen zu Hamburg im August 1791; nebst einigen Reflexionen über Zunftgeist und Zunfterziehung: Aus dem Journal von und für Deutschland [8, no. 7].* Frankfurt a.M. and Leipzig, 1792.

———. *Ueber die Einrichtung der mit der Hamburgischen Allgemeinen Armenanstalt verbundenen Kranken-Besuch-Anstalt.* Leipzig, 1793.

———. *Ueber Leibrenten, Witwen-Cassen, und ähnliche Anstalten, und besonders über die im Jahre 1778 zu Hamburg errichtete allgemeine Versorgungs-Anstalt.* Hamburg, 1788.

———. *Versuch einer Geschichte der Hamburgischen Gesellschaft zur Beförderung der Künste und nützlichen Gewerbe in den ersten 25 Jahren.* Hamburg, 1790.

———. *Versuch einer Geschichte der hamburgischen Handlung, nebst zwei kleineren Schriften eines verwandten Inhalts.* Hamburg, 1797.

———. *Versuch einer vollständigen Untersuchung über Wucher und Wucher-Gesetze, und über die Mittel, dem Wucher ohne Straf-Gesetze Einhalt zu thun; in politischer, justizmäßiger und mercantilistischer Rücksicht.* Hamburg, 1790.

Haeberl, Franz Xaver von. *Abhandlung über öffentliche Armen- und Krankenpflege mit einer umständlichen Geschichte der in dem ehemaligen Krankenhause zum heil. Max bey der barmherzigen Brüdern gemachten Erweiterungs- und Verbesserungs-Versuchen und den hiervon in neuen allgemeinen Krankenhause zu München gemachten Anwendungen.* Munich, 1820.

Hagen, Theodor Philipp von der. *Plan zur besseren Einrichtung der Armenkasse und Verteilung der Almosen in Berlin.* Berlin, 1787.

Hecker, August Friedrich. "Welche sind die bequemsten und wohlfeilsten Mittel, kranken Armen in den Städten die nötige Hülfe zu verschaffen?" *Neues Hannoverisches Magazin,* nos. 83–85 (1793).

Heß, Jonas Ludwig von. *Agonieen der Republik Hamburg im Frühjahr 1813.* Hamburg, 1815; rev. ed., Altona, 1816.

———. *An das Große Armen-Collegium.* Hamburg, 1806.

———. *Hamburg, topographisch, politisch und historisch beschrieben.* 3 vols. Hamburg, 1787–92; 2nd ed. (slightly different title), 3 vols. Hamburg, 1810–11.

———. *Was darf und darf nicht in Hamburg geschehen?* Hamburg, 1799, 1800.

Hudtwalcker, Johann Michael. *Bemerkungen über die Schrift: Wünsche bey Hamburgs Wiedergeburt.* Hamburg, 1814.

[Hudtwalcker, Martin Hieronymus]. *An die Hamburgische Allgemeine Armenanstalt im Mai 1833.* Hamburg, 1833.

Justi, Johann Heinrich Gottlob von. *Grundsätze der Policeywissenschaften, in einem Vernünftigen, auf den Endzweck der Policey gegründeten, Zusammenhänge und zum Gebrauch Akademischer Vorlesungen, abgefasset.* 3rd. rev. ed. Göttingen, 1782. Rpt. Frankfurt a.M., 1969.

Kerner, Georg. *Über das Hamburgische Entbindungshaus und das Entbindungswesen der Armenanstalt.* Hamburg, 1801.

Kiehn, Meno Günter. *Das hamburgische Waisenhaus: Geschichtlich und beschreibend dargestellt.* Hamburg, 1821.

Koch Sternfeld, J. E. von. *Versuch über Nährung und Unterhalt in zivilisierten Staaten: insbesondere über Wohlfeilheit und Teuerung. Gekrönte Preisschrift.* Munich, 1805.

Listert, Joseph. *Ursachen des Verfalls des Wohlstandes der Hanse-Städte und Mittel diesen Uebeln auf die zweckmäßigste Weise abzuhelfen.* Hamburg, Bremen, and Lübeck, 1808.

Lloyd, Hannibal Evans. *Hamburgh; or, a particular Account of the Conduct of the French in that City.* London, 1813.

MacFarlan, John. *Inquiries Concerning the Poor.* Edinburgh, 1782.

Markus, Adalbert Friedrich. *Von den Vortheilen der Krankenhäuser für den Staat.* Bamberg and Würzburg, 1790.

Martens, Andreas Ehrenfried. *Das Hamburgische Criminal-Gefängnis genannt: Das Spinnhaus und die übrigen Gefängnisse der Stadt Hamburg nach ihrer innern Beschaffenheit und Einrichtung beschrieben, nebst einigen Ansichten und Ideen über Verbesserung ähnlicher Anstalten überhaupt.* Hamburg, 1823.

———. *Das Hamburgische Kurhaus und dessen Einrichtung.* Hamburg, 1822.

Menuret, J.J. *Essai sur la ville d'Hambourg considérée dans ses rapports avec la santé au lettres sur l'Histoire médico-topographique de cette ville.* Hamburg, 1797.

Merkel, Georg. *Briefe über einige der merkwürdigsten Städte im nördlichen Deutschland.* Leipzig, 1801.

Meyer, Friedrich Johann Lorenz. *Johann Arnold Günther: Ein biographischer Umriß.* [Hamburg], 1806.

———. *Johann Arnold Günther: Ein Lebensgemälde.* Hamburg, 1810.

Minder, Johann Arnold. *Briefe über Hamburg.* Leipzig, 1794.

Möller, Kurt Detlev and Annelise Tecke, eds., *Caspar Voght und sein Hamburger Freundeskreis: Briefe aus einem tätigen Leben.* 3 vols. Hamburg, 1959, 1964, 1967.

Möglichst spezielles und richtiges Tagebuch vor allem, was in den unruhigen Tagen in Hamburg im Monat August 1791 bei dem Aufstand der Handwerksgesellen Tag vor Tag vorging. Hamburg, 1791.

Neues gemeinnütziges Magazin für die Freunde der nützlichen und schönen Wissenschaften und Künste. Hamburg, 1761.

[Nicolai, Friedrich]. *Beschreibung der Königl. Residenzstädte Berlin und Potsdam.* 3rd ed. Berlin, 1786.

Nicolai, Friedrich. *Beschreibung einer Reise durch Deutschland und die Schweiz im Jahre 1781. Nebst Bemerkungen über Gelehrsamkeit, Industrie, Religion und Sitten.* 12 vols. Berlin and Stettin, 1783–95.

Niemann, August C. H. *Uebersicht der neuen Armenpflege in der Stadt Kiel Sr. Königl.*

Hoheit des Kronprinzen Befehl vorgelegt von der Gesellschaft freiwilliger Armen-freunde in Auftrag derselben abgefasset von ihrem Wortführer, Prof. Niemann. Altona, 1798.

———. *Von der Industrie, ihren Hindernissen und Beförderungsmitteln, ein Bruckstück aus der Polizeiwissenschaft.* Altona, 1784.

Nolting, J. H. B. *Johann Georg Büsch: Professor der Mathematik an dem Gymnasium in Hamburg.* Hamburg, 1801.

Ohnmasgeblicher Vorschlag eines Volksfreundes um einer durch die Sperrung der Elbe ausser Arbeit gesetzten Menge Menschen in Hamburg baldigst Arbeit zu verschaffen, und sie vor Mangel und gänzlichen Verarmung, noch vor Eintritt des nahen Winters, zu schützen. Hamburg, n.d. [1803].

Pauli, J[ohann] [Ulrich]. *An alle wahre Patrioten Hamburgs gerichtete Ermahnung, zur Aufrichtung einer ähnlichen Patriotischen Gesellschaft, zur Aufnahme der Handlung, der Künste, der Manufacturen und des Ackerbaues, wie die zu London und Paris ist; nebst einer Beylage: Auszug aus der Handlungszeitung von Paris genannt, den gegenwärtigen Zustand beyder Gesellschaften betreffend.* Hamburg, 1765.

Pehmöller, Christian Nicolaus. *Über den gegenwärtigen Zustand der Armen-Anstalt. Eine Untersuchung, in den Sitzungen des großen Armen-Collegii von 15ten und 22sten September 1808 vorgetragen, von einem Mitgliede desselben.* Hamburg, n.d. [1808].

Pestalozzi, Johann Heinrich. *Sämtliche Werke.* Ed. Artur Buchenau, Eduard Spranger, and Hans Stettbacher. Berlin, 1927–.

Rambach, Johann Jakob. *Versuch einer physisch-medizinischen Beschreibung von Hamburg.* Hamburg, 1801.

Rathgeber für Conscribirte und deren Verwandte. Enthalten: das Verfahren der Conscription: die Gesetze und besondern Vorschriften darüber, nebst Angabe derjenigen Fälle, in welchen die Befreiung statt hat. Aus dem Französischen übersetzt. Hamburg, 1811.

Reimann, Johann Friedrich. *Beschreibung der Rekanschen Schule.* Berlin and Stettin, 1781. 2nd ed., 1792.

Reimarus, Johann Albert Heinrich. "Anrede an die den 10ten October 1765 zum erstenmal von den Vorstehern zusammenberufenen Mitglieder der Gesellschaft." *VS* 1 (1792): 9–17.

———. *Entwurf eines allgemeinen Staats-Unterricht für künftige Bürger.* Hamburg, 1803.

———. *Die Freiheit des Getraidehandels nach der Natur und Geschichte erwogen.* Hamburg, 1790.

[———]. *Handlungs-Grundsätze zur wahren Aufnahme der Länder und zur Beförderung der Glückseligkeit ihrer Einwohner aus der Natur und Geschichte untersucht.* "Cosmopolis" [Frankfurt am Main and Leipzig], 1768.

———. *Untersuchung der vermeinten Nothwendigkeit eines autorisirten Kollegii medizi und einer medizinischen Zwangs-Ordnung.* Hamburg, 1781.

———. *Die wichtigen Fragen von der freyen Aus- und Einfuhre des Getraides, nach der Natur und Geschichte untersucht.* Hamburg, 1771.

Reyher, Johann Georg. *Ueber die Einrichtung kleiner Hospitäler in mittlern und kleinern Städten.* Hamburg and Kiel, 1784.

Richey, Michael. "Anmerckungen über die bey Rengern in Halle herausgekommene Nachricht von Hamburg nebst einer Anleitung zur Hamburgischen Histoire." [Hamburg], 1758. [In StAHbg, *HS* 273].

Rochow, Friedrich Eberhard von. *Der Kinderfreund, ein Lesebuch zum Gebrauch für Landschulen.* 2 vols. Berlin and Leipzig, 1776, 1780.

————. *Materialien zum frühen Unterricht in Bürger- und Industrieschulen.* Berlin and Stettin, 1797.

————. *Versuch über Armenanstalten und Abschaffung aller Betteley.* Berlin, 1789.

Rulffs, August Friedrich. *Ueber die Preisfrage der Königliche Societät der Wissenschaften in Göttingen: Von der vortheilhaftesten Einrichtung der Werk- und Zuchthäuser.* Göttingen, 1783.

[Schacht, Johann Justus]. *Entwurf zur Errichtung einer Credit-Casse für die Erben und Grundstücke in der Stadt Hamburg und deren Gebeit, zur Sicherheit und Aufrechterhaltung des Werths derselben.* Hamburg, 1772.

Schleiden, Jacob. *Bemerkungen über die jetzige Einrichtung der Einquartierung in Hamburg nebst Vorschlägen zur Verbesserung derselben in einem Schreiben an ein Mitglied des Collegii der Herren Sechziger.* Hamburg, 1808.

Sextroh, Heinrich Philip. *Über die Bildung der Jugend zur Industrie: Ein Fragment.* Göttingen, 1785.

Sieveking, Georg Heinrich. *Fragmente über Luxus, Bürger-Tugend und Bürger-Wohl für hamburgische Bürger, die das Gute wollen und können; am 17ten November 1791 in der Gesellschaft zu Beförderung der Künste und nützlichen Gewerbe gelesen. Mit Beiträgen und Bemerkungen von zweien seiner Freunde* [*J. M. Hudtwalcker, J. A. Günter*]. Hamburg, 1797.

Steltzner, Michael Gottlieb. *Versuch einer zuverlässigen Nachricht von dem kirchlichen und politischen Zustande der Stadt Hamburg.* 6 vols. Hamburg, 1731–39.

Süssmilch, Johann Peter. *Die göttliche Ordnung in den Veränderungen des menschlichen Geschlechts, aus der Geburt, dem Tode und der Fortpflanzung desselben erwiesen.* 2 vols. 2nd ed. Berlin, 1765.

Thiessen, Johann Otto. *Dem Andenken meines verewigten Freundes des Herrn Johann Klefekers.* Hamburg, 1786.

————. *Versuch einer Gelehrtengeschichte von Hamburg nach alphabetischer Ordnung mit kritischen und pragmatischen Bemerkungen.* 2 vols. Hamburg, 1780.

Über das Prinzip, die Gränzen und den Umfang der Polizei. Leipzig, 1808.

Unparteiische und deutliche Beschreibung der in Hamburg entstandenen Handwerksunruhen, die den 19. August 1791 ihren Anfang nahmen und erst ab den 26. August beendigt wurden. [Hamburg, 1791].

Voght, Caspar. *Account of the Management of the Poor in Hamburgh Since the Year 1788 in a Letter to Some Friends of the Poor in Great Britain.* Edinburgh, 1798; London, 1796.

————. *Auszug aus dem der patriotischen Gesellschaft abgelegten und dem Armen-Kollegium mitgetheilten Bericht über Flachsgarn-Spinnerey und Weberey.* Hamburg, 1834.

————. *Gesammeltes aus der Geschichte der Hamburgischen Armen-Anstalt während ihrer fünfzigjährigen Dauer.* Hamburg, 1838.

————. "Geschichte des ersten Zeitraumes der hamburgischen Armenanstalt, von Jahre 1788 bis zum Jahre 1798." *Jahrbücher der Straf- und Besserungs-Anstalten, Erziehungshäuser, Armenfürsorge, und anderer Werke der christlichen Liebe,* no. 9 (1833): 260–364.

————. *Lebensgeschichte.* Hamburg, 1917.

————. *Ueber die ersten Fortschritte der Anstalt, deren Zweck es ist, zu untersuchen, inwiefern es möglich sei, durch angemessene Verausgabung die Spinnerei zu einem dauernden Erwerb für die arbeitslosen Armen Hamburgs zu machen.* Hamburg, 1835.

———. *Ueber die hamburgische Armen-Anstalt v. J. 1788 bis 1794. In einem Brief des Herrn Baron von Voght an einige Armenfreunde in England. Aus dem Englischen übersetzt von J. J. Eschenburg (1796).* 2nd ed. Lüneburg, 1832.

Voigt, Johann Friedrich, ed. *Aufzeichnungen des Senator und Landherrn Lic. Wilhelm Amsinck über seine Verwaltung der Landherrenschaft von Bill- und Ochsenwärder 1800/1801.* Hamburg, 1911.

Vorläufige Nachricht von der einzuführenden Neuen Hamburischen Armen-Ordnung. Hamburg, 1788.

Wagemann, Arnold. *Ueber die Bildung des Volkes zur Industrie.* Göttingen, 1794.

Wagemann, Ludwig G., ed. *Göttingisches Magazin für Industrie und Armenpflege.* 1788–1805.

Wagnitz, Heinrich. *Historische Nachrichten und Bemerkungen über die merkwürdigsten Zuchthäuser in Deutschland.* 2 vols. Halle, 1791–94.

Weber, Friedrich Benedict. *Staatswissenschaftlicher Versuch über das Armenwesen und die Armenpolicey mit vorzüglicher Hinsicht auf die dahin einschlagende Literatur.* Göttingen, 1807.

Westpahlen, Johann. *Hamburgs tieffste Erniedrigung.* [Hamburg, 1814].

Willebrand, Johann Peter. *Grundriß einer schönen Stadt, in Absicht ihrer Anlage und Einrichtung zur Bequemlichkeit, zum Vergnügen, zum Anwachs und zur Erhaltung ihrer Einwohner, nach bekannten Mustern entworfen. Nebst einer Vorrede von der Wirkung des Climas auf die Gesinnung und Gesetzgebung der Völker.* 2 vols. Hamburg and Leipzig, 1775–76.

[Wohlwill, J.] *Beiträge zur Theorie des Armenwesens, veranlaßt durch des Herrn Carl Godeffroy "Theorie der Armut".* Hamburg, 1834.

Ziegenhagen, Franz Heinrich. *Lehre vom richtigen Verhältnisse zu den Schöpfungswerken, und die durch öffentliche Einfürung derselben allein zu bewürkende allgemeine Menschenbeglückung.* Hamburg, 1792.

Zincke, Georg Heinrich. "Abhandlung von der Wirtschaftskunst der Armen und Dürftigen, sammt denen allgemeinen Regeln ihrer Wirtschaft." *Der Duisbergischen gelehrten Gesellschaft Deutsche Schriften.* Duisberg and Düsseldorf, 1759.

Secondary Literature

Abel, Wilhelm. *Massenarmut und Hungerkrisen im vorindustriellen Europa: Versuch einer Synopsis.* 2nd ed. Göttingen, 1977.

Aigner, Josef. *Der Volks- und Industrieschulen-Reformator Bischof Ferdinand Kindermann.* Vienna, 1867.

Ahrens, Gerhard. *Caspar Voght und sein Mustergut Flottbek: Englische Landwirtschaft in Deutschland am Ende des 18. Jahrhunderts.* Hamburg, 1969.

Albrecht, Peter. "Die 'Braunschweigischen Armenanstalten.' Ein Beitrag zur städtischen Armenpolitik in der ersten Hälfte des 19. Jahrhunderts (1796–1853)." *Diplomarbeit,* Hamburg 1966.

———. "Die Übernahme der Prinzipien der Hamburger Armenreform für die Stadt Braunschweig." *Jahrbuch der Sozialarbeit* 4 (1982): 181–203.

Altmann, S. P., et al., eds. *Die Entwicklung der deutschen Volkswirtschaftslehre im neunzehnten Jahrhundert.* Leipzig, 1908.

Amburger, Erik. "Aus dem Leben und Wirken von Hamburgern in Rußland." In Peter Classen and Peter Scheibert, eds. *Festschrift Percy Ernst Schramm zu seinem 70. Geburtstag von Schülern und Freunden zugeeignet.* 2 vols. Vol. 1, pp. 3–25. Wiesbaden, 1964.

Amsinck, C[aesar]. *Die niederländische und hamburgische Familie Amsinck: Ein Versuch einer Familiengeschichte.* Hamburg, 1886.

Arndt, Carl. "Die Einwohnerzahl der Niederdeutschen Städte von 1550 bis 1806." Ph.D. diss., Hamburg, 1946.

Augner, Gerd. *Die kaiserliche Kommission der Jahre 1708–1712: Hamburgs Beziehung zu Kaiser und Reich zu Aufang des 18. Jahrhunderts.* Hamburg, 1983.

Aust, Alfred. *Mir ward ein schönes Loos: Liebe und Freundschaft im Leben des Reichsfreiherrn Caspar von Voght.* Hamburg, 1972.

Baasch, Ernst. "Der Einfluß des Handels auf das Geistesleben Hamburgs." *Pfingstblätter des hansischen Geschichtsvereins.* Vol. 5. Leipzig, 1909.

———. *Geschichte Hamburgs, 1814–1918.* 2 vols. Gotha, 1924–25.

Baasch, Ernst. "Hamburgs Seeschiffahrt und Waarenhandel vom Ende des 16. bis zur Mitte des 17. Jahrhunderts." *ZVHG* 9 (1894): 295–420.

———. *Die Handelskammer zu Hamburg, 1665–1913.* 3 vols. Hamburg, 1915.

———. "Zur Geschichte einer hamburgischen Groß-Tabaksfirma [F. Justus] im 18. und 19. Jahrhundert." *ZVHG* 29 (1928): 1–60.

Bake, Rita. *Vorindustrielle Frauenerwerbsarbeit: Arbeits- und Lebensweise von Manufakturarbeiterinnen im Deutschland des 18. Jahrhunderts unter besonderer Berücksichtigung Hamburgs.* Cologne, 1984.

Baumeister, Hermann. *Die halb-öffentlichen milden Stiftungen in Hamburg.* Hamburg, 1869.

Bavendamm, Dirk. *Von der Revolution zur Reform: Die Verfassungspolitik des hamburgischen Senats 1849/50.* Berlin, 1969.

Becker, Carl L. *The Heavenly City of the Eighteenth-Century Philosophers.* New Haven, Conn., 1932.

Becker, Ludwig. *Die Geschichte des Hamburger Zuckerhandels (Von den Anfängen bis zum Weltkrieg).* Rostock, 1933.

Behrends, Ludwig. *Die Entwicklung der direkten Steuern in Hamburg und die Errichtung der Steuerdeputation am 9. März 1815.* Hamburg, 1915.

[Beneke, Otto]. *Der Hamburgische Bürgermeister Johann Heinrich Bartels: Ein Abriß seines Lebens und Wirkens, nebst Fragmenten aus seinen Schriften.* Hamburg, 1850.

Beneke, Otto. *Hamburgische Geschichte und Denkwürdigkeiten.* 2nd ed. Berlin, 1886.

———. *Hamburgische Geschichten und Sagen.* Hamburg, 1854. 3rd ed. Berlin, 1886.

———. *Von unehrlichen Leuten: Culturhistorische Studien und Geschichte aus vergangenen Tagen deutscher Gewerbe und Dienste.* 2nd rev. ed. Berlin, 1889.

Bergmann, Klaus. *Agrarromantik und Großstadtfeindschaft.* Miesenheim a. Glan, 1970.

Berlin, Jörg, ed. *Das andere Hamburg: Freiheitliche und demokratische Bestrebungen in der Hansestadt seit dem Spätmittelalter.* Hamburg, 1981.

Beutin, Ludwig. "Aus der Wirtschaftsgeschichte der Hansestädte und der Niederlande [rev. art.]." *VSWG* 38 (1949): 69–78.

Biedermann, Karl. *Deutschland im achtzehnten Jahrhundert.* 4 vols. Leipzig, 1867–80.

Biensfeldt, Johannes. *Johann Georg Büsch: Ein Beitrag zur Geschichte der Nationalökonomie.* Erlangen, 1910.

Billerbeck, Paul. "Sozialpolitische Ideen in der deutschen kameralistischen und pädagogischen Literatur des 18. Jahrhunderts." Ph.D. diss., Cologne, 1938.

Bing, Wolf. "Hamburgs Bierbrauerei vom 14. bis zum 18. Jahrhundert." *ZVHG* 14 (1909): 209–332.

Bippen, W. von. "Die Ausbildung der bürgerlichen Armenpflege in Bremen." *Bremisches Jahrbuch* 11 (1880): 143–61.

Biraben, Jean-Noel. "La Population de Reims et de son arrondissement, et la vérification statistique des recensement numériques anciens." *Population* 16 (1961): 722–30.

Blackbourn, David. *Populists and Patricians: Essays in Modern Germany History.* London, 1987.

Blackbourn, David, and Geoff Eley. *The Peculiarities of German History: Bourgeois Society and Politics in Nineteenth-Century Germany.* Oxford and New York, 1984.

Blaich, Fritz. *Die Epoche des Merkantilismus.* Wiesbaden, 1973.

Blanning, T. C. W. *The French Revolution in Germany: Occupation and Resistance in the Rhineland, 1792–1802.* Oxford, 1983.

Bleek, Wilhelm. *Von der Kameralausbildung zur Juristenprivileg: Studium, Prüfung und Ausbildung der höhern Beamten des allgemeinen Verwaltungsdienstes in Deutschland im 18. und 19. Jahrhundert.* Berlin, 1972.

Böhme, Helmut. *Frankfurt und Hamburg: Des deutschen Reiches Silber- und Goldloch und die allerenglischste Stadt des Kontinents.* Frankfurt, 1968.

Boehart, William. "... *nicht brothlos und nothleidend zu hinterlassen: Untersuchungen zur Entwicklung des Versicherungsgedankens in Hamburg, insbesondere zur Entstehung der Hamburgischen Allgemeinen Versorgungsanstalt von 1778.* Hamburg, 1985.

Böhmert, Viktor. *Das Armenwesen in 77 deutschen Städten und einigen Landarmenverbänden.* Dresden, 1886.

Böttiger, K. W., ed. *Schilderungen aus Karl Aug. Böttiger's handschriftlichen Nachlasse.* 2 vols. Leipzig, 1838.

Böttiger, Theodor F. *Hamburgs Patrioten 1800–1814.* Berlin and Leipzig, 1926.

Bolland, Jürgen. *Die hamburgische Bürgerschaft in Alter und Neuer Zeit.* Hamburg, 1959.

———. *Senat und Bürgerschaft: Über das Verhältnis zwischen Bürger und Stadtregiment im alten Hamburg.* Hamburg, 1954.

Bourdieu, Pierre. "Sur le pouvoir symbolique." *ASEC* 23 (1977): 405–11.

Bracher, Karl Dietrich, et al. *Deutscher Sonderweg: Mythos oder Realität? Kolloquien des Instituts für Zeitgeschichte.* Munich, 1982.

Brachmann, Friedrich. *Johann Hübner. Johannei Rector 1711–1731: Ein Beitrag zur Geschichte der deutschen Literatur.* Hamburg, 1899.

Bramst, Klaus. *Das hamburgische Strafrecht im 17. Jahrhundert: Der Übergang vom städtischen zum gemeinen Strafrecht.* Hamburg, 1958.

Brandt, Martin. *Die Bestrebungen der Hamburgischen Armenanstalt von 1788 zur Erziehung der Armenbevölkerung: Ein Beitrag zur Geschichte der Industrieschule.* Hamburg, 1937.

Bredel, Willi. *Unter Türmen und Masten: Geschichte einer Stadt in Geschichten.* Berlin, G.D.R., 1968.

Breuer, Stefan. "Die Evolution der Disziplin zum Verhältnis von Rationalität und Herrschaft in Max Webers Theorie der vorrationalen Welt." *Kölner Zeitschrift für Soziologie und Sozialpsychologie* 30 (1978): 409–37.

Briggs, Asa. "The Welfare State in Historical Perspective." *Archives Européenes de Sociologie* 2 (1961): 221–58.

Brügmann, Ursula. "Die öffentliche Armenpflege der Stadt Hannover in den Jahren 1770–1824." *Hannoversche Geschichtsblätter,* n.s., 24 (1970): 89–146.

Bruhn, Hans. "Hamburger Studenten auf der Universität Göttingen 1734 bis 1837." *ZNF* 30 (1955): 117–29, 168–70.

Brunner, Otto. *Neue Wege der Verfassungs- und Sozialgeschichte.* 2nd enl. ed. Göttingen, 1968.

———. "Souveränitätsproblem und Sozialstruktur in den deutschen Reichsstädten der frühen Neuzeit." *VSWG* 50 (1963): 329–60.

Brunner, Otto, Werner Conze, and Reinhart Koselleck, eds. *Geschichtliche Grundbegriffe: Historisches Lexikon zur politisch-sozialen Sprache in Deutschland.* Stuttgart, 1972–.

Buek, Friedrich Georg. *Genealogische und Biographische Notizen über die seit der Reformation verstorbenen hamburgischen Bürgermeister. Bey Veranlassung des Vereins für hamburgische Geschichte gesammelt.* Hamburg, 1840.

———. *Die hamburgischen Oberalten, ihre bürgerliche Wirksamkeit und ihre Familien.* Hamburg, 1857.

———. *Handbuch der hamburgischen Verfassung und Verwaltung.* Hamburg, 1828.

Cassedy, James H. *Demography in Early America: Beginnings of the Statistical Mind.* Cambridge, Mass., 1969.

Chisick, Harvey. *The Limits of Reform in the Enlightenment: Attitudes Toward the Education of the Lower Classes in Eighteenth-Century France.* Princeton, N.J., 1981.

Chrisman, Miriam, and Otto Gründler, eds. *Social Groups and Religious Ideas in the Sixteenth Century.* Kalamazoo, Mich., 1978.

Cockburn, J. S., ed. *Crime in England, 1550–1800.* Princeton, N.J., 1977.

Comminchau, Gerhard. "Zur Geschichte der hamburgischen Jugendfürsorge im 18. Jahrhundert." Ph.D diss., Hamburg, 1961.

Conze, Werner. "Vom 'Pöbel' zum 'Proletariat'—Sozialgeschichtliche Voraussetzungen für den Sozialismus in Deutschland." *VSWG* 41 (1954): 333–64.

———, ed. *Staat und Gesellschaft im deutschen Vormärz, 1815–1848.* Stuttgart, 1962.

Crum, Frederick S. "The Statistical Work of Süssmilch." *American Statistical Association,* n.s., 55 (September 1901): 22–25.

Dalgård, Sune. "Hamburg-Iberian Trade, 1590–1625." *SEHR* 9, no. 2 (1962): 195–204.

Dankert, Werner. *Unehrliche Leute: Die verfemten Berufe.* Bern and Munich, 1963.

Dann, Otto, ed. *Lesergesellschaften und bürgerliche Emanzipation: Ein europäischer Vergleich.* Munich, 1981.

Daur, Georg. *Von Predigern und Bürgern: Eine hamburgische Kirchengeschichte von der Reformation bis zur Gegenwart.* Hamburg, 1970.

Davis, Natalie Zemon. *Society and Culture in Early Modern France: Eight Essays.* Stanford, Calif. 1975.

Deerr, Noel. *The History of Sugar.* 2 vols. London, 1949–50.

Dilcher, Liselotte. "Der deutsche Pauperismus und seine Literatur." Ph.D. diss., Frankfurt, 1957.

Dorwart, Reinhold August. *The Prussian Welfare State Before 1740.* Cambridge, Mass., 1971.

Dreyer, Karl-Joachim. "Hamburg als Mitglied des Deutschen Bundes." Ph.D. diss., Hamburg, 1976.

Duda, Detlev. *Die Hamburger Armenfürsorge im 18. und 19. Jahrhundert: Eine soziologisch-historische Untersuchung.* Weinheim and Basel, 1982.

Dülmen, Richard van. *Die Gesellschaft der Aufklärer: Zur bürgerlichen Emanzipation und aufklärerischen Kultur in Deutschland.* Frankfurt, 1986.

Eckardt, Hans Wilhelm. *Privilegien und Parlament: Das Auseinandersetzungen um das allgemeine und gleiche Wahlrecht in Hamburg.* Hamburg, 1980.

Ehlers, Joachim. *Die Wehrverfassung der Stadt Hamburg im 17. und 18. Jahrhundert.* Boppard am Rhein, 1966.

Ellermeyer, Jürgen. "Zu Handel, Hafen und Grundeigentum Hamburgs im 17. und 18. Jahrhundert." In Jürgen Ellermeyer and Rainer Postel, eds., *Stadt und Hafen: Hamburger Beiträge zur Geschichte von Handel und Schiffahrt,* pp. 58–79. Hamburg, 1986.

Ellermeyer, Jürgen and Rainer Postel, eds. *Stadt und Hafen: Hamburger Beiträge zur Geschichte von Handel und Schiffahrt.* Hamburg, 1986.

Elsas, Moritz J. *Umriß einer Geschichte der Löhne und Preise in Deutschland von ausgehenden Mittelalter bis zum Beginn des 19. Jahrhunderts.* 3 vols. Leiden, 1936, 1940, 1949.

Emminghaus, C. B. Arwed, ed. *Das Armenwesen und die Armengesetzgebung in europäischen Staaten.* Berlin, 1870.

———, ed. *Poor Relief in Different Parts of Europe.* London, 1873.

Endres, Rudolf. "Das Armenproblem im Zeitalter des Absolutismus." In *Aufklärung, Absolutimus und Bürgertum in Deutschland: Zwölf Aufsätze,* edited by Franklin Kopitzsch, pp. 220–41. Munich, 1976.

Engelsing, Rolf. "Lebenshaltungen und Lebenshaltungskosten im 18. und 19. Jahrhundert in den Hansestädten Bremen und Hamburg." *IRSH* 11 (1966): 73–107.

———. *Zur Sozialgeschichte deutscher Mittel- und Unterschichten.* 2nd enl. ed. Göttingen, 1978.

Erichson, Kurt. *Die Fürsorge in Hamburg: Ein Überblick über ihre Entwicklung, ihren gegenwärtigen Stand und dessen gesetzliche Grundlagen.* Hamburg, 1930.

Eschenberg, Theodor, ed. *The Road to Dictatorship: Germany, 1918–1933.* London, 1964.

Essig, Olga. "Caspar Voght über Pestalozzi. Ein Brief aus Yverdun an die Patriotische Gesellschaft." *HGH* 8 (1935): 177–80.

Eulen, Focko. "Vom Gewerbefleiß zur Industrie: Ein Beitrag zur Wirtschaftsgeschichte des 18. Jahrhunderts." Ph.D. diss., Hamburg, 1966.

Eulenberg, Franz. "Zur historischen Bevölkerungsstatistik in Deutschland." *Jahrbücher für Nationalökonomie,* 3rd ser., 29 (1905): 519–27.

Evans, Richard J. *Death in Hamburg: Society and Politics in the Cholera Years, 1830–1910.* Oxford, 1987.

———. *Rethinking German History: Nineteenth-Century Germany and the Origins of the Third Reich.* London, 1987.

Ewald, Martin. *Der hamburgische Senatssyndicus. Eine verwaltungsgeschichtliche Studie.* Hamburg, 1954.

Fairchilds, Cissie C. *Poverty and Charity in Aix-en-Provence, 1640–1789.* Baltimore and London, 1976.

Felsing, Ferdinand. *Die Statistik als Methode der politischen Ökonomie im 17. und 18. Jahrhundert.* Borna-Leipzig, 1930.

Feuchtwanger, Ludwig. "Geschichte der sozialen Politik und des Armenwesens im Zeitalter der Reformation." *Jahrbuch für Gesetzgebung* 32 (1908): 1423–60; 33 (1909): 191–228.

314   Bibliography

Fiege, Hartwig. *Geschichte der Hamburgischen Volksschule.* Hamburg, 1970.
Finder, Ernst. *Hamburgisches Bürgertum in der Vergangenheit.* Hamburg, 1930.
Fink, G. "Die Frage des Lübecker Patriziats im Lichte der Forschung." *ZVLG* 29 (1938): 257–80.
Fischer, Alfons. *Geschichte des deutschen Gesundheitswesens.* 2 vols. Berlin, 1933.
Fischer, Thomas. *Städtische Armut und Armenfürsorge im 15. und 16. Jahrhundert: Sozialgeschichtliche Untersuchungen am Beispiel der Städte Basel, Freiburg im Breisgau und Strassburg.* Göttingen, 1979.
Fischer, Wolfram. *Armut in der Geschichte: Erscheinungsformen und Lösungsversuche der "Sozialen Frage" in Europa seit dem Mittelalter.* Göttingen, 1982.
Ford, Franklin L. *Strasbourg in Transition, 1648–1789.* Cambridge, Mass., 1958.
Foucault, Michel. *The Birth of the Clinic: An Archaeology of Medical Perception.* New York, 1973.
———. *Discipline and Punish: The Birth of the Prison.* New York, 1977.
———. *Madness and Civilization: A History of Insanity in the Age of Reason.* New York, 1965.
Fox-Genovese, Elizabeth, and Eugene D. Genovese. *Fruits of Merchant Capital: Slavery and Bourgeois Property in the Rise and Expansion of Capitalism.* New York, 1983.
Frankel, Ernst. *Deutschland und die westlichen Demokratien.* Stuttgart, 1964.
François, Étienne. "De l'uniformité à la tolérance: Confession et société urbaine en Allmagne, 1650–1800." *Social History–Histoire Sociale* 16 (1983): 7–33.
———. "Unterschichten und Armut in rheinischen Residenzstädten des 18. Jahrhunderts." *VSWG* 62 (1975): 433–64.
Freundenthal, Herbert. *Vereine in Hamburg: Ein Beitrag zur Geschichte und Volkskunde der Geselligkeit.* Hamburg, 1968.
Frevert, Ute. *Krankheit als politisches Problem, 1770–1880: Soziale Unterschichten in Preußen zwischen medizinischer Polizei und staatlicher Sozialversicherung.* Göttingen, 1984.
Friedrichs, Christopher R. *Urban Society in an Age of War: Nördlingen, 1580–1720.* Princeton, N.J., 1979.
Fritz, Paul, and David Williams, eds. *City and Society in the 18th Century.* Toronto, 1973.
Frohneberg, Erich. *Bevölkerungslehre und Bevölkerungspolitik des Merkantilismus unter besonderer Berücksichtigung des 17. und 18. Jahrhunderts und der Länder Deutschland, England, Frankreich und Italien.* Gelnhausen, 1930.
Funk, F. X. "Die Auffassung des Begriffs der Polizei im vorigen Jahrhundert." *Zeitschrift für gesamte Staatswissenschaft* 19 (1863): 489–555.
Gabrielsson, Peter. "Klopstocks Schwager Hartman Rahn als Entrepreneur der Hamburger Kattundruckerei, 1763–1770." *ZVHG* 70 (1984): 37–72.
Gaedechens, C. F. *Historische Topographie der Freien und Hansestadt Hamburg und ihrer nächsten Umgebung von der Entstehung bis auf die Gegenwart.* 2nd ed. Hamburg, 1880.
Gallois, Johann Gustav. *Geschichte der Stadt Hamburg.* 3 vols. Hamburg, 1853–64.
———. *Hamburgische Chronik von den älteren Zeiten bis auf die Jetztzeit.* 4 vols. Hamburg, 1861–63.
Gay, Peter. *The Enlightenment: An Interpretation.* Vol. 1, *The Rise of Paganism.* Vol. 2, *The Science of Freedom.* New York, 1966–69.
Gernet, Hermann Gustav. *Mittheilungen aus der älteren Medicinalgeschichte Ham-*

burgs: Kulturhistorische Skizze auf urkundlichem und geschichtlichem Gründe. Hamburg, 1869.

Gerth, Hans H. *Bürgerliche Intelligenz um 1800: Zur Soziologie des deutschen Frühliberalismus.* Edited by Ulrich Herrmann. Göttingen, 1976.

Glass, David Victor. *Numbering the People: The 18th-Century Population Controversy and the Development of the Census and Vital Statistics in Britain.* Franborough, England, 1973.

Grab, Walter. *Demokratische Strömungen in Hamburg und Schleswig-Holstein zur Zeit der ersten französischen Republik.* Hamburg, 1966.

Grager, Erich. *Kiel und die Gesellschaft freiwilliger Armenfreunde 1793–1953: Ihr soziales, kulturelles und wirtschaftliches Wirken.* Kiel, 1953.

[Gravenhorst, Heinrich Wilhelm]. *Das Hamburgische Allgemeine Krankenhaus.* 2nd enl. ed. Hamburg, 1848.

Grebing, Helga. *Der "deutsche Sonderweg" in Europa, 1806–1945: Eine Kritik.* Stuttgart, 1986.

Grimm, Harold. "Luther's Contributions to Sixteenth-Century Organization of Poor Relief." *ARG* 61 (1970): 222–34.

Gutton, Jean-Pierre. *L'État et la mendicité dans la première moitié du XVIIIe siècle: Auvergne, Beaujolais, Forez, Lyonnais.* Saint-Etienne, 1973.

———. *La Société et les pauvres en Europe: XVIe–XVIIIe siècles.* Paris, 1974.

———. *La Société et les pauvres: L'Exemple de la généralité de Lyon, 1534–1789.* Paris, 1970.

Habakkuk, H. J. *Population Growth and Economic Development Since 1750.* Leicester, Eng., 1971.

Haesenne-Peremans, Nicole. *Les Pauvres et le pouvoir: Assistance et répression aux pays de Liège (1685–1830).* Liège, Belgium, 1983.

Hahn, Julius. *Aus Hamburgs Schreckentagen.* Hamburg, 1909.

Hall, Basil. "The Reformation City." *Bulletin of the John Rylands Library* 54 (1971): 103–48.

Hallema, A. *Geschiedenis van het gevangeniswezen hoofdzakelijk in Nederland.* The Hague, 1958.

Hamerow, Theodore S. *Restoration, Revolution, Reaction: Economics and Politics in Germany, 1815–1871.* Princeton, N.J., 1958.

Hampson, Norman. *The Enlightenment.* Harmondsworth, Eng., 1968.

Hartung, Fritz. "Der Aufgeklärte Absolutismus." In *Die Entstehung des modernen souveränen Staates,* ed. Hans Hubert Hofmann, pp. 152–72. Cologne and Berlin, 1967.

———. *Deutsche Verfassungsgeschichte vom 15. Jahrhundert bis zur Gegenwart.* 7th ed. Stuttgart, 1959.

Hauschild-Thiessen, Renate. "Hamburg um die Wende vom 18. zum 19. Jahrhundert. Tagebuchaufzeichnungen Ferdinand Benekes." *HGH* 9, no. 8 (December 1974): 181–208.

———. *Die Niederländische Armen-Casse: "Hamburgs stille Wohlthäterin." Ihre Geschichte von 1585 bis zur Gegenwart.* Hamburg, 1974.

———. *Theodor Hasche: Das Leben eines Hamburger Apothekers. Erinnerungen aus der ersten Hälfte des 19. Jahrhunderts.* Hamburg, 1981.

Heckscher, Eli. *Mercantilism.* 2 vols. London, 1935.

Heckscher, J. "Lebensmittelpreise in Hamburg während der Belagerung durch die Franzosen." *MVHG* 7 (1900): 405–6.

Heere, Paul, ed. *Politisches Handbuch*. Leipzig, 1923.

Henderson, W. O. "The Berlin Commercial Crisis of 1763." *EHR* 15 (1962–63): 89–102.

Henning, Friedrich-Wilhelm. *Das vorindustrielle Deutschland 800 bis 1800*. 3rd ed. Paderborn, 1977.

Herrmann, Ulrich, ed. *"Die Bildung des Bürgers": Die Formierung der bürgerlichen Gesellschaft und die Gebildeten im 18. Jahrhundert*. Weinheim, 1982.

———, ed. *"Das pädagogische Jahrhundert": Volksaufklärung und Erziehung zur Armut im 18. Jahrhundert in Deutschland*. Weinheim, 1981.

Herzig, Arno, Dieter Langewiesche, and Arnold Sywottek, eds. *Arbeiter in Hamburg*. Hamburg, 1983.

Hitzigrath, Heinrich. *Hamburg und die Kontinentalsperre*. Hamburg, 1900.

Hollingsworth, T. H. *Historical Demography*. London, 1969.

Hübbe, Heinrich. *Die kaiserliche Commission in Hamburg*. Hamburg, 1856.

Hubrig, Hans. *Die patriotischen Gesellschaften des 18. Jahrhunderts*. Weinheim, 1957.

Hufton, Olwen H. *The Poor of Eighteenth-Century France 1750–1789*. Oxford, 1974.

Huhn, Fred-Conrad. "Die Handelsbeziehungen zwischen Frankreich und Hamburg im 18. Jahrhundert unter besonderer Berücksichtigung der Handelsverträge von 1716 und 1769." Ph.D. diss., Hamburg, 1952.

Humbert, Magdalene, ed. *Bibliographie der Kameralwissenschaften*. Cologne, 1937.

100 Jahre Statistisches Amt Hamburg, 1866–1966. Hamburg, 1966.

165 Jahre Patriotische Gesellschaft: Ein hamburgisches Jahrbuch 1930. Hamburg, 1930.

Hunecke, Volker. "Überlegungen zur Geschichte der Armut im vorindustriellen Europa." *GG* 9 (1983): 480–512.

Imbert, Jean. *Les Hôpitaux en France*. Paris, 1974.

Imhof, Arthur. "Die Funktionen des Krankenhauses in der Stadt des 18. Jahrhunderts." *Zeitschrift für Stadtgeschichte, Stadtsoziologie und Denkmalpflege* 4, no. 2 (1977): 215–42.

Im Hof, Ulrich. *Das gesellige Jahrhundert: Gesellschaft und Gesellschaften im Zeitalter der Aufklärung*. Munich, 1982.

Ingrao, Charles. "The Problem of 'Enlightened Absolutism' and the German States." *JMH* 58, suppl. (1986): S161–80.

Iven, Kurt. *Die Industrie-Pädagogik des 18. Jahrhunderts: Eine Untersuchung über die Bedeutung des wirtschaftlichen Verhaltens für die Erziehung*. Berlin and Leipzig, 1929.

Jantke, Carl, and Dietrich Hilger. *Die Eigentumlosen: Der deutsche Pauperismus und die Emanzipationskrise in Darstellungen und Deutungen der Zeitgenössischen Literatur*. Freiburg and Munich, 1965.

Jeannin, Pierre, ed. *Gekräuselt, gepudert, mit untadeliger Anmut: Hamburg und die französischen Revolution*. Hamburg, 1977.

———. "Die Hansestädte im europäischen Handel des 18. Jahrhunderts." *HGH* 89 (1972): 41–73.

Jeserich, Kurt G. A., Hans Pohl, and Georg-Christoph Unruh, *Deutsche Verwaltungsgeschichte*. Vol. 1, *Vom Spätmittelalter bis zum Ende des Reiches*. Stuttgart, 1983.

Jetter, Dieter. *Geschichte des Hospitals*. Vol. 1, *Westdeutschland von den Anfängen bis 1850*. Wiesbaden, 1966.

Joachim, Hermann. *Handbuch für Wohltätigkeit in Hamburg*. Hamburg, 1901; 2nd ed. [*Handbuch der Wohltätigkeit in Hamburg*] Hamburg, 1909.

———. *Historische Arbeiten aus seinem Nachlaß*. Hamburg, 1936.

Jobst, Dionys. "Der Polizeibegriff in Deutschland." Ph.D. diss., Munich, 1953.

Jolles, Oskar. *Die Ansichten der deutschen nationalökonomischen Schriftsteller des 16. und 17. Jahrhunderts über Bevölkerungswesen.* Jena, 1886.

Jones, Colin. *Charity and Bienfaisance: The Treatment of the Poor in the Montpellier Region, 1740–1815.* Cambridge, Eng., 1982.

de Jong-Keesing, Elizabeth. *De economische crisis van 1763 te Amsterdam.* Amsterdam, 1939.

Joulia, Antoinette. "Les Institutions administratives des départements Hanséatiques." *RHMC* (July-September 1970): 880–92.

Julius, Nicolaus Heinrich. *Dem Andenken des Königl. dänischen Etatsrath und Ritters Caspar Freiherrn von Voght.* Hamburg, 1839.

Jütte, Robert. *Obrigkeitliche Armenfürsorge in der frühen Neuzeit: Städtisches Armenwesen in Frankfurt am Main und Köln.* Cologne und Vienna, 1984.

Katz, Michael. *The Irony of Early School Reform.* Cambridge, Mass., 1968.

Kayser, Rudolf. *Die Oberalten: Festschrift zum vierhundertjährigen Gedächtnis der Einsetzung des Kollegiums.* Hamburg, 1928.

Kellenbenz, Hermann. *Sephardim an der unteren Elbe: Ihre wirtschaftliche und politische Bedeutung vom Ende des 16. Jahrhunderts bis zum Beginn des 18. Jahrhunderts.* Wiesbaden, 1958.

———. *Unternehmerkräften Hamburger Portugal- und Spanienhandel, 1590–1625.* Hamburg, 1954.

Kellinghusen, Hans. *Geschichte der Familie Kellinghusen.* Vol. 1, *Die Stammfolge der Familie von Hans bis Jürgen Kellinghusen, 1507–1686 (1757).* Hamburg, 1919.

Kirchenpauer, Gustav Heinrich. *Die alte Börse, ihre Gründer und ihre Vorsteher: Ein Beitrag zur hamburgischen Handelsgeschichte.* Hamburg, 1841.

Klein, Gottfried. *400 Jahre Hamburger Börse: Eine geschichtliche Darstellung.* Hamburg, 1958.

Klessmann, Eckart. *Geschichte der Stadt Hamburg.* Hamburg, 1981.

Kluth, Otto. "Un ami allemand de Mme de Staël." *Alma Mater* 15 (December 1945): 489–98.

Knudsen, Jonathan B. *Justus Möser and the German Enlightenment.* Cambridge, Eng., 1986.

Koch, Herbert. "Handelsbeziehungen zwischen Hamburg und Jena 1768 bis 1786." *HGH* 17 (1959): 1–9.

Koch, Lotte. *Wandlungen der Wohlfahrtspflege im Zeitalter der Aufklärung.* Erlangen, 1933.

Kocka, Jürgen. "Bürgertum und Bürgerlichkeit als Probleme der deutschen Geschichte vom späten 18. bis zum frühen 20. Jahrhundert." In Jürgen Kocka, ed., *Bürger und Bürgerlichkeit im 19. Jahrhundert,* pp. 21–63. Göttingen, 1987.

Kocka, Jürgen, ed. *Arbeiter und Bürger im 19. Jahrhundert: Varianten ihres Verhältnisses im europäischen Vergleich.* Munich, 1986.

———, ed. *Bürger und Bürgerlichkeit im 19. Jahrhundert.* Göttingen, 1987.

———. *Bürgertum im 19. Jahrhundert: Deutschland im europäischen Vergleich.* 3 vols. Munich, 1988.

Koester, Johanna. *Der rheinische Frühliberalismus und die Sozialfrage.* Ed. Walther Peter Fuchs. Berlin, 1938.

Köhler, Ernst. *Arme und Irre: Die liberale Fürsorgepolitik des Bürgertums.* Berlin, 1977.

Kollmann, Paul. "Ueberblick über die Wirksamkeit der 'Allgemeinen Armenanstalt' der Stadt Hamburg von 1788 bis 1870." *Statistik des Hamburgischen Staats* 3 (1871): 99–136.

Kollmann, Wolfgang. *Sozialgeschichte der Stadt Barmen im 19. Jahrhundert*. Tübingen, 1960.

Kopitzsch, Franklin. *Grundzüge einer Sozialgeschichte der Aufklärung in Hamburg und Altona*. Hamburg, 1982.

———. "Die Hamburgische Gesellschaft zur Beförderung der Künste und nützlichen Gewerbe (Patriotische Gesellschaft von 1765) im Zeitalter der Aufklärung: Ein Überblick." In Rudolf Vierhaus, ed., *Deutsche patriotische und gemmeinnützige Gesellschaften*, pp. 71–118. Munich, 1980.

———. "Johann Georg Büsch oder von hamburgischen Tradition der Sozialarbeit." In *Jahresbericht der Hamburgischen Gesellschaft zur Beförderung der Künste und nützlichen Gewerbe (Patriotischen Gesellschaft von 1765) für das Geschäftsjahre 1981/82*, pp. 35–40. Hamburg, 1982.

———. "Sparkassenrealität und Sozietätsbewegung im Zeitalter der Aufklärung." In *Historische Marktanalyse, Frühe Sparkassenideen: Utopie und Realität*, pp. 123–56. Neustadt a.d. Aisch, 1984.

———, ed. *Aufklärung, Absolutismus und Bürgertum in Deutschland: Zwölf Aufsätze*. Munich, 1976.

Köppen, Heinrich Franz. *Die Handelsbeziehungen Hamburgs zu den Vereinigten Staaten von Nordamerika bis zur Mitte des 19. Jahrhunderts*. Cologne, 1973.

Koppmann, Karl. *Aus Hamburgs Vergangenheit: Kulturhistorische Bilder aus verschiedenen Jahrhunderten*. 2 vols. Hamburg and Leipzig, 1885–86.

———. "Die Berechnung der Einwohnerzahl aus den Listen der Neubürger." *MVHG* 3 (1880–81): 122–25.

———. *Hamburgs kirchliche und Wohltätigkeit-Anstalten im Mittelalter*. Hamburg, 1870.

Kostanecki, Anton von. *Arbeit und Armut: Ein Beitrag zur Entwicklungsgeschichte sozialer Ideen*. Freiburg, 1909.

Kowalewski, Gustav. *Die Aufgaben der hamburgischen Patriotischen Gesellschaft während der Franzosenzeit*. Hamburg, 1913.

———. *Geschichte der Hamburgischen Gesellschaft zur Beförderung der Künste und nützlichen Gewerbe (Patriotische Gesellschaft)*. 3 parts in 7 vols. Hamburg, 1897–1913.

———. "Die Gründung der Patriotischen Gesellschaft im Urteile der Zeitgenossen." *Jahrbuch der Hamburgischen Gesellschaft zur Beförderung der Künste und nützlichen Gewerbe (Patriotische Gesellschaft, gestiftet 1765)* (1907/09): 1–5.

———. *Die Hamburgische Patriotische Gesellschaft und die Wirtschaftssysteme des 18. Jahrhunderts*. Hamburg, 1910.

Kraus, Antje. *Die Unterschichten Hamburgs in der ersten Hälfte des 19. Jahrhunderts: Entstehung, Struktur und Lebensverhältnisse—Eine historisch-statistische Untersuchung*. Stuttgart, 1965.

Kresse, Walter. "Die Auswirkungen der Handelsverträge der Hansestädte mit den amerikanischen Staaten auf die Hamburger Schiffahrt." *ZVHG* 60 (1974): 139–46.

———. *Materialien zur Entwicklungsgeschichte der Hamburger Handelsflotte, 1765–1823*. Hamburg, 1966.

Kressin, Arthur. "Vom alten Hamburger 'Krankenhof' zum neuen 'Allgemeinen Krankenhaus' in der Vorstadt St. Georg." Typescript, Hamburg, 1961.

Kriedte, Peter. *Spätfeudalismus und Handelskapital: Grundlinien der europäischen Wirtschaftsgeschichte vom 16. bis zum Ausgang des 18. Jahrhunderts*. Göttingen, 1980.

————, Hans Medick, and Jürgen Schlumbohm. *Industrialisierung vor der Industrialisierung: Gewerbliche Warenproduktion auf dem Lande in der Formationsperiode des Kapitalismus.* Göttingen, 1977.

Krieger, Leonard. *The German Idea of Freedom: History of a Political Tradition.* Boston, 1957.

————. "The Idea of the Welfare State in Europe and the United States." *JHI* 24 (1963): 553–68.

Lackemann, L. *Die Geschichte des hamburgischen Armenschulwesens von 1815 bis 1871.* Hamburg, 1910.

Ladurie, Emmanual LeRoy. "Chanu, Lebrun, Vovelle: La Nouvelle Histoire de la mort." In Emmanuel LeRoy Ladurie, *Le Territoire de l'historien,* pp. 393–403. Paris, 1973.

Landau, Johann. "Die Arbeiterfrage in Deutschland im 17. und 18. Jahrhundert und ihre Behandlung in der deutschen Kameralwissenschaft." Ph.D. diss., Zurich, 1915.

Landwehr, Götz. "Johann Georg Büsch und die Entwicklung des Handelsrechts im 18. Jahrhundert." In Hans-Dieter Loose, ed., *Gelehrte in Hamburg im 18. und 19. Jahrhundert,* pp. 57–105. Hamburg, 1976.

Lane, Frank P. "Johannes Bugenhagen und die Armenfürsorge in der Reformationszeit." *BJ* 64 (1983): 147–56.

Lappenberg, Johannes Martin. *Die milden Privatstiftungen zu Hamburg.* Hamburg, 1845.

Laufenberg, Heinrich. *Hamburg und die französische Revolution.* Hamburg, 1913.

————. *Hamburg und sein Proletariat im achtzehnten Jahrhundert: Eine wirtschaftshistorische Vorstudie zur Geschichte der modernen Arbeiterbewegung im niederelbischen Städtegebiet.* Hamburg, 1910.

Laufer, Otto. *Hamburg.* Leipzig, 1912.

Laufs, Adolph. *Die Verfassung und Verwaltung der Stadt Rottweil, 1650–1806.* Stuttgart, 1963.

LaVopa, Anthony J. *Prussian Schoolteachers: Profession and Office, 1763–1848.* Chapel Hill, N.C., 1980.

Lebrun, François. *Les Hommes et la mort en Anjou aux XVIIe et XVIIIe siècles: Essai de démographie et de psychologie historiques* Paris, 1975.

Lehe, Erich von. "Überblick über die Geschichte der hamburgischen Verwaltung vom Mittelalter zur Neuzeit." Typescript, Hamburg, 1950.

————, Heinz Ramm, and Dietrich Kausche, *Heimatchronik der Freien und Hansestadt Hamburg.* 2nd ed. Cologne, 1967.

Lehmann, Oskar. *Die deutschen moralischen Wochenschriften des achtzehnten Jahrhunderts als pädagogische Reformschriften.* Leipzig, 1893.

Lehr, Hans Walther. *Das Bürgerrecht im hamburgischen Staate.* Hamburg, 1919.

Leith, James. "The Hope for Moral Regeneration in French Educational Thought, 1750–1789." In Paul Fritz and David Williams, eds. *City and Society in the 18th Century,* pp. 215–29. Toronto, 1973.

Liebel, Helen. *Enlightened Bureaucracy versus Enlightened Despotism in Baden, 1750–1792.* Philadelphia, 1965.

————. "Laissez-faire vs. Mercantilism: The Rise of Hamburg & the Hamburg Bourgeoisie vs. Frederick the Great in the Crisis of 1763." *VSWG* 52 (1965): 207–38.

Lindemann, Mary. "Bürgerliche Karriere und patriotische Philanthropie: Armenpolitik in Hamburg vor und nach der Reform von 1788." In Christoph Sachße and Florian Tennstedt, eds., *Jahrbuch der Sozialarbeit* 4 (1981): 157–80.

————. "Maternal Politics: The Principles and Practice of Maternity Care in Eighteenth-Century Hamburg." *JFH* 9, no. 1 (Spring 1984): 44–63.

Lis, Catharina. *Social Change and the Labouring Poor: Antwerp, 1770–1860.* New Haven, Conn. and London, 1986.

————. "Sociale politiek te Antwerpen, 1779. Het controleren van de relatieve overbevolking en het reguleren van de arbeidsmarkt." *TVSG* 5 (1979): 146–66.

————and Hugo Soly. *Poverty and Capitalism in Pre-Industrial Europe.* Brighton, Eng., 1979.

Loose, Hans-Dieter. "Die Jastram-Snitgerschen Wirren in der zeitgenössischen Geschichtsschreibung." *ZVHG* 53 (1967): 1–20.

————, ed. *Barthold Heinrich Brockes (1680–1747). Dichter und Ratsherr in Hamburg: Neue Forschungen zu Persönlichkeit und Wirkung.* Hamburg, 1980.

————, ed. *Gelehrte in Hamburg im 18. und 19. Jahrhundert.* Hamburg, 1976.

————, and Werner Jochmann, eds. *Hamburg: Geschichte der Stadt und ihrer Bewohner.* vol. 1, *Von den Anfängen bis zur Reichsgründung.* Hamburg, 1982. vol. 2, *Vom Kaiserreich bis zur Gegenwart.* Hamburg, 1986.

Luhrs, W. "Der Hamburgischer Senat von 1815 in englischer Sicht." *ZVHG* 48 (1962): 103–10.

McKeown, Thomas, and R. G. Brown. "Medical Evidence Related to English Population Changes in the Eighteenth Century." *PS* 9 (1955): 119–41.

McManners, John. *Death and the Enlightenment: Changing Attitudes Toward Death Among Christians and Unbelievers in Eighteenth-Century France.* New York, 1981.

Maier, Hans. *Die ältere deutsche Staats- und Verwaltungslehre (Polizeiwissenschaft): Ein Beitrag zur Geschichte der politischen Wissenschaft in Deutschland.* Neuwied am Rhein and Berlin, 1966.

Marchtaler, Hildegard von. *Aus Alt-Hamburger Senatorenhäuser: Familienschicksale im 18. und 19. Jahrhundert.* Hamburg, 1959.

Marcks, Erich. *Hamburg und das bürgerliche Geistesleben in Deutschland.* Hamburg, 1907.

Marquardt, Frederick. "Pauperismus in Germany during the Vormärz." *CEH* 2 (1969): 77–88.

Martens, Wolfgang. *Die Botschaft der Tugend: Die Aufklärung im Spiegel der deutschen Moralischen Wochenschriften.* Stuttgart, 1968.

Marzahn, Christian. *Das Zucht- und Arbeitshaus: Die Kerninstitution frühbürgerlicher Sozialpolitik.* (Arbeitspapiere des Forschungsschwerpunktes Reproduktionsrisiken, soziale Bewegungen und Sozialpolitik, no. 5). Bremen, 1980.

Matthaei, Henning. *Untersuchungen zur Frühgeschichte der deutschen Berufsschule dargestellt am Wirken der Patriotischen Gesellschaft zu Hamburg im 18. Jahrundert.* Hamburg, 1967.

Matti, Werner. "Bevölkerungsvorgänge in den Hansestädten Hamburg und Bremen vom Anfang des 19. Jahrhunderts bis zum Ersten Weltkrieg." *ZVHG* 69 (1983): 103–55.

Mauersberg, Hans. *Wirtschafts- und Sozialgeschichte zentraleuropäischer Städte in neuerer Zeit: Dargestellt an den Beispielen von Basel, Frankfurt a.M., Hamburg, Hannover und München.* Göttingen, 1960.

Mayr, Joseph Karl. "Zwei Reformatoren der Wiener Armenfürsorge: Eine sozialgeschichtliche Studie." *Jahrbuch des Vereins der Geschichte Wien* (1951): 151–86.

Mehnke, Bernhard. *Armut und Elend in Hamburg: Eine Untersuchung über das öffentliche Armenwesen in der ersten Hälfte des 19. Jahrhunderts.* Hamburg, 1982.

Melhop, Wilhelm. *Alt-Hamburgische Bauweise: Kurze geschichtliche Entwicklung der Baustile in Hamburg, dargestellt am Profanbau bis zum Wiedererstehen der Stadt nach dem großen Brand von 1842 nebst chronistisch-biographischen Notizen.* Hamburg, 1908.

Melle, Werner von. *Die Entwicklung des öffentlichen Armenwesens in Hamburg.* Hamburg, 1883.

Melton, James Van Horn. *Absolutism and the Eighteenth-Century Origins of Compulsory Schooling in Prussia and Austria.* Cambridge, Eng., and New York, 1988.

Menck, Friedrich W. C *Synchronistisches Handbuch der neuesten Zeitgeschichte.* Hamburg and Leipzig, 1826.

Menke, Christoph Friedrich. "Die wirtschaftlichen und politischen Beziehungen der Hansestädte zu Rußland im 18. und frühen 19. Jahrhundert." Ph.D. diss., Göttingen, 1959.

Merk, Walther. *Der Gedanke des gemeinen Besten in der deutschen Staats- und Rechtsentwicklung.* Weimar, 1934.

Metz, Karl. "Staatsraison und Menschenfreundlichkeit. Formen und Wandlungen der Armenpflege im Ancien Regime Frankreichs, Deutschlands und Grossbritanniens." *VSWG* 72 (1985): 1–26.

Mintz, Sidney. *Sweetness and Power: The Place of Sugar in Modern History.* New York, 1985.

Mollat, Michel. *The Poor in the Middle Ages: An Essay in Social History.* New Haven, Conn., 1987.

Möller, Bernd. *Imperial Cities and the Reformation: Three Essays,* ed. and trans. H. C. Erik Midelfort and Mark U. Edwards. Philadelphia, 1972.

Möller, Kurt Detlev. "Caspar von Voght. Bürger und Edelmann 1752–1839." *ZVHG* 43 (1956): 166–93.

———. "Johann Albert Fabricius, 1668–1736." *ZVHG* 36 (1937): 1–64.

Mönckeberg, Carl. *Hamburg unter dem Drucke der Franzosen, 1806–1814.* Hamburg, 1864.

Möring, Maria. "Die Englische Kirche in Hamburg und die Merchants Adventurers." *HGH* 20 (1963): 93–112.

Möring, Walther. *Die Wohlfahrtspolitik des Hamburger Rates im Mittelalter.* Berlin and Leipzig. 1913.

Mörke, Olaf. *Rat und Bürger in der Reformation: Soziale Gruppen und kirchlicher Wandel in den welfischen Hansestädten Lüneburg, Braunschweig und Göttingen.* Hildesheim, 1983.

Mommsen, Hans and Winfried Schulze, eds. *Vom Elend der Handarbeit: Probleme historischer Unterschichtenforschung.* Stuttgart, 1981.

Moore, Barrington, Jr. *Society and Democracy in Germany.* London, 1967.

Münsterberg, Emil. *Das Elberfelder System: Festbericht aus Anlass des fünfzigjährigen Bestehens der Elberfelder Armenordnung.* Leipzig, 1903.

Nahrstedt, Wolfgang. *Die Entstehung der Freizeit zwischen 1750 und 1850. Dargestellt am Beispiel Hamburgs. Ein Beitrag zur Strukturgeschichte und zur strukturgeschichtlichen Grundlegung der Freizeitpädagogik.* Göttingen, 1972.

Neddermeyer, F. H. *Zur Statistik und Topographie der Freien und Hansestadt Hamburg und deren Gebietes.* Hamburg, 1847.

Neumann, Carl. "Die deutsche Versicherungsliteratur des XVIII. Jahrhunderts." *Zeitschrift für die gesamte Versicherungswissenschaft* 12 (1912): 317–34.

Nipperday, Thomas. "Verein als soziale Struktur in Deutschland im späten 18. und frühen 19. Jahrhundert." *Geschichtswissenschaft und Vereinswesen im 19. Jahrhundert: Beiträge zur Geschichte historischer Forschung in Deutschland.* edited by Harmut Boockmann et al., pp. 1–44. Göttingen, 1972.

Nirrnheim, Hans. "Johann Georg Büsch, (Mitbegründer und der erste Vorsteher der Patriotischen Gesellschaft.) Vortrag, gehalten im Verein für Hamburgische Geschichte am 3. December 1900. . . ." *Hamburgische Correspondent,* 12 December 1900.

Oestreich, Gerhard. *Geist und Gestalt des frühmodernen Staates: Ausgewählte Aufsätze.* Berlin, 1969.

———. "Strukturprobleme des europäischen Absolutismus." *VSWG* 55 (1969): 329–47.

Otruba, Gustav, ed. "Bericht über eine im Auftrag der Mährischen Lehensbank durchgeführte Kommerzialreise—Eine zeitgenössische Bestandsaufnahme zur Wirtschaftslage mitteleuropäischer Städte um die Mitte des 18. Jahrhunderts (Teil III)," *JFW* (1976/II), 253–78.

Parry, Geraint. "Enlightened Government and its Critics in Eighteenth-Century Germany." *HJ* 6 (1963): 178–92.

Die Patriotische Gesellschaft zu Hamburg 1765–1965: Festschrift der Hamburgischen Gesellschaft zur Beförderung der Künste und nützlichen Gewerbe. Hamburg, 1965.

Payne, Harry. *The Philosophes and the People.* New Haven, Conn., 1976.

Peter, Joachim Heinrich. *Die Probleme der Armut in den Lehren der Kameralisten: (Eine dogmengeschichtliche Studie).* Berlin, 1934.

Petersen, Christina. "Die Teutsch-übende Gesellschaft in Hamburg." *ZVHG* 2 (1847): 533–64.

Plessner, Helmuth. *Der verspätete Nation: Über die politische Verführbarkeit bürgerlichen Geistes.* Stuttgart, 1959.

Poel, Gustav. *Bilder aus vergangener Zeit: Nach Mittheilungen aus großentheils ungedruckten Familienpapieren.* Hamburg, 1884.

Pohl, Hans. *Die Beziehungen Hamburgs zu Spanien und dem spanischen Amerika in der Zeit von 1740 bis 1806.* Wiesbaden, 1963.

Pollard, Sidney. "Factory Discipline in the Industrial Revolution." *EHR,* 3nd. ser., 16 (1963–64): 254–71.

Postel, Rainer. "Obrigkeitsdenken und Reformation in Hamburg." *ARG* 70 (1979): 169–201.

———. *Die Reformation in Hamburg, 1517–1528.* Gütersloh, 1986.

———. "Reformation und bürgerliche Mitsprache in Hamburg." *ZVHG* 65 (1979): 1–20.

———. "Sozialgeschichtliche Folgewirkungen der Reformation in Hamburg." In Wenzel Lohff, ed., *450 Jahre Reformation in Hamburg: Eine Festschrift,* pp. 63–84. Hamburg, 1980.

Prange, Ruth. *Die bremische Kaufmannschaft in sozialgeschichtlicher Betrachtung.* Bremen, 1963.

[Prell, Marianne]. *Erinnerungen aus der Franzosenzeit in Hamburg.* Hamburg, 1963.

Puhle, Hans-Jürgen. *Politische Agrarbewegungen in kapitalistischen Industriegesellschaften Deutschland, USA und Frankreich im 20. Jahrhundert.* Göttingen, 1975.

Quaderni storici. Special issue on "Sistemi di carità: esposti e internati nella soceità di antico regime." 53 (1983).

Raeff, Marc. "The Well-Ordered Police State and the Development of Modernity in Seventeenth- and Eighteenth-Century Europe: An Attempt at a Comparative Approach." *AHR* 80 (1975): 1221–43.

———. *The Well-Ordered Police State: Social and Institutional Change Through Law in the Germanies and Russia, 1600–1800.* New Haven, Conn. and London, 1983.

Ramcke, Rainer. *Die Beziehungen zwischen Hamburg und Österreich im 18. Jahrhundert: Kaiserlich-reichsstädtisches Verhältnis im Zeichen von Handels- und Finanzinteressen.* Hamburg, 1969.

Rathje, Jürgen. " 'Der Patriot,' eine hamburgische Zeitschrift der ersten Hälfte des 18. Jahrhunderts." *ZVHG* 65 (1979): 123–43.

Redeker, Heinrich. *Die Reorganization der hamburgischen Polizei im 19. Jahrhundert.* Saalfeld, 1932.

Reichmann, Eberhard. *Die Herrschaft der Zahl: Quantitatives Denken in der deutschen Aufklärung.* Stuttgart, 1968.

Reidel, Manfred. "Bürger. Staatsbürger. Bürgertum." In *Geschichtliche Grundbegriffe: Historisches Lexikon zur politisch-sozialen Sprache in Deutschland,* edited by Otto Brunner, Werner Conze, and Reinhart Koselleck. Stuttgart, 1972–.

Reincke, Heinrich. *Forschungen und Skizzen zur hamburgischen Geschichte.* Hamburg, 1951.

Reincke, Heinrich. "Hamburgs Bevölkerung." In Heinrich Reincke, *Forschungen und Skizzen zur hamburgischen Geschichte,* pp. 167–200. Hamburg, 1951.

Reincke, Johann Julius. *Das Medizinalwesen des Hamburgischen Staats: Eine Sammlung der gesetzlichen Bestimmungen für das Medizinalwesen in Hamburg.* 3rd rev. enl. ed., Hamburg, 1900.

Reißmann, Martin. *Die hamburgische Kaufmannschaft des 17. Jahrhunderts in sozialgeschichtlicher Sicht.* Hamburg, 1975.

Reith, Charles. *The Police Idea: Its History and Evolution in the Eighteenth Century and After.* Oxford, Engl., 1938.

Riedel, Karl Veit. *Friedrich Johann Lorenz Meyer 1760–1844: Ein Leben in Hamburg zwischen Aufklärung und Biedermeier.* Hamburg, 1963.

Riis, Thomas, ed. *Aspects of Poverty in Early Modern Europe.* Alphen aan den Rijn, 1981.

Ritter, Gerhard A. *Deutscher und britischer Parlamentarismus: Ein verfassungsgeschichtlicher Vergleich.* Tübingen, 1962.

———, ed. *Vom Wohlfahrtsausschuss zum Wohlfahrtsstaat: Der Staat in der modernen Industriegesellschaft.* Cologne, 1973.

Rodegra, Heinrich. *Das Gesundheitswesen der Stadt Hamburg im 19. Jahrhundert unter Berücksichtigung der Medizinalgesetzgebung (1586–1818–1900).* Wiesbaden, 1979.

———. *Vom Pesthof zum Allgemeinen Krankenhaus: Die Entwicklung des Krankenhauswesens in Hamburg zu Beginn des 19. Jahrhunderts.* Münster, 1977.

Rösch, Friedrich. *Die Mainzer Armenreform von Jahre 1786.* Berlin, 1929.

Rohr, Donald. *The Origins of Social Liberalism in Germany.* Chicago and London, 1963.

Roosbroeck, Robert van. "Die Niederlassung von Flamen und Wallonen in Hamburg (1567–1605): Ein Überblick." *ZVHG* 49/50 (1964): 53–76.

Roosen, Berend Karl. *Geschichte unseres Hauses.* Hamburg, 1905.

Rosen, George. *From Medical Police to Social Medicine: Essays on the History of Health Care.* New York, 1974.

Rothman, David. *The Discovery of the Asylum: Social Order and Disorder in the New Republic.* Boston and Toronto, 1971.

Rotzoll, Ursula. "Kastenordnung der Reformationszeit: Von der mittelalterlichen zur neuzeitlichen Armenpflege." Hausarbeit, Phillipps Universität, Marburg-Lahn, Fachbereich Philosophie, 1959. (Cited as StAHbg, *HS* 695).

Rückleben, Hermann. *Die Niederwerfung der hamburgischen Ratsgewalt: Kirchliche Bewegungen und bürgerliche Unruhen im ausgehenden 17. Jahrhundert.* Hamburg, 1970.

Rüdiger, Otto. *Die ältesten Hamburgischen Zunftrollen und Brüderschaftsstatuten.* Hamburg, 1874.

————. *Caspar von Voght: Ein hamburgisches Lebensbild.* Hamburg, 1901.

————, and Georg Hermann Sieveking. "Kleine Studien über Caspar Voght." *MVHG* 7 (1902): 147–48, 161–64, 399–44, 356–65, 394–97.

Sachße, Christoph, and Florian Tennstedt. *Geschichte der Armenfürsorge in Deutschland.* vol. 1, *Vom Spätmittelalter bis zum 1. Weltkrieg.* Stuttgart, 1980. vol. 2, *Fürsorge und Wohlfahrtspflege 1871 bis 1929.* Stuttgart, 1988.

————, eds. *Bettler, Gauner und Proleten: Armut und Armenfürsorge in der deutschen Geschichte, ein Bild-Lesebuch.* Reinbek bei Hamburg, 1983.

————, eds. *Jahrbuch der Sozialarbeit* 4 (1982). Special issue: *Geschichte und Geschichten.*

————, eds. *Soziale Sicherheit und soziale Disziplinierung: Beiträge zu einer historischen Theorie der Sozialpolitik.* Frankfurt, 1986.

Scherpner, Hans. *Die Kinderfürsorge in der Hamburgischen Armenreform vom Jahre 1788.* Berlin, 1927.

————. *Theorie der Fürsorge.* 2nd ed. Göttingen, 1974.

Schilling, Heinz, and Hermann Diedriks, eds. *Bürgerliche Eliten in den Niederlanden und in Nordwestdeutschland: Studien zur Sozialgeschichte des europäischen Bürgertums im Mittelalter und in der Neuzeit.* Cologne and Vienna, 1985.

Schillinger, Ruth. *Die wirtschaftliche Entwicklung des Stoffdrucks: Langfristige Tendenzen und kurzfristige Einflüsse.* Cologne, 1964.

Schmidt, Wilhelm. "Die wirtschaftlichen Folgen des 30-jährigen Krieges für Hamburg." Ph.D. diss., Hamburg, 1921.

Schmoller, Gustav. *Die Entstehung der deutschen Volkswirtschaft und der deutschen Sozialreform.* Munich and Leipzig, 1914.

Schönfeld, Gustav. *Beiträge zur Geschichte des Pauperismus und der Prostitution in Hamburg.* Weimar, 1897.

Schrader, Theodor, ed. *Hamburg vor 200 Jahren: Gesammelte Vorträge.* Hamburg, 1892.

Schramm, Percy Ernst. *Deutschland und Übersee. Der deutsche Handel mit den anderen Kontinenten, insbesondere Afrika, von Karl V. bis zum Bismarck: Geschichte der Rivalität im Wirtschaftsleben.* Braunschweig, 1950.

————. *Gewinn und Verlust: Die Geschichte der Hamburger Senatorenfamilien Jencquel und Luis (16. bis 19. Jahrhundert): Zwei Beispiele für den wirtschaftlichen und sozialen Wandel in Norddeutschland.* Hamburg, 1970.

————. *Hamburg, Deutschland und die Welt: Leistung und Grenzen hanseatischen Bürgertums in der Zeit zwischen Napoleon I. und Bismarck: Ein Kapitel deutscher Geschichte.* Munich, 1943.

————. *Hamburg, ein Sonderfall in der Geschichte Deutschlands.* Hamburg, 1964.

————. "Die von den Hamburgern bevorzugten Universitäten (Ende des 17. bis Anfang des 18. Jahrhunderts)." *ZVHG* 52 (1966): 83–90.

————. *Kaufleute zu Haus und über See.* Hamburg, 1949.

————. *Neun Generationen: Dreihundert Jahre deutscher "Kulturgeschichte" im Lichte der Schicksale einer Hamburger Bürgerfamilie, 1648–1948.* 2 vols. Göttingen, 1963–64.

Scheibe, Jörg. *Der "Patriot" (1724–1726) und sein Publikum: Untersuchungen über die Verfasserschaft und die Leserschaft einer Zeitschrift der frühen Aufklärung.* Göppingen, 1973.

Schreckenstein, Karl Heinrich Roth von. *Das Patriziat in den deutschen Städten besonders Reichstädten, als Beitrag zur Geschichte der deutschen und des deutschen Adels.* Tübingen, 1885. Rpt. Aalen, 1970.

Schubert, Ernst. *Arme Leute, Bettler und Gauner im Franken des 18. Jahrhunderts.* Neustadt a.d. Aisch, 1983.

Schultheiss, Carl. "Die philanthropische Pädagogik in Hamburg." *MVHG* 14 (1826): 197–200.

Schultz, Helga (with Jürgen Wilke). *Berlin 1650–1800: Sozialgeschichte einer Residenz.* Berlin, G.D.R., 1987.

Scribner, Robert W. "The Reformation as a Social Movement." in *Stadtbürgertum und Adel in der Reformation: Studien zur Sozialgeschichte der Reformation in England und Deutschland [The Urban Classes, the Nobility and the Reformation: Studies on the Social History of the Reformation in England and Germany],* edited by Wolfgang Mommsen, pp. 49–79.

Seelig, Geert. *Die geschichtliche Entwicklung der hamburgischen Bürgerschaft und der hamburgischen Notabeln.* Hamburg, 1900.

Sellin, Thorsten. *Pioneering in Penology: The Amsterdam Houses of Correction in the 16th and 17th Centuries.* Philadelphia and London, 1944.

Sharlin, Allen. "Natural Decrease in Early Modern Cities: A Reconsideration." *PP* no. 79 (1978): 126–38.

Sheehan, James. *German Liberalism in the Nineteenth Century.* Chicago, 1978.

Shepansky, Ernst W. "Ein Beispiel zur Sozialgeschichte der Fremden: Mennoniten in Hamburg und Altona zur Zeit des Merkantilismus." *HJWG* 24 (1979): 219–34.

750 Jahre Hospital zum Heiligen Geist mit Oberalten-Stift und Maria-Magdalenen-Kloster. Hamburg, 1977.

Sieveking, Heinrich. *Georg Heinrich Sieveking: Lebensbild eines hamburgischen Kaufmanns aus dem Zeitalter der französischen Revolution.* Berlin, 1913.

————. "Die Hamburger Bank 1619 bis 1875." In *Festschrift der Hamburger Universität ihrem Ehrenrektor Herrn Bürgermeister Werner von Melle . . . zum 80. Geburtstag am 18. Oktober 1933 dargebracht,* pp. 21–110. Gluckstadt and Hamburg, 1933.

————. "Hamburger Gefängnisfürsorge im 18. Jahrhundert." *AZ* 3 (1933–34): 94–106.

————. "Das Handlungshaus Voght und Sieveking." *ZVHG* 17 (1912): 54–128.

————. "Der Hamburger Armenfreund Caspar von Voght in seiner internationalen Wirksamkeit." in *Festgabe für Emil Zürcher zu seinem siebzigsten Geburtstag,* pp. 73–108. Bern, 1920.

————. "Das Handlungshaus Voght und Sieveking." *ZVHG* 17 (1912): 54–128.

————. "Johann Albert Heinrich Reimarus als Philosoph, als Patriot und als Volkswirt." *Vorträge und Aufsätze herausgegeben vom Verein für Hamburgische Geschichte* 5 (1930): 8–20.

———. "Vom Leben auf dem Hammerhofe vor 100 Jahren." *HGH* 14, no. 3 (1853): 191–98.

Sievers, Kai Detlev. *Volkskultur und Aufklärung im Spiegel der Schleswig-Holsteinischen Provinzialberichte*. Neumünster, 1970.

Sieverts, Rudolf. "Die Patriotische Gesellschaft und ihre Bedeutung für die Geschichte der sozialen Fürsorge." in *Die Patriotische Gesellschaft zu Hamburg 1765–1965: Festschrift der Hamburgischen Gesellschaft zur Beförderung der Künste und nützlichen Gewerbe*, pp. 77–90.

Sigsworth, E. M. "Gateways to Death? Medicine, Hospitals and Mortality, 1700–1850." In Peter Mathias, ed., *Science and Society, 1600–1900*, pp. 97–110 Cambridge, Eng., 1972.

Sillem, C. H. Wilhelm. "Zur Geschichte der Niederländer in Hamburg von ihrer Ankunft bis zum Abschluß des niederländischen Contracts 1605." *ZVHG* 1 (1841): 241–48.

Skalweit, Stephen. *Die Berliner Wirtschaftskrise von 1763 und ihre Hintergründe*. Stuttgart and Berlin, 1937.

Small, Albion W. *The Cameralists: Pioneers of German Social Polity*. New York, 1909.

Soetbeer, Adolph. *Ueber Hamburgs Handel*. Hamburg, 1840.

Soliday, Gerald L. *A Community in Conflict: Frankfurt Society in the Seventeenth and Early Eighteenth Centuries*. Hanover, N.H., 1974.

Soly, Hugo. "Economische ontwikkeling en sociale politiek in Europa tijdens de overgang van middeleeuwen naar nieuwe tijden." *TVG* 88 (1975): 584–97.

Sontheimer, Kurt. *Antidemokratisches Denken in der Weimarer Republik*. Munich, 1962.

Sothmann, Marlene. *Das Armen-, Arbeits-, Zucht- und Werkhaus in Nürnberg bis 1806*. Nuremberg, 1970.

Stekl, Hannes. *Österreichs Zucht- und Arbeitshäuser 1671–1920: Institutionen zwischen Fürsorge und Strafvollzug*. Vienna, 1978.

———. "Soziale Sicherung und soziale Kontrolle: Zur österreichischen Armengesetzgebung des 18. und 19. Jahrhunderts," *Bericht über den 14. österreichischen Historikertag in Wien* (1979): 136–51.

Stern, Fritz. *The Politics of Cultural Despair: A Study in the Rise of the German Ideology*. Berkeley, Calif., 1961.

Stigler, Stephen. *The History of Statistics: The Measurement of Uncertainty Before 1900*. Cambridge, Mass., 1986.

Stobbe, Otto. *Geschichte der deutschen Rechtsquellen*. Braunschweig, 1864.

Strauss, Gerald. *Nuremberg in the Sixteenth Century: City Politics and Life Between Middle Ages and Modern Times*. 2nd. rev. ed., Bloomington, Ind. and London, 1976.

Streng, Adolf. *Geschichte der Gefängnisverwaltung in Hamburg von 1622–1872*. Hamburg, 1890.

Stuhlmann, C. A. "Erläuterungen zu den Tabellen über die Bevölkerungszustände Hamburgs und seiner Vorstädte." *Beiträge zur Statistik Hamburgs* (1854).

———. *Die Hamburgische Credit-Casse für Erben und Grundstücke, nach ihrer Entstehung, Natur und Wirksamkeit und ihrer Umformung durch die revidirten Artikel von 1846*. Hamburg, n.d.

Sydow, Paul G. A. "Die pädagogischen Bestrebungen der Patriotischen Gesellschaft." In Gustav Kowalewski, ed., *Geschichte der Hamburgischen Gesellschaft zur Beförderung der Künste und nützlichen Gewerbe (Patriotische Gesellschaft)*. vol. 2, pp. 447–76.

Toellner, Richard, and Paul R. Blum, eds. *Studien zur Thematik des Todes im 16. Jahrhundert.* Wolfenbüttel, 1983.

Thomas, Keith. "Work and Leisure in Pre-Industrial Societies: Conference Paper." *PP* 29 (1964): 50–62.

Thompson, E. P. *The Making of the English Working Class.* London, 1963.

———. "Time, Work-Discipline, and Industrial Capitalism." *PP* 38 (1967): 56–97.

Traphagen, Wilhelm. *Die ersten Arbeitshäuser und ihre pädagogische Funktion.* Berlin, 1935.

Tribe, Keith. "Cameralism and the Science of Government." *JMH* 56 (1984): 263–84.

Troitzsch, Ulrich, ed. *Technologischer Wandel im 18. Jahrhundert.* Wolfenbüttel, 1981.

Trost, Fritz. *Die Göttingische Industrie-Schule.* Berlin, 1930.

Uhalde, Steven D. "Citizen and World-Citizen: Civic Patriotism and Cosmopolitanism in Eighteenth-Century Hamburg." Ph.D. diss., University of California, Berkeley, 1984.

Uhlhorn, Gerhard. *Die christliche Liebestätigkeit.* 3 vols. Stuttgart, 1882–90.

Unger, Eike Eberhard. "Nürnbergs Handel mit Hamburg im 16. und beginnenden 17. Jahrhundert." *Mitteilungen des Vereins für Geschichte der Stadt Nürnberg* 54 (1966): 1–85.

Urlaub, Hildegard. *Die Förderung der Armenpflege durch die Hamburgische Patriotische Gesellschaft bis zum Beginn des neunzehnten Jahrhunderts.* Berlin, 1932.

Valjavec, Fritz. *Die Entstehung der politischen Strömungen in Deutschland, 1770–1815.* Munich, 1951.

———. *Geschichte der abendländischen Aufklärung.* Vienna and Munich, 1961.

Venturi, Franco. *Utopia and Reform in the Enlightenment.* Cambridge, Eng., 1971.

Vierhaus, Rudolf. *Deutschland im Zeitalter des Absolutismus (1648–1763).* Göttingen, 1978.

———, ed. *Bürger und Bürgerlichkeit im Zeitalter der Aufklärung.* Heidelberg, 1981.

———, ed. *Deutsche patriotische und gemeinnützige Gesellschaften.* Munich, 1980.

———, ed. *Kultur und Gesellschaft in Nordwestdeutschland im 18. Jahrhundert.* Forthcoming.

Voegt, Hedwig, ed. *Georg Kerner, Jakobiner und Armenarzt: Reisebrief, Berichte, Lebenszeugnisse.* Berlin, G.D.R., 1978.

Vogel, Walther. "Handelskonjunkturen und Wirtschaftskrisen in ihrer Auswirkung auf den Seehandel der Hansestädte." *HGH* 74 (1956): 50–64.

———. *Die Hansestädte und die Kontinentalsperre.* Munich and Leipzig, 1913.

Voigt, Johann Friedrich. *Beiträge zur Hamburgischen Verwaltungsgeschichte.* Vol. 3., *Die Protokolle der am 27. Mai 1814 erwählten Reorganisationsdeputation von zwanzig Bürgern.* Hamburg, 1918.

———. "Der Schuldenbestand der Stadt Hamburg im Jahre 1814." *MVHG* 12 (1914): 57–63.

Walker, Mack. *German Home-Towns: Community, State, and General Estate, 1648–1871.* Ithaca, N.Y., 1971.

———. "Rights and Functions: The Social Categories of Eighteenth-Century German Jurists and Cameralists." *JMH* 50 (1978): 234–51.

Wallerstein, Immanuel. *The Modern World-System.* 2 vols. Chicago, 1974, 1980.

Wehler, Hans-Ulrich. *Deutsche Gesellschaftsgeschichte.* Vol. 1, *Vom Feudalismus des Alten Reiches bis zur Defensiven Modernisierung der Reformära, 1700–1815.* Munich, 1987.

Weis, Eberhard. "Absolute Monarchie und Reform in Deutschland des späten 18. und frühen 19. Jahrhunderts." In *Aufklärung, Absolutismus und Bürgertum in Deutschland: Zwölf Aufsätze,* ed. Franklin Kopitzsch, pp. 192–219. Munich, 1976.

Weitzman, Arthur J. "Eighteenth-Century London: Urban Paradise or Fallen City?" *JHI* 36 (1975): 469–80.

Westphalen, Nicolaus A. *Hamburgs Verfassung und Verwaltung in ihrer allmähligen Entwickelung bis auf die neueste Zeit.* 2 vols. Hamburg, 1841. 2nd rev. and enl. ed., Hamburg, 1846.

Whaley, Joachim. "The Protestant Enlightenment." In Roy Porter and Mikuláš Teich, eds. *The Enlightenment in National Context,* pp. 106–17. Cambridge, Eng., 1981.

———. *Religious Toleration and Social Change in Hamburg, 1529–1819.* Cambridge, Eng., 1985.

———, ed. *Mirrors of Mortality: Studies in the Social History of Death.* New York, 1981.

Williams, Raymond. *The Country and the City.* London, 1973.

Winkelmann, Friedrich. *Wohnhaus und Bude in Alt-Hamburg: Die Entwicklung der Wohnverhältnisse von 1250 bis 1830.* Berlin, 1937.

Wiskemann, Erwin. *Hamburg und die Welthandelspolitik von den Anfängen bis zur Gegenwart.* Hamburg, 1929.

Wohlwill, Adolf. *Georg Kerner: Ein deutsches Lebensbild aus dem Zeitalter der französischen Revolution.* Hamburg and Leipzig, 1886.

———. "Zur Geschichte des Gottorper Vergleichs vom 27. Mai 1768." *Jahrbuch der Hamburgischen Wissenschaftlichen Anstalten* 13 (1895): 1–42.

———. *Hamburg während der Pestjahre, 1712–1714.* Hamburg, 1893.

———. *Neuere Geschichte der Freien und Hansestadt Hamburg insbesondere von 1789 bis 1815.* Gotha, 1914.

Wolff, Hans M. *Die Weltanschauung der deutschen Aufklärung in geschichtlicher Entwicklung.* 2nd ed. Bern and Munich, 1963.

Wolzendorff, Kurt. *Der Polizeigedanke des modernen Staats: Ein Versuch zur allgemeinen Verwaltungslehre unter besonder Berücksichtigung der Entwicklung in Preußen.* Breslau, 1918. Rpt. ed., Aalen, 1964.

Woodward, John. *To Do the Sick No Harm: A Study of the British Voluntary Hospital System to 1875.* London and Boston, 1974.

Woolf, Stuart. *The Poor in Western Europe in the Eighteenth and Nineteenth Centuries.* London and New York, 1986.

Wurm, C[hristian] F[riedrich]. *Der europäische Hintergrund der Snitger-Jastram'schen Wirren in Hamburg 1686.* Hamburg, 1855.

Zachau, Monika. *Zwangsläufig oder Abwendbar? Auffassungen von Armut in Hamburg innerhalb und außerhalb der "Hamburgischen Gesellschaft zur Beförderung der Künste und nützlichen Gewerbe" zwischen 1788 und 1840.* Hamburg, n.d. [1988].

Zobel, Karolina. "Polizei. Geschichte und Bedeutungswandel des Wortes und seiner Zusammensetzungen." Ph.D. diss., Munich, 1952.

Zobst, Dionys. "Der Polizeibegriff in Deutschland." Ph.D. diss., Munich, 1933.

INDEX